THE NATION'S ADVOCATE

THE NATION'S ADVOCATE is one of a list in the cultural history of Western Pennsylvania made possible through a grant-in-aid from The Buhl Foundation of Pittsburgh.

EPITAPH—on a Lawyer

The Lord works wonders now and then,
Here lies a lawyer—AN HONEST MAN.

—*Westmoreland Republican* (Greensburg, Pa.)
May 22, 1819

HENRY MARIE BRACKENRIDGE

CAROLINE MARIE BRACKENRIDGE

Courtesy of Helen Brackenridge Painter

The
NATION'S
ADVOCATE

Henry Marie Brackenridge and Young America

By
William F. Keller

UNIVERSITY OF PITTSBURGH PRESS

Library of Congress Catalog No. 56-6426

© 1956
University of Pittsburgh Press
Printed in the United States of America

To DOROTHY SMITH KELLER

Preface

In Philadelphia in 1787 the delegates to the Constitutional Convention fashioned a new government for the United States. In backwoods Pennsylvania the year before H. M. Brackenridge was born, and he grew into manhood in the years his countrymen pushed westward toward the Pacific. Brackenridge became better acquainted with his expanding nation than most of his contemporaries and wrote more authoritatively about it for the pleasure and instruction of his fellow citizens. His biography, therefore, as it relates the events of his long life (1786-1871), records the growth of the United States. The story of his life—and the theme of this book—is epitomized by an "ORIGINAL ANECDOTE" which appeared in the *Pittsburgh Gazette* in 1798:

> A FRENCHMAN was travelling in one of the lower counties, not long since.—He met one of our men with a musket and furniture going to attend muster.—"Pray, young man," says Monsieur, "be you one ARISTOCRAT or one DEMOCRAT?" "Why," replied the youth, "I am SUPERIOR TO EITHER, I am an AMERICAN."

This book is the first published biography of H. M. Brackenridge, a lawyer and a judge by profession, an author by avocation. In his own day he was a controversial figure, often the victim of calumny. My purpose in writing his biography is to set the record straight by according him the recognition his achievements merit. I tried to portray him honestly, although I wrote with a sympathetic pen. It was, in fact, my concern to document the mental turmoil which distressed him for years until he overcame a deep-seated sense of inferiority in an extraordinary way.

I solely am responsible for the interpretations in the book—of Brackenridge's writings, of the events of his life, and of the American history connected with his life. In an attempt to make this work readable and authoritative I kept scholarly trappings to a minimum without neglecting to cite all sources of information. Likewise, I constructed the bibliography and the index with the general reader as well as the scholar in mind.

The kindnesses of many people—only a few of whom I can thank here—made the writing of this book possible. Dorothy Smith Keller, my wife, and William C. Wilkins, my stepson, were unfailing in the encouragement, expressed in many ways, which they gave me through all the stages of this project. To my parents, George J. and Florence Keller of Erie, Pennsylvania, I owe a similar debt of gratitude. Here, also, I wish to express a special word of appreciation to Dr. John W. Oliver, Mrs. Lois Mulkearn, Mrs. P. B. Massey, Mr. Fred Shelley, and Mrs. Helen Brackenridge Painter, the great-granddaughter of H. M. Brackenridge. The late Franklin F. Holbrook was of great assistance to me in my research at the Historical Society of Western Pennsylvania. Mrs. Agnes L. Starrett, director of the University of Pittsburgh Press and University editor, was a wise and kindly counselor in the preparation of my book. I received invaluable aid from the personnel of many libraries, particularly University of Pittsburgh; Carnegie Library of Pittsburgh; Historical Society of Western Pennsylvania; Historical Society of Pennsylvania; American Antiquarian Society; New York Public Library; University of Virginia; Library of Congress; National Archives; Maryland Historical Society; Missouri Historical Society; Historical Society of Delaware; Harvard University; Boston Public Library; Department of Archives, Louisiana State University; and the William Henry Smith Memorial Library, Indiana Historical Society.

To the University of Pittsburgh and to The Buhl Foundation I am deeply appreciative for making possible the publication of my writing.

I have permission to publish materials from many sources. Credit is given in the citation to every quotation.

WILLIAM F. KELLER

Pittsburgh, Pennsylvania
March 4, 1956

Contents

I	Birthright	1
II	Father and Son	16
III	Ste. Genevieve	29
IV	The Student	43
V	*The Law Is a Jealous Mistress*	56
VI	The Bar of Pittsburgh	68
VII	The Attorney at Law	82
VIII	*Sketches of the Territory of Louisiana*	96
IX	The Race to the Arikara Village	112
X	A Man of Some Importance	128
XI	Grass in the Streets of New Orleans	142
XII	The Garret	155
XIII	Peregrine Bochinjochelus	168
XIV	The Secretary of the Mission to South America (1)	184
XV	The Secretary of the Mission to South America (2)	198
XVI	*If I Err, I Will Err with Them*	214
XVII	Return to Missouri	230
XVIII	Andrew Jackson's Private Secretary	246
XIX	The Alcalde of Pensacola	264
XX	Judge Brackenridge of West Florida	280
XXI	*Freedonia*	298
XXII	Judge and Mrs. H. M. Brackenridge	316
XXIII	Deer Point and Tarentum	331
XXIV	The Fall from Grace	349
XXV	The Sage of Tarentum	364
	Notes	381
	Bibliography	425
	Index	435

List of Illustrations

HENRY MARIE BRACKENRIDGE   *Frontispiece*
CAROLINE MARIE BRACKENRIDGE

PITTSBURGH ABOUT 1800: (31) H. H. Brackenridge home,
      Market Street between First and Second Streets
                                            Opposite Page 8

JUDGE HUGH HENRY BRACKENRIDGE   *Opposite Page 9*

MAP OF MISSOURI RIVER REGION, a territory sparsely settled
      when Henry Marie Brackenridge and John Bradbury
      took their trip in 1811. Map engraved for Bradbury's
      Travels in the Interior of America.   *Opposite Page 330*

BRACKENRIDGE'S PROPERTY on Santa Rosa Peninsula across
      from Pensacola. Map of the Western Part of Florida
      made by John L. Williams about 1827.   *Opposite Page 331*

THE BRACKENRIDGE HOME, "Oak Grove," Tarentum, Penn-
      sylvania   *Opposite Page 346*

HENRY MARIE BRACKENRIDGE in the late years of his life
                                            Opposite Page 347

I: Birthright

For the appreciative audience gathered at Nassau Hall in Princeton on commencement day, September 25, 1771, Hugh Henry Brackenridge signalized the course of future events as he neared the end of his exercise, a poem on "The Rising Glory of America":

> ... Hail, happy land,
> The seat of empire, the abode of kings,
> The final stage where time shall introduce
> Renowned characters, and glorious works
> Of high invention and of wond'rous art
> Which not the ravages of time shall waste
> Till he himself has run his long career.[1]

The words echoed the patriotic sentiment already prevailing among the incipient rebels at Dr. John Witherspoon's College of New Jersey. Hugh had collaborated with Philip Freneau, his classmate and perhaps closest friend, in writing the poem,[2] an epic expressive of their pride of country. But long before their senior year, they had nourished thoughts of political freedom with such fellow students as James Madison and William Bradford, Jr.

There was reason for Hugh to glorify America. Of these four Princeton Whigs, only he was an immigrant to the colonies. His father, an impoverished farmer, had brought him as a child of five years from Scotland to York County, Pennsylvania, where the entire Brackenridge family worked hard on the land leased near the Maryland border. Hugh had, however, the opportunity of attending a country school near by, for his parents believed in the value of education. Here began his lifelong search for knowledge, particularly in the classics and in the law. About the age of fifteen he successfully applied for the position of teacher of a small free school in Maryland; and at eighteen he won admission to college. Poverty, nevertheless, had dogged his steps the whole way to Princeton.[3]

It was already manifest that he possessed a touch of genius in addition to perseverance. A whim had caused him to change the usual spelling of his family name from Breckinridge to Brackenridge.[4] This act was but a precursor of countless others to come, many of which were so original as to earn him early in life the reputation of eccentricity. When Hugh continued at college after graduation to serve as a tutor and to study theology,[5] the esteem of his friends increased. "Mr. Brackenridge's illness gives me great uneasiness; I think he would be a loss to America," wrote a worried Madison to Bradford in 1774. "His merit is rated so high by me that I confess, if he were gone, I could almost say with the poet, that his country could furnish such a pomp for death no more."[6] Madison, however, could be critical of some of Hugh's attempts at versifying, on one occasion finding the subject of a poem "fright-

1

ful" and the phraseology "antiquated," although admitting the presence of "many real beauties in it, and several strokes of a strong original genius. . . ." Brackenridge had, in fact, purposely written the poem "to raise the character of his academy by the fame of its teacher,"[7] for on the eve of the Revolution he was the master of a school on the Eastern Shore of Maryland.[8]

The outbreak of hostilities found Hugh a patriot destined not to bear arms but to minister to the minds of men. He soon had occasion to write a play of five acts in the heroic style, entitled *The Battle of Bunkers-Hill,*[9] which his pupils recited for their parents.[10] In 1777, he served a regiment of Washington's army as chaplain, going to the battlefield of Brandywine wearing a cocked hat and carrying a pocket Bible in a saddlebag.[11] His usual sermon, or discourse, to the troops stressed politics unashamedly, for the independence of the colonies had to be achieved: "Let [the soldier] be of the mind to fight from hill to hill, from vale to vale, and on every plain, until the enemy is driven back, and forced to depart — until the tyrant shall give up his claim, and be obliged to confess, that free men, that Americans are not to be subdued."[12] Hugh aided the revolutionary cause in another way — as the editor of the *United States Magazine: A Repository of History, Politics and Literature,*[13] published in Philadelphia in 1779. Patriotism was the keynote of this journal. To its pages Freneau frequently contributed both poetry and prose.[14] These former Princetonians were two of the most inspiring penmen of the Revolution.

Brackenridge had in the meantime resolved an inner conflict concerning his religious beliefs and the ministry as a career. Unable to harmonize all of his views with the doctrines of Scotch Presbyterianism, he could not consider the idea of ordination in his own, or any, church. Orthodoxy was alien to his temperament. In this unsettled frame of mind, a condition persisting for two years, he shifted his attention from the study of theology to the pursuit of law, a transition completed by his removing to Annapolis to read under the supervision of Samuel Chase.[15]

At first Hugh intended to practice his profession in Philadelphia. There he won admission to the bar in the Court of Common Pleas.[16] But he had quickly decided that the prospect of success was unpromising: ". . . I saw no chance of being any thing in that city, there were such great men before me, Chew, Dickenson, Wilson &c."[17] Born in 1748, Hugh was now thirty-three years old — no age to encourage him to take the arduous and uncertain road toward the head of the bar. The situation in the West, he reasoned, would be different, for there no one would stand in his way as he sought clients and political preferment. Thus in the spring of 1781, the year of Yorktown, Hugh began the journey to the headwaters of the Ohio.

2

His destination was the village of Pittsburgh, which lay on the other side of the Allegheny Mountains, nestled in the angle of land at the confluence of the Allegheny and Monongahela rivers. The actual surveying of the town of Pittsburgh was not completed until 1784. The traveler at this time was apt to notice only the squalor of the place with its "paltry log-houses"[18] and the brisk trade in flour and skins exchanged for goods transported from the eastern cities of Philadelphia and Baltimore. But many pioneer families bound for Kentucky floated by the new town on boats loaded with all their possessions without stopping to purchase supplies. The traveler might well remark, as Arthur Lee did,[19] that this settlement of predominately Scotch and Irish inhabitants would never become an important center of commerce and industry in the western country.

Lee had also noted that the townsmen possessed the services of four lawyers and two doctors, although they lacked a minister of religion. One of these attorneys at law was Brackenridge, whose practice was increasing to such an extent that he stood at the head of the bar by 1786, a claim[20] which he could later make without fear of contradiction. He drew his clientele from the counties of Fayette, Washington, and Westmoreland.[21] Litigants of the backwoods trusted this witty and eloquent counselor, who believed that Pittsburgh "would one day be a town of note. . . ."[22]

The beauty of its situation beguiled Hugh.[23] Until torn away by a flood, a tree stood at the point of land where the rivers met. Here he had often left his clothes in the shade while he bathed, or sometimes he had leaned against the trunk observing the "conflict" of waters. Only a gentle rippling was noticeable when the rivers were equal in height; but when they were not, the current of one or the other was the master. In Hugh's opinion this junction of the Allegheny and the Monongahela was truly lovely. He could not resist the lure of these waters. With a group of friends he enjoyed moving up or down the rivers in a barge, then resting, or perhaps picnicking, in the shade of a bower of ash or oak at a spring. Fishing in the vicinity of Pittsburgh was likewise a popular pastime. Many an evening found anglers distributed along the banks hoping that the nibble of a perch or a pike or a sturgeon would become a sudden bite. According to Brackenridge, there was "not a more delightful spot under heaven to spend any of the summer months than at this place." Why people visited the Warm Springs in Virginia puzzled him, for here at Pittsburgh the town and country blended together. Breezes came off the rivers, the sun never sent down "its beams concentrated as in a burning glass," and everyone shared "the prospect of extensive hills and dales, whence the fragrant air brings odours of a thousand flowers and plants, or of the corn and grain of husbandmen, upon its balmy wings."

3

In 1786, the outlines of Fort Duquesne were still visible at the Point, the ditch and mound overgrown with vegetation. A small garrison was stationed at Fort Pitt which stood in fair condition above the old French works. Hugh believed that the fortification, noteworthy for its stone magazine, no longer was necessary for the defense of the town. Adjacent to Fort Pitt was an orchard of apple and pear trees lining the bank of the Allegheny. Before the Revolution, in the heyday of the garrison, this spot was known as the King's Artillery Gardens, then, as now in Hugh's time, a popular resort for an evening stroll. The bank of the Monongahela was ordinarily the scene of noisy activity, for here many lively business places extended up the river for nearly half a mile. Behind them lay the main part of town, with Grant's Hill rising eastward. Flanking this elevation were Quarry Hill on the northeast and Ayres Hill on the southeast. The town proper actually stood on the third level of ground above the water of the Allegheny.

Brackenridge viewed Pittsburgh and its inhabitants in a sentimental light. With pride he noted a hundred dwellings, ignoring the mean log construction of most of them and the filth of the streets on which they fronted. More important in his mind was the fact that in the winter the buildings were warm, heated by an abundance of fuel, both coal and wood. New construction he could mark every day along with the improvement of existing structures. The population, about fifteen hundred people according to his estimate, was growing apace from births in the town and from the influx of strangers who decided to reside there. A temporary accession to the population occurred in the fall and winter months when many travelers tarried in Pittsburgh before descending the Ohio or resuming their journey elsewhere. Winter was consequently not a season of dreary solitude for the inhabitants but one of conviviality: "It must appear like enchantment to a stranger, who after travelling an hundred miles from the settlement, . . . to see, all at once, and almost on the verge of the inhabited globe, a town with smoking chimnies, halls lighted up with splendor, ladies and gentlemen assembled, various music, and the mazes of the dance."

Hugh did not consider such a description of Pittsburgh too fanciful, for he was avowedly a self-appointed publicity agent for the place. Among his first contributions to the *Pittsburgh Gazette,* established by John Scull and Joseph Hall in July, 1786, was a lengthly piece entitled "On the Situation of the Town of Pittsburgh, and the State of Society at That Place." Brackenridge boasted about the salubrity of the climate, over-estimated the population and the number of dwellings, and rendered a crude and bumptious community too glamorous. To "induce emigration to this particular spot" was his explanation for writing the article. "Who knows," he asked the reader, "what families of fortune it may induce to emigrate to this place?" He had written a model of promotional literature.

In this summer of 1786, Hugh's mind was so preoccupied with plans for the improvement of the town of Pittsburgh and the western country generally that he barely noticed his son Henry Marie, born on May 11.[24] To Hugh the event was of little consequence in comparison with the excitement of launching the first gazette to be published west of the Alleghenies: "I had an ambition; or rather I obeyed the impulse of my mind in being among the first to bring the press to the west of the mountains. . . ."[25] The encouragement of such an undertaking was his intention when he had left Philadelphia in search of a career. As the former editor of the *United States Magazine,* he understood the power of the public press. A newspaper established in Pittsburgh would be an effective agency for promoting the interests of the entire western country. Before the first issue of their gazette, the young printers Scull and Hall had therefore received his active support. Brackenridge, in turn, was now to have at hand a vehicle invaluable for communicating with the citizenry of his section of Pennsylvania.

How he planned to utilize this new medium of expression was soon apparent. Standing at the head of the bar in the western counties, Hugh considered the time propitious for his entry into the political arena. The idea of holding a public office derived from his hopes and aspirations formed during the Princeton days and the Revolution; it was, moreover, a basic principle of the concept of democracy evolving gradually in his mind. But the driving impulse was the desire to get ahead in the world and to make a name for himself by fostering the progress of the United States as well as Western Pennsylvania and Pittsburgh—

> . . . glorious works of high invention and of wond'rous art . . .

a thought which still tantalized its author. His decision to place himself before the public as a candidate for the state assembly at the next election was accordingly not reached on the spur of the moment. A resident of Pittsburgh and thereby of Westmoreland County, he penned a letter to his fellow electors on September 7, announcing his candidacy; signed his name; and sent it to the printing office for publication.[26]

As an electioneering device the letter was clever. This statement Brackenridge had prepared as carefully as if it were the argument for an important cause which he was pleading in court. Consequently, he intended to insinuate a few significant ideas in the minds of the electors by relying on a casual manner of expression and by a direct appeal to their self-interest before advocating measures of civic improvement. He had no intention, furthermore, of appearing too eager for a seat in the assembly.

5

He had thought a bit about the approaching election, he apprised his fellow citizens; and then he mentioned specific matters to which they would undoubtedly want their legislators to attend. First he recommended an extension of the period established for taking out patents for land, offering other proposals designed to settle the whole land problem. He suggested also the passage of a law permitting judges to receive testimony in cases involving the settlement of titles to real property, a measure which would tend to prevent injustice being done to parties as had occurred in the past. "I conceive it to be a public good to this country that the town of Pittsburgh be encouraged, that it be made a borough, that it have a seat of justice, that it have a school endowed in it," he averred next. Another telling point, one that would engage the attention of the commercial and agricultural interests in the entire region, was his insistence on the free navigation of the Mississippi. The United States, he held, must never relinquish that right for twenty-five years in return for a free trade with all the Spanish ports in American vessels. It therefore behove the representatives from Western Pennsylvania to protest against such an agreement in the state assembly. Thus did Brackenridge oppose the Jay-Gardoqui negotiations then in progress between the United States and Spain.

Hugh's statement now struck a personal note. As one interested in the foregoing matters, he had wondered what he might do to promote them. As a result, he had decided that "it may be convenient for him to serve during the ensuing year as a representative in the assembly. . . ." Because attention to his law practice did not leave him time enough to discuss his candidacy with various individuals, he had adopted "a mode not usual, viz. to signify it in the Gazette." In this manner Hugh had found it possible to offer himself for election. "If after this declaration," he concluded, "it should so happen that he is not elected, there is no harm done, he will be perfectly satisfied."

Brackenridge's technique for winning office proved successful. This letter to prospective constituents was a demonstration of his manner of wooing popular support when not harassed by political enemies. As a democrat he believed in the fundamental goodness of his Westmoreland neighbors, and as reasonable and fair-minded people he had offered them his program. What he advocated would benefit the entire county. Evidently this was the general belief among the electors, for on October 10, the day of the annual general election for selecting their representatives in the state legislature, they chose him along with William Findley and James Barr to sit in the assembly.[27]

Hugh now considered the *Pittsburgh Gazette* as his own personal channel of communication with the public. He sent a notice[28] to the printers on October 30, informing them that he would return from Philadelphia, where the assembly sat, in time to attend to his law business at the next meeting of

the county courts. Brackenridge wanted his clients to know that he had no
intention of neglecting their interests because of his election to the legislature.
Such favors as the insertion of this notice by the printers he reciprocated in
full measure. Soon after his arrival in Philadelphia the news of Hall's death
came and also a plea for help from Scull who needed assistance in the printing
establishment. By December 16, Hugh had the problem solved. He had
arranged for the purchase of Hall's share of the equipment by a certain John
Boyd, who "now sets out to settle in our town." This information and much
more besides the new partner carried with him in a letter[29] of that date which
Brackenridge had prepared for publication in the *Gazette*. He owed an explanation, Hugh had written, for not appearing at the county courts as promised, although he planned to attend them in the spring and had meanwhile
arranged his legal affairs so that none of the clients would be injured by his
remaining in Philadelphia. Two factors detained him—the expected impass-
ability of the Susquehanna River when he would reach it and the "business"
which he had "instituted" in the assembly.

The proceedings in that house concerning the western country lay close to
Brackenridge's heart. He briefly described the transactions for the benefit of
his constituents. There was a bill published for the erection of a new county,
with Pittsburgh temporarily at least the seat of justice. Hugh hoped that this
arrangement would become permanent. Another bill published was one incorporating trustees for an academy to be established there. Hugh thought that
he might possibly obtain part of the reserved tract opposite Pittsburgh as
endowment for the school, because a bill providing for the sale of that land
had likewise been published. He himself had introduced a bill to establish
also in that town what he designated as "a religious Christian Society." He
was interested, moreover, in a plan for constructing a road between the Susquehanna and Allegheny rivers. He mentioned, too, a further object which he
had in mind: "I am about to try my hand in having all caveats tried by juries
of the county, and not in Philadelphia, at such immense distance. To deprive
of trial by jury, in the most essential right, is against the constitution." He
could report nothing concerning the excise laws, for that matter was still in
the hands of a committee. His "great object"—the Mississippi question—he
intended to submit for debate within several days. As the prime mover behind
much of this legislative activity Hugh had confidently rendered the electors
of Westmoreland a detailed account, which in his day was an innovation.

The report, however, contained a surprise for his fellow citizens. He had
opposed the measure permitting the use of certificates—depreciated paper
currency—in payment of patent money on old land rights: "This is a point I
had at heart, but on more knowledge of the subject, I saw it was not the

interest of the western country, nor perhaps the general interest of Pennsylvania." Hugh's stand shocked his constituents; it was well-nigh unthinkable. In the opinion of the irate inhabitant of Westmoreland whose land was at stake further explanation of Brackenridge's position was unnecessary.

In the eyes of his colleagues from Western Pennsylvania, Hugh was also a grievous sinner. He refused, for example, to operate according to the principle of party regularity, a determination which became evident at the outset of his legislative career. The bill for the establishment of a new county naturally aroused opposition from the representatives of the counties from which it would necessarily be carved. In order to win support for this measure Brackenridge had to join the opposite party in the legislature, becoming an "anti-constitutionalist"; whereas Findley and the other members from the West were "constitutionalists."[30] Hugh likewise differed with his western associates on the issue of the Bank of North America. Knowing how severely they condemned his independence, he accordingly resolved to defend himself through the columns of the *Gazette*.

But Hugh well knew that his defense in the public press could not wait until the end of the second session of the assembly and his return home in April. Already political opponents were attacking him scurrilously through pieces published in the *Gazette*, sufficient proof that he did not control its editorial policy. In mid-February, the issue of January 20, 1787, reached him in Philadelphia, containing a letter signed "A FARMER." This correspondent —"who insinuates that I have sold the good will of my country for *stockholders beef*"[31]—infuriated Brackenridge with the imputation of dishonesty in his voting against the use of certificates in the patenting of land under the old rights. Hugh was consequently in no judicious frame of mind when he wrote Scull and Boyd from his room in the Old Indian Queen on February 19. Because a representative must follow the instructions of his constituents, he explained, the electors of Westmoreland should send him directions for guidance in future debate on that subject if they disapproved of his vote. "At the same time they ought to be certain that they understand their own interest, and that they do not destroy the influence of their representative in the house, and disgrace themselves . . . ," added this candid legislator.

The attitude of the citizens of Pittsburgh was also inexplicable to Brackenridge. He therefore lectured them in a letter[32] written for publication at the same time as the one to Scull and Boyd. The people there, he had learned, were annoyed with him because he had referred to them in the assembly as "Christians" without mentioning any sect and had in addition introduced the bill for the incorporation of their church without calling it Episcopal or Presbyterian or anything else. "Now I am of the Christian faith as you are;

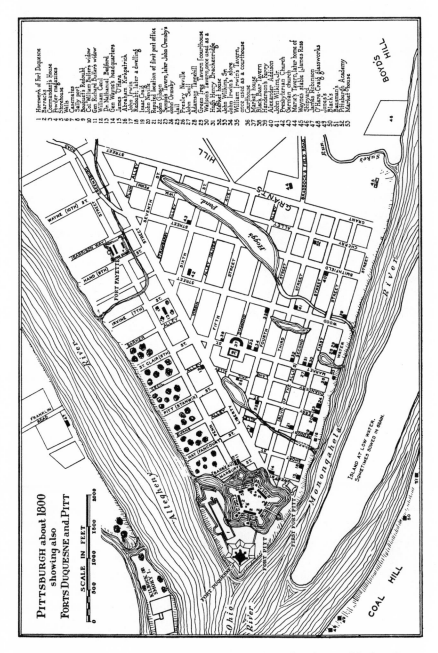

PITTSBURGH about 1800

showing also

FORTS DUQUESNE and PITT

SCALE IN FEET

0   500   1000   1500   2000

1 Horsework of Fort Duquesne
2 Barracks
3 Commandant's House
4 Powder magazines
5 Storehouse
6 Wells
7 Casemates
8 Sally port
9 Bouquet's Redoubt
10 Col. William Butler's widow
11 Gen Richard Butler's widow
12 William Cecil Bedford
13 Dr. Nathaniel Bedford
14 Gen Wayne's headquarters
15 James O'Hara
16 Abraham Kirkpatrick
17 John Irwin
18 Redoubt, later a dwelling
19 Isaac Craig
20 John Neville
21 Reputed location of first post office
22 John Gibson
23 Semple's Tavern, later John Ormsby's
24 John Ormsby
25 Jail
26 Presley Neville
27 John Scull
28 Adamson Tannehill
29 Green Tree Tavern (courthouse
30 Watson's Tavern, once used as a
31 Hugh Henry Brackenridge
32 Market house
33 John Wilkins, Sn.
34 John Irwin's store
35 William Irwin's tavern,
    once used as a courthouse
36 Courthouse
37 Market house
38 Black Bear Tavern
39 Henderson's Ferry
40 Alexander Addison
41 John Wilkins, Jr.
42 Presbyterian Church
43 German church
44 Marie's Tavern, later home of
45 Wayne's stable (James Ross
46 Shipyard
47 James Robinson
48 O'Hara-Craig glassworks
49 Jones's
50 Dick's
51 Bausman's
52 Pittsburgh Academy
53 Market house

BOYD'S HILL

PITTSBURGH ABOUT 1800: (31). H. H. Brackenridge home, Market Street
between First and Second Streets.

JUDGE HUGH HENRY BRACKENRIDGE
Portrait by Gilbert Stuart. Owned by University of Pittsburgh

but with respect to mode of church government, or mode of worship, they are with me of no moment," he asserted. "Having the same good opinion of your understanding that I have of my own, I had believed you would have thought so likewise." He could not resist making a sally:

... I had hoped that seated on the utmost verge of the inhabited globe, and separated from the Old World by a great mountain, you would have taken up things on the first principles, and presented a church like those in the time of the first apostles, distinguished by the name of *Christian* only, and have left it to divines in future times to dispute, as they now do, about those of Smyrna or Ephesus, whether you were Presbyterian or Episcopal.

This penchant for lacing his speech and correspondence with witticisms and a frequent resort to satire—or even sarcasm—put his career in the public service in jeopardy. Such outspokenness was not, however, a reliable indication of political naiveté, for Hugh enjoyed the give-and-take of disputation whatever the circumstances. An honorable man, he willingly admitted that he could be wrong on a particular issue, although he would never tolerate any implication that he had acted in bad faith or dishonesty. As Brackenridge sat in the assembly on March 5, somebody handed him a copy of the Pittsburgh newspaper containing in this instance a publication by Findley, who justified his own position concerning the matter of certificates and accused his fellow member from Westmoreland of saying that *"the people were fools"* and of claiming that he "would set things right in the *Pittsburgh Gazette*. . . ." Hugh immediately sent a hasty note[33] from the legislative chamber to Scull and Boyd, announcing that he had bowed to public opinion on the issue of the certificates and that with regard to his "vanity," to which Findley had referred, he promised to "be a little more modest for the future." Hugh realized his chief failing as an elective officeholder—indeed, as an active participant in public life—and acknowledged it: ". . . I am not the most guarded person in my speech. . . ." Anybody, he informed them, could take advantage of him by removing an expression of his from its context and then deliberately concealing the attendant circumstances which gave meaning to what was said— that is, any individual who was "malignant enough" to do so. In Brackenridge's opinion, Findley resented the "severity" with which he had been treated in their controversy about the Bank of North America. Finally, Hugh wrote that he would elaborate upon the entire situation after his return home: "In the mean time it will be fair [for the public] to suspend their judgment."

Ironically, this scholar-lawyer had apparently created the agent of his own ruin by encouraging the establishment of the first newspaper beyond the Alleghenies. At home in Pittsburgh that April, he saw at once the seriousness of his predicament. His first move in an attempt to restore himself in the public favor, however, was a warning note[34] to Scull and Boyd about the possible consequences of printing defamatory material, as the publication of a libel brought the printer within the pale of the law equally with the author.

Brackenridge's next step was the preparation of a series of articles for publication in the *Gazette*. They promptly appeared in eight installments[35] under the general heading of "To the INHABITANTS of the WESTERN COUNTRY." He presented a comprehensive review of the whole proceedings in the assembly, with emphasis on his own conduct and the origin of the enmity existing between Findley and himself. The series was a tour de force of sustained argument, with the first installment alone occupying about two and one-half pages of the four-page newspaper. His great object, of course, was to demonstrate how Findley had used a chance remark to defame him. Hugh charged John Smilie, of Fayette County, with complicity in this design to link two unrelated things—*"that the people were fools,* (God knows what people) and for this reason *I would write in the Pittsburgh Gazette"*—in order to destroy a political career: "Every candid person must see the violence of these men, when one of them retails a sentence of a conversation overheard, and the other splices it with what had no relation to it." No decent man could criticize Hugh's attitude, which was simply this: "I am willing that my judgment should be questioned, but not the rectitude of my intentions." He discussed every major issue which had arisen during the two sessions of the assembly—then he dropped his "pen for the present."

Findley, a weaver, a farmer, a shrewd politician, and the idol of backwoods democracy, was now unmistakably the leader of the opposition to Brackenridge. He was Hugh's bête noire. He was intent on destroying Hugh as a force in Westmoreland politics. Findley therefore published a series of eight articles[36] in the *Gazette,* entitled "OBSERVATIONS upon the ADDRESS of H. H. BRACKENRIDGE, Esq; to the INHABITANTS of the WESTERN COUNTRY." He was determined to implant in the minds of the electorate the idea that Hugh was a double-dealer—a person who courted the backwoodsmen for political advantage while his sympathies lay with the moneyed interests of the East. This learned lawyer was nothing but a political trickster, Findley cleverly insinuated. As his articles appeared one by one, Brackenridge could not remain silent, publishing in the *Gazette* two articles[37] with the title of "NOTES on the OBSERVATIONS of WILLIAM FINDLEY." Here he related how Findley during the bank debate had alluded to Hugh's private life "in low and illiberal language, and for this reason I treated him with *indignity."* Findley was, nevertheless, proving to be an efficient assassin of character.

But there were also admirers of Hugh's conduct in the legislature. He himself had solicited a certificate from Thomas Mifflin, the late speaker of the assembly, stating that Hugh had never spoken derogatorily of the inhabitants of Western Pennsylvania in the debate on the bank or at any other time. Mifflin complied at once with the request.[38] He could not recall any expressions disdainful of the people, adding that he had always regarded Brackenridge as their enthusiastic public servant. This statement quashed the accusation that Hugh had in debate referred to the backswoodsmen as "prowling wolves." Few of his friends and supporters, however, cared to sign encomiums with their own names, especially if they resided in Westmoreland County or in its vicinity. In the *Gazette,*[39] "A FARMER," who lived on the Conemaugh River, denounced Findley's attack on Hugh's character as "unwarrantable" and "unjust" and then effectively compared the conduct of both men in the assembly, with his remarks based on personal observation. This anonymous correspondent had divined the purpose of Findley's writings in the public press—they were "principally calculated to blacken the character of his colleague. . . ." The farmer wanted to know why the other representatives had not helped the back country as Hugh had done: "viz-Academy at Pittsburg; Incorporating the society there; Has a prospect of obtaining land for the academy; Five hundred pounds for laying off a road to the Canamaugh, laying off a town on the lake Erie, and several other things." There was evidence which Findley could not conceal! A Philadelphian[40] noted that Brackenridge had been so successful in aiding the western country because he had earned the good will of the eastern members in the assembly by voting to accommodate them in several instances. Hugh's addresses on the bank and the Mississippi problem, the correspondent observed too, were considered "equal to any of the speeches of Pitt and Fox in the house of commons in England." The Mississippi speech actually moved another person to express his esteem in poetry:

> OHIO's son thou well deserv'st the praise,
> Of genial fervor for thy western flood,
> For in the party vapour of these days,
> Thy noble object is the public good.[41]

On an issue of even greater moment than the Mississippi question—that of remodeling the national government—Brackenridge had also differed with his colleagues from the West. When he favored the calling of a convention for this purpose, he compounded his crimes of the past months according to their view. They became violent Anti-Federalists upon the completion of the Constitution of 1787 and its transmission by Congress to the states for ratification. Sectional in outlook, they feared the creation of a stronger central government which might threaten their particular interests. In a vain attempt to delay the summoning of a ratifying convention in Pennsylvania, Findley and the other Anti-Federalists had on one occasion absented themselves from the assembly, hiding from the sergeant at arms and the clerk. In that way the western members protested the haste with which the eastern conservatives were pushing the ratifying process.

These proceedings in the assembly Brackenridge recounted in prose and verse in the *Gazette*. In the crucial contest over the ratification of the Constitution, he was its most powerful defender in the western counties. His writings on the subject included not a single assay on government comparable to the articles which James Madison, Alexander Hamilton, and John Jay wrote to assist ratification of the Constitution in New York. Hugh used satire in his effort to demolish the Anti-Federalists' position and lampooned their conduct in the assembly in Hudibrastic verse. He concentrated his attack on Findley personally. Brackenridge published an account of the transactions in the assembly concerning the Constitution, concluding with the thought that if the people rejected it he could only say ". . . in the language of the prophet, 'O Israel thou art destroyed for lack of knowledge.' "[42] He framed a series of questions—"QUERIES to the ASSEMBLYMAN"[43]—designed to embarrass his chief antagonist, beginning in this humorous vein: "SIR, are you not Findley? Did you not abscond from the house the last two days of the session? Did you not *hasten your pace* when the serjeant at arms pursued you to take you?" Question by question Hugh gradually revealed the ludicrous happenings in Philadelphia as the Anti-Federalists tried to delay the calling of a ratifying convention. Their astonishing performance he retold in verse—"On the running away of the Nineteen Members of Assembly from the house, when it was proposed to call a convention to consider the new system of congressional government; and on the apology made by them in their address, &c. A Hudibrastic."[44] Brackenridge relied on ridicule to discredit the opposition to the Constitution.

This spirited defense of the new plan of government wrecked Hugh's hopes for an active political career, and it ruined his law practice. His colleagues from the western counties had little difficulty in convincing their constituents that the adoption of the Constitution would increase their taxes and endanger their cherished backwoods freedom. The farmers, furthermore, resented Hugh's jesting, particularly at the expense of Findley, who was after all one of them. They callously overlooked Hugh's exertions in their behalf, distrusting his statesmanlike attitude in considering not only the prosperity of his district but also the welfare of the state and country. They shunned Brackenridge. Newcomers to the bar, like James Ross, got his legal business.[45] Hugh would not leave Westmoreland because "pride and good policy" forbade such an easy solution to the problem. He would soon decide instead to keep silent on all public matters until the popular enmity for him had abated. "It was the first experience, I had ever had in life, of unpopularity, and I found it a thing more painful to sustain, and more difficult to remove, than I had thought it to be," he admitted in retrospect.[46] How galling it was to him when Findley was re-elected to the assembly along with James Barr in the general election for Westmoreland County in October of 1787.[47] The third representative chosen was John Irwin—not H. H. Brackenridge as had been the case the year before. On November 6, another blow fell as the citizenry of the county selected their delegates to the state ratifying convention. Three stanch Anti-Federalists were the victors—William Todd, John Baird, and Findley.[48]

Hugh's feelings were understandably bitter. His reward for zeal in the public service was condemnation. He believed that democracy required an enlightened electorate which valued the exercise of judgment by its representatives. But Findley, who flattered his constituents and therefore popular, was incapable of initiating policy. Brackenridge pondered his fate. Then he put his thoughts again in Hudibrastic verse, publishing in the *Gazette*[49] a satire entitled "On the Popularity of ...." This poem was a scathing characterization of his former colleague:

> WHENCE comes it that a thing like this,
> Of mind not bigger than a fly's,
> Should yet attract the popular favor,
> Be of his country thought the saviour,
> Sent to *assembly* and *convention*
> With votes almost without dissention.

In the poem Findley became "Traddle," a weaver who should have stayed busy at home instead of meddling in government. Much of the work was undeniably coarse, for in Hugh's opinion Findley—"this Teague Regan"—was indeed vulgar. The verses dripped venom because Hugh was subject to the same passions as all of his neighbors. But the poem was not solely the product of spite, for already he was beginning to plan a commentary on frontier manners and politics. Not even he knew what form it would eventually take.

Brackenridge was dispirited, although he had sufficient reason for boasting of his accomplishments. It was high time that a Westmoreland assemblyman had had the betterment of his town and county at heart, for, during the period from October 10, 1786 to May 12, 1787, the movement of immigrants to Kentucky was great: by actual count there had passed down the Ohio River "177 boats, 2689 people, 1333 horses, 766 cattle, 102 waggons, and 1 phaeton" and others unobserved during the night.[50] Hugh had realized the significance of Pittsburgh's location and the importance of exploiting it as well as fostering the cultural growth of the community. The measures which he had sponsored in the assembly were now one by one bearing fruit—in 1787, the incorporation of the Pittsburgh Academy (the future University of Pittsburgh[51]) and the Presbyterian Congregation; and in 1788, the erection of Allegheny County.

When Hugh read in the *Gazette* of February 23, 1788, that the Academy trustees were requested to meet at the home of David Duncan the next month for the consideration of important business, he knew that the school in particular was at last a reality.

Hugh's triumph was soon complete. The struggle for the ratification of the Constitution in the various states had continued throughout the winter of 1787-88 and into the following spring. The first three states to ratify were Delaware, Pennsylvania, and New Jersey—in that order and all in December. Then came Georgia, followed by Connecticut, Massachusetts, Maryland, and finally South Carolina late in May. Only one more state needed to ratify the Constitution in order to render it operative, an action which New Hampshire took on June 21. Virginia did not ratify until five days later. So intense was the fight generally, in some states desperate, that countless rumors flitted about the land, with a good many coming directly from Philadelphia to Pittsburgh over the road which Hugh thought resembled "the way to Heaven, rough, rugged, and difficult to pass."[52] On June 20, a false report reached town that Virginia was the ninth state to ratify the Constitution. Brackenridge and the Pittsburgh Federalists were exultant, not knowing that on the morrow New Hampshire would actually have the honor of casting the decisive vote.

A celebration[53] was in order. Early on Saturday evening, June 21, about fifteen hundred Pittsburghers and inhabitants of the surrounding country—men, women, and children—streamed up Grant's Hill, where, overlooking the junction of the rivers forming the Ohio, they awaited the festivities to begin and the words of the orator on this momentous occasion. Brackenridge, the attorney at law and ex-legislator, addressed them as follows:

> Oh my compatriots; I have great news to give you. A union of nine states has taken place, and you are now citizens of a new empire: an empire, not the effect of chance, nor hewn out by the sword; but formed by the skill of sages, and the design of wise men. Who is there who does not spring in height, and find himself taller by the circumstance? For you have acquired superior strength; you are become a great people.

Hugh did not speak long. When he had finished, the crowd cheered three times and tossed hats wildly in the air. The managers of the celebration kindled nine piles of wood symbolizing the ratifying states, leaving four intermediate piles, representing the states which had not yet adopted the Constitution, unlighted. But to these four they applied the torch, only to smother the flames at once with green leaves and branches. The pile of New Hampshire, nevertheless, blazed with remarkable splendor, as did that of Rhode Island which had tar and feathers and brimstone tossed into it because this state had not sent delegates to the convention in Philadelphia. Then the New York and North Carolina piles burst into flame. The thirteen crackling fires united in one

14

gigantic blaze lighting the night sky. As the young people danced about their roaring bonfire on the green, the Indian chiefs present grunted in astonishment and "concluded this to be a great council. . . ."

Was little Henry Marie Brackenridge, two years old now, somewhere in this throng clapping his hands in delight at the high jinks? He was likewise a citizen of the new nation.

II: Father and Son

As a child Henry was a homeless wanderer. He paid the price of Hugh's preoccupation with politics and literature and a dwindling law practice. Almost from the time of his birth, Henry was "cast upon the charity of an uncharitable world."[1]

Henry was so young (less than eighteen months old) when his mother died that he could not recall her appearance in later years.[2] The Christmas season of 1787 found him motherless, living apart from his father. Hugh had become a lodger at the home of John and Jane Marie, where Albert Gallatin spent the holiday with him.[3] But chance[4] was responsible for placing his son in the care of a cobbler's wife.

She lived in a log cabin rented from Henry's father, a circumstance, however, which did not ensure the boy a decent upbringing.[5] The cobbler and his wife, although a respectable enough couple, paid scant attention to Henry, having neither the means nor the desire to keep him well fed and clothed. But their son Joe took Henry in charge, the two boys becoming inseparable companions. Joe was an accomplished idler and mischief-maker, but on their escapades he guarded Henry "from all harm with the affection and ferocity of a tiger."

When Jane Marie visited Henry in the cobbler's house, his life there shocked her. She obtained Hugh's consent to bring the boy to her home, where kindly treatment resulted in a marked improvement in Henry's appearance and conduct.[6] This change in his situation was a happy one and fitting too, for Hugh had named his son "Henry Marie."

Jane and her husband were thrifty and industrious, already on their way to prosperity. In 1789, John was the owner of lots in the town of Pittsburgh, one or two of which he advertised for sale.[7] A few years later he was a merchant, displaying chintzes, calicoes, and shawls at his dwelling; and he was in the market for the purchase of rails, logs, posts, and clapboards.[8] In 1795, he sold brandy, Jamaica spirits, Madeira, loaf and brown sugar, coffee and chocolate.[9] Finally, on November 8, 1797, he announced the opening of his famous tavern, "the Sign of the BELL, on the Point of Grant's Hill, Fourth Street, in the Borough of Pittsburgh."[10] Busy though Jane obviously was, working hand in hand with John to achieve success, she lavished the attentions of a fond mother on Henry, having no children herself at the time of his arrival in her household.[11]

He was an impressionable child. When Hugh discovered this fact, that his son really had "an improvable intellect"[12] at the age of two, he at last showed some interest in him. Henry's imitation of the clergyman whom he had seen at church fascinated his father. Once when Henry played near his chair, Hugh could not resist looking up from his book and saying:

"Well, boy, can you do anything for your living?"

"I can make shoes," Henry answered, imitating the motions of a cobbler at his bench.

"You must learn to read," was Hugh's ominous reply.

Fortunately for Henry, Jane was usually near to intercede for him whenever he opposed the will of his father. Hugh was now determined to teach his son reading and gave him a hornbook for this purpose. Frequently Jane had to rescue a screaming, recalcitrant Henry from the switch in the hand of an equally resolute parent.[13] Naturally the boy was afraid of his stern father. But to this child Hugh also presented a fearsome appearance, with his large nose, florid face, and "clear and polished forehead"[14] from which he raised his spectacles when taking his eyes off a book and about to speak. He was, moreover, a powerfully built man, muscular from athletic training in his youth.[15] On one occasion an assailant clubbed Hugh on the shoulder without warning, never expecting him to take up the fight. Another time a fellow named Simpson made the mistake of drawing a sword on Brackenridge in the back room of an inn, finding himself suddenly dropped by a hurtling chair and his weapon smashed to the floor by the impact. Hugh completed the job by tossing the man onto the fire, where his clothes began to burn. Brackenridge was no weakling, nor was he an indulgent parent.

Excepting the lessons with the hornbook, Henry's life in the Marie home was pleasant. Hugh was generally kept busy at his office in the town leaving the boy free to absorb a variety of enduring impressions,[16] of which several were not agreeable to recall in later life. Henry once had to swallow some of Dr. Nathaniel Bedford's disgusting medicine—the taste lingered nauseously. A dog bit Henry under the left eye on another occasion. The treatment consisted of applying a bit of its hair to the wound. There was an Indian scare one night, with the whole town astir. These were all incidents vivid to Henry but still commonplace. He listened to the tinkling of the cowbells in the valley of Suke's Run—"the lonely, mournful sound." From the Marie house on Grant's Hill the boy saw the meeting of the rivers, the scene unobscured by smoke. Henry could, in fact, watch much that was happening in town.

Pittsburgh was a close-knit community. In Hugh's opinion, the inhabitants were "stowed away like persons in a jail, or on board a man of war,"[17] a situation fraught with explosive possibilities should gossips not restrain themselves. During the winter of 1788-89, talebearing appeared in town to his dismay. Hugh knew how quickly scandal could destroy the happiness of people in a small community. Because no clergyman capable of attacking this evil effectively had settled in Pittsburgh, Brackenridge decided to write a sermon[18] on the subject and then to publish it in the *Gazette*. He thought that the result of its publication in March of 1789 was beneficial to the village society.

"I know thy works, and where thou dwellest, *even* where Satan's seat *is*." Rev. 2:13. That was the text on which Hugh based his sermon. At the beginning he pointed out how ancient and widespread was the doctrine of the devil. The Biblical text "where Satan's seat *is*," Brackenridge explained, would indicate that the devil lived on the earth in some definite abode: "but our consolation is, that it cannot be in this town, for in that case, he would be too great a distance from the centre of his vast dominions; being on the very verge of the settled globe, I mean of close settlement and population." Why, then, were there evidences of his activity in Pittsburgh? Was he such a zealous devil that he did not wish to overlook this settlement in the western country? He undoubtedly had assistants to help manage his affairs: "It may therefore be set down as certain, that tho' this town cannot be the seat, or pandemonium of Satan himself, yet it may be the residence of some intendant, or sub-devil." Hugh assured his readers that he could speak with some authority, having studied the subject of the demon's character and his operations as assiduously as any astronomer ever probed the mysteries of the skies. In conducting his investigations, Hugh had tried to determine the one evil most prevalent in his community. "I have found this vice to be *tale bearing*," he reported confidently. He had also discovered that the subordinate demon responsible for inspiring it was a "little insignificant cur that could find no employment at the court or pandemonium of the great devil, or the more important parts of the empire, but was dispatched to this quarter as a remote situation." When Hugh analyzed the nature of this despicable vice, the subscribers to the *Gazette* ought to have blushed from shame. He concluded by giving them a few rules for dealing with scandalmongers and for avoiding the practice themselves.

For a time at least the townsmen mended their fault. But their morals needed a constant toning-up treatment. In this respect Pittsburgh was no different from most frontier towns in history. Talebearing, drinking, gambling, brawling, and dueling made up only a small part of the catalogue of questionable practices indulged by a majority of its inhabitants. Who would not drink whisky when it was a natural product of Western Pennsylvania? Who could resist betting on a favorite horse at the gala Pittsburgh Races when as early as September 5, 1786 —and no doubt even earlier—the Jockey Club announced attractive purses and track rules which included the warning that "No Jocky will be permitted to ride unless he has some genteel Jocky Habit"?[19]

About the same time that the appearance of scandal had disquieted Hugh, he met his match in repartee during a discussion which suddenly shifted to the subject of morals. So rarely did anyone thus best him that the *Gazette*[20] reported the following to its readers:

BON MOT
Of DAVID SAMPLE, Esquire

At the last county court of Westmoreland, the conversation turning on Indians, treaties, &c. it was observed by Mr. Brackenridge; an Indian of spirit loves his squaw, builds his cabbin, and goes to hunt: it is only the indolent and worthless that lurk about agents, come to towns, and go to treaties and pass for chiefs. The Cornplanter for instance, was a clever fellow some time ago, but loitering so much about Pittsburgh, particularly of late, that he has lost his character among his own people. I never had a high opinion, said Mr. Sample, of the morals of Pittsburgh, but I had not supposed them so utterly abandoned, that a savage losses character by associating with them.

Many Pittsburghers were certainly lax in the application of moral principles to the conduct of business. They did not practice the golden rule. Grasping merchants were fast giving the town a bad name by the exorbitant prices put on their wares. What Pittsburgh needed, of course, was an adequate supply of labor, especially of artificers whose products made here in the western country would be unencumbered with heavy transportation charges and could therefore be sold more cheaply. The printer Scull, aware of this need, published an "Invitation to Emigrants"[21] in the spring of 1789. "Every office except that of the president of the United States, is open to the meanest and most indigent emigrant, if he possesses talents, industry and virtue to assist his progress," Scull mentioned as an important inducement to settling in Pittsburgh. The artisan or laborer, he continued, could earn a good living here: a shoemaker, for example, could buy 180 pounds of wheat, making 120 pounds of flour, or more than 60 pounds of pork or beef with a pair of shoes worth 11*s*. 3*d*. Scull believed that his fellow citizens should employ workmen who lived in their own town or county rather than those at a distance: "We want people, we want sober and diligent tradesmen; hatters, button makers, rope makers, weavers, &c. . . . ." The merchants meanwhile profited from the scarcity of labor—and some outrageously.

Of this fact John Pope was convinced. On June 1, 1790, he had left Richmond, Virginia, on the first stage of a tour which would eventually take him to Kentucky, Louisiana, and the Floridas.[22] He had crossed the Alleghenies and had then taken a boat bound for Kentucky at the junction of the Redstone and the Monongahela, reaching Pittsburgh from this point in twenty-three hours in the month of October.[23] Here he spent ten days, ample time in which to visit all parts of the town and adjacent country and to interview the leading citizens. "Goods of every Description are dearer in *Pittsburg* than in *Kentuckey,* which I attribute to a Combination of pensioned Scoundrels who infest the Place," Pope charged.[24] Hugh had taken this traveler to see Fort Pitt and other spots of interest in the vicinity.

But to Pope, Brackenridge was the outstanding attraction in Pittsburgh. The night of his arrival in town, he had composed a poem in honor of Hugh's recent marriage and had sent it to him hopefully as a means of introduction—"*To H. H. BRECKENRIDGE, Esq; on his being fairly NOOS'D.*"[25] So laughable was this production that Hugh not only forwarded it to the *Gazette* for publication but struck up an acquaintance with its author immediately.

The circumstances of Hugh's courtship and marriage of Sabina Wolf fascinated Pope, whose version of the affair subsequently became the best known. According to his account, one day a storm had forced Brackenridge, who was riding the circuit, to seek shelter at the home of a German farmer in Washington County. Hugh had asked to have his horse fed and had then waited for the rain to stop. The downpour had been so heavy that he requested his horse be brought to the door of the house in order to avoid getting wet feet. Jacob Wolf told his daughter to do this—much to Hugh's astonishment, for

> Nut brown were her Locks, her Shape was full strait,
> Her Eyes were as black as a Sloe;
> Milk white were her Teeth, full smart was her Gait,
> And sleek was her Skin as a Doe.

Brackenridge himself went to the stable for the horse and continued on his way. But Sabina had so enamored him that before long he turned back to revisit her home, where he at once solicited Wolf with a request to marry her. Hugh had to plead his cause carefully, for his reputation had led the farmer to believe that this wit was now jesting. Still the farmer hesitated to give his consent because the girl cleared his meadow of shrubbry growth every year, saving him about ten dollars each time. Such a situation did not discourage Hugh who promptly paid Wolf money to cover his loss, won Sabina's approval, and married her. At the time of their marriage Brackenridge was about forty-two years old.

For Henry this event was portentous. Not for many years would he realize how much it would affect his future; when he did, the knowledge of it would make his heart bleed. In 1790, however, his father re-established the Brackenridge home, removing Henry from the care of Jane Marie.[26] Hugh soon sent Sabina "to *Philadelphia,* where she . . . is under the Governance of a reputable female Character, whose Business will be to polish the Manners, and wipe off the Rusticities which Mrs. *Breckenridge* had acquired whilst a *Wolfe.*"[27]

Squire Wolf, a justice of the peace, liked his stepgrandson. He took Henry to the farm,[28] where the boy quickly learned to speak the German dialect used in the household. He also went to school, which was only two or three miles from the Wolf homestead but far enough for him to freeze his fingers and toes on the way back one cold day. The grandparent, who had hurried Henry to the distillery, thawed them there in cold water. Wolf, incidentally, closed his distillery long before the rise of the temperance movement in the belief that he had no right to produce an intoxicating liquor ruinous to healthful and moral living. The most exciting incident during Henry's stay at the farm was the successful attempt of his older schoolmates to win a Christmas holiday of two weeks from their teacher. When he and his pupils had reached what seemed like an impasse, they managed to bar him from the log-cabin school. The indignant master started down the chimney only to retreat upward when confronted with fire, hot ashes, and menacing firebrands pointed at him. Reluctantly he granted the vacation period demanded.

This absence of both his wife and son from Pittsburgh, temporary though it was, proved a blessing to Hugh. He was busy rebuilding his law practice, destroyed by his forthright opposition to the politics of Findley and the other legislators from Western Pennsylvania. Any person interested enough in the official conduct of these representatives could subscribe to the *Proceedings and Debates of the General Assembly of Pennsylvania,* which Thomas Lloyd recorded in shorthand and promptly published, beginning with the third session of the eleventh assembly.[29] Consequently no one was solely dependent on the gazettes for such information. But who in the western counties cared to examine the record objectively? ". . . I had thought to have defended myself by writing, but only made the matter worse," Hugh reasoned later, "for the people thought it impossible, that plain simple men could be wrong, and a profane lawyer right."[30] Hugh, nevertheless, sought nomination as a candidate for a seat in the new Congress of the United States, being himself very active in the canvass.[31] But neither party—Federalist or Anti-Federalist—would support him.[32]

Brackenridge at last surrendered his ambition to serve the public in an elective office. He now devoted himself to legal business and to literature, the latter pursuit gradually monopolizing his attention as he reviewed his brief political career and then sought to give meaning to his experience by use of the pen.

He first employed Hudibrastic verse in the manner of his castigation of Findley in the satire "On the Popularity of ...." In 1788-89, Hugh wrote a lengthy narrative poem entitled "The Modern Chevalier,"[33] again transmogrifying Findley into "Traddle." In this work Hugh directed his knight to a cabin inhabited by a "weaver who had serv'd the state," but who was at that moment working at his loom. The chevalier, seized with a desire to know why any man was content to labor in a cellar and to be of no importance in society, moved to the window and addressed him, damning the weaver's lowly occupation and exhorting him to

> Arise and shake your slumber off;
> You have capacity enough;
> Assume your place in state affairs,
> And get up to the top o' th' stairs.

The knight who had thrust his head through the window in the excitement of his speech did not see the approach of the weaver's wife but felt instead the blow of her cudgel upon his rump. Resisting the impulse to strike with his sword, he beseeched her for an explanation of her anger. Experience had taught her, she replied, that Traddle was better off busy at his loom than engaged in politics as he had once been, much to the knight's surprise. She did not want anyone to entice her husband from his work again, although

> . . . there is not far off a writer
> To whom I bear a little spite here,
> Because he laughs at Traddle's nonsense
> Which is not equal to his own sense,
> And says it is a vile state slur
> To chuse him for a senator . . . .

The knight found this rhymester in a garret, where the two immediately discussed the role Traddle should play in political affairs. Later the knight addressed a group of people on the same subject, insisting that only the qualified person should be chosen for public office. Next he consulted a conjurer on the matter, and also a philosopher who explained the phenomenon why the people elected the worst candidates to represent them in government—thereby ending the story.

This poem inspired[34] Hugh to write his novel *Modern Chivalry: Containing Adventures of Captain John Farrago, and Teague O'Regan, His Servant,* the first book by a back-country author. He naturally progressed from the one literary form to the other as he viewed his political experience more and more from a less personal standpoint, the Westmoreland voters, for example, becoming the American electorate in his mind. He was like the painter whose work required a broader canvas.

Thus in 1790,[35] Brackenridge was already at work satirizing the manners of his fellow citizens. He had the leisure for this project; as a matter of fact, "It is a good deal owing to my solitary residence in the western country, at a distance from books and literary conversation, that I have been led to write at all. It was necessary to fill up the interstices of business."[36] Hugh frankly wanted his novel to be a paying proposition, selling at least enough copies to defray the cost of printing. In 1792, he himself read the proof sheets of the first volume in the shop of John M'Culloch, No. 1, North Third Street, in Philadelphia, at the same time applying successfully for admission as a counselor in the Supreme Court of the United States.[37] The second volume also issued from this press the same year. But the third was an altogether different matter, for its publication by Scull in Pittsburgh in 1793 was a significant literary event in the western country. On February 23, the printer inserted a notice in his *Gazette* advertising the volume as ready for sale at 3*s.* 9*d.;* and in his issue of April 13, he noted that a "few copies of the first and second Volume may be had in this town." Brackenridge in subsequent years added to his work, a fourth volume, for instance, appearing in 1797.[38]

Hugh's wit as evidenced in *Modern Chivalry* was irrepressible. Responsible for this propensity for satire, he claimed, was his habit of reading Lucian in the original Greek as a student and of acquainting himself with the modern satirists like Cervantes and Swift. He soon thought and wrote as they did, a practice which involved him in "broils with individuals" and rendered him "obnoxious to public bodies. . . ." He therefore tried to avoid the use of satire: "It may be said of satire, what was said of anger by some philosopher, It never pays the service it requires . . . I never knew any good come of wit and humour yet."[39] In writing this work, Hugh proved himself to be a master practitioner of the satiric style.

Likewise with tongue in cheek, he averred that the purpose of his writing *Modern Chivalry* was to furnish a model of "good language"—and of "good writing"—useful to authors and orators and conducive to fixing "orthography, choice of words, idiom of phrase, and structure of sentence. . . ."[40] His sole object, in short, was "the giving an example of a perfect stile in writing. . . ."[41] This aim precluded any attempt to write a work containing some thought or some degree of sense: it would necessarily be "a book without thought, or the smallest degree of sense. . . ." as Hugh considered the maxim—one thing at once—the soundest ever devised by man.[42] "The truth is, as I have said, I value this book for little but the stile," he reiterated. "This I have formed on the model of Xenophen, and Swift's Tale of a Tub, and Gulliver's Travels. It is simple, natural, various, and forcible. I hope to see it made a school book; a kind of classic of the English language."[43] His style actually possessed these characteristics—and authenticity. A real westerner, Hugh excelled in the use of the ribald and exaggerated language of the American frontier.

This byplay involving the matter of style Brackenridge found useful as a means for introducing witty comment on a variety of subjects, as, for example, on the literary critics and more especially on the savants of the academies. In the introduction to the third volume, Hugh discussed style and critics at length, in an ingenious way conveying the idea that his own work was written "in the same pure, simple attic taste"[44] as that of such authors as Swift and Addison. Into the text of this section he incorporated Hudibrastic verses on

The critic, sir's, the natural father
Of every snifling, snuffling author;[45]

an oration[46] on Liberty to serve as proof that he could "rise to the swell of the highest pipe of diction";[47] and a poem,[48] a Hudibrastic also, on the Society of the Cincinnati. By interspersing this particular kind of subject matter among the chapters containing the tale of Captain Farrago and his servant Teague, Hugh obviously hoped to entice his reader into a careful reading of the whole work, a treatment resulting, however, in a lack of balance. But such a defect in his novel did not trouble him.

There was no reason why it should. Hugh intended *Modern Chivalry* to be discursive so that he could comment on various foibles of his fellow man as he led the Captain and Teague from one adventure to another. With such a construction, of course, Hugh could always add chapters or even volumes to the work whenever a new idea worth exploiting occurred to him. The favorable reception of one volume by the public encouraged him to proceed with the next,[49] continuing his narrative which was in the style of Cervantes' *Don Quixote*.

The tale begins with a singular thought striking John Farrago, a bachelor aged about fifty-three, at one time of his life an insignificant captain of militia, and now as most of his life a kind of gentleman farmer. His servant at the moment happened to be an Irishman named Teague O'Regan. An urge one day suddenly seized Farrago "to saddle an old horse that he had, and ride about the world a little, with his man Teague at his heels, to see how things were going on here and there, and to observe human nature."[50]

The two adventurers had not gone far, perhaps twenty miles, when they approached a racecourse. Here the jockeys assumed that Farrago planned to enter his lean nag for the purse, an intention which he denied having; but upon his denial, they believed that the horse was surely a "bite"—that notwithstanding an ungainly appearance, it was fast. Not caring to be bit by a bet, they questioned the Captain insistently about the animal's pedigree. Farrago, annoyed, addressed them on the subject, contending that a pedigree, whether it be in horses or in men, was of no consequence: "The jockeys thought the man a fool, and gave themselves no more trouble about him."[51] The race over, a fight broke out concerning the winner. The fact that gentlemen could be so indecent impelled Farrago to tell them about the courtesy characteristic of the Olympic games in ancient Greece. At this point somebody pushed the Captain off his horse, but fortunately Teague was at hand to help him on again. Farrago, sustaining only a slight bump on the head, finally drank a quantity of grog and retired for the night after undergoing a vexatious examination by a surgeon.

As Hugh indicated[52] for his reader's benefit, certain reflections occur to a person familiar with the Captain's experience. Farrago was a man of sound judgment because he had not entered his nag, a satisfactory plow horse only, in the race. The proverb—let the cobbler stick to his last—expresses the idea involved in the decision which the Captain had to make. But he was a naive man, untutored in the ways of the world, to think "that jockeys and men of the turf could be composed by reason and good sense. . . ." Another reflection is "the professional art of the surgeon to make the most of the case, and the technical terms used by him." But Hugh observed in addition that Farrago was "wrong in declining his prescriptions; for the maxim is, *Unicuique in arte, sua perito, eredendum est;* every one is to be trusted in his profession."

The experience of the Captain the next day was still more astonishing. He arrived at a place where an election for choosing a member of the state legislature was in progress. The contest for the seat involved a weaver (Traddle, Findley!) and an educated man who warned the crowd about the incompetence of his opponent. Farrago saw a chance to address the people in the same tenor: ". . . to rise from the cellar to the senate house, would be an unnatural hoist . . . There is no analogy between knotting threads and framing laws."[53] Then the Captain drew Traddle aside in an attempt to persuade him to withdraw as a candidate. At this moment Teague decided that he had the qualifications to be a legislator; and the crowd seemed to agree with him, at least not opposing his unexpected candidacy. Informed of this startling development concerning his bogtrotting servant, Farrago addressed the people again:

. . . A free government is a noble possession to a people: and this freedom consists in an equal right to make laws, and to have the benefit of the laws when made. Though doubtless, in such a government, the lowest citizen may become chief magistrate; yet it is sufficient to possess the right; not absolutely necessary to exercise it. Or even if you should think proper, now and then, to shew your privilege, and exert, in a signal manner, the democratic prerogative, yet is it not descending too low to filch away from me a hireling, which I cannot well spare, to serve your purposes?[54]

The angry Captain did not mince his words. Resentful, the electors were insistent regarding their rights to choose Teague to represent them.

Consequently Farrago's only hope was to remonstrate effectively with his servant where the crowd could not overhear the conversation. He explained to Teague the qualifications and the onerous duties of the legislator. Farrago reminded him also of the unpleasantness of public criticism and ridicule: "It is the devil in hell to be exposed to the squibs and crackers of the gazette wits and publications." The Captain (Hugh!) could vouch for the truth of this. "You have nothing but your character, Teague, in a new country to depend upon," Farrago admonished him. "Let it never be said, that you quitted an honest livelihood, the taking care of my horse, to follow the new fangled whims of the times, and to be a statesman."[55] The whole argument was too persuasive for Teague to ignore. When he declined their proffered honor, the people elected the weaver as their representative instead.

25

The Captain's troubles incident to Teague's aspiration to rise in the world, unforeseen at the start of their journey, had now begun. The servant could not seem to avoid some form of honor almost day by day as they proceeded toward Philadelphia, then the capital of the United States. They quarreled, for instance, when a philosopher proposed Teague as a member of the American Philosophical Society. But the bogtrotter was really a rascal much given to falsehood—a rogue who would accuse a clergyman of attacking an innkeeper's daughter in order to shift suspicion from himself. Teague, nevertheless, decided to become a candidate for the ministry. Farrago had to work hard to frustrate him in such efforts to get ahead. There was a scheme to make the servant a king of the Kickapoos, a plan which the Captain had to ruin. When Teague wanted to be a lover, to woo a certain Miss Sally, the Captain had him whipped through artifice. Farrago had to hoodwink him time after time in order to rid his mind of silly notions. But the pushing servant nearly married a gentlewoman, a maiden easily persuaded; he did become an actor in a theater, although quickly dismissed because of an indiscretion. He wished to be a lawyer, actually attended a presidential levee, and undertook a course of training in manners, including dancing lessons, to fit himself for a post in government, a process which inspired "a kind of Teagueomania, amongst the females"[56] of Philadelphia.

At this point in the tale, Hugh ended the third volume, which was the first book both written and published west of the Alleghenies. He himself read the proof sheets furnished by Scull. This fact Hugh confided in a separate section entitled "Conclusion of the Third Volume." Brackenridge also felt obligated to tell his reader something about Teague's future: "As to the fate of the bogtrotter, I must leave the matter in suspence until the fourth volume, when I shall dispose of him to as much advantage as possible."[57] There was another matter for the reader to consider, Hugh advised: ". . . I wish I could get this work to make a little more noise."[58] Why did not somebody either praise it or condemn it? Was every critic in Philadelphia asleep?

Hugh had only to be patient, for what he had written was so clever and so provocative that it would always be meaningful and appreciated in a democracy no matter what the age. Time would prove that he had composed a classic satire ridiculing the follies of his day. He poked fun at the general state of morals, the stupidity of most people, and their irresistible urge to push themselves forward in society and in government. He left no doubt about his dislike of such things as orthodoxy, Hamiltonian finance, the pomposity of the erudite, and the levees of President Washington. Hugh's work, born of disillusionment, effectively satirized the manners not only of the boorish backwoodsman but also of the eastern politician who was invariably one of the "fat swabs, that guzzle wine, and smoke segars."[59] Hugh's theme, therefore, was not provincial, although he pilloried primarily the shortcomings of his neighbors in Western Pennsylvania.

Brackenridge's contest with Findley had thus become a personal war against demagoguery. Hugh saw clearly the defects of democracy, that in particular it could raise too easily the unprincipled and the unfit to posts of high power. Democracy therefore required an enlightened electorate insistent on selecting only the qualified for public service. There was no place for selfish and pushing politicians who did not have the welfare of their country at heart, nor was there any reason why sectional interests should prevail over the national. Hugh himself had tried to translate political theory into political action by playing the part of a legislator who, although bound by the collective will of his constituency, was an initiator of policy, an independent thinker. By detecting and exposing the weaknesses of democracy in the new and struggling nation, Hugh had performed a magnificent service for his fellow citizens.

Modern Chivalry grew fast in the public estimation. "Twenty years ago this work . . . was the humorous text book of all classes of society, here away," wrote the editor of Pittsburgh's lively journal, the *Literary Examiner, and Western Monthly Review*, in 1839. "It was to the West what Don Quixote was to Europe—a satirical lash to whip the follies of the times and excoriate mendacious ignorance." Hugh's wit, wrote this critic, was as "keen as a Damascus scimitar."[60] The first edition of the entire work eventually went out of print, with proud owners of copies rarely parting with them. *Modern Chivalry* also survived the twentieth-century criticism, indeed was enhanced by it. Vernon Louis Parrington read the whole book with immense satisfaction, dubbing its author the "Free-Lance Democrat."[61]

But for Hugh's son Henry the greatest thrill imaginable was reserved when, as a young man, he was addressed by a gentleman in New Madrid on the Mississippi:

"From your name, sir," said he, "may I ask whether you are related to the author of 'Modern Chivalry'?"

"I felt an indescribable emotion when the question was put, and replied with a degree of satisfaction which was not concealed, 'Sir, I am his son.'"

"What!" said he, "the son of the author of 'Modern Chivalry'!"

"The exclamation reminded me of the honor done to Grotius, although that sage had the satisfaction of enjoying it in person."[62]

As a child, however, Henry had returned to Pittsburgh from Squire Wolf's farm before Scull published the third volume of the work. The farmer and his young charge rode on horseback into town, descending Coal Hill where the smell of smoke was strong. The boy took especial note of the sycamores with their bark white as milk lining the bank of the Monongahela.[63]

Pittsburgh was much the same as when he had left it, with one exception. The hogs which many of the people owned but neglected to pen were becoming more and more of a nuisance by destroying one garden after another. Finally, irate inhabitants consulted Henry's father on the matter. Hugh held that the keeping of swine was indictable under the common law because Pittsburgh was not only a market town now but a county town as well and the seat of a law court.[64]

But Henry did not remain long in Pittsburgh, which was still so countrified, playing with his friend Joe. That his son had learned to speak some German impressed Hugh favorably, for he subscribed to the saying "that a man doubles himself by learning another language."[65] The elder Brackenridge soon announced his intention of sending Henry to a village in Louisiana where he could live with a French family and quickly learn their language also. This was certainly a novel idea no matter what plan of education Hugh was forming in his mind for Henry's benefit—sending his son on a dangerous journey fifteen hundred miles through the wilderness to learn French! Henry himself would write years later that although "I escaped many dangers, both physical and moral, yet I think it probable that a direction was given to my feelings rather unfavorable to my success in life."[66] The truth was that Hugh had another reason for sending him away in addition to his learning a new language. In one respect, and not an uncommon one, Hugh lacked courage. But this cause of Henry's early wanderings—the objections of Hugh's new wife—the father would not confess until near death.

III: Ste. Genevieve

Hugh surely realized the enormity of his decision to send Henry to Louisiana in 1793. But the menacing situation on the American frontier—from Canada to the Gulf of Mexico and the Floridas—did not deter him from seizing the opportunity presented by a French trader who offered to place the boy in the care of a family residing in the Mississippi village of Ste. Genevieve.[1] The spring and summer months of this year proved to be among the most critical ever experienced in the whole history of the new republic.

The crosscurrents of international politics were threatening to tear the United States asunder. Hurriedly the Washington administration had to devise a definitive foreign policy for a government only four years old with little standing in the world community. Revolutionary France, whose leaders had decapitated Louis XVI in January and shocked many Americans, but not Hugh nor Thomas Jefferson, confronted the First Coalition as summer began. The French aimed to spread the principles of republicanism—the Rights of Man—over the face of the earth, to assist the oppressed everywhere who dragged the chains of tyranny, including their former brothers in Louisiana. Would the people of the United States aid their old ally of 1778 in defiance of the monarchs of Europe? That was the awesome question which the American citizenry began to debate in the spring. Was there to be war or no war?

The problem of neutrality split the American populace in two. The Anti-Federalists, who now in 1792-93 were the opponents of Alexander Hamilton's financial policy and his pro-British attitude, wanted to help France in her time of trouble. They advocated either outright aid to the sister republic on the continent or a neutrality benevolent to her. These Francophiles under the leadership of Jefferson, the secretary of state, were small landholders, urban workers, southern merchants, and frontiersmen primarily, with a few professional men included in their ranks; all were republicans and some, zealous democrats. The Federalists, marshaled by Hamilton, the secretary of the treasury, were bankers, planters, merchants, clergymen, and land speculators; all were Anglophiles, favoring a strict neutrality beneficial to their own commercial interests and to Great Britain. In April the arrival of Edmond Charles Genet, the first minister to the United States from the Republic of France, threw the entire country into an uproar which did not abate until late summer and early fall when it became apparent that his mission would shortly be a total failure. The American people, meanwhile, had gone mad in their fervent advocacy of the one cause or the other; the nation was near disruption by party spirit.

Hugh was an out-and-out Francophile. He linked the preservation of democracy in America with the success of France. On July 4, Grant's Hill was the scene of a patriotic celebration[2] at which a number of Pittsburghers heard an oration[3] by Brackenridge. "Shall kings combine, and shall republics not unite?" he asked dramatically. "We have united. The heart of America feels the cause of France . . . Can we be indifferent? Is not our fate interlaced with hers?" The celebrators seated themselves at the festive board in a booth near by when Hugh had concluded his remarks with the order to "pour out libations to sentiments of liberty, and let the loud mouthed artillery be heard on the hill." The toasts which followed echoed his sentiments.

When Hugh spoke, the American people had still to evince their collective will. No one dared to predict whether the Federalists' policy of impartial neutrality would win popular favor or not. In July the situation was touch and go, with the officers of the federal government striving desperately to steer the ship of state into a safe channel.

But the westerners, for whom Brackenridge was in this instance a spokesman, were no longer interested in the development of an American policy which might conceivably allay their distress in the future. They demanded that their grievances be redressed at once. The Spanish control of the Mississippi enraged them. They denounced the British retention of military posts on the northern and northwestern frontier. The Indian policy of Spain infuriated them. They hated the Hamiltonian excise law. The West, seething with discontent, was astir with preparations for direct action, a resort to force. Sympathetic with the principles of her Revolution, the frontiersmen had sought the aid of France and promptly received it.

The Girondist government had sent Genet to the United States with instructions to negotiate a new treaty of mutual assistance and alliance, seeking to liberate Spanish America, to open the navigation of the Mississippi to American trade without restriction, and to assist the Canadians to overthrow British rule. An extraordinary assignment the visionary leaders of France had given their envoy, a young and impetuous man. As soon as he had landed at Charleston, South Carolina, he had launched the vast enterprise against the Spanish by planning a co-ordinated attack on the Floridas and Louisiana. Already in February, George Rogers Clark, a neglected hero of the Revolutionary War, had solicited French support for a descent on New Orleans. The minister had subsequently accepted his proposals and commissioned him a major general in command of the Independent and Revolutionary Legion of the Mississippi, authorized to raise and direct troops for their design.

Genet chose André Michaux, a French botanist, to act as his political agent in the West. This Frenchman had obtained the backing of the American Philosophical Society for a proposed expedition to explore the country along the Missouri River and thence to the Pacific, receiving official instructions from

Jefferson himself. The minister saw in his compatriot an excellent emissary to send to Kentucky with a message for Clark and with French commissions to distribute to westerners desirous of joining the project. On July 15, Michaux left Philadelphia at ten o'clock in the evening to avoid the stifling heat as much as possible, reaching Pittsburgh twelve days later. On July 28, the day after his arrival, he visited Brackenridge,[4] undoubtedly discussing the political outlook in the West with him. Michaux spent the next week botanizing in the vicinity, particularly on the banks of the Monongahela, although not resuming his journey until August 14. While in Pittsburgh he noted that the townsmen were demolishing Fort Pitt "to use the bricks in building the houses that are being erected every day. . . ."[5] In this fashion, talking politics and studying plants, Michaux made his way westward. Genet had also empowered this agent to treat with the Indians in the Mississippi region and with the French in Louisiana.

The frontiersmen were convinced that the British instigated the Indian depredations in the Ohio country. They accused the British also of supplying the red men with arms and ammunition. The Indian policy of Spain the westerners likewise condemned for the same reason. The savages persistently plundered the whole frontier from north to south. The Washington administration had tried to ease the menace by negotiating treaties whenever practicable, by garrisoning various part of the borderland, and by sending expeditions under General Josiah Harmar and Governor Arthur St. Clair of the Northwest Territory into the Ohio region. But in 1790, the Indians defeated Harmar ignominiously; and the next year, they destroyed St. Clair's army.

The red men grew bolder, and the westerners angrier and more impatient. In 1792, President Washington gave General Anthony Wayne the task of eradicating the Indian threat in the Ohio Valley. Wayne's first problem when he reached Pittsburgh was to assemble an army from the assorted recruits and regulars available, his second was to train them in the art of Indian fighting. He established a camp at a place which he named "Legionville," on the Ohio nineteen miles from Pittsburgh. Plagued by desertions and faced with organizing his Legion of the United States to suit the demands of Indian warfare, Wayne became a strict disciplinarian. In February, 1793, Captain John Finley, an assistant quartermaster stationed at Legionville, requested Major Isaac Craig in Pittsburgh to "send down some whip cord for cats,—they have no cats to whip men with."[6] The General, not intending to meet the fate of Harmar and St. Clair, would devote nearly two years to the preparation of his army for the struggle. Detachments of men meanwhile passed through Pittsburgh on their way to the encampment.[7] With Wayne seemingly inactive, the Indians became more impudent than ever, in mid-May stealing "seven horses belonging to Elliot and Williams, from the west side of the Allegheny" and only about two miles from Pittsburgh. [8]

The Indian danger did not discourage the western trader, who continued his activities determinedly. Nothing, in fact, could block the movement of settlers into the wilderness—neither the policies of Great Britain and Spain nor the depredations of the red men. The situation served as a challenge to Jacob Myers of Pittsburgh who established a packet line to Cincinnati in the fall. Launching his service with two boats operating on a fortnightly schedule —the first to leave Pittsburgh on October 21 and the second on November 5— he had two more on the ways nearing completion. Myers constructed his vessels with the Indian menace along the Ohio in mind. "No danger need be apprehended from the enemy, as every person on board will be under cover, made proof against rifle or musket balls, and convenient port holes for firing out of," he claimed in his *Gazette*[9] announcement. "Each of the Boats are armed with six pieces carrying a pound ball; also a number of good muskets, and amply supplied with necessary ammunition, strongly manned with choice hands, and the masters of approved knowledge." The vessels boasted separate cabins for the lady passengers, conveniences which made landings in dangerous places unnecessary, and an abundance of food and liquor at a fair price. Besides passengers the boats carried freight and letters. Persons using the service could if they wished insure their property at offices maintained at Pittsburgh, Limestone, and Cincinnati.

Any business venture in the West at this time was hazardous. Frequently a trader encountered an appalling amount of misfortune. Some merchants, for instance, built a sloop on the Ohio not far from Pittsburgh and then loaded it with tobacco and peltry for Philadelphia. They unloaded their cargo at New Orleans, paid the duty on its value, reloaded the goods, and paid the charge for that privilege. To get clearance for their vessel, they converted her into a Spanish bottom, obtaining a Spanish captain and crew, and they themselves sailed as mere passengers. But a privateer, outfitted at Philadelphia and with Pennsylvanians in her crew, captured their sloop! "Instead of erecting a monument, which they rather deserve, to the honour of men who teach us how easily our commerce may be extended by shipping from the Western Waters, even to the distance of Pittsburg," wrote an incensed correspondent to the editor of a Philadelphia newspaper, "our Privateers' men are like to send those men home broken merchants, a monument of the effects of faction or a government within a government."[10] If the sloop in question was the "Alodia," which happened to be captured by the famous Genet privateer, the "Little Democrat," the incident had a happy ending, for this prize, seized by the Pennsylvania militia, was restored to the owners.[11]

Despite the risks involved in trading on the western waters, John B. C. Lucas, a Frenchman who had settled on a farm near Pittsburgh, had planned a voyage down-river in the spring of this year, 1793. He was an admirer of Hugh, having "cultivated his acquaintance without interruption, as a literary and a philosophic man."[12] Brackenridge in turn had befriended Lucas from the time of his coming as an immigrant to the forks of the Ohio.[13] Thus it was that Hugh entrusted his son to him on the long voyage to Louisiana, knowing Lucas to be a person experienced in traveling through the wilderness.

The chances were not slight that the boy, now seven years old, would get an arrow shot into his chest or a ball in his head, especially in the sparsely settled region beyond Wayne's training ground. On April 30, the army had left the winter quarters at Legionville for Fort Washington[14] (which became modern Cincinnati). The actual site for his encampment Wayne named "Hobson's Choice," the place being as good as any other which he might have selected.

With his young charge[15] Lucas began the voyage down the Ohio in late spring after the army had moved from Legionville to its new quarters. When Michaux arrived in Pittsburgh not long afterward, he noted in his journal that Lucas, known as "an excellent Democrat," was "now absent. He passes for an educated man with legal knowledge."[16] As long as Hugh's son was fated to make this journey through the Indian country, he could not have had a more trustworthy guardian.

At the start of the voyage Henry was a bewildered boy, sad and unlucky.[17] The six shillings in silver, "which had purchased my consent to depart from my native spot," he locked carefully in his trunk. Joe accompanied Henry to the flatboat, sobbing and hugging his playmate affectionately when told that he could not go along. Besides Lucas and the boy the vessel carried thirty soldiers and their officer as passengers. Not far down-river, somebody, probably a soldier, stole the money from Henry's trunk. A search under the officer's direction did not uncover the vanished coin but produced instead a brief altercation between him and a noncommissioned officer on board who had used disrespectful language. With his sword he struck the offender on the head, causing blood to flow. To this incident Henry later attributed his aversion to military discipline. The boy asked in vain to be returned home. But his tribulations were only beginning, because for supper he received fat pork, ship biscuit, and chocolate, food which so revolted him that he slipped it overboard. Hunger eventually overcame his nausea for the stuff.

The high spring waters enabled the flatboat to make faster progress than ordinarily. At Legionville Henry noticed garden flowers growing wild, being no longer tended.[18] The whole ten-day descent from Pittsburgh to Hobson's

Choice, which was actually four hundred yards beyond the settlement of Cincinnati, was through a wilderness where the forests began at the edge of the river.[19] Wayne's encampment stood in a clearing surrounded by towering trees and a tangle of vines. Lucas and his charge remained here several days, "the beating of drums, the clangor of trumpets, and the movements of horse and foot" leaving a lasting impression in Henry's mind.

The passage from Hobson's Choice to New Madrid, the Spanish post on the west bank of the Mississippi below the mouth of the Ohio, was dangerous.[20] A man and a small boy accompanied Henry and his guardian on this stage of the voyage. In the past Indians had massacred entire families on the stretch between Pittsburgh and Louisville, knowledge of which prompted the party to keep as close to the Kentucky shore as possible. Almost silently they floated down the river to the Falls of the Ohio (Louisville), where the high waters carried them easily over the rapids. From this point to the Mississippi they heard no human voice other than their own. The descent, marked by a fearful storm, was rapid. Finally, the current of the Mississippi swept them down to New Madrid, where an official brandished a sword by way of indicating a spot for them to land—and their voyage was safely over.

While preparing for the journey to Ste. Genevieve, Lucas placed Henry temporarily in the care of a family resident in this dismal settlement controlled by the Spanish.[21] The boy found himself left alone with people whose language he was unable to understand and whose diet of black bread and catfish soup seasoned with pepper and garlic almost sickened him. How glad he was to see his guardian return with a guide, two horses, a little pony, and such equipment as a hatchet, coffeepot, and tin cups. Each person had a blanket for bedding. With the boy astride his pony, they traversed the swampy country to their destination, reaching it in a week or ten days. The whole way they had not seen a single house, although they passed through an Indian village. The redskins treated them civilly, nevertheless causing Henry to tremble as he had "learned to look upon these people as demons." Entering the village of Ste. Genevieve, the party proceeded straight to the house of Vital Beauvais where Henry was to make his home. That night Lucas departed, not to return for the boy until a long time later.

But here in this household the wanderer received the warm affection which he craved.[22] The well-to-do Beauvais, "a tall, dry, old French Canadian," won Henry's respect at once. A solemn man, not at all inclined to merriment, Beauvais smoked a pipe incessantly as if he always had weighty problems to ponder. He dressed, however, like the other men of the village, "with a blue cotton handkerchief on his head, one corner thereof descending behind and partly covering the eelskin which bound his hair, a check shirt, coarse linen pantaloons on his hips, and the Indian sandal or moccasin" on his feet. His wife contrasted pleasantly with him, for she was a big and buxom lady and very pious. Because she "felt some repugnance at putting a little heretic into the same bed with her own children," she insisted on having Henry baptized a Roman Catholic by the village curate, Père St. Pierre, acting as a sponsor with her husband. The boy now knelt beside her every night to pray; and then, as she tucked him in bed, he listened gratefully to "those gentle admonitions which sink deep into the heart."

In no time Henry was transformed into a happy French lad. The thoughtfulness of his playmates helped much to produce this change in his nature. When he first ventured into the street and up to a group of boys playing, he was the master of only two French words—*oui* and *non,* whereas nobody in Ste. Genevieve, except Père St. Pierre, knew a single word of English.

> "Where have you come from?" the children asked.
> "Yes," Henry answered.
> "What is your name?"
> "No."

Not one boy sneered. They made Henry a member of their group instantly. At school he quickly learned their language; and then imperceptibly, he forgot his own. All *le petit Anglais* could say after some months had passed was simply *yes* and *no.* He would return to the United States as "a French boy to learn English."

The people of Ste. Genevieve could not resist his bright-eyed appeal. Once at school there was a public contest to determine the best reader, the prize being a set of miniature teacups and saucers. To the astonishment of everyone the winner was not a girl of the village but Henry, who received the caresses of the parents present. Proudly he gave his prize to Zouzou, the Beauvais baby at home in the cradle. Père St. Pierre selected Henry to serve as an altar boy. After the afternoon mass on Sunday, the boy enjoyed going to the ball where the children from both rich and poor families gravely learned how to comport themselves in polite society. The minuet was the main dance which they were taught. On these occasions Henry was undeniably a village favorite; and as the recipient of much affectionate attention, he sometimes incurred the displeasure of the Beauvais children, whose jealousy, though, was fortunately only a fleeting manifestation. There was no trace of it left when a bilious fever attacked him the second summer of his stay in their home. His foster mother and her eldest daughter nursed him back to health without the aid of a physician because Ste. Genevieve lacked one. During this illness Henry preferred the ministration of the Beauvais daughter, for she had become his heroine.

A keen observer from infancy, Hugh's son now began to evince a questioning mind as well as an imaginative one. On a Christmas Eve about an hour before the colorful midnight mass was to begin, he sat alone in church on a chair before the altar holding a cross in his hand: "My imagination was at first filled with an indescribable awe at the situation in which I was placed, and I gazed upon the sacred images about the altar as if they were in reality what they represented. . . ." When this feeling gradually disappeared, Henry was troubled, for he asked himself "many questions, *to which I could find no satisfactory answers.*" As a matter of fact, his experience had made him old beyond his years.

But living with the Beauvais family had satisfied Henry's need to belong to someone who would care for him with compassion and understanding. Love and the feeling of security which was a part of it was what he had longed for in the past as his "affections, like the young tendrils of the vine, had fastened" on persons closer to him than his father, for whom there existed only a feeling akin to terror. To Beauvais and his wife and children Henry owed

much for the care they had taken of my person, and still more for the pains with which they had preserved the health and purity of my mind. I left them with a heart innocent and virtuous, and with impressions which, if not indelible, were yet sufficient to carry me a long distance through the temptations of vice and folly. I was taught to reverence my parents, to respect the aged, to be polite to my equals, and to speak the truth to every one. I was taught to restrain my temper, to practice self-denial, to be compassionate to man and beast, to receive without murmur or complaint what was provided for me, and to be thankful to God for every blessing.

Henry therefore exhibited a massive flow of tears when Lucas arrived in Ste. Genevieve to return him to his native land. One last lingering look the boy took of the Beauvais dwelling as he left the village—a low and long house of whitewashed clay with a porch in front and a shed in back. A huge chimney divided the building in two, each part having a fireplace. One half of the house served as the kitchen, and the other contained the dining room, parlor, and master bedroom. Henry would never forget the appetizing soups, gumbos, and fricassees which appeared regularly on the table, nor the exciting farmyard and the beautiful garden from which they derived. But now he could only see the giant fencing of cedar pickets which enclosed it all.

Henry took sorrowful leave of the village also. Its inhabitants, many of whom worked in the lead mines of the district or trafficked with the Indians, had all liked him. He would miss the Kickapoo boys who had taught him how to shoot correctly with the bow and arrow. Often they had come into town to play with their white friends. He would miss watching the farmers going back and forth between their homes in the village and their fields on the outskirts, "with their working cattle, carts, old-fashioned wheel-plows, and other implements of husbandry." Life in Ste. Genevieve was unhurried and pleasant, enlivened by church processions and public balls. Politics was not the concern of the people, only the province and worry of the commandant.

While Hugh's son sojourned peacefully in Ste. Genevieve, the anxious officials of Spanish Louisiana from New Orleans to St. Louis had feverishly prepared for attacks on their territory. In particular they feared an invasion by the force which Clark was reported to have forming in Kentucky under the authorization of the French minister himself. Early in 1794, the Spanish had actually sent Thomas Power there "to keep an eye on the movements and progress of what is generally known by the name of Genet's expedition against Louisiana. . . ."[23] Had the French envoy not been the victim of adversity, for which his own misconduct was partly responsible, Henry might well have seen the end of Spanish rule in Ste. Genevieve. But by summer Genet's frontier design had collapsed on account of a lack of money for Clark's needs, the unavailability of the French fleet for support of his expedition by land, and the decisive proclamations issued by Citizen Fauchet, the new Jacobin minister to the United States, and by President Washington. These proclamations prohibited the recruitment of French and American citizens for such an enterprise. As indicated by their addresses and resolutions, the citizenry of the United States had, meanwhile, accepted the policy of strict neutrality in relation to the belligerents.

To Hugh's credit, he had maintained an enlightened view of the entire episode. Aid to France was just in his opinion—the fulfillment of a debt to an ally and the encouragement of a people who emulated the American experiment in democracy. Genet's courtship of the public in the United States disturbed Brackenridge not at all, although he thought the minister "ill-used in the noise that was made about his saying *'That he would appeal to the people.'* Why not? *Have not the people a right to receive his appeal?* If so, he has a right to make it." As long as there was no interference in the internal affairs of the nation, Genet had done nothing illegal by making such an appeal. The matter was external, between the governments of the United States and France. "I was angry at him," Hugh declared, "that he should consider it as a slander to have it reported of him; I say he had a right to appeal; but he ought to have been sure that when the appeal was made, it would not be decided against him."[24] Hugh was not, however, an advocate of Jacobin violence.

He could not stomach any conspiracy which endangered the Union. As the result of a series of conversations with various individuals, Hugh had concluded that a design was afoot with the purpose of delivering a part of the United States, if not all of it, to France. He made notes of what he had learned from Michaux, for example; and he would do the same when "the late Spanish commandant of St. Genevieve, with one Powers, an Englishman, called on him."[25] How shocked Hugh would have been had he known at the time of the conversation with Power the disreputable character of the man! A paid agent of Spain, Power was a participant in the Spanish Conspiracy which aimed to detach Kentucky from the Union. Power had spied on Clark. Later the traitorous General James Wilkinson *"employed"* Power *"as a spy, for the United States...."*[26]

But more astonishing still, this same Power, unknown of course to Hugh, was the single companion of his son Henry for two days and nights on a desolate riverbank in the summer of 1795.[27] The keelboat which Lucas had obtained for the trip upriver to Pittsburgh was really not large enough for the cargo of lead and peltry and the party on board, which included both Henry and Power. The boat first had to descend the Mississippi to the mouth of the Ohio before the second stage of the voyage could begin. When the Kaskaskia was reached on the way down, Lucas deposited the bulkier articles on the shore and then with his vessel and boatmen started up the river to the village of that name for a load of furs, leaving Power and the boy behind to guard the goods.

Until Lucas returned they had little to do except to make the time pass as pleasurably as possible. In the shade of some trees at the edge of the Kaskaskia they made beds from the vine of the wild pea. The handsome Power, a courtly man who spoke French and Spanish fluently, slept a lot, even during the day, when the lulling warm air made him drowsy. Chattering parakeets and hummingbirds flashing about entertained Henry while his companion was asleep. When the time began to drag for the boy, Power let him play with a handkerchief filled with dollars. Henry jingled them on the smooth rock which lined the shore of the stream. But he soon became desperately lonesome when "the stillness of the wilderness rung in my ears! In fact, the two days and nights I passed here appeared among the longest of my life."

But when the voyage was resumed, life was no longer dull for the boy.[28] On a hot day before reaching the mouth of the Ohio, the party observed a phenomenon which Henry at least was never to see again in all of his subsequent traveling—the water about the boat afoam from the lashings of countless fish which hurled themselves in all directions. Men shot them with rifles. There was no lack of food on this stage of the journey, the descent of the Mississippi. The ascent of the Ohio was a different matter, for the provisions ran low and the hunters often bagged no game. All the way to the Falls of the Ohio the party sighted only two log cabins and no boats descending the river. One day—two days sometimes—they would be without food, and then providentially wild life appeared which could be shot. From a herd of buffaloes— by now rarely encountered in the Ohio region—the hunters managed to kill a sizable calf, although unable to bring down a splendid bull at which they had fired. On another occasion they encamped near a grove and lighted their fires for the night; there, above them, they perceived a flock of turkeys at roost. The party devoured ten or twelve of the birds for supper and breakfast. There were times, however, when an attempt to assuage hunger proved unsuccessful, such as the experiment of frying river mussels and seasoning them with pepper and salt. No one could eat them without vomiting.

Nothing eaten the whole distance from Ste. Genevieve to Louisville tasted better to Henry than the roasted bear which the party prepared after an exciting brush with the animal. They descried him one afternoon swimming across the river to the Kentucky side. The boatmen, maneuvering their vessel skillfully, blocked his retreat to shore. There he swam in the middle of the Ohio, with all the guns on board trained on him. Henry was spellbound when the beast received the fire and badly wounded headed for the boat, "champing his teeth, and his eyes red with rage." There was no time to reload the guns, because he reached the vessel in an instant and started to climb aboard. It was then that somebody seized an axe and brought a smashing blow down on his head. The party feasted that night and the boy found a roasted paw succulent and savory.

The manner of living on this boat, with the meals dependent more and more on the bounty of nature, weakened Henry's health.[29] Sleeping was a difficult problem, because the hull was packed with peltry. One stormy night when rain lashed down accompanied by lightning and thunder so many persons squeezed into the canvas-covered cabin that they crowded Henry out. He had to sleep in the open on the footway, or running board, at the edge of the boat, lying there awake under a thin and soaking capote. At Louisville a fever and ague gripped Henry, a condition not helped by his succumbing to the temptation of eating unripe watermelon.

Lucas soon realized that his charge was too ill to complete the voyage to Pittsburgh. The trader had sold much of his cargo in Louisville, transferred the remainder of the furs to a canoe, and hired a lad named Duncan from the Monongahela country to help him with the poling upriver. The three of them made a striking picture as they slowly ascended the Ohio—the future congressman and judge at the stern pushing with a pole, his hand Duncan at the bow, and Henry seated between them on the peltry. Whenever the ague shook Henry, the others in consequence were in constant danger of losing their balance. The poor boy could not forestall such seizures no matter how vigorously his guardian swore at him—and Lucas's "temper was none of the sweetest." The party encountered a lot of rain and also some early snow. With the weather bad and Henry's ague recurring every day, Lucas finally decided to leave him at Gallipolis, the first settlement reached where he could receive proper care.

Henry's sojourn[30] here did not begin auspiciously. Lucas had taken him immediately to the house of Dr. Antoine Saugrain, a physician who delighted in conducting experiments in chemistry and physics. He was a lively Frenchman, short and jolly. But the boy did not realize all of this until later, for upon his arrival he had lain wrapped in a blanket in an inconspicuous corner for several hours until an attack of the ague had run its course. Then he jumped up, eager to stretch his legs after the confinement of the canoe, dashing from the house to the bank of the river and up to a boy whom he had espied playing there. Henry tried to wrestle with him in fun, only to receive a severe thrashing in return. This lad had mistakenly believed that Henry sought a fight instead of friendship.

But after this unhappy meeting, Henry had no trouble in making friends in Gallipolis. His problems were of a different kind. His ague persisted throughout the winter and into the spring. The day after Henry's arrival Saugrain directed him to drink enough warm water—a gallon or two—to rinse his stomach thoroughly, in the hope that this treatment would prove effective in combatting the disease. The straitened circumstances in which Lucas had left the boy might have delayed the recovery of his health. Henry had no money with which to clothe himself, nor did Saugrain have any to offer. "Money had been sent for my keeping, but unfortunately it never reached its destination," the boy learned afterward. Meanwhile in cold weather he did chores without a hat, and barefoot, being unable to wear a pair of wooden shoes given him. In Gallopolis also he experienced sustained hunger when the following summer all the families had scarcely anything to eat. At this time, moreover, an epidemic cast a pall over the community. Henry, no longer attacked by the ague, was one of the few persons immune from the scourge.

He shared in whatever befell the Saugrain household, whether good or bad. The physician and his wife, a cheerful woman, treated Henry as a member of the family, not as an object of charity. Her brother was Henry's companion. The two boys, who were of the same age, not only played together but also performed their duties in the kitchen and about the log cabin together. Henry was especially fond of Saugrain: ". . . I used to sit by him as often as I could, watching the curious operations of his blowpipe and crucible." Visitors to the small laboratory would watch the experiments suspiciously, fearful of black magic; but some could not resist buying the phosphoric matches which Saugrain offered for sale. Henry admired the barometers and thermometers which the little physician fashioned, puzzled over the mystery of the peach enclosed in a bottle with a narrow neck, and stared happily at the swans swimming in

40

basins of water. Once Saugrain took Henry with him on a visit to a neighboring settlement. Here the boy had his first taste of wine, a liking for which he never lost, although he later developed a dislike to rum, brandy, and whisky. In spite of the lack of money and the frequent presence of hunger, his life in the Saugrain home was pleasant.

Henry's favorite occupation was weeding the garden planted by the physician in the spring. One day Henry noticed a young woman, not over twenty years old, on the other side of the fence and similarly engaged. Undoubtedly there were covert glances exchanged at first, followed by a few words—then she told her new acquaintance, who listened enraptured, the tale of Bluebeard. They became fast friends; and he, her hero. One day, alone on the bank of the river, Henry had watched a man bathing move into deeper and deeper water and suddenly thrash about in obvious distress. The sight of the flailing arms sent Hugh's son leaping into a canoe which he maneuvered into reach of the man's grasp. The man hung on with deathlike grip until Henry's screams brought aid. Subsequently this person married the girl who had picked weeds with Henry. Their daughter married an enterprising lawyer, named Samuel F. Vinton, who became a well-known congressman from that district in Ohio. For his quick-wittedness Henry "earned the civic crown" of Gallipolis.

Gallipolis was an odd village, carved out of the wilderness. The inhabitants were mainly French royalists antagonistic to the Revolution, as Saugrain himself was. They were also artists and craftsmen—for example, "carvers and gilders to the king, coachmakers, frizeurs and perukemakers"—who were unsuited to the rough and unpredictable life of the American frontier. Once Henry saw "half a dozen at work in taking down a tree, some pulling ropes fastened to the branches, while others were cutting round it like beavers." In addition to their various trades the villagers cultivated garden plots, never attempting large-scale farming. They lived in long log barracks which were divided into rooms about sixteen or twenty feet wide, although some persons like Saugrain were fortunate enough to dwell in separate cabins. When Henry left their settlement, the Gallipolitans were a frustrated people.

Late in the summer of 1796, the ten-year-old boy learned that his father had at last arranged for the completion of the voyage to Pittsburgh. By the time an army officer had arrived in Gallipolis to take Henry in hand, he had recovered his use of the English language, although he did not lose his foreign accent for a long time. The officer bought him shoes and respectable clothes and then took him on board a boat. Travel between Cincinnati and Pittsburgh was now quite safe because Wayne had defeated the Indians at Fallen Timbers in 1794, and signed the Treaty of Greenville with them the next year.

Early in October, Wayne's military rival, General Wilkinson, left Cincinnati for Pittsburgh and the East with his family. They traveled ostentatiously up the river on a barge managed by twenty-five or thirty boatmen and were entertained by a band of musicians on board. Before long this craft overtook the boat carrying Henry, whereupon he changed vessels in order to become the playmate of Wilkinson's son, Joseph Biddle, who was nearly eleven years old. The grandeur of the General's mode of travel overwhelmed Henry: "The splendor of the furniture—the elegance of the dresses—and then the luxuries of the table, to a half-starved creature, produced an effect which cannot be easily described."[31] Wilkinson's joviality—"it seemed to be his business to make every one happy"—impressed Henry who also grew particularly fond of his soft-spoken wife. One day this quiet lady discovered the two boys sticking minnows with pinhooks and gently but effectively reproved them for destroying life without reason.

The barge finally arrived at Pittsburgh on October 20.[32] A salute of artillery welcomed the General. After watching the boat approach the landing, Joe, who had thought he would never see Henry again, embraced him, and accompanied him home, where they found Hugh, as might be expected, "sitting in his office, unmoved by the uproar which had disturbed the whole village."[33]

Henry was frightened as he faced his father.

"Well, boy, can you read French?" Hugh asked, and then gave his son a copy of Fénelon's *Télémaque* to read.

Henry stuttered.

"Sir, your progress does not equal my expectations," Hugh remarked. "Joe, take him to Fenemore, the tailor, to get a suit of clothes, and then to Andrew Willocks, to have his measure for a pair of shoes."

IV: The Student

The evening of his return Henry visited Jane Marie, with Joe leading the way to her house. Joyful at seeing Henry again, she hugged him and caressed him and then put in his arms "her infant daughter, her first and last born child, and caused my face to be suffused with blushes, by telling me that the *innocent babe was to be my wife. . . .*"[1] There in the Marie home that fall night, the wanderer held with embarrassment the tiny Caroline whom he would eventually marry. But his companionship with Joe ended abruptly.

Joe was now an odd boy whose "propensities were almost entirely animal. . . ."[2] He had a low and wrinkled forehead; he was pug-nosed and thick-lipped; he was mentally dull. The older Brackenridge had tried in vain to improve Joe's mind and to develop morality in him. The cobbler's son, however, excelled in mastering various vices, having a special fondness for whisky, tobacco, and obscene literature. Among a group of boys Joe inspired emulation because he was fearless and in his own way a leader. No one could beat him playing marbles except Andy, a Negro boy belonging to General John Neville. Joe invariably commanded the boys of the upper town in their mimic battles with those of the lower town. He was rough and tough and, as always, devoted to Henry's protection.

Nevertheless Joe was no longer a fit companion for Henry.[3] He revealed his secrets to young Brackenridge and eagerly initiated him in unwholesome practices. Once he took Henry to a clandestine meeting of juvenile delinquents who specialized in raiding gardens and orchards, although not disdainful of other possible plunder. While the "swinish herd" watched breathlessly, Henry tasted the whisky in the tin cup placed at his mouth and then rejected it in disgust. This was the only time he attended a meeting of the club. Somehow his father discovered Joe's true nature, whereupon he gave the boy a thrashing, money, and a new suit of clothes, ordering him away from the Brackenridge home and forbidding any further association with Henry. The boys never saw each other again until once in later life when they met in a frontier settlement where Joe had become a constable.

Except for the escapades with Joe, Henry lived under the strict supervision of his father, in whose company he now spent most of his time. The boy was thus in a situation to hear much talk concerning the political affairs of the day. In particular he learned a great deal about the uprising in Western Pennsylvania in 1794 (the Whisky Insurrection), which had occurred during his absence in Louisiana, and about his father's conduct in it: "I heard all the circumstances related by eye witnesses, and heard it universally admitted, that by his address and activity, the town (of Pittsburgh) was saved from destruction by the mob which marched in from Braddock's Field."[4]

43

Hugh had undergone a harrowing experience in that affair. In Western Pennsylvania opposition to the Hamiltonian excise had originally manifested itself in condemnatory resolution and occasionally in resistance to the collection of the tax on whisky. In 1793-94, the formation of democratic societies throughout the United States was indicative of a strong feeling against the Washington administration on the part of many citizens. Dedicated to the preservation of republicanism in America, a purpose which required keeping a careful watch on government, the clubs had advocated the cause of France, advising and aiding Citizen Genet. It was not surprising, therefore, that such an organization in Western Pennsylvania—the Mingo Creek society with ultrademocratic principles—became "the cradle of the insurrection," at least in Hugh's opinion.[5] Although he had represented the distillers of whisky in court on different occasions, he did not intend to become a leader in the opposition to the excise, nor would he countenance the use of violence in the movement. He tried to serve as a mediator between the parties involved, only to meet with hostility from all sides. Enemies grossly misrepresented his position—with a dire result, as revealed by the following handbill[6] which was quickly reprinted in the *Pittsburgh Gazette* of November 1, 1794:

> *Citizens of the Army advancing to the Western Country.*
>
> SERIOUS intimations are given me, that I am considered by you, as greatly criminal in the late insurrection in this country; and that though I may have shielded myself from the law, by taking advantage of the terms of the amnesty proposed by the commissioners, and sanctioned by the proclamation of the President, yet that I shall not escape the resentment of individuals. It would seem to me totally improbable, that republican soldiers would sully the glory of their voluntary rising, by a single intemperate act. Nevertheless, as it would wound me with exquisite sensibility, to be treated with indignity, by words or looks, short of violence, I beg leave to suggest to you, that it is a maxim of reason, that a man "shall be presumed innocent till the contrary is proved;" and I give you a strong presumption of my innocence, viz. that though having an opportunity of relinquishing the country, I stand firm, and will surrender myself to the closest examination of the judges, and put myself entirely on the merit or demerit of my conduct, through the whole of the unfortunate crisis.
>
> H. H. BRACKENRIDGE.
>
> *Pittsburgh, October 26, 1794.*

Hugh stood firm and soon had the satisfaction of being exonerated from the charge of insurgency by Secretary of the Treasury Hamilton himself,[7] who at the time was also acting as secretary of war.

But Brackenridge was more unpopular than ever with the people of Western Pennsylvania. Before his involvement in the affair, he had offered his name as a candidate for Congress to the electorate of the district composed of Washington and Allegheny counties. As the election day approached, in October, 1794, Hugh had announced his intention to remain in the contest to counteract a rumor that he had withdrawn. He was not afraid to submit his conduct to public scrutiny: "I may at present have less popularity than I had, but the time will come when I shall be considered as having deserved well of the country, in all the delicate conjunctures in which we have been situated."[8] Then, as the army neared Pittsburgh, he had published a notice in the *Gazette*[9] stating his determination to write a history of "the late convulsion . . . as may satisfy all reasonable men of the uprightness of my intentions, and the purity of my conduct, with regard to individuals, or the public, in the whole of this business." In the following months Brackenridge collected vouchers from many prominent persons who were willing to testify in his behalf; he planned to include the documents as evidence in the proposed book. The work, entitled *Incidents of the Insurrection in the Western Parts of Pennsylvania, in the Year 1794*, appeared in 1795, printed by M'Culloch in Philadelphia. Written hastily, this explanation of Hugh's conduct was accurate —and honest;[10] and it certainly provided a vivid account of the backwoods protest against the excise.

Although the *Incidents* constituted his formal defense, Brackenridge also added a fourth volume to *Modern Chivalry*, satirizing aspects of the insurrection and continuing his commentary on political philosophy. At the beginning of the story Teague received the appointment of an excise officer from the President and immediately departed for his post in Western Pennsylvania. This development caused Farrago to employ another servant, a Scotchman named Duncan Ferguson who was a Covenanter in faith and much given to theological disputation. The Captain and his new valet set out on the road west discussing religion animatedly; and on the fourth day of their journey, they unexpectedly came upon Teague. The two bogtrotters wrangled as the way was resumed, wearying Farrago, who suggested that O'Regan proceed ahead. But the exciseman came to a quick and inglorious end in his brief career when a mob, shouting *"Liberty and no excise, liberty and no excise; down with all excise officers,"*[11] tarred and feathered him. Looking like "a wild fowl of the forest,"[12] he finally found himself locked in a cage, a hapless creature exhibited to the public as an animal of an unidentified species and subjected to an investigation by representatives of the Philosophical Society. Brackenridge concluded his tale with Teague's arrival in revolutionary France as a scientific exhibit. There, however, the rabble welcomed the bogtrotter as a sans-culotte and released him, for he had accidentally lost part of his tar and feathers at the nick of time. The Captain (and Duncan) had meanwhile reached home safely.

In the eleventh chapter of this amusing volume, the author interrupted his narrative to give his reader some serious reflections on the qualifications of legislators and the necessity of informed voting by the people. Hugh considered the proper use of the suffrage to be "the first spring of happiness in a republic."[13] If this part of the governmental machine was tampered with in any way, its operation as a whole would be affected. Positive legislation was necessary to promote good government, but "the system of family and scholastick education" was important, too. Consequently, there was advice which every father should give to his son, prefaced by this thought: "Young man, you have the good fortune to be born in a republic. . . ." He therefore had "a right *to elect,* and a right *to be elected."* Hugh stressed the principle of honor as a guide in exercising the right of suffrage and the matter of talent as the prime consideration in seeking a public office. "Lay in a stock of knowledge by reading in early life," the father might well recommend. "Your old age, by these means will acquire dignity; and appointments will readily follow. You will be under no necessity of soliciting inordinately the suffrage of men."[14]

Brackenridge meant this advice for his son in particular. He was probably planning the book, or perhaps actually writing it, when Henry returned from Louisiana because M'Culloch published it in Philadelphia in 1797. Father and son together read about the adventures of Farrago and his two servants, Henry at times being unable to check his laughter over some incident in the work.[15] Often Hugh laughed too, for he was as proud as Punch that the boy understood the satire. Before reading *Modern Chivalry,* however, Henry had first to finish Defoe's *Robinson Crusoe.*

That very fact—the order in which Henry read books—indicated the pains which his father took to give him a sound basic education. The boy studied his lessons from early morning, almost from the moment of awakening, until his bedtime in the evening.[16] For two hours before breakfast a small man with a long nose, named Visinier, taught Henry French, or rather sought to improve his pupil's command of the language by having him read *Télémaque* and a translation of Vergil's *Aeneid.* The boy liked this reading, but he also enjoyed watching the teacher use his gold snuffbox. After breakfast Henry read works in English—several in translation—under the direction of his father. After *Modern Chivalry* they turned to Cervantes' *Don Quixote*—then came Le Sage's *Gil Blas,* Fielding's *Tom Jones,* and Goldsmith's *Vicar of Wakefield.* Henry even read volumes of the *Spectator,* the paper which Addison and Steele had conducted together. Sometimes at night Henry slipped out of bed and lay "before the slacked coal fire, using the faint light emitted through the bars of the grate" to continue a story which had excited him during the day. A man named Tod, an expert calligrapher, gave him lessons in penmanship. Henry did not like the study of arithmetic, in which he was tutored by one of his father's law students every day for an hour or two. Memorizing the multiplication table was difficult for him, although he managed to learn fractions and square root and algebra—all of this he did with loathing. But he gradually became an admirer of Euclidean geometry "as furnishing the anatomy of the reasoning powers. . . ."

Henry disliked lessons which he had to memorize.[17] An assignment which involved the use of creative thought was a different matter because such a task provided a challenge for him. His father sometimes would give him a passage to read in a work like Cook's *Voyages* or Hume's *History of England* with the warning to prepare himself for questioning. The keenness of Henry's observations based on this reading frequently surprised Hugh, causing him "to suspend his unfavorable prognostics of my capacity." In other respects the boy's progress was discouraging, for Hugh's insistence that his son read the classics—the masterpieces of ancient Greece and Rome—in the original and commit them to memory killed his enthusiasm for study. Henry learned by heart "grammer after grammer, and whole vocabularies and conjugations of irregular verbs. . . ." When his father lost his temper, Henry's memory became more wretched than ever. Hugh was as dictatorial now as he had been with the hornbook before.

Henry suffered because his father was a brilliant classicist who overvalued a mastery of Latin and Greek. Hugh characterized Franklin as a "strong-minded, imperfectly-educated man" whose achievements would have been greater had he attended college. In Brackenridge's opinion, an education was incomplete without a thorough knowledge of the classics. He therefore had hoped that his son would excel in this field of study and was grievously disappointed when he did not. Unfortunately Hugh did not realize that Henry's temperament was responsible for the lack of progress: "It was only when self-taught, that I relished the classics." In teaching them to his son, Hugh used the wrong method by demanding undue memorization of the lessons and by relying on the ever-present threat of punishment as an incentive to diligent study.

Such treatment soon made Henry a refractory pupil.[18] Infrequently he received permission to leave his particular assignment for an hour or so before dinner when he could play outside, although he never had sufficient time to make real friends among the boys of his age. Application to his lessons became more and more irksome, with the result that his "attention was thus often called off from the sufferings within doors, to the consolations of hoops and marbles without." Because punishment followed neglect of his work, Henry resorted to "deception, evasion, and other tricks" whenever a reprimand appeared imminent. An inner conflict began to torment him, for what he had learned with the Beauvais family in Ste. Genevieve now clashed with a growing inclination to disobey his parent. Sent to the garret for the purpose of undisturbed study, Henry instead read countless books and magazines which were gathering dust there; when discovered at this pastime he returned forthwith to his desk in his father's office, after being duly chastised. Then he hunched over his work, but in its place covertly read passages in a pocket-size Bible, creating the appearance of a boy busy with his lesson. It was no wonder that when he was granted a respite he could not resist stretching a "moment of liberty" into half a day. On his return home, however, he was always afraid, hesitating near the door while desperately thinking of an excuse for his tardiness. "I became, in fact, a bad boy, and a fit subject for the corrupting influence of any depraved associate," Henry admitted years later.

Likewise, in retrospect he was certain that attendance at a public school from the time of his return from Louisiana would have benefited him more than the tutelage of his father.[19] The feeling of shame which often possessed Henry was a harmful influence to the development of his character. To do his best work, moreover, he required the competition of other students because with him the urge to excel was "a powerful stimulant. . . ." He also concluded that constant application to study, unbroken by periods of recreation, was injurious to any student, convinced that the "boy among his playfellows, even while at play, is not uselessly employed; he is rehearsing, in miniature, the part he will be called to act on the more extended theater of life." He believed that his father was remiss in failing to inculcate moral and religious principles more than he did. Reason, in Hugh's belief, dictated honesty on the part of an individual. When his son gave him a six-cent piece found in a pair of trousers in the garret, he therefore pocketed it without a word of commendation: "I instantly resolved to make a different use of the next that should fall in my way, and even to indemnify myself when an opportunity might offer."

Despite the glaring flaws in this course of study, it was praiseworthy in other respects. Henry, for example, never lost his love of reading[20] which his father had fostered by their spirited discussions of the books regularly assigned for perusal. Their reading of *Modern Chivalry* together was a high light in Henry's education. As a boy and as a man he esteemed this frontier classic and maintained that Sir Walter Scott himself never delineated a finer character—that is, of that type—than Farrago's servant, Duncan Ferguson.[21] In their discussions Brackenridge always talked to his son as to a man, with the result that "by far the most valuable portion of my education consisted in his conversation, or rather lectures. . . ."[22] Obviously the mere association with such an intellect was an invaluable experience for an impressionable boy, and Hugh excelled in the communication of his vast fund of knowledge. Henry also had the priceless privilege of sitting at a desk in his father's study, observing there the irascible lawyer's relations with his clients, and constantly admiring "his love of justice, his sterling integrity, and perfect disinterestedness."[23] Cruel

Hugh was in driving his son toward an impossible perfection and culpable, too, for not striving to be more humane in his dealing with him, but he was nevertheless the dominating influence in Henry's whole long life—feared and respected.

About three years this clash of two strong-willed personalities continued when at last Brackenridge decided to send his son to the Pittsburgh Academy. It was a wise decision.[24] Henry accomplished little toward the end of the period, managing to thwart his father's wishes at every turn. He finally reached the fourth book of Vergil, "not led up the steep ascent by the gentle hand of Minerva, but driven like a laden ass with a cudgel." To Hugh such progress was not only inexplicable but disheartening.

For Henry attendance at the Academy was a release from bondage. The school had two capable teachers in James Mountain and the Rev. John Taylor. Mountain,[25] who taught Greek and Latin, had served in the classical department of the Canonsburg Academy until May, 1797, when he left upon the refusal of the trustees to increase his salary. In addition to his reputation as a classicist—having memorized most, if not all, of Homer's *Iliad,* he could recite passages from it at random—Mountain soon achieved recognition as a lawyer at the Pittsburgh bar. Taylor was in charge of the other subjects offered at the Academy when Henry was a student there.[26] Noted particularly as a mathematician and astronomer, Taylor, however, also became the first rector of Trinity Episcopal Church in Pittsburgh. These two men were not harsh disciplinarians. They put Henry in the second class with James O'Hara, Fayette Neville, Wilkins Tannehill, and James C. Wilkins. At once Henry realized that he had progressed rapidly in his studies at home in spite of all the heartache. But he was not a bookworm who hated to see his class dismissed at the end of the day. He played in all the games organized by his friends at the school, although "from the peculiarity of the circumstances of my life, [I] would often pass hours entirely alone, or in rambles over the hills, enjoying a kind of dreamy solitude, deeply tinged with sadness."

Much to his surprise and anguish Henry was responsible for a whipping administered to Christopher Magee, a friend and fellow student.[27] In doing his chores one morning, Henry climbed to the hayloft to toss fodder down to the Brackenridge horse, when the head of a Negro suddenly appeared out of the hay and whispered, "Don't be scared, young massa, I'se a po' nigga run away last night from de boat, come down from Figginy on de Monigehale, and gwine to Kentuck; pray, massa, only let me stay, and tell nobody till de boat go away." This the boy did, going so far as to smuggle bread and meat to the hungry fugitive until the vessel had gone. The Negro came out of hiding, found a job as a hostler, but returned about a week later in the hope that his protector might know the whereabouts of any old but still serviceable trousers. Henry, of course, remembered the pair in which he had discovered the six-cent piece. He gave them to the grateful Negro, receiving a dollar in return. What to do with so much money presented a problem which Henry solved by giving this vast sum to young Magee "under a promise of secrecy," "Christy" having won his esteem by curing him of fear in swimming in the river. (Reputed the most daring boy in town, Christy had simply taken Henry into deep water, let him sink, and then pulled him out, magically no longer afraid of drowning.) Christy blundered, however, by thoughtlessly exhibiting the dollar in his father's sight. Magee, a strict Presbyterian, accused his son of larceny when the source of his wealth remained unaccounted-for. One whipping after another did not force him to reveal his secret. Christy finally was allowed to keep the money, provided that he restore it to the owner. After the incident Henry "seemed to feel the stripes" on his own body and resolved never again to sell trousers which were not his and to shelter fugitive slaves. This episode was related to his father's constant "inveighing against speculators, misers, and avaricious people. . . ."

The education of boys like Henry and Christy was not considered complete until they had taken lessons in dancing and fencing. Henry himself had learned the minuet in Ste. Genevieve. In 1796, the year of his return to Pittsburgh, a dancing teacher, named R. Davenport, not only taught the popular English dances but also introduced some reels to his classes conducted in a large room in a house on Second Street, between Market and Wood.[28] When Henry attended dancing school, his instructor chose him and Morgan Neville to demonstrate a hornpipe, at that time considered the height of achievement in dancing.[29] His lessons in fencing with the small sword Henry took with a Frenchman by the name of De Lisle.

Henry was certainly not a clumsy boy, nor one lacking in sufficient courage and determination to perform such a feat as walking the wire and slack rope.[30] He taught himself the trick, although his companions had given up the hope of mastering it. After watching an exhibition of wiredancing, the boys had strung a wire on which to practice in a stable. When Passamonte, the acrobat, came back to Pittsburgh for another performance after half a year had passed, Henry was prepared to startle his friends by a daring act of showmanship. Passamonte leaving the room temporarily to investigate a disturbance caused by some boys who tried to watch the exhibition without paying for the privilege, Henry took "his place on the wire, to the infinite amusement of the spectators." But on his return the acrobat, furious at Henry's impudence, sent him scurrying among the benches.

Entertainers like Passamonte now visited Pittsburgh regularly, for in a decade it had become the "Gateway to the West." In 1786, the elder Bracken-ridge had optimistically stated that about 1,500 people lived in the town; in January, 1796, however, the population of the borough of Pittsburgh was only 1,365, as determined by the official count of the assessors.[31] Enterprising townsmen, nevertheless, had reason to expect a bright future for their community. Wayne had ended the Indian menace in the Ohio Valley. It was thus not alarming when two red men appeared on the west bank of the Allegheny several miles from town in late March, 1795. They looked peaceable enough, although probably willing to steal horses whenever given the chance, as the editor of the *Gazette* warned the "frontier people to keep a good look-out."[32] In November of that year Scull noted jubilantly that the "emigration to this country this fall surpasses that of any other season—and we are informed, that the banks of the Monongahela, from M'Kee's Port to Redstone, are lined with people intending for the settlements on the Ohio, and Kentucky."[33] He added, moreover, that as "an instance of the encreasing prosperity of this part of the state, land that two or three years since was sold for ten shillings per acre, will now bring upwards of three pounds." The progress of settlement on the lands west of the Allegheny but within Pennsylvania was a fact which heartened all Pittsburghers who thought of the future. Early in March, 1796, Scull reported "that upwards of 1,200 persons have crossed that river within this month past, with the express intention of fulfilling the law by making an actual settlement."[34]

As if to dramatize the importance of Pittsburgh as the metropolis of Western Pennsylvania, the townspeople held a fair, beginning on Monday, June 6. An announcement in the *Gazette*[35] more than three weeks before the opening day gave the merchants and farmers ample time to apply to the clerk of the market for booths in which to display their wares and produce. Equal foresight was manifest in the arrangements made for the entertainment of the crowds expected to attend, for in mid-May horses were in training for the races—the special attraction for the people who like to wager. But for the enjoyment of everyone, Saunders, an acrobat, and "his man Merryman," were engaged to perform "astonishing feats of Slack Rope, Wire Dancing, Balancing, Tumbling, the Italian Shades, &c. &c, &c." every evening while the fair was in progress.

Henry, of course, could not attend this gala event in 1796, but in the years following both he and the other boys of the town impatiently awaited the opening of the county fair and the commencement of the races. The racecourse occupied part of the plain which lay between Grant's Hill and the Allegheny.[36] On racing days business came to a standstill in Pittsburgh, as the inhabitants— of high and low estate and "of all ages and sexes"—streamed toward the track surrounded by stands at which refreshments were sold: "where every fifteen or twenty minutes there was a rush to some part, to witness a *fisticuff*—where dogs barked and bit, and horses trod on men's toes, and booths fell down on people's heads!" At one spot a group about the fiddler Crowder raised the dust with a reel, and not far away Dennis Loughy, "the blind poet, like Homer, casting his pearls before swine," chanted "his master-piece, in a tone part nasal and part guttural,—

> 'Come, gentlemen, gentlemen all,
> Ginral Sincleer shall remem-ber-ed be,
> For he lost thirteen hundred men all,
> In the Western Tari-to-ree!' "[37]

When the cry of "To horse! to horse!" was heard above the din, the spectators hurried to the starting post or to another vantage point, while above them on a platform the judges of the race prepared for action.

Henry always watched Loughy and listened to his songs entranced. The poet was eccentric and gifted. Dennis never wore shoes because it was convenient for him to feel "his way with his toes!"[38] By this method he could go anywhere in Pittsburgh unattended. Often Henry saw him approach a corner, groping.

"A little farther on, Dennis," some kind person would at that moment remark.

"I thank you—I thank you—I know my way," Loughy, indignant, would reply in his characteristic twang.

But he had won the affection of his fellow citizens, who expected him to appear at all major functions in the town as well as at the fair and the races. How impressed Henry was when he saw the "Judges of *Nisi Prius* and *Oyer and Terminer*" going to and from court on horseback, wearing black suits and cocked hats, and led by the High Sheriff with a white wand—the little procession moving solemnly behind Dennis who wore a tattered uniform without the red lapels and marched barefoot to the "rr-ran-rr-ran-tan" of his drum!

Henry was old enough to appreciate the talent of this ballad maker, for Dennis had achieved recognition as the Blind Poet of Pittsburgh by the turn of the century. There was published in the *Gazette* of March 8, 1800, a humorous document entitled "A Taylor's Will!!" in which a certain Joseph Haigh bequeathed to Dennis the "sum of *Nineteen Shillings and Ten Pence half penny,* as a trifling compensation for his trouble in composing the lamentation on the death of General George Washington. . . ." This was the time, in fact, when Dennis began to advertise his work for sale in the form of broadsides. He memorialized every significant event of his day in verse, composing and selling a ballad, for example, "In Praise of Our Present Governor" after the election of Thomas McKean to that office.[39] Few Pittsburghers, whether Federalist or Republican in politics, could read this advertisement about another ballad with equanimity:

A NEW SONG,

On THOMAS JEFFERSON'S *election to the Presidency of the United States*, Composed by DENNIS LOUGHHY, and sold by him—price *Six Cents*.

Pittsburgh, March 23, 1801.[40]

Dennis's rival in the esteem of Henry and his friends was the Chevalier Gabriel Dubac, a French *émigré* who had settled in Pittsburgh to become a storekeeper. From time to time he advertised new assortments of dry goods and groceries for sale, such as wines, teas, sugars, snuff, tobacco, mould candles, and castile soap. He sold lead in pigs and bars at a low price but "for cash only."[41] Dubac handled the products of near-by farms, also, at one time offering to sell the house which he himself occupied in exchange for "approved country produce."[42] Whenever a farmer asked him what was the lowest price acceptable for certain goods, he invariably "consulted" a pet raccoon, to the delight of any bystanders.[43] The ownership of this animal, of course, was the chief reason for his popularity with the boys of the town. Sometimes the raccoon escaped to the street, only to be discovered immediately by them and his offense reported: "M. Dubac, M. Dubac, your raccoon has got loose—your raccoon has got loose." Their insistent clamor never really angered him, for, according to Henry, Dubac "would rather petulantly, yet slowly, and with a most polite motion of the head and hands, repeat, *'Late eem go—late eem go.'* "

Loughy and Dubac were but two of the many "original characters"[44] who lived in Pittsburgh during this period of Henry's life; the location of the town also resulted in his meeting a number of famous travelers who stopped there to prepare for the voyage down the Ohio. Some of them hoped to visit the elder Brackenridge, considering him, now more than ever, the foremost attraction of the place. Many were guests in his home. He entertained, for example, the exiled Duke of Orleans, who became the king of France, and his two brothers—three gracious and unassuming young men in Henry's opinion, and not at all like the "showy city gentlemen, with fair top-boots and ratan, and who found nothing good enough for them at the tavern. . . ."[45] Unless a traveler carried letters of introduction to the leading families in Pittsburgh society—the Craigs, the Butlers, the O'Haras, the Nevilles, the Kirkpatricks, the Stevensons, the Wilkinses—he obtained hospitality in one of the local taverns.

Henry held the tavern-keepers in high regard, for they not only dispensed the hospitality of his town, but several of them made his welfare their special

53

concern. Until his death in January, 1797,[46] Patrick Murphy operated the finest tavern in Pittsburgh, frequented by the most respected gentlemen. His wife Mary, or "Molly" as most people affectionately called her, then became the proprietress of the Sign of General Butler, located on Market Street, although, after several years had passed, she advertised it to be let to a new management.[47] She was Henry's staunch friend,[48] and in the future she became the protectress of Jane Marie and her daughter, Caroline. "Many an orphan," wrote Henry as a man, "many a friendless one, many a wretched being has shed, in secret, the tear of gratitude over the memory of Molly Murphy!" The Marie tavern, the Sign of the Bell, was an increasingly popular haunt of the Republicans as the old century ended and the new began.[49] The Maries worked prodigiously to make their property on Grant's Hill the loveliest spot in Pittsburgh, planting it with a variety of flowers and shrubs. Occasionally, however, the Republicans met at the tavern of Captain John Smur to discuss politics and to enjoy refreshment.[50] Tavern keeping as an occupation in Pittsburgh even appealed to William Peter Eichbaum, a glass cutter to Louis XVI until the French Revolution, although he maintained a glazing business after the opening of his "house of Entertainment at the Sign of the INDIAN QUEEN, in Front street, near Market street" in the spring of 1800.[51]

Exciting a place as Pittsburgh obviously was for an Academy student, Henry still looked forward to visits with his grandmother in the country, several times a year spending a week or two with her.[52] Hugh's mother liked to tell Henry stories about the unusual talent which his father had frequently manifested as a boy: "She doated on him—he was the constant theme of her discourse, excepting when it turned on Scripture and religion." From his grandmother Henry learned the Scotch dialect, a process aided by his reading her the poems of Allan Ramsay and Robert Fergusson. On other occasions she captivated the boy with her graphic description of the castle of the Duke of Argyle.

Henry's knowledge of Scottish writings was suddenly broadened when his father removed him from the Academy—his classical education uncompleted —and put him under the tutelage of a relative named John Gilkison, who favored the works of such authors as the philosophers Reid and Stewart in his reading.[53]

Gilkison was the first proprietor of a bookstore and circulating library in Western Pennsylvania. He had studied law for a time under the elder Brackenridge, besides tutoring Henry in arithmetic. When Gilkison abandoned the thought of law as a career, Hugh helped him establish the store in one wing of the Brackenridge house just before Christmas in 1798. Gilkison's stock, which contained works for sale and rental ("for a reasonable time, at a reasonable price"), was especially strong in schoolbooks.[54] In addition to his book and stationery store, he maintained a scrivener's office, prepared to draw various legal instruments. How important this service could be in a town like Pittsburgh, where Frenchmen and other foreigners either resided or visited continually, was evident when Congress enacted the Alien and Sedition Acts. The law of June 18, 1798, increased the period of residence in the United States for an alien aspiring to citizenship from five to fourteen years. Gilkison drew petitions under this Naturalization Act and advertised them in the spring of 1799, with the warning that "Foreigners who have not been Naturalized, must apply before June next, or they will be prevented from becoming citizens for fourteen years."[55]

As his work was light, Gilkison had sufficient leisure to read the books right at hand in the store. He studied the writings of Locke, Newton, and Bacon, displaying on occasion a noticeable aptitude for advanced mathematics.[56] Gilkison habitually read until midnight, a practice which proved ruinous to his health, for finally at the age of thirty he succumbed to tuberculosis.

At the commencement of his studies with Gilkison, Henry discovered that the bookseller was not a severe taskmaster. "I was always at his side, and trimmed the same lamp, but in very different reading," Henry recalled appreciatively long after his mentor had died. "I luxuriated on the sweetmeats of the bookstore, running through novel after novel, and searching out every light or amusing work in the store or library, until at last I became completely surfeited."[57] Then the boy turned to poetry and biography and works on political affairs, reading books on the French Revolution avidly. Gilkison, happy to have Henry's companionship, never held him to a rigid course of study but instead discussed many subjects with him. Henry tried to win any argument which might arise, relying on an overpowering flow of words whenever handicapped by a lack of knowledge. Henry liked to declaim, particularly if he had an audience. One night he startled Gilkison and several townsmen who were present in the store by the vigor of his speech, which increased in intensity as the moments flew by. Standing on the hearth without shoes, Henry had waxed eloquent as the bricks grew hot underneath his feet. Despite the neglect of his lessons, this association with Gilkison benefited Henry. Not only did he assimilate an amount of useful information, but he acquired self-confidence when consistently treated more as an equal than as a pupil.

Certainly Brackenridge had little time now to devote to the upbringing of his son, having embroiled himself again in party faction. But he was thereby enabled to teach Henry the art of practical politics.

V: *The Law Is a Jealous Mistress*

When the elder Brackenridge wrote in *Modern Chivalry* that every male citizen in a republic had "a right *to elect,* and a right *to be elected,*" he expressed a belief which was one of his guiding principles. Not popular enough himself to win an elective office, he had to work for the election of candidates who shared his political views. Consequently, Henry, at the age of twelve years, saw his father establish the Democratic-Republican party in Western Pennsylvania and become its recognized leader.[1]

His experience in the Whisky Insurrection had not impaired Hugh's fighting heart. As soon as he had published the defense of his conduct in that affair, he re-entered politics,[2] resolved to attack his Federalist opponents, some of whom were his personal enemies, in an attempt to weaken their strength in Pittsburgh and the surrounding country. In the town there were less than fifty Democrats eligible to vote. The Federalists, of course, controlled the political offices. So determined was Brackenridge to injure their party that he gave up his law practice and in prose and verse "wrote with the pungency and force of a Junius, and spoke with the inspiring eloquence of a Henry. . . ." No longer practicing in the court presided over by Judge Alexander Addison, a fanatical Federalist, Hugh was safe from involvement there in any dispute designed to discredit him. The struggle between the Federalists and the Democrats quickly became rancorous, destroying friendships and ending all dealings—business and social —between members of the two parties.

In November, 1797, Brackenridge indicated anew his interest in active politics by voicing his esteem for Lucas, Henry's former guardian and now a member of the state legislature, and for Gallatin, the congressman. In a letter to Scull, Hugh denied having written some essays which Lucas had published and taken credit for, although he admitted having had a hand in Lucas's election. He praised Lucas's independence and integrity, adding that he "is a man of information and of sentiment; speaks the Latin with elegance; the French like a scholar and a gentleman, and the English at least as well as Albert Gallatin who for seven years led the assembly of this state, and for three years has been considered as the first in congress, and if not always right, yet at least always eloquent."[3] Both men as Democrats deserved Hugh's support. It was Gallatin, however, who would have to run again in the next congressional election. This was also the time of the "X Y Z Affair," when a distrust of French sympathizers like Lucas and Gallatin was prevalent. But Hugh left no doubt about his regard for them, presaging his effort to return Gallatin to his seat in Congress.

By the time the campaign began in 1798, most people had forgotten that Brackenridge had already, in effect, endorsed the candidacy of Gallatin. Few therefore fathomed Hugh's strategy to split the Federalist party in his district. When John Woods, the Federalist lawyer whom Gallatin had defeated in the two previous elections, entered the lists again, Hugh denounced him in the most sarcastic terms in a letter[4] addressed to the Citizens of Greene, Washington, and Allegheny Counties, challenging his fitness for the office. Then Brackenridge revealed what had always irked him the most about this candidate: in 1781, "I pushed my way to these woods whence I thought I might emerge one day, and get forward myself in a Congress or some other public body. But what has been my surprise to find a youth of Bedford county in my way. . . ." As a matter of fact, the last time they had met in friendship had been in 1788, "over a dinner of bacon and greens at Monroe's tavern in Canonsburgh. . . ."[5] In that year Woods had wrecked Hugh's hope of winning a seat in the first Congress to meet under the new Constitution; now, a decade later, Hugh planned to thwart him in a like manner and, in addition, to damage the Federalist cause.

Brackenridge's next move came at a meeting in Pittsburgh called for the purpose of nominating a candidate to represent the district in Congress.[6] Not a candidate himself, he said, he was free to consider the qualifications of other men. The meeting then proceeded to nominate Colonel Presley Neville, in the belief that Gallatin might refuse to run for the office again; or if willing, he might find the prevailing anti-foreign sentiment impossible to overcome. Gallatin was not even a resident of the district, furthermore. A committee, of which Hugh was a member, published these reasons in a signed statement, dated August 4. His part in the proceedings dumfounded the Federalists, for Neville was one of them and a member of a family and political alliance—"the Neville Connection"—which Brackenridge hated. "As to stiling myself a PRIME MOVER, in the case of Nevill," Hugh declared, "I had thought I was, because no person had mentioned his name to me before I mentioned it to some; but it appears that he had been in the contemplation of many."[7] When an astute individual comprehended Hugh's tactics—"Woods and Neville he pitches to the devil . . . Gallatin is his man"[8]—he replied: "As to any thought or language of mine, savouring of deceiving Col. Neville, or 'gulling' as they will have it; let who will have said it is false, and who will believe it is a fool."[9]

The Federalists tried too late to mend their fences. It was not until September 28 that "an honorable accommodation" between Woods and Neville could be announced to the electorate of the congressional district.[10] The leaders agreed to support Woods after Neville had been persuaded to withdraw his name as a candidate. Brackenridge's stratagem of introducing Neville's name in the campaign to divide the Federalist party succeeded, for Gallatin retained his seat in Congress.[11]

The outcome of this election was proof that Hugh had the making of a shrewd politician in him. No one was happier about his father's successful essay than Henry, who read everything which Hugh wrote concerning politics "with great delight, and often committed to memory, being of course a violent Democrat as well as himself."[12] His course of reading, which included the great satires and books on history—and above all *Modern Chivalry,* helped Henry to understand the political maneuvering and to appreciate the discomfiture of the Federalists.

Their party was responsible for the passage by Congress in 1798 of the Alien and Sedition Acts. Of the blunders which the Federalist leaders committed both nationally and locally, none was greater than this attempt to stifle all criticism of the administration policies. The Democrats damned the Sedition Act in particular as unconstitutional. It was Scull's unhappy lot as a Federalist editor to defend the law. "The sedition law was designed for the purpose of impressing upon turbulent and unprincipled men some respect for the government of our country," he reminded the readers of his gazette.[13] His statement was a bald threat to any person who doubted the constitutionality of the act and said so in public, or who dared to evince dissatisfaction with the Federalist leadership in national and local government. Hugh was a prime target for Federalist zealots; but he conducted his affairs so carefully that one party member could only write: "A thief hates the eighth commandment. So does Mr. Brackenridge a law against sedition. It is a restraint on his corrupt nature."[14]

But this legislation which was inimical to free speech and a free press did not save the Federalists from defeat in Pennsylvania the next year, 1799—a defeat more humiliating and serious than the re-election of Gallatin to Congress. In the gubernatorial election James Ross, a United States senator, was the Federalist candidate pitted against Thomas McKean, the chief justice of Pennsylvania and a signer of the Declaration of Independence. Scull announced the candidacies of both men in late March, and at the same time declared his support of Ross on the ground that he was a citizen of the western country.[15] Several days later there occurred in Pittsburgh the launching of the United States Galley "Senator Ross," a vessel carrying a cannon in her bow and swivels on her quarter-deck. When she was safely afloat in the Allegheny, her crew fired a salute, which Fort Fayette returned immediately. Because the launch was accomplished without mishap, Scull heralded it as "A GOOD OMEN" in his paper.[16]

The Federalists, nevertheless, lost this election, noteworthy for the vehemence with which charges were hurled at the candidates. In the *Gazette* of October 5, for example, Scull gave up the entire second page to an attempted refutation of the assertions that Ross was "an open Reviler of Religion; a Deist;

an Atheist; a Speculator; a Landjobber; an active Agent in exciting the Western Insurrection; and that in Public life he has been altogether under Foreign Influence." Over a hundred Pittsburgh Federalists had signed the statement. To agitate their opponents even more the Democrats bandied Hugh's name about as a candidate to represent Allegheny County in the next assembly, for, as "A FARMER" put it, "if it is necessary to have a good Governor, it is not less so to have a wise and virtuous Legislature."[17] But "A REAL FARMER" believed that Brackenridge was responsible for that observation and the letter in which it had appeared: ". . . many are wicked enough to ascribe the piece to old Hugh himself."[18] Brackenridge, whose candidacy was not pushed vigorously, was unsuccessful; but in the state-wide contest for governor McKean was victorious. Not fully apparent as yet was the ultimate doom of the Federalist cause, and the triumph of Jeffersonian Republicanism.

At six o'clock on Saturday evening, October 26, the joyous Democrats— "the friends of Thomas M'Kean"—gathered at Smur's tavern to celebrate the victory.[19] Numbering between forty and fifty, they were a convivial group for whom Hugh acted as president, or chairman, and Samuel Ewalt as vice-president. McKean was the subject of an enthusiastic toast, naturally. Then, at nine o'clock, Hugh left the assembly: "Volunteer on the occasion. H. H. Brackenridge, the friend of his country, of the poor and of the oppressed." A half-hour later the celebrators were ready to depart for their respective homes, having in reality acclaimed Hugh their leader. Outdoors in the street armed men, fearful that McKean's followers intended to incite a riot, accosted some of them. The Democrats held another meeting at noon the following Monday, at which time under Hugh's chairmanship they disavowed any intention of disturbing the peace. An investigation proved that a nasty rumor had caused the incident.

After McKean's victory the intense pre-election feeling between the parties in Pittsburgh and Allegheny County did not abate. Hugh himself was not through tormenting his Federalist adversaries, and he had a special surprise reserved for Scull. On November 18, Brackenridge was the chairman of an important meeting held by the supporters of McKean at Smur's tavern. Angered by the abuse dealt them in Scull's paper, they resolved "that we will encourage another Press, and that a committee be appointed . . . for this purpose."[20] Hugh personally informed Scull that a press which could print pamphlets at a reasonable price was desirable; moreover, he told the editor frankly that he "did not like the general spirit" of the *Gazette* "for some time past."[21] Brackenridge's argument was unassailable:

. . . Indeed there seems to be a use for two presses, it is so little that one weekly paper can communicate. In the city there is scarcely a householder but takes a daily paper, and some two, which is six or more in the week. The people of the country have as much need of information as the town, in a government founded on opinion, and where the sentiments of the people govern. In a contest for power, or difference of opinion upon principle, it is difficult for a press not to have a leaning or be suspected of it. And the party in whose interest it is not thought to be, will naturally look to another!

Scull was furious: "He [Brackenridge] knows his talk about plenty of intelligence and cheapness of printing, is only to GULL those he can make tools of. What Printer prints cheaper than I do? What sheet is better filled than mine?"[22] But such outbursts did not deter Hugh from proceeding with his plan for the establishment of another newspaper.

He bought the types and a press and named the gazette himself before obtaining an editor for it.[23] The *Tree of Liberty* was to be the title, accompanied by a motto taken from the Scriptures, Rev. 22:2—"And the leaves of the tree were for the healing of the nations." When the paper first issued from the press on August 16, 1800, there appeared above the motto a picture of the "tree of life" with the heads of people visible beneath its spreading branches. But most readers, especially the curious Federalists, at once thought of the French Revolution and the guillotine and shuddered as they eyed this rebus at the top of the first page. Brackenridge had persuaded John Israel, the Jewish publisher of the *Herald of Liberty,* in Washington, Pennsylvania, to become the editor of the new organ of the Democratic-Republican party in the western counties.

"Brackenridge of late seems to have a hankering after the *Jews,*" a subscriber to the *Gazette* wrote to Scull on the appearance of the *Tree of Liberty.* This statement[24] was typical of many scurrilous references to both Brackenridge and Israel which now began to appear in the Federalist journal. There was unquestionably a considerable amount of anti-Semitism in Western Pennsylvania, as reflected by the nature of the publications in that one paper alone. Israel was made to feel his Jewishness. But the hatred which many individuals felt for Hugh was without bound, for he contributed material regularly to the columns of the *Tree of Liberty,* attacking the Federalists in his inimitable way. By the end of September, 1800, Scull boasted that flooding his office were communications concerning Brackenridge, promising his subscribers to consider for publication those which contained "truth, decency and good sense. . . ."[25] At the same time, however, Israel received a flow of communications "relative to Mr. Scull. . . ."[26] The *Tree of Liberty,* Israel informed his correspondents, must not imitate Scull's "general system of scurrility and abuse," adding that "his stupidity and ignorance are so proverbial, that all we think necessary, is to continue, as we have begun, *shaving him with a feather.*"

This journalistic warfare in which his father planned much of the strategy had its effect on Henry,[27] for, at the age of fifteen, he "became a writer. . . ."

The idea of submitting an article to the editor of the *Tree of Liberty* flashed into Henry's mind, but difficult he found the actual work of expressing his thoughts on paper. He strove for perfection, copying and recopying the article twenty times or more until at last he could find no further changes to make. Israel published the production which the young author sent him anonymously.[28] When Henry saw "the first-born" of his brain in print, he "trembled like an aspen leaf. . . ."

His father had meanwhile received his reward for establishing the Jeffersonian party in Western Pennsylvania, backed by a powerful agency of propaganda, the *Tree of Liberty*. A despondent Federalist drew up a petition addressed to "H. H. B....................., Esq. President of the Jacobin Society, Professor of Chivalry, Privy Counsellor to the Governor of Bantam, Poet Laureat to the Herald of Sedition, Biographer to the Insurgents, Auctioneer of Divinity, and Haberdasher of Pronouns, &c. &c.," and sent it[29] to the *Gazette* for publication, or perhaps Scull himself was the author. The "Two Thousand" petitioners begged forgiveness for their offense of voting for Ross; and they hoped to avoid punishment "by laying their petition on the lower end of the lower step" of Brackenridge's law office. It was here, in fact, on the east side of Market Street in their clapboard houses that Hugh and some of his closest associates had conducted the campaign against the Federalists. Here operated the "Clapboard Democracy," a name becoming so significant that Thomas Baird, a member of this potent junto, proudly advertised the firm of Fulton and Baird as located in the "Centre of Clap-Board Row."[30] The leader of these Democrats now capped his political career by accepting the appointive office of a justice of the Pennsylvania Supreme Court from Governor McKean, whose victory in the election had created a vacancy on the bench.[31]

"We learn, that Captain Farrago has returned home from his journey to the eastward, laden with more SUBSTANTIAL HONOURS than those acquired in his expeditions with his Irish servant Teague O'Regan," Scull reported to his subscribers on January 25, 1800. That was true. Besides his appointment as a judge Hugh had had the satisfaction of seeing Governor McKean remove James Brison from the office of prothonotary of Allegheny County and replace him with the bookseller Gilkison. Once during the period of the Whisky Insurrection, Brison, a Federalist, had snubbed Hugh and Sabina Brackenridge by not inviting them to a ball in honor of General Henry Lee, who commanded the army sent by the President to quell the uprising. By favoring the dismissal of Brison, Hugh had repaid him in full for the slight, although Scull gave as the reason for the action the fact that the prothonotary had voted for Ross in the election.[32]

Shortly after undertaking the duties of his office, the sickly Gilkison died.

Hugh's sympathetic hand was evident throughout Gilkison's short-lived career, from the moment he had entered the law office as a student and as Henry's tutor to the appointment as prothonotary. Through Hugh's influence also Tarleton F. Bates received the position of clerk in Gilkison's office.[33] Brackenridge decided to let his son remain under the bookseller's wing, with, however, the stipulation that Henry serve a kind of apprenticeship in the office before beginning a serious study of the law. Then, on Friday night, March 21, 1800, the new prothonotary died.[34]

Hugh settled Gilkison's affairs with dispatch. Fortunately for him his relative had kept a careful record of the business transacted in the bookstore and scrivener's office. Entries on every page of Gilkison's account book[35] provided evidence that Brackenridge had financed the venture and, incidentally, that his son had been a regular customer—"Stock for 1/4 Quire paper for Henry .... 1.3" (December 9, 1799). As Gilkison's creditor, therefore, Hugh was in a position to dispose of the bookstore to Zadok Cramer, who, as early as March 29, advertised his intention of establishing a bookbindery.[36] Within a few months Cramer was ready to begin his business of manufacturing blank and bound books, in addition to selling stationery and the works of noted authors, including the classical. Likewise, Hugh had quickly attended to another matter, as his fellow citizens soon discovered when they read the *Gazette* on April 19:

TARLETON F. BATES, ESQ.
Is appointed Prothonotary of this County—Vice JOHN C. GILKESON, Esquire, deceased.

Although this appointment of Bates to the county office was part of Hugh's reward, conceivably an instance of patronage, he took his seat on the supreme bench of the state resolved to be independent of special interests which might seek to influence his decisions. He no longer accepted invitations to dinner or to other social affairs, thereby avoiding obligation to various hosts who might sometime appear before him as suitors in court.[37] "It is not in the natural order of things, for men in authority who have *discipline* to support, to become *guests;* much less who have controversies to determine between man and man," he stated near the end of his judicial career. "There is a repugnance in a mind of *sensibility* in deciding against your *host*, if you can help it; and you will at least have a wish when his cause comes to trial, *that it may turn out good.*"[38] Hugh was aware, too, that "wine will put a judge in good humor," occasionally perhaps "into too good a humor with one counsel *at the expense of another; or at least of the cause* which he supports." Although Hugh was a convivial person who drank whisky and other liquor like most people at the time, he faithfully followed the precepts which he himself had framed for the impartial administration of justice. His personal enemies and the Federalists, however, circulated the most preposterous tales concerning his conduct, both official and unofficial. A citizen dependent on the gazettes for information had no way of ascertaining the truth concerning this eccentric judge.

In the minds of his opponents, of course, Brackenridge sinned damnably by continuing his political writing after his appointment to the bench. So determined was Hugh to strengthen the Jeffersonian party in Western Pennsylvania that even on circuit he replied vigorously to Federalist criticism. He also saw to it that the *Tree of Liberty* began operations smoothly, assisting Israel in every possible way. The fact that Hugh remained in Pittsburgh with his family after appointment as judge had angered his critics because they had "raised a cry that now he was provided for himself, he would leave the country, and *desert the people.*"[39] His adversaries therefore altered the charge against him to one which was really complimentary—"that the people are more under his influence than is consistent with their own independence; they are spoken of in a late publication as *'those under his command.'* " As Israel declared in the *Tree of Liberty*, if Hugh left Pittsburgh to establish residence elsewhere, the same enemies would spiritedly deny that he had had any power or political influence whatever while living in the town. Actually wanting to move to a more central location in the state,[40] Brackenridge bided his time until well after the inauguration of Jefferson. "He [Brackenridge] leaves this place with his family for Carlisle on Monday next," Israel announced in his paper on Saturday, August 22, 1801.

When the Brackenridges set out for their new home in Cumberland County, they left Henry behind in Pittsburgh to continue his clerkship in the law. After receiving his appointment as prothonotary, Bates had employed the boy to work in the office, giving him board and clothing in return for services which were poorly performed.[41] Like any boy who was fifteen years old, Henry had to attend to business of his own, a multitude of projects which constantly popped into his mind and tantalized him unmercifully while he copied legal documents. Bates was a tolerant man, who reproved Henry frequently for carelessness in transcribing names and dates—whenever, for example, Henry unconsciously wrote the name of Pocahontas for the name of Smith on a deed—but who never resorted to severe punishment out of anger: "If he had not been one of the mildest and most indulgent men in the world, he would have knocked me down twenty times a day." Henry was always chagrined by his inefficiency after Bates had rebuked him, resolving to do better in the future.

This boring work disrupted Henry's practice of reading everything at hand at all hours of the day and night. When Bates realized the boy's frustrating situation, he agreed to effect a compromise, whereby Henry kept on his desk in the office only a small collection of books for perusal in spare time—the *Elegant Extracts in Prose and Verse,* Cicero's *De officiis,* the Abbé Maury on "Eloquence," the *Lectures* of Hugh Blair, the *Speeches* of John Philpot Curran —and promised to read other works in their lodgings. Some books caught Henry's interest at the beginning and held him captive until he had finished reading them. Chained to a bench he soon found himself on one occasion after he had espied a dog-eared volume in the barroom of a tavern and had begun reading. Wanting a number of pages, including the title page, the book proved to be Dr. Johnson's *Rasselas.*

Certain enthusiasms also gripped Henry from time to time.[42] One was his zeal for drawing and painting, which was so strong a feeling that willingly, he thought, would he spend the rest of his life in jail if permitted "to do nothing else but copy drawings." Into the night he sat copying painstakingly the three hundred or so engravings in the magnificent volume which Bates owned on the subject of physiognomy—the work of Johann Kaspar Lavater, the Swiss theological writer who believed that facial characteristics held the secret of a person's nature. Henry became a proficient copyist, a fact which led some people to think mistakenly that he had a talent for painting. Although he had read every available book in town on painting and bought crayons, India ink, and water colors, he could never create an original work of art. Eventually he discovered his lack of ability in this respect himself and returned, not dispiritedly, to his books. Another fleeting passion was to excel in playing a musical instrument, with the result that he took violin and flute lessons to no avail on account of a "very bad ear." But Henry never lost his love of music.

When these two enthusiasms had run their course, another took their place in his high estimation—the theater. One of the projects, therefore, which monopolized Henry's thoughts to the detriment of his work as a law clerk was the organization of a Thespian club by the young men of Pittsburgh.[43] Thomas Butler, Morgan Neville, George Wallace, and William Wilkins played the leading roles in their dramatic productions, although Henry appeared in two parts on the stage of the improvised theater in the courthouse: "I had the honor of delivering a letter to Captain Glenroy, and of appearing as a Scotchman in Dick the Apprentice." The performances did not smack of the amateurish, for the acting was polished and the staging clever. To enhance the quality of their production in February of 1803, the actors spent "several hundred dollars for music from Philadelphia. . . ."

With such elaborate arrangements the venture had to be a financial success, for otherwise the organization would be in embarrassing straits and face

immediate extinction. The actors picked a Saturday night for their performance in the large room in the courthouse, gave an order to Scull for a supply
of tickets, and then advertised the double bill in the gazettes, the program
featuring plenty of comedy to attract a large audience:

TO-MORROW EVENING
Will be Performed, at the Court House,
BY THE YOUNG GENTLEMEN
Of this town,
THE
COMIC OPERA
OF THE
POOR SOLDIER,
AND THE
APPRENTICE,
A FARCE.
BOX and PITT 3-4 of a Dollar.
GALLERY 1-2 Dollar.
Tickets may be had at Mr. Scull's Printing Office.
The Curtain will rise precisely at half after Six.
FRIDAY, FEBRUARY 18TH, 1803.[44]

The performance was a hit. It was repeated a few weeks later, on Wednesday
evening, March 9, "FOR A BENEVOLENT PURPOSE."[45] The activities
of the Thespian society evidently created a favorable impression in the minds
of most Pittsburghers, especially those who were not strict Presbyterians and
consequently not puritanical in point of view. But Henry's father did not
appreciate the efforts of the club to popularize drama in Pittsburgh because
he "had the greatest contempt for village play-acting, and no great respect
for actors on any stage (although he possessed the talents to be one of the
greatest both in tragedy and comedy). . . ."[46] The elder Brackenridge undoubtedly read the notices of the production in the gazettes and received
accounts of his son's performance from friends "who thought they were
giving him some agreeable news. In consequence of this I received a very
strict injunction to attend to my law books, *'as the law is a jealous mistress, and
will not abide a rival.'* " Although Hugh lived in Carlisle now, he kept check
of Henry.

That Henry was not blameworthy for his interest in dramatics his father
would have realized had he considered the matter objectively. Henry lodged
with Bates at Mrs. Earle's boardinghouse in Market Street, and here he also
stayed off and on after he had left the prothonotary's employ. But at this
time in 1803, the "house furnished the principal *dramatis personae*" for the
productions of the Thespian club.[47] It was thus Henry's good fortune to associate with a group of talented young professional men, sophisticates whose
knowledge and polite manners charmed him: "The conversation at dinner was

65

almost always interesting, turning on general politics, history, military events of Europe, or public characters; while the most rigid observance of good breeding prevailed, and the most gentlemanly tolerance of opposing opinions."[48] Indeed, as Henry likewise recalled, "It was not a hasty meal snatched at a *table d'hote*, but the 'feast of reason and the flow of soul.' " The diners at Mrs. Earle's table subsequently advanced to some of the highest offices in the land—to Congress and the Supreme Court of the United States. Sometimes an army officer or a famous traveler joined the lively company; and on occasion, too, an odd person like Francis Scachi appeared, who took profiles with his "physiognotrace" and sold plain, black, and gilt frames in which to put them.[49]

The miscellaneous reading which Henry did in his room at the boarding-house, or elsewhere except in the office, somewhat reflected the substance of the conversations at the table. He therefore studied the works of such writers as Voltaire and Helvetius and Paine—devotees of reason who "pulled down religion" and "put up nothing in its place."[50] He came to believe that his acquaintanceship with their writings was actually harmful to his mental growth, not having been at once counteracted by the views of thinkers like Cicero and Grotius and Locke on the same subject. Heavy fare this was for a boy hardly seventeen years old.

But Henry was a fast learner if not coerced in his studying or work, and particularly so if self-instructed. Bates well understood this trait of his clerk, remonstrating mildly with him whenever justified by inefficient work and gradually enlarging the scope of his experience at the same time by trusting him with more and more duties outside the office. Consequently Henry began to attend the court where he not only observed the proceedings, listening attentively to the speeches of opposing counsel and to the charges of the judge presiding, but also participated in them by swearing the juries and witnesses and performing other similar services: ". . . I picked up much law, in the way a child acquires its vernacular tongue."[51]

In spite of his acceptance as one of them by the circle at Mrs. Earle's and the friendship of the elegant Bates, Henry needed the companionship of a boy with whom he could share his youthful interests. Joe, the cobbler's son, had been Henry's protector in childhood, although he was not a wholesome influence for him as they grew older. But Henry had found a real friend to replace the luckless Joe in the person of an ambitious and intelligent lad named John Nicholson, who studied medicine diligently under the tutelage of an experienced practitioner, undaunted by the lack of a formal education.[52] They had become such close companions that they "almost renounced all other society. We walked, and read, and talked together, and even kept up an episto-lary correspondence, once a day, while he was confined to the shop and I to the

66

office." This friendship was of the utmost importance to Henry, for even in the midst of a multitude he could feel lonesome. With his family two hundred miles away in Carlisle, he felt insecure, although his landlady was as kind to him as a mother.

The West now beckoned more than ever to the inhabitants of the East, particularly to the young like Nicholson. Since the Treaty of San Lorenzo, 1795, the frontiersmen had enjoyed the free navigation of the Mississippi and the right of deposit at New Orleans. Commerce on the western rivers flourished as the inhabitants of the region promptly exploited the situation, often in an ingenious way. One company formed by twenty farmers, according to the editor Israel's information, built the brig "Monongahela Farmer" an ocean-going ship, which "left her natal stream" in May of 1801 with eight hundred barrels of flour on board.[53] Each member had invested one hundred dollars in the vessel besides owning a share of the cargo consigned to the New Orleans market. The master, however, carried orders to "proceed from thence to one of the islands" if that port had an oversupply of the commodity. "That the profits may be worthy of the undertaking, to stimulate them and others to future enterprises, we wish, and have very sanguine hopes that they will be," Israel observed editorially in his notice of this venture. It was the same speculative spirit which soon prompted Nicholson to go "down the river to seek his fortune as a physician."[54]

The decisive event which determined Nicholson's action, and countless others similar, was the Louisiana Purchase. A crisis had arisen in 1802, when the acting intendant of Louisiana, Juan Ventura Morales, had arbitrarily revoked the American right of deposit at New Orleans, infuriating the westerners but also producing the negotiations with Napoleon's government resulting in the acquisition of the whole vast province. The purchase was a master stroke in diplomacy, which Israel lost no time in applauding: "The cession of Louisiana, including the island of New Orleans, to the United S. at once puts a stop, to the bellowings of federalists, and obliges them, contrary to their wishes, *to praise the administration.*" The editor stressed the fact that Jefferson and his ministers, Robert R. Livingston and James Monroe, had obtained advantages for the American people in general and especially for the inhabitants of the western country without war or prejudicial commitments. Henry and Nicholson undoubtedly read this editorial in the *Tree of Liberty* of July 16, 1803, and discussed it together. Within a year Nicholson went down the Ohio.

Not many years later Henry, too, went down-river to the land of promise. But for the moment he had to pursue the law with unflagging attention as his father had commanded.

VI: The Bar of Pittsburgh

In 1814 the elder Brackenridge climaxed his career by publishing a book entitled *Law Miscellanies,* in which he suggested—or rather "hinted at"— a course of study for the law student to follow, designed to facilitate "the ascent to the summit. . . ."[1] He made the arduous preparation necessary to reach this goal, the admission to practice at the bar, seem like an exciting adventure: ". . . the citadel of the law must be taken . . . by regular approaches; the difficulties of it must be encountered at long shot."

Brackenridge's advice to prospective law students, as far as it went, was to the point. The chief qualification of a lawyer, he wrote, was integrity—*"the love of truth and justice."* Another qualification was a liberal education, whereby a student acquired a knowledge of literature, science, and a mastery of his own "vernacular tongue." To become proficient in the proper use of words— to have the ability to select the best term in every instance—he needed some knowledge of the languages, particularly Greek and Latin and French and German. Brackenridge recommended, moreover, the study of the finest models of writing to acquire an appreciation of style. Obviously he hoped to encourage students of promise, and not dunderheads, to enter upon the pursuit of law. Nevertheless, he advocated a gradual approach, or introduction, to the subject by the study of history, ethics, and politics first, followed by jurisprudence itself, especially municipal law. He believed that the student required supervision in his course of reading, reserving Blackstone's *Commentaries* as a final task. Abridgments and reports must never be read "flush through" in his opinion, for little of the contents was ever remembered.

Brackenridge also indicated a handicap under which many students labored —*"the want of application in early years,"* observing that few were able to regain the ground lost then. In elaborating on this idea, he gave a nice demonstration of placing the proper word in the proper place:

> . . . Owing to the indulgence of parents, and family education, there is a want of tone in the mental system, which it is not easy to restore in the academies, or produce . . . And after leaving the academies, sufficient preparation is not enjoined, or allowed for the gaining a knowledge of a profession; and this from an impatience to get forward, and to fly unfledged from the nest. *Boys are men too soon,* and therefore, *always boys.*

Thus he disclosed the reason he had directed Henry's pre-law studies himself. He had seen that his son did not suffer from a lack of "tone in the mental system"; and in spite of his unfeeling treatment of the boy, he had succeeded in this purpose. Henry, therefore, began his law course prepared to tackle the most difficult treatises with confidence. Brackenridge, furthermore, had determinedly refused to let his son "fly unfledged from the nest."

He had decided, too, the exact place where Henry should commence his study of the law. In July, 1803, the Governor appointed William Ayres to the office of prothonotary, register, and recorder of the newly created county of Butler, which lay north of Pittsburgh.[2] Ayres, like Gilkison, had read law in Brackenridge's office; but unlike Gilkison, he had completed his studies successfully and begun his attorneyship before receiving the appointment as a prothonotary. Desirous of continuing his practice as well as enjoying the prestige of public office, Ayres employed Henry to attend to the routine duties of the position, with the understanding that he read law in his free time. But the elder Brackenridge was the one who perceived the special advantage of this arrangement: "It was thought by my father that the solitude of Butler would be more favorable to application than the society of Pittsburg."[3]

Henry's life in Butler was idyllic.[4] The county seat was hardly even an outpost in the wilderness, consisting of several unfinished log cabins, when he arrived there, although a store, two taverns, and a blacksmith's shop were soon erected and opened for business. He had brought Ayres' library with him from Pittsburgh as well as his own reading matter. He plunged immediately into Blackstone's *Commentaries*, not saving it for a last task; but for relaxation he turned to the plays of Shakespeare or of Molière or to a work like *Plutarch's Lives*. Henry studied in the morning and evening, performing his few duties in the office as speedily as possible so that "generally the day was sacred to liberty." With gun in hand and a book in his pocket he rambled about the countryside day after day and month after month. Glade Run became his favorite haunt because there somewhere he could always find the edge of a cliff on which to sit and gaze "on the silent waste, giving wing to fancy, and weaving a thousand rainbow tissues of the brain." Once, when he rested under an oak and looked dreamily down the meadow which sloped away beneath him, a huge buck with branching antlers approached slowly up the hill. Finally, at the last moment, the deer raised his head and stared into Henry's eyes and, startled, sprang into the brush. Then, reluctantly, Henry returned to the office.

Henry spent almost a year in Butler, during which time he attended the earliest courts held in the county.[5] The first court, attended by the bar of Pittsburgh, was a hilarious exhibition of frontier justice, drawing the inhabitants, predominantly Scotch-Irish, from all corners of the county to the new "hall of justice," a "log-cabin just raised and covered, but without window-sash, or doors, or daubing. . . ." When Judge Jesse Moore, the president of the Court of Common Pleas, and the two associate judges took their seats in chairs placed on a carpenter's bench, a number of curious spectators hastily climbed to the rafters where they hung, "suspended like enormous Madagascar bats," with John McJunkin astride the joists "directly over the heads of their honors. . . ." Before the presiding judge, who was the quintessence of judicial dignity, could organize the court and proceed with the business, he had to order the sheriff to pull these strong-willed frontiersmen down from their perches. Afterward Henry watched intently on this February day in 1804 as some of the leading Pittsburgh attorneys at law were admitted to practice before the court—Steele Semple, William Wilkins, Henry Baldwin, and the same James Mountain who had been his teacher at the Academy at home. [6]

Henry returned to Pittsburgh to enter Mountain's office as a law student beginning a supervised course of study. [7] Despite the attraction of the outdoors in Butler, Henry had managed to read Blackstone and John Reeves' *History of the English Law,* acquainting himself generally with the subject. On his arrival in Pittsburgh he went immediately to the boardinghouse of Mrs. Earle to arrange for his meals and lodging. Nicholson, he knew, had gone down the Ohio, thereby leaving him without a close friend as he began his serious preparation for admission to the bar.

But one day not long after his return Henry happened to enter Baldwin's office when the lawyer was absent, finding there instead a broad-shouldered and long-visaged youth reading a law book—"It was unnecessary to inquire whether he was a student." [8] Walter Forward glanced at the caller, a slender person of his own age, an animated figure, well-dressed, and plainly eager for a conversation. Soon they were arguing a point of law, with Henry, who was losing, becoming so impassioned that passers-by gathered at the window.

Forward was determined to succeed in his preparation for the bar. Born in Connecticut, he had as a boy moved with his family to Ohio, where he helped his father on their farm and eventually taught a night school. Deciding to become a lawyer, he had set out for Pittsburgh on foot and without money. Fortune led him to Baldwin's office, where the attorney was at that moment about to go on the circuit. Having heard Baldwin's name mentioned as a lawyer and hoping to read law with him, Forward now frankly explained his penniless situation and likewise his ambition. Baldwin gave him the office key and directed him to start reading Blackstone in his absence. That Baldwin had instantly taken a liking to him was the only encouragement Forward needed to attempt a difficult course of study with no preparation whatever.

For this law student Henry was a stimulating companion. Forward, in turn, "became more than a brother" to Henry. [9] After their meeting they had strolled up Grant's Hill and beyond to a small waterfall, one of Henry's favorite spots, on a Saturday afternoon. [10] Here, deep in a glen and out of sight of curious eyes, they had bathed under the chill, cascading water and Forward had washed his trousers while expressing bitter annoyance at his lack of funds. When he became the editor of the *Tree of Liberty* in December of 1805, however, he was able to prosecute his studies without financial worry. His life during this period was otherwise uneventful, whereas Henry's continued full of unusual incident.

Henry's protectress, Jane Marie, was now in dire trouble.[11] Raised in Philadelphia, she had married John Marie in her seventeenth year. The ceremony was performed by Bishop White in Philadelphia in October, 1779. Born sometime in the year 1727-28, Marie was so many years older than his wife that from time to time he made a will or an agreement designed to protect her rights in their marriage. In Philadelphia, for example, on September 13, 1786, he signed, sealed, and published his will[12] bequeathing all of his possessions to her and appointing her the sole executrix of it. In Pittsburgh on February 12, 1797, Marie signed an agreement, duly witnessed and recorded,[13] by which he promised never to sell or alienate in any way "No. 6, outlot"—their beautiful property on Grant's Hill—without her prior consent. But Jane, nevertheless, lost her home with its parklike setting in an extraordinary manner.

Early in 1803, the wife of Steele Semple warned Jane that the loss of her home was imminent. Marie, who longed to visit France, his native land, before he died, had left Pittsburgh on January 3 of that year in the company of Senator Ross, who stood at the head of the bar. That night they stayed at an inn twenty miles away, at which time Marie agreed to sell his property on Grant's Hill to the lawyer, violating the agreement with his wife. On January 14, Marie signed not only a power of attorney empowering Jane to act for him legally but also a deed conveying to Ross the home and the six acres of land—as well as the gardening tools, the grates in the house, and a young cow—for a consideration of two thousand dollars and two bonds totaling sixteen hundred more. Both documents were in Ross's handwriting—the deed officially recorded on June 10.[14] Jane was dumbfounded when Mrs. Semple informed her of the transaction, recalling later that no "dispute, no anger, no difference on any matter whatever, preceded [her husband's] departure; as he grew in years he was occasionally peevish, but my disposition was not to notice it, nor indeed to reply or aggravate a petulance that many good people are not free from."[15]

Jane was a plucky fighter, as Ross soon learned. Marie had continued on his way to France, whereas the lawyer had returned to Pittsburgh to attend court in the spring. At that time Ross unceremoniously inspected the Marie home and informed Jane of his purchase. She reminded him confidently that her husband was unable to sell the property without her approval: "Mr. Ross then assumed a soothing tone—he condescended even to complaisance—but this course was no more successful with me than the other, and he departed menacing me with the utmost vengeance of the law."[16] Ross followed up his visit with a threatening letter,[17] dated April 1, in which he refused her offer to reimburse him for any money given her husband in return for a cancellation of the transaction of January 14. Jane was determined to preserve the place on Grant's Hill for her daughter's inheritance. When Ross's threats of impending misfortune began to materialize—"my reputation was now assailed; the people of the neighbourhood gradually withdrew or became shy of me," she decided to sell her furniture with the purpose in mind of renting the house, keeping an apartment in it, however, for herself and Caroline as a haven until Marie returned from France. The sale of the household effects began on August 2.

Jane herself had no way of anticipating what was now about to happen. On that day John Johnston, who witnessed the transaction of January 14, and Semple told her that they had received a power of attorney from Marie in France to be exercised jointly with Thomas Collins and John Lucas, superseding hers. She later proved to her own satisfaction at least that their power of attorney was a forgery.[18] But on this August 2, she refused to stop the sale as they had requested. The next day about ten o'clock in the morning, when Jane was in the process of washing her linen and clothes, a band of ruffians, claiming to have received orders from Ross, appeared on the scene and forced their way into her house. As the elder Wilkins and Baldwin, the lawyer, watched, the intruders hurried up the stairs; smashed open the door of the bedroom to which Jane had fled frightened; seized her by the legs; and with her head banging helplessly against the steps, dragged her down into the street. There they left her lying unconscious in a shockingly disheveled state under a blazing sun: about sunset, "Old Mr. Wilkins, who would not interfere in the morning, now came, and after I had been tore thus out of my house, wanted to know where I meant to lodge! And no doubt this was humanity, since he was Mr. Ross's bosom friend."[19] But Wilkins did obtain lodging for her at a tavern, where she remained three weeks nursing her cuts and bruises. Baldwin never surrendered to Jane the affidavits of witnesses in his possession, nor made them public.

Jane's troubles were not over because she refused to legalize Ross's seizure of her home. A bricklayer named Gray gave her lodging: ". . . Mr. Steele Semple, one of Mr. Ross's friends, a man who had spent days and months at my house, who, in fact, married his wife out of my house, interfered to deprive me even of this shelter; but the magnanimity of Mr. Gray resisted. . . ."[20] Ross expressed willingness to return her furniture—that is, the pieces not broken— if she deeded the property to him. Consequently Jane, in her forties, had only six hundred dollars to her name—realized from a sale of damaged goods and the liquors left in the tavern cellars—an amount which Ross begrudged her.

The following spring, sometime after Henry's arrival from Butler, Jane had a well-nigh incredible experience as she walked past her former home on a balmy evening with little Caroline and a servant girl:

... my child exclaimed *"O mama, see what beautiful paper they have put on our entry."*
... I glanced my eye involuntarily in the direction which my child had directed it ...
James Ross, himself, sprung forth upon me, in his hand he bore an enormous whip of
cowhide ... and with horrid imprecations fell upon me with this weapon; he beat my
child, and not contented with the lash which he had broken upon me, he clubbed it ...
I made an effort to escape, but insensible and blinded by the blows and wounds that I
had received on my face and eyes, I ran against a fence and there fell. ...

Mr. Henry Brackenridge, son of the judge, Mr. Mountain the attorney, Mr. Ayres
the attorney, Mr. Samuel Smith, carpenter, and Mr. Osborne, saw the transactions, and
saw Ross pursue me across the street.[21]

How hard it must have been for Henry to concentrate his attention on the
law books in Mountain's office after witnessing such a deed by the omnipotent
leader of the Pittsburgh bar! Or could this scene have been exaggerated by Jane's
imagination, devised for the purpose of injuring Ross in the gubernatorial
election of 1808? During the heated campaign her account of how she had lost
her lovely home was circulated throughout the state in pamphlet form—*The
Case of Jane Marie, Exhibiting the Cruelty and Barbarous Conduct of James
Ross, to a Defenceless Woman. Written and Published by the Object of His
Cruelty and Vengeance, and Addressed to the PUBLIC OF PHILADELPHIA
and the Whole of PENNSYLVANIA.* Her lurid story certainly contributed to
Ross's defeat in the election. Whether embellished or not, her account was
fundamentally true, as the documents on record proved.

On his return from France the eighty-year-old Marie perfected the agreement
of January 14 with Ross, an act officially recorded on August 28, 1807,[22] having
previously applied for a divorce and having also published a notice in the newspaper[23] announcing that he was not responsible for any debts contracted by
his wife. But at the very time when he was beginning his course of study under
Mountain, in May, 1804, Henry saw his benefactress leave Pittsburgh, a
despairing woman who had lost her home, resigned to doing needlework to
support herself and Caroline in Philadelphia.

Although Jane's departure was a heavy personal blow for Henry, no matter
under what cloud she had left Pittsburgh, he resolutely attended to his law
studies. He tackled the law of tenures and read the books of reports, a course
of study involving "distinctions so refined and subtle as to require to be seen
through the microscope of mental vision."[24] An unprofitable task this wearisome work seemed to him at the time. In 1842, however, he was the author of
*An Essay on Trusts and Trustees: In Relation to the Settlement of Real Estate
—The Power of Trustees—and Involving Many of the Most Abstruse Questions in the English and American Law of Tenures,* a treatise suggested by the
analysis of a deed of trust which had reserved a large tract of land for the
support of Caroline, with Ross himself named as one of the trustees!

Henry did have some diversion from this tedious study. He found the reading of historical works to be relaxing as well as interesting.[25] He read Edward Gibbon's *History of the Decline and Fall of the Roman Empire* and William Robertson's *History of the Reign of the Emperor Charles the Fifth*. He read *The Federalist*. He had, in fact, a predilection for books on American history. It was not surprising, therefore, that he began reading *The Life of George Washington* by John Marshall as soon as the first volumes appeared in the bookstores. He enjoyed, too, the exciting conversation every day at the table in Mrs. Earle's boardinghouse. But indispensable to his happiness was the companionship of Forward.

They spent their spare time together whenever possible. But their friendship irritated another young Pittsburgher, Ephraim Pentland, who had established the *Commonwealth* on July 24, 1805, to further the interests of that branch of the Democratic-Republican party in Pennsylvania which opposed Governor McKean. Pentland's gazette, which supported Simon Snyder against McKean in the gubernatorial election that year, was thus the rival of the *Tree of Liberty*. Pentland taunted Bates and Baldwin especially in the columns of his paper, and bitter he was when their candidate McKean was re-elected governor. "Virtue, Liberty, and Independence" was the slogan which Pentland had chosen for the *Commonwealth,* although as a belligerent editor he frequently slipped from the path of rectitude. After the election he vented his spleen against his political enemies. There were no libel laws to protect the victims.

We understand, from good authority, that Israel has sold the establishment of the *Tree of Liberty* to Messrs. BATES & BALDWIN—and that—*Forward,* a young student of morality from Connecticut, and who for three months preceding the late election, in company with a spurious branch of the *Brackenridge* family, employed his leisure hours in pasting obscene caricatures on the market house in this borough, will shortly commence his editorial career, immediately under the patronage of these gentlemen.[26]

By this time, the end of 1805, Pittsburgh had certainly become a demoralizing place for a sensitive youth like Henry. Pentland, as one instance, carried his dislike of the Brackenridges, father and son, too far. The editor delighted in referring to the judge as "Teague O'Regan," always in conjunction with a pointed phrase like "when sober,"[27] "a little more sober,"[28] or "a certain *drunken judge.*"[29] Perhaps this situation had influenced Hugh in deciding to send his son to Jefferson College at Canonsburg for six months in the fall of 1805, although Henry later stated that the reason he went there was to have the experience of studying under Samuel Miller, the well-known professor of mathematics and natural philosophy.[30] He attended the college, nevertheless, at the behest of his father.

This brief interval in his law studies passed pleasantly for Henry. Attendance at the small institution in Western Pennsylvania, chartered in 1802 and named in honor of the President of the United States,[31] was to be Henry's only experience as a college student. Here he studied such subjects as geography, Euclidean geometry, and natural philosophy under Miller's inspiring instruction: "He never took a book in his hand while we were demonstrating on the board, or when examining us in the most abstruse branches."[32] He was a favorite of the students because he not only had his knowledge at his finger tips, as Henry himself said, but also was a man who never belabored them for poor recitations—he believed in the efficacy of sweet reasonableness. Henry had three roommates, two of whom he liked well enough—Richard Coulter, a future congressman, and a youth named Graham, fated to die later in a duel. The third roommate, a New Englander, was, in Henry's opinion at least, a "bore of the first order," given to asking the silliest questions imaginable.[33] None of them frittered time away, for, as students of modest means, they hoped to acquire as much knowledge as possible during their days in college. These roommates, in fact, rose habitually an hour or two before sunrise. Henry participated in the activity of the literary societies, the Philo and the Franklin, as his extracurricular interest, on one occasion writing a prize composition.

But a somber event had meanwhile occurred in Pittsburgh, casting a pall over his carefree life in Canonsburg—the death of Bates, the prothonotary, in a duel. Pentland, who came originally from Philadelphia to establish the *Commonwealth,* had made a number of enemies in Pittsburgh by defaming his political opponents in editorial comments. Pentland's aspersions finally led Bates to cowhide him, the editor fleeing ignominiously to the house of a friend.[34] But as fate decreed, Bates actually fought Thomas Stewart, a merchant, who was the bearer of Pentland's challenge. Bates had refused to fight the editor, not considering him a gentleman and condemning him also for having appealed to the civil authority for protection. The duel with pistols— and the distance ten steps—took place on January 8, 1806, three miles from town and near the Monongahela. On the second fire Bates "received the ball of his antagonist's pistol, in the upper part of his breast, and expired in an hour."[35] Friends carried his body into Mrs. Earle's dining room and laid it on the carpet. Henry felt his death deeply, and many a person shed a tear at his passing.[36]

Therefore, when young Brackenridge returned to Pittsburgh, another friend was no longer a part of the familiar scene. But there was still Forward, who proved to be as apprehensive about his progress in preparing for the bar examination as Henry was about his own. With another candidate named McDonald, they met nearly every day to quiz each other on points of law, hoping at the same time to sharpen their wits.[37]

More valuable, however, was their activity in the law society which they now helped organize, for the incentive to prepare formal arguments on a particular question was provided as well as the opportunity to speak in public.[38] The membership consisted of ten or twelve young lawyers and law students, who at once elected William Wilkins as their president. Henry, Forward, and Charles Wilkins framed the constitution. Organized on a Saturday, the society decided to meet on the one following to debate a question involving the "subject of the admissibility, or credibility of the witness. . . ." The members divided themselves into two teams, assigned to each its side of the argument, and then adjourned the meeting.

The prospect of a debate in which members of the bar participated served as a powerful stimulus for Henry to perfect his oratory, both in content and delivery. His experience in debating at Jefferson College had revealed his chief weakness, an inability to develop a sustained argument on some question. He accordingly resolved to correct this deficiency that he might surprise the society with the quality of his performance. In his room at night he mastered the case which had suggested the question for debate and studied other cases to which the original referred, "following, like an antiquarian, or rather explorer, every little streamlet to its source." He noted various topics which might provide examples to illustrate his argument. In the daytime he practiced delivering his speech in the unfrequented oak grove atop Watson's Hill, at first finding few ideas—"only a few shabby recruits"—to string together. More work he did on the cases that night, and the next day back to his outdoor study he went to try again to construct a speech without recourse to pen and paper; and finally before the end of the week, he was successful. Euclid's logic and the orations of Demosthenes were his models. He finished the final rehearsal of his speech before noon on the Saturday of the debate. "When my turn came to speak," he recalled in later life, "I had only to open my mouth, and my words seemed to run out of themselves like the water from a Dutch pump, for I knew nothing of gesture, or the management of the voice." But he had made a satisfactory impression on his fellows, convincing himself at the same time that the habit of solitary declamation was worth while to form.

Besides his law studies and his interest in this society, Henry took lessons in German from Christopher Frederick Schewe, a Prussian whose eccentricity fascinated him.[39] This was in reality the beginning of an unusual friendship which ended abruptly years later in Florida under tragic circumstances. But at this time in 1806, the German added a touch of jollity to Henry's otherwise severe life. Ten years earlier Schewe had opened a store in a yellow house in Second Street in partnership with Frederick Hanckel, dealing in a variety of merchandise which included mirrors, tumblers, smelling bottles, Russian and West Indian rhubarb, loaf sugar, linen, ribbons, and yarn.[40] The venture was short-lived, however, lasting less than a month: the partnership was dissolved

76

by mutual consent, with Hanckel continuing the business alone.[41] Schewe eventually became a teacher of French at the Academy in town and a lodger at Mrs. Earle's boardinghouse.

Here he regaled the company with his jokes and anecdotes. Schewe asserted that he had toured Europe as the tutor of a young nobleman and that he had witnessed the storming of the Bastille in Paris, exhibiting a bullet scar on his leg as proof of his presence in the mad throng before the fortress. No one, of course, unless he did so in jesting at the festive board, wanted to doubt the truth of Schewe's wonderful stories, some of which concerned Frederick the Great and his generals. But more astonishing than his tales was the fact that he had recently become the minister of the German Lutheran church in Pittsburgh while teaching languages and drawing at the Academy. The hotheaded Pentland felt Schewe's spell, observing editorially in the *Commonwealth* that such an eloquent, learned, and tasteful gentleman should be encouraged to remain in town—"that whilst many men without talents, are patronized in Pittsburgh, this gentleman will not be under the necessity of leaving the town, exclaiming 'virtus laudatur, sed alget.' Or in the words of Dryden, 'for virtue is but drily praised and starves.' "[42]

Schewe had one unfortunate failing, an addiction to drink. He was unmistakably a chronic alcoholic. The most important things in his life finally became beer and tobacco. According to Henry, Schewe "used to express philosophically, the same sentiment which I have heard from Achilles Murat in jest, that *whisky was the* BEST PART *of the American government.*"[43]

Evidently Schewe was a bachelor with little or no interest in women, whereas this was the time when Henry became more and more conscious of feminine charms. Was the kindhearted Schewe his confidant in this matter? Or was it Forward? Henry, nevertheless, was now a secret admirer of pretty girls, although he appeared very timid in their company. Consequently, at the moment when he needed to use all of his power of concentration in preparing for the bar examination, "delightful visions too often took possession of my mind."[44]

There was also another distraction for him that summer and fall of 1806—the constant speculation about town concerning the mysterious plans of Aaron Burr, and then the sudden appearance of the man himself in Pittsburgh. "His projects were discussed in our little senate, and at the dinner-table, for months, before the attempt was made to carry them into execution," Henry wrote in retrospect.[45] It seemed clear to him at the time that Burr's design was the instigation of a revolution in Mexico and its subsequent liberation. That was Burr's great object, in Henry's view—certainly not the separation of western states from the Union, a scheme which was impossible of fulfillment after the Louisiana Purchase. As they enlisted men for the cause, Burr's agents, whom

Henry saw, maintained that President Jefferson had given tacit approval of their efforts; and they stated, furthermore, that the armed forces of the United States would aid them, should war with Spain be the result of their project.[46] What fortunes were in store for them upon the liberation of Mexico, the emissaries never said precisely. They were intentionally vague.

In mid-August Burr himself arrived in Pittsburgh incognito. Henry passed the adventurer in the street, recognizing him immediately.

"Who is he?" Burr asked his companion, by chance Henry's friend.

"That is young Brackenridge," he replied.

"He must be one of us," Burr then said.

This conversation Henry overheard,[47] although that might well have been Burr's intent.

Burr's real objective, even his destination, did not become a matter of public knowledge. After Burr's departure Pentland noted this fact in his gazette: "Our fellow-citizens, generally, feel anxious to know the object of Mr. Burr's journey, at this time—and as he was perfectly *taciturn* during his stay, many conjectures are afloat."[48] There were indeed innumerable rumors about him circulating in town and up and down the rivers. Pentland hoped that editors farther west would be in a better position than he was to inform the public concerning the object of this suspect enterprise. Four months later, near the end of December, he reiterated the same idea, but added that "while we are staring to the westward, we are surprised with budgets from the east."[49] It was an odd situation in his opinion because Pittsburgh was, after all, the place where the conspirators had rendezvoused first.

Notwithstanding the paucity of information from the West, Pentland had collected some information about "this desperate and detestable plot" for his subscribers.[50] He was fearless enough to publish the names of the conspirators from Pittsburgh who had flirted with treason. Between fifteen and fifty young, unmarried men, some of whom were "of *conspicuous* parentage," had gone down the Ohio in boats filled with provisions and military equipment, declaring *"that they were engaged to go on some MILITARY expedition, of which Col. BURR was to be the chief."* He named Thomas Butler, Morgan Neville, and William Robinson as members of the first families in town. He named others as "young men of desperate fortunes—and inimical to the general government." All had descended the river without examination by borough officials. Pentland pointed an accusing finger at Presley Neville, the new prothonotary, as the major general of the militia who had encouraged youths, including "his son *Morgan,* an ignorant, inconsiderate young man, full of vanity and pomposity," to join Burr to make their fortunes. *"James Ross, James O'Hara,* and *John Wilkins jun.* there is no doubt, are also intimately acquainted with the whole business—though they have had cunning enough to conceal it," wrote the editor, reckless of danger. "Burr staid at Mr. O'Hara's when in Pittsburgh—and, of course, did not depart without seeing and communicating with the high toned aristocrats of the town." Thus Pentland pinned the label of insurrectionist on the coats of the Pittsburgh Federalists. To his joy, not one Jeffersonian Republican had succumbed to "the wiles of the deceitful. . . ."

There was good reason why Henry did not join the expedition, which collapsed straightway when President Jefferson issued a proclamation against it, followed by the arrest and trial of Burr. Henry and Forward associated with a different group of young men than the sons of the Federalist leaders, therefore never coming in close contact with Burr on his visits to Pittsburgh. As Henry listened to the discussion of the affair at Mrs. Earle's table, moreover, he remembered his father's condemnation of all clandestine enterprises which might conceivably jeopardize the safety of the Union. But above all Henry was determined to pass his bar examination, which had approached with dismaying rapidity, and to begin his career in the law without further ado.

Exactly twenty and a half years old, Henry sustained this test without difficulty; and in open court the next day, November 12, 1806, he took the oath admitting him to the bar to practice law in Allegheny County.[51] Success at first intoxicated Henry: "Now thought I to myself, I am at length on the great stage of action, and must soon perform wonders."[52] But quickly came the realization that he "had hardly touched the threshold" of the law profession, and that he had much more to learn than had ever occurred to him before. He wisely decided not to postpone his maiden appearance as an attorney at law, knowing from the experience of others how one is apt to shrink from making the first speech in court. That same evening of November 12, Henry, therefore, participated without preparation in a case of libel, the opposing counsel happening to be his teacher, Mountain! The candles lit and the speech of Mountain finished, Henry began to address the judges and the jury, obviously embarrassed, until he noticed the "malicious pleasure" which the opposite party took in his discomfort, whereupon he "broke forth, at once, into a tremendous philippic against him and his counsel."[53] Mountain paid Henry a visit the next morning, congratulated him, and engaged him to help in some cases. Henry spoke in court six more times that week to "keep the ice open. . . ."

He was always proud of the fact that he had served his apprenticeship in a shop filled with such talented craftsmen as the members of the Pittsburgh bar,[54] of whom Ross was the acknowledged leader, feared and respected. As a Federalist member of the Senate, Ross had achieved a national reputation, but he was also a powerful politician in the state, despite his lack of success in winning the governorship. Locally, only a Jane Marie fighting for her home had the courage to thwart him in any way. His colleagues at the bar knew that not only their reputations but also their careers were at stake if they challenged him in an important matter, especially if they belonged to the Federalist party—a political opponent could afford to be less heedful. Jane described the situation in her pamphlet addressed to the citizens of Pennsylvania: " . . . the courts and lawyers, and indeed all the people at and near Pittsburgh, are in terror of James Ross. . . ."[55] In 1807, after Henry had gone to Carlisle, Jane returned to Pittsburgh with Caroline for a period of four months to battle for her rights, at which time only Mary Murphy dared to give them lodging.[56] Ross, in short, was a shrewd land speculator and real estate operator[57] whose mastery of the law made him unusually successful in this business. In court the presence of Ross, with his "large and noble frame, and a head of Homerian cast,"[58] overawed the younger practitioners like Henry and intimidated the older as well. Ross's arguments were clear and forceful and appealing to reason: "He never tripped, or appeared at a loss for an expression. . . ." Ross, according to Henry, was certainly one of the best speakers in the United States.

Ross married the sister of the well-to-do John Woods who stood next at the bar. Woods was that same "youth of Bedford county" whom the elder Brackenridge had always found in his way whenever a chance of political advancement presented itself. Knowing the enmity which existed between his father and the Federalist lawyer, Henry studied carefully the manner in which Woods managed a case in court. Woods was an authority on the law of tenures, with more business than he cared to handle; an aristocrat, he selected his clientele. His shrill voice, however, did not match his handsome figure: "but, like John Randolph, his ear-piercing voice often gave effect to a powerful invective."[59]

Other members of the Pittsburgh bar were distinguished men in their own particular way. The newcomers to the profession like Henry and Forward enjoyed most of all to hear the huge Steele Semple plead a cause, for his speech abounded in classical allusions and witticisms, although he hesitated, often even stammered, in its delivery. But Semple was a timid and lazy man who died early, scarcely in his forties.[60] Henry naturally had an affectionate regard for his preceptor, Mountain. This teacher-lawyer had few, if any, innate gifts: "Nature had left him to do everything for himself."[61] Mountain, however, had become a learned man, and gradually a polished advocate, also, as he gained experience at the bar. Henry's father liked him. In contrast to Semple and Mountain, men of local prominence only, were Henry Baldwin and William Wilkins, who were now rising fast to the top of their profession and who were in the future to achieve high national office. [62] Baldwin, who became a congressman and eventually an associate justice of the United States Supreme Court, was an unpretentious scholar and a logical speaker. The well-bred Wilkins, whose speeches lacked depth and force, "knew those whom he addressed, as the musician knows the instrument he touches." He became a federal judge, a senator, and a minister to Russia.

The elder Brackenridge had once headed the bar of Pittsburgh. His son ranked him above them all—above Ross and Woods, Semple and Mountain, and Baldwin and Wilkins—as an advocate of remarkable ability:

. . . His imagination ascended the "highest heaven of invention." When he began to speak he frequently appeared to labor under great embarrassment, like an eagle rising from the level ground; but as he proceeded he rose by degrees, and when he poured himself upon his career, he seemed . . . to range through heaven, earth and sea. [63]

VII: The Attorney at Law

In late November, 1806, not long after his admission to the bar, Henry mounted a Canadian pony, previously burdened with heavy saddlebags, and kicked the beast in the side as the signal to start the journey over the mountains to Carlisle.[1] Muffled in an overcoat to protect against the cutting cold of the morning, he quit Pittsburgh—the scene of his triumph—now a bustling place where the pungent smoke of soft coal issued from hundreds of chimneys and blanketed the valleys. He considered himself a knight-errant seeking adventure, although a tear came to his eye as he thought of the friends he was leaving. But contemplation of the future cleared his eye, for "I was to remain some time at Carlisle, and then either return to take up my residence in the West, or go to the blooming South in search of fortune. And then, what wonders to be wrought by me at the bar!" Thus inspired he addressed the jury loudly, at the same time urging his plodding pony onward along the lonely road. In the middle of his speech Henry came upon a wagon train with its horse bells jingling; and high-spirited, he shouted, "The glasses sparkle on the board." The wagoners—"the *lords of the road*"—did not hear him. Therefore, he passed them carefully, nodding his head in polite greeting, for they were a rude and arrogant lot.

Henry crossed the mountains almost without incident, although not far beyond Bedford he had a startling encounter with a woodsman.[2] When Henry stopped at a streamlet called Bloody Run to water his pony, out of the forest burst a tall mountaineer with hair uncut, an axe on his shoulder, and a butcher knife in a sheath at his side. One hand he carried in a sling. Using the other hand as a cup, he drank from the brook and disquieted young Brackenridge momentarily with the sudden remark, "Well, stranger, I kilt seventeen o' them." He added mysteriously that he had saved the life of another. Then Henry learned to his relief that the queer fellow had merely wiped out a den of rattlesnakes, sparing one, however, to carry in the crown of his hat. But the snake had bitten him in spite of a charm, in which he still had much confidence. To earn a living the woodsman hunted bee trees in the mountain country. After their leave-taking Henry continued on his way, thrilled by the scenery as his pony bore him on the rutty road over the high hills. From the summit of the last mountain he gazed down upon the plain where Chambersburg lay and instinctively was glad of his American birth: "It was then I felt that I was in feelings as well as birth, a native of the Ohio—a Western man—and I involuntarily resolved within myself that this should not be the last time of my crossing the mountains." The mountain barrier behind him, Henry decided to take the stage the rest of the journey to Carlisle, and he sold his nag to the innkeeper at Shippensburg.

Carlisle, the capital of Cumberland County, was a town containing about three hundred houses, a post town and a college town which favorably impressed travelers[3] and visitors like Henry. The markethouse, brick courthouse, and stone meetinghouse stood at the intersection of the two main streets. There were other churches in the town, several inns, and the tavern where the stagecoaches and wagon trains stopped. Most notable of the edifices in Carlisle, of course, was the stone building of Dickinson College with its cupola. The streets were wide, the sidewalks paved or made of flagstones, and the houses built of wood, brick, and stone.

Here in Carlisle the elder Brackenridge awaited his son anxiously. He was afraid that Henry had joined Burr's expedition.[4] Hugh had known Burr as a fellow student at Princeton and had watched his career closely in the years following. Hugh realized how strong the temptation to join Burr's project must be for adventuresome youths living in Pittsburgh where talk about it had long been on the tip of almost every tongue.

Hugh, in fact, had much advice to give Henry. The elder Brackenridge, for example, had just seen his *Gazette Publications* issue from the press of Alexander & Phillips in Carlisle, a volume in which he had collected some of his fugitive writings—"this trash,"[5] he called them—to amuse and inform the reader. Although Hugh had enjoyed writing the verse and prose in the collection, he believed that authorship was not the way to earn a living or to gain fame in the United States: "I would warn therefore a son of mine against too much attention to some parts of what may be called polite literature, as not fashionable in our present state of society, and as a seducing syren from the more profitable pursuits of life."[6] But certainly he never discouraged Henry to write whenever and whatever he wished, providing he gave first thought to his profession of the law. On the other hand Hugh was firm in his condemnation of puppyism as evidenced by young lawyers. On this subject Henry was sure to receive a lecture. The newcomer to the bar ought not to imitate the practitioners already there, for, in Hugh's opinion, imitators were "contemptible everywhere. . . ."[7] He remembered how young members of the Philadelphia bar had worn spectacles not because they needed them to see but because they imitated the famous lawyers there—"Wilson, Lewis, Coxe, and Wilcox"— who did need them. The one bad habit with which Hugh had no patience whatsoever was the smoking of cigars, for "the segar excites thirst and leads to intemperance. When the mouth is parched, you must wet the whistle . . . I never see a young person with a segar in his teeth, but I give him up, as one that will never come to much." That his father intended to discuss the avoidance of bad habits with Henry was a certainty.

"The situation of the greatest danger to a young practitioner of law is a

83

remote county town, where amusements are few, and a literary society is wanting," Hugh was convinced.[8] Indeed, having pondered the matter of his son's career, he expressed his thoughts on the subject several days after Henry's arrival.[9] Hugh himself regretted, as he now said, that he had made the mistake of leaving a large city to seek his fortune in a new land—the West. He detailed the disadvantages of a country practice and then suggested Baltimore as the most promising place for Henry to begin his law career: "If you have but a pig, carry it to the middle of the market." He warned his son, however, that he needed a thorough knowledge of the law merchant and admiralty law and a mastery likewise of "the chancery practice and the science of special pleading" if he decided to venture upon the Baltimore stage. The father estimated the time required for such preparation to be at least a year, and possibly six months longer. Besides this specialized study, Henry could relax his mind—and broaden it too—by pursuing a course of general reading.

Henry received his father's advice with mixed feelings. The younger Brackenridge realized that he had a lot to learn despite his legal training and admission to the bar. He had no quarrel with his father on that score—the need for further study, he readily admitted.[10] But he agreed to the Baltimore proposal "through respect, although against my instinct, which drove me to the West, as the young turtle, after being hatched by the sun, takes to the water."[11] Henry was not confident that he could fashion a successful career in Baltimore.[12] It galled him, furthermore, that he himself had not charted the course to follow.

But Henry plunged into the work as outlined and supervised by his father, studying thirteen or fourteen hours every day in a household dedicated to the pursuit of knowledge. "All my wants were kindly attended to by my step-mother, leaving me nothing to think of but my books," Henry averred at a later time.[13] Cornelia, his half sister, was reading the gazettes at the age of three; and his half brothers, Alexander and William, were receiving a rigorous classical education directed by their father. During the day few visitors interrupted the routine of study in the Brackenridge home; but after teatime, when not on circuit, Hugh welcomed calls by literary or professional men because from them he derived information or instruction.[14]

Henry often served as his father's amanuensis, for Hugh's handwriting had degenerated into an illegible scrawl.[15] The son liked to tell how a certain gentleman once received a letter from the elder Brackenridge and, finding it impossible to decipher, resolved to trick him. The correspondent deleted Hugh's signature, substituted his own, and mailed the letter back: "my father attempted in vain to make out the scrawl!" At a fast clip Hugh dictated to Henry new chapters for *Modern Chivalry* as well as articles for newspapers and even verse, fixing the punctuation of each sentence as he proceeded. For Henry this secretarial work helped relieve the tedium of his study.

His course of reading was difficult.[16] He began by studying the treatises of Jean Jacques Burlamaqui on general law, then read the great authorities on international law like Vattel, Martens, and Pufendorf, and moved on to the standard works on the law merchant, insurance, shipping, bills of exchange and promissory notes, and the law of equity. At the same time he read all the books of reports which were pertinent to his study, and available. But Henry's intellectual curiosity, which was already insatiable, led him to peruse other volumes, both prose and verse, unrelated to the law. He continued the study of German, begun under the tutelage of Schewe in Pittsburgh, and became so proficient that he could read Gellert, Schiller, and Goethe in the original. To aid in learning the language he occasionally wrote a piece in English for a German gazette, edited by a clergyman who translated Henry's contribution before its publication. Henry also tackled an Italian grammar, tutored in pronunciation by a Roman Catholic priest.

To practice solitary declamation and to read outdoors in pleasant weather, Henry resorted to a spot west of Carlisle where huge rock formations resembling ancient works ready to fall stood starkly on the plain.[17] He named the place the Ruins of Palmyra. Here he came day after day in the afternoon after teatime, and he stayed usually until sunset and sometimes until dark. One night, however, Henry became so frightened that never again did he stay there late. In the darkness a voice had cried to him to stop, as he memorized aloud passages from English poetry. Henry heard the words repeated and, thinking he heard footsteps, too, he hurried into town. He never hit the explanation of this mystery, nor did he ever forget the incident.

Henry attended court at Carlisle to observe the members of the Cumberland County bar in action.[18] He was an admirer of the two leading lawyers, Thomas Duncan and David Watts, the acknowledged rivals on this particular circuit. Henry marked the interesting contrast presented by the men in court: Watts was a powerful person, "a singular instance of the union of great strength of mind, with bodily powers equally wonderful," who hammered a telling point home with impressive vehemence; whereas Duncan was a small, spry man with a large head, who developed his arguments systematically and, being a keen student of human nature, managed his cases well. Duncan, Henry learned, "perused Coke on Littleton as a recreation, and read new books of reports as a young lady reads the new novels." Henry also thought well of the gifts possessed by the young attorney at law, John Gibson, who eventually became the chief justice of Pennsylvania. Judge James Hamilton, who presided in 1807, Henry deemed an elegant man and considered him learned, although excessively minute in his charges to the jury. For Henry attendance at court was as much a part of the preparation for going to Baltimore as solitary declamation and the reading of law books.

He followed this grueling course in earnest throughout the winter and into the summer and autumn of 1807. The more he studied the more aware he became of how little knowledge he had at his command. From time to time he bridled his impatience to begin his career in the city, wisely postponing his departure. As an attorney at law he even deferred the business of a client to press his studies the harder. "I shall not go to Baltimore this spring, as I expected, but in the fall or beginning of winter; intending to remain at home and make myself better acquainted with the merchantile branch of Jurisprudence, and somewhat with the local laws of Maryland," he wrote Dunning McNair in June. As a result, Henry added, "I am very sorry that I cannot give you that satisfaction in your business that I could wish."[19]

But when Henry had completed a year of preparation, he could no longer control his restlessness.[20] The elder Brackenridge reluctantly consented to his departure, placing in his son's hand, however, a book which advocated the age of thirty as an ideal time to enter the law profession: "It might do in England, I thought; but the plan was not suited to America, at least to me." Then, realizing Henry's impatience, his father gave him some advice which stressed the value of constant application to his practice and the harm of allowing politics to interfere with work until well established in the profession. "I will make you up a small library and a purse of a hundred dollars or so," Hugh told Henry. "As my salary is almost my only dependence, for I have committed a great error in not attending sufficiently to the main chance, you must now swim without a cork jacket." He concluded his advice with a warning about the danger of falling into debt, for "the man who is in debt is no longer free— he is a slave." In spite of his eagerness to be off to a larger scene of action than Carlisle and out from under the parental wing, Henry felt that his success depended on a generous measure of good fortune besides an adherence to his father's counsel.

The first sight of Baltimore staggered Henry, who was, after all, a youth from the country.[21] Early in December, about eight o'clock at night, he stepped from the stagecoach, which had carried him and a companion from Carlisle, into the Indian Queen. The bright lights everywhere nearly blinded him, and the people hurrying by on the sidewalks—the throngs—astonished him. Henry and the other young gentleman from Carlisle supped in the hotel, whereupon the latter suggested they attend the performance of *Hamlet* at the theater that evening. In the theater, later, Henry sat in his box as if stunned, for the lights, the music, the audience below had dazzled him. Then he felt himself lost in the crowd because not one person knew or cared that he sat there—he was lonesome. But when the curtain rose, the mood vanished. About midnight the two gentlemen returned to their hotel and there found a cold after-theater snack prepared for them. While Henry ate the wing of a boiled fowl, he watched his friend consume "a dozen or two of *horrid-looking things* called oysters!" Henry slept fitfully this first night in Baltimore.

Fortunately, the son of the celebrated Dr. Charles Nisbet, the former president of Dickinson College, practiced law in Baltimore and immediately came to the aid of young Brackenridge who called on him the morning after his arrival in the city.[22] Alexander Nisbet introduced Henry to many prominent people, moved his admission to the bar, and gave him the use of his office. For several months Henry went to Nisbet's office daily, and from this vantage point surveyed the law profession in Baltimore. He had to admit to himself that he was not ready to practice there because he lacked a mastery of the peculiarities of Maryland law. He did not, in short, know the local statutes. Nisbet advised Henry to spend a year with him as a clerk, certainly an apprenticeship worth while although it would pay him nothing.

But Henry declined the offer and thereby put himself in an embarrassing position.[23] He could not impose himself upon Nisbet indefinitely. It occurred to Henry, furthermore, that the expense of renting his own office and furnishing it would be prohibitive. There was, too, the gnawing question whether he would have any business if he did have an office. Complicating his situation was the fact that he could no longer afford to live at the hotel. But luckily his cousin, James Clark, was the proprietor of a store in the Baltimore suburbs. There Henry repaired and arranged to board and lodge, in return giving Clark most of what money remained: "Here I felt myself as snug as a squirrel in his hole; and when I chose to peep out into the great world, it was no longer with the horror of want, misery, or starvation, which I had begun to feel."

His problem of where to live solved, Henry decided to learn how successful lawyers in Baltimore had risen to the top of their profession.[24] What steps had they taken in their climb? He noticed at once the full dockets in the courts and the large number of lawyers to handle this business; but he soon perceived that only a few had lucrative practices and that many more barely earned a living. The few, in other words, monopolized the business of the courts. Clients sought the lawyers with the biggest practices, invariably ignoring the attorney at law who struggled stoutheartedly to establish himself in the profession. Henry estimated that two-thirds of all the lawyers stood at the rear of the bar, some of whom might possibly move to the head after years of attendance in court and the dogged pursuit of clients. Henry met certain young advocates whose methods of building a clientele were not ethical. One had a father, a justice of the peace, who supplied him with clients. Another had furnished his office on credit: "He told me that his plan was to establish the *relationship* of debtor and creditor; that is, to become in debt to as many as he could, and by this means make it the interest of his creditors to patronize him and push him into practice, in order to secure the payment of their debts." Henry stayed in Baltimore long enough to see the failure of this scheme—the lawyer's creditors so harried him that he left town.

His study of the law profession in Baltimore led Henry to conclude that the chance of success was not good unless he was willing to endure years of drudgery and frustration first.[25] He realized, also, that he did not wish to practice law there anyhow. The thought of the dull routine year after year until he reached the top, where the financial reward, he found, was not great, repelled him. There was the possibility, moreover, that success might elude him, leaving him a miserable hanger-on at the rear of the bar. He resolved instead to spend his time in the city adding to his knowledge of the law and observing "the ways of the world by extending my intercourse with all kinds of people."

But, admittedly, his zeal to further his law career abated.[26] His reading in the law became haphazard. For the purpose of instruction the courts did not offer much. Henry had, as a matter of fact, seen more talented lawyers in Pittsburgh and Carlisle than he could observe in the county and criminal courts of Baltimore. The admiralty court, however, was different, for several noted lawyers practiced there. The courthouse itself was an old structure, at this time resting on a foundation of stilts necessitated by leveling the adjacent streets. There was danger of the building collapsing whenever crowded. Once, when Henry was present in court, a German merchant suddenly announced that the stovepipe had sunk noticeably: "spectators, witnesses, parties, lawyers, bailiffs, judges, went pell-mell, tumbling over each other, into the street." In addition to attendance at court, Henry went to the meetings of a law society in Luther Martin's office. One of Martin's students, Richard Magruder, became Henry's lifelong friend.

Less interested in mastering the subtleties of the law than formerly, the zest of launching himself in the profession having gone for the moment, Henry devoted himself to becoming a well-read city gentleman. This was a natural development as his circle of friends and acquaintances grew larger, no longer limited to the law society and the profession itself. At first, however, his life fell into a deliberate pattern: in the morning he studied the Italian and Spanish languages; in the afternoon he practiced solitary declamation whenever possible and visited the city library and the bookstores; and in the evening he read in his room.[27]

His time was spent, therefore, in reading and "in *thoughtful idleness* out of doors."[28] Henry read ravenously, as if he had a starving mind to stuff. Every morning he read in bed until breakfast. A friend had given Henry the use of a share in the public library, with the result that he could take books to his room. This library of fifteen to twenty thousand volumes was especially strong in the classics. Henry read the Roman writers in the original Latin, but the Greek in translation as much as possible. He knew the booksellers of Baltimore so well that he could read any of the recent publications without charge, although he, in turn, gladly performed small services for them. Thus Henry had at hand two splendid sources of knowledge to tap—the public library and the bookstores: they "were resorts as natural to me as the waterbrook to the thirsty wild deer of the forests." When a friend once asked the elder Brackenridge where to find his son in Baltimore, Hugh advised him that Henry could be found easily by an inquiry at the library or at the bookstores. What he read there Henry pondered as he walked aimlessly about town in the afternoons.

This interest in literature brought Henry several cherished friendships. One was with James Sloan, the son of a wealthy boot and shoe manufacturer.[29] Henry considered Sloan, a Princeton graduate, the most gifted and polished young gentleman in Baltimore. Sloan lived in a suite of rooms in his father's mansion, where he strove to master the accomplishments of the elegant gentleman of that day. He studied languages and general literature assiduously in the mornings and at that time saw only a few callers, one of whom was Brackenridge. The two of them discussed weighty subjects as they strode back and forth in the apartment. Sloan's library, in Henry's opinion, was particularly good, as was the library of Dr. James McHenry, a secretary of war in the administrations of Washington and John Adams. Henry visited the McHenry home more and more as he became friendlier with the nephew, John McHenry, a lawyer who was preparing for publication reports of cases in the court of appeals.[30] Young McHenry soon was Brackenridge's most intimate acquaintance in the city.

In accordance with his father's advice, however, Henry shunned the pleasures of a social life with a seductive round of gay parties. He avoided the temptation for months—then chance tossed him into the whirl of high society.[31] He began to spend an evening now and then at the home of the old and gouty Judge Chase, who had been the elder Brackenridge's preceptor in the law years before and who now enjoyed the company of young men. He invited Henry to dinner, an invitation unfortunately forgotten when the appointed time arrived. Unaware of his blunder Henry visited the Chase home later; and an explanation of the breach of etiquette being demanded by his host, he did not lie. "What, sir, forget an invitation to dine with me; I admire

your candor, sir, but d--n your politeness!" roared the judge. His daughter
Mary laughed in delight, and told Henry that she had picked him as her
escort to a party that night. To a *friseur* he hurried, then to his room to dress
formally, and back to the Chases to hand into a carriage the vivacious and
"celebrated"—Mary. At the ball that evening Henry met Madame Bonaparte,
the wife of Jerome, who "stood leaning upon a marble slab under a large
looking-glass, and although quite small and delicate, was Venus herself. She
gave a gentle inclination of the head as I made my bow, while I immediately
backed my topsails, filled away, and fell to leeward."

After his introduction to Baltimore society by Mary Chase, Henry, although
inwardly protesting, was swept into an idle life as a fashionable young man,
eligible to be invited to dinner and to parties. He now received invitations to
all important functions in the city.[32] As he attended each one, he lost more and
more of his rustic demeanor; but it required no less a gallant than General
Wilkinson himself to teach him to rise when addressed by an older gentleman.
"The general, happening once to recognize me in a ball-room, on being told
by some one who I was, came up to me where I was seated, and took me by
the hand; instead of rising, as was proper for me to do, I sat still," Henry
always remembered to his chagrin. "He gave me a gentle squeeze of the hand,
at the same time lifting it up; the hint was enough, I sprang upon my feet
and stood upright before him."[33] But at heart Henry disliked much of the
social activity which had engulfed him.[34] Large affairs where intelligent conversation was lacking bored him, and annoyed him if he were asked to help
entertain with a story or a song:

. . . I had the misfortune on one occasion, when harassed to do or say something for
the amusement of the company, to take it into my head to give the celebrated speech of
Logan in the original Indian. What was still more unfortunate, my Indian happened to
take wonderfully, and as long as I remained in the city it was a continual tax upon me,
at the same time that it probably procured me numerous invitations which I should not
otherwise have received. It is true, I had heard the speech recited by General Gibson, by
whom it was taken from Logan and delivered to Lord Dunmore, but I only recollected
a few words of it; the rest was an imitation of the sounds, with which I used to amuse
my playfellows when a boy.

Henry loathed, too, the custom of drinking healths. He preferred smaller and
informal dinners to encourage conversation. Baltimore, like Mrs. Earle's boardinghouse, nevertheless, was an excellent school of manners for Henry.

Also, at this time in 1808, Henry found Baltimore an exciting school of
politics.[35] There he observed demagoguery as practiced in a city. But in Baltimore as in other ports along the coast, Jefferson's embargo had heightened the
interest of the populace in political affairs, especially as the ranks of the unemployed grew with the decline in commerce. Henry and his friends, always

enthusiastic supporters of the President, advocated retention of the measure
without bothering to consider its soundness in all respects. On one occasion
Henry heard the embargo and the Jefferson administration defended by the
speaker at a barbecue held several miles from town. Henry had never before
attended a political rally like this meeting in a grove, where the people gorged
on roast ox, bread, whisky, and beer. He discovered quickly that his mood
differed from that of the crowd, for, whenever he was apt to question a statement of the speaker, the people about him thundered their applause. The
speaker flattered them shamefully. More frightening to Henry than this exhibition of demagoguery, however, was the burning of casks of gin, all imported
and British licensed, in a huge bonfire on a hill near Baltimore. As the flames
licked the casks, bursting them, the scum of the city and Fell's Point scooped
up the blazing liquor which spouted forth and in some places collected in
puddles; and unemployed idlers—sailors—jostled citizens in the streets in
town. Henry even attended the meeting of a radical, or Jacobin club, the
members of which he despised, however, for their intolerance of views not
their own. Everywhere he went in Baltimore to observe political activity, he
saw the manipulation of the masses for selfish ends—demagogues courting
the people.

Back home in Pennsylvania the embargo was an issue in the gubernatorial
contest between Ross and Simon Snyder. The Federalists denounced the
embargo, according to the editor Pentland, as a means to further the candidacy
of Ross.[36] But this was the same election in which Jane Marie's pamphlet circulated throughout the state. In William Duane's *Aurora* of Philadelphia,
moreover, her account of the treatment received from Ross had first appeared
as a campaign document. Other editors reprinted her charges as ammunition
to ruin the Federalist cause. Thus it happened that Hugh and Sabina Brackenridge and their neighbors could read the story in the extra edition of *Kline's
Carlisle Weekly Gazette* of October 4, with this headline:

JAMES ROSS
*A Candidate for the first magisterial
office of Pennsylvania,*
versus
Mrs. JANE MARIE.

Named in the account as a witness of Ross's attack on Jane, Henry was fortunate to be in Baltimore where the curious were unable to ply him with
questions.

But Henry was fast tiring of his life in Baltimore, although he lingered
indecisively.[37] He had become a man about town who was much in demand
socially, a young attorney at law, however, with no professional future. He

knew the leading members of the bar personally, and even hobnobbed with one or two—Robert G. Harper, the acknowledged head of the profession; Luther Martin, the uncouth but clever lawyer; William H. Winder, a "first-rate slang-whanger"; and the somewhat lesser lights like Jennings, Purviance, and Kell.[38] Their speeches in court had occasionally given Henry ideas to develop by solitary declamation. But like "a blind horse in a bark-mill, although in motion there was no progress."[39]

Troubled by his failure, and discontented, Henry welcomed the chance to leave Baltimore when a man from Somerset, in Pennsylvania, apprised him that both the town and county had the services of only one resident lawyer.[40] The thought that his failure would humiliate his father did not deter Henry from making speedy preparations to leave the city, although for that reason he was regretful. Two weeks later he reached Somerset.

The morning after his arrival in the mountain town Henry met the lawyer who would now be his opponent at the bar.[41] He visited Henry at his tavern to welcome him to Somerset, to offer advice, and subtly to put him in his proper place. Forthrightly he explained to the newcomer that little profitable business could fall to him, for he himself *"booked* about five hundred dollars a year" as the only lawyer in the county. The matter of insufficient income Henry considered as no stumbling block at all to success in Somerset, for at last he could appear regularly at the bar as a practicing attorney at law. Henry had no intention to argue about his share of the business because he planned to be "the Cicero of the place. . . ." The lawyer's use of the term "booked" shocked Henry who naively believed that members of the profession served society without thought of gain—that they accepted honoraria and nothing more!

Later the same day Henry investigated the state of his wardrobe to determine what garments discarded for city wear might be repaired for use in the mountains.[42] He was economical despite his unconcern about the size of his income. He took the clothes to the tailor and then walked to the edge of town and into the country, where shortly he came upon a swift stream backed by a pine forest, a spot suitable for declamation. As he had often done elsewhere when addressing an imaginary jury, Henry talked louder and louder as he neared the climax of his speech—and suddenly he stopped, for racing toward him were the tailor, his journeyman, and a good part of the population of Somerset. Henry was able to start singing "Hail Columbia" as they arrived on the scene and, puzzled, stood looking at him. But without comment they turned about and retraced their steps into town. When the tailor brought Henry's trousers back to the tavern that night, he asked for "the young mon that's *troubl't in mind.*"

The prompt payment of his tailor bill and the renting of an office, however, convinced the people of Somerset that Henry was really an attorney at law and not "a yelling madman," as they might first have thought upon surprising him engaged in declamation.[43] He was lucky enough to obtain the office, including the furnishings, of a lawyer who recently had died. Henry was ready for business when his books arrived from Baltimore. The interim between sessions of the court he planned to devote to a review of the elementary works in the law, a task reserved for the morning, and in the afternoon to reread the writings of English historians. He hoped that his sojourn in Somerset would prove more rewarding professionally than his stay in Baltimore, both in quiet study and in actual practice at the bar.

But he grew more and more uneasy as the time for court approached.[44] There was a prodigious amount of work for him to do in preparation—and likewise for his experienced rival—because they alone were named as opposing counsel in the hundreds of suits on the docket. Any person indicted by the grand jury Henry intended to defend, also, providing his services were requested. One heartening thought was the fact that he knew Judge John Young personally, as he had long been a close friend of the elder Brackenridge. Walter Forward had married Judge Young's niece and immediately built a practice in the most businesslike fashion, whereas Henry was now trying to establish himself in the profession high atop the Alleghenies. More nervous as each day passed, Henry persuaded Forward to attend court to assist him in the management of the cases.

Henry spent the whole term of almost a week "in a painful and feverish state of excitement."[45] Forward's presence in court, as well as his assistance, was invaluable to Henry, who soon realized that his own speeches were too ornate and complex for the plain Germans and Scotch-Irish in attendance. Forward, poised and persuasive, opened every case: "He marked out the course, filled up the valleys, leveled the mountains, paved the way, while I drove my vehicle over it with a thundering noise." This first term of court revealed Henry's chief weakness as an advocate, his lack of ease at the bar, which, however, practice could cure. But conquering the temptation to exhaust the subject matter of his speeches was difficult for him, as evidenced at the next term of court when the length of one, a three-hour affair, obviously irritated the judge. Responsible for the failing was Henry's ambition to become a great orator.

When court was not in session, he found life in Somerset uninteresting. Henry missed the sparkling society of Baltimore, for in Somerset "almost the only social people were a few who met now and then to drink apple-toddy and sing songs, Irish, Dutch or Welsh."[46] On winter evenings he studied French literature, a diversion made possible by the death of a Frenchman whose books had passed into Henry's hands.[47] Another effective way to relieve the tedium of life in the county town was to talk with the travelers who stopped at the inn.[48] Because the stagecoach did not run on Sunday, in consequence of the mail arrangements, the passengers had to spend the day in Somerset; and disgruntled, they appreciated Henry's fellowship. That is how he first met Philip Doddridge, the eloquent lawyer-politician who, in time, represented a Virginia district in Congress.

For Henry, in fact, the people who passed through Somerset were a constant source of amazement. The West lured the most original characters imaginable, many of whom thus spent a moment of their lives in his company. Henry never could forget the evening the innkeeper called him to act as an interpreter for an excited Frenchman who had arrived with an impressive entourage—a wife, a monkey, parrots, and a servant.[49] He was a nobleman— "the first one I had seen *alive*"—the son of an *émigré* to Russia; and animated he was, as he turned to Henry in fury: "Ah! monsieur, *vous avez un vilain pays.*" The traveler had to stop in Somerset to have his barouche repaired, for wagoners had broken one of its wheels in passing him on the muddy road. Had not men on horseback happened by, the lords of the road would have murdered the Frenchman, who had demanded their help in dragging his carriage out of the mud by waving money and pointing cocked pistols at them. Henry surmised at once that the Frenchman's arrogance and temper had caused most of his troubles—that there was reason for landlords of the inns to give him soiled sheets and good American democrats to manhandle him as he sought to discipline his servant. Henry's astonishment, however, was boundless when the nobleman visited the law office later, "happened to see an elegant copy of Tasso, which he admired, said it was of no use there, and actually put it in his pocket!"

Incidents such as this encounter with the Frenchman, by relieving some of the monotony of Henry's existence, often made him desirous of a complete change of scenery, even if only for a short time. He therefore visited friends in the neighboring counties whenever an opportunity arose.[50] The high light of his excursions was the week in which he enjoyed the companionship of Walter Forward as the guest of Judge Young in Greensburg.

After a residence of eight months in Somerset, Henry resolved to abandon his practice in the town and county.[51] No longer a novice in court and now first at the bar, he had little incentive to remain. He was not ready, furthermore, to root himself permanently anywhere. Imaginative and adventurous, he felt the lure of the West until it became irresistible. There he was certain to find fame and fortune: "I mused continually on the project of seeking the distant, magnificent West, and of attaining, on the Ohio or Mississippi, distinction and wealth with the same rapidity, and on the same scale, that those vast regions were expanding into greatness."

More and more, too, the attorney at law dreamed of Ste. Genevieve and Gallipolis—of the Beauvais family and Dr. Saugrain.

VIII: *Sketches of the Territory of Louisiana*

On a sunny April morning in 1810, a young man, slim and wiry, appeared on the bank of the Monongahela at Pittsburgh and boarded a keelboat.[1] He was, obviously, to be a passenger on the voyage down-river, for, dressed neatly in black, he sat on a chest on the afterdeck as two polers pushed the vessel from the shore. His hair was auburn; and his eyes under the long and thick brows were hazel—a "dark hazel." His nose was long, but his face was round. This person was Henry, who, in May, 1809, not quite a year before, had won admission to the bar of Westmoreland County.[2] But now in the spring of 1810, his law career in the Pennsylvania mountains was behind him. Henry was about to revisit the scenes of his childhood.

Henry had actually just visited the place of his birth.[3] Although his stay in Pittsburgh was brief, he was able not only to see his friends and acquaintances again after an absence of more than three years, but also to visit "with something like religious enthusiasm, every spot, every rock, every tree, and every hill, where I loved to wander when a boy." As the boat glided past the Point, Henry turned on his seat to watch his native town recede into the distance. A tear of sentiment clouded his vision momentarily when he thought that he might never again see his Pittsburgh friends nor the town itself: "Grant's Hill, the spot endeared by infant recollection, and the grove on Watson's Hill, my *alma mater,* were the two last objects to fade from my sight. Farewell, my native town!"

Henry was unabashedly a romantic, whereas his companion, with whom he shared the chest as a seat, was a prudent, but cheery Quaker named Greaves.[4] Henry had met Greaves at the inn in Somerset one Sunday and instantly liked him. Greaves was an Irishman, aged twenty-three, bound for the South to manage a cotton plantation. His preparations for leaving Somerset already made, Henry had quickly decided to join the Quaker for the voyage down the Ohio. In Pittsburgh they had bought all the necessary provisions for the entire party of five persons aboard the boat as payment for the passage, although the captain had refused to fix any charge whatever.

Henry, of course, had not forgotten to dispose of his personal library in the most beneficial way possible—by sending most of his books ahead to Ste. Genevieve with the baggage and keeping only a few at hand to read on the journey.[5] One work which he had reserved for perusal in this fashion was the *Essay on Population* by Malthus. In Pittsburgh Henry had added to his collection for the voyage by buying books concerning the country which he was about to see for the second time—works like George Imlay's on Kentucky. Henry also carried with him a deistic book which attempted "to prove that

Christianity was all an imposture. . . ." When Pittsburgh had passed from his view, Henry showed the work to his friend Greaves and indicated the nature of its contents. Then they threw the book into the river.

Their progress down-river to Gallipolis was fast and uneventful.[6] At first Henry found the passing scene unfamiliar; in fact, he was unable to associate any particular spot with the voyage of his childhood until he recognized Legionville. He noticed with pleasure what inroads civilization was making on the wilderness—in place of rude clearings there were now neat farms. Beyond Legionville the party encamped for the night. To his surprise Henry discovered that he did not know how to make tea: "I filled the coffee pot with boiling water, and then put a handful of leaves into it, but they remained on the top, and refused to sink in spite of all I could do." Embarrassed, Henry finally made the attempt again under the captain's direction. After a simple meal of broiled beefsteak and tea the party retired for the night to get an early start the next morning. That day they reached Wheeling. Evidences of spring began to appear on the banks of the river as they proceeded—the air became balmy, tree buds swelled, shrubs blossomed, and the mockingbirds sang. The party soon reached Marietta, and not long after glided past the lovely Island of Blennerhassett. On Sunday they watched the people on shore going to and from church. In contrast to this peaceful scene Henry recalled how the fear of Indians had dominated the mind of everyone who voyaged down the Ohio at the time of his first passage.

Henry was anxious as the boat approached Gallipolis, remembering the happy months which he had spent in the Saugrain household as a boy; he waited impatiently to step ashore.[7] But the thought had never occurred to him that Gallipolis might now be an American town, with few traces of the French settlement remaining: "I hastened to the spot where I expected to find the abode, the little log-house, tavern, laboratory, and garden of the doctor; but they had vanished like the palace of Aladdin." He saw instead some logs left from Saugrain's tenement. As Henry, whose heartache was almost unbearable, returned to the boat, he noticed the new brick courthouse standing on the green, the brick and frame houses, the gardens, and the shade trees: "This was too much; I hastened my pace, and with sorrow once more pushed into the stream."

This poignant experience, however, did not lessen Henry's pleasure in the voyage one whit.[8] After all, not every place reached or incident met was associated with the events of his boyhood in a dispiriting way. Cincinnati, he soon discovered, had developed into a beautiful town with a market rivaling the one in Philadelphia. Not only was the produce as good in Cincinnati, but cheaper—a turkey, and perhaps a goose with it, for sixteen cents. The growth

97

of Louisville likewise was an agreeable surprise, although beyond there evidences of civilization rapidly disappeared. One day the vastness of the flights of wild pigeons overhead astounded everyone on board the boat. But the number and size of the mosquitoes encountered at the mouth of the Wabash seemed also remarkable to Henry—and there the party was detained for half a week. He escaped much misery by sleeping with Greaves, for "the cannibals found his flesh more tender, and more appetizing." Beyond the Wabash the Ohio carried the boat through heavily timbered country.

In this wild stretch of the river the captain disclosed his plan to open a store in New Madrid, an intention which Henry and his companion at first did not consider alarming.[9] But then the captain began to cook for the entire party, at the same time confiscating the provisions which Henry and Greaves had furnished in Pittsburgh in lieu of passage money. The captain served only cakes of Indian meal fried with bacon and hoarded the other supplies, including the tea and coffee, to sell in his store. He threatened Henry and Greaves with pistols when they objected to the lack of food. They had to submit, for Greaves, the Quaker, would not fight and Henry was unarmed. Henry, indeed, had resolved earlier in life never to wear arms of any kind when traveling in a peaceful region, hoping thereby to avoid attacks. When the boat arrived at New Madrid, the two passengers hurried ashore with their baggage and to an inn without speaking to the captain—"a stupid boor"—who had undoubtedly enjoyed his game.

But Henry, unfortunately, was not done with the captain.[10] The day after their arrival Greaves continued on his way south, whereas Henry had to tarry in New Madrid to prepare for the long journey overland to Ste. Genevieve. At this time the two boatmen called on Henry to complain that the captain had not only pocketed the money which they had given him for safekeeping on the voyage but had also withheld the wages due one of them. Henry advised them to see the captain once more; and if they obtained no satisfaction, to go to a justice of the peace. Consequently, Henry soon received a summons to appear in court as a witness in the case. The decision pronounced against him, the captain cursed Brackenridge and threatened him and, moments later, challenged him to a duel by putting two butcher knives at his feet. The magistrate, happening upon this scene outside his office, ordered an officer to jail the offender unless he departed immediately; and then, taking Henry's arm, he took him into his house for a late breakfast.

This unexpected fracas upset Henry, who now experienced a gamut of emotions. As they were eating, the magistrate, whose name was Humphreys, suddenly asked Henry if he were a relative of the author of *Modern Chivalry*. Henry proudly acknowledged himself to be the author's son, to Humphreys' delight. When Henry revealed his intention to proceed shortly to Ste. Gene-vieve, the magistrate offered him the use of his horse. Accepting the offer, Henry brought his baggage to Humphreys' house and there repacked every-thing for the journey through the wilderness. He set off on foot, for the two boatmen, who wished to accompany him, were to follow with the horse and baggage. At once Henry began to review the events of the morning and con-cluded reproachfully that he ought to have accepted the challenge. When the boatmen overtook him, they reported, not without pleasure and some exaggeration, too, that the captain was publicly branding him as a coward: "Yes, coward! that term of reproach which, in the West, included at that time every other." This intelligence set Henry's brain afire. He hurried back to town and, happily, there encountered Humphreys who forced him to drink lemonade in the inn and to collect himself. The magistrate persuaded Henry not to degrade himself by noticing the captain. But Humphreys, in addition, strolled about town with the agitated young man, introducing him to in-fluential persons, and afterward invited him to dinner. In this way the people of New Madrid saw Henry in town and had no reason to accuse him for fleeing in fright. Thus in good spirits and "with a light elastic tread" Henry hastened that evening to overtake the boatmen.

It was a splendid night in late May, with the air brisk.[11] Henry expected to meet his companions at a settler's house about eight miles away. The sun set and night came on as he walked along a clean trail which led him through an enchanting glade. Then the wood swallowed him up—it was dark. But Henry heard dogs barking in the distance, and before long the crackling of a fire, for the boatmen and the settler and his family (the wife and fourteen children!) were sitting around it waiting for him to arrive from town. The settler, a native of Connecticut and now a squatter on public land, won Henry's admiration and the family charmed him, even the "half dozen flaxen-haired rogues" who pestered him with questions. There followed supper in the cabin, more conversation back under the tree where the fire still burned, and finally a period of religious worship indoors. The two boatmen, young Ralph Higgen-botham and tough Bill Hulings, did not disdain the invitation to join the family service. "The scene will never pass from my memory—it was a scene of moral beauty which I have never seen surpassed," Henry declared many years later.

During the rest of the journey to Ste. Genevieve he recollected more and more the scenes of his sojourn there.[12] As his party neared the town, his remembrances grew fanciful, although the thought that his godparents might not be there, or might even be dead, troubled him. After leaving the settler and his family, Henry's party had made satisfactory progress, although they

99

never were free from hunger. One night beyond Cape Girardeau they reached an Indian village; and, fatigued and hungry after wading through swampland much of the day, they sought lodgings from the chief, who unceremoniously refused them shelter. But at another village a mile away they were luckier, for at last an Indian received them in his cabin in spite of his wife's protests. Meekly the travelers went to sleep on bearskins on the floor, thankful for a place to rest but "hungry enough to digest nails." The following day, however, they assuaged their hunger at the next Indian village where a chief offered them as much hominy as they could eat and also venison. That night Henry retired joyously with the thought that on the morrow he would reach Ste. Genevieve. But he could not help wondering whether he would find Ste. Genevieve as changed as Gallipolis by the incursion of his fellow Americans.

Although dark when Henry arrived in Ste. Genevieve, he saw enough that was familiar to cause him to anticipate a happy reunion with his friends.[13] The house of the commandant still stood; the picket fencing, the farmyards, and the gardens dominated the scene as before; and the cattle as always mooed in the streets. The next morning Henry dressed in his best clothes—"a neat summer suit, with silk stockings and pumps"—and then inquired at the inn about the Beauvais family. Learning that the marriage of Zouzou, the baby to whom he had given his prize of miniature teacups and saucers, was to occur that night, he decided to delay his appearance at the Beauvais home until the time of the wedding. Meanwhile, he busied himself by checking his baggage and the books shipped ahead and renewing friendships. The people of Ste. Genevieve had not forgotten *le petit Anglais,* he found.

That evening Henry approached the Beauvais house, from which came the cheerful noise of revelry, and asked a servant for Madame Beauvais.[14] Now came the supreme moment as the "hale old woman of sixty" appeared at the door:

"Madame," said Henry, "do you recollect the little English boy?"

She looked at him: *"Comment—est il possible? Oui—oui—c'est lui—c'est lui—c'est Henri!"*

According to Henry himself, "such a bussing frolic took place as was never surpassed even in Ste. Genevieve" when the whole situation was explained to the wedding guests. Then Zouzou, the bride herself, showed everyone the gift which Henry had given her so many years before.

The week which followed his arrival was a period of uninterrupted pleasure for Henry.[15] His godparents, whose children were now all married, insisted that he live with them: "you have come to console us in our old age—*restez, Henri; restez avec nous."* Madame Beauvais, of course, brought him up-to-date on everything that had happened in Ste. Genevieve during his long absence, assisted by her husband who supplied information and anecdotes of his own. They plied him with questions, too. Henry left their home many times to wander about the village and the countryside, revisiting his former haunts alone; and as he did this, he felt sad occasionally. But the melancholy was fleeting. The young people of the town, particularly the friends of the couple just married, accepted him without question as a member of their set. One day that first week, suitably chaperoned, they ascended the Mississippi in barges to the picturesque ruin of the Fort de Chartres, where they strolled about and danced until nightfall.

By the second week in Ste. Genevieve Henry had to consider the matter of earning a living, at least of adding to the dwindling amount of cash in his purse.[16] He resolved to begin a law practice immediately, for a session of the territorial court was about to be held at Ste. Genevieve. The preparation for his first case involved a study of French law in relation to the settlement of estates—he had to investigate the custom of Paris, a copy of which Beauvais himself owned. Henry prepared his case very carefully because he wanted to please his friends in town by an exciting display of his talent. But there was a more impelling reason, for sitting on the bench as the presiding judge would be John B. C. Lucas, Henry's guardian on the first voyage to Ste. Genevieve! As part of his strategy Henry decided to flatter him: "my former guardian could hardly contain his satisfaction, especially when I indulged in some compliments to the sagacity of the President of the United States in selecting men so peculiarly qualified to decide a case like that before the court." The judges —there was another—decided the case in favor of Henry's client. At this term of court Henry had considerable success, especially in cases concerning the right of soil on lands containing deposits of lead ore. When the term ended, he had cash on hand and owned a horse.

Despite this success in court and the wish of his godparents that he live with them, Henry had no intention of settling permanently in Ste. Genevieve, or anywhere else in the Missouri country.[17] One characteristic of the way of life in that region irked him: "On the first day of the term I remarked the number of armed people about me—some with pistols behind them, under their coats; nearly all with dirks peeping from their bosoms; even the judges on the bench had their pistols and ataghans by their sides!" It was still a rude and dangerous society which he saw about him, although he did learn that bloodshed was not as great as the stranger might think. Henry, however, believed that the New Orleans scene presented a better opportunity for a successful career in the law than that of either Ste. Genevieve or St. Louis. But to St. Louis he wanted to go before descending the river to New Orleans.

First Henry visited the village of Mine à Burton, about forty miles from

Ste. Genevieve, as the guest of the Perry family, intending to proceed from the lead diggings directly to St. Louis.[18] Many years before Henry's father had had the elder Perry as a client in Pennsylvania, and the younger Brackenridge had represented the sons of that man at the recent court held in Ste. Genevieve. The Perrys, consequently, welcomed Henry to their home, which was an unpretentious cabin on the bank of a stream running through a gorge, in contrast to the imposing residence of Moses Austin, "the nabob of the place. . . ." Henry, who spent several weeks in the village, was struck particularly by the quarrelsome and fierce nature of the inhabitants, as they were always ready to defend their claims by violent means. He watched the diggers working at the pits and the smelters extracting the lead. He toured the whole district, interesting himself, as a result, in the study of geology and chemistry.

The village of Mine à Burton itself was not far from St. Louis, a distance which Henry covered leisurely on horseback in a few days.[19] Although he carried letters of introduction with him, he looked forward to seeing certain friends again—Graham, his roommate at Jefferson College; Saugrain, the physician of Gallipolis; and Schewe, the teacher-minister of Pittsburgh. All three, he knew, had settled in St. Louis. As Henry entered the town, he met a religious procession led by two beautiful young ladies; he waited respectfully in an alleyway until it had passed, and then went to the inn.

Henry rejoiced when he saw the easy circumstances of the Saugrain family.[20] The physician, now the father of little girls, lived in a pretty cottage near the edge of town. His wife was still as good-natured as she had been in Gallipolis. Henry dined with them, and over glasses of claret they recalled the trying life on the Ohio. With his happy home and a good medical practice, Saugrain was content.

Schewe, too, led a contented life in St. Louis. Fortescue Cuming, a traveler who was on his way to the western country on an extended tour which eventually took him down the Mississippi River and as far as West Florida, had met the eccentric Prussian in Pittsburgh in 1807, and described him as "a man of liberal morality, and a lively social companion."[21] The Lutheran pastor, however, not long after Cuming's visit to Pittsburgh abandoned the pulpit in the sincere belief that he was unfit for the ministry. According to Henry, Schewe had said once that "when he first proposed to his father to let him study divinity, the old man indignantly said to him: 'You be a minister!— you rashkel, you have not an ounce of minister's flesh on your rashkelly pones.' "[22] Pentland, the editor, had hoped that the people of Pittsburgh would patronize this jovial and learned man and encourage him to stay in town, a wish that did not materialize. By a notice inserted in the *Commonwealth*,[23] Schewe had informed the townsmen that "his engagement with the

German congregation" was to expire on March 12, 1808, at which time he planned to leave Pittsburgh. He wanted to settle accounts promptly with the people indebted to him or holding demands against him, the notice read; and when the response to his request was slow, he published another,[24] which threatened a resort to the law to force payments. By the turn of the year Schewe had settled in St. Louis, where he started a grammar school.[25] He painted miniatures in his spare time to add to his meager income as a teacher, and finally he "opened an establishment for the sale of small wares, beer, soap, candles, salt-fish, and a variety of other huckstery. . . ."[26] Of Schewe's activities Henry was generally aware, "yet I knew, let his occupation be what it might, he could not cease to be the same philosopher, original genius, and inimitable jester, whether over a tankard of beer or in the pulpit."

But Schewe had changed startlingly in appearance, as Henry discovered on locating him in his dirty, smelly, and cluttered shop.[27] The Prussian was slovenly dressed, no longer "black-coated, ruffle-shirted, and silk-stockinged (and well-shapen was that leg, and well did its owner know). . . ." The new Schewe, who embraced Henry and "applied his unshaven, and pershaps un-washed face, to mine," was a small, bald man. Schewe was overjoyed to see his former student: "And then he capered, and danced, and sung, and laughed, and cried."

Schewe's store, especially the back room containing a small library, a mineral collection, and chemical apparatus, acted as a magnet on Henry, drawing him there often in the ensuing weeks.[28] Young Brackenridge valued his friend's conversation, for Schewe's talk was never senseless and often penetrating in thought. But the inhabitants of St. Louis had lost their esteem for the school-teacher and miniature painter who had sunk so low on the social scale as to become the proprietor of a little shop which reeked with the smell of beer, tobacco, fish, and onions. Henry decided to rectify the situation by going about town and referring to the storekeeper as *"Doctor Schewe,"* who, as a matter of fact, did boast a variety of diplomas. After some persuasion by Henry, Schewe agreed to the plan. In no time at all people who had never troubled to notice him before began to address him respectfully.

Although Henry spent much idle time at the store, he was in daily attendance at Graham's law office. Henry's former roommate had become a lawyer after his student days in Canonsburg and established a practice in St. Louis, where the citizenry thought well of him.[29] Henry helped in the preparation of cases and made himself as useful as possible to his friend in return for the privilege of sharing the office.

Graham, who was a fashionable dresser and, in Henry's opinion, had "an exalted sense of honor, with not a little of military instinct," lacked the literary and scientific interests of his office companion.[30] They passed little time together in the evenings as a consequence, Graham frequently playing cards with a group of young army officers. Watching a game as a spectator one night, he saw a lieutenant cheat and immediately accused him of the dishonorable act. The outcome, of course, was a challenge, followed by the duel. Because a question arose over a point of honor, precisely like the one at issue in the Bates-Stewart duel, Graham did not confront his challenger on the field but the second instead, a physician who happened to be, ironically, the lawyer's best friend in St. Louis. This duel, likewise, was to be a *combat jusqu'à la mort*. "The fatal morning having arrived, the whole party proceeded, after daylight, in the same boat across the river to Illinois," Henry wrote in later life. "Excepting a surgeon, no one accompanied them. I was the only person who attended them to the boat. . . ." Henry, sick at heart, strained his ears to catch the reports of the gunfire—without avail. But Graham was so badly wounded—a ball in his side, a ball through the calves of his legs, and a ball through the hand which held the pistol—that within half a year he died.

How Henry hated dueling! To him the practice involved "false honor" and "barbarous and irrational morality."[31] The westerners on the whole tolerated dueling. Joseph Charless, the publisher of the *Louisiana Gazette* of St. Louis, was an exception, however. He informed his subscribers that they could expect no account of " *'an affair of honor!'* which took place here last week," because dueling was a "barbarous custom, hooted at by civilized society, falling daily into merited contempt. . . ."[32] But another promising lawyer among Henry's friends—first Bates and now Graham—was dead.

Before the duel—in fact, two months after his arrival in St. Louis—Henry had gone on circuit to replenish his purse.[33] He had spent much of his time learning Spanish, an occupation which brought him no money. But he considered the acquisition of knowledge to be more important than the amassing of wealth: "Yet, I must candidly admit, that fame was a more powerful motive with me than avarice. . . ." He had thus to desert his books for attendance at the courts.

He started on the circuit in September, traveling on horseback. During court week at Ste. Genevieve, he enjoyed the hospitality of his godparents. Although not involved in the matter in any way, Henry witnessed the evil effect of dueling when a lawyer and a physician fought each other as the direct result of a case of slander tried in the Ste. Genevieve court. The first fire felled the physician, who left a widow and seven children to mourn him. Another tragedy Henry encountered after he had attended the court at Cape Girardeau and set off for New Madrid. On the way he felt an urge to visit the squatter and his family with whom he had spent that happy night a few months before.

To his horror Henry found the settler a broken man, who had buried his wife and four of his children, the victims of a bilious fever. Sorrowfully Henry rode into New Madrid.

Here in New Madrid, in what leisure hours he could find during court week, Henry examined the library in the home of Madame Peyroux, the widow of the former commandant.[34] Peyroux himself not only had appreciated literature but had written essays on geological subjects. Henry, obviously, could never resist the attraction of strange books, or the temptation to investigate the nature of a library new to him. He was rapidly becoming the authority on the subject of western libraries, of which all were private. But the year of 1811 had hardly begun when several gentlemen in St. Louis "expressed a wish to commence a public library, and attach thereto a cabinet, for the reception and preservation of such natural curiosities as might be found in the country."[35] Unquestionably this statement in the *Louisiana Gazette* represented Henry's interest in literary and scientific subjects at work for the advancement of learning in the West. William Clark, who had voyaged up the Missouri with Meriwether Lewis and who now served as the Indian agent stationed at St. Louis, showed Henry a magnificent collection of Indian curiosities.[36] Furthermore, Frederick Bates, the brother of the ill-fated Tarleton and the secretary of Louisiana Territory as well as the acting governor, opened his "extensive" library to Henry's use.

But the most impressive library in St. Louis belonged to Auguste Chouteau, the leading citizen.[37] Henry visited this wealthy man, who lived in a stone and galleried mansion, and saw there "one of the largest private libraries I had seen, chiefly consisting of folio and quarto, from which circumstance I conjectured they had once belonged to the Jesuits, who, half a century before, had a college at Kaskaskia." Chouteau permitted Henry to take books to his lodgings for study at night—works like Lahontan's *New Voyages to North-America,* Lafitau's *Moeurs des Sauvages Ameriquains,* Hennepin's *Description de la Louisiane,* and Charlevoix's *Histoire et description generale de la Nouvelle France.* Access to such a library, especially in the West, was a rare privilege, of which Henry took full advantage, even devoting time during the day to examine the collection thoroughly.

Henry's preoccupation with literature was contrary to the advice of his father. But the elder Brackenridge had always begrudged work when it interfered with his literary pursuits. His son's attitude was the same: "The drudgery and sameness of mere business, I felt as waste of time, and interference with reading, and the solitary meditation in my walks."[38] Now, in the fall of 1810, Henry took up the pen to share his knowledge with his fellow Americans; with the enthusiasm and confidence of youth, he sought fame by his writing.

Charless was the person responsible for the beginning of Henry's literary career.[39] Henry early made the publisher's acquaintance, for, with St. Louis lacking a bookstore, he had gone to the print shop to read the exchange papers received there. The place soon became a regular resort for Henry. Here he could watch the *Louisiana Gazette,* a four-page affair, issue from the press every week. Small though his paper was, Charless often found it difficult to fill the columns with interesting matter. On September 27, 1810, for example, in an editorial he deplored the fact that the "present times" were "uncommonly dull for printers, and uncommonly busy for the farmers. Nothing that can excite a shade of interest is transpiring in the American atmosphere, and nothing effecting national concerns is transacted abroad." Henry, who appreciated the chance to read the papers on the exchange list, now reciprocated Charless' favor by writing articles for the gazette, enlivening its columns with informative—and provocative—material.

Henry's first contribution, the work of a well-read, traveled, and ebullient youth, appeared in Charless' paper in mid-October.[40] He cast his material, which concerned the topography of St. Louis, in the form of a letter to the publisher, signed "Z".[41] Charless printed it in two installments. Henry's opening paragraph surely caught the eye of the reader and fixed his attention: "It is scarcely worth enquiring, whether the site of this town, was chosen by the flight of birds, by the advice of [an] oracle, or from accident or design: it is certain the selection of this spot was a fortunate one, and evinces taste and judgment. I wish I could say as much of the plan and Improvement of the town itself." He chided the inhabitants of St. Louis for permitting the town to grow without improving the narrow and crooked cross streets, which ran east and west. There was not a single row of houses in the whole town, he complained; and, furthermore, many residents hid their gardens and orchards behind stone walls or cedar pickets. Cincinnati's site, he advised them, was similar—but how elegantly that town was laid out! "There is another thing with which I must accuse the public spirit of St. Louis," Henry continued. "On approaching the town, I came to the rivulet . . . which empties into the Mississippi, below the town; and where I expected to see a bridge. I found myself stopped by a deep canal, forty or fifty feet wide. . . . Why is there not a bridge thrown across here?" This anonymous correspondent gave the St. Louisans with public spirit food for thought.

They were, nevertheless, proud of their town; and some of them were really civic-minded. Most of the inhabitants were French Canadians, although the Americans were fast increasing in number; and there were some Spaniards and other Europeans, also.[42] Because the people of St. Louis were mainly traders and government employees, the town itself was more bustling than

Ste. Genevieve and less rural in appearance. In January, 1811, Charless published the latest census figures with a brief commentary, indicating an actual population for Louisiana of 22,000 persons at least.[43] The district (county) of St. Louis, in particular, contained 5,667 inhabitants; the district of Ste. Genevieve, 4,620. "The district of St. Louis," Charless commented, "is next to the upper or most northern in the territory, and when it is remembered that we form the extreme N.W. frontier of the Union, the following enumeration of domestic industry &c. will be highly interesting to the friends of America." In the district, as a matter of fact, there were already nine water mills, six sawmills, fifteen horse mills, twelve distilleries, two breweries, two shot towers, four saltworks, and hundreds of looms and spinning wheels. Charless himself was ever alert for news concerning his town, district, and territory, and brimful, too, with ideas for their improvement. Henry was likely the "gentleman from Pittsburg" who had told the publisher in late August of 1810, that a steamboat[44] for the Mississippi trade was under construction at the forks of the Ohio, information which inspired Charless to note "that no speculation could reward the capitalist more than 2 or 3 Steam Boats to ply regular[l]y from Orleans to St. Louis, the falls of Ohio and the intermediate towns."[45] Charless, moreover, advocated the erection of a steam mill to manufacture flour in the St. Louis area, waxing enthusiastic over the advantages of the place: "What a field for an enterprising merchant! The finest soil for any kind of grain (or hemp) in the world, with a navigation unimpeded by *falls* or *shoals* commanding a choice of season to transport our surplus produce to market."

Henry's second contribution to the gazette was an unsigned article, entitled "American Antiquities,"[46] a production not only manifesting a serious intellectual interest on his part but also an attempt to make the St. Louisans, including the hard-bitten fur traders, conscious of the ancient past. "What! has America antiquities?" he asked the reader enthusiastically. "Is she not the child of yesterday?" Henry cited evidence—geological, biological, and archaeological—to prove that America was not of recent origin: "Grant then, that America has existed for some thousands of years. . . ." Henry constructed his argument carefully to indicate the possibility of the existence of a highly developed civilization in North America long before the advent of the white man:

I have observed that civilization, is the necessary result of a numerous, and condenced population. This cannot be easily attained in cold climates. . . . In America we perceive, that civilization, began in the warmest climates; where nature with little assistance from man produced abundance of food. From these observations I think it not unreasonable to say, that if the northern part of this continent, ever was at any time, or ever would have been civilized, if left to itself by Europeans, it had been through the aid of the southern. Why may not great revolutions have taken place in Mexico and

South America? Is it certain that Mexico, Peru and Chili, when visited by Europeans exhibited only the first dawn of civilization? . . . .

If we calmly review that period in History called the dark ages, when so much learning was lost, and so many arts perished, we will be satisfied, that but for the invention of letters, Europe would have returned to a state of barbarism. But if Europe had returned to this state, should we not still see the monuments of her former greatness; edifices of stone, acquaducts, canals, pavement, and the earth perforated, in the working of mines? Do we find any of these things in the northern part of this continent?

I am not contending the probability of such a state of society ever having existed in this country. I am only speaking of its possibility. . . .

America may have been less fortunate than Europe, in those happy inventions, that serve to perpetuate improvements; and yet she may have attained in some of the sciences a greater excellence. The character of her civilization, may have been different from any of which we have a knowledge; and her relapse produced by causes of which we can form no conjecture. But we are acquainted with such as are amply sufficient to produce these effects; there are pestilence, war, and the convulsions of nature.

This theory never lost its fascination for Henry. He had begun a lifelong study of American antiquities.

But the St. Louisans, except a few men like Bates, Clark, and Chouteau, had never interested themselves in such a subject. They were indifferent to the fact that in the vicinity of their town were astonishing evidences of antiquity, especially the great mounds across the river on the American bottom in Illinois: "I could meet with no one that had the curiosity to visit them."[47] Not even Graham consented to accompany Henry to the site.[48] Henry crossed the Mississippi alone, determined to test his conjectures on American antiquities by personal observation: "If we should look for a numerous population of the aborigines any where in America, it would be here."[49]

Never had Henry read a description of the place which he was about to see. His reward for crossing the river was, therefore, ample.[50] On the Illinois side he walked across a bridge over a creek, passed through a small wood, and came upon the open prairie. He followed a road along the south side of the creek and shortly arrived at the first group of mounds, from fifteen to forty feet high. A chain of mounds connected this group to the Cantine mounds about five or six miles away: "These are all the work of human hands, what a field for fanciful conjecture! their form and size vary considerably: at the first glance they look like enormous haystacks scattered through a meadow." But he was thrilled when he saw the largest mound, which stood on the bank of the Cahokia. He calculated the circumference of this "most stupendous pile of earth" to be about 3,500 feet; and its height, about eighty. The mound was oblong, running from north to south. Henry discovered that the top was sowed in wheat and that part of the terraced south side was a kitchen garden. Many other mounds, perhaps fifty, encircled this awesome one. Not far away the Trappists occupied temporary cabins erected on a small mound, their other structures dotting the plain below. Henry of course, visited the monastery before returning to St. Louis.

He promptly wrote an account of his visit to the site of the magnificent tumuli which stood literally at the front door of the St. Louisans. Charless published the unsigned article, entitled "Cantine Mounds, and the Monastery of La Trappe," in two installments in January of 1811. But Henry did not intend to lay down his pen when the essay was written and published. Between the installments of this essay Charless printed another unsigned article which Henry had written on the "Limits of Louisiana."[51] The author predicted that sometime "national difficulties" would occur because of the indeterminate boundary of the huge territory, stressing the point that "the accumulating wave of American population, will disdain every boundary but that of nature or of necessity." To this article Henry appended a list of the sources consulted in its preparation—maps, histories, and the "documents accompanying the president Jefferson's communications."

By these four anonymous articles in the *Louisiana Gazette,* Henry proved himself to be a young writer of promise—certainly an essayist with a clear and vigorous style. His legal training enabled him to present facts in a convincing way, for he revealed the source of his information and strengthened it by personal observation whenever possible, knowing the books which he had consulted teemed with inaccuracies. For the same reason, too, he excelled in argument and exposition. Henry was an observant person, who usually caught every detail of a scene at a single glance. This characteristic was already apparent in the vividness of his description. Highly imaginative, he tended to embellish his account, although he had no intention of misleading the reader. His writing evidenced, also, the cockiness of a confident youth who had something worth-while to say and knew how to say it effectively. Charless, consequently, had welcomed Henry's contributions.

But as the editor of a paper in a territory about which little was known in the United States, Charless now encouraged Brackenridge to prepare a general description of Louisiana for publication. In that way the editor knew he could best satisfy the many "queries" which he had received concerning the region, realizing that such a detailed account would be particularly useful to people "desirous of emigrating" there. Thus it happened that Henry wrote the "Sketches of the Territory of Louisiana," the first number of which appeared in the *Louisiana Gazette,* January 31, 1811. In a brief introduction, printed in italics, Charless announced his indebtedness for the essays "to the pen of H. M. Brackenridge, Esq. We considered it a tribute, due to Mr. Brackenridge, to say, that the fullest reliance can be placed upon the accuracy and impartiality of his descriptions."

Henry had undertaken the task with the responsibility of the scholar and the inspiration of the artist. In the introductory essay he declared that his object was "to state facts unadorned," not wishing "to amuse, merely, but to give information." He mentioned the disadvantages as well as the advantages of the territory for the prospective settler. He supplied footnotes for the learned reader. But there was a delightful personal touch, for Henry did not hesitate to draw on the experience of his own travels for pertinent and up-to-date information.

The titles of the sketches read like the chapter headings of a book:

No.   II: Rivers—Face of the country, &c.[52]
     III: Soil—Climate, &c. From New Madrid to the Missouri.[53]
      IV: The country, North of the Missouri.[54]
       V: Natural productions, animal, vegetable, and mineral.[55]
      VI: Political divisions of the Territory, Inhabitants, Settlements.[56]
     VII: Towns and Villages.[57]
    VIII: Manners and customs of the ancient Inhabitants—Government—Historical epocha—comparison between their situation under the former and the present governments.[58]
      IX: Lead Mines in the district of St. Genevieve.[59]
       X: A general view of the country west of the Mississippi, and of the Rocky Ridge. Indian nations of the Missouri.[60]
      XI: Resources of the Territory—in agriculture—manufactures and trade.[61]

Henry had, in effect, produced the making of a book.

Instantly upon the publication of the essays Henry won a modicum of fame. Editors throughout the United States reprinted them, generally giving Henry credit as the author. In the spring of 1811, for example, the Carlisle paper published several, with this acknowledgment: "Extracted from Mr. Brackenridge's valuable 'Sketches' of Upper Louisiana—published in the L. Gaz. at St. Louis."[62] In Baltimore Hezekiah Niles, who began publishing his *Weekly Register*, that famous repository of information, in September of 1811, the same year, immediately reprinted extracts from the sketches in his "Geography" department.[63] The one printed in the issue of December 7, significantly, carried the editorial note—"Corrected and communicated by the author."

The popular demand for copies of the sketches began as soon as the first numbers in Charless' gazette reached the East. In May, when the Philadelphia merchant, Joseph Herzog, wrote a long letter to his partner in St. Louis, he asked that "the series of statistical papers published by your printer on Louisiana" be sent with the first goods shipped eastward.[64] For a man like Herzog, engaged in the western trade, the informative sketches had immense value.

But one man more than any other in the whole United States was certain to find Henry's work of interest—Thomas Jefferson, the author of the celebrated *Notes on the State of Virginia* and the President whose statesmanship resulted in the Louisiana Purchase and the Lewis and Clark expedition as well. Richard Wash of St. Louis not only forwarded the first numbers to Monticello but also prepared a crude map so that Jefferson "might read Mr. Breckenridge's remarks with more satisfaction. . . ."[65] The copies of the *Louisiana Gazette* unfortunately going astray, never reaching Jefferson, Wash tried again:

I herewith enclose you seven nos & will forward the rest in the course of a week or two. The Author I fear, has been rather too desirous of obtaining a reputation for writing truths with facility: But of his merit in this respect you are the better Judge. One thing tho' is most certain,—we need not blush at the colour of his praise.

IX: The Race to the Arikara Village

"We this week finish Mr. Brackenridge's Sketches,[1] and cannot but regret the loss of his literary contributions," Charless announced in his gazette of June 27, 1811. "Mr. B. is now making a tour of the N.W. and Western border of Louisiana and will perhaps visit the city of Mexico, and return by the province of Texas to New Orleans. We understand he intends to publish the result of his travels." After returning to St. Louis, Henry read this statement and did not like the second part of it at all, as he immediately notified the editor.

The previous winter, when he was busy writing the essays for Charless' paper, Henry had become friendly with John Bradbury and Thomas Nuttall, two naturalists who were botanizing in the vicinity of St. Louis. Nuttall, an Englishman, was only a few months older than Henry; whereas Bradbury, a Scotchman, was more advanced in life than his associate and at the time better known in the scientific world. Bradbury held a commission from the botanical society in Liverpool to investigate plant life in the United States. When he received an invitation to ascend the Missouri River with an expedition led by Wilson P. Hunt, Bradbury accepted it with pleasure and without hesitation, canceling his plan to proceed to the Arkansas for botanical research.[2]

Hunt was the right-hand man, the chief agent, of John Jacob Astor, who had conceived a fabulous undertaking to control the fur trade in the Far West by the establishment of a fortified post at the mouth of the Columbia River.[3] The merchant-capitalist had enlisted several able but discontented employees of the Northwest Company, which had its headquarters in Montreal, and also obtained the services of Hunt, an American citizen from New Jersey. Then on June 23, 1810, Astor and his partners signed the articles of agreement forming the Pacific Fur Company. As head of the firm Astor agreed to manage the New York office and to supply the capital required to launch the enterprise. The partners appointed Hunt to be the first agent of the company at their trading center on the Pacific coast. Astor sent the "Tonquin," commanded by Jonathan Thorn, on the long voyage to the Columbia loaded with supplies for the post, including seeds for planting there, and goods for the Indian trade. Hunt, however, was to proceed to St. Louis and up the Missouri, across the Rocky Mountains, and thence to the Pacific. It was his duty to determine suitable sites for the erection of company posts along the route.

Hunt proceeded to St. Louis with the greatest dispatch possible.[4] He was an honest, polite, and easygoing person who had previously engaged in trade at St. Louis. But he was no ranger of the woods—not a *coureur des bois*. Donald McKenzie, a partner who accompanied him, was a master of woodcraft, a veteran formerly in the service of the Northwest Company. They needed to exercise all their wits and to draw upon their combined experience when hiring *voyageurs* at Montreal, for the Northwest Company kept the most experienced and trustworthy in its own employ. After the purchase of supplies for the expedition, the party embarked at St. Anne's in a huge canoe made of birch bark and fitted with a sail. Their progress up the Ottawa River and then to Michilimackinac was disappointingly slow because of the unreliable crew, indifferent to work. At Mackinaw, Hunt employed more *voyageurs* and welcomed a young and capable Scot, named Ramsay Crooks, as a new partner in the firm. The party, numbering now more than thirty, reached St. Louis on September 3, 1810.

Their arrival created a sensation among the St. Louisans engaged in the Indian trade, and especially among the partners of the St. Louis Missouri Fur Company.[5] Hunt's competitors tried everything to frustrate his plans, managing to delay his departure for the upper reaches of the Missouri until the following spring. He wisely decided to establish winter quarters in the hunting country upriver, where the expense of supporting his augmented party was not as great as in St. Louis or in the other settlements. By mid-November, as the Missouri rapidly became icebound, they encamped about 450 miles from the Mississippi. At this place Robert McClellan, an intrepid trader who had fought bravely under General Wayne against the Indians, joined the party as a partner in the company at Hunt's invitation. McClellan was a slight but strong man, dark-eyed and often ill-tempered. Here, too, John Day, a tall hunter of middle age, became a member of the expedition. But Hunt was still not satisfied with the strength of his party. He wanted to employ more hunters and an interpreter who understood the language of the warlike Sioux. Hunt hoped to obtain the men in St. Louis, for there in the fall he had persuaded Joseph Miller to join the expedition as a partner and had also hired some boatmen and hunters despite the opposition of rival traders. Hunt, therefore, returned to St. Louis in January, arriving on horseback in the company of two associates.

Hunt's mission proved difficult, requiring the nicest management.[6] The St. Louis Missouri Fur Company, which was in serious financial straits, planned an expedition up the Missouri to save itself from bankruptcy and, if possible, to determine the whereabouts of Andrew Henry, a partner who had to desert the company post at the Three Forks of the river and to cross the Rocky Mountains after constant bedevilment by the Blackfeet. The partners deputed one of their number, Manuel Lisa, to lead the enterprise. With two expeditions readying for the ascent of the Missouri, the competition for employing hunters and *voyageurs* was fierce. Hunt, as a result, had to offer generous advances of pay and to overlook defects in the character of prospective employees. He was lucky enough to hire an interpreter in the person of Pierre Dorion, a half-breed in the service of Lisa's firm until an unquenchable thirst for whisky—at ten dollars a quart—had left him hopelessly in debt on its books, and made him willing to sign with another company. After negotiations lasting almost two weeks and the promise of two hundred dollars as an advance of pay, an embittered Dorion, ignoring Lisa's threats, agreed to accompany Hunt. Then, to Hunt's discouragement, as he was on the point of departure from St. Louis, five American hunters arrived from the Missouri encampment with stories of mistreatment by the partners in charge there. Two of the hunters finally consented to return with Hunt; but the other three, remaining obdurate, so frightened the new employees with tales about the perils of the voyage that they refused to leave the town. With but one hunter, consequently, and some *voyageurs,* Hunt embarked at last. He had on board Dorion's squaw and two children, for the interpreter insisted on their presence as part of his bargain!

"Mr. Wilson P. Hunt, left, this place last Monday, with a well equipped barge, to join his associates, at the Otto village, to proceed on his expedition to the Columbia river," reported Charless' paper in mid-March. "His party amount to about seventy able bodied men, nerved to hardship."[7] The news item added that Hunt was "accompanied by Mr. Bradbury and a Mr. Nuttall, who are deputed to this country, to explore and make known its riches, in the Animal, Vegetable and Mineral Kingdoms. . . ."

Fortunately for Dorion and Hunt, Bradbury decided to remain in St. Louis until the arrival of the mail, which was expected the next day from Louisville.[8] The botanist stowed his baggage in the boat, however, for at St. Charles he intended to join the party. But that night after Hunt had left, Bradbury learned that Lisa had obtained a writ for debt against Dorion and intended to serve it at St. Charles. To warn the interpreter of the danger, Bradbury and Nuttall left town precipitately at two o'clock in the morning and were able to head the boat as it began the ascent of the Missouri. Dorion and his family scurried into the woods after promising to meet the party above St. Charles. The expedition left there on the morning of March 14, the Canadian *voyageurs* "measuring the strokes of their oars by songs, which were generally responsive betwixt the oarsmen at the bow and those at the stern: sometimes the steersman sung, and was chorused by the men."[9] Bradbury was struck by the "frivolity" of their songs, one of which began like this (in his translation of the French):

> Behind our house there is a pond,
>> Fal lal de ra.
> There came three ducks to swim thereon:
> All along the river clear,
> Lightly my shepherdess dear,
>> Lightly, fal de ra.

As he had promised, Dorion suddenly appeared on the bank and waved to the singing boatmen. He boarded the barge without his wife, for, after a quarrel and a thrashing from him, she had fled with her two papooses. But on March 15, several hours before daybreak, she hailed the party from the opposite shore and waited contentedly until she could go aboard. At last Hunt felt that his expedition had really started its voyage.

In St. Louis Henry had watched the rivalry between the two fur companies increase and, as a fascinated spectator friendly with the principals of both expeditions, he soon succumbed to a desire to go up the Missouri himself. A law career in New Orleans could wait! Bradbury and Nuttall had stimulated Henry's interest in natural science to the point where he took to the fields to botanize with them. Therefore, when asked to join Lisa's party, Henry accepted the invitation gladly, with little thought of the Indian danger: "The pleasure of being in company with Mr. Bradbury, whom we expected to overtake, was not a light consideration."[10] But his single motive, as he expressed it, was "the mere gratification" of "an idle curiosity."[11] This reason for making the hazardous voyage seemed so slight to Henry that it troubled him. He convinced himself, however, that he was justified in making the trip, although his position as Lisa's guest and as an observer only—not as a hunter or boatman— might mean that he could never perform any useful service for the expedition: "It was a good opportunity to improve my Spanish, as we spoke the language exclusively, and read Don Quixote together, at such intervals as we would snatch for the purpose."[12]

But the indomitable Lisa, who was Spanish, had fired Henry's imagination. "He was about five feet eleven, of a Herculean frame, possessed of a powerful mind, of that cast which is formed for action; his eye was all fire . . .," Henry pictured him nearly thirty years later. "Lisa, in short, unlike the slow, procrastinating, solemn Spaniard, was all action and fire, which joined to his personal prowess, reminded me of the heroes of Cortes, Sandoval, Ohd, or Alvarado."[13] Lisa had spent his youth at sea in the service of the king and then in merchant ships, and finally had appeared in the upper Mississippi region, where he became a magnate in the Indian trade. He related his adventures among the red men on the Missouri to Henry, who listened in wonder and longed to visit the scenes, too, and

be able to say I had been near the source of the Missouri; had seen Indians and buffaloes, and like other travellers, earn the enviable privilege of making people stare by dealing a little in the marvellous. Besides, I might make a book, filled with exciting incidents, which might be read; and thus, instead of being a mere atom of the nebulus and undistinguished galaxy, I might stand out a separate star, bearing a name, and shining with my own light. I therefore proposed to accompany him, in the spring, in his voyage up the Missouri, and to this he cheerfully assented.[14]

115

His curiosity and the quest for fame were, of course, the basic considerations inspiring Henry to accompany Lisa. Whether Henry had forthrightly asked Lisa's permission to become a member of the expedition is uncertain, however, in the light of contradictory evidence[15]—a mere hint of his wish to voyage up the Missouri might have sufficed to win him the invitation.

To Henry, as well as to other confidants, Lisa expressed the hope that he could negotiate a peace with the Blackfeet and establish a profitable trade with them.[16] But to attempt such a project, Lisa had first to lead his party safely through the country of the hostile Sioux. He took every possible precaution against the menace.[17] The barge, manned by twenty oarsmen, was the "best that ever ascended this river," according to Henry, for Lisa had rigged it with a mast and two sails for navigation, and for defense had fitted it with a swivel at the bow and two brass blunderbusses in the cabin—"one over my birth, and the other over that of Mr. Lisa." Every man in the party of twenty-five was fully armed. But as an additional safeguard against robbery, Lisa hid most of the merchandise in a false cabin. He resolved, furthermore, to overtake and join Hunt's party before it reached the Sioux country.

Lisa made no secret of his hope to overhaul the rival expedition. There was a possibility that marauding bands of Sioux might not prove troublesome, for the fall of the year was the customary time for their appearance along the river.[18] But Lisa announced publicly his intention of bending to the oars to overtake Hunt, with the result that Charless commented in his paper that should "Mr. Lisa join Mr. Hunt's party, on the head waters of the Missouri, they will form an army able to oppose any number of Blackfeet which may attack them."[19] Lisa, surely, did not want Hunt to have the advantage of trading with friendly redskins alone—a reason for haste, however, which was best left unsaid.

Lisa began the voyage the beginning of April—his destination, as Charless informed the public, was Fort Mandan.[20] The departure from St. Louis and St. Charles was difficult to effect until all the hands had wearied of carousing.[21] On April 2, the barge pushed into the subsiding floodwater at St. Charles, moved a few miles upriver, and stopped. Some men on board were roistering still; and others lingered in the village, reluctant to leave civilization without a satisfying fling. Not until two o'clock the next afternoon could Lisa get his party under way.

At the village of Cote sans Dessein, they learned for the first time the kind of progress Hunt was making.[22] Henry made brief notes of what interested him as they proceeded up the Missouri—nothing seemed to escape his eye. The blustery Canadians and half-breeds earned his respect immediately because they worked hard on a disagreeable diet of hominy for breakfast, fat pork and biscuit for lunch, and mush with tallow in it for supper, food, however, which was better than the usual fare for such people. From the start of the voyage heavy storms lashed the party repeatedly. At first navigation was easy, for the sails proved their worth in a breeze and only occasionally did the oars and poles give way to the towing line. Henry took special note of the Tavern Rocks, where travelers could find shelter in a cave; he measured a cottonwood one evening and found its circumference to be thirty-six feet. He studied the problem of navigating the river, impressed by the rapidity of the current, which in some places became violent as it rushed around *"embarras,* or rafts, formed by the collection of trees closely matted, and extending from twenty to thirty yards." Now navigation was maddeningly slow, and dangerous. The party passed the Gasconade River on April 9, and again could use the sails; but the following day an embarras caused a delay. The country was rich, as Henry discovered on April 11, when he crossed the fertile land to Cote sans Dessein with an interpreter, having gone ahead of the barge for the pleasure of a two-mile walk in pleasant weather. At the village they "inquired with eagerness after the party of Mr. Hunt; we were informed that he had passed this place twenty-one days ago. Thus far, it appears that we have gained but two days upon him."

Bradbury, meanwhile, had experienced something which was denied Henry because of the need for haste to gain on the advance party. On March 17, before Lisa's expedition began its ascent of the river, Bradbury's party had stopped briefly at Charette, a tiny French village, and the same afternoon had continued the voyage: "On leaving Charette, Mr. Hunt pointed out to me an old man standing on the bank, who, he informed me, was Daniel Boond, the discoverer of Kentucky."[23] Bradbury, who carried a letter of introduction to the pioneer, went ashore, planning to overtake the boat later in the day. The botanist talked at length to the venerable woodsman: "He informed me, that he was eighty-four years of age; that he had spent a considerable portion of his time alone in the back woods, and had lately returned from his spring hunt, with nearly sixty beaver skins." In passing this same stretch of the river Henry also wished to visit Boone,[24] but, alas, did not even get a glimpse of him.

Determinedly the Lisa party strained every muscle to gain in the race.[25] At Cote sans Dessein, Lisa employed Castor, a Kansas Indian, as a hunter; repaired the cabin; and once more got his expedition started on its way. They soon passed the Osage River; and two days later they reached the saltworks managed by Braxton Cooper, where there was a settlement of seventy-five families: "We inquired for the party of which we were in chase—they had passed by *nineteen* days before us." On April 17, Lisa's party under sail swept by the mouth of the Grand River, and then had their progress slowed by bad

117

weather. But on Sunday, April 21, they stopped for the night "above an encampment of Mr. Hunt, which appeared not more than ten or twelve days old."

Fort Osage, high on a bluff overlooking the Missouri, was a welcome sight to Henry, for driving rains, adverse winds, and annoying mosquitoes made the ascent of the river still difficult.[26] On Thursday, April 25, his party arrived at the fort, where a soldier awaited them on shore. He led Lisa and Henry to the officer in command, who greeted them cordially. While Lisa attended to the business of the expedition, George Sibley, the factor, took Henry to visit Sans Oreille, the Osage warrior who was more powerful than Young White Hairs, the chief of this Siouan tribe. Henry presented a pipe to Sans Oreille, sent him by Clark, the Indian agent. The handsome warrior, a gracious recipient of the gift, intrigued Henry, who learned all he could about him: "No demagogue—no Cataline, ever used greater art and finesse, or displayed more policy than this cunning savage." Fort Osage itself, Henry noted, was small and triangular; and the factory, where Sibley carried on the Indian trade, consisted of a cluster of buildings. The circular lodges of the Little Osage band stood near by. Sibley, as he told Henry, was about to depart for the Grand Saline in the company of Osage warriors. At the fort, also, Henry obtained news about the rival expedition: "Thus far we have gained about one hundred miles upon the party of Hunt—we are in good spirits, and will renew the pursuit with augmented vigor."

The distance from the mouth of the Missouri to Fort Osage was 306 miles, according to the calculation of William Clark.[27] The post, in reality, marked the outermost limit of American settlement. This sobering thought occurred to everyone on Lisa's barge after the departure from Fort Osage late in the morning of April 26:

> We have now passed the last settlement of whites, and probably will not re-visit them for several months. This reflection caused us all to think seriously of our situation. I almost repented of having undertaken this voyage, without an object in view, of suitable importance. Our men were kept from thinking too deeply, by the cheering songs, which were encouraged by Mr. Lisa, and the splashing of the oars, which kept time with them. So far removed, I seemed to look back, as from an eminence; thus abstracted, I fancied that I contemplated my country with more accuracy than I could while protected in its bosom.[28]

There was a chance of trouble, however, for the men began to murmur beyond the earshot of Lisa.[29] Henry did not attribute their attitude to discouraging progress. On April 27, his party met a group of traders descending the river and learned from them that unfavorable winds had handicapped Hunt's expedition. The traders, who had met Hunt's party five days previously, believed that it could be overtaken at the Platte River: "The good news we have heard, animates our men very much." The next day Lisa's expedition passed the Kansas. The morning of April 29, the members breakfasted aboard the barge as a breeze moved it steadily upriver. Long stretches of open water cheered them, although sometimes the Missouri became crooked and narrow and sand bars proved a hindrance. There could be no fear of hunger, for deer and turkeys abounded; and on April 30, both Lisa and Henry killed a deer with little effort. That day their party made thirty-three miles; and May 1, twenty-seven miles. There was beautiful weather the two following days. Henry, consequently, was shocked to hear men grumble about their lot as he warmed himself at the fire on the night of May 4. They complained that the voyage was the most rigorous in their experience. "This discontent was of course excited by some Thersites of the party," Henry was sure. "Great exertions have certainly been made and no moments lost, in advancing our voyage, but much of the time we were carried along by the wind, when there was no need for any labor on the part of the men." Henry could not sympathize with them. "The weather is now fine, and their labor diversified, when there is no wind, by the pole, the oars, or cordelle, which is little more than a promenade along the sand bars." He tried to placate them with such reasoning.

They did not meet Hunt at the Platte.[30] On May 5, in fact, two men coming down-river from Hunt's party told them he had passed there almost a week before. This information was not disheartening because "it seems we have gained upon them as much as we expected." By May 9, a few men in Lisa's party were sick, the victims of coughs and fevers; and there was a case of pleurisy. The next day they reached the Platte. When bad weather detained them on May 11, Henry walked into the country and viewed the river, impressed, for it looked as wide as the Missouri and was filled with many islands and sand bars. Passing the Platte, in the minds of the Missouri boatmen, was comparable to crossing the equator, providing an occasion for merrymaking. Anyone who had never passed the river had to be shaved unless he "could compromise the matter by a treat." Beyond the Platte the party entered the Upper Missouri.

The ascent of the river now became harder.[31] The men had to use the towing line, or *cordelle*, often. Driftwood impeded their progress. On May 13, Henry thought they had "reached the highest point to which settlements will probably extend on the western side for many years." That evening they passed the Council Bluffs, the meadows where Lewis and Clark had once conferred with the Indians. Then one day the Lisa party ran into a downpour; and one night they were unable to sleep when a crashing storm broke over them. They came to an encampment of Hunt on May 16 and noted the buffalo bones "strewed about. If it be their encampment at the time we were at the river Platte, it is not more than six days since they were here."

The gap between the two expeditions narrowed slowly.[32] Early on the morning of May 18, the Lisa barge began winding its way around the base of Blackbird Hill, named after the Maha chief who was buried astride his horse on the summit. From this vantage point the warrior hoped to see the traders ascending the Missouri. According to Henry, Blackbird had been as feared in this country as Tamerlane was in Asia: "Yet, the secret of his greatness was nothing more nor less than a quantity of arsenic, which he procured from some trader. He denounced death against any one who displeased him, or opposed his wishes . . . ." At the Maha village the party expected to overtake Hunt and his men. But at that place Lisa learned that four days before the rival expedition had left the Mahas and continued on its way. Lisa decided to send his interpreter and an Indian overland to the Poncas to ask Hunt to wait at their village. On May 20, Lisa's party passed the Big Sioux River. Then, three days later, the barge sailed by the Burning Bluffs, where Henry observed great masses of pumice. That same day, May 23, the party espied men standing on a sand bar, one of whom was the factor stationed at the Mandan village by the St. Louis Missouri Fur Company: "He tells us that the Indians are ill disposed to the whites, every where on the Missouri. Mr. Henry is in a distressed situation over the Rocky mountains. . . . They did not see the boats of Hunt." Indeed, during the night Indians had fired on this little company which was bringing peltries down the river.

Lisa's party, discouraged, resumed the voyage with the factor accompanying them.[33] The next day they saw the first live buffalo—a bull standing on a bluff above the river. As if to bolster their spirits, the weather turned warm and the scenery became more and more beautiful. On May 25, the prairie with its blue grass and wild flowers lured Henry ashore, although he was "forbidden to wander far, on account of the Indians, who it is thought may be near." That night the scenery bewitched him, and the sky appeared to him "as clear as in a Chinese painting . . . ." At dawn the following morning, the interpreter and the Indian returned from their mission with the intelligence that Hunt would await them at the Ponca village. They reached there in the early afternoon of May 27, as naked men and dirty women and children—"filthy and disgusting" in Henry's eyes—lined the bank in welcome. But here two men from Hunt's party, evidently deserters, "informed us, that as soon as he heard of our approach, which was quite unexpected, he had determined to exert himself to the utmost, to get out of our reach. The fact is, there does not exist the greatest confidence between the two commanders." Henry divined the situation: "Ours seems to think, that it is the intention of Hunt, to pass the Sioux, who may wish to detain him, by telling them that their trader is coming on with goods for them. While on the other hand, Hunt may believe that Lisa intends to pass him, and tell the same story."

This was a pretty state of affairs. If Henry's conjecture were correct, and distrust motivated the conduct of both leaders, a meeting of the rival expeditions in the desolate upper Missouri region was unwise. But Lisa, not a prudent man ordinarily, could think of only one thing to do: ". . . push our voyage, if possible, still more than before."[34]

Then, within a week, Lisa's party overtook Hunt.[35] The afternoon of May 29, they arrived at Little Cedar Island, and at its point found an encampment of his with the fire unextinguished. They proceeded under sail until eleven o'clock that night, making seventy-five miles in twenty-four hours. The next evening the pursuers passed the White River and heard "several gun shots, which we supposed to have been from the party of Hunt." But on the last day of May the sudden appearance of three buffaloes swimming toward them caused a firing of their own guns in sport for a half-hour in spite of an agreement to pass up this stretch of the river in silence for fear of an Indian attack. At the noise an Indian came to the riverside to investigate the disturbance. At daybreak firing began on the opposite side of the Missouri and red men waited there on the shore until Lisa's party rowed across to them. Henry, like everyone else, was ready for violence: "Each rower had his gun by his side— Mr. Lisa and myself, besides our knives and rifles, had each one a pair of pistols in our belts. On reaching the shore we discovered twelve or thirteen Indians on a log. Mr. Lisa and I, leaped on shore and shook hands with them." Lisa gave the Sioux a convincing story of hard luck—that he was their unfortunate trader whose peltry had burnt and who now was on his way to rescue his men at the head of the Missouri, whereupon he would return to trade with them and their whole nation—and he gave them a gift, also. The Sioux, therefore, hesitated to molest his party; and he did not linger to invite attack. Only two days before Hunt had passed this spot. At the Great Bend of the river, which was, as Henry noted, "twenty-one miles around, and only one and an half across," Lisa sent two men ahead "to notify the boats of our near approach." The next morning, Sunday, June 2, Henry himself set off on foot and, after a four-mile walk, saw Hunt's boats in the distance—admittedly a joyous sight.

The joining of the two expeditions was colorful.[36] Henry, of course, hurried back to his party with the news. At once they got under way; and arriving opposite the place where Henry had seen Hunt's boats, they discovered a band of three hundred Arikaras, whom they thought Sioux, signaling them to cross: "We suffered them to shout, to gallop their horses, and to wave their robes unnoticed." In reality, the Indians were a friendly party, desirous of escorting

Lisa's expedition the rest of the distance to Hunt. Lisa had actually passed raiding bands of Sioux unobserved. At eleven o'clock that same morning[37] the chase ended, although the race was not over: "It was with real pleasure I took my friend Bradbury by the hand; I have reason to believe our meeting was much more cordial than that of the two commanders." Henry was not wrong.

Hunt had never trusted Lisa, who, after all, did succeed in delaying the ascent of the Missouri until spring. But fanning Hunt's dislike of his rival was the hate which Crooks and McClellan harbored for him as a consequence of his keen competition in the Indian trade.[38] On the basis of personal experience they considered Lisa tricky and treacherous, accusing him of having instigated "the Sioux to treat them ill the preceding year."[39] McClellan had sworn that if he ever met Lisa in the Indian country he would kill him; and he did not hesitate to repeat the threat when Lisa's party came into view. Hunt, therefore, had tried desperately to evade his rival, having had no intention to wait for him at the Ponca village. But now that Lisa had overtaken him, Hunt was afraid that he would lose the race to the Arikara village. He expected Lisa to resort to any deceit to obtain the advantage in the Indian trading.

Thus, suspicious of each other and wary, the two parties proceeded "in company the rest of the day, forming a handsome little fleet of five sail."[40] At dusk the expeditions encamped together—alone in the wilderness twelve hundred miles from the Mississippi.

Aside from Henry, the two people in whom resentment did not smolder for one reason or another were Bradbury and Nuttall. The men of science, Henry could see, were having a happy time engaged in their botanical pursuit. Already Bradbury had discovered about one hundred plants not yet described in scientific literature.[41] But in April he had narrowly escaped death when a rattlesnake struck at him from the top of a rock as he busily collected plants at the base: "The noise of its rattle just gave me sufficient notice to withdraw my head."[42] Nuttall was heedless of danger; and in his zeal for botanizing occasionally delayed the party, causing them to wait anxiously for his return to the boat after an excursion into the country. "To the ignorant Canadian boatmen, who are unable to appreciate the science, it affords a subject of merriment; *le fou*, the fool, is the name by which he is commonly known," Henry learned after the two parties had joined. "No sooner does the boat touch the shore, than he leaps out, and when his attention is arrested by a plant or flower, every thing else is forgotten. The inquiry is sometimes made, *où est le fou?* where is the fool? *il est après ramasser des racines,* he is gathering roots."[43] Henry, an enthusiast himself, thought that Nuttall was too absorbed in his scientific interest for his own good. Henry, naturally, was a bit condescending in forming his judgment of the young Englishman.

The outburst of the pent emotions, confined by both parties for three long days, occurred on June 5, late on a rainy afternoon.[44] While Henry and Bradbury were walking at some distance from the Missouri and observing antelope, wolves, buffaloes, prairie dogs, and a hare, Lisa tried to inveigle Dorion by inviting him to the barge, offering him whisky, and reminding him of the obnoxious debt. But Dorion was not tractable—nothing could tempt him to desert Hunt's party. Dorion returned to his camp and reported the incident to Hunt, no doubt embroidering it considerably. At the moment of Bradbury's arrival there, Lisa appeared to borrow a towing line from Hunt. When he saw Lisa, the interpreter confronted him in a fury and struck him at least once. Lisa, enraged, rushed to his camp and returned with a knife buckled to his girdle. Henry, unable to appease Lisa's anger, accompanied him, fearful of senseless slaughter. Dorion, in the meantime, had grabbed a pair of Hunt's pistols; and McClellan and Crooks had indicated their intent to enter the fray. Hunt restrained McClellan from turning his rifle on Lisa, who, however, now insulted the rival commander, provoking him to issue a challenge—a duel with pistols. In an attempt to mediate, Henry stepped between Lisa with his knife and Dorion with his guns. Lisa, in answer to the challenge, hastened to his camp to prepare for the duel. There Henry and Bradbury succeeded in dissuading him from any immediate action, which was certain to be bloody.

As both camps seethed, Henry and Bradbury served as go-betweens for the two parties, striving to allay suspicions and to resolve differences to prevent an outbreak of violence. Each was loyal to his respective commander, although Henry believed that Lisa was "imprudent" in soliciting Dorion with whisky and thereby putting himself "in the power of a worthless fellow . . . ." Henry blamed Hunt for manifesting "but little disposition" to avert a clash, except his successful effort to control McClellan. The next day the expeditions continued the voyage up the Missouri, usually keeping to opposite sides of the river but always in sight of each other. For three days there was no contact between the parties, a circumstance which annoyed Bradbury, for it "deprived me of the society of my friend Brackenridge. I regretted this circumstance, and purposed to join him this morning, but was prevented by our stopping on an island to breakfast, where our hunters killed two buffaloe and two elks."[45]

Before the parties reached the Arikara village, the two friends had met again for strolls into the country for botanizing. Both expeditions passed the Cheyenne River on June 8,[46] and the day following Henry and Bradbury took a short walk together. Then, on June 11, the two parties encamped near the former site of the Arikara village, about six miles below where it was now located.[47] That night Henry visited Hunt's camp as an ambassador to arrange the "manner of arriving at the village, and of receiving the chiefs. This is the first time our chiefs have had any intercourse directly or indirectly since the quarrel." At this time Henry, who perceived how much the rival party distrusted Lisa, pledged himself for the good conduct of his commander in trading with the Arikaras. If Henry managed the negotiations well, and everyone involved kept his word, the race to the Arikara village would end peacefully in a tie.

That night both parties huddled in their tents in their respective camps while rain beat upon them, drenching the beds and the baggage and dampening spirits generally.[48] In the morning at nine o'clock two Arikara chiefs and an interpreter boarded Lisa's barge, which proceeded to the shore opposite the village. Hunt's party landed near. The men of both expeditions quickly spread their effects on the bank to dry. The time was now ten o'clock. Across the river, a half mile wide at this point, there was a bustle as a chief ordered the council lodge prepared for a conference. Soon he invited the two parties to join him whenever they were ready, his words carrying distinctly over the water. The situation was ticklish, as Bradbury well knew: "It was evident that Lisa was still suspected; and M'Clellan, in particular, carefully watched his motions, determined to shoot him if he attempted to cross the river before us, to attend the council of the Indians, contrary to what had been previously agreed upon with Mr. Brackenridge on his behalf."

But at the council Lisa comported himself tactfully, a pleasant surprise for everyone. About two o'clock in the afternoon two delegations, fourteen men in all from the expeditions, crossed the river and went directly to the lodge, where they sat on mats—buffalo skins—placed on the floor. The chief, named Le Gauche because he was left-handed, passed the pipe about for smoking, and directed his herald to summon the other chiefs to the conference. Upon their arrival Le Gauche took the pipe again and ceremoniously opened the meeting "by blowing a whiff upwards as it were to the sky, then to the earth, and after to the east and west, after which the pipe was sent round." Henry noticed that etiquette required a person to hold the pipe until his neighbor, to whom he passed it, had puffed several times. When the speechmaking began, the high light was Lisa's address to the chiefs. The gist of it was this, according to Henry: Lisa "observed, that the strangers in company with him were going a long journey to the great Salt lake to the west, and ought to be treated well, that any injury done to them, he should consider as done to himself; that in this respect they were as one people." There were other speeches, including one by Hunt. But Lisa's speech at once had eased the tension between the two expeditions.

After the council their relations became harmonious and even amicable. It did not seem to disturb Hunt's party at all when both expeditions that night crossed the Missouri and encamped below the Arikara village, with Lisa's camp nearer to it than his rival's. The trading did not begin immediately because the chief had first to consult his subordinates about conditions to regulate the traffic.[49] They finally agreed with Lisa that one buffalo robe was worth twenty balls and twenty loads of powder.[50] The Arikaras, who planned a foray against the Sioux, were anxious to obtain carbines and ammunition, knives and tomahawks. Hunt, in turn, was in the market for a sufficient number of prime horses to carry his expedition overland from the Arikara village to the Columbia River.[51] At the price fixed, such a horse cost ten dollars worth of goods. On June 16, Bradbury returned to his camp after a visit to the village and found Hunt and Lisa busy negotiating an exchange of three boats and surplus Indian goods for some horses which were in the possession of the St. Louis Missouri Fur Company at its fort near the Mandan village almost two hundred miles further up the Missouri.[52] Lisa was undeniably a wily competitor in the fur trade, but not unwilling to lend a helping hand to a rival in need—and with the Arikaras reluctant to part with many of their best horses, Hunt needed horses.

During this extended period of trading between the fur companies and the Arikaras, Henry and Bradbury visited the Indian village, consisting of distinct upper and lower towns separated by a stream, and they botanized in the vicinity.[53] The filthy village, which swarmed with children and dogs, disgusted Henry, who concluded that the "lovers of Indian manners, and mode of living, should contemplate them at a distance." The village was a quagmire after the heavy rains and, as Henry himself put it, not much better than a "hog pen." The children, who looked upon Henry as a savage, invariably fled afraid whenever he approached them. He noted the construction of the lodges, covered with earth on the outside; and with Bradbury, he entered several, one of which the medicine man occupied. They watched a war party set off and others return, and witnessed the reception accorded a deputation from the Cheyennes. The daily activity of the village fascinated Henry: "We here see an independent nation, with all the interests and anxieties of the largest: how little would its history differ from that, of one of the Grecian states!"

Henry and Bradbury now parted company for a time. On June 19, after a breakfast of dog meat, Bradbury left the Arikara village on horseback for Fort Mandan with a party led by Crooks.[54] They went on this risky journey through the Sioux country to obtain the horses which Lisa had promised Hunt. They reached their destination in three days, welcomed at the fort by Reuben Lewis, who was Meriwether's brother.[55] Fort Mandan was a square blockhouse with several outbuildings, enclosed by a high palisade.[56] Here, in the neighborhood of the fort, Bradbury collected plants until the arrival of Lisa's boat with Henry on board a few days later. They stayed at Fort Mandan until July 6, making excursions into the country and also to the Indian villages some distance below the outpost, which was 1,640 miles from the Mississippi.[57] On June 28, the two of them visited White Wolf, a Minnetaree chief, and then continued on their way to the Mandan town, where they feasted on a dish of jerked buffalo meat, beans, and corn with the fat and loquacious She-he-ke, or Le Gros Blanc, who had once journeyed to the United States and received a medal for befriending Lewis and Clark on their expedition.[58] On the Fourth of July, in celebration of the day, Lisa invited a party to dine aboard his boat— Henry, Bradbury, Nuttall, Lewis and two Minnetaree chiefs named Le Borgne and Black Shoe.[59] This was the last event of Henry's stay at Fort Mandan, for, several days after, he and Bradbury and Lisa were back at the Arikara village, where Crooks had already arrived with the horses.[60]

Lisa now demonstrated his confidence in Henry.[61] The fur trader, who still had business to conclude on the Upper Missouri, decided to send two boats filled with peltry to St. Louis; and he put them under Henry's command with orders to travel as fast as possible without stopping for Indians. Henry merited this charge, for it was his diplomacy—and Bradbury's too—which had averted carnage on the Missouri, far from civil authority.

The descent of the river began on July 17.[62] Bradbury, who carefully packed several thousand living plants in seventeen trunks, returned to civilization with Henry. Six men manned the oars of each boat. As the party passed Hunt's camp, he "caused the men to draw up in line, and give three cheers, which we returned"—a farewell which Bradbury never forgot. He was disappointed, however, that the rapid descent afforded little time to botanize. The party passed the Cheyenne River the first day, and soon reached the Great Bend, where they saw many herds of buffalo. Then came the White River. The night of July 20, a severe thunderstorm discomforted them. Bradbury looked compassionately at Henry, who lay next to him on the deck in a soaking blanket: "For myself I felt but little: two years, in a great measure spent in the wilds, had inured me to hardships and inclemencies; but I felt much for my friend Brackenridge. *Poor young man*, his youth, and the delicacy of his frame, ill suited him for such hardships, which, nevertheless, he supported cheerfully."

The next day the weather cleared, and the sun was pleasantly warm. The two boats swept by the Ponca village. That night the party saw thousands of buffaloes on the hills; and from a woods, where a herd of males had encountered females, they heard an awesome roaring which neither Henry nor Bradbury could describe. They passed the Maha village the following day. Then came the Blackbird Hill, the Platte River, and Fort Osage, renamed Fort Clark, to which Sibley, the factor, had just returned from the salines on the Arkansas. He showed Henry and Bradbury some salt procured there. Henry's party continued its descent; and, as he proudly recorded, "We arrived at St. Louis early in August, having made fourteen hundred and forty miles in little better than fourteen days."

On his arrival in St. Louis, Henry went to the post office for his mail.[63] Then on August 2, he wrote the editor of the *Louisiana Gazette* a letter, thanking him for his flattering comment concerning the essays on the topography of the territory, but taking exception to the "statement of my having set out, on a journey to the westward, with the intention of visiting the city of Mexico, and of publishing the result of my travels, on my return to my own country."[64] That Henry had a flair for publicity was obvious: "It is true, I have more than once expressed an opinion, that such a tour, in case of the independence of the Mexican colonies, & of an amicable intercourse between them and the United States, would be highly interesting; but having devoted myself to a different pursuit, and besides feeling deficient in the qualifications which a person undertaking such a tour ought to possess, I never had any serious thought of it." Henry wanted his acquaintances to understand that he had not abandoned his practice of the law in the United States.

X: A Man of Some Importance

The voyage up the Missouri with Lisa and the descent with Bradbury proved that Henry wore well under the most trying conditions, for he had won the trust of the rival commanders upriver, and now in St. Louis he still retained the respect of Bradbury. Their friendship, indeed, was stronger than ever despite the fact that Lisa had compromised Henry, by first agreeing with Bradbury to have the boats land him at suitable places for botanizing and then, in an about-face, by ordering Henry to descend to St. Louis as rapidly as possible. Bradbury, who blamed Lisa's "breach of faith" for losing the chance of collecting "a great number of new plants" on the return voyage,[1] from the outset had appreciated the difficulty of Henry's position: ". . . although I found that Mr. Brackenridge felt sensibly for my disappointment, yet I could not expect he would act contrary to the directions given by Lisa: I had in consequence the mortification . . . of passing a number of plants that may probably remain unknown for ages."[2]

But Henry and Bradbury had brought to St. Louis the first authentic report concerning the two expeditions which were so far up the Missouri. Charless, of course, interviewed them immediately upon their arrival and then published the result in his paper[3] under the heading—*"From Mr. Bradbury & Mr. Brackenridge, lately arrived from the Mandan village, we learn the following particulars."* The account related how Hunt's party had unexpectedly passed the Sioux country without trouble and how Lisa's had had the same good fortune. The statement contained the exciting intelligence that by now—August 8, to be exact—Hunt had started overland to the Pacific. The news concerning Andrew Henry, the member of the St. Louis Missouri Fur Company whom Lisa sought, was hopeful, for evidence pointed to his eventual return to the Mandan village from the waters of the Columbia, where he had collected a quantity of beaver after crossing the mountains while beset by the Blackfeet and the Crows. Henry and Bradbury also reported to Charless that the Blackfeet and the Assiniboin "appeared extremely well provided with arms & ammunition, perhaps by the British establishments, in order to annoy the Missouri traders." But in the entire statement, strikingly, there was not a single hint of the rivalry which had endangered the two expeditions.

Their exploit of passing the Sioux safely thrilled people everywhere in the United States. Papers about the country reprinted the account in Charless' gazette *in toto*, giving Henry and Bradbury widespread publicity. The *Commonwealth* of Pittsburgh, for example, printed the complete story on September 23, 1811—but the bellicose and anti-Brackenridge Pentland no longer was the editor! About the same time the *Weekly Register* of Baltimore published[4] a brief paragraph on the attempt of the St. Louis Missouri Fur Company to extend its trade "to the uttermost branches of that mighty river," in those few words alone capturing the excitement—and the promise—of the frontier for eastern readers.

On October 21, Lisa himself arrived in St. Louis, accompanied by Reuben Lewis and Andrew Henry, who returned to civilization after an absence of almost three years.[5] Henry had suffered severely in his flight to the Columbia, subsisting much of the time on roots; and he had "like another Crusoe dressed himself from head to foot in skins. . . ." On the descent from the Arikara village Lisa had contacted Sioux bands and satisfied them at least temporarily by establishing a trading house for their use. Lisa's expedition, in fact, had improved the financial condition of the company. But the three veterans of the fur trade expressed grave concern about Hunt, whose party had left the Arikara village on July 18: "It is the general opinion that he will encounter great difficulties before he reaches the Columbia, if it be possible for him to succeed in the attempt this fall."

Hunt reached Astoria, the company post at the mouth of the Columbia near Cape Disappointment, on February 15, 1812.[6] The hardship which Hunt's party endured in crossing the Continental Divide justified the apprehensions of Lisa and his partners. Hunt left the Arikara village with eighty-two horses, an insufficient number; and consequently, most members of his expedition— even Dorion's squaw—began the perilous journey afoot. The expedition divided into separate parties at the Snake River, accounting for the fact that McClellan and McKenzie arrived at Astoria in January, Hunt in February, and Crooks in May. Crooks had undergone the severest privations. The whole heroic story Crooks and McClellan and Robert Stuart carried to civilization when they left the Pacific coast with dispatches for Astor in New York and reached St. Louis in the spring of 1813. Newspapers throughout the United States printed a firsthand account of their experiences under the headline, "American Enterprise."[7] The onset of the War of 1812, however, sealed the fate of Astor's undertaking, unfortunately rendering it a failure.

For his courageous role in this drama of the wilderness, as mediator between the camps of Lisa and Hunt, Henry received an accolade many years later from Washington Irving, the historian of the daring project, who was commissioned to write *Astoria; or Anecdotes of an Enterprise beyond the Rocky Mountains* by Astor himself.[8] Irving gave Henry the credit for resolving "the delicate point of management; how the two rival parties were to conduct their visit to the village with proper circumspection and due decorum. . . . Seeing the jealousy entertained of Lisa, Mr. Breckenridge, in his negotiation, had arranged that a deputation from each party should cross the river at the same time, so that neither would have the first access to the ear of the Arickaras."[9] After his return to St. Louis in 1811, Henry's acquaintances had accorded him immediate praise for his achievement upriver—he was a leading light of their town.

The St. Louisans, as well as Henry and others in the territory, now realized the folly of depending on the trade in skins and furs for prosperity. The "spirit of enterprise and industry is every day manifesting itself among the people of this Territory," Charless had observed enthusiastically in his paper while Henry was with Lisa on the Missouri. "They begin to be convinced that the Peltry and Fur trade is diminishing in value, and that it is necessary to give up in part the old staple, and turn their attention to the more important one of Lead."[10] Several parties, according to the editor, had just left St. Louis by boat for the place known as "the Spanish Mines" on the Mississippi, where Julien Dubuque had established mining operations years before. This attempt to enlarge some of the mines and to put them into production excited much interest in St. Louis, especially after the hiring of nearly one hundred laborers for the work. It was not surprising that Henry wrote a brief description of the mines for the readers of the *Louisiana Gazette* soon after his return to town. His article, entitled "Dubukes Mines," appeared in the issue of August 22, 1811. Less than a column in length, the article was not an addition to his "Sketches of the Territory of Louisiana"; it was instead a hasty essay written to inform the general public about the lead mines, a main topic of conversation at the time of his arrival in St. Louis.

In the same issue of Charless' paper as the article on the Dubuque mines there appeared a report of the trial of an Indian murderer, in which Henry participated as one of the counsel for the defense. The editor printed the account under the headline of

CURIOUS CASE,
Of an Indian tried for the murder of an Indian woman.

Charless described the case as "important and interesting."

The trial betokened the problem created by the drunken Indians who frequented St. Louis. Charless used the word "infest" in righteous annoyance— "Indians who infest this town and neighborhood"—when he reported how an unruly party had burned a barn owned by Pierre Chouteau.[11] The Indians were vermin, he thought. Responsible for their degradation, however, were the unprincipled retailers of whisky, who sold it to them openly by the bottle in defiance of the law. In May, when Henry was absent from town, they had paraded the streets swinging their bottles in drunken revelry; and "during these orgies, an Indian of the name of Squinoai, attacked an Ottoway woman, in the most populous part of the town, and at mid-day, and put her to death by thrusting an arrow into her neck and down her body. . . ."

But the facts of the case were confusing. As Charless wrote in reporting the trial to his subscribers, there "was some material contrariety in the evidence as to the manner in which the blow was given; some doubts also remained as to the identity both, of the accused and of the deceased."[12] It now seemed, however, that Askmava, a member of the Mascouten tribe, had struck Othepya "over the shoulder of another Indian, with a bunch of arrows, but not spiked," as they walked along the street arguing. Askmava and Othepya were intoxicated, witnesses stated. After receiving the blow, Othepya ran into the shop of James Beard, a blacksmith, where she fell on pieces of iron—"sharp and broken"—and died. The physician, who examined the body, found "a wound in the neck by which the jugular artery had been opened, four or five inches in depth, and in his opinion with a sharp instrument." Nobody had witnessed the entire incident, although some witnesses had seen the blow struck and others had watched the death of an Indian woman in the smithy.

The trial of Askmava began on Monday, August 2. Thus Henry had resumed his practice of the law almost as soon as he arrived in St. Louis. Happening to walk by the old Fort shortly after his return, Henry noticed an Indian, naked except for a blanket at his waist, sitting behind an iron grating imprisoned and signaling him to approach. The prisoner then invited Henry to play a game of checkers. Henry sat down on a stone, after glancing first at the Indian: "There was no paint on his body, his head had none of the adornments of the warrior, but his wire tweezers had not been idle, for his beard was plucked as clean as usual." The prisoner easily won every game they played. Through an interpreter Henry learned later that this Mascouten Indian had married a Kickapoo, who had subsequently left him for another red man. A chance meeting of Askmava and Othepya on a St. Louis street, therefore, had ended in her murder. Henry volunteered his services as a lawyer to the prisoner, who accepted the offer gratefully but who clearly expected no miraculous rescue from his predicament. "Tell the chiefs," the Indian requested Henry, "that I am a warrior, and wish to be shot, and not hung like a dog." Askmava explained "that the breath, or *spirit,* which was to live in the other world, not being able to come out of the mouth, the windpipe being choked up, would be obliged to make its escape in another direction, and that it would then be ashamed to appear among other spirits!"

Askmava's case was tried at the Court of Oyer and Terminer for the district of St. Louis, with John B. C. Lucas, the presiding judge, and Auguste Chouteau, his associate, sitting on the bench. They assigned Henry and another lawyer named W. O. Allen as counsel for the defendant. The case seemed hopeless to everybody—the Indian was certain to be convicted of murder in the first degree. The chief of Othepya's tribe had actually demanded the custody of Askmava for the execution of the *lex talionis* in Kickapoo fashion. But Henry confidently predicted the acquittal of the Indian.

"The council for the prisoner contended at great length," Charless noted in his account of the trial which lasted three days. Henry had not conquered his predilection for exhausting the subject matter of his speeches; he still liked to milk it dry. But he startled his former guardian and everyone else with the originality of his argument, the same course of reasoning later sanctioned by the Supreme Court of the United States. In his address Henry admitted the guilt of the defendant, who had committed the crime, however, "under the influence of passions which, even in the case of a civilized man, might plead some mitigation of the offense." The prisoner was, nevertheless, guilty of murdering Othepya. But because an Indian was not an alien, a citizen, nor a denizen, Henry argued that he could not be tried in an American court for a crime committed against another Indian. No law of Congress, or of the territorial legislature, applied to such a case. "In acquitting the prisoner, gentlemen of the jury," Henry assured them, "you do not pronounce him innocent—you simply declare that the punishment of his offense, and the responsibility of that punishment, do not devolve on you. He will not escape the punishment due to his crime." Tribal laws, based on the principle of the law of retaliation, would determine the punishment.

Another argument by the defense counsel was equally ingenious, and of special moment to the territory itself. Henry and his associate displayed a neat bit of showmanship when they challenged the prosecutor to prove that the district named in the indictment was in existence: "It was contended, that unless it could be shewn that there was a district of St. Louis, and that, by some public act making it such, this material allegation in the indictment would be altogether unsupported by proof, and consequently that neither the court (which is a district court) nor the jury, could have any right to adjudge the case of the prisoner." This was an embarrassing question, which, as Charless reported, the court "told the jury they would reserve. . . ." The defense counsel had demanded that the act of division, which created the districts as required by the organic law of the territory, be produced in court. But as Charless explained to his subscribers, the "territory was divided into districts by proclamation which is said to have been lost."

The defense counsel did not rest their case at this point, of course. They stressed the uncertain evidence presented to the court as well as the "novelty of the case," which "was in itself a cause of doubt. . . ." The prosecutor replied to their arguments, in Charless' opinion, "in an ingenious but candid manner," and then Judge Lucas charged the jury. There was an adjournment of court for an hour: "The jury were but twenty minutes in their room until they were agreed, and when the court met returned a verdict of *not guilty.*"

The time was now Wednesday evening. Because the Kickapoo deputation had waited patiently three days for a chance to seize Askmava, the court temporarily remanded him to prison for his own protection. He obtained his freedom in a few days. But Henry, one of Askmava's counsel, never learned what finally happened to him.

Despite this victory, which he shared with Allen, Henry could not interest himself in a law career in St. Louis. Literature again preoccupied his mind.[13] But he did not become a man of fashion and an idler who read books only for the sake of amusement. A work like William Robertson's *The History of America*, first published in London in 1777, Henry studied with a critical eye. The eight books, into which the work was divided, recounted the history of the discovery of America and the conquest of Mexico and Peru. Robertson's writing was justly famous for its descriptive style, although it contained certain inaccuracies and faults of omission. The most popular feature of the work, perhaps, was Robertson's treatment of the aboriginal society of the New World, which he considered so extraordinarily rude as to know nothing about the arts man first employed in his attempt to improve his lot.

The notion shocked Henry. He rushed into print in Charless' paper with an essay entitled "Observations on a passage in Dr. Robertsons America."[14] Henry quoted the offensive statement at the beginning of his article, indicating his intention to refute it: "This idea is certainly unsupported by the facts." He emphasized the fact that civilized nations exhibit differences—that each one has "a marked and distinct character." Henry understood the cultural approach to history, an interpretation which fosters a tolerant and appreciative view of mankind; and he therefore had no patience with evidences of intolerance: "Because Mexico differed from China or France, forsooth it must be barbarous! It was a narrow and bigoted prejudice, which influenced the Greeks, when they gave the term of barbarians, to all that were not like themselves." Henry described some Mexican antiquities—the palace of Montezuma, the floating gardens, and the mines. He pictured the pattern of life in ancient Mexico. "This hasty view of the state of society in Mexico, sufficiently refutes the assertion of Dr. Robertson," Henry contended. "The reputation of this great man, is deservedly high, but it is thought that his History of America is the least valuable of his works." Finally, Henry condemned Robertson for entering "upon the subject with a prejudiced mind; like other Europeans, he could not think it possible for the human mind to expand its powers on this side the Atlantic."

Henry's attitude in this instance was reminiscent of Jefferson's determination to refute the assertion of Buffon, the French naturalist, that animals in America were degenerate. Fittingly Charless published Henry's castigation of the learned principal of Edinburgh University in the *Louisiana Gazette* of October 12, the very day Columbus had landed on a Bahama island in 1492. Significant, also, was the fact that Henry signed his essay with a "B."; whereas he used "H.M.B." as the signature for his article on the Dubuque mines, published less than two months before.

But it did not matter how well-known Henry had become in St. Louis or attractive the opportunities which he had found there—"my destiny called me to Lower Louisiana."[15] He, therefore, collected letters of introduction from important St. Louisans to their friends in the South. Charles Gratiot, the well-to-do chairman of the board of trustees of St. Louis, gave Henry an excellent recommendation to Julien de Lalande Poydras,[16] one of the most cultured and public-spirited residents of the Lower Mississippi as well as one of the wealthiest. Poydras was the best possible person to introduce Henry to the world of New Orleans.

In November,[17] Henry boarded a keelboat, having said good-by to his friends in St. Louis. Schewe accompanied him "to the river with a basket of apples from his little huckster-shop; but the poor fellow, in his haste, stumbled and fell on the gravelly beach, cutting his face, and scattering his farewell present."[18] Schewe wept at the parting, as the boat moved into the river to begin the voyage to New Orleans, where Henry arrived late in December.

Bradbury soon followed Henry down-river.[19] Near the end of November the botanist had received an unexpected remittance from the backers of his research, a gratifying windfall inasmuch as a bilious fever had confined him to bed for weeks after his return to civilization. Upon his recovery he engaged to superintend a shipment of lead to New Orleans. On December 5, he left St. Louis with one passenger on board and a crew of five French Creoles. The voyage was hazardous because the weight of the lead would cause the boat to sink instantly in the event of an accident, like the striking of a submerged tree. On the way down to Natchez, Bradbury's party in mid-December experienced a frightening earthquake, which Charless in St. Louis described as "one of the most violent shocks . . . recorded since the discovery of our country."[20] Bradbury reached Natchez on January 5, 1812; and there the next morning he boarded the steamboat from Pittsburgh, which had passed his party "at the mouth of the Arkansas, three hundred and forty-one miles above Natchez; she was a very handsome vessel, of four hundred and ten tons burden, and was impelled by a very powerful steam engine, made at Pittsburg, whence she had come in less than twenty days, although nineteen hundred miles distant."

On January 13, the botanist was in New Orleans, where he "again met with my friend Brackenridge, and on the 20th set sail for New York."

Besides the reunion with Bradbury in New Orleans, Henry met Zadok Cramer, the Pittsburgh publisher, who had bought Gilkison's bookstore from the elder Brackenridge over a decade before. Cramer suffered from what Henry called a "pulmonary complaint," the effect of overwork on a delicate constitution.[21] His health impaired, Cramer had taken to traveling, descending the Mississippi in 1811 to Natchez and New Orleans, where he found some relief for his condition. When Henry proposed the publication of his "Sketches of the Territory of Louisiana" with the journal of his voyage up the Missouri, Cramer agreed, "on condition that I would extend it, and add something relative to the state of Louisiana."[22] Before the publisher left New Orleans for his home in Pittsburgh, Henry had begun work on his first book.

Henry was so conditioned that he engaged in literary endeavor with compunction. The favorable reception of the essays on Louisiana had given him a taste of the heady wine of fame, specially pleasing to youth. But as Henry realized after a sip from the goblet, the effects could be unfortunate for any novice who had tasted success, for he might wish to become a professional writer—and "a professed author in our country, alas! is pitiable indeed." Such a person in the United States was a "mere abstract man, without any degree of importance, or consequence, attached to him; he is not ranked as having any employment in the state, ecclesiastical, civil, or military, and necessarily takes up his abode next door to starvation."[23] This sentiment in the preface to Henry's first book—*Views of Louisiana; Together with a Journal of a Voyage up the Missouri River, in 1811*—is sufficient proof that his father, as fearsome and forbidding as ever, still lived in Carlisle in full possession of his critical faculties. No one, Henry insisted, must think that he had abandoned the law profession to wander instead "about the western country, writing geography, philosophy, history, and the Lord knows what. . . ."[24]

Recalling a parental injunction of an earlier day, Henry in his preface attributed his lack of proficiency in natural history to a devotion to the "profession, which my lord Coke, observeth, 'is a jealous mistress, and will not abide a rival.' "[25] Henry, in other words, had not had the time to become a specialist in any of the sciences: "I have therefore been compelled to content myself with admiring merely the face of nature, without attempting to analize, or seek out her hidden character."[26] His work, consequently, was not a scientific treatise at all, consisting only of the "cursory observations of an ordinary traveller. . . ."[27] Although Henry was familiar with the available literature on Louisiana, and had borrowed some of his ideas, he now presented much fresh material, original with him, to the reading public.[28]

His work took the form of a book of travels. Henry collected his contributions to Charless' gazette and revised them. The sketches on Louisiana constituted the framework of the book, although requiring some alteration as a result of the admission of Louisiana to the Union in 1812, the first state carved from the Purchase, and the creation of the Territory of Missouri in the same year. To the *Views of Louisiana,* divided into two books, Henry added the journal of his Missouri voyage and an appendix of eight items. To both the *Views* and the *Journal* he attached explanatory footnotes. He prefaced the *Journal* with an acknowledgment of his obligation to William Clark, "who politely favored me with every means of information in his power," and a wish that "Mr. Bradbury will favor the world with the result of his observations."[29]

The eyewitness motif naturally predominates throughout the entire volume. Henry, therefore, was the author of a very personal book, and not the compiler of a dry-as-dust compendium. He himself enjoyed reading books of travel, finding nothing "more pleasing and instructive than the testimony of eye witnesses. . . ."[30] As an eyewitness himself, he strove to present truthful testimony in his work, for, as he averred, "I have no higher aim in these 'Views,' than to be considered one of those who furnish materials for abler hands."[31] The text of the *Views* Henry deliberately peppered with personal observations: "I found strawberries ripe about the fourth of that month [July], near the Mandan villages."[32] Henry's happy use of his own eyewitness testimony thus characterized the *Views* as well as the original essays in the *Louisiana Gazette.*

The *Journal* was a sprightly narrative comprising the notes which Henry had made on the voyage up the Missouri. He did not revise this material as he at first intended, "not regarding my voyage of as much importance as I had imagined it would be, when I undertook it. . . ."[33] His notes, however, needed no polishing, so charming were they. Observing the customs of the Arikaras, for example, Henry concluded that chastity

appeared to be unknown as a virtue. Yet this may not have been universal; a more minute acquaintance with these people, might have enabled me to explain this strange phenomenon. From the remnant of a singular custom which prevails amongst them, one might suppose that this had not always been the case. On a certain occasion, a great number of young girls were collected before the medicine lodge or temple, prizes were exhibited, and a cedar bough was stuck on the lodge; the old men who reside in the temple, proclaimed, that whoever was yet a virgin, should come forward and touch the bough, and take the prize; that it was in vain to think of deceiving, the *manitou* would reveal every thing; the young men were moreover required to declare against any one who should attempt it, all they knew. A young metiff, daughter of the interpreter, a beautiful girl of sixteen, came forward, but before she could ascend to touch the bough, a young fellow stepped out and bade her remember a certain place! She withdrew, confused and abashed. There was a pause for a considerable time; I began to tremble for the maidens of Arikara, when a girl of seventeen, one of the most beautiful in the village, walked forward and asked, "where is the Arikara who can boast of having received favors from me?" then touched the bough, and carried off the prize. I feel a pleasure in adding, for the honor of the ladies of Arikara, that others followed, though I did not take the trouble of noting the number.

Seeing the chief one day in a thoughtful mood, I asked him what was the matter— "I was wondering" said he "whether you white people have any women amongst you." I assured him in the affirmative. "Then" said he, "why is it that your people are so fond of our women, one might suppose they had never seen any before?"[34]

Although Henry usually disparaged savage society as he had seen it, he was, plainly, a sympathetic observer who wanted to understand its customs. The ways of a people strange to him had always interested Henry, who instinctively identified himself with them. As the godson of Vital and Madame Beauvais, he could describe the character of the French inhabitants of Louisiana with greater sympathy and understanding—and with more accuracy—than any contemporary commentator on the American West. He discerned the effects of the transfer from the Spanish rule to the American, declaring in the *Views* that the "silent but subtle spirit" of the United States government "is felt in every nerve and vein, of the body politic."[35] He gloried in the magic process:

. . . Louisianians, you have now become truly Americans; never will you again be transferred from one nation to another; IF YOU ARE EVER SOLD AGAIN, IT WILL BE FOR BLOOD.

At the same time, let us allow, for those emotions which must naturally be felt. Like two streams that flow to each other from remote and distant climes, although at length, included in the same channel, it is not all at once that they will unite their contributary waters, *and mingle into one.*[36]

Both the *Views* and the *Journal* abound with Henry's shrewd judgments and conjectures, his opinions enlivening the whole work. Although little seemed to escape his notice, history confirmed most of his predictions. Occasionally it proved him wrong—such was his belief that white settlement would "probably" not extend above the region about Omaha "for many years."[37] He had, accountably, ignored the steamboat as a factor in transforming the wilderness of the Missouri Valley into a center of civilization, for the "New Orleans" had just inaugurated steamboating on the western waters in 1811, the same year as his voyage upriver with Lisa.

It was appropriate that the firm of Cramer, Spear and Eichbaum, Booksellers & Stationers, published Henry's lively book on Louisiana and the Missouri country. After Cramer had reorganized the Gilkison establishment, he installed a press and began the printing of schoolbooks, including the primer and the catechism.[38] No longer were the arithmetics and the grammars and the readers carted laboriously over the mountains to Pittsburgh and neighboring settlements. Cramer soon was in a position to supply schoolbooks to retailers throughout the West. To aid the boatmen on the western rivers, he compiled the *Navigator,* to the later editions of which he appended a brief account of Louisiana, "and of the Missouri and Columbia Rivers, as Discovered by the Voyage under Captains Lewis and Clark."[39] Cramer took pride in the constant revision of his handbook for navigators and traders—he could judge the worth of Henry's work for publication.

His health declining steadily, Cramer lived long enough to see Henry's book through the press. The "Proposals," which advertised the intended publication of the work and indicated the nature of its contents, appeared in the newspapers[40] in the summer of 1812. The price of the *Views* was set at $2.00 in boards; "neatly bound," at $2.50. A free copy was promised for every ten subscribers a person might obtain. The notice stated, also, that the "work will be put to press in the winter of 1812-13, and be ready for delivery the spring following." There was a delay in publication, however, for Henry did not register the title with the clerk of the District of Pennsylvania until November 24, 1813.[41] At last, on January 5, 1814, Cramer's firm announced that it had just published the *Views:* "In this work, there will be much to gratify the curious and inquisitive; but it will be principally useful, as a compend, of such information, as may be desired, by those who are disposed to emigrate."[42] Cramer, in the meantime, had again sought the milder climate of New Orleans. During the summer of 1814, he proceeded to Pensacola, where he died on August 1.[43] "He had for a long time been conscious of his approaching dissolution, but preserved his cheerfulness to the last: even his severe disease could not sour a temper so mild and pleasant; nothing fretful, peevish or ill natured," wrote Henry in tribute to the publisher of his first book.[44]

Cramer's Pittsburgh Magazine Almanack, for the Year of Our Lord, 1815 carried an advertisement of Henry's work on its front cover. The notice stated that his book had "excited considerable interest and attention. . . ." The almanac, incidentally, was an excellent advertising medium, for its useful information and the weather forecasts of the Rev. John Taylor had made it popular throughout the western country—in Henry's own words, the "most popular"[45] publication of its kind. "As a statistical and historical work," the advertisement read, too, the *Views* stood "pre-eminent to any thing yet published" on Louisiana.

The same opinion William Darby held. As a deputy surveyor for the United States and a member of Jackson's topographical staff in the 1814-15 campaign, Darby was qualified to comment authoritatively on Henry's book. Darby, moreover, was collecting material for the publication of a statistical account to accompany his proposed map of Louisiana when the first edition of the *Views* appeared. The *Views* aided Darby in his research, for he considered it the one book on Louisiana which both instructed and amused the reader "in an eminent degree." According to Darby, there was no evidence of youthful exaggeration in the *Views*—it was the work of a responsible author:

. . . Mr. Breckenridge wrote from personal observation, unshackled by preconceived opinions in religion, politics, national distinctions, or physics: . . . . This enlightened young man described men as he found them, represented objects without distortion; and as far as his descriptions extend may be considered correct, chaste, and natural. If Mr. Breckenridge had accompanied his work with a map correctly drawn from actual admeasurement and observation, he would have left but little for his successors to execute, in giving to the literary world a clear, comprehensive, and finished picture of Louisiana.[46]

Darby thus indicated the one weakness of Henry's work—it lacked a map.

There is a hazard involved in authorship as Darby, and Henry, eventually learned—the exposing of oneself to public notice and possible attack. Darby published *A Geographical Description of the State of Louisiana . . . Being an Accompaniment to the Map of Louisiana* in 1816, in its preface praising Henry's book, as noted, but misspelling his name, a mistake corrected in the second edition[47] printed the next year. But in 1817, also, Darby had to resort to the newspapers in a spirited defense of his own work and the *Views*.[48]

Niles, the publisher of the *Weekly Register,* had printed a communication concerning the "Prairies of Louisiana," in which the writer asserted that the "accounts published by Brackenridge and Darby are most to be relied on; but neither of those writers have been sufficiently explicit, though each enjoyed opportunities of acquiring better information." When Darby, who was in New York at the time, read this slighting remark as reprinted in the *Morning Chronicle* of Savannah, he was furious, for he knew the wide currency it would get as paper after paper extracted the original letter, signed "A Louisiana Planter," from Niles' publication. Immediately Darby wrote a letter of protest to Alden Spooner, proprietor of the New York *Columbian,* hoping that editors elsewhere would reprint it. In denouncing the "rude compliment" paid Brackenridge and himself, Darby, who was to become one of the foremost geographers of his day in the United States, chided Niles for his negligence in publishing inaccurate material: "If the expressions of this writer had not gained a power of malignant mischief against Mr. Brackenridge and myself, as well as some claim to credit from the publication from which it originated, it might have followed covered with contempt to the grave of oblivion, the thousand other bombastic descriptions given to the public every day on Louisiana, and also upon all other parts of the south and west."

Niles' reaction to Darby's charge was decent. The Baltimore editor promptly published Darby's letter to Spooner *"unasked,"* with pertinent comments "inserted, enclosed in brackets," expressing regret for any injury done the geographer and, inferentially, Henry. Because Niles was personally acquainted with the author of the offending piece, therefore

possessing my confidence, his article was very slightly *looked* over, and I do not recollect that I *read* it until this day. This was accidental—a similar circumstance never occurred but *once* before since I have published the REGISTER, in respect to a piece from manuscript; else, I think, that I must have noticed the wild mistake as to the superficial extent of the country spoken of. *It was sufficient for those who read the proof that it was according to the copy;* and so it is, a few unimportant and immaterial errors excepted.— This is an *excuse* though it is not a *justification,* on my part—it was my business to have *read* it. But a charitable disposition would overlook *two* things of this sort in *six* years!!

No wonder Niles acquired a reputation of publishing a trustworthy repository of news!

Except the aspersion by the Louisiana planter, Henry's work received a favorable, even warm, reception by the public and the critics. Evidently there was a continuing demand for the book because Henry soon was busy preparing a new edition, although thereafter he published the *Views* and the *Journal* separately. The work, also, appeared in a German edition printed in Weimar in 1818.[49] Some time elapsed, of course, until the book was reviewed in the periodicals. The *Edinburgh Review* did not notice the first edition, published in Pittsburgh, until the summer of 1819, when it carried a lengthy article on Louisiana, reviewing four different books on the same subject. The critic mentioned indebtedness to Henry's work "for much various and useful information" and then from the *Views* quoted his vivid description of a breach in the Mississippi levee.[50] But Henry's *Journal,* after he had rewritten it and published it separately from the *Views,* received the immediate attention of the critics.

Meanwhile, as soon as his book issued from the press of Cramer, Spear and Eichbaum early in 1814, Henry forwarded a copy to Jefferson at Monticello, receiving a gracious note of thanks in return. In thanking the author, Jefferson explained, he rendered "his portion of the general gratitude due for this valuable contribution towards the knolege of a great country which nature has destined to become the most interesting portion of the Western world. he salutes mr Brackenridge with great respect and esteem."[51]

This note from the ex-President elicited a reply[52] from Henry, who was anxious to account for the errors in his book. To Jefferson, at least, Henry believed he owed an explanation. The mistakes, almost inevitable in a pioneering work, troubled him so much that he now contemplated a second edition, if the first sold well. The new sources of information constantly opening to him had "disclosed many errors," he informed Jefferson. "I regard the work," Henry added, however, "merely as a contribution towards something of a higher kind, which, I hope, may be undertaken by some one, possessed of the necessary qualifications: should this be the case, instead of attempting a second edition, I will be content, to become a correspondent, and a contributor; in this way, as far as my information will enable me." Henry did not intend to apologize for the defects of his volume, for he realized, as he admitted to Jefferson, that an author must never publish his work until satisfied he cannot make it better: "Indeed, I have done wrong in publishing so soon, but I was actuated [by] a belief that a regular work on such a subject could not be expected from one whose pursuits were of a different nature, and in some degree incompatible with the undertaking." As Henry discovered errors in his book, both factual and typographical, he obviously magnified their import, for the moment finding authorship a frightening experience. He hoped that Jefferson would be sympathetic, for, after all,

. . . My essays were hastily written, and in irregular desultory manner, often in the bar room of a country tavern, or in a boat as I passed along, and not composed in privacy and retirement. They were printed at the distance of two thousand miles from me, the manuscript forwarded by mail generally as it was written.

An authority on Louisiana, nevertheless, Henry considered his letter a good chance to bring his correspondent up-to-date on the deplorable situation there in the spring of 1814. "The pressure of war has been more severely felt here than in any other state of the Union," he apprised Jefferson. Conditions were worse in the city than in the country, for in the country there was always food to eat. But in both the city and the country, property, no matter what kind, had diminished greatly in value. Many firms and banks had already failed, and the remaining banks had stopped paying their notes—"commerce ceasing their credit no longer buoys them up." Bank notes no longer circulated freely— unless offered at a sizable discount, people refused to accept them. Henry noted, too, that New Orleans had "undergone a surprising depop[ulation] within the last eighteen months."

At this point Henry ended his letter to Jefferson on a personal note: "I contemplate passing through Virginia this coming Autumn or the Spring following, and hope to have it [in] my power to [pay] my respects in person at Monticello."

XI: Grass in the Streets of New Orleans

Henry was not presumptuous—certainly the thought that he was never occurred to him—when he wrote so familiarly to Jefferson and invited himself to Monticello. He had already begun a correspondence with the ex-President, whom he venerated. Henry was now accustomed to associate with important people and even to communicate directly with officers of the federal government. An enterprising young man, he met with considerable success on the Lower Mississippi.

New Orleans was a surprise to Henry, for he had not anticipated the "wild confusion, of all nations and tongues"[1] which he found there on his arrival in December, 1811. The city, he said, was "a place of speculation, dissipation, debauchery, and revel; but not much for books." But he located a library in the old government house, a large, although haphazard, collection of books which did not antedate the transfer of government to the United States: "I was almost the sole visitor, and roamed through it in pursuit of old authors relating to the colonization of Louisiana, to garnish the work on which I had been engaged in St. Louis, and some valuable ones were found, unknown to me before." Here, then, he did much of the work necessary to prepare the *Views* for publication.

His quiet study in the library was interrupted soon; he received an appointment as a deputy attorney general for the Orleans Territory within a month or two after his arrival.[2] His letters of introduction, which he brought from St. Louis, had given him immediate entree to the highest political circle in the territory. But the office which he consequently obtained was no sinecure—nobody, as a matter of fact, had wanted it until his appearance on the scene![3] The position took Henry on a circuit of a thousand miles through a country inundated with the spring floods. There was wearisome travel by horseback, and "some dangerous work in prosecuting robbers and outlaws, especially on the west side of Red River, and the border of Texas." In the fall, after the lands had drained, Henry made the circuit again, this time plagued by mosquitoes and a bilious fever.

The organization of the state government of Louisiana, of course, wiped out Henry's territorial post. But during the winter of 1812-13, he helped establish the new judicial system.[4] Leading Louisianians like Julien Poydras, who had served as president of the constitutional convention of the Orleans Territory, consulted Henry as the work progressed. He, too, had become acquainted with Eligius Fromentin, the secretary of the convention, an odd individual whom he would know better some years hence in West Florida. For his contribution to the establishment of the Louisiana judicial system,

Henry was appointed a judge of one of the districts into which the state was divided—"for it was my work, that is to say, through others."

Henry settled in Baton Rouge, "a quiet and pleasant place for a student, and abundant leisure from business."[5] Here he became a friend of the elderly bibliophile, Don Juan Lopez, "who resembled Don Quixote in person. . . ." Henry dined regularly with the Spaniard, a bachelor, who could not understand English. Their conversation, therefore, was in Spanish, and undoubtedly in a Spanish of an elegant style. Henry admired his friend's library which contained rare books, including editions published by the Spanish Academy. Henry read Mariana's *History of Spain* and Ercilla's heroic poem, *La Araucana;* he delighted in the illustrations of a beautiful edition of Cervantes. Henry thus had the opportunity to become the master of the most polished Spanish.

As a judge in Louisiana Henry had to know the Roman civil law thoroughly; he had to study a legal system altogether different from the English common law.[6] He found it "no child's play" as he studied the *Corpus Juris Civilis,* the great code of Roman law, and the *Institutes.* He examined the *Code Napoléon.* He read the legal digest of Jean Domat, the French jurisconsult of the seventeenth century—*Lois civiles dans leur ordre naturel.* There was the *Partidas*—and much more, too.

Henry had leisure, nevertheless, in which to indulge a special interest—speculation on the population and tumuli of the North American aborigines. He had not forgotten the mounds near St. Louis. But the subject engrossed his attention in the summer of 1813, in Baton Rouge, for about this time he had prepared for publication the last chapter of the *Views,* entitled "Antiquities in the Valley of the Mississippi." On July 25, he wrote Jefferson a long letter[7]—the first that he had ever written to the ex-President—communicating his reflections on the significance of the tumuli in the western country.

"From a knowledge that research into the history of the primitive inhabitants of America, is one of your favourite amusements, I take the liberty of making this communication," Henry began. Then he explained the origin of his own interest in the same study:

. . . My attention to the subject, was first awakened on reading, when a boy, the observations contained in the "Notes on Virginia," and it has become, with me, a favourite theme of speculation. I often visited the mound, and other remains of Indian antiquity in the neighbourhood of Pittsburgh, my native town, attracted by a pleasing interest, of which I scarcely knew the cause, and afterwards read, and heard with delight, whatever related to these monuments of the first, or rather earlier, inhabitants of my native country. Since the year 1810 (without previously intending it) I have visited almost every thing of this kind, worthy of note on the Ohio and Mississippi; and from examination and reflection, something like hypothesis, has taken the place of the vague wanderings of fancy.

Henry now gave Jefferson four conclusions resulting from his observation of the Indian remains in the West. I. The great valley of the Mississippi, he stated, contained evidences of once having a population much larger than commonly believed. II. In the valley there were "traces of two distinct races of people, or periods of population, one much more ancient than the other." III. The huge tumuli marked the more ancient period. IV. The most impressive remains, both in number and size, stood "precisely in the part of the country where the traces of a numerous population might be looked for, to wit, from the mouth of the Ohio (on the east side of the Mississippi) to the Illinois river, and on the west side from the St. Francis to the Missouri."

Supporting evidence accompanied the conclusions. Henry noted, for example, that many districts on the Ohio and the Mississippi rivaled the valley of Mexico, the center of an "astonishing population" at the time of the Spanish conquest, in beauty as well as in fertility. If they had never supported a large population, he reasoned, "such a fact would form an exception to what has usually occurred, in every other part of the globe." He was certain, moreover, that the later period of population, of which the traces were more numerous, marked a people much less advanced in civilization than the one more ancient. He compared the extraordinary mounds of the earlier period with the more recent, and less awesome, barrows and palisaded towns: "I have been sometimes induced to think that at the period when those mounds were constructed, there existed on the Mississippi, a population as numerous as that which once animated the borders of the Nile, or of the Euphrates, or of Mexico and Peru." Almost opposite St. Louis, indeed, were tumuli which he considered as evidence for the existence of two ancient cities only five miles apart on the bank of the Cahokia.

But for Jefferson's benefit Henry enumerated the larger mounds on the Ohio and the Mississippi, most of which he had examined personally. He listed fifteen notable sites of the gigantic tumuli, although he placed those at Grave Creek and at Marietta, located on the Ohio, in a second or third class as compared with the others farther west. Because groups of mounds distinguished every site, Henry concluded that each was "probably" once the location of an ancient city: "But the principal city and center of population was between the Ohio, Mississippi, Missouri, and Illinois." He stressed the resemblance of the tumuli to those of New Spain, both in appearance and probable purpose, even inferring a possible intercourse between the two centers of population. "The *Adoratorios* of New Spain, like all works of the kind, answered the three purposes, of the temple, the fortress, and the mausoleum," Henry maintained. Then he asked Jefferson, who had studied only the unpretentious barrows of his native Virginia: "Can we entertain a doubt but that this was also the case with those of the Mississippi?"

144

Henry's letter was sure to interest Jefferson, one of the nation's first archae-
ologists. Although Henry apologized for the length of his letter—and "perhaps
tiresome," too—his youthful enthusiasm, as characterized by the repetition of
"astonishing" and its forms, was winning. Jefferson could appreciate his
correspondent's reference to the European custom of belittling everything
American: the philosophers of Europe called America "the *New World,* as
though its formation was posterior to the rest of the habitable globe." He
considered the letter from Brackenridge a significant communication, the contents of which merited publication.

At Monticello Jefferson had read Henry's letter "with pleasure" and answered it at once.[8] He had never realized, he informed Henry, that the mounds
and fortifications in the western country were "so numerous." Jefferson added
that he had forwarded the letter to the American Philosophical Society in
Philadelphia, "deeming it well worthy their attention. . . ."

At their meeting the first week in October, 1813, the members of the Society
listened to a reading of Henry's letter and then referred it to a committee to
determine its suitability for publication.[9] The committee reported[10] favorably
in March, 1815. Finally, the letter appeared as a philosophical paper in the
Transactions of the society published in 1818. The *Analectic Magazine,* which
took prompt notice of the *Transactions,* observed that about nine years had
elapsed since the publication of the previous volume and suggested that the
society "follow the usual practice of similar societies in Europe, and present
to the world an annual volume of their reflections and discoveries."[11] The
magazine praised Henry's paper, in particular, as "curious and entertaining;
and will well repay an attentive perusal to a reader who feels interested in the
antiquities of this continent."[12] Niles did not overlook the letter either, reprinting it in his *Weekly Register.*[13]

Henry's life in Baton Rouge in 1813 was not a secluded one, consisting only
of quiet dinners with his friend Lopez, the bibliophile; the study of Roman
civil law necessary for the performance of his judicial duties; and diligent
research on American antiquity. He was remarkably active—an extrovert, apparently, who mingled in all ranks of society, thoroughly enjoying himself.

Henry had met William Shaler, whom he liked immediately. Close was their
friendship, which Henry expressed in this way: "I respect and love him as a
father."[14] Shaler, about thirteen years older than Henry, was worthy of his
esteem. Born in Bridgeport, Connecticut, Shaler became an adventurous sea
captain who eventually engaged in the China trade. In 1810, however, he
received an appointment as consul and agent for commerce and seamen at
Havana, a post which he left in less than two years to serve officially as an
agent to watch the movements of Mexican revolutionists.

Conversation with Shaler, who had proceeded from New Orleans to the Texas frontier, intensified Henry's interest in the Spanish American struggle for independence. But Henry was especially attentive to developments in the Mexican provinces, which were so near. Shaler told him about the activities of the chief Mexican agents, José Bernardo Gutiérrez de Lara, José Alvarez de Toledo, and Dr. John Hamilton Robinson, and the policy of Secretary of State Monroe toward them. Monroe's attitude proved so uncertain, however, that the hopes of the revolutionists for aid in their revolt against Spanish authority—as France had assisted the American colonies in the war with Great Britain—were soon dashed. The result was a period of filibustering in the borderland.

Although Henry was aware of the devious and frantic operations of the Texan insurgents in 1813, knowing many of them personally, he viewed their conduct in the light of the independence movement of the Spanish colonies as a whole. Henry and Shaler, in fact, had seriously discussed the idea of collaborating on a work narrating the events in the Mexican provinces, which they deemed of great significance. They decided to call their proposed book *The History of the Revolution of Texas*. Shaler, who held a commission as a commercial agent to Mexico, arranged to have Henry join him in the mission, but which failed to materialize upon the outbreak of the counter-revolution there.[15] Before the year 1813 had ended, Shaler left Louisiana for the city of Washington where he received a new assignment, this time to Europe. In Baton Rouge, therefore, Henry was faced with the task of starting the book alone.

The production of such a volume as they envisaged involved a special difficulty—the acquisition of the essential source material from the very participants in the events which they planned to describe. The problem, of course, confronted Henry at the outset of his work. "You will be surprised when I inform you that I have in vain and every means to procure the necessary documents for the History of the revolution of Texas; neither, Johnston, Fisher, Sibly, nor Murray have yet given me the least assistance," Henry complained in a letter[16] of November 29, 1813, to Shaler. "I took pains to interest, Kemper, Ross, Luckette, and Smith in the affair; they were all convinced of the policy of the measure, but from what cause I know not, the documents which you put into my hands are the only ones, I have yet procured." Thwarted momentarily in his work, Henry could merely record the latest activities of the adventurers and attempt to fix their role in the independence movement. There was, for instance, the Napoleonic exile, General Jean Humbert, about whom Henry gave Shaler the latest information: "Humbert whom we saw at Natchez is making a great noise in this lower country, but I am inclined to think he will blow out in a few weeks. He is a hedlong, unprincipled, lying adventurer."

But hardly a week had passed when Henry was able to send more cheerful news about the book to Shaler and also, in spite of his busy life, to confess having a feeling of boredom.[17] Word had come to Henry from Natchitoches, he informed his friend, that the documents needed for the history would shortly be forwarded to Baton Rouge: "when they come into my hands, I will endeavour to make the best of them." He believed that it would then take six or eight weeks to prepare his part of the manuscript. As to the insurgents themselves, Henry reported that he had heard nothing from Toledo; that Humbert was "falling fast into contempt," although the French at Natchitoches respected him; and that Samuel Kemper refused to associate with him at all. "There is nothing new in this part of the world," Henry continued. "People growing poor as fast as they got rich some years ago; I am becoming heartily tired of the mud banks of the Mississippi. It is truely *le bord du Monde,* the lands end." A fit of restlessness had seized him again: "How I should be delighted to be a lakey or *valet de chambre,* to some Embassador to some of the republicks of South America! But I am too far out of the way here to think of such promotion."

Another week actually found Henry busy at work on the book, for he had received enough material to begin the first chapters.[18] Now, in mid-December, he wrote Shaler, outlining the way he planned to treat their subject:

. . . I have sketched an introductory chapter, something in the declamatory style, on the propriety of our feeling an interest in the great events, events to us truely important which are now taking place in the Spanish Colonies—on the nature and tendency of Colonies—the treatment which they experience, and particularly those of Spain—the notice of the revolt of the colonies, the probable consequences of a seperation—the advantages we should reap from it &c &c.[19]

The pen flew across the page of his letter:

The History begins in the second Chap. for which I have also sketched an exordium, and have chosen a key neither to high nor too low—but such as to raise the narrative to a sufficient degree of dignity. "The Revolution of Texas, is one of those occurrences on the theatre of the world, which merits the attention of the historian, as well when we consider the instructive and interesting incidents to which it has given rise, as its connexion with that mighty struggle, in which the whole of America is at the present moment engaged, in throwing off the dominion of Europe, and in establishing their independence" &c—The American volunteers are compared to La Fayette, Kocsiusco &c—

The great distance separating Henry and Shaler, however, made collaboration on their book increasingly difficult and at last stopped the project altogether. If Henry desired his friend's opinion on some matter, months had to pass before a reply was possible. When Shaler left Washington, he placed the notes which Henry had given him in the care of John Graham, the chief clerk of the Department of State. "But for the difficulty of conveyance I would request that the notes furnished by me might be returned in order to enable me to complete the work, as Mr. Shaler will not be in situation to attend to it," Henry wrote in explanation to Graham. "The notes can be of little service to any one but himself or me, or who is not intimately acquainted with the minutiae of the affair."[20] But *The History of the Revolution of Texas,* which Shaler and Henry had enthusiastically planned, was never published.

The Texan rebellion, in truth, had collapsed by the end of 1813. As Henry reported to Shaler, the filibusterers bickered among themselves instead of uniting against the Spanish foe. But the War of 1812 disrupted the situation, for many of the adventurers joined the forces of the United States against the British. In December, Reuben Kemper showed Henry a letter from Toledo, who wanted to join Andrew Jackson, at the time engaged in fighting the Creeks.[21] The war against Great Britain undoubtedly was responsible for the failure of the revolt in Texas.[22]

John Windship, a young Harvard graduate who had come to Louisiana to practice law and had met Brackenridge, like him studied the Mexican events with fascination. From the frontier parishes of Rapides and Natchitoches, Windship wrote William Plumer, Jr., once a fellow student at Harvard, an interesting series of letters[23] in 1813 and until his untimely death in 1814, vividly describing the Texan insurgents—their rivalry and their prospects: "These Revolutionists being disappointed in their grand object will become Brigands of the whole interiour. Already this is the case—Murder & Plunder are already too common."[24] Scarcely two months after he had written those words, Windship died. But before his death he had furnished his New England correspondent with an excellent account of the situation in the new state of Louisiana, emphasizing the unpatriotic attitude of the people toward the war. All the factions, he found, were discontented and contentious—the American Party, the French Party, the Spanish Party, the Creoles, the Negroes, and the Indians. "What political Chemist will ever unite us?" he asked Plumer.[25]

In the *Views,* Henry had answered the same question by indicating his faith in the operation of the United States government as a unifying agency in the transformation of the Louisianians into Americans. But the process was gradual, distressingly slow in time of war. Both Henry and Windship considered the prevailing indifference of the population to the defenseless condition of the state, wide open to attack by the British, as shameful. Windship, the transplanted Yankee, modestly acknowledged the inadequacy of his portrayal of the situation to Plumer: "Perhaps I may amuse but cannot flatter myself to instruct or inform you."[26] But he thought that a copy of Henry's *Views* would prove a useful present for his correspondent in New England, if one were obtainable. "This author is a young man of talents, information & great excentricity," wrote Windship in describing Henry. "He knows the country from actual observation. He speaks the French Spanish English & Indian, & has devoted years to his favourite pursuits." In Windship's opinion there was no better authority than Brackenridge on Louisiana affairs.

As an American citizen whose country was at war and had already tasted defeat, Henry tried to bestir the people of Louisiana to preparing a defense against a British attack. But they seemed hopelessly apathetic. Business had stagnated after the start of the war in the North. To Henry, at least, Louisiana "appeared almost a solitude," with the grass growing in the New Orleans streets.[27] There, in the city, he delivered a speech favoring the war; but he discovered "no enthusiasm or American feeling." The attitude of the Napoleonists among the French element of the population angered him most of all: "Some of them even called him 'our emperor.' This made me hate him." Henry and Windship were not alone in their feeling, although a handful, in this instance, was helpless in swaying the multitude.

Perhaps a military movement against Louisiana by the enemy, actually endangering the people, might rouse them from their lethargy. But to hope for such a development unprepared, Henry knew, was to court disaster. As the months passed in 1813, whoever thought as Henry did became more and more uneasy, afraid that the seat of the war might suddenly shift to the deep South, "the weakest part of the Union."[28] In mid-September, Henry decided to communicate directly with responsible officers of the federal government concerning the deplorable, and the disgraceful, state of affairs in Louisiana with respect to the conflict.

Henry sent his information to Secretary of State Monroe himself in a lengthy letter, dated Baton Rouge, September 14, 1813.[29] "I fear the moment is approaching, when this country, thus far exempt from the immediate calamities of the war, will begin to attract the more serious attention of the Government," Henry wrote, not mincing any words. "I will venture to assert, that it is the most vulnerable part of the United States; the population is absolutely incapable of self defence."

Henry now sought to convince Monroe, and President Madison also, of the validity of this charge, which persons unacquainted with conditions in Louisiana might well doubt. The population of Louisiana was unlike any other in the entire United States, he insisted at the beginning of his letter. Along the Mississippi from Natchez to New Orleans, there were possibly one thousand effective men, unhappily unarmed and "deeply sunk in apathy": "There are no musters or reviews; the young men amble as usual from one plantation to another, and scarcely know that the American nation is at war." Their attitude had made him undeniably bitter, for he believed that American freedom was worth the effort to preserve it. Their single fear—the "one thing which can rouse them to serious exertion"—was the apprehension of a negro insurrection. Henry disclaimed any intention to win popularity on the Lower Mississippi when he pictured the planters generally in this unflattering light: "Besides being ignorant, careless, indifferent as to the National Government, they are *selfish;* provided one family is secure, it cares not for the situation of others." It was his contention that the federal government must not look to the banks of the Mississippi for a force to repel invasion.

That area, according to Henry, contained the largest body of effective men in the state. The residents of the Attakapas and the Opelousas could be of no use either, although they numbered more Americans among them and had a little military spirit. But the presence of slaves and Choctaws, who might rise in their absence, kept the white men close to home. Henry was certain that an invading force of five hundred regular troops would encounter no opposition in the Opelousas or the Attakapas. In West Florida the situation was no better. The settlers there lacked an organized militia and, moreover, had the Creeks to fight. The Americans of West Florida, nevertheless, were "by far the most effective portion of the state"; but they had few men to spare for service out of their district. After his analysis of the population of Louisiana, Henry concluded that "No considerable force can be embodied, and marched to a distant point. As an American whose feelings are interested in the safety, and honor of his country, the prospect is painful to me."

The outlook was dismal. The eastern frontier of Louisiana and the Mississippi Territory was in danger after a massacre on the Tombigbee River, Henry asserted. There now existed a declared war with the Creeks, who undoubtedly counted on obtaining arms from the Spanish and British. If the British attacked New Orleans at this time, September, 1813, they would meet slight resistance, Henry predicted: "In a few days six or eight hundred men might ascend the lake of Barataria, and cross from thence to the Mississippi; an equal number could ascend the river, and by this means possess themselves of the city." In New Orleans there was "no bond or cement in the conglomeration of all nations" which composed its population; and not many people there felt a loyalty to the American nation anyhow.

Henry feared, furthermore, that the United States might face a new enemy on the borders of Louisiana—the Spanish. He reminded Monroe that the Spanish resented the American annexation of West Florida and the aid which American citizens gave the Mexican insurgents. The end of the Peninsular War at home and success in their colonies, too, would alter Spanish policy, he believed. In Mexico the royalists already appeared to have the upper hand: "I have been watching the progress of the Mexican revolution with great anxiety, and I must confess I do not feel that confidence in its success, that I did a year ago." He mentioned the defeat of the Mexican patriots, as the insurgents were called, at San Antonio, so recent a battle that the full particulars had not yet reached Baton Rouge. Many Americans whom Henry knew had fallen in the engagement: "No disaster in the course of our war—even the surrender of Hull, affected me so sensibly."

He had volunteered his observations on the situation in Louisiana, Henry stated in conclusion, in the belief that the government in Washington needed all the information obtainable on the subject of national defense. Then he expertly summarized the contents of his long letter:

. . . The state is threatened on one side by the Spaniards of Mexico,—on the other side by Spaniards, English and Indians, and is filled with combustible materials within; the situation of the inhabitants is not the most secure: and they are less capable of self defence than any other part of the Union.

Six weeks later, at the end of October, Henry addressed another letter[30] to the secretary of state, for new information had come to hand. The situation, he told Monroe, was not quite as black as he had described it in his other letter, written at the moment when the massacre perpetrated by the Creeks had alarmed the whole state and rumors were prevalent that the Spanish royalists were approaching Natchitoches. The battle at San Antonio was not as disastrous as originally thought: "I have conversed with a number of persons who were in the engagement, and with prisoners who have lately come in." The Spanish force had suffered severe losses despite the fact that the patriots had fled at the first onslaught, leaving the American volunteers to fight alone. At the end the Americans actually had victory snatched from them when an officer of the patriots and about fifty men unexpectedly deserted to the royalists. What conditions were like in the Mexican provinces as a result of the battle, Henry had no way of knowing. Aside from this intelligence, the outlook had not changed in his opinion. He reiterated his observation that the British would find Louisiana "the most vulnerable part of the United States."

After another six weeks had passed, by mid-December, the British threat had become real in the minds of most Louisianians. Henry wrote Shaler that the people were in a state of constant alarm over reported landings of British troops.[31] "War with them, it seems to me must be inevitable," he added. Operations against the Creeks proceeded slowly. Responsible individuals now entertained one thought only: Was time running out on the defenseless people of Louisiana to the jeopardy of the Union?

Henry, meanwhile, was more than ever ambitious to get ahead in the world.

151

At the age of twenty-seven he aspired to a higher position in the public service. He sought the office of district attorney for Louisiana, "which my friend Tully Robinson declines accepting,"[32] going so far as to write the secretary of state about the matter. Henry was confident that his candidacy would receive the support of the members of Congress from Louisiana besides the encouragement of Adamson Tannehill and Abner Lacock, "from the district of Pennsylvania, from which I emigrated."[33] But Thomas B. Robertson, a Louisiana congressman, gave Henry hopeful news straight from Washington. President Madison had authorized Robertson to thank Henry for his reports on conditions in Louisiana and to request that he continue them, "at the same time intimating a desire to engage my services in a diplomatic capacity."[34]

Nothing could detain Henry in Louisiana after the receipt of such intelligence. But the uncertainty of his health was a factor in the decision to return to the North, where he hoped to recover his full strength.[35] Therefore, in September, 1814, after resigning his judgeship, he left Louisiana with the intention of proceeding directly to Washington to solicit a diplomatic assignment.[36] On the way he fell ill in Kentucky.

But when Henry was well enough to travel again, he went to Pittsburgh and there opened a law office on the west side of Market Street between Diamond and Fourth.[37] At this address he had begun a practice of the law in time to be listed in *The Pittsburgh Directory, for 1815*, the first publication of its kind in the town. Had Henry given up his ambition to win a diplomatic post, and to begin a career in the foreign service, now that he was at home among the friends of his boyhood and youth? Had he at last overcome that restlessness which never had let him fasten his roots anywhere? On February 15, 1815, he was admitted to practice in the courts of Butler County,[38] a fact indicating that he did not consider himself a mere transient in Pittsburgh who intended to proceed to Washington as soon as he had filled his purse.

To acquaintances, especially those younger than he, Henry appeared a glamorous figure on his return to his native town. Everyone knew him as the author not only of the "Sketches of the Territory of Louisiana" but also of the recently published *Views*. He was the man who had voyaged up the Missouri with Lisa and who had subsequently descended the Mississippi to Natchez and New Orleans. To the boy who frequented the landing to stare at the vessels there and the boatmen and the travelers—the hubbub was wonderful—Henry was a person to envy. In the late fall of 1815, a clergyman from New England, named Timothy Flint, gazed at the same scene and found the great cluster of boats a "singular, whimsical, and amusing spectacle. . . ."[39] Appreciatively he noted the huge barges, the slender keelboats, the Kentucky flatboats, and the "ferry-flats," "Allegany-skiffs," and pirogues and listened to the music of the fiddles to which the boatmen danced on board their vessels: "The boatmen are dancing to the violin on the deck of their boat. They scatter their wit among the girls on the shore who come down to the water's edge to see the pageant pass."[40] As a boat disappeared behind a wooden point and its bugle blared, a youth watching it might feel a mysterious pulling at him—he wanted to run after the boat and to disappear with it into the West.

Pittsburgh's prosperity, it seemed to Flint, was fast slipping down-river.[41] The steamboat, in effect, transferred much of the business and wealth of Pittsburgh to Cincinnati and Louisville as rapidly as it drove the other craft off the rivers: "Her decline is not much regretted, for she used to fatten on the spoils of the poor emigrants that swarmed to this place." But as Pittsburgh lost her pre-eminence in business, the New England minister thought, she gained in virtue. The improvement in morality was so marked that the traveler was no longer inclined to think of the town "as immersed in 'sin and sea-coal'. . . ."

Returning home after his travels in the West and the South, Henry certainly was questioned by his friends in Pittsburgh on the subject of the war, which had taken an inglorious turn. The war with Great Britain was unpopular in many parts of the United States notably in New England where opposition to the conflict had appeared at the outset. As Henry had feared, the defeat of Napoleon in Europe had permitted the British to prosecute the war in America more vigorously. They even entered Washington and burned the Capitol. The chief American commissioners—John Quincy Adams, Henry Clay, and Albert Gallatin—who began their negotiations for peace at Ghent in the summer of 1814 had a weak position for bargaining at the conference table, although, fortunately, they proved more astute than the members of the British commission. But as every patriotic American had to admit, the depressing situation was a far cry from the days of 1811 when the War Hawks had advocated war to chastise the British and to conquer Canada. "As for our part, we are prepared for the worst that can happen, and our resources will protect us for years in a contest with Great Britain," the *Commonwealth*[42] had trumpeted confidently months before the declaration of war. "They have every thing to lose and nothing to gain. We shall lose nothing and retain our rights and legitimate sovereignty." But could Henry offer encouragement to disillusioned Pittsburghers after what he had seen in Louisiana?

The American people were demoralized. Aside from Thomas Macdonough's decisive victory in the Battle of Lake Champlain in September, 1814, nothing had occurred to restore the national honor in the contest with Great Britain. In the South, however, Jackson had won the Creek War, defeating the Indians at Horseshoe Bend in March. Appointed a major general and put in command of the American troops in the Mobile-New Orleans district, he stood as the lone guardian of his country against another British invasion.

That was the posture of events as known by the people of Pittsburgh when an extra express rider galloped into town from Washington on the morning of February 18, 1815.[43] He was on his way to Erie and Detroit with dispatches of the greatest importance—"Peace is concluded with England." The postmaster general had issued orders for the utmost speed in delivering the intelligence, promising an extra allowance to every rider who performed his duty well. The dispatches were on their way north before the townsmen had caught their breath. When the *Commonwealth* issued from the press that same day, the reader saw the news item about the express rider beneath the matter-of-fact heading—"Peace." But there was a headline that stirred the blood,

GLORIOUS NEWS!
General Jackson's Official Letter,

and beneath it appeared his report of the Battle of New Orleans, January 8.

The news of the peace and of Jackson's victory reached Pittsburgh at the height of the theatrical season. On Monday evening, February 13, the talented Mrs. Emma Turner had starred in a comedy of five acts, called

Wives as they were,
AND MAIDS AS THEY ARE,

besides singing a song—"Bless my heart, how cold it is"—and dancing the Polish Minuet with Mr. Jefferson.[44]

To another member of the company playing at the Pittsburgh Theater, however, fell the honor of reciting a poem[45] in tribute to the hero of New Orleans. At a subsequent performance the actress, Mrs. Barrett, recited the "Ode on Jackson's Victory, 8th January, 1815," composed by H. M. Brackenridge, Esq. For the occasion Henry had written a poem of seven stanzas, of which this was the last:

The brok'n clouds of the terrible fray
From our country have all rolled away,
In shameful defeat
Th' invaders retreat,
Even time shall hold sacred that day.
Latest star of the union rejoice,
'Mid the spheres ever bright be thy course;
Let Britons beware
Invasions who dare.
And let Jackson's bright fame with ages go down
In the land young in story, now great in renown.

XII: The Garret

The "Ode on Jackson's Victory" represented Henry's immediate reaction to the unexpected news from New Orleans. The poem was his contribution to the rise of the Jackson Legend in the West but, more important, it was an indication that, if given the chance, Henry would strive to assist in the recovery of the national honor, and the national morale, by his writings. For it was a melancholy fact that the signing of the Treaty of Ghent had preceded Jackson's victory.

"War being now over, and peace once more honorably restored, it will be well to breathe awhile, and look around us, in order to form a just idea of the situation in which we stand, in this western country," Henry began his article, entitled "The Western Country," which appeared in *Cramer's Pittsburgh Magazine Almanack, for the Year of Our Lord 1816*.[1] At the moment of his writing, however, the Indian allies of Great Britain had not ceased their hostilities: "These *blood hounds,* cannot all at once be withdrawn from the scent upon which they have been put, but I trust it will not be long before a stop will be put to their murders."

The war, Henry now observed, had benefited the people of the western country, although he was careful to note that "the popularity of the war in the west, has been considered as originating in the most unpatriotic and selfish views." No one, he argued, could have foreseen the actual course of the war as well as the advantages it happened to bestow on the West as a section. The westerners had suffered, too, as a consequence of the hostilities. It was Henry's intent, however, to remind the farmer reading the almanac before his fire that the blessings of the war preponderated in the balance and his prospect was therefore brighter than ever. During the conflict necessity had led the westerners to the discovery of new ways of supplying their wants—both in manufacturing and the opening of more channels in trade. No longer would cotton and sugar, for example, be brought overland from the eastern coast to Pittsburgh for shipment down the Ohio to Kentucky; instead, the steamboats and barges would supply the towns upriver with such articles shipped directly from the Lower Mississippi. The war had given an amazing impetus to manufacturing in the West, freeing it from a dependence on the East for glass, iron, coarse cloths, earthenware, and other merchandise: "Not that I consider, a total independence of the eastern section as a desireable thing—no, the more closely we are connected by mutual interests and wants, the better, but there ought to be something like an equilibrium, and doubtless, there still exists and will ever exist, a sufficient dependence for the purpose of reciprocity."

The movement of population during the war, Henry explained, had strengthened not only the region beyond the Alleghenies but also the entire country.

The West, which was less exposed to attack than other parts of the United States, drew settlers and businessmen with capital to invest, thus accounting for the astonishing amount of machinery and the number of steam engines there. But the war, he added, "served the union, as well as the western country; a considerable population had been flowing into Canada, from the northern states, which would have been worse than lost to us, but this was compelled by the war to go to the westward." Kentucky and Tennessee, moreover, had received a sizable accession of population from the South, an emigration which Henry believed would continue although the conflict had ended.

All in all, he predicted the continuation of prosperity in the West. He disagreed with the opinion of some people that the end of hostilities would "materially check the western country." In the immediate prewar period the region had flourished and, according to him, the conflict had accelerated the progress already apparent. The states of Ohio, Kentucky, and Tennessee and the territories of Missouri and Mississippi would lure more and more emigrants from less prosperous areas of the United States and also from Europe. Indeed, Europeans would seek security and happiness "in our favored country (which now stands so proudly pre-eminent in Christendom)" in ever greater numbers; and most of them would head for the fertile lands in the West.

But Henry, who had read his evidence logically enough and optimistically (as a westerner would), was mistaken in his prediction of prosperity, for he did not anticipate the Panic of 1819. He had overlooked the dangers of easy credit and inflated prices and speculation. He did not foresee the collapse of the foreign market for cotton. He had, of course, no way of knowing that the Second Bank of the United States, chartered in 1816, would eventually curtail its loans under the presidency of Langdon Cheves. Although a failure in this instance as a prognosticator, Henry's attempt to inspire a pride of country was effective.

For the same number of the almanac which contained his article on the western country, Henry prepared a brief biographical essay on Zadok Cramer.[2] His death in the summer of 1814 was a blow to Henry, who remembered the time fourteen years before when his father had sold Cramer the little Gilkison bookstore "on the most favorable terms." Henry sketched the publisher's career and described his character, elaborating the theme that this kindly and enterprising man, who had not reached his fortieth year, "was worthy to be remembered, as well on account of his usefulness as a citizen, as for his private worth."

Henry did not remain long in his native town in 1815, content to practice law and to write occasional pieces like the two essays in *Cramer's Pittsburgh Magazine Almanack* or the "Ode on Jackson's Victory." The thought of a career in diplomacy still interested him. He went to Washington where he obtained an introduction to President Madison, who, in turn, introduced him to Secretary of State Monroe. The President thanked Henry for the reports sent from Louisiana and said: "Your father and I were in the same class at Princeton; he was the first and I was the last." The compliment to his father rendered Henry speechless: "Having no words for a suitable reply, I could only make a very low inclination of the head and remain silent."[3] When no diplomatic post seemed available for him, he spent several months in Philadelphia browsing in the Franklin Library and the bookstore of Mathew Carey. Then Henry returned to Baltimore, determined to make a second attempt to establish himself in the legal profession there.

The prosperous Baltimoreans who wanted a war with Great Britain in 1812 had their wish granted in full measure, for they and their sons had to defend the city against a British attack two years later, on September 12-13, 1814. Their heroic defense inspired Francis Scott Key to compose the "Star-Spangled Banner." Jackson's victory at New Orleans was specially significant to the Baltimoreans who themselves had successfully resisted invasion. "The war is terminated at a moment the most auspicious to the United States; it has finished with the most brilliant success on the part of our fellow citizens at New-Orleans, who have completely repulsed the invading foe," wrote William Gwynn, the editor and publisher of the *Federal Gazette & Baltimore Daily Advertiser,* upon receiving the first news of peace.[4] But two weeks later, after the flush of excitement had gone, he frankly asked his subscribers, *"What have we gained by the war?"*[5] To help them answer the question, he referred them to the *Daily Courier* of Petersburg, Virginia, which stated "very pointedly that 'we have not in the treaty gained a *single point* we contended for'!"

Nevertheless, the defense of Baltimore was a high light in the history of the city. Months before the first anniversary of the event, plans were made to commemorate it by the erection of a monument in memory of the Baltimoreans who had fallen in the fighting—in the battle at North Point and at the bombardment of Fort McHenry. September 12 was the day set for the civic procession to the site of the proposed monument for the laying of its cornerstone. The day before, September 11, Gwynn published an eleven-stanza poem, "On the Monumental Procession,"[6] which Henry had written in honor of the solemn occasion:

> Behold, the pious city bend
> In holy gratitude to tell
>   the valor of her sons;
> And bid that monument ascend,
> To speak of those that bravely fell
>   Whose fa[t]ed loss she mourns.

Then let this monument arise,
Our city's ornament and pride
And ev'ry freeman's boast;
And bid it tell, *he* never dies,
Who fighting on his Country's side,
His fleeting breath is lost.

In Baltimore, now called "The Monumental City,"[7] Henry promptly resumed his former habits.[8] There he again haunted the library and the bookstores. He attended the courts more frequently than he had during his first residence in the city. But Baltimore in 1815 boasted an institution, a year old, which was certain to arouse his curiosity—Rembrandt Peale's Museum and Gallery of Fine Arts.[9] Among the oddities on display in the museum Henry could gaze at the skeleton of the mammoth, and in one room he could see the proprietor's own paintings. In June, the next year, Peale gratified the Baltimoreans by using "carburetted Hydrogen Gas" to illuminate his picture gallery.[10]

When Henry wearied of diversion in town, he walked into the country seeking pleasant spots to practice solitary declamation.[11] On Whetstone Point, the peninsula on which Fort McHenry stood, he found a thicket ideally suited for a lone orator fashioning a speech—a high hedge enclosing five or six separate "grassy apartments." Here he practiced declamation without fear of being overheard and becoming a laughingstock of Baltimore.

But one evening as he approached his retreat, a voice startled him. In his sanctum sanctorum someone was talking. Henry edged to the thicket, spread aside the branches, and saw his friend, William Pinkney, the great advocate and leader of the American bar, "ventilating his oratory according to my own practice!" Henry listened intently, careful to make no sound to disturb the orator as he rehearsed a speech. The following morning Henry hurried to the courthouse where he found everyone waiting for Pinkney, who arrived late and then apologized for his tardiness and unpreparedness as well: "I beg your honor's pardon, it really escaped my recollection that this was the day fixed for the trial." Henry stared at the lawyer in astonishment, for he looked like a man of fashion dressed for a morning stroll: "His hat, beautiful and glossy, in his hand, his small rattan tapping the crown. He drew off his gloves, and placed them on the table. . . . His coat was of blue broadcloth, with gilt buttons; his vest of white Marseilles, with gold studs, elegantly fitting pants and shining half boots. . . ." It was a hushed courtroom when Pinkney spoke: "When he began, his tones were low and even somewhat plaintive, like the sound of the coming wind through a forest, or the humming of a swarm of bees." Slowly he warmed to his subject, the words and sentences of his speech flowing "into each other in perfect musical harmony. . . ." Henry, who had

heard the speech in the rough, listened as enchanted as all his neighbors were
—they were "in a glow of rapture, like persons entranced."

Pinkney's display of eloquence was an inspiration to Henry, who said to
himself, "I, too, am a painter," although he realized the impossibility of ever
matching the performance.[12] But during his second residence in Baltimore,
the creative impulse was strong in him. Henry was the victim of an inward
struggle in which the forces of the Law and of Literature contended for the
mastery of his affections. Neither was as yet dominant.

Authorship was no longer easy for him to resist. His *Journal,* which he had
published in 1814 without first revising the notes made on the voyage up the
Missouri, was worth publication separately from the *Views.* A rewritten and
enlarged *Journal* could not fail to amuse a large part of the reading public,
as Henry well knew. But he believed, also, that such an edition would prove
useful "in conveying something like an exact idea of the extent to which the
immense regions west of the Mississippi are susceptible of population. This is
a consideration to the statesman of no small moment."[13] He, therefore, prepared a new edition in which he not only revised the original material but
added to it. The Baltimore firm of Coale and Maxwell published the second
edition of the *Journal* in 1815, and reprinted it the next year.

The revised *Journal* was proof that Henry was indeed a painter. While preparing the new edition for the press, he naturally relived the entire voyage—
the ascent and descent of the Missouri. He remembered now the story which he
had heard of a female maniac who lived in the wilderness near the Gasconade
River, seen and befriended by a number of people. Although Henry had never
glimpsed the maniac, and had even doubted the story, he felt sympathetic
toward her. In his mind he identified her plight with his own misfortune in
life and composed the "Lines on an Unfortunate Female Maniac, Seen on the
Missouri, beyond the White Settlements":

> What strange—what spectre shape art thou,
> The terror of this savage scene,
> That glid'st beneath the poplar bough,
> With looks so wild, and haggard mien?
> Far, far, the haunts of men are past,
> Mid silent hills, and lonely woods,
> Where Nature rules the dreary waste,
> Missouri, pours his turbid floods.
>
> Speak—whate'er thou art declare—
> The spirit of the gloomy groves,
> Unreal vision of the air,
> Or daughter of the oozy waves?
> And yet, that loose dishevell'd hair,

159

Those rent and tatter'd weeds, betray
A human form, in deep despair,
    Some wretched child of misery.

Ha! the sad, the silent tear—
    Mayhap, some lost distracted maid,
By anguish torn, pursued by fear,
    From friends and dearest home hast stray'd;
Forlorn, amid these dreary shades,
    The haunt of ev'ry savage thing,
Where death on ev'ry side invades,
    And hope no more may comfort bring?

Lo! see, with hollow shriek she flies—
    'Tis the poor maniac of the wild:
Soon, soon, she vanish'd from our eyes,
    The lost—the heav'n protected child.—
In wonder, long the shore we gaze,
    And still we hear the piercing cry—
Our blood still curdles with amaze,
    As when red lightning flashes nigh.

Alas! poor hopeless, phrenzied maid,
    Who has thus sadly injur'd thee?
Perhaps, by falsehood's tongue betray'd,
    Or stung by vip'rous cruelty.
Sad maniac of the wilderness,
    May heav'n still in safety keep,
And when thy darken'd ray shall pass,
    The silent grove o'er thee will weep.[14]

The spirit of the poem was autobiographical, for in a state of depression Henry could only think of himself as a "wretched child of misery." From thoughtless and cruel persons he had already received a full measure of scorn, which he was finding harder and harder to contain. He poured the hurt in his heart into his verse. But at the same time he sensitively depicted the wretch of the Missouri wilderness whom the superstitious boatmen conjured fearfully in their minds.

The critics acclaimed the new edition of the *Journal*, commenting particularly on Henry's talent for description. "His description of the Indians, and of such scenery as he could see from the banks of the river, for he was seldom able to stray far from it, are given with animation, and will repay for the trouble of perusal," stated the *North-American Review and Miscellaneous Journal* in a favorable notice of the book.[15] The magazine, which quoted generous passages from Henry's work, mentioned the life imparted to its pages by the account of the exertions of Lisa's party to overtake Hunt.[16] The review in the *Analectic Magazine, and Naval Chronicle* was much more laudatory. The critic commended the "candour and simplicity" of Henry's statement of the motives which induced him to accompany Lisa.[17] The *Journal,* according to this re-viewer, was not a dry recital of the happenings on the toilsome ascent of a river: "It abounds with descriptions of natural scenery, and savage manners, given with spirit and vivacity, and derives additional interest from the party being in pursuit of Mr. Wilson Hunt. . . ."[18] Henry, in short, was a young author deserving encouragement: "It is seldom that the hardihood and spirit necessary to such an undertaking are combined with the powers of observation and description possessed by this writer, and wherever they are so found united, we feel a peculiar gratification in lending our aid to honour and reward the possessor."[19]

This review in the *Analectic Magazine,* of February, 1816, without doubt increased Henry's reputation as an author of promise among the literati of Baltimore. Some months later, in June, he received an interesting bit of pub-licity when Niles published in his *Weekly Register*[20] reports of an inunda-tion threatening New Orleans as the result of a breach in the levee at a plan-tation six miles above the city. Within two days the crevasse was one hundred yards wide, the rising water inundating a fourth of New Orleans. To provide his subscribers with information on the Mississippi and its embankments, Niles printed an extract from the *Views,* "written," as he noted, "by H. M. Brackenridge, esqr. late holding a judicial office in that country, and now a member of the Baltimore bar."

The news in Niles' publication about the catastrophe at New Orleans dis-turbed Henry so much that he wrote a letter[21] to the editor on June 19, hoping to allay widespread fears that the city was destroyed. In his *Views,* he explained to Niles, he had tried to bring the need of safe embankments to the public attention, "but the unhappy feuds which prevailed, and the apathy to every thing which did not concern their interest as individuals, rendered it useless." Now disaster had struck the inhabitants of the city, although, in Henry's opinion, there was no reason to suppose its total destruction, as the exaggerated reports seen in the gazettes and heard in conversations might lead one to believe. The flood, however, would produce intense suffering, especially among the poorer people living in the back streets and in the suburbs. Their distress was tragic enough; but, he reasoned, something worse than misfortunes which could be assuaged menaced the city itself:

. . . she cannot so easily change the character which she will acquire abroad, of being unavoidably subject to the recurrence of so dreadful a calamity. It is this which will endanger her prosperity, much more than the floods of the river: and it is with a view of encountering the public opinion, on this subject, that I take the liberty of coming forward to suggest a few ideas, the result of my observations while in that country.

Henry believed that there was a possibility of action at last from an aroused and united population, for the "closing scene of the last war, in which Louisiana covered herself with glory, has produced a total change in the character of the people, who begin to entertain a just pride of country. . . ." As the first step in securing the vicinity of New Orleans from an inundation, he recommended the organization of a company attracting investors throughout the United States and receiving aid from the federal government—the reclamation of overflowed land was a useful and profitable operation. The company must open the larger natural sluices, make some artificial sluices, and then erect satisfactory embankments. It was not a hopeless task because the Mississippi, in spite of its mightiness, was one of the "most gentle and easily guided" rivers. By his letter to the editor of an influential publication, Henry entertained the hope that he might counteract the unfavorable opinion prevailing of "a permanent and irreparable injury to the city of New-Orleans; an opinion which might materially affect her future prosperity . . . ." In conclusion he urged his fellow Baltimoreans, and Americans everywhere, to send "assistance to the poor and distressed inhabitants of a sister city, which has been visited by a deluge almost as dreadful in its effects, as a general conflagration."

Only six days after Henry wrote this letter concerning the inundation of New Orleans, he suffered a personal loss—the death of his father. The winter of 1815-16, the elder Brackenridge had attended to his judicial duties as faithfully as ever, much of the time spent on circuit. His work as a justice of the Supreme Court of Pennsylvania was heavy and an increasing tax on his constitution. But despite his lack of leisure he wanted to compile a volume of the writings of his friend James Mountain—Henry's preceptor in the law—who had died in 1813, "not with any view to emolument for his family, but as a small monument of his own fame & reputation; and these published with an introduction which I had proposed to draw up, might be of this nature, and serve as a memorial of my friendship."[22] To this end he had sorted a box of Mountain's papers, selecting from them "all that were worth anything, the greater part being but rubbish, and sweepings of the office. Th[es]e I threw into the fire." He had not progressed further in his project because in all of 1815 and in January and February of 1816, he could spend a total of five weeks at home in Carlisle—"and that at short stay a time; say, not more than a week or ten days." Then time ran out on Hugh Henry Brackenridge.

Between three and four o'clock on Tuesday morning, June 25, 1816, he died in Carlisle. The local paper stated he was the victim of "a tedious illness."[23] George Kline, the publisher, eulogized him as a scholar, paying tribute to the originality of his thought and to his "playful talent of wit and humor," and adding: "But he was more than this: his family will have to deplore the loss of an affectionate husband, a kind and attentive parent; the

Commonwealth will regret in his decease, a good citizen, and a faithful public servant." Judge Brackenridge died at the age of sixty-seven.

Henry had hurried home from Baltimore to attend his father in the last moments of his illness. It was a time of the deepest gloom for the son, for he had long considered himself an unwanted child—a castoff. As Henry confided to Thomas Butler, a friend who lived in St. Francisville, Louisiana, his father once told him that the "jealousy of my step-mother, and fear that he would think of me in his last moments, was the cause of my many wanderings in early infancy; at least this was the reason which he assigned to me, but which may be mistaken."[24] The despondency arising from the death of his father forced Henry to share this miserable confidence with someone.

But Henry did not share in his father's estate. The elder Brackenridge, who had avoided amassing a fortune, owed nothing nor did anyone owe him at his death, "except the State for a quarter's salary."[25] He bequeathed all his possessions to his wife Sabina, "that thereby she be able to retain some authority over the children . . . ."[26] Her possession of his property, he made clear in his will, was to serve as a "check upon them": "Doubtless if I had not a perfect confidence in her prudence as well as sense of all the duties of humanity, I would not put them then in her power . . . ." Henry was unable to decide whether his father had done right in willing everything to his stepmother, "but it did not proceed from any injustice on his part, for it was in consequence of my positive declaration that I would accept nothing of his estate."[27]

Brackenridge's legacy to his children was not a fortune but an education. Long after the death of his father Henry delighted in recalling the days when they had read *Modern Chivalry* together; and he liked, also, to picture the Brackenridge home in Carlisle as a happy place of quiet study where Alexander and William and Cornelia had done their lessons under parental guidance and he himself had read the law in preparation for a career in Baltimore. "He was honestly of opinion that good education was a better gift to his children than fortune, and no father ever devoted himself more anxiously to accomplish that object," Henry once asserted in defense of his parent.[28]

Henry cherished no ill will for his stepmother. He admired her estimable qualities as his father's wife and the mother of their three children—"an excellent woman,"[29] he called her. But he returned to Baltimore heartsick and penniless.

There he received a letter[30] from Walter Forward, which was written to cheer him but, in fact, could only depress him more than ever. "It was told me that after the death of your Father, you received from your Step-mother $800, as your share of his estate," wrote Forward. "This was cheering news but rather *apocryphal*, at least to my mind." Henry's situation was ironic.

Alexander Brackenridge had just told Forward in Pittsburgh that his brother was making a living in Baltimore, whereas Henry was on the verge of quitting the city in despair, having acquired no paying clientele whatsoever. Forward, unknowing, advised Henry not to be dissatisfied as long as his profession provided him with an income:

. . . In so large a place you can only win your way by slow degrees. What a damn'd thing it is that a person must wait so long upon fortune. She is the most unfeeling silly coquette that ever haunted the poets dream. And withal she has no *Caste*. Some stupid dirty Ass or boar has all her carresses, while the high minded youth is cast off.

Then Henry read this in Forward's letter:

I wish you were here to feed my ambition. I am too great a lover of ease & not sufficiently patient of labor. I resolve & re-resolve & yet do nothing. What is a mere living, or even wealth—the chance of eating loads of provisions or drinking the sea, or riding in a coach with a black bear on each horse. Then to die & rot like a fat hog, remembered only by the stye & trough left behind. I load myself with permanent reproach, & still cant mend. Writing to you does a little good.

But Forward had business, and Henry had none.

Luckily Henry had the chance to turn to authorship to stave off the danger of going into debt. He became a hack. Joseph Cushing, a bookseller, offered him six hundred dollars for a history of the late war with the British, providing the book could be written and published in six weeks—in time for the fall trade.[31] Henry accepted the proposal, found a garret in which to live and write, and began the task in the heat of summer. Cushing supplied his author with the source materials—newspaper files, pamphlets, official reports, letters. Henry had not a moment to spend on research. He studied during the day and arranged his documents, and at night he wrote: "My task was thirty pages of foolscap, which I had ready in the morning with the corrected sheets (sixteen pages octavo) when the printer's devil paid me his visit."

Henry completed the work in the allotted time. He hardly had finished writing the book when it issued from Cushing's press on September 28, 1816. The *History of the Late War, between the United States and Great Britain. Containing a Minute Account of the Various Military and Naval Operations* was illustrated with plates and sold for $1.50 bound. Henry did not receive the credit of authorship, for "by an American" graced the title page instead of his own name. On the day of publication Cushing advertised[32] the book for sale at his Town & Country Book and Stationery Store, No. 6, North Howard Street. The two thousand copies of the first edition sold quickly, encouraging the publisher to plan another.[33] The second edition of four thousand copies, bearing Henry's name as the author, appeared in 1817. Cushing paid him three hundred dollars for revising and correcting the first edition. Then there was a third edition published in the same year, and a fourth in 1818. An immensely popular work, the *History of the Late War* went into ten editions at least, including the French and the Italian.

Brackenridge, the hack, had accomplished a small miracle by writing a creditable history of the war with Great Britain in six weeks. Any critic of the first edition had to consider the conditions of the performance and to allow for the inaccuracies which he might find. The author had time neither for painstaking research nor for the deliberate weighing of his evidence. But he had the opportunity to correct and revise his text in preparation for a second edition, and for many subsequent editions. In comparison with the sweep of Brackenridge's narrative, its pace, its clearness, and the provocative opinions animating it, Francis F. Beirne's *The War of 1812,* published in 1949, is dull.

More than a century and a quarter intervened between the publication of the two books, both written in a popular style with no attempt to display erudition. Each narrated the events of the war and assigned the responsibility for its origin. Beirne, in accordance with the modern interpretation of the conflict, stressed the role of the War Hawks in instigating it, whereas Brackenridge, the westerner, blamed the British for causing the war. Brackenridge never changed the patriotic theme of his book as it went through edition after edition. "England was not fighting the battles of the world, but of her ambition; she was not the bulwark of our religion, but the instigator of the savages; she was not the world's last hope," he maintained. "That last hope is America; not as the pretended champion in the cause of other nations, but as a living argument that tyranny is not necessary to the safety of man; that to be degraded and debased, is not the way to be great, prosperous and happy."[34]

The *History of the Late War* gripped the reader, eager to discover instances of American heroism. He sought a glorification of the war effort which, as the author left no doubt, was crowned by victory, all the more remarkable in view of the youth of the nation. The reader did not mind the author's frequent flights in rhetoric nor the polemical nature of his work, for he was the advocate of a cause. The reader could appreciate the "barbarity" of the British in occupying Washington and burning the Capitol and the President's House, a scene of destruction which the author depicted vividly—an ugly action by the enemy which no amount of rationalization could ever efface. But by the end of the book, the reader, carried swiftly along by his natural interest in the subject and by the energetic style of writing, knew that Brackenridge was not a preacher of hate but the proponent of friendly and constructive relations between Great Britain and the United States.

Although the book was rhetorical and polemical, it did not lack facts. It was a skillful synthesis of a huge mass of source material—an exhibition, too, of the large fund of knowledge which Brackenridge commanded. It was a solid work despite the absence of scholarly trappings. James Parton, the biographer of Andrew Jackson, finding the *History of the Late War* useful, pronounced it "excellent" and then quoted from it in his own work to illustrate "the angry feeling of both nations" during the war.[35] This commendation of Brackenridge's book appeared in the text of Parton's biography of Jackson; but in his annotated bibliography Parton was more precise: "One of the earliest, and much the best, of the shorter histories of the war of 1812. Judge Brackenridge was an old acquaintance of General Jackson, and served as his secretary and translator when the general was Governor of Florida."[36] Parton used an 1846 edition of Brackenridge's history.

Lafayette, a hero of the American Revolution, likewise valued the *History of the Late War*. He read the two-volume French edition, containing a map of the theater of the war, which was presented to him by the translator, A. de Dalmas, in 1820. "I have received the excellent translation of a work, interesting to me from so many considerations," Lafayette replied. "Our young American army, and the invincible navy of the United States, have given great satisfaction to the old soldiers of independence."[37] One thought in particular struck Lafayette: "The battle which closed this war, that of New Orleans, is one of the most curious phenomena of military history, and one of the best arguments in favor of the employment of militia to resist the attacks of regular troops."

Here, in Lafayette's own words, was proof that Brackenridge had done his part well in the restoration of the national honor. Lafayette could speak with pride of the army and navy of the United States after reading this history of the War of 1812; and Lafayette, also, referred to Jackson's victory at New Orleans as the "battle which closed this war . . . ." In his book Brackenridge had not noticed the conclusion of the Treaty of Ghent until he had first treated the subject of the "Memorable Battle of the 8th of January." The fact that a translation of the book (the second edition) was soon undertaken in France seemed important to Niles, the editor: "The undertaking to publish such a work in France proves of itself, that the history of our country, and its onward march, excite no little attention there."[38]

The feat of producing in the required time a popular history of the war, which, however, could interest readers like Lafayette and Parton, exacted a heavy toll from the author. The ordeal was too great for him to endure without injury. The intense concentration necessary for the task upset his mind— "and it seemed to me that I must go mad."[39] For weeks he languished in his garret mentally ill, thinking only of "blood, and battles, and politics." One of his symptoms he described as "a nervous twitching, like St. Vitus's dance." Aggravating the condition, of course, was the death of his father, although the distress occasioned by this loss, in effect, rendered his performance in writing the book all the more spectacular. Slowly he regained his health.

Brackenridge was not one to complain to his family or friends whenever fortune treated him ill. He never looked for sympathy at home. Instead of grumbling about his lack of success in the law in Baltimore, he gave his family to understand that he was earning a living, if not as yet near the head of the bar. Nor did he care to have his discouraging situation known among his Pittsburgh friends—not even Walter Forward. "It gives me much pleasure to hear of your good prospects in Baltimore," wrote Henry Baldwin, the Pittsburgh lawyer who had just won a seat in Congress ("I have turnd fool in my old age and been elected to Congress . . . .").[40] Thus, in the fall of 1816, Forward could happily count on acquiring some of Baldwin's practice ("When he is gone the full harvest will be ripe for me."),[41] whereas Brackenridge had no practice at all in Baltimore.

It was no wonder that Brackenridge was dispirited. In November, when, sitting alone in his garret, he recalled the pleasant times he had spent in the company of his Louisiana friends, the recollection seemed to "gild" his gloom. "I have said *gloom,* for such it has been for a year past, for I have lived that length of time in this city in a kind of painful obscurity," he wrote at once to a Louisiana friend, Thomas Butler. Brackenridge told how he had strived to move forward at the bar, even avoiding a social life in his zeal to get ahead. But as he had discovered during his first residence in Baltimore, he could not hope to build a practice there without years of hard work and patient waiting for success. Then he told Butler how the illness of his father had called him home to Carlisle. "On my return to Baltimore, being without means, I unfortunately turned author for two months during the summer, and wrote a history of the war for a bookseller, on the proceeds of which, I am now living," he continued despondently, "but the fears of continuing an author in this miserable garret which I now occupy, haunts me: in any country, it is a most wretched business."[42]

XIII: Peregrine Bochinjochelus

"What is the matter that you have not written to me for so long a time;
I think something has happened to make you forget me," Cornelia Brackenridge wrote anxiously to Henry, her half brother, exactly two weeks after he
had written morosely to Butler. "I have various conjectures on the subject,
sometimes I think you are married, and are so much occupied with your wedding that you have not time to write. If it is so I shall quarrel with you, and
think you might have invited me to your wedding."[1]

Cornelia was aware of Henry's hurt—that feeling of not belonging to the
family circle. As his little sister she tried all her wiles to get him to write and
to come home to Carlisle for a visit; she loved and admired him. Surely he
did not leave Baltimore without telling her, she chided him: "wherever you
are, do pray write; and tell me if you intend coming to see us, every person is
enquiring when Henry will be here, it is all they can talk about when they
come to see us." Then, in her letter Cornelia took another tack: "Mrs. McCoskry
has been in Baltimore, when she returned she had a great deal to talk about;
she told me something about seeing you but she talked so fast, that I could
not make out what she meant." Obviously, Cornelia was glad that Mary
Hamilton had gone to Baltimore for the winter: "I suppose you will see her.
she is a very fine girl and is rich." Cornelia closed her letter with the advice
that Henry "had better write soon or I will conclude, you have run off with
an heiress from boarding school."

Cornelia had now attained the age when she delighted in thinking of her
brothers as the suitors of eligible young ladies. But in this respect Henry was
her chief concern. "Have you seen Miss Mary Hamilton yet?" she asked him
playfully after a few months had passed—in March, 1817. "I think you are
not much of a galant, you are forgetting yourself; you must marry some rich
lady, and bring her to see us. Mr Hamilton is very polite to Mama, perhaps
you might fancy Mary, she is a very amiable, fine girl."[2] Cornelia thought it
was a capital idea that Henry should marry.

But in Baltimore he read his sister's last letter sadly. Then he took to verse
to express a troubling thought:

To a Lady Who Advised Him to Take a Wife

I

Rising from wildest ocean's bed
  Think on some desert rocky isle;
Amid the waste it rears its head,
  Was never cheer'd by human smile.

II

Then think on some poor wretch forlorn
  Condemn'd by chance, or tyrants' hate
From all that's dear here rudely torn
  To meet a lonely exile's fate.

III

Some voice now whispers in his ear
    "Go cross that sad and trackless deep,
"See all again thy heart holds dear:"
    Ah! cruel voice, thou mak'st him weep.

IV

His eye is o'er the wat'ry waste,
    No barque to bear him thence appears;
The joys of home thou ne'er shalt taste,
    Give to the barren rock thy tears.

V

Fair one, believe, such fate is mine—
    With soul to finest feeling tun'd,
Shall I, an untaught heart incline,
    A soul, that ne'er with soul, commun'd.

VI

Dare I some gentle maid to woo
    With every charm adorn'd like thee,
Soon, on the rock, I'd wake, of woe
    Amid the wildly rolling sea.—[3]

The poem, however, was not meant for Cornelia's eye. Brackenridge dramatically submitted the verse as the literary exercise required for admission into the Delphian Club, a select group of Baltimoreans whose purpose was to promote the cultural life of their city and the progress of American literature. [4]

On Saturday evening, August 31, 1816, seven men, all of whom were fond of literary and scientific pursuits and conviviality, too, had met to form their fellowship, "the ancient and reputable Delphian Club," named after the oracle of ancient Greece. At this meeting the members adopted a constitution for their governance and elected officers. Dr. John D. Readel, a physician, served briefly as vice-president of the organization and then became the secretary who kept the minutes with astonishing devotion. His club name was Blearix von Crambograph. Each member had a similar pseudonym. Dr. Tobias Watkins, denominated Pertinax Particular, was chosen president upon the resignation of William Sinclair, called Muggius Sin-clear, several weeks after the Delphians had organized their club. Never did the membership exceed nine at a time, and only sixteen had the honor of having their names recorded under the constitution in Dr. Readel's minute book. Brackenridge's name stands tenth on the list, his signature beautifully inscribed; and the name of John H. B. Latrobe, the son of the architect of the Capitol in Washington, is last.

The members intended to have a festive time when they met on Saturday evenings. They banished the cares of the workaday world from their minds with witty conversation and a light repast provided by the host—bread and cheese, whisky and cigars on one occasion and partridges on another. They joked, they punned, and they told stories—manly stories. According to Article

IX of the Delphian Constitution, which was rigidly enforced, any member "convicted of retailing to the Club" a stale "joke or jest, bon mot or witticism" was liable to a fine of twenty-five cents, although an accuser was subjected to the same penalty if unable to prove his charge. But the Delphians also engaged in serious talk and zestfully criticized the literary productions of their fellow members. Article X of their constitution made it "lawful" to introduce into the conversation "any subject of Literature, Science, Arts, Belles Lettres, Moral or Natural Philosophy, or any of their respective branches." There was the understanding, furthermore, that the Delphians were to contribute to the *Portico,* Dr. Watkins' literary magazine.

It was, therefore, an exclusive company of congenial men which Brackenridge joined. Akin to the Tuesday Club of Annapolis, which had thrived in the mid-eighteenth century, the Delphian Club helped to inspire a burst of literary activity in Baltimore, creating the intellectual atmosphere Edgar Allan Poe came to know.[5] The Delphians were professional men with a strong taste for literature. Their fellowship had suffered a temporary setback in the first months of its existence when the membership was reduced to five; but, in the secretary's words, it quickly "recovered from its depression" and soon flourished again.[6] When the Delphians admitted Brackenridge to their lively coterie, Dr. Watkins was president; John Pierpont, a member of a dry-goods company and a poet, the vice-president; Dr. Readel, the secretary-treasurer and laureate; and John Neal, the prolific novelist, Joseph D. Learned, a lawyer, and Edward Denison, a poet, members. But before the first anniversary of the club, two others after Brackenridge won admission—the newspaper editors, Paul Allen and William Gwynn.

As a candidate for admission into the club, Brackenridge followed the prescribed procedure, which required submitting either an essay or a poem to the secretary, along with a petition for membership and the payment of a fee of five dollars, although, being impecunious at the time, he delayed paying it. Election to the club was only by the unanimous vote of the members. On January 25, 1817, the Delphians gathered in the office of Dr. Watkins.[7] That evening the conversation was desultory until "agreeably interrupted by a visitor —and the club having passed several hours in social colloquy with the author of 'Views of Louisiana,' and partaken of the President's supper, separated at a late hour, and in excellent order." As a visitor to one of their meetings was, then, the way Brackenridge met the Delphians; but shortly after he had received his sister's second letter in March, he became a formal candidate for membership. On March 29, the club held its meeting at Dr. Readel's office,[8] at which time Brackenridge's poem was read, "and Mr. B was unanimously elected a member—The Secretary was ordered to preserve the poem in the archives."

The new member, aptly designated Peregrine Bochinjochelus, from the first enjoyed the merrymaking of his fellow Delphians. He was not backward in participating in the give-and-take of the conversation. At the meeting on April 12, for example, when the talk turned to the subject of punning, "member B remarked that if punning were made pun-ishable he would recommend that all the puns, pun-y or pun-gent ever extorted from the groans of writhing vowels, or consonants, monosyllables or polysyllables should be collected into one huge folio, if practicable; and that the forced perusal of it should constitute the pun-ishment of every punster." [9] To say that in a group of witty conversationalists took courage; but in trying to outdo the others in the repartee, Peregrine Bochinjochelus recovered his morale, which had almost disappeared a few months before. This association with the Delphians was for him the best possible release from the confinement of his garret. Peregrine Bochinjochelus became the official historiographer of the Delphian Club.

By now, the spring of 1817, Brackenridge again viewed life optimistically. He had emerged from his retreat to play an active part in the world about him. He had become so busy that once he was forced to neglect the obligations of his Delphian membership. He did not attend the meeting[10] of May 3, when it was his turn to receive questions to be answered in the form of an essay for presentation at the following meeting. Pertinax Particular, the learned Tripod (or president), had prepared three questions for Peregrine Bochinjochelus:

1. What is the greatest vice to which man is subject?
2. If the Articles of the Decalogue were to be reduced in number, which of them could be dispensed with in civil society?
3. What writer in the English Language has rendered the greatest benefits to Literature?

But at the next meeting,[11] May 10, Peregrine Bochinjochelus, arriving at the moment when the Tripod had just completed an epigram, had to apologize for not having his entire essay ready to present to his fellow Delphians. He read, however, the unfinished answer on the first subject: "Professional business had prevented the completion of it, and he was ordered to deliver it finished into the hands of the Secretary before the next meeting."

The questions[12] caused Brackenridge no trouble at all. In his answer to the second, he asserted that the Fourth Commandment could be considered "as chiefly political," and that society could dispense with the Sabbath without suffering inconvenience. After all, he reminded the Delphians, the Greeks and Romans never observed one. But he did not wish to imply that such a day set aside for rest and "holy meditation" was an unwise institution. "There is another commandment, however, which may be entirely dispensed with: 'love thy neighbour as thyself'—for that which is never practised, which is impossible, considering human nature, to be put in practice, ought to be dispensed with. In the words of the great orator Pinkney, 'useless legislation is vicious legislation.' " Brackenridge believed that only one answer was possible for the third question—Shakespeare.

Neither did any doubt exist in Brackenridge's mind about the answer to the first question. He was positive in his belief that one vice above all others was the most wicked. "Some would say that the most pernicious of all vices, or habitual commissions of moral offences, is falsehood," he began his argument. "That this is the foundation on which every other vice is built, that this is, in fact, the chief ingredient of all immorality . . . ." But some people, he noted, insisted that habitual drunkenness was worse than habitual falsehood. He detailed the evil effects of strong drink, observing that "Alexander was drunk when he killed his friend, and Nero must have been drunk when he set fire to Rome." He agreed emphatically, however, with the persons who condemned incontinence as the worst vice of all—and for the reason that

seduction must necessarily involve more than one in ruin. The seduction of a married woman must necessarily involve two; but in all probability the circle will be wider.—The injury thus inflicted is worse than murder, because an end is put to every hope of happiness. I am inclined upon the whole to think that this vice is the most atrocious that Hell has let loose upon the world. This horrid vice persuades us to wallow with the brute, and to commit acts at which reason trembles with more horror than at the sight of the most cruel murder. It has tempted the guardian, the schoolmaster, the clergyman to take advantage of the situation in which they have been placed. When the Devil has failed to entrap mankind by every other bait, he puts lust on his hook, and never fails to drag the deluded wretch down to Hell!

Whether he realized it or not, Brackenridge had reached a crisis in his life. He was now striving to convince himself that his lot was not without hope and that he was not condemned to everlasting unhappiness. He was not to blame for his misfortune! The loneliness, indeed, had made him a finer man. In verse he recited the melancholy circumstances of his childhood and youth and expressed that very thesis:

The Genius of the Hills, an Elegy

I

How mournful is that mellow light
 The speeding morn so gently throws,
Belov'd by spectres wan of night,
 While nature lies in deep repose.
Now silence on each sloping hill
 And thro' the vale in sadness reigns.
All save the leaf and stream are still
 Or in wild note 'poor-will complains.

172

II

Where fairies by yon silver fount,
   'Mong pearly dews their revels keep
A wanderer came, the stars to count
   Or rankling sorrows mourn and weep
His gnawing griefs refused controul;
   Awhile, he gazed the moon's pale light,
Then pour'd his melancholy soul
   Upon the listening ear of night.

III

"Hard is my fate" the wanderer cried,
   "Nor home, nor kindred now are mine;
"Affection's glowing smile denied,
   "Oh! born to suffer and repine.
"Does Mem'ry paint my infant scene
   "Gilded by warm parental love?
"Ah no! the world bestow'd its frown
   "And cruel scorn then bade me rove.

IV

"Now rudely torn from place to place
   "In sorrow still my childhood pass'd;
"Sometimes saw fortune's smiling face,
   "Felt oft'ner Mis'ry's keenest blast.
"Witness ye stars and gentle moon
   "How chequer'd was my scene of life,
"How much endur'd till manhood's noon
   "Gave strength to brave the dangerous strife.

V

"Oft driv'n from this my native spot,
   "A wand'rer on some distant strand,
"My native tongue almost forgot,
   "A stranger in my native land.
"Like some poor weed, or tender blade,
   "The stream has swept from neighbouring plains
"And bears along the swoll'n tide,
   "Nor rests till fate or chance ordains.

VI

"And yet these vales and swelling hills
   "And streams that o'er the pebbles glide,
"Are like to me a mother's smiles,
   "More dear than all the world beside.
"Oh! wild lov'd haunt of early day
   "Alone in melancholy mood
"Once more I yield to fancy's sway
   "Among thy rocks and sounding wood.

VII

"Thou aged tree, I know thee well,
   "O'erhanging still the rocky steep,
"Here mem'ry fondly loves to dwell,
   "While 'neath thy ruin'd bows I weep.

"My soul in every object sees
  "A lovely form, oh! once how dear!
"Her voice in every swelling breeze
  "Comes in soft musick to mine ear.

VIII

"Once felt my bosom friendship's glow,
  "In boyhood's visionary day,
"O'er hills and rocks we'd often go
  "Lone pair! to dream the hours away.
"Alas! aspiring generous youth,
  "Thy spirit bland has ta'en its flight
"Bright angels call'd, and led thee forth
  "From earthly gloom, to light and life.

IX

"Yet science fair her ample store
  "Op'd to my youthful mind, and smil'd,
"And Nature's Book with richest lore
  "Replete 'mongst rocks and forests wild.
"Ah! why not form'd of meanest clod
  "And cast in Nature's rudest mould,
"So with blest dulness I might plod,
  "Like Africk slave be bought and sold.

X

"With genius why inspire my mind
  "Or why plant virtues in my breast
"If cruel scorn yet stand behind
  "And fate decrees thou'lt ne'er be blest."
Thus spoke the deep desponding mind,
  Till softening grief to sadness grew—
His sighs—he gave them to the wind,
  And tears commingled with the dew.

XI

Sudden, see him with wonder start,
  His tears and sighs at once suppress'd,
The blood runs thrilling to his heart,
  Amaz'd, alarm'd, himself he bless'd:
For some ethereal sound was heard
  That did such magick wonders bring
The aspen's trembling leaf scarce stirr'd
  The gliding rill ceas'd murmuring.

XII

The Genius thus: "Beware young man
  "Of this despondency beware;
"Hear me, and follow wisdom's plan
  "Nor tempt the demon of despair.
"Misguided youth thy mourning cease,
  "Think of the pangs that thousands feel,
"And see them suffer all in peace
  "Tho' Hope despair their wounds to heal.

XIII

"Then grieve for sufferings past no more
  "To Providence give thanks, not blame,
"Since thou from sage experience' store
  "Hast more receiv'd than years might claim.
"Think what fell disappointments wait
  "The vain, the proud insatiate soul,
"Where sits ungovernable hate,
  "And temper fierce that spurns controul.

XIV

"Who looks with unforgiving scorn
  "Nor feels the charities of life
"As spots where virtues may adorn
  "While in himself wild weeds are rife.
"Hast thou not arrogance observed
  "With haughty mien and tyrant frown
"Provoke the blow so well deserved
  "Yet the gross fault will never own?

XV

"Mark that slothful wayward elf
  "Whose humor, flattery scarce can please
"Whose narrow thought, and love of self
  "But feel contempt for all he sees:
"Mark yon degraded abject wretch
  "His heart to fiends of guilt a prey;
"No touch of tenderness can reach
  "No sympathetick feeling sway.

XVI

"Hear this one boast himself, his deeds,
  "Benevolence he never knew;
"Mild gratitude indignant bleeds
  "To hear her name profan'd by you.
"Had opening life, affection nurs'd,
  "And press'd thee to her bosom warm
"While anxious care and love caress'd
  "Shielding thy tender years from harm.

XVII

"Wanderer thou wouldst like these have been
  "Or fallen worse debas'd and lost,
"Wrung by remorse of conscience keen
  "Hating all, by all accurs'd.
"Shudder thou wouldst should I impart
  "What vices are subdued in thee,
"What wickedness would fill thy heart
  "Untam'd by harsh adversity.

XVIII

"Blush not thy destiny obscure—
  "To be, God does not vainly give;
"Freely the frown, and scorn endure
  "If thy own conscience bids thee live.

"Prosperity a frequent ill
"Or passions gives, or makes them worse;
"Misery's oft a wholesome pill
"And fortune's smile a gilded curse."

XIX

The voice divine no more was heard
Yet seem'd around still lingering
Till leaf of aspen trembling stirr'd
And gliding rill 'gan murmuring.
And now each goblin, fay or sprite
On fleecy cloud, or moonbeam fled,
Before the rays of golden light
The rising sun o'er Grant hill shed.[13]

Consequently, May, 1817, was a triumphant month for Brackenridge, marking a personal victory. But it is not certain whether the Delphians caught the significance of the poem when, in the absence of Peregrine Bochinjochelus, Pertinax Particular read it to them at the meeting of May 24, held in the office of Blearix von Crambograph. They received the elegy, however, "with applause, and the Secretary was ordered to record it."[14] The crisis, precipitated by the death of the elder Brackenridge, was over for his son, who had, in effect, exorcised his mind from a demon. Henry Marie Brackenridge was now precisely thirty-one years old.

Also, the Delphian Ledger[15] indicated that Brackenridge was not without funds—that he had money in his purse:

Dr. .... to Club May 31st 1817 .... Cr.
Member B.
    You too for fines and fee
    Are debtor Member B.,
    Six dollars and a quarter, altogether—
    Which, paid with t'others, Brackenridge,
    Would at a single thwack enrich
    The Club, and be a fund for rainy weather!
    "Six dollars and a quarter!
    "Ecods! the Bill's a snorter!
    "What! Club of cognoscenti
    "Trust quarters five and twenty."
    B. cash paid as he said it,
    For which I give him credit!

But despite earnest effort to build a lucrative law practice, Brackenridge, as late as mid-April, 1817, had to admit failure—"I have never yet received one dollar of a fee."[16] He had no real competition to fear, for, excepting Robert G. Harper, the Baltimore lawyers were men of ordinary ability; but as he found again during his second residence in the city, the citizens habitually employed the services of a few established practitioners, never thinking to patronize the newer men at the bar. Brackenridge who never quite reached the point of leaving Baltimore and thereby acknowledging defeat, seized every chance to put himself in the public notice and to gain recognition from his fellow lawyers. For example, in 1816, in the case of *M'Kean* v. *Bruff,* he delivered an argument,[17] prepared with the greatest pains, before the Chancellor of Maryland—an argument on the chancery powers of that state. At the beginning Brackenridge asserted that the question involved was one "of some novelty, and, I think, of some importance."[18] He proved how injustice often resulted from the practice of permitting witnesses themselves to decide whether or not to withhold testimony essential to cases being tried in court. He sought to establish this proposition: "that a party has a distinct and perfect right to the testimony of his fellow-citizen, when legally required, unless it is withheld on the ground of some sufficient legal excuse."[19] Not content to rest his case at this point, however, he announced his intention "to ascend to higher ground, whence I may be enabled to overlook the whole of this intricate subject."[20] In a lengthy argument of this kind Brackenridge excelled, for he could display his skill in research as well as his power of logic.

Paying clients, however, continued to elude him. Early in 1817, when he was still despondent, he went to Washington to represent a French gentleman before a committee on land claims. Six weeks he spent there trying in vain to obtain the passage of a report which the committee had finally issued in favor of his client. But the client could only defray Brackenridge's expenses, promise him something more, and introduce to him "several clients of the same kind, who have large claims to bring before Congress next winter, but it was not in their power to advance me any cash."[21] Then, in spite of such frustration, Brackenridge engaged in several criminal cases in Baltimore; and to his surprise his "speeches made considerable noise in the city, and placed me high (so I have been told) in the opinion of the bar."[22] Alas! he collected no fees.

Brackenridge, meanwhile, had not abandoned authorship in his desperate pursuit of the law. He conceived three projects likely to enhance his reputation as a writer.

Brackenridge believed that the public would welcome a revised edition of his father's novel, *Modern Chivalry,* with a biographical sketch of the author. Accordingly, he wrote James Ross on January 16, 1817, requesting materials for the work—anything which he might wish to contribute to the proposed memoir. But the request did not strike a responsive chord in Ross, who had no desire to honor his old rival in the law and in politics: "I have a lively recollection of his wit, of his playful fancy, of his eloquence when roused by a subject that touched him, and of the felicity of thought and expression which so strongly marked his character; but I cannot recal any particular specimen, nor give an authentic report of any argument, conversation, or literary disquisition which would explain or illustrate the structure of his mind."[23] Ross was most apologetic in his attitude, giving several reasons to account for his inability to offer anything of value to the work, and especially—"During the last eighteen years, I saw him but seldom, & then only under the restraint & circumspection of political estrangement, so that it is impossible for me to give even a tolerable sketch, when a perfect deliniation, an exact likness, must constitute the principal value of the memoir, when given to the world." Brackenridge broached the matter of a new edition of *Modern Chivalry* to his brother Alexander, who, however, delayed so long in replying—favorably to the proposal, it developed[24]—that they never did collaborate on the project. Alexander edited the two-volume edition of the novel, published by the Pittsburgh firm of R. Patterson & Lambdin in 1819, having obtained "the Copyright with Consent of my mother. . . ."[25] But many years passed before his brother Henry wrote a biographical essay honoring their father.

But another project, the publication of a second edition of the *Views* separately from the *Journal*, Brackenridge completed successfully. He revised the material, appending to the chapter on "The Levees, or Embankments of the Mississippi," which was the last chapter, his letter to Niles concerning the inundation of New Orleans in 1816. He dedicated the book to the celebrated Abbé José Francisco Corrêa da Serra, who had praised the original essays which appeared in Charless' gazette in St. Louis as the "Sketches of the Territory of Louisiana." In his dedication Brackenridge called Corrêa "one of the most enlightened foreigners that has ever visited the United States." Corrêa, whom Brackenridge knew personally, was a botanist, historian, philosopher, diplomat—in 1816, appointed the Portuguese Minister at Washington.[26] In Baltimore, in 1817, Schaeffer and Maund published the second edition of the *Views,* now entitled *Views of Louisiana; Containing Geographical, Statistical and Historical Notices of That Vast and Important Portion of America.*[27]

Brackenridge's third project was an article on foreign affairs, "The Florida Question Stated," written for the *American Register; or, Summary Review of History, Politics and Literature.*[28] It was an essay of nearly twenty-one pages upholding the policy of the American government concerning the conflicting claims of the United States and Spain to that part of Florida lying between the Mississippi and the Perdido. The question of the Louisiana boundary had long disturbed Spanish American relations, a dispute which Monroe, first as secretary of state and then as president, labored to settle by the conclusion of a Florida treaty. As stated in the opening paragraphs, the purpose of Brackenridge's essay was to re-examine the American position: "If we have been led into error, let us retrace our steps, and endeavour to make atonement; if right, let us persist in our course with the confidence and courage of self-approba-

tion; but let us first examine the ground on which we stand, fairly and dispassionately." Brackenridge aimed, therefore, to present the facts of the case
to his reader, who then could form his own conclusions. The author related the
history of Florida as it pertained to the boundary question and both quoted
and interpreted the articles of pertinent treaties. But in the end the reader had
to conclude that Brackenridge was not in sympathy with the "advocates of
Spain." His article was well-written.

Now, in April, 1817, something extraordinary happened to Brackenridge,
the new member of the Delphian Club. Fortune began to tantalize him, as if
his prodigious efforts in the law and in literature of the past few months—his
means of making a mark in the world—were at last to be crowned with
success. But there was something more astounding still: the happy concatena-
tion of events had placed him in an embarrassing situation.

To Thomas Butler, and none other, Brackenridge owed an immediate and
detailed explanation. Now living in the house of an elderly French lady in
Baltimore, he wrote Butler excitedly on April 10: "Fortune within the last
ten days seems about to play one of her unaccountable freeks with me."[29]
Not only had he suddenly risen high in the estimation of the local bar, but
there was this, too:

... My essay on the Florida question, is at this moment a subject of general conversation, and this has brought my "Views of Louisiana" and history of the war, into notice.
What is still more strange, Mr. Brown who passed this place last week, told me that I
was mentioned at Washington as the successor of Walter Jones, the present district
attorney of Columbia, who will succeed Rush as Attorney General! I do not know what
to think of this. It may all be the contrivance of the devil to keep me here in poverty
and obscurity. I am advised to go down to Washington and have some conversation
with Mr. Monroe—To turn my back on fortune when she is about to do something for
me would not be prudent, and yet I fear my conduct cannot be reconciled with propriety
in having taken advantage of your permission which was intended only in case of my
being able to return immediately to the Mississippi.

Butler had given Brackenridge permission to draw on New Orleans, providing
he used the money to return to Louisiana to practice law. At the City Bank in
Baltimore, as a result, he received an advance of two hundred dollars, part of
which, perhaps, paid his Delphian fines and fee. But he assured Butler that
he would not lightly give up his intention to return to the South—"Do not
suppose, however, that a mere phantom deceives me."

Brackenridge ended his letter on a jubilant note. "My mind," he wrote,
"under the pressure has acquired much greater energy. Secluded from all gay
society, my whole time has been taken up in a series of mental exertions." He
might have added that no longer did the nervous twitching—the St. Vitus's
dance—torment him.

There was abundant evidence coming to hand to convince the aspiring

lawyer-writer that fortune was really smiling on him. Early in June he received
a letter from his sister in Carlisle. "The history of the war, has made a great
noise here, there was nothing else talked of from the first mention of it,"
Cornelia informed him. "Mrs McCoskry pretends to be very anxious to see it,
whether she is or not, I can not tell."[30] In the afternoon of May 30, just before
writing her brother Henry, Cornelia had taken a walk "in the country to see the
locusts, they are very pretty, they have W on their wings the vulgar say it is
for war, you may write another history." Poor Cornelia! she hoped that her
brother would come home soon. When he did come, she directed him, he
must bring her a "piece of music called the Tyrolese war song as a piece
offring for not coming sooner . . . ." But, busier than ever, he lacked the time
for a visit to Carlisle. No less a person than Richard Rush, Madison's attorney
general and now Monroe's acting secretary of state (pending the arrival of
John Quincy Adams to take the post), had written Brackenridge in May,
actually courting his favor. Rush's letter[31] was gracious. The young official—
about six years older than Henry—sent him a copy of a tract on jurisprudence,
which he had written more than a year before and which the elder Brackenridge had read and commended before his death. "You will allow me to use
this occasion of saying, that I possessed, for many years, the pleasure and
advantage of your father's acquaintance, and latterly that of his occasional
correspondence; always having been charmed with his genius and learning,"
Rush told the son.

Two months later, on July 11, Rush addressed Brackenridge again, but this
time in his official capacity as acting secretary of state. It was an exciting
letter,[32] and somewhat mysterious, for, in spite of its enigmatical nature, it
clearly indicated that perhaps Brackenridge's hope of obtaining a diplomatic
assignment, or some other government post, might be fulfilled. "Thinking it
possible that I may have occasion to address you on some public business in
the course of a week or ten days, I am induced to ask the favor of your remaining in Baltimore during that time, should this letter find you there," Rush
wrote. But he had to add that it was not at all certain whether there would be
any necessity for his writing Brackenridge on such a matter, and, therefore,
he did not wish to put him "to the least personal inconvenience."

There was not the slightest chance that the request could inconvenience Brackenridge, for he was ill. He had attended the regular meeting of the Delphian
Club on July 5,[33] but he was absent the next week on account of sickness.[34]
On July 19, the entire membership was present in Dr. Watkins' office, "except,
B, who was still sick."[35] For the same reason he was unable to attend the
meeting of July 26.[36] But the ill Delphian had recovered enough by the morning of July 16 to leave his room and the house for a walk to the post office,

where he found Rush's letter. Brackenridge answered it when he returned to his lodgings, apprising Rush of the state of his health and expressing gratification over the possibility of public employment.[37] As the days slowly passed during his convalescence, he busied himself by reading, by tending to his correspondence, and by that means managing some legal business.[38]

But soon Brackenridge received another letter[39] from Rush in the Department of State, marked "Confidential" and dated July 17, 1817. "The President having determined, for objects not necessary to be here stated in detail, to send three commissioners to different parts of South America, thinks proper to connect with them a secretary, and is desirous to avail himself of your services in that capacity," Brackenridge read, and surely with elation, for here was a respectable post made to order for him. Rush hoped that his correspondent's health would enable him to begin the voyage in a week or ten days on a ship sailing from New York. According to Rush, the voyage probably would be completed by the following January. As secretary of the mission Brackenridge would receive two thousand dollars as compensation, one half to be advanced upon his acceptance of the post.

The ailing Brackenridge, who was now gradually recovering his health, accepted the appointment with alacrity. Although he was still very weak, he wrote Rush, he considered the offer so advantageous that he could not think of declining it without making every effort to prepare himself for the service.[40]

A few days later he received two letters from Rush indicating that everything was being done to expedite the sailing of the mission. In one letter Rush included a word of caution concerning Brackenridge's duties: ". . . it will not be necessary to say more, than that you will be pleased to consider yourself as under the direction of the commissioners."[41] This statement caused Brackenridge no concern at all, as subsequent events proved. "Great confidence is felt in the fidelity and diligence with which you will perform them, as well as in the useful zeal which you will carry with you for the public service in all respects," Rush continued. There was a possibility, he mentioned also, that John Graham, one of the commissioners, on his way to New York might join Brackenridge in Baltimore. Rush urged him, moreover, to speed his preparations for an early departure of the ship, which was to sail as far south as the Plata River and on her return to visit the countries on the Spanish Main: "The ship is the Ontario, Captain Biddle." There was no need for the secretary of the mission to provide stores for the voyage as everything necessary for a comfortable passage was already aboard the vessel. In the other letter[42] Rush stated that an advance of one thousand dollars of Brackenridge's compensation was to be advanced to him immediately.

The matter of an advance was important to Brackenridge, for he again

181

lacked cash. It is true that his great labors in the law and in literature yielded him little financial profit, but it is also probable that his handling of what money he had was careless. Like his father he was indifferent to its proper management. Late in life the elder Brackenridge had regretted his own lack of frugality, having despised miserliness; and his son Henry later blamed himself for having been "all my life culpably careless in money matters."[43] But now, in July, 1817, a one-thousand-dollar advance was promptly forthcoming, collectible at the Franklin Bank in Baltimore.[44]

"My health is improving rapidly, in a few days I shall consider myself well," Brackenridge advised Rush on July 28. "I feel in high spirits . . . ."[45] With money on hand, his health better, and the prospect of an interesting voyage, he was happy—and, as he wrote Rush, anxious to forward the business of the mission. Therefore, he visited the bookstores in Baltimore, seeking informative works on South America for the use of the commissioners and himself. "My mind having been very much tuned to the affairs of South America and Mexico, for these six or seven years, every book of travels or statistics relating to them has been read by me with great attention," he asserted. This was not idle boasting, for Brackenridge shortly earned the reputation of being one of the best informed citizens of the United States on Latin American affairs— and possibly the best informed. He presumed, however, that Graham, the former chief clerk in the State Department, would himself have the standard authorities on South America—like Humboldt, Depons, and Molina—to take on the voyage. The other commissioner appointed was Caesar A. Rodney, whom Brackenridge knew slightly, as he told Rush. But as he also told Rush, he had learned that Theodorick Bland, a Baltimore judge, might become the third commissioner: ". . . I know Judge Bland well. He is a man of plain unaffected yet agreable manners, of a sound judgment and excellent discrim[in]ation. I do not think the government could select a more suitable person, he seems to me to possess the very cast of mind adapted to it." The enthusiastic secretary of the mission had more to say about Bland: "His general information is extensive, he is indefatigably inquisitive, and as careful to treasure up all the information he can gain. He has besides turned his attention to the subject for several years past in a very particular manner." It never occurred to Brackenridge in his zeal that his praise of Bland was excessive. This was one time he made a grievous error.

But by the end of July Bland had not received the appointment, although the post of commissioner, declined by one appointee, was vacant.[46] Rush notified Rodney of the situation on July 29, stating that he and his colleague, Graham, would "be attended, in capacity of secretary, by Mr. Brackenridge, a gentleman of great merit from Baltimore, and who to other accomplishments adds that of being master of the Spanish language."[47] This reference to Bracken-ridge's knowledge of Spanish was significant, for, before long, enemies called him an incompetent translator.

The end of July thus found Brackenridge, now considered a Baltimorean, ready to leave the city on his diplomatic assignment to South America. Word arrived from Graham that he anticipated the pleasure of the secretary's company on the trip to New York, their point of departure, and that the State Department had provided a fund for the purchase of books useful to their mission.[48] On his arrival Graham handed Brackenridge a message from the acting secretary of state, dated July 30: "From the date of this letter, you will perceive that I make it rather personal than official, our matters of business being all closed."[49] Rush wished him *bon voyage!*

The Delphians met as usual Saturday, August 2, and Blearix von Crambo-graph noted in his minute book: "Present all except Member B absent from town."[50] But that was no reason why the Delphians could not enjoy a quip at his expense, turning on the question—"What is the most rational relaxation for a scholar, from the fatigues of study?"—

. . . The most rational relaxation from the fatigues of study for him, is, after a hard day's labour in correcting foul proof, to be seated in his elbow chair, contemplating his increasing fame, having just received a letter from his bookseller, in the following words: "Dear Sir! Your history of the war will immortalize you. It is the best production of the kind from any American authour. The first edition is all sold—and the publick expects with impatience, a second for which you shall be handsomely paid, Yours &c."

XIV: The Secretary of the Mission
to South America
(1)

For some years—six or seven, he told Rush—Brackenridge was a student of Latin American affairs and a sympathetic observer of the independence movement in the countries to the South. He favored the patriot cause. Now, in 1817-18, he became its foremost advocate and chief propagandist, recognized as such in the United States and in Europe.[1]

But in midsummer, 1817, the newspaper press bombarded the American public with claim and counterclaim, charge and countercharge, made by both royalists and patriots. Muddling the situation, of course, were the factors of political expediency (the politician) and financial profit (the privateersman). "Many of the accounts and rumors respecting the operations of these people [the South American patriots] must go upon trust," Selleck Osborn declared editorially[2] in his Wilmington, Delaware, paper, the *American Watchman,* of which he had just become the publisher on July 19. "There is reason to believe that corruption is busily at work on the behalf of the Spanish royalists, to misrepresent the prospects and operations of their antagonists." He could have said as much about the patriot cause, except that he was a patriot sympathizer. Baltimore was the center of privateering activity, where rival patriot factions fought each other in a war of propaganda for recognition and support, to the detriment of the whole independence movement. Because Osborn had faith in the slogan of his paper, "Intelligence is the life of Liberty," he printed the royalists accounts, letting his subscribers themselves judge their authenticity. There was, in short, a paucity of accurate information about the developments in South America. In this respect the United States government was no better off than the American public.

The main duty of the mission to South America, consequently, was to collect facts on the state of affairs in the rebellious colonies of Spain. In his official instructions[3] to Rodney and Graham, Bland not being appointed until late November, Rush not only stated the *raison d'être* of the mission but also described the kind of information desired and indicated where to look for it. Upon this new and comprehensive information the Monroe administration hoped to base its future policies. Rush reminded the two commissioners that the United States government considered the struggle between Spain and her colonies "a civil war, in which the parties were equal," and the warring parties injurious to the lawful commerce of American citizens: "Acting with impartiality towards the parties, we have endeavored to secure from each a just return." Administration policy, according to Rush, was founded upon the belief that the United States must solicit the friendship of every independent government erected in Spanish territory. "The contest, by the extension of the revolutionary movement and the greater stability which it appears to have acquired, becomes daily of more importance to the United States," he continued. The President, therefore, needed accurate and detailed information about the situation in South America. Go to the Plata River first, Rush ordered the two commissioners, to visit Buenos Aires and Montevideo, on the way stopping at Rio de Janeiro to deliver dispatches to Thomas Sumpter, the United States minister to the Portuguese Court in Brazil. On the return voyage, if circumstances were propitious, the mission was to touch at São Salvador and Pernambuco, and from thence to go to the Spanish Main, "as far westward as Carthagena, looking in at any other convenient ports or places as you coast along." Observe at every place visited, he directed also, the form of government in operation, the population, and the resources "of the contending parties, wherever a contest exists." Note, furthermore, the nature of military forces, the names as well as characters of leading men, the attitudes prevailing toward the United States and the great European nations, the articles of commerce and the possibilities of trade, and ports and harbors and defense works. Determine—and this was very important—the "real prospect, so far as seems justly inferable from existing events and the operation of causes as well moral as physical in all the provinces where a struggle is going on, of the final and permanent issue." How durable were the new governments and what was the extent of their authority? was a question particularly applicable to Buenos Aires, Rush stressed. At Caracas, which seemed at the moment to lack a government, investigate General Bolivar. The commissioners, finally, were not bound to fixed rules of conduct but were left free to exercise their own judgment in all contingencies.

The U.S. Corvette "Ontario," commanded by James Biddle, awaited the mission at New York. But once there Brackenridge did not embark, for Rodney's son became desperately ill and plans for an immediate departure were canceled—as Brackenridge himself said, "for his father to leave him in his present state would be utterly impossible."[4] The time did not drag, however, as Brackenridge met his fellow lodgers and became friendly with them. John Quincy Adams, who was on his way to Washington to take charge of the Department of State, arrived with his family from England and stayed in the same house. "He is a plain good looking man baldheaded, short thick, rather awkward, but possessing a countenance highly intelligent," Brackenridge described him. "His lady is a sharp nosed little thing."[5] Commodores Stephen Decatur and John Rodgers and Captain Lewis Warrington lodged there, also.

When there seemed no likelihood of sailing for some time, Brackenridge returned to Baltimore; and there he surprised the Delphians by his unexpected attendance at the meeting of September 6, held at the home of Pertinax Particular. After a cordial welcome, "Member Bochinjochelus, Historiographer of the Club then related the following fact concerning a German Delegate to the Pennsylvania Legislature. This Solon being asked what the Legislature had been doing during the session, replied: 'Toing, hon? Dey has peen talking und-und-und-nexseht Sadurtay dey owes me dree hoonnert Tâlers!' "[6]

But the delay in departure deranged Brackenridge's finances. His one-thousand-dollar advance dwindled quickly, although he had miscalculated his needs from the beginning. Then, in New York, he learned to his dismay that it was advisable to take at least five hundred dollars with him on the voyage. Therefore, he borrowed two hundred dollars more from the account of his friend Butler, "trusting that on explaining the matter to you, you would indulge me a little longer."[7] When September and October had passed without the start of the voyage, Brackenridge addressed Secretary of State Adams himself on the matter of waiting for the mission to begin while his original advance was almost "melted away."[8] As he explained to Adams, he was not practicing law in the meantime—he had no income. He requested another advance from the government, not specifying any sum. But Adams understood Brackenridge's predicament and promptly arranged a five-hundred-dollar advance for him.[9]

The frugal Adams, however, was aghast when he discovered the nature of the stores put aboard the "Ontario" for the benefit of the commissioners to South America and their secretary on their long voyage. The Secretary of State could only register dismay, for the delicacy of the situation made him hesitate to order changes in the list of supplies.[10] The "Ontario" might have a tedious voyage but the members of the mission could dine sumptuously if stormy seas did not ruin their appetites:

15 Gallons Cogniac Brandy	12 bottles Anchovies & a few
10 Gallons old Jamaica Rum	Pots of assorted Pickles
2 quarter casks Madeira wine	24 baskets Salt
2 " " Sicily wine	12 lbs Black pepper
20 dozen first quality Claret	2 bottles Cayenne pepper
20 " second " "	large
12 bottles Lime Juice	10 lbs English Mustard
12 dozen American Porter	1000 Pickled Oysters
12 " Brown Stout	100 lbs Bourbon Coffee
12 " Cider	20 lbs Souchong Tea
4 " Olive Oil	100 lbs Loaf Sugar
6 bottles ketchup	100 lbs Lump "
12 " capers	1 Barrell St. Croix Sugar
24 " olives	10 Gallons Sugar House Molasses

1 lb Nutmegs
2 lb Cinnamon
6 bushels Split Peas
12 Kegs crackers
1 Box Vermicelli
40 Hams best quality
50 lbs Smoked Beef
1 Quintal Salt Fish
50 Pickled Tongues
24 Smoked "
20 lbs Bologna Sausages
6 lb Salmon
2 English Cheese
2 American Cheese
15 Gallons white Wine Vinegar
50 lbs Fresh Butter, put up in small stone pots & covered with Salt Petre
1 Keg of 40 lbs well packed with salt

on the top put into a large keg perfectly tight & filled with strong pickle & Salt Petre
3 boxes Muscatel Raisins
40 lbs Almonds
20 bushels Potatoes (part new)
3 bushels Russia Turnips
50 bunches Onions
4 dozen Fowls
6 " Ducks
50 " Eggs packed in sand after being dipped in hot oil
6 Hogs
2 Sheep
Herbs (quantum sufficit)
20 bushels Corn
2 barrels kildried Meal.

The members of the mission were sure to sleep comfortably, too:

3 Matrasses of the best quality, thick & soft, & adapted to the births or cots for which they are intended

3 pair feather Pillows
9 pair of sheets & pillow cases
3 pair blankets.

To make matters worse from Adams' point of view, the "Ontario" now received orders to proceed to the Pacific Ocean and the Columbia River, whereas the "Congress" frigate was ordered to take the gentlemen of the South American mission on board at Annapolis. He could not decently direct the transfer of the stores from the one vessel to the other, so that in the end Captain Biddle dined well on his voyage[11] and the passengers on the "Congress" enjoyed the same fare as he did! Adams had requested the navy agent at Baltimore to procure an identical list of stores for the "Congress," "but he desires it to be expressly understood that this list is not to be considered as a precedent upon any future occasion in which this Department has any concern."[12]

Thus Brackenridge and the commissioners did not sail to South America on the "Ontario" but on the "Congress," a frigate commanded by Commodore Arthur Sinclair. Before embarking on his own voyage, however, Captain Biddle of the "Ontario" arranged to have Brackenridge's possessions returned to him— books, a mattress, and a bandbox.[13]

Brackenridge spent most of his time in Washington while he awaited the start of the voyage. There he frequented the Library of Congress, enlarged not long before by the library of Thomas Jefferson which the federal government had purchased—"the librarian and myself being about the sole occupants for several months."[14] Jefferson's collection was strong in works concerning the periods of the American and French Revolutions, according to Brackenridge, and contained books which he "attacked like a ravenous wolf." The result of his study was an anonymous pamphlet—"BY AN AMERICAN"—entitled *South America: A Letter on the Present State of That Country, to James Monroe, President of the United States,* of which the Washington edition of fifty-two pages issued from the office of the *National Register* on October 15, 1817.

The anonymity of the letter was necessary. As secretary of the proposed mission to South America, a fact-finding commission, Brackenridge was daring enough in addressing the President anonymously on the great subject of the day, the independence movement in South America, and in presenting a case for the recognition of the new republics. But he did not dare to admit publicly the authorship of the pamphlet, for that would jeopardize, if not at once destroy, the supposedly impartial character of the mission. He was, however, one American citizen trying to convince another, who happened to be the President, of the merit of a particular cause.

Brackenridge proved a brilliant advocate. He wrote the pamphlet "in the spirit of an *advocate,*" as he later told his friend William Shaler.[15] His theme, as expressed in the words of Pope, Brackenridge printed on the title page:

> More powerful each, as needful to the rest,
> And in proportion as it blesses, blest.

From the beginning of his work Brackenridge tried to persuade his reader that "like a decrepid and worthless hag" Spain had been "an incubus on South America."[16] He began his argument with the discovery of America by Columbus and the subjugation of the inhabitants of Mexico, Peru, and part of Chile by the cruel Spanish invaders, who lusted for gold and silver. "Nothing can be more true than that the discovery, settlement, and conquest of America, was the work of private enterprise, but the advantages have been reaped by the different sovereigns," he contended.[17] Everything they subordinated to the selfish acquisition of wealth by mining, forbidding manufacturing and restricting agriculture and commerce. The country of a Spanish colonist became, in effect, a prison. Then Brackenridge showed why the British colonies in the New World, which were actually inferior in soil and climate and later in establishment, outstripped the Spanish and eventually won their independence: "In us the birth of a nation was hailed, by the rest of mankind, with enthusiastic joy, we are now about to behold the birth of empires. Eighteen millions of souls are now struggling to be free. . . ."[18] Their aim was "to shake off the European yoke." Their revolutionary movement filled Brackenridge with sublime anticipation: "The dawn of that glory which the discovery of America will shed upon the world, is but just beginning to appear. Hitherto it has been a discovery locked up."[19]

Spain's attempt to quell the uprisings was folly, in Brackenridge's opinion.

He believed that the separation of the colonies from the mother country was inevitable, due, in part, to "the offensive arrogance of the European, who fancies himself a superior being. . . ."[20] As in North America, now in South America, patriots defended their native soil against an oppressor who fought at the greatest disadvantage. Then he made a telling point: if Spain "should be successful for the present, can she produce a change in their minds? She might as well think of making war on the elements."[21]

Brackenridge was certain that the enmity between Spain and her colonies, already so deep-rooted, could only increase. To counteract the tendency toward separation, he asserted, the royal family of Spain might wisely have transferred its court to Mexico, like the Portuguese Court in Brazil. But Spain had unwittingly encouraged the desire of her colonies for independence by aiding the British colonies in North America in their struggles for freedom: "The imprisoned are tormented by the desire to escape, as much by the natural love of liberty, as by the sight of others in the enjoyment of it."[22] The revolutions in South America were not accidental in nature but the "natural consummation of what had been long and gradually preparing. . . ."[23] It was unjust, therefore, to insist that the South Americans as a whole were not fit to govern themselves, a favorite argument of their enemies. Brackenridge, in fact, vigorously attacked the slanderers of the South Americans: "Persons who have never seen a South American are in the habit of condemning them all by the wholesale, as stupid, depraved, and worthless."[24] Again and again he reminded his reader that the enemies of the American people, and of the United States, had cast similar aspersions at them. His enlightened argument was indisputable: "Man is every where a noble and lofty being, and if the burthen which bows him to the earth, be taken away, if the slavish bands in which he is fastened are burst, he will suddenly rise with ease to the natural standard of his character."[25]

"It is not always safe to reason from what has been, to what will be," Brackenridge continued.[26] But it was not fair to doubt the ability of the patriots to erect mild and stable governments after the overthrow of foreign despotism. He cited the proclamations, political writings, and the newspapers of the patriots as proof of their knowledge of self-government. According to Brackenridge, the patriots inculcated a love of country in their youth: "I have been told by a gentleman who has frequently questioned the boys of the most common class, 'what are you?'—'a patriot'—'why are you a patriot?'—'because I will defend my country against invaders, because I do not like that my country should be governed by strangers, and because I wish to be free.' "[27] As a matter of fact, wherever the patriots succeeded in expelling the Spanish, they established newspapers for the dissemination of political information, almost every word published obviously inspired by a genuine admiration of their American brothers to the North. The patriots, furthermore, were fast gaining ascendency over their Spanish masters: "The united provinces of La Plata, as well as Chili and Peru, are already lost to Spain for ever."[28]

At this point in his argument in favor of the patriots, Brackenridge made another prediction which also stood the test of time: *"The time will come when Europe will visit America for the double purpose of enjoying her vast commerce and of finding a passage to the east; America will then be the centre of commercial attraction to the whole world."*[29] He agreed with the advocates of a canal across the Isthmus of Panama that such a project was both feasible and desirable, although they realized that Spain aimed to thwart the plan. In Brackenridge's mind there was nothing visionary about a canal connecting the two oceans nor about the benefits it would bestow on the world in general and the United States in particular.

Brackenridge now forcefully stated the concept of the two spheres which later found its way into the Monroe Doctrine:

> . . . There may be in many things, *a common American continental interest, in opposition to an European interest.* I am no advocate for the visionary idea of a great American congress on the isthmus, but there may exist an understanding, upon a variety of subjects of general concern. The weight and importance of each state, will be wonderfully increased by this vicinage of independent states, even if there should be no alliance. The United States are at present, a single isolated power, and the monarchs across the Atlantic, are under no apprehensions that other nations will make a common cause with us, when our rights are violated. Suppose, for example, the existence of several governments on this continent, entirely free from any connection with Europe and completely beyond her control—beyond the vortex of any of her primary interests—would the British, or any other government, in this case, have set at naught the rights of neutrals? No, she would have placed too high a value on the good will of America, to have sported with them so lightly.[30]

Brackenridge elaborated upon this concept and, moreover, outlined an American foreign policy. "The independence of America from Europe, is the first great object to be attained," he declared. "Compared to this, every consideration is of minor importance."[31] His contention that the form of government adopted by the countries of Latin America little concerned the United States, of course, infuriated extreme republicans. But his contention was founded on common sense and fair-mindedness: "It would be highly offensive and insulting on our part, to dictate to any people, the kind of government they ought to adopt. True republican liberality forbids it. . . . Let us cherish our own institutions; but we may do this with less boasting of ourselves, or fault-finding with others."[32] Therefore, he advocated friendly relations with the Brazilian Court, although, in the recent war between the United States and Great Britain, "the king of the Brazils *leaned rather to the side of our enemy."*[33] Likewise, the United States had no right to interfere in the insurrection at Pernambuco, for "whatever we may think of the *form,* the Brazilians had already obtained the great object for which the Americans are contending, *a government within themselves;* the affair of Pernambuco was nothing more than the revolt of an adjoining province. . . ."[34] Such a confounding of things, he warned, could only injure the entire patriot cause.

Although Brackenridge foresaw cooperation with Great Britain in support of the South Americans, he was convinced that the *"United States will be the natural head of the New World."*[35] The United States, after all, was "the elder state" in the western hemisphere and dedicated to justice and peace; and he added sincerely that if *"all the nations in the world were governed by the same principles that we are, there would be an end to wars."*

He became more and more specific concerning policy as he proceeded with his argument. *"It is very evident that we must be, and should be proud to be, the first to acknowledge the independence of South America, or any part of it, whenever it may be achieved, now, or ten years hence."*[36] He pooh-poohed, and effectively, any danger to the United States inherent in such a policy. But he insisted that the United States government should not intermeddle in party faction in the countries to the South, which was a natural development—"If Puerrydon has been called a tyrant, Mr. Madison has been called a Caligula. . . ."[37] He discussed the fortunes of South American leaders—Pueyrredón, Carrera, and San Martin. He did not advocate, however, joining the patriots in a war with Spain: "What then ought we to do? I say at once, *to establish official relations with the republics of La Plata and Chili."*[38] Nothing in international law, Brackenridge asserted, forbade their recognition as independent states.

Finally, he ended the letter to President Monroe on this note: "It was given to our immortal Washington, to achieve the independence of one half of America, and I most sincerely hope, it may be yours to acknowledge the independence of the other."[39]

In his pamphlet, which was eminently quotable, Brackenridge "foreshadowed not only the Monroe Doctrine but the Monroe Doctrine in its Pan-American interpretation of 1940."[40] But the idea of hemispheric solidarity, or the doctrine of the two spheres, was not original with him, for, from as early as 1810 at least, several references to it had appeared in the Baltimore press.[41] It was Brackenridge, nevertheless, who exploited the concept in a powerful way.

Both in the United States and abroad, the public reaction to the pamphlet was immediate and great. Its popularity in the United States and its cheap price caused Sir Charles Bagot, the British minister, to report to his government a suspicion that the Monroe administration had subsidized its publication.[42] In 1818, the pamphlet was republished as a book in London and also reprinted there in the *Pamphleteer*,[43] a periodical serving as a repository of the best pamphlet writings of the day. The Abbé de Pradt was the translator of the French edition.[44]

Brackenridge's advocacy of the patriot cause naturally displeased the Spanish authorities, who appreciated the forcefulness of his argument. In 1818, an anonymous pamphlet[45] appeared in London, written by "An Englishman" and addressed to "His Catholic Majesty, Ferdinand the Seventh, King of Spain"— an unimpressive attempt to refute Brackenridge's reasoning in support of the South Americans. Perhaps this was the production of the English writer whom the Spanish minister himself was reputed to have employed to frame a reply to Brackenridge's *Letter*.[46]

But in the United States the Brackenridge pamphlet provoked—really hurt —no one more than it did Antonio Gonçalves da Cruz, the agent of the rebellious Pernambucans who sought American aid in their revolt against the royal government of Brazil. Permitted to ship supplies to the provisional government of Pernambuco, he tried in vain to win recognition as well from the United States. Thus Brackenridge's dismissal of the Pernambucan cause as being of no interest to the American government was a blow to the envoy. Da Cruz counterattacked at once with an anonymous sixteen-page pamphlet, in the form of a letter, entitled *Reply to the Author of the Letter on South America and Mexico, By an American, Addressed to Mr. James Munroe, President of the United States, Printed at Washington, in This Present Year, 1817*, dated Philadelphia, November 6, and signed "C****."[47] The author declared himself in hearty accord with everything in the *Letter* except the inexplicable condemnation of the Pernambucan revolt. Da Cruz seemed to find a flaw in Brackenridge's argument: "This discourse of yours supposes that the right of resistance against despotism is given only to nations governed colonially, or by a power removed from their center: that is to say, however oppressed a people may be by a central or domestic government, it cannot take the alarm to escape from oppression."[48] The Pernambucans, he contended, had revolted against an arbitrary monarchy—"the arbitrary power of the house of Braganza," which was "no longer in Lisbon, but at the court of Brazil."[49] According to Brackenridge, however, the Pernambucan problem was subordinate to the one great object—the separation of America from Europe. The royal government of Brazil soon dashed the hopes of the Pernambucan agent by smashing the new republic.

Brackenridge had no intention of keeping his authorship of the *Letter* secret, although he would not acknowledge it publicly, for he desired the prestige which its success would bring. Therefore, he sent copies of the pamphlet to friends and acquaintances and to strangers who were important people.

One copy in particular he presented to Commodore David Porter, commissioner of the Navy Board. Porter, significantly, was a partisan of the Chilean exile, José Miguel Carrera, who hoped to regain control of his homeland. Carrera was an enemy of the Chilean royalists; of Bernardo O'Higgins, a rival Chilean patriot leader; and of José de San Martin, the Buenos Aires general who favored O'Higgins. Besides Porter, Carrera had the support of John Stuart Skinner, the Baltimore postmaster, who wrote a series of anonymous letters, signed "LAUTARO," to the newspapers advocating the recognition of Chile, actually a Carrera-dominated Chile. Skinner was the son-in-law of Judge Theodorick Bland, whom Brackenridge had recommended so effusively to Richard Rush as a prospective member of the mission to South America. But now, in October, 1817, Brackenridge in his pamphlet had challenged the Carrera interests by insisting that the independence of South America as a whole was more important than the success of a single faction. What would Commodore Porter say about that?

As soon as Porter had received the pamphlet and studied its contents, he invited the author to visit him immediately at his beautiful home, "Meridian Hill," which stood on the heights north of the White House—"I have sent my carriage in the hope that you might favor me with your company to day."[50] The day was Ocober 26. Considering his connection with Carrera, Porter's attitude was surprising:

. . . My ideas accord precisely with yours on the subject of S American affairs, and as to the conduct this Government should adopt in regard to the Independents—The conclusions you draw from facts, and your reasonings, are so just that I have no doubt your production will attract, not only the attention of the "wise and upright Statesman" to whom it is addressed but that of the people of the United States generally, put the public mind in a proper train of thinking, and settle the opinions of those who were undetermined.

Was Porter sincere in making such a statement? Or was he flattering Brackenridge in the hope of enlisting him in Carrera's cause? "Since reading your book I feel myself a better 'patriot,' " Porter assured Brackenridge. "My opinions are more correct, and my zeal in favor of a political connection between the United States and South America has greatly increased." Then Porter came to the point: "an interchange of sentiments may elicit new lights, and it is not impossible that by concert a greater effect may be produced on the government and on the public." Porter, also, requested a copy of the *Letter* to send to Joel Poinsett and advised Brackenridge that "a plate will allways be laid for you whenever you will do me the favor to take your dinner with me *unceremoni-*

ously." But certain it is that Porter, if indeed he made the attempt, never persuaded Brackenridge to join the Carreristas.

Newspaper editors, especially those who championed the cause of South American independence, printed reports attributing authorship of the *Letter* to Brackenridge. Thomas Ritchie, the publisher of the *Richmond Enquirer,* promptly informed his subscribers about the pamphlet which he had received in the mail from Washington: "We understand it is from the pen of Mr. H. M. Brackenridge, author of 'Views of Louisiana'—who was said to have embarked in the Ontario as one of the Commissioners to South America; but who, we conjecture, is still at Washington."[51] Ritchie's conjecture was correct. But the reference to Brackenridge as a commissioner was indicative of the unreliability of the reports circulating about the country concerning this mission which had not yet sailed for South America. The publisher announced his pleasure to find Brackenridge writing on the patriot side: "Mr. B. writes with ability, in a chaste and perspicuous style." Ritchie extracted paragraphs from the pamphlet to prove that Brackenridge's "views of the course which the United States ought to take are the same which have been sketched in this paper—his *reasons* are nearly the same." In Ritchie's paper in September and October, however, the "Lautaro" letters, written by Skinner, had first appeared, urging the immediate recognition of Chile—Skinner, the investor in privateering ventures and the personal creditor of Carrera in the amount of four thousand dollars![52] There was, consequently, a difference in views noticeable to the careful reader comparing certain articles in the paper with the pamphlet.

As the days passed in November without the departure of the mission, the rumors afloat increased in number. But it was the influential editor Niles who provided his readers with accurate information, although it was unofficial. "Though the fact is not officially stated, it appears to be acknowledged, that *Caesar A. Rodney, John Graham* and *Theodorick Bland,* esqs. as commissioners, with *H. M. Brackenridge,* esq. as their secretary, are immediately to proceed in the Congress frigate to South America," he reported in mid-November. "The object of their mission is rather guessed at than known—but it seems agreed that their purpose is only to obtain a knowledge of the state of things on which government may rely for its future direction."[53] The editor, long a keen observer of the patriot struggle for independence and a sympathizer, approved Brackenridge's views on the South American question and emphatically said so in noticing a "very ably written pamphlet . . . lately . . . published at Washington, addressed to the President of the United States, and of which Mr. *Brackenridge* is said to be the author. . . ."[54] Then Niles indicated the significance of Brackenridge's work, the product of hours of study in the Library of Congress: "Considerable importance has been ascribed to this pamphlet, on account of the present situation of its author."

But the composition of the mission had suddenly become public knowledge because from some person in authority, or with the proper contacts with government, the facts leaked out. Osborn printed a Baltimore report, dated November 10, in his *American Watchman* five days later. The facts squared with Niles' account, although the source of the news thought "it proper to remark, that our information is not derived from either of the gentlemen above named, or any one connected with them, yet it may be entirely relied on." In other words, neither Rodney, Graham, Bland, nor Brackenridge had provided the information.

Although Bland, the third commissioner, was still unappointed, the frigate "Congress," being readied for sailing, had received its surgeon for the voyage in the person of Dr. William Baldwin. He was a gentle man with a puckish sense of humor—he was shrewd and humane. In the opinion of his friend, Dr. William Darlington, Dr. Baldwin was a man of "child-like simplicity."[55] The son of Thomas Baldwin, a member of the Society of Friends, he had become the teacher of a country school near his birthplace in Chester County, Pennsylvania; and interested in the sciences, he aspired to be a practitioner of medicine. He served as an apprentice to Dr. William A. Todd, a physician of Downington, in Chester County, and also began attending the medical lectures at the University of Pennsylvania, where he was William Darlington's classmate. At this period in his life Baldwin became an avid botanist, haunting the Marshallton Botanic Garden. He sailed to China as a surgeon on a merchant ship before obtaining his degree in medicine. But on his return from the Orient he completed the medical course at the university and earned his diploma, the title of his thesis being, *A Short Practical Narrative of the Diseases Which Prevailed among the American Seamen, at Wampoa, in China, in the Year 1805; with Some Account of Diseases Which Appeared among the Crew of the Ship New Jersey, on the Passage from Thence to Philadelphia.* In the years following, he practiced medicine and botanized, all the time handicapped by a frail constitution predisposed to tuberculosis. But it was his botanical zeal which brought him the appointment as surgeon on the "Congress"—the United States government ordered him to investigate the plants of the places which the mission visited.[56]

Late in October, Dr. Baldwin had discussed the matter of this assignment at the Navy Department. To his surprise he found "among the great folks, at Head Quarters, some lovers of science. . . ."[57] Moreover, they informed him that his knowledge of natural history was an important factor in his selection for the post of surgeon on this particular voyage. The chance to botanize in South America and the advice of his friends to accept the appointment—Rodney, the commissioner, was anxious for him to go—decided Dr. Baldwin, although another consideration was the possible beneficial effect of the voyage on his health. By November 10, he was ready to leave his family in Wilmington, Delaware, and to proceed to Norfolk, there to join the "Congress."[58] On the way to Baltimore he met Corrêa da Serra, the Portuguese minister, and enjoyed some botanical talk with him.[59] In Baltimore he spent one day, "becoming acquainted with NILES,—and our *Secretary*, BRACKENRIDGE, who, I have no doubt, will prove as interesting, as I am very certain he will be amusing, and eccentric, on the voyage. He will lay in (he says) *ample stores for the mind:* and I am told that he sings an excellent song,—and can, if we require it, give us the *Speeches* of G****, exactly."[60] But, as he wrote Dr. Darlington, Dr. Baldwin also thought Brackenridge's "knowledge of the Spanish language may be of much importance. He translated the Exposition, of PUEYRREDON, —which you may have seen in the papers."

Dr. Baldwin's assignment to the "Congress" and the appointment of Bland as the third commissioner[61] on November 21 at last brought the mission to the point of departure. On that day Secretary of State Adams gave the commissioners supplementary instructions,[62] which, however, did not greatly alter the original orders issued to Rodney and Graham in July. But now the gentlemen of the mission were directed to protest to the various revolutionary authorities their indiscriminate commissioning of privateersmen who formed nests of adventurers at Amelia Island and Galveston and plundered the commerce of the United States and violated its laws. The practice of commissioning the unprincipled freebooters, they were to remind the revolutionists, did not help the cause of South American independence but only tended to deter the recognition of the new governments by other countries. Adams authorized one or more of the commissioners to proceed by land from Buenos Aires to Chile, if such an undertaking seemed expedient at the time—in reality, a concession to Bland and the Carreristas. The compensation for each commissioner, Adams stated, was fixed at six thousand dollars. Their stores for the voyage, he added, were already on board the ship.

Brackenridge had received his instructions—all that were necessary—from Rush in July. Although the delay in the sailing of the mission had upset his finances, Brackenridge had gained, nevertheless; for the publication of his pamphlet, which he could not have written had he departed immediately for South America, brought him quick recognition as an authority on the independence movement of the southern peoples. The voyage, therefore, was full of promise for him. He was in the best of spirits. The evening of November 22, he attended the meeting of the Delphian Club to announce his departure for South America, having been absent since Session LIV in September. But he had no time to fraternize with his fellow Delphians:

> . . . When his Ludship had ceased to read, the Historiographer rose from his seat, took his hat, and then took leave of the Club. "My Lud!" said he, "I have an engagement this evening, which prevents me from remaining longer in your august presence: in other words, I have left at the Theatre two ladies, whom I accompanied thither about two hours ago: they are under the protection of one of my friends;—but as they must undoubtedly sigh for my return, I am forced to tear myself from you. But, before I go, My Lud, I must inform you, that before the next hebdomadal Session of this ancient and Reputable Club, I shall be absent from the United States on my way to South America. It is unnecessary to tell you why I go thither. My Lud, I shall not forget the Club; and I hope that the Club will not forget me.—I shall be absent but a few months."
> Having spoken thus, Peregrine Bochinjochelus left the Hall.[63]

The following Thursday, November 27, the three commissioners and Brackenridge, their secretary, left Baltimore on the Norfolk steamboat. William T. Read, the private secretary of Rodney, accompanied them,[64] as did Rodney's son, Thomas.[65] A delay in the transmission of orders held the "Congress" at Norfolk, where, however, the members of the mission enjoyed the hospitality of the citizens. Then, on the morning of December 4, the frigate sailed from the Chesapeake, clearing the capes at nine o'clock.[66]

According to Brackenridge, there were four hundred persons on board the "Congress," more than the usual number, for this particular voyage, sure to be interesting, had attracted a considerable number of lieutenants and midshipmen who ordinarily would not have gone.[67] "We have in the wardroom, six Lieutenants, one Lieut. of Marines, one Sailing-master, one School-master, and one *Chaplain;*—the latter great character has been transferred to my department," Dr. Baldwin had written Dr. Darlington a few moments before sailing, while the ship still stood in Hampton Roads. "I shall station him in the cockpit, and teach him a different *duty* from that of *commanding our consciences,* —which he said he was authorized to do!"[68] The chaplain faced a hopeless task if he tried to command the consciences of the members of this mission to South America.

XV: The Secretary of the Mission to South America

(2)

From the beginning of the voyage the mission was torn by dissension, which the members effectively concealed from the public eye. In his lowly station as secretary Brackenridge was the storm center.

The passage to Rio de Janeiro took fifty-five days.[1] At the outset the weather was cold and disagreeable until the entrance into the Gulf Stream brought warmer air. Then, on December 17, a gale began buffeting the frigate, keeping Brackenridge below deck. But he admired the efficiency of the sailors as they prepared the vessel for riding out the tempest. Their discipline was superb. After the storm a period of steady progress ensued until January 5, 1818, when a calm set in that lasted beyond the middle of the month. "This was one of the most disagreeable periods of my life," Brackenridge avowed later. "It appeared as if we had been condemned to perish in this dismal region: a black sea around us, and above us generally a gloomy sky; dark shapeless clouds continually gathering as if to contend with the sun, whose fierce vertical rays occasionally bursting forth seemed almost to burn. The arch of the horizon was diminished in a most surprising manner, as if presaging a dreadful storm."[2] He was despondent; and his colleagues looked equally low-spirited, at least to him. But as they neared the equator and crossed the line, a breeze grew stronger by the hour and the jollity of the traditional ceremony obliterated the general depression. On January 27, the "Congress" made Cape Frio; and the next morning, all on board could descry the Sugarloaf Mountain which stood at the entrance to the harbor of Rio de Janeiro.

Moored in the majestic harbor, the ship at once became the object of admiration by the visitors who came aboard, especially to the delight of Brackenridge, for whom such a reception was a novel experience.[3] A Portuguese officer, wearing a magnificent uniform and speaking excellent English, "strutted about, repeating the expression, 'd—d fine ship, sir—very fine ship indeed.' " This functionary, actually one of little importance as Brackenridge soon discovered, joked without inhibition, drank a glass of wine, and finally in line of duty asked Commodore Sinclair a few questions about his vessel. There followed visits by the commanders of warships anchored in the harbor—the captain and several officers of an Austrian frigate and the captains and officers of the British men-of-war. "We could easily see one thing, that secretly nourished our pride, which was the homage universally rendered to our superior excellence in nautical concerns," Brackenridge noted happily. "This could not be concealed; we could see it in every look and action of our proud cousins of the family of John Bull; and as to the Portuguese and others, they pretended no competition."

But, sea-weary, Brackenridge was impatient to go ashore.[4] A boat from the "Congress" carried him and other eager sight-seers through the busy harbor to the queen's stairs, the landing place not far from what Brackenridge described as "a prodigious dung heap, the accumulation of ages from the stables of the city." As a matter of fact, the republicans from the United States, Brackenridge, Dr. Baldwin, and the others connected with the mission, including the commissioners themselves, found little to their liking in the capital of Brazil, a monarchy. The populace impressed Brackenridge unfavorably despite his rule never to judge people hastily and by wholesale, and he found the appearance of their city mean. The general custom of wearing uniforms and decorations about town astonished him: "Contrasted with the habits and opinions of our country, where man is by nature a noble and dignified being, this idle and silly display produced in my mind the very reverse of respect." The party from the "Congress" fell in with two countrymen, temporary residents of Rio de Janeiro, who offered to act as guides. In walking about the city, Brackenridge observed many things which reminded him of New Orleans. But his knowledge of the Portuguese capital, the royal government, and the politics of South America was broadened considerably when Sumpter, the American minister, invited the mission to dinner at his residence. It was on this visit that Brackenridge had a glimpse of royalty when the queen and several princesses passed Sumpter's house in a cavalcade, pausing momentarily to exchange words of greeting. "Although I had read a great deal of kings, and queens, and princesses, I had no idea that I should feel so little of that awe and dread, supposed to be produced by *the irradiations of majesty*," Brackenridge admitted later. Once Sumpter himself had caused a diplomatic incident by refusing to dismount from his horse and showing sufficient deference to royalty upon encountering the queen's cavalcade—he never submitted to the practice, as had other foreign representatives at the court.

Sumpter did not present the commissioners to King John VI, for they were in Brazil only as private citizens, although custom decreed that Commodore Sinclair, as the commander of a foreign warship, undergo the ceremony.[5] From him Brackenridge obtained a description of the short and fat and black-eyed ruler, who professed a friendship for the United States.

Brackenridge never wasted a moment, it seemed, in his efforts to collect a variety of information about Brazil for the use of the commissioners. Even when he ascended part of the Parrot's Head, a mountain near the city, in the company of Read and Dr. Baldwin, he noted minute details of everything he saw, whereas the surgeon-botanist looked for new plants to study. When the three tired climbers gave up their goal of reaching the top of the mountain, they followed an aqueduct back into town.[6] They arrived there in the evening, exhausted and hungry, only to have well-bred ladies pelt them from doors and windows with wax balls containing scented water.[7] But there was no use to protest a drenching during the three-day period of merrymaking, the carnival, which the Portuguese happened to be observing with their customary enthusiasm. The mission remained long enough in Rio de Janeiro for Brackenridge to witness the colorful ceremonies of the king's coronation on February 6.[8] "Such is the first coronation of a king in America—will it be the last?" Brackenridge wondered afterward.

But he had watched the coronation ceremonies, like the illuminations, from the deck of the "Congress." He had no desire to go ashore for a closer view of the celebration, listening that entire evening to the ringing bells and the cannon. "How much of this nonsense does it take to make a King!" he exclaimed the next day in a long letter to His Ludship Pertinax, "Pres't of the A. & R.D. Club."[9] Pertinax Particular read this letter from Peregrine Bochinjochelus to the Delpians on April 25, 1818. It pleased the Delphians, for they had appointed him at their "XLIX Session, Clubicular Collector of Curiosities—of which the present letter is the first specimen that he has transmitted to this here ancient and reputable Club."

By the spring of 1818, in fact, a flood of letters and official dispatches began pouring into the United States from members of the mission as well as men associated with it, like Read and Dr. Baldwin. Each commissioner reported the events of the voyage according to his particular sympathies respecting the revolutionary factions in South America. Some letters written to private correspondents found their way into the columns of newspapers, whereas others were written especially for publication in the press.[10] Readers of the gazettes could thus follow the progress of the mission almost day by day.

Dr. Baldwin, who kept his friend Dr. Darlington well informed about the mission, fast became an admirer of Brackenridge, whom he had met in Niles' office in Baltimore. This was to prove a fortunate circumstance for the secretary of the mission. But while they were becoming boon companions on the voyage, the circumstances of their meeting in Baltimore had resulted in embarrassment for Niles! The editor had once referred to Dr. Baldwin as a former member of Congress from Georgia. The statement immediately elicited a reply from Selleck Osborn, who reminded his own subscribers in Wilmington that the surgeon's family resided in their borough and that he had never sat in Congress: "Doctor B. is a naturalist of the first order, and as a botanist, especially, is believed to be without an equal in this country."[11] Niles, however, was quick to acknowledge his mistake:

> I am glad that the error was made, seeing it has been the cause of more fully introducing to the public a most amiable gentleman. The error occurred thus—Dr. B. brought letters to me from a friend in Wilmington, and I had the pleasure to introduce him to Mr. Breckenridge, secretary to the commissioners, in my own office. Immediately after which, Mr. B. *seemed* to recognize him as having been formerly in congress from *Georgia,* to which Dr. B. as I thought, assented. The facts furnish additional evidence of the momentous truth, how easy it is to be deceived by *appearances* of things, as we suppose that we see and hear them.[12]

Dr. Baldwin, meanwhile, was finding that Brackenridge was not such an eccentric person after all.

The "Congress," sailing from Rio de Janeiro in friendly company with the British sloop of war, "Blossom," Captain Hickey, next proceeded to Montevideo without untoward incident.[13] Before the departure on February 9, however, there was an unpleasant occurrence involving an American seaman who absented himself from the boat without leave and later was seen on the street by two lieutenants. When they tried to apprehend him, the deserter protested loudly that he was a Portuguese subject impressed into the American navy. Two soldiers rescued him; but, according to Brackenridge, the "affair had been buzzed abroad through the city, and was no doubt represented in the most unfavorable light with respect to us." No longer was it wise for a person attached to the "Congress" to go on shore. The Portuguese minister heightened the ill feeling by demanding the release of all the Portuguese aboard the American frigate, thereby implying the detention of impressed seamen there. Commodore Sinclair resolved to pay no further attention to the affair; and he sailed his ship past the forts, with the "men called to quarters, and the matches lighted, determined to give Santa Cruz a broadside or two, at least, before she could sink us." The "Congress" shortly overtook the "Blossom," whose commander had graciously offered to share his knowledge of the Plata River where navigation was known to be hazardous. On February 22, the "Congress" anchored in soft mud off Montevideo.

As Brackenridge expressed it, the business of Montevideo was war.[14] A Portuguese force had captured the town from the patriots. When a boat from the "Congress" put ashore, a lieutenant made an immediate call on the Portuguese general in command, Carlos Frederico Lecor, a tall and handsome man who invited the members of the mission to dine with him the next day. At this interview Brackenridge was present, for he had watched Bland climb into the boat, taking advantage of the chance to visit the town, and "I determined to accompany him." Afterward, at an inn on the plaza, they met Carrera, the Chilean revolutionary; and leaving him with Bland, Brackenridge walked about Montevideo, noting the ravages of war in a once prosperous community. Although it was soon time for the siesta, Brackenridge continued his stroll through the quiet streets: "Happening to peep into a meat shop, I observed a kind of Indian lying on his poncho on the earthen floor, in the midst of myriads of flies, who covered his bare legs, face, and hands, without causing him the slightest uneasiness." That scene, somehow, represented the decline of Montevideo, the commercial center of the vast Banda Oriental del Uruguay.

The following morning Carrera conducted a party from the "Congress," including Brackenridge, on a ride beyond the walls of Montevideo but within the Portuguese lines.[15] Beyond the lines roved bands of Gauchos, the followers of the patriot leader, José Artigas, who fought the Portuguese and at the same time challenged the authority of the revolutionary government at Buenos Aires. Brackenridge called him a "barbarian" and likened his partisans to the Missouri Indians. The country about Montevideo was laid waste by these herdsmen, or Gauchos, in spite of General Lecor's presence in the town. On their ride by horseback the party of Americans saw a band of Gauchos steal horses from the Portuguese. When the listless Portuguese neglected to pursue the adversary, Brackenridge concluded they could never conquer the country; but he also believed that the "respectable" part of the population did not support Artigas: "The simple fact is, that if his name had not been used to give sanction to privateers, we should have heard little in his praise."

But here in Montevideo, Brackenridge had an opportunity to watch Carrera attentively—to study him as a patriot leader.[16] At the dinner given by General Lecor in honor of the company on board the "Congress," Brackenridge met an agent of the Buenos Aires government, who sought to counteract any favorable impression the Chilean might have made on the minds of the American commissioners. He reminded Brackenridge of the "deadly enmity" which Carrera entertained for the government and even the people of Buenos Aires: "My business was that of a listener—I could only answer, that I thought his observations worthy of being attended to." Then, on the day after the dinner, Carrera boarded the "Congress" with Bland and stayed as a guest overnight when a northeast wind made a trip back to shore risky. "As the fortunes and character of general Carrera had excited considerable interest in the United States, I was induced to observe him closely, in order that I might form an opinion for myself," Brackenridge stated subsequently. "I had been highly prepossessed in his favor, on account of the generosity of himself and family towards commodore Porter, after his desperate battle on the coast of Chili. I had seen him in the United States, and was much pleased with his modest unassuming deportment. But doubts had been raised in my mind as to the true

character of his patriotism." As he listened to the conversation of this aristocratic Chilean, an exile from his country, Brackenridge was convinced that
he was not a true patriot:

> . . . I concluded, therefore, that his seeming candor and liberality, was merely intended
> to enable him the more effectually to prejudice our minds against the chief magistrate
> of Buenos Ayres. There was one sentiment uttered by him, which, in my conception,
> was incompatible with genuine patriotism. He observed, in substance, that as long as
> the country was still in danger from Spain, it would be well enough to accept the aid
> of the army of San Martin; but, that as soon as the Spaniards were driven off, the army
> of Buenos Ayres might be expelled in turn! From this, it was natural for me to infer,
> that he had already endeavored to excite his partisans in Chili to raise the standard of
> civil war; but that on the approach of a new danger from the common enemy, he had
> resolved to postpone his design, until they were a second time driven out by San Martin.
> For my part, I could see no object to be answered by such an act, but that of placing
> the family of Carrera in power.

Revenge, Brackenridge decided, was Carrera's chief motivation.

On the evening of February 26, the commissioners and their secretary, and
others attached to the mission, embarked on an hermaphrodite brig, a dirty
and unfinished boat appropriately named the "Malacabada," for the difficult
passage upriver to Buenos Aires, happy to leave the depressing atmosphere of
Montevideo.[17] Several women occupied the cabin: "Thus crowded together
on deck, with scarcely room to turn round in this crazy vessel, no one would
have suspected that the *Malacabada* carried a mission from the great republic
of the north, to the rising republic of the south." The owner of the "Malacabada," however, was proud of his boat, which a pampero had never yet
seriously damaged. In conversation with him Brackenridge soon learned that
he was a Buenos Aires patriot, a member, incidentally, of a most respectable
family. The young patriot had once lived in the United States, a fact which
explained his command of the English language. From him Brackenridge
obtained a mass of information, especially opinions on political affairs, including an unflattering characterization of Carrera. Brackenridge plied his new
acquaintance with questions before wrapping himself in his overcoat and
falling asleep on the deck in the chill air.

In the morning the southern shore of the Plata was visible in the distance.[18]
The heat became oppressive as midday approached, almost unbearable to the
passengers on the exposed deck. But Brackenridge made the time pass faster
by engaging several residents of Buenos Aires in conversation—in Spanish.
As patriots the news of the mission from the United States elated them. The
people of their country, they assured Brackenridge, hoped to establish a government like that of the United States. In the evening, after a festive glass,
they entertained the company on board with a national song. That night, too,
Brackenridge had his first taste of maté, the herb of Paraguay, which, being

pleasantly bitter, reminded him of Chinese tea. At dawn the "Malacabada" reached the outer roads before Buenos Aires, six miles from shore, but glided slowly to within a half-mile of land before casting anchor. The fog lifted, and "our impatient eyes beheld *the celebrated seat of liberty and independence of the south.*"

There, in Buenos Aires, on March 3, Brackenridge and Dr. Baldwin happened to sit side by side attending to their correspondence and joyously imbibing the air of freedom. "I will say," Dr. Baldwin wrote to Dr. Darlington, "that already I feel myself more at home, than I did at Rio de Janeiro: and Mr. BRACKENRIDGE, who is writing along side of me, concurs with me in opinion. We feel that we are among a people more like ourselves."[19] Dr. Baldwin, furthermore, advised his correspondent that he himself had caught the spirit of a people fighting for their independence: "There is,—as Mr. BRACKENRIDGE has just observed,—an union of sentiments, and interests, felt between the members of *Republics,* which the subjects of despotism never can feel,—even towards each other." In Rio de Janeiro, Dr. Baldwin's great interest was botany, which, he now found and was willing to admit, had given way to his enthusiasm for the patriot cause, although not completely.

Unknown to Brackenridge sitting beside him, Dr. Baldwin paid him a compliment in the letter to Dr. Darlington. "By the bye—I will just *quietly* hint, that I think Mr. B. will be likely to do as much service, in this commission, as the commissioners themselves," wrote the good-natured surgeon, who shortly was even more positive in expressing his admiration for Brackenridge's ability and zeal—and for a special reason.

A few days earlier they had come on shore together in company with the owner of the "Malacabada," a lieutenant from the "Congress," and the purser.[20] From the river Buenos Aires had looked to Brackenridge like a massive fortification stretching along the bank for several miles. When shallow water stopped the boat from the "Malacabada" about a hundred yards from the wharf, the party transferred to a two-horse cart with huge wheels. At the edge of the river washerwomen were busy, and some onlookers on the wharf viewed the landing without much interest. But this advance party from the American mission had surprised the government and people of Buenos Aires by arriving without fanfare. In Brackenridge's opinion, the unostentatious arrival of the mission gave them an example of real republicanism, which was characterized by simplicity and humility.

As soon as he had secured lodgings in a hotel, Brackenridge was eager for a walk about the city.[21] He quickly learned why Buenos Aires had no use for fire engines—the houses had but little wood in their construction. But he was particularly taken by the charming patios and the iron gratings at all the windows. The whole town, he noted, formed a fortification which could be easily defended: ". . . I do not know a worse situation in which an enemy could be, than in one of these streets." The streets, however, were filthy and generally in disrepair. But the people on the streets breathed an air of freedom. As he walked up one street and down another, he felt more and more that he was in a land of freedom, observing "an independence, an ingenuousness in the carriage, and an expression in the countenance of those I met, which reminded me of my own country. . . ." No trappings of royalty, or signs of nobility, could be found anywhere in the city. Even the women of Buenos Aires strolled about breathing the air of freedom. He remarked the Gauchos on horseback clustering about the grogshops, the enormous wagons drawn by oxen, the peddlers of fruit and milk, the priests and monks, the market place, the plaza, and some pampas Indians: "Buenos Ayres may very justly be compared to the bust of a very beautiful female, placed upon a pedestal of rude unshapen stone."

The next day, a Sunday, Brackenridge was still as fascinated by the sights of the city and its vicinity as the most avid tourist.[22] He visited several churches, including the cathedral which covered nearly an entire square. As a young man, however, the beauty of the women of Buenos Aires, dressed in their Sunday finery, fixed his attention—"They walk more elegantly than any women I ever saw." But he also watched the regular troops and the civic militia parade. In the afternoon he was not too tired to stroll into the country with Dr. Baldwin and a citizen of Buenos Aires whom they had met. They passed the arena where bullfights were held. Brackenridge was pleased to learn that the revolutionary government frowned on the brutal entertainment and that it was less popular than formerly. Another reform which the new regime had promoted was the abolition of "the silly custom which prevailed here, as well as at Rio, of throwing waxballs filled with water, at people in the street" during the carnival. On their walk in the country the two sight-seers and their escort called at a mansion where the owner, a supporter of the revolution although a native of Old Spain, engaged them in a lively political discussion. Here Brackenridge was informed that the mission from the United States was the subject of much conjecture in Buenos Aires.

On the morrow, Monday, the commissioners directed Brackenridge to wait on Gregorio Tagle, the secretary of state, to request an official interview for them.[23] Brackenridge was accompanied to the offices of government at the fort by the American consul, Thomas L. Halsey. As a citizen of the United States, Brackenridge took an unfavorable notice of the guards stationed about, the display of bayonets, which he considered a barbarous remnant of pageantry left from the days of the viceroys. He found Tagle at work in his office: "I stated to him the occasion of my visit, and at the same time, presented a newspaper containing the president's message, in which the objects of the mission were succinctly set forth." Tagle, "a small well set man, about forty years of age, of a dark complexion, with a keen penetrating eye," being polite in the Spanish style, insisted that Brackenridge designate the time of the commissioners' visit, whereupon the following Wednesday was named. Their reception by Tagle, however, was formal and brief, for, after paying their respects to him, they requested a meeting with Juan Martín de Pueyrredón, the Supreme Director of the state.

About noon the next day Pueyrredón received the mission cordially.[24] The members, accompanied by their secretary, were welcomed at the fort and at the director's apartments by several hundred smiling people. The commissioners and Brackenridge went again through various offices to reach the one occupied by Tagle, who then conducted them upstairs, where they passed between two lines of officers standing at attention in a large hall before Pueyrredón's apartments. The Supreme Director favorably impressed Brackenridge, being a dignified man of middle age, of medium height, but a bit stout. He was fair in complexion and blue-eyed. Although a revolutionary, Pueyrredón was temperate in his conduct. He was known as a hard worker in his office. This was the man, then, to whom Rodney stated the object of the mission. In reply, the Supreme Director expressed the friendliest sentiments, stressing the natural sympathy existing between the Americans of the North and the Americans of the South. "You will see many things amongst us, to excite your surprise. *We are a people who are just beginning to be,*" he added. To assist the commissioners in collecting information, Pueyrredón recommended waiving all diplomatic forms. Rodney answered the address briefly—then the American mission departed.

Despite the willingness of both parties to dispense with diplomatic falderal, an embarrassing incident occurred.[25] After the meeting with Pueyrredón, the commissioners received a number of callers, some of whom were returning the visit to him. A general and other distinguished officers, in fact, repaid the call on the Supreme Director immediately—"The general made a long harangue, which did not amount to much, and then took his leave." Then came members of the city council, and even the secretary of the treasury. But that evening an honor guard and a band unexpectedly appeared in the patio of the place where the commissioners were lodged. The officers in charge stated the Supreme Director had sent them. The commissioners, nevertheless, politely refused the guard of honor, although welcoming the musicians who played for several hours to a gathering of ladies and gentlemen of Buenos Aires and to many, also, "that could not with propriety be ranked under either of these denominations." The following morning Rodney and Bland visited Pueyrredón to explain the dismissal of his guard. He anticipated their explanation by saying agreeably that he had merely executed the wishes of his fellow citizens —the guard was a mark of respect to the mission. It was the right of the commissioners, he said also, to accept or decline the guard as they chose. This custom of posting a military guard, Brackenridge conjectured later, was a remnant of Spanish show.

But the matter of housing was a vexatious problem from the moment the mission had landed in Buenos Aires.[26] No one was satisfied with his temporary lodgings. A few gentlemen attached to the mission were anxious to move into other quarters "in order to avoid being teazed to death by a certain race, not to be named in good house-wifery." The general belief, as Brackenridge reported, was that the brick floors of their rooms favored "the multiplication of these tormentors." A search for a furnished house, large enough to accommodate everyone and fair in rent, meanwhile proved futile. Finally, Halsey, the consul, offered his own residence, which the commissioners reluctantly accepted, not wanting to inconvenience him. Brackenridge refused to join his colleagues in the new quarters because for twelve dollars a month he had rented a furnished room opening on a patio, a jessamine on one side of the door and an aromatic shrub on the other. His landlady, a widow, kept her home immaculate; and, best of all, she knew the important people in Buenos Aires, many of whom visited her frequently.

With the formalities of their arrival over and settled in comfortable quarters, the members of the mission received visitors and returned their calls, a duty which took much time but yielded some information, and keenly observed the life about them in the city and in the country.[27] Brackenridge noticed the preponderance of the military and the clergy among the callers, although he subsequently learned that many of the officers were not professional soldiers. He often saw the aged Dr. Gregorio Fuñes, the historian and dean of the Cordova cathedral, indeed cultivating "his acquaintance with assiduity, and through him became acquainted with a number of others, who frequented his house." Brackenridge spent many delightful evenings at the home of San Martín's father-in-law, where he danced the minuet; and Dr. Baldwin was overjoyed to meet Aimé Bonpland, the French naturalist who now lived with his family only two miles from town. But Brackenridge was disappointed to discover that some of his own countrymen, resident in Buenos Aires, unjustly belittled, and even damned, the work of the men in power there, seeking to prejudice the minds of the commissioners: "As the secretary of the mission, I was particularly exposed to this kind of importunity, from a supposition that I would be a convenient channel . . . ." Many of the critics, of course, were involved in privateering and desirous for a war with the Portuguese. They naturally favored the cause of Artigas—and likewise Carrera's interest.

Now, in March, however, it seemed certain to most people in Buenos Aires that Carrera's enemies were triumphant—that his was a dying cause. In January, 1818, O'Higgins and his supporters had written a Chilean Declaration of Independence. Then, on February 12, freedom from the Spanish monarchy was proclaimed in the plaza of Santiago. When this intelligence reached Buenos Aires, about ten days after the arrival of the American mission, there was public rejoicing for three days.[28] Brackenridge watched the exercises and the illuminations appreciatively, but he was most interested in the patriotic exhibitions performed by the youth of the city at the pyramid of the revolution in the plaza. Each commissioner from the United States received a printed copy of the Chilean declaration and medals in commemoration of the event, which was the outcome of San Martín's scaling the Andes with an army—a brilliant feat in itself—and then defeating the Spanish.

Despite the proclamations and the celebrations, Chilean independence was not yet a certainty. Brackenridge sympathized with the inhabitants of Buenos Aires when the disheartening news of the march of the royalist army on Santiago replaced the glowing report of Chilean independence—and San Martín's army appeared in great danger across the mountains.[29] How gloomy was Buenos Aires! San Martín's enemies worked to discredit him; Carrera's friends were gleeful, full of "secret satisfaction, which they could with difficulty conceal." Their conduct disgusted Brackenridge. But their day was short, for soon came the authentic account of San Martín's victory over the royalists, April 5, on the plains of Maipú, thereby insuring the independence of Chile from Spain. Never had Brackenridge seen such an expression of popular feeling as the exhibition of joy which now erupted in Buenos Aires.

After witnessing such scenes—a whole people "one day depressed, and the next extravagantly elated"[30]—and for weeks experiencing life among them, Brackenridge was homesick. Buenos Aires was interesting enough, as was the whole country, and the people likable. But there were various customs, and certain conditions, which irritated the visitor from the United States—bullfights, for example. Although losing popularity, according to Brackenridge's information, they were still barbarous, as he discovered when the amusement was resumed after Lent.[31] The picadors, he was astounded to note, actually arrived at the arena in irons, for they were criminals condemned to amuse the public by fighting bulls. Armed with pikes, their function was to wound the bull. Others teased the bull by waving colored flags before him and by thrusting firecrackers into the orifices of his body and exploding them: "The crackers being consumed, the animal stood still, his tongue lolling out, with panting sides and eyes blind with rage." Then the matador killed him with a sword thrust. As far as Brackenridge could tell, only coarse people attended the spectacle—no public officials were present as spectators. Countless such impressions as this gruesome one of the bullfights, and the Carreristas' hatred of San Martín as another, finally convinced Brackenridge that "THERE IS BUT ONE AMERICA LIKE OURS."[32]

Indeed, everyone attached to the mission was impatient to return to his native land. But Bland, the friend of Carrera, first wanted to cross the Andes for a visit to Chile. On April 15, he left Buenos Aires on the long journey, arriving at Santiago early in May.[33] Bland, who sailed from Valparaiso in July and reached the United States in October, was the only commissioner who traveled to Chile. Late in April the other members of the mission had departed from Buenos Aires to return to the "Congress," which had not risked going up the river for them.[34] The frigate weighed anchor off Montevideo on April 29. There was a stop at Maldonado for supplies, where a pampero endangered the ship—as Brackenridge wrote later, "we considered our escape peculiarly fortunate." A passage of twenty-five days brought the "Congress" in sight of Bahia, or São Salvador.

Commodore Sinclair took his ship into the harbor without a pilot. At the approach the harbor had appeared a "forest of masts" to the watchers on deck.[35] The American consul, Henry Hill, welcomed the mission to this part of Brazil, where the members found São Salvador a pleasant contrast to Rio de Janeiro, another Portuguese city, being better constructed and cleaner. After the loading of supplies, the "Congress" was ready to put to sea again on June 5, and the next day gained the open water. The frigate now made a fast run along the coast to the island of Margarita, where the mission obtained information favorable to the cause of Venezuelan independence.[36] During their brief stay on the island, the members made a short trip inland to the village of Assumption to interview the governor, on the way noticing many fortifications. It was the American mission which brought the first news of the victory of Maipú to the inhabitants of Margarita.

"We spent but two days at this interesting Island," Dr. Baldwin reported to Dr. Darlington on July 7, as the "Congress" approached the United States south of Cape Henry.[37] With "joyful hearts, after so long an absence," the company on board impatiently waited for the frigate to arrive in Hampton Roads and at Norfolk. Brackenridge, however, came home with a bitter heart, although he was happier after Bland had left his fellow commissioners for the trip to Chile. Dr. Baldwin, who knew the treatment accorded the secretary on the mission and was sympathetic, praised his work unqualifiedly. "I cannot, however, but add," Dr. Baldwin wrote to Dr. Darlington, "that this mission to South America will derive a great deal of its importance from the talents, acquirements, and indefatigable exertions of Mr. BRACKENRIDGE, —of whom I have spoken in my former letters. He has taken up the cause of the South Americans with a zeal which does equal honor to his head and his heart."

Dr. Baldwin had certainly spoken of his friend Brackenridge in previous letters. But there was no hint of any Brackenridge eccentricity. Dr. Baldwin was determined to give Brackenridge his due in an obvious attempt to counteract any unfavorable reports which Bland, or perhaps Graham, might have sent to the United States to tarnish his reputation. From São Salvador Dr. Baldwin had written to Dr. Darlington "that Mr. BRACKENRIDGE, from his knowledge of the Spanish language, is eminently qualified for obtaining useful and correct information,—and he has lost no time in attending to it. He has unquestionably added greatly to the importance of the mission . . . ."[38]

After the "Congress" had reached Norfolk, Selleck Osborn printed in his Wilmington gazette a letter, written in Buenos Aires, March 11, "by a gentleman attached to the Congress Frigate, was designed for his Correspondent in this country; but as, from some circumstances, it is supposed to have miscarried, it has since been obligingly communicated, by the writer."[39] The writer was undoubtedly Dr. Baldwin, who, in concluding the letter, had expressed his belief that both the mission itself and the general public would be benefited immensely by Brackenridge's labors on the voyage: "His talents, industry, and complete knowledge of the Spanish language, have enabled him to amass a vast fund of the most interesting information, which I hope he will lose no time in making public." This statement, with its reference to Brackenridge's conscientious attention to business and his mastery of Spanish, was another deliberate refutation of charges which Bland had made against him as secretary of the mission. "He was among the first of his countrymen, who began to entertain correct views of the South Americans; as his letters addressed to the President of the United States, before he visited Buenos Ayres, will testify," Dr. Baldwin asserted in defense of Brackenridge. In Baltimore Niles promptly reprinted[40] the letter from Osborn's *American Watchman*. Thus, before the end of August, 1818, Brackenridge's conduct on the mission, as viewed by one observer, was made a matter of public record, although the name of the author of the testimonial was not revealed.

But in the meantime, on July 24, President Monroe "in confidence" had shown Secretary of State Adams a letter written by Bland in Buenos Aires to Skinner, in which the commissioner was highly critical of both Pueyrredón and Tagle.[41] Bland, moreover, had indicated that he was dead-set against the recognition of the Buenos Aires government by the United States. In this confidential letter which had fallen into Monroe's hands (that is, been "communicated to him"), Bland had written disparagingly about Brackenridge, or in the words of Adams himself: "It appears from Bland's letter to Skinner that he quarrelled with Brackenridge on board the ship, and that they had no intercourse with each other after they landed."[42]

Brackenridge, however, subsequently described the situation to William Shaler, insisting that the mission had been "wretchedly composed."[43] In his characterization of the three commissioners, Brackenridge was scathing, although indicating a high regard for Rodney. Graham, in the secretary's opinion, was "a lazy, well meaning, kind of man, much afflicted with the affectation of dyplomacy—secret as a mouse—possessing no original views, and not capable . . . of forming an opinion about any thing." Brackenridge did not have to say more, for, as he reminded Shaler, "Graham you know. . . ." Bland, the secretary of the mission had to admit, was industrious and "had mind, but of such a kind that it had been better to have had none—he is a wrongheaded man, totally unqualified for the business on which he was sent." Brackenridge considered Rodney "a good man, but a mere child."

There was nothing disloyal about such a characterization of the commissioners, for, at the time of his writing to Shaler in April, 1819, Brackenridge was really the late secretary of the mission, as it no longer existed. But Bland's treatment of him still rankled in his breast. Always, Brackenridge informed Shaler, Rodney was kind and friendly; and Graham was not a cause for complaint, "although he is a heartless selfish man."[44] Bland was the troublemaker: ". . . Bland, actuated by a despicable jealousy, took great pains to convince me, that he entertained a contemptuous opinion of me. The situation I assure you was rendered by this beast, one of the most unpleasant."

The animosity between the commissioner and the secretary increased after the mission's return to the United States. The controversy in which they were involved continued for several years. To clear his name in this struggle with the Carreristas and the privateersmen, in which they besmirched his character and challenged his fitness for the post of secretary on the recent mission, Brackenridge appealed to Read to answer the charges. Read, whom Selleck Osborn once described as "a young gentleman of singular intelligence and acquirements,"[45] was happy to undertake this service. "You have requested me to state what I know as to the charges preferred against you, and your general conduct and services while secretary of the late mission to South America. This statement I have neither the right nor the inclination to withhold."[46]

Read's statement vindicated Brackenridge's conduct and his honor as well:

211

Holding no official station in the mission, I accompanied, I was, of course, as to it not an actor but a spectator.

Soon after the Commissioners left the United States I perceived among them jealousies, little honourable to those who entertained them, and highly detrimental to the public service. I perceived that disgust was caused by the independence with which you maintained your opinions in all discussions, an independence, however, tempered by due respect for the seniority and rank of your associates. A determination to regard you as a mere underling, and to treat you as nothing more than a *copying machine,* speedily became apparent. Your situation was most trying. You displayed integrity and firmness, and, though sometimes betrayed into asperity when mildness would have been better, I may add, you displayed prudence.

Brackenridge, therefore, had not been insubordinate.

According to Read, there was no foundation to the charge—"want of veracity"—made against Brackenridge:

> The charge—*want of veracity*—appears to be entirely made with reference to the *party-disputes,* which, unfortunately, have agitated, and still embroil the infant republics of South America. We citizens of the United States are very prone to become partisans; as soon as we heard of these disputes we became San Martin-men or Carrera-men, sided with Buenos Ayres, or swelled the ranks of Artigas and the provinces. More importance has been ascribed to these and other South Americans than they deserved. We have been led falsely to believe that the liberties of South America must stand or fall with San Martin and Puerreydone, or Artigas and the Carreras. . . . From what I learned in South America, and since my return, I have concluded that Buenos Ayres, though too grasping, is not a tyrant, and the provinces, though unreasonably jealous of her influence, and not sufficiently grateful for her superiour exertions and sacrifices in the common cause, are not anarchical; in short, I am convinced that, as in all controversies, there are faults on both sides, and that on questions, obscured by the weakness of fools, and artifice of knaves, rendered also difficult of elucidation from the remoteness of the country to which they relate, men may express opinions diametrically opposite, and yet not be liars.

Likewise, Read refuted the spiteful accusation that Brackenridge was a sot:

> The charge of *intemperance* is rather insinuated than broadly made. It seems as if a transient feeling of compunction had made your calumniator falter in the very act of preferring this accusation. Intemperance, a vice which numbers among its victims men of the brightest intellects and most generous feelings, cannot be hidden from intimates. Hypocrisy may hide envy, malice and revenge from all eyes but those of the omnipotent, but it can be no mask to the drunkard. However furtively the glass may be quaffed, sparkling eyes, flushed cheek, tottering gait, and unwonted loquacity will proclaim the potation. I was for six months with you on shipboard; had you been a sot I must have known it; during this period I never saw you intoxicated. But I know the sole ground on which your adversaries rely in support of this charge. Sandy indeed is the foundation on which they have builded it. During the evening of that day, on which, the despatch, announcing the victory of Maipu, was received at Buenos Ayres, her most respectable citizens flocked to the house of the Commissioners to pay them their respects. Group succeeded group until a late hour. All were received with a courtesy befitting representatives of our government. These visitants hailed us as brethren—embraced us —called upon us to join them in toasting our country—our constitution—San Martin, the Washington of the South—Had any man attached to the mission declined a single toast proposed on this joyous occasion by these warm-hearted South Americans he would have proved himself not only a very phlegmatic being but a sorry diplomatist. You need not,

surely, blush at having infringed on that evening one of the laws of temperance, which even ascetics would think, on such occasion, more honoured in the breach than in the observance.

Now Read disproved the charge that Brackenridge had been an incompetent secretary because he was "so ignorant of Spanish as to be unable to hold a conversation in that language." Such an accusation was unbelievable in Read's opinion: "I was, of course, never present at the interview between our Commissioners and Don Gregorio Tagle, but I heard you, almost every day, converse in Spanish; you always spoke fluently, appeared clearly understood by those to whom you addressed yourself, and to comprehend what they said without difficulty." But Read said more about this particular charge:

> I never heard, while in Buenos Ayres, that the Commissioners employed Mr. Niglos, or any other gentleman, to act in your stead as their interpreter. Had so gross an indignity been offered you, is it probable that you would have borne it in silence, or that others would not, at least, have whispered it? The sister of the Carreras, who were under sentence of death, requested the Commissioners to use their influence with the Supreme Director to obtain the pardon of her unfortunate relatives. The Commissioners refused, very properly, to interfere as representatives of our government, but, humanely, determined to request the pardon as a favour to themselves. Mr. Bland took the management of this business, and, for what reason I know not, employed Mr. W. G. Miller as his interpreter.

There was one other allegation which Read could not believe—that while Brackenridge labored zealously for the success of the mission, at the same time he had aspersed "the Commissioners in idle conversations. . . ."

Read thus dismissed every charge as groundless. Like Dr. Baldwin, Read appreciated the work Brackenridge had done as secretary of the mission to South America: "For the benefits, and they are numerous, which have resulted from the mission, the citizens of the United States are, I firmly believe, chiefly, Sir, indebted to you." Despite this zeal in the public service, Brackenridge found himself the victim of character assassination. But now he proved himself a fighter, as his father had been in similar situations!

XVI: *If I Err, I Will Err with Them*

In mid-July, 1818, immediately after landing at Norfolk, Brackenridge had continued his campaign for the recognition of the Buenos Aires government by the United States. With Bland still abroad, the time was opportune—to be sure, there was not a moment to waste in the struggle with the Carreristas.

Brackenridge's ally was Rodney, the commissioner, a fact which Secretary of State Adams at once surmised. He wondered whether they had given the President the idea of promoting the independence movement in South America, for, one day late in July, Monroe had startled Adams by directing him to propose to the British government a policy of cooperation for that very purpose.[1] When the Secretary of State had asked the President what part of South America he meant, he replied: "All South America, and Mexico, and the islands included." The shrewd Adams probed Monroe's mind, finding that "it was a crude idea, which he immediately abandoned. But I conjectured that either Rodney and Brackenridge, or the Richmond Enquirer, had put it into his head." The Secretary of State, also, dampened Monroe's enthusiasm by observing that Great Britain was not ready to entertain such a proposal. A few days later, in discussing South American affairs with John Calhoun, the secretary of war, Adams learned from him that Rodney and Brackenridge disagreed with Bland on the subject of recognizing the Buenos Aires government. The two cabinet members, furthermore, noted the activity of Rodney and Brackenridge in "filling the newspapers, through the Delaware Watchman, with publications to operate on the public opinion in favor of the recognition."[2] No commissioner, of course, had as yet submitted a report to the government—a report in which he was expected to present facts impartially and not to deliver opinions.

But Adams and Calhoun were correct in naming Osborn's *American Watchman* as Brackenridge's principal organ of propaganda. While the mission was in South America, the Wilmington editor had printed material favorable to the cause of South American recognition, whereas other editors had published reports of patriot disasters. Then to Osborn's joy, Dr. Baldwin and Thomas Rodney, the commissioner's son, arrived home in Wilmington and forthwith provided him with accurate intelligence for his subscribers, confirming a Norfolk dispatch about patriot successes. After interviewing Dr. Baldwin and young Rodney, Osborn enthusiastically predicted—"it is now next to certain"— that "the report of the Commissioners must furnish the desiderata required by our people and government for the acknowledgment of the independence, at least of Buenos Ayres, Chili, and Venezuela." The Fifteenth Congress, Osborn wrote, would have the glory of "embracing a first born sister, and lighting her path to the happiness which we have attained!"[3] Moreover, Read gave his translations of several Chilean documents to Osborn for publication.[4]

Another valuable channel of communication with the public for Brackenridge's purpose was Niles' respected repository of news. In his *Weekly Register* the Baltimore editor had long advocated the cause of South American independence and favored especially the Buenos Airean interest.[5] Niles and Brackenridge both opposed the Carrera faction.

The chief proponent of recognition in Congress was Henry Clay, the friend of Niles and Brackenridge. Clay's interest in the cause, however, did not antedate theirs. But it was the Kentuckian who had brought the question of recognition to the floor of the House of Representatives early in the spring of 1818, when the commissioners were in Buenos Aires. On March 24, during a consideration of the clause in the appropriation bill providing thirty thousand dollars as compensation to the commissioners, Clay had voiced his disapproval of such a mission to South America, which, he declared, could not obtain authentic information.[6] According to him, the right method was to send an intelligent and observant person whose purpose in visiting the southern countries was concealed. Clay proposed an amendment to appropriate eighteen thousand dollars for the outfit and the salary for one year of a minister from the United States to the United Provinces of Rio de la Plata. That same day, March 24, Clay initiated a debate on the question involved in his motion—the formal recognition of the independence of the Buenos Aires government. In his great speech,[7] lasting more than an hour, Clay echoed the sentiments which Brackenridge had expressed earlier in his anonymous *Letter* addressed to President Monroe. The next day, March 25, Clay concluded his argument in favor of recognition, speaking for three hours. The exciting debate continued until Saturday, March 28, when his motion was rejected by a vote of 115 to 45. Although the vast majority of the members voting sympathized with the patriot cause, they feared the possibility of a war with Spain.

His defeat in the House, however, did not discourage Clay, who had joined Brackenridge in the contest to win recognition for the South Americans. "I made . . . the proposition to Congress about which I conversed with you last fall," Clay explained to Brackenridge in midsummer, 1818, soon after the return of the mission to the United States. "Although opposed by the whole weight of the Executive, we had in support of it a respectable vote of pure and unmixed Republicans. I did not expect it to succeed, and my main object was to awaken and interest public attention in the great struggle to the South. That object, notwithstanding the efforts to misinterpret and misrepresent my motives, has been fully accomplished."[8] In this letter of August 4, Clay thanked Brackenridge for the letters he had sent him from Buenos Aires and Norfolk: "Without presenting to the public your name or mine, I took the liberty of having published so much of your letter from B. Ayres as I thought it was proper for the public to see. It has been every where read with great avidity. I shall not allow to be published any part of your letter from Norfolk that will commit you, not even with the Judge." The Kentuckian, therefore, was using every possible means to arouse the public to the support of the Buenos Airean cause. But he frankly did not expect the Monroe administration or the public to benefit much from the work of the commissioners, for Brackenridge's account of the dissension in the mission served to convince Clay of the futility of sending several men to one or two large cities to gather information, as he had maintained in the House in March. "My opinion has constantly been that we were to look to you for any interesting collection of facts that might be made, and I yet promise myself much satisfaction from conversing with you, which I am eager to do as soon as possible," he assured Brackenridge. "Where will you be in October & November? Do you mean to favor the public with any account of your travels? Or are we to expect nothing but what being reported to the President will be communicated by him to Congress?"

As it happened, Brackenridge had written Clay from Carlisle on August 3; their two letters, consequently, crossed in the mail. In Lexington Clay answered[9] his correspondent's latest letter on August 18, noting that Brackenridge now admitted having written from Norfolk when his mind had not "recovered its tone and whilst you were yet smarting with the recollection of undeserved treatment. I thought so from the tenor of it, and altho' I shewed it confidentially to one or two friends, I did not permit any part of it to be published." Clay certainly had no intention to compromise his friend and ally. But at this time in mid-August, Clay put several more questions to Brackenridge:

> You obligingly offer to answer any enquiries I may make. I do not wish prematurely to lift the veil which may cover the transactions of your mission; but if it should not be improper I should like to know whether the Commissioners have made any report to Government, and if any of what tenor? whether it was prepared at Buenos Ayres before the separation of the Commissioners, or since the return of two of them?
> I learn from a friend at Washington that the "long and short of Mr. Graham's opinion is that the affairs of the Patriots are not in a situation to justify any change in the course our Government has hitherto pursued towards them, nor would their affairs in his opinion be benefited by our interference." Is this an opinion formed at Buenos Ayres or at Washington since Mr. G's return?

There was another question which Clay added as a postscript: "Could you not favor the public with a pamphlet presenting your own views and observations during your late mission?" But elsewhere in his letter, Clay, who had learned that Brackenridge had been nominated at Baltimore as a candidate for the Maryland legislature, wished him success in the race.

But what chance did Brackenridge have in seeking election to the House of Delegates as a member from Baltimore, the privateering center? Despite his controversy with Bland and the Carreristas, he had made many friends in the city through his legal and literary endeavors—he was well-known in the most fashionable circles. In his walks about town in the past, he had formed a wide acquaintanceship among the citizenry: "But still more important was the practice of stump speaking among candidates, which had recently been introduced, and it so happened that I became almost immediately successful and popular in that line."[10] The candidates—and Brackenridge as one of them—delivered their harangues from a small elevation before the courthouse.

A victory in the election likely meant public approval of Brackenridge's South American policy. This was undoubtedly the chief reason he became a candidate for the legislature. Six candidates—one Federalist and five Republicans—contested for the two seats. Although not recommended by the Republican ward committees, Brackenridge was a victor on election day, October 5. He received 2,986 votes in comparison with the 3,739 cast for the other winner, but the candidate next highest had only 1,845.[11] Brackenridge himself considered his election a rebuff to the privateersmen engaged in plundering the Portuguese commerce. "The great majority by which I was elected . . . to the legislature, in spite of all the efforts of these men, sufficiently prove that publick opinion is in my favour," he wrote Shaler afterward.[12]

"There are men in this place, whom the whole community are satisfied have participated in the infamous plunder of the Portuguese commerce; although no admirer of that nation, I have not hesitated to declare my abhorrence of the practice," Brackenridge informed Shaler. "This is a cause of ill will between me and Bland, whose son in law Skinner, is implicated; but these men are supported by some influential men at Washington *who have the ear of the President*."[13] The problem of the Artigan privateers, of course, was a constant harassment for Corrêa, the Portuguese minister at Washington. The Baltimore election was hardly over when Corrêa in desperation tried to employ Brackenridge "in a legal capacity,"[14] without doubt as a counsel in cases to win indemnity for losses sustained by Portuguese commerce. But until that matter was arranged, providing Brackenridge were willing, Corrêa hoped that his friend would publish the facts about the freebooters: "In the mean time I am sure your own honorable feelings, and love of truth have made you exert your abilities as a writer."

As early as mid-August, in fact, Brackenridge was planning to write an account of his experiences on the voyage to South America, for at that time Dr. Baldwin, who happened to be in Philadelphia, wrote Dr. Darlington that the late secretary of the mission was in Wilmington "and will remain there until he prepares for publication."[15] Then, directly from Wilmington in late October, Dr. Baldwin reported to Dr. Darlington that Brackenridge was about to return to Baltimore, having expressed a wish "to see you, and have some conversation on S. American Politics."[16] Aside from any time spent in Baltimore electioneering, Brackenridge had worked in the congenial atmosphere of Wilmington on the documents collected for the mission in South America.

"Since my return from South America, in July last, I have been almost continually engaged in making translations, copying papers &c, belonging to the business of the mission," Brackenridge advised Secretary of State Adams the first week in November. "I may therefore consider myself, as having been, at least eighteen months, instead of eight months, in the service of the government of the United States."[17] After all, Brackenridge had left for New York the end of July, 1817, although the mission did not sail until December. The period seemed a long time to him to be without a regular income. The government still owed him five hundred dollars of his stipulated compensation. Because the commissioners had received an additional compensation by reason of the delay in sailing, Brackenridge now claimed an extra allowance *"in the same proportion"*—one thousand dollars more.

Brackenridge addressed this request to Adams in the form of a letter, dated November 4, instead of waiting on him personally, knowing that only two days before the Secretary of State had received word of his mother's death. Brackenridge could not stay longer in Washington, where he had been with Rodney, whose report at last was ready to submit to the government. Perhaps it was well that Brackenridge did not see Adams at this time, for the President, as the Secretary of State had discovered on November 2, was unhappy about the apparent reluctance of the commissioners to agree on a report which all three could sign.[18] Bland had just arrived in the United States from Valparaiso, opposed as ever to the Buenos Aires government; whereas Rodney and Graham, who had originally thought a joint report possible, learned otherwise when they were unable to compromise certain differences in opinion. "Rodney, the President hinted, is under the influence of Brackenridge, the Secretary to the Commission, who is a mere enthusiast, and so devoted to South America that he has avowed the wish to unite all America in conflict against all Europe," Adams recorded in his diary. "Rodney, therefore, traces the South American to the North American revolution, and identifies them together in a manner which the President thinks will be offensive to the European allies; and he hinted that Rodney's report would be purposely adapted to the views rather of Clay and the opposition than to those of the Administration." The President was certain, according to Adams, that Rodney's report would paint "everything at Buenos Ayres as he saw it, couleur de rose, and that it will be used as a weapon of party." Barely a week before this meeting of Monroe and Adams, Niles had published a lengthy editorial on the new republics of the South, predicting confidently that the commissioners' report would be favorable to a policy of recognition.[19] Although an impassioned editorial, excellently written, it represented wishful thinking!

But Rodney's report itself[20] could not have been an outright disappointment to Niles. Although the document bore the date of November 5, probably to accord with the date of Graham's, Adams actually received it two days earlier. In his opinion, the report stamped Rodney as "an enthusiastic partisan of the South American cause," consisting "of a very superficial historical review of the South American Revolution, and an apologetic eulogium upon the present Government of Buenos Ayres."[21] Osborn, of course, praised the report in his newspaper and characterized Rodney's course as "manly" and statesmanlike for advocating the recognition of the United Provinces in his covering letter to Adams. In spite of his sympathy for the patriots, Niles felt constrained to correct his fellow editor by printing Osborn's editorial with the comment: "We have reason to believe that Mr. Rodney has not offered any opinion as to the expediency of acknowledging the independence of Buenos Ayres."[22] Niles was not mistaken, although Rodney had implied in his report that Buenos Aires deserved recognition.

The morning of November 4, the day after he had received Rodney's report, Adams discussed the embarrassing disagreement among the late commissioners with Daniel Brent, who was Graham's successor as chief clerk in the State Department. Brent was a civil servant with long experience in the office there and a respectable man whose opinion carried weight with his superior.[23] Brent informed him that the dissension among Rodney, Graham, and Bland was greater than ever. "Purviance, lately returned from Baltimore, says it is currently reported there that Bland was concerned in the South American privateering with Skinner, the Postmaster at Baltimore, and that he went to Chili on that business, upon the pretence of his public trust," Adams noted. "Rodney and Brackenridge countenance these reports, but Graham has entire confidence in Bland's integrity."[24] That same day Bland himself visited Adams at the State Department and promised to have his report ready within ten days.

But Graham, meanwhile, submitted his report[25] to the Secretary of State. In his covering letter to Adams, Graham declared that he and Rodney could not compromise their views in certain instances, although they differed on no really important fact. Graham decided to present his own report, as he explained to Adams, in order not to change the tenor of Rodney's by introducing observations on what his colleague had already written. Graham's report was naturally shorter, for the repetition of the general facts as stated by Rodney was unnecessary—originally, Rodney had undertaken the task of framing a joint report. The procedure adopted by Rodney and Graham, involving the production of separate reports, resulted in comparisons being made by many people, especially newspaper editors. Osborn, for example, advised his subscribers that Graham's report, though well written, was "more speculative in its style than practical, containing more reflections than fact, and is therefore not so replete with information and interest, as that of Mr. Rodney, nor does it bear those marks of research and observation which are visible in the latter."[26] Less partisan in his comments[27] was Morgan Neville, the acting editor of the *Pittsburgh Gazette,* who had anticipated a discrepancy in the reports, knowing the characters of the two men. He noticed the enthusiasm of Rodney and the caution and doubt of Graham as manifested in the documents.

However, it was Bland's report,[28] dated November 2, which Adams considered the best of the three submitted to him. Bland divided his lengthy document into two parts—the first concerning Buenos Aires and the second, Chile. "Bland alone, though he went out perhaps as great an enthusiast as any of the rest, saw the whole truth, and did not shrink from telling it out," Adams stated in his diary seven months after he had received and studied the three documents. "His report contained more solid information, and more deep and comprehensive reflection, than all the rest put together; but he is now attacked for it."[29] But Adams shortly had his faith in Bland's integrity shaken when, in the line of duty, he confronted the late commissioner with seeming evidence of his complicity in privateering.

The Carreristas, sharing responsibility for the divided commission and the production of three reports to the government instead of one, were for the moment victorious in the struggle with the Rodney-Brackenridge-Clay faction, which failed to win the administration for the Buenos Airean cause. Long before the second session of the Fifteenth Congress began, the partisan gazettes had devoted more and more space to the South American issue—as in 1793, when the Genet affair split the nation, editors now found themselves unable to discuss the question of the day dispassionately, although some of their writing, like Osborn's editorials, "A Broad View of Our South American Relations, Public and Private,"[30] "General Artigas,"[31] and "The Exiles from Buenos Ayres,"[32] was masterly. The Carrera press, represented by journals like the *Maryland Censor,* financed by Skinner as a counterbalance to Osborn's *American Watchman,* the *Baltimore Patriot,* and William Duane's Philadelphia *Aurora,* printed powerful propaganda against recognition of the South Americans. Osborn never hesitated to lock horns with the opposition editors. When the *Aurora* suggested that a monarchist faction in Buenos Aires aimed to establish a *"nobility hole"* there and a king on a throne, he counterattacked vigorously.[33] Nor did Osborn neglect to answer anonymous writers who challenged him from the columns of rival gazettes: "The letter which appeared in the Watchman, and upon which this writer has commented as the production of Mr. Brackenridge, was not written by that gentleman, but by another gentleman of talents and information, who has so little desire to *conceal* his name, that if the New York writer will come forward and request it, he may obtain it without difficulty. Will *he* do the same?"[34] When the editor of the *Aurora* attributed to Brackenridge the authorship of the editorial articles on South American affairs in the *American Watchman,* Osborn announced that he himself had written them.[35] But Osborn's devoted labors in the South American cause were in vain.

The Monroe administration, which viewed the South American question in the light of European developments as well as domestic politics, refused to alter its cautious foreign policy after the commissioners had reported to Adams. Monroe and his Secretary of State did not intend to jeopardize the negotiation of the Transcontinental Treaty—and a cardinal aim of Spanish policy was to prevent the recognition of the South American patriots by the United States. The split commission, therefore, was an administration victory, for a united commission representing the Rodney viewpoint and submitting reports in accordance not only might have forced a change in the neutral policy, disrupting the negotiations with Spain, but also would have enhanced the prestige of Clay. After the commissioners had touched at Rio de Janeiro and Sumpter had reported the stir caused by their visit, particularly in the diplomatic corps, Monroe himself wrote ex-President Madison: "Mr. Sumter thinks that our movements will be watched by all the allies. . . . This experiment, so far, shews that if a step, involving no very serious consequences, is viewed with such unfavorable eyes, in what light one of a bolder character would be seen. I have no doubt that it will produce a strong sensation among all the allies."[36] The President, fearful that a bold move might precipitate foreign intervention in the struggle between Spain and the colonies and an interposition not limited to a mere expression of views, sought the advice of Joel Poinsett, who had long resided in South America as a special agent for the United States. But, significantly, during his residence in Chile, Poinsett had become an intimate of the Carrera brothers! Monroe, nevertheless, had another report[37] to consult on the condition of South America. The upshot of Monroe's investigation of the state of affairs there by means of the mission was simply his satisfaction with the course already pursued by the United States government and a determination to continue it, as he declared in a message to Congress, dated November 16, 1818.[38] He hoped to promote the recognition of South American independence by the European allies as quickly as possible without a change in policy, believing that his mission to South America had helped to give the former colonies of Spain the advantages of recognition "without any of its evils."[39]

Only three days before Monroe sent his message to Congress, Niles published the first of two "Letters from South America,"[40] the second of which carried a by-line crediting the essay to Brackenridge. The late secretary was not expected to submit a written report to Adams, nor was he invited to present his views on South American affairs at a conference. Indeed, there is no mention of Brackenridge in the collection of reports and documents of the mission as communicated by Monroe to the Fifteenth Congress on November 17 and December 15. On the voyage, however, Brackenridge had kept a private journal which he later delivered to Rodney.[41] On this record Brackenridge must have depended for many of the countless details which made the two letters in the *Weekly Register* so colorful. The subject matter of both was a relation of his experiences in Buenos Aires, enlivened by provocative comments on what he saw and heard. No doubt Clay's hope that Brackenridge would publish a pamphlet about his voyage was an inspiration to him—but his determination to weaken, if not destroy, the Carreristas was productive of a two-volume classic, of which the two essays in the form of letters were extracts.[42]

By this time in mid-November Brackenridge's enemies were busy defaming him with the dual purpose of ruining him as an effective propagandist for the patriot cause and of nipping his political career in the bud. In his *Aurora* Duane charged Brackenridge with incompetence as secretary of the mission, especially as an interpreter.[43] This was a slander which, astonishingly, the editor of the *Federal Gazette & Baltimore Daily Advertiser* promptly picked up as ground for questioning Brackenridge's character as a representative in the next Maryland legislature. The late secretary refused to notice the charge, except to reply that any "gentleman who feels an interest in my character as a representative, and who thinks the charges brought against me of sufficient importance, will, by calling on me, obtain every necessary information."[44]

Such defamation did not injure Brackenridge's reputation at all, nor impair his usefulness as a representative of the city of Baltimore to the December session of the House of Delegates at Annapolis. Not only did he serve with honor, but also the following August, 1819, he confidently announced his candidacy[45] as a Republican for re-election to the legislature: "I lost no popularity in the legislature, but before the second election, the Missouri question arose, and as I took the side of Missouri against restriction, my Quaker friends left me, and in consequence my majority fell off to one thousand."[46] But it was during his first term that Brackenridge, summoning all his powers as an advocate, delivered his speech on the Jew Bill.

"On reading yesterday the Baltimore Telegraph I found the report of a Committee in favour of Judaism which is infinitely more disagreeable to my feelings than either Catholicism Mahometanism or Gentilism," wrote Judge John Young of Greensburg, shocked but not surprised, to Brackenridge. "It has occurred to me that you were one of that Committee and probably drafted the report."[47] Young, long a friend of the Brackenridges, father and son, knew their penchant for advocating unpopular causes, which usually meant being ahead of their times. The judge, a Swedenborgian,[48] had intended to write Brackenridge for information about his voyage to South America, being particularly interested in the state of morals and religion there; but with this startling development in the Maryland legislature, the reporting of a bill to extend to the Jews the same rights and privileges enjoyed by Christians, he waited no longer in addressing his young friend. He reminded Brackenridge of all the familiar arguments against giving the Jews the vote in Maryland, although he did not want them—"that unfortunate but stiff necked & rebellious people"—persecuted. In the judge's opinion, Brackenridge would be wise to remember that Christians elected him to his seat in the House of Delegates.

In his long speech in favor of the bill Brackenridge, in effect, answered the judge's letter—the speech "was indeed mainly prompted by that letter."[49] The entire speech[50] was composed without benefit of putting a single thought on paper, or having an outline to follow. But after its delivery Brackenridge wrote it out for preservation. He spoke for religious liberty, viewing the subject politically as another proponent of the bill had already discussed it theologically. Brackenridge attacked the provision in the Maryland constitution requiring a religious test for holding public office in the state. He framed three questions and answered them, thereby ascending to the first principles:

1. Have the Jews a *right* to be placed on a footing with other citizens?
2. Is there any urgent reason of state policy which requires that they should be made an exception?
3. Is there anything incompatible with the respect we owe to the Christian religion, in allowing them a participation in civil offices and employments?

He aimed the shafts of his argument at Judge Young and others who thought like him: "An odious exclusion from any of the benefits common to the rest of my fellow-citizens, is a persecution, differing only in degree, but of a nature equally unjustifiable with that whose instruments are chains and torture." He pointed out a monstrous inconsistency whereby a Jewish citizen of Maryland, who was ineligible to hold even the most insignificant office in his own state, could be elected the President of the United States—and in developing that idea, he rose in the highest flight of oratory. But the gist of his great speech was simply this: "Where the matter is a mere difference of opinion, I HOLD MY RIGHT UNQUESTIONABLE TO DIFFER FROM ANY OTHER MAN, OR FROM ALL MANKIND, BE THE SUBJECT WHAT IT MAY."

Had Judge Young heard Brackenridge deliver this speech at Annapolis, he would have thought old Hugh was speaking.

The debate on the Jew Bill, as the measure was popularly called, lasted three days.[51] But on January 22, 1819, the bill was defeated by a vote of 50 to 24. Both members from Baltimore, Brackenridge and Thomas Kell, voted for it, however. According to Niles, one important cause for its defeat was the near balance of parties in Maryland—political expediency killed a measure "which reason says is right, and which revelation does not forbid."

"I have warmly advocated the Jew bill in this House, because I beleive, *that governmet is tyrany, whenever it intermeddles with religion,*" Brackenridge replied to Judge Young from Annapolis. "In this, I am supported by the wisest assemblage of men this country ever witnessed; the framers of the Constitution of the United States. If I err, I will err with them."[52]

Thus Judge Young, whose opinion of the Jews was the accepted one in his day, had his answer. But Brackenridge's speech was immediately recognized for what it was—a noble one. Niles pronounced it "excellent" and admitted having "much pleasure in laying it before our readers, as honorable to the head and heart of the delegate from Baltimore."[53] The grateful Jews printed the speech in a pamphlet[54]—containing also the committee report, the bill itself, and Thomas Kennedy's speech—and circulated it throughout Maryland. Kennedy, really the originator of this move to enfranchise the Jews of the state, did not lose heart at the setback, nor did his supporters, for, after Brackenridge had departed for the West, they continued to work for the cause and eventually succeeded.[55] Then came the first fruits of victory in 1826, when S. Etting and J. I. Cohen were chosen members of the Baltimore city council: "They are such as we would (in the language of Henry the IV.) introduce either to the friends or the enemies of our city. They are the first Jews ever elected by the people to office in Maryland, being until lately denied the rights of citizens, by the constitution of the state."[56]

As indicated by his speech on the Jew Bill, Brackenridge had reached full stature as an advocate. But not many months after its delivery, Secretary of State Adams made a discreditable entry—that of June 4, 1819—in his diary, putting Brackenridge, and Rodney too, in a class with Baptis Irvine, a fanatic republican and a journalist, and W. G. D. Worthington, the United States agent at Buenos Aires and Chile, both of whom irritated him: Irvine "and Worthington and Rodney and Brackenridge all stand looking in ecstatic gaze at South America, foretelling liberty to it as the Jews foretell the Messiah."[57]

Brackenridge was not "a mere enthusiast" for the South American cause as the President had characterized him to Adams, or some kind of a fanatic as Adams himself had now intimated. Brackenridge could recognize tyranny in Maryland where the Jews lacked the vote as well as in South America where the colonists of decadent Spain aspired to freedom. In each instance his argument was the result of careful observation and sound judgment. "I assure you it was with reluctance I undertook to write, but it was a thing expected, and the ungenerous attempt to undervalue my services on the mission, urged me to the task," were the two reasons Brackenridge gave Peter S. Du Ponceau, the Philadelphia lawyer, for writing a report on South America, an unofficial report to the nation rather than for the government. "It has turned me aside from my profession. I was bred a lawyer, and it is by the profession of the law I must subsist—it is in the profession of the law that I wish to excel."[58]

But writing an account of the mission did not turn Brackenridge aside from his profession a long time. Early in April, after he had sounded Rodney on the idea of publishing proposals for the contemplated book, he received a caution in reply: "But in no event slight your professional business. You now occupy high ground, & you must improve it."[59] Such an admonition, of course, was not wise. Shaler understood Brackenridge's temperament better than Rodney; and he remembered, too, the fate of *The History of the Revolution of Texas,* which never saw publication. "I am now engaged in writing an account of the voyage," Brackenridge had written Shaler. "How this will turn out I know not. I had hoped that I should write no more books, but my destiny must be fulfilled."[60] Shaler, who was now the American consul general at Algiers and, incidentally, unhappy about his lot in the government service— "I find myself confounded with the common herd, and might probably be permitted to go quietly to sleep in Numidia, unregretted, and even unremembered"—received Brackenridge's letter at Gibraltar on July 4 and answered it the next day. "Your book I shall wait for with impatience, and I will repeat to you what I have often said, that you should not write it with too much precipitation, one good and well written book is worth a thousand hasty ones," Shaler advised him. "From what you have done, I conjecture that you might with care and patience immortalize your name."[61] Had Shaler's letter reached Brackenridge before the completion of the work on South America, the advice it contained could not have had any effect on him, for he was an impatient man anxious to get the task finished.

Brackenridge completed his work at a breakneck pace, continuing it in the style of his two "Letters from South America," which had appeared in the *Weekly Register* the previous November. But he took time to ask Clay to suggest questions on various topics which he thought should be treated in a discussion of the political, religious, and commercial conditions of the United Provinces. Clay, however, had taken a trip to Louisiana and could be of no help, except to say on his return that he trusted Brackenridge's "good sense" to select the proper subjects.[62] In April various literary notices announced to the public that Brackenridge's latest work, the *Voyage to South America, Performed by Order of the American Government, in the Years 1817 and 1818, in the Frigate Congress,* was being prepared for the press. Osborn[63] and Niles,[64] in particular, stressed the author's fitness for the task—in their opinion, his production would likely be the most interesting ever published about South America. Niles pointedly mentioned Brackenridge's command of the Spanish language as a special qualification for the work. By July the author, so fast had he written, actually finished the first volume. But near the end of the second volume he confessed to the reader in a footnote[65] that the tremendous undertaking had exhausted him: "I have omitted many interesting particulars, which I intended to have stated, suffering somewhat from indisposition, and being worn out by continual application for several months." Nevertheless, late in October, Niles heralded the completion of the *Voyage to South America* and its publication:

This interesting work is just now published in two neat 8vo volumes, price five dollars. Some extracts from it have been presented to the readers of the REGISTER, and we venture to say that it contains a greater mass of important information respecting the countries visited, than ever before, and all together, was known to the people of the United States. Every body is acquainted the fitness of Mr. B. for a work like this; and he has executed the task in his very best manner.[66]

But as soon as he had completed the first volume, Brackenridge sent a copy to Adams at the State Department.[67] This was the correct thing to do, for the Secretary of State was thereby given the opportunity to suggest changes in the book or even the removal of anything embarrassing to the Monroe administration. Because of his connection with the mission as secretary, Brackenridge realized that more importance would be attached to his statements in the work than they would otherwise merit; and accordingly, as he informed Adams, he limited himself as much as possible to observations on noncontroversial subjects like geography, history, and statistics of the places visited. There were certain differences of opinion noticeable between this new work and the pamphlet addressed to President Monroe, he also advised the Secretary of State, for in the earlier production his information was not as good and he wrote more as the advocate. "I have not touched on the conversations held with the officers of the government of Buenos Ayres," Brackenridge assured him. The author added that the second volume would have been completed within the week "but for a slight attack of bilious fever. It will be forwarded in the course of a fortnight."

There was something else which Brackenridge wanted Adams to know about the book:

> In the preface I allude to the attack made upon me in the Aurora, but I have reason to beleive originating much nearer home. Although as much of a South American patriot as a man ought to be, my zeal fell far short, or perhaps was of a different kind from that, of the patriots here. My patriotism rested on no foundation of private specu- lation, *in conjunction with M'Greggor, or with Carrera, or with Commodore Taylor.* It may be said that I allude to others in my preface, and in my book. I certainly do, and should those persons call upon me for a more particular explanation they will not find me backward in giving it. I have perhaps been actuated by false delicacy towards them. To speak more explicitly, I beleive in my heart, that the intimacy of Mr. Skinner and Mr. Bland, with the *patriot people,* has not been such as an American of high and honourable feelings could be proud to acknowledge. To my own knowledge Skinner corresponded with that blackguard ruffian Macgreggor, until he took his leave of Amelia island, and while here, he was their constant intimate. To Carrera, Skinner advanced five thousand dollars, in the prospect of future contracts and advantages in case of the success of Carrera. It was the business of his father in law Mr. Bland to recover this money at Montevideo, and afterwards in Chili. He made a demand of the money from the government of Buenos Ayres, according to the acknowledgment of Skinner to me in the presence of Mr. Rodney. The truth is, their ideas of gentlemanly propriety and delicacy of conduct, differs entirely from mine. Since my return I have not been on speaking terms either with Skinner or Bland, and I beleive never shall. The subject is a disagreeable one to me and I feel no wish to pursue it.

Secretary of State Adams certainly had a bit of intelligence to ponder now!

Brackenridge's preface, in which he publicly challenged the Carreristas, was a sparkling essay justifying the publication of the *Voyage.* "A common complaint is, the want of information on the subject of South America, but the meaning of all who make it, is not precisely the same," he began.[68] It was a mistake, he asserted, to think that the lack of knowledge was due to a deficiency of published works on the subject, for there was a plenitude of writings, ancient and modern, some of which were easily procurable for study, although others in their original editions were rare but still available in compilations. He listed the most prominent authorities whose works treated the geography, history, and statistics of New Spain and the lands to the South. According to Bracken- ridge, one explanation was, simply, that the study of South America had "not yet become fashionable. . . ."[69] The complaint that the available information was not up-to-date, however, was just. But he cited the recently published *Outline of the Revolution in Spanish America,* "By a South-American,"[70] as a meritorious contribution to the fund of knowledge. The reports of the three commissioners to South America, furthermore, provided many new facts for the interested public. "Why then it will be asked, do I swell the pile of unap-

227

propriated, neglected information, by the addition of two octavo volumes?"
was the question he now put to his readers.[71]

Brackenridge warned his readers not to expect an account of everything
known about the huge continent to the South. He described his task succinctly:
"I have undertaken to give a narrative of a voyage of nearly twenty thousand
miles, with all that I saw and heard, or could collect from authentic sources,
at the places where I touched. . . ."[72] The greatest need—and how well he
stated it!—was not a work which contained all the requisite information on
the general subject of South America but one "that should create a desire to
be informed."[73] Although he modestly denied having the capacity for such
an undertaking, he produced a stimulating work. As the author of the *Views*
and the *Journal,* he had learned the art of writing entertaining books of travel.
But, also, he boldly threw down the gantlet to the Carreristas in his preface:
"I am aware . . . that I have enemies—few in number, indeed, but malignant
—their attempts to injure me, whether open or concealed, I hold in equal
contempt. To the American public, to whom *I make my report,* I address myself
with confidence, fully convinced that its sentence will be just, even if against
me."[74] Then he told his readers how he had acquired a knowledge of the
French and Spanish languages by living on the borders of New Spain—a
knowledge, too, of the Spanish character and institutions and literature—and
how he had early sympathized with the patriots without becoming a partisan
of any particular faction. As for privateering, he had always condemned it—
"I consider it as an abominable abuse. . . ."[75] At this point his readers could
tell—that is, if they read the preface—that the *Voyage* would at least be provocative, if nothing else.

Also in the preface Brackenridge informed his readers about the research
necessary for the *Voyage.* "It is not by remaining a few months in a strange city,
or running full speed over uninhabited plains, that much profound knowledge
is to be obtained," he admitted candidly.[76] He himself talked with people
who had traveled in South America, and from them he extracted as much
information as possible. Then, on the mission, he became acquainted with all
classes of society, aided greatly by his situation as secretary without being
hampered in his pursuit of information by diplomatic formalities. In Buenos
Aires he collected every document imaginable: "I had the good fortune to
make an extensive collection of pamphlets, files of newspapers, and political
tracts. . . ."[77] He used Commodore Sinclair's papers and the commissioners'
reports. Despite the excellence of his materials and his effort to weigh the
evidence carefully, he pleaded guilty to the commission of many errors,
"alleging in mitigation, that authorship in this country is not a profession, that
it has been engaged in by me at the expense of the occupation by which I must

earn my bread."[78] After all, he was forced "to keep pace with the printer"—
there was no chance to correct and polish, the penalty for completing the work
in less than three months.[79]

The *Voyage* was a remarkable mass of information about South America,
related, of course, to the grand theme of the independence movement. The
author documented his material thoroughly and in the appendices printed the
reports of Rodney and Graham and his own *Letter* to President Monroe. But
nowhere in the entire work, not even in the lengthy introduction or in the
chapters descriptive of the places visited by the mission, was there tedious
reading. His style, as a reader familiar with the *Views* and the *Journal* might
expect, was informative but lively and colorful and personal. Brackenridge's
observations recalled the trenchant writing of his father:

A people must be educated and prepared for freedom.[80]

Lands are better cultivated by freemen in all climates; AND SLAVERY IS EVERY
WHERE A CURSE.[81]

Man is a moral agent, governed by intelligence, and urged forward by the impulse
of his feelings and passions. This is the fountain and secret of his strength and power.
All the worth and value of man, in society, is made up of honor, character, estimation
and opinion.[82]

What after all are forms of government, or political institutions, unless supported
by the education, habits, and virtues of a people? Without these the most perfect forms
that were ever conceived will be inefficient; *anarchy and despotism will merely change
hands, and hold an alternate sway.*[83]

Brackenridge was, obviously, a Jeffersonian like his father; and like his father,
Madison's classmate, he sang of the glory that was America. No wonder he
saw the American Revolution as the inspiration for the patriots of the South—
which it was. No wonder he doubted the patriotism of Carrera as he did, and
labeled the chieftain Artigas a barbarian. No wonder he attacked Bland and
the Carreristas throughout his work—more by innuendo than by blunt accusation—for, as he had told Adams, he did not wish to embarrass the Monroe
administration.

But how would the public receive Brackenridge's spirited report?

XVII: Return to Missouri

When Clay read in the gazettes about the publication of the first volume of the *Voyage* and then received a letter, dated August 5, 1819, from the author announcing publication, he was "eager to see it, and doubt not that I shall derive much pleasure and instruction from the perusal of it."[1] Not long before, the Kentuckian had read the *Letters on the United Provinces of South America, Addressed to the Hon. Henry Clay* by Vicente Pazos, a Buenos Airean exile. A native of Upper Peru, Pazos had written a short work which, as Clay assured Brackenridge, "has left to you an extensive field wholly unoccupied." But some months earlier, when Selleck Osborn learned of the publication of Pazos' book, he had advised his subscribers of his relief that "Mr. Brackenridge's 'Voyage to South America' has not yet passed the press, and may detect any imposition which may have been attempted."[2] The publication of Brackenridge's work was sure to cause a stir among his friends as well as his enemies.

In July Brackenridge sent Rodney a copy of the first volume of the *Voyage.* "I am delighted with your introduction," Rodney replied enthusiastically. "It supports, in detail, with the weight of authority, what I have stated in a general manner. In the texture of your work, you have interwoven a number of anecdotes, as I knew you would, equally entertaining & instructive. I shall be impatient to peruse the second volume."[3] Such encouragement helped Brackenridge to finish the *Voyage,* although his determination to best his calumniators was alone sufficient to drive him to its completion. William P. Brobson, who became an influential newspaper editor and a banker in Wilmington,[4] saw this first volume in Rodney's office and then informed the author that only favorable comments about it had appeared as yet in the papers but—"You do not, however, expect to escape the ordeal of Colonel Duane's criticism, as he will certainly return the fire you gave him last year."[5]

Some people tried to be helpful and encouraging to Brackenridge as he labored to complete the *Voyage.* His half brother, William, had seen an announcement of the work in a newspaper and immediately requested several subscription papers, offering to obtain subscribers. At the time of his writing, William was practicing law in Indiana, Pennsylvania, a county seat where, as the prosecutor ("not on account of merit but owing friends at the seat of Government"), he hoped to learn the ins and outs of the profession.[6] But, in turn, he asked a favor of Henry:

. . . You do not write? I discover in your letters to me (when you do write) that you write as if you were writing to a child, in the same style precisely, trifling circumstances which you think will suit my taste,—but that taste has altered since you last saw me, and I wish you hereafter to write to me as to one, who has left off his boyish tricks—

I now consider myself a *man,* (at least I wish to be considered as such) and shall endeavor to behave as a *man* through life.

William's proposal was fair enough! Peter S. Du Ponceau, also, not only sub-scribed to the *Voyage* but promised to try to induce his friends in Philadelphia to do likewise: "The times, however, are unfavorable, as Bank notes, now, are more fought after than Books."[7] He was not exaggerating the situation, for Brackenridge published his work in the year of the panic—1819—which was followed by several years of depression.

But when both volumes had issued from the press, the author was generous in distributing copies to friends and acquaintances. Copies, for example, he sent to President Monroe himself and to Stephen Pleasonton, a government clerk.[8] Brackenridge presented his work to Calhoun, who, however, was so busy with official duties, which disrupted his habit of reading, that many months, possibly two years, passed before he read it. In thanking Brackenridge at that late date, Calhoun complimented him on the excellence of the *Voyage* and praised his efforts to make his fellow citizens better acquainted with the state of affairs in South America.[9] Calhoun sympathized with the independence movement and confidently predicted its ultimate success. The Secretary of War, like Brackenridge, advocated a policy by which the United States would "take a lead in the affairs of the world," a "noble destiny" greatly accelerated by the revolutions on the southern continent.

There was, of course, one man above all in the United States whom Bracken-ridge wanted to have his work and to commend it—Jefferson. Although Brackenridge had not hesitated to send the ex-President a copy of the *Views* five years before, he now lacked the confidence to forward the *Voyage* directly to Monticello. But Rodney was willing to perform the office of transmitting a copy to Jefferson.

"Your's of Dec. 19. is recieved," Jefferson replied promptly to Rodney. "a letter from an antient friend and fellow-laborer in good works is like refreshing showers to a thirsty plant."[10] During a term in Congress Rodney had stanchly supported the Jefferson administration and then had become Jefferson's and Madison's attorney general. Rodney's letter accompanying the *Voyage,* therefore, had recalled pleasant memories in Jefferson's mind:

. . . but they must not make me forget the duty of thanking you for mr Brackenridge's book: and altho South America is a matter of prospect and for the new generation only, yet the old may indulge a little peep into futurity, and some curiosity respecting it's destinies. this book is the more acceptable as I never read a word in the newspapers of what they pretend to be passing in those countries, unless it be sanctioned by government, or by a responsible name. ignorance is preferable to error, and he who has no ideas is less distant from truth than he who has false ones. the former has only to learn; the latter to unlearn, to retrace and obliterate his steps & set out anew. I have begun to read the work, and already percieve an impenetrable mist dissipating and clearing off. I do sincerely wish our brethren there may acquire self government. but I fear they have much to go thro', and much to unlearn before they get into the right tract. I think, with mr Brackenridge, that "a people must be educated and prepared for freedom." this will require the period of one generation at least, during which they must expect hard domestic probations, as well as some interruptions of foreign conflict. but these are not for my time; and, from an old man, they can recieve no aid but his prayers. those on your own behalf are offered up sincerely that you may be happy while you live, and live as long as you wish.

For the encouragement of the author, who still smarted from the treatment accorded him on the mission, Jefferson's sentiments could not have been more inspiring. When informed of Jefferson's opinion of the *Voyage,* Brackenridge was unable to resist telling him about the circumstances of its composition, exactly as he had done after the publication of the *Views.* "I am but too sensible that in point of execution it bears the marks of haste, and has many blemishes," Brackenridge explained modestly to Jefferson. "My habit, is, to think much, to write rapidly, and to polish at leisure; but in this instance, I was compelled by a contract between the bookseller and printer, to complete it in ninety days, when I had not more than forty pages written—It was completed in a little more than two months."[11] Then, in this letter to Jefferson, Brackenridge penned a Jeffersonian expression—"The *truth* has been my guiding star." According to Brackenridge, he had tried to view his subject as a philosopher— impartially: "It was unfortunate for me that I was compelled to differ from some men who have private interests to gratify, and who have discovered hostility to me, because the accounts which I give tend to falsify theirs."

Consequently, a counterattack by the Carreristas was certain. It came in the form of a 175-page pamphlet, entitled *Strictures on a Voyage to South America, as Indited by the "Secretary to the [Late] Mission" to La Plata: Including Observations on the Capability of the Spanish Americans for Civil Liberty.— On the Principal Events (Civil and Military,) of the Revolution in Buenos Ayres, Chili, the Oriental Banda, Etc. And on the Importance of Friendly Relations, Political and Commercial, with the Independent States of South America. In a Series of Letters, Addressed to a Gentlemen of Distinction at Washington* and written "By a Friend of Truth and Sound Policy."[12] There were anonymous letters attacking Brackenridge printed in the Carrera press, particularly in the *Baltimore Patriot*; but this pretentiously titled and vituperative pamphlet, the production of a disordered mind, was intended to be the chief means of his ruin. The author was Baptis Irvine, who had returned from a brief mission to Venezuela as an agent of the American government. As he told Secretary of State Adams, Brackenridge believed that the pamphlet was the joint effort of Bland, Skinner, Irvine, and Manuel Moreno, a Buenos Airean exile.[13] Irvine, however, publicly claimed the authorship of the work, although he obviously obtained assistance from all three of his fellow Carreristas.

Aside from an introductory "Advertisement" and curious addenda like the "Apologetical Postscript" and "Opinions of the 'Voyage,' &c.," the pamphlet consisted of two long letters, dated Baltimore, January 10 and 20, 1820, and a note of January 25, all addressed to a personage in Washington, presumably Commodore David Porter. From the beginning of his work Irvine leveled his preposterous attack at Brackenridge personally—vindictively: "Yes, it *is* true that a *genius* must work like a *ditcher* or a *dray-horse,* unless like the Secretary he can be 'deep learned and shallow read.' I must not dispute about *inspiration!*"[14] But Irvine, also, asserted that he would undo the mischief which Brackenridge had perpetrated by the publication of his book, "a scandalous *book;* but I might have added, morally and politically corrupt."[15] In his criticism of the *Voyage* and in his castigation of its author, Irvine employed ridicule with little success; he succeeded only in making himself appear ridiculous. Nevertheless, Irvine, criticizing Brackenridge's work page by page, did manage to catch him in the commission of various errors and contradictions which, however, were trivial in light of the magnitude of the *Voyage* and the speed of its composition.

When he caught Brackenridge in a slip, Irvine was merciless. In his description of a bullfight in Buenos Aires, for instance, Brackenridge had made a careless mistake on which his adversary pounced delightedly. Irvine quoted the relevant passages from the *Voyage* and then added his sarcastic comments:

"At one side of the *toro* [bull] there was a seat appropriated to the city authorities." p. 60.

That seats should be assigned to the city authorities in contact with a furious beast is remarkable, because the Spaniards are strict in ceremonies of respect, and proverbially tenacious of etiquette. But, our Secretary was present, and saw for himself!

"Their irons [viz. the criminals,] were not taken off until immediately before *entering* the *toro.*" p. 61. How? did the combatants go down his throat? . . .

If there were 45 persons *on* this terrific bull, and the combatants within him, how much did he weigh? To our deep regret the Secretary is silent as the grave about it. The bullocks exhibited in Baltimore last year weighed about 1500 lbs.—How is this? how could a Spanish scholar so accomplished as Mr. Secretary, happen to confound *La Plaza de Toros* with *toro,* the *building* with the *beast?* He who began his accidence in Louisiana, and finished the philosophy of language in La Plata! An ordinary school boy could not have made and repeated the mistake; but great minds, intent on great speculations will forget words, though they are perfectly master of their elements—the alphabet.[16]

Such scoffery at his expense always tortured Brackenridge, an unhappy fact which Irvine undoubtedly realized. In cautioning Brackenridge to write his book slowly and painstakingly, Shaler had hoped his friend would avoid such a pitfall as this in which he was now trapped.

Jefferson's eloquent letter to Rodney, of January 2, 1820, even became a
point of contention between the author of the *Voyage* and his critic. According
to Irvine, Brackenridge, "being deeply stung by the first number of the
'Strictures,' " had quoted from the letter as a testimonial of his work and
published it in a Washington newspaper.[17] Then Irvine had published a
rejoinder in the *Baltimore Patriot,* later reprinting it as an addendum to the
Strictures. To a thinking reader, Irvine's piece discredited its author rather than
Brackenridge:

> As to the sanction of the illustrious, the admirable *Jefferson,* I freely declare my
> disapprobation of besieging great men, for the purpose of trepanning them into *ex parte*
> decisions and hasty opinions.—Jews and Gentiles throng his halls, jostling and *capsizing*
> one another to touch the hem of his garment, or obtain, as a relic, the scrawl of his
> pen.—Could kings see and feel the glory of such homage, they would *almost* be tempted
> to resign crowns and break chains, rise to the rank of men, and leave the stage amidst
> their plaudits. While the great *Jefferson* draws towards the frontiers of another world,
> it is unfair, it is ungenerous and cruel, to distract his attention in favour of undeserving
> objects.

This was a poor estimate of Jefferson who had the University of Virginia
still to build!

But Irvine's counterattack harmed Brackenridge's reputation not at all. Although Irvine was able to make a valid criticism here and there in the two
volumes of the *Voyage,* he could not present evidence in the *Strictures* to
refute Brackenridge's characterization of Carrera and his intimation of an
unsavory connection between Carrera and Bland. Nowhere in his *Strictures,*
which upheld the Latin American policy of the Monroe administration, did
Irvine present a serious charge against Brackenridge that was convincing. In
their newspaper controversy, which accompanied the publication of the *Voyage*
and the *Strictures,* Irvine had no better luck in effecting the downfall of his
adversary.

In reality, Brackenridge had written the best and the most popular work of
his day on South America. The critic who reviewed it for the *Analectic Magazine,* however, was "in a measure disappointed, and dissatisfied" when he read
the *Voyage,* for, as an admirer of the *Views* and the *Journal,* he believed the
new work contained too much information of a geographical and political
nature and not enough of "the usual piquant ingredients of books of travels."[18]
That was the reason, in his opinion, why most people found the commissioners'
reports dull reading and turned hopefully to the *Voyage* for material on the
scenery and local customs of South America and for a collection of anecdotes.
The critic, therefore, regretted Brackenridge's attention to the party spirit on
the southern continent—"He writes as one who had earnestly taken a side, and
is drawn into discussions somewhat unjust in reference to the individuals

whom he arraigns, and not a little fatiguing for the reader. . . ."[19] The critic called the discussions "worse than useless"; in fact, he thought the two volumes might well have been "compressed into one stout octavo." He was not a captious critic, for he welcomed their publication: "They certainly constitute a plentiful fund of useful and agreeable knowledge concerning the countries of which they treat; they are written, besides, in a style, which, if not always neat and correct, is generally clear, easy, and characteristic of a lively, vigorous mind, familiar with good models of authorship." He attributed the occasional errors and anything "objectionable" in the organization and substance of the work to the haste of its composition. He liked Brackenridge's survey of conditions in South America before the outbreak of revolution and described the Introduction, which concerned that subject, as "an instructive, pregnant digest."

In 1949, over a century and a quarter later, an authority on the background of the Monroe Doctrine acclaimed the *Voyage* more positively than the *Analectic* critic. This modern student stated without reservation that Brackenridge's work "remains a far more notable publication than any of the Commissioners' official reports; it is a document of first-rate importance in Latin American history."[20] Thus, like his father's *Modern Chivalry*, Brackenridge's *Voyage* met the standard of twentieth-century criticism—in 1819-20, his "publication, though unofficial, was both more readable and more widely read than any piece of literature on South America since his own *Letter* to James Monroe."[21]

Following publication of the *Voyage* in Baltimore in 1819, Brackenridge had immediately prepared an improved edition for John Miller, the London publisher, who had it off the press the next year. The author dedicated this English edition to Sir James Mackintosh, the professor of law and general politics at Haileybury. Rodney thought Miller had published the *Voyage* "in a very handsome manner."[22] As he told Brackenridge, Rodney "saw however, taking only a glance, nothing new except a pretty dedication to that learned & excellent man McIntosh. I have no doubt the edition will soon be disposed of in England, & will be productive of great good to the S. American cause."

Fitting it was that Richard Rush happened to be the American minister to the Court of St. James's when the *Voyage* appeared in London in the English edition, for he had originally arranged the appointment of Brackenridge as secretary of the mission to South America, and eventually he handled the negotiations leading to the enunciation of the Monroe Doctrine. "When the work came out, I procured a copy and read it through," Rush informed Brackenridge. "It yielded me both pleasure and instruction; the latter from the knowledge it gave me of many things that I was before ignorant of; the former from the enlightened attachment to the institutions and character of our own country, which displays itself wherever you had the opportunity. Other merits it also had."[23] Rush praised the work of his compatriot in the diplomatic circles in London and in other circles where he mixed and had "reason to suppose that a few copies were, in consequence, taken." But Rush warned his friend not to hope for a large sale of the *Voyage:*

> Whenever an American will undertake to write a "Sketch Book", ingeniously selecting from the surface of things in England every topick of praise, whilst he hides every thing of an opposite description, praising also the whole while as ingeniously as he selects, he may expect that his book will be popular in England, and sell well. But when he writes on any other subject, no matter with what skill, he must publish at his peril, if he publishes in England.

Both Rodney and Rush saw copies of the Miller edition of the *Voyage* before the author himself did, much to his surprise. When Rodney notified him of the arrival of the work in the United States, Brackenridge was disappointed that the publisher had seemingly overlooked him, especially after having sent to London a corrected copy with additional material for the new edition.[24] Brackenridge, consequently, not only wrote Miller himself about the matter but also Rush, who promptly communicated with the publisher.[25] Astonishingly, Miller was not the only London publisher to issue the *Voyage* in 1820, for R. Phillips printed an abridged edition and F. and J. Allman published an abbreviated edition in Spanish, entitled *Artigas y Carrera* and translated by Carlos A. Aldao. A reprint of Aldao's translation appeared in Buenos Aires in 1927, published by L. J. Rosso. There was even a German translation printed in Leipzig in 1821.

But it was an edition in English, published by the Allman firm in 1820, which the *Monthly Review* of London noticed in its pages.[26] The critic reviewed the *Voyage* chapter by chapter, noting that a "copious introduction" included "original remarks on the population, the state of learning and information, the Spanish system of finance, commercial policy, and colonial government." The journal reprinted lengthy extracts from both volumes. The critic, significantly, agreed with Brackenridge's views concerning privateering.

The nefarious practice, however, was now on the wane. In 1819, the year before, William P. Brobson had realized it, for he believed the people of the United States had come universally to condemn the "privateering patriotism" which marked the supporters of Artigas; "and this result," as he observed to Brackenridge, "may be dated from the return of the Commissioners from B. Ayres, since when it has daily lost ground."[27] If Brobson were correct, and he was, Brackenridge's efforts to discredit the privateersmen had unquestionably helped turn public opinion against them.

Clay, who meanwhile had labored doggedly in Congress in behalf of the patriot cause, at last met with a measure of success, to the joy of his loyal supporters, including Brackenridge and Rodney. His achievement was accomplished despite the preoccupation of its members with the Missouri question. The first compromise involved in its settlement—admitting Maine as a free state, empowering Missouri to form a constitution without restriction on slavery, but prohibiting it north of 36° 30′ N. Lat.—was effected by March 6, 1820. "The settlement of the Missouri question I think a happy thing; and I believe the arrangement which has been made a very good one," Clay wrote Brackenridge the next day.[28] Clay also expressed the belief that his fellow legislators would proceed immediately "to the other business of the session, which I hope we shall do well, without regard to our bickerings and the loss of time." In May he introduced in the House of Representatives a resolution[29] on sending a minister to South America, which was passed by a vote of 80 to 75, surprising many persons who had predicted its defeat. Clay was justified in considering its passage a personal victory, for he had won the first majority in Congress for recognition. The vote, however, was not a decisive matter because qualifying words in the resolution enabled a backer of the Monroe administration to vote for it. "Clay has succeeded at last and he is much elated, and I am glad of it on his account, for let Mr Adams friends say of him what they will he is a noble minded American, and we ought not to cast him off for a few faults," Brackenridge opined to Rodney,[30] who concurred heartily.[31]

But Clay was unable to force recognition of the South American states by his tireless campaign in Congress. In February, 1821, his motion to provide an appropriation for the outfit and salary of an envoy to South America did not carry, although he obtained majority votes on his twofold resolution expressing sympathy with the patriots and approval of recognition when the President did act on the matter. Clay now retired from Congress.

Monroe and his Secretary of State, however, resolved the question of recognition only a year after the Kentuckian's departure from the legislative chamber where he had fought so determinedly for the patriot cause. In 1821, Spain had finally ratified the treaty of 1819 annexing Florida; and by the end of the year, her armies had suffered disaster after disaster, both in South America and in New Spain. "I look to the news from the Spanish Main and from Mexico with much interest," Brackenridge had written Rodney in mid-May, 1820, under the spell of a vision. "What a glorious thing to make journey to the City of Montezuma without the least obstacle or restraint! We are on the eve of great things. A free intercourse with New Spain would be of incalculable advantage to us."[32] Brackenridge, in fact, elaborated this idea and discussed the consequences certain to "flow from the final overthrow of the Spanish colonial system" in an undated, fifteen-page memorandum, entitled "Notes on Spanish American Affairs," which came into the possession of Monroe himself.[33] By 1822, with the independence of the South American states an established fact, the time was ripe to encourage commercial relations with them, as Brackenridge contended, before British interests captured control of the trade. Thus no longer did the Monroe administration hesitate to recommend recognition to Congress—early in May the President signed an act appropriating money for the expenses of diplomatic missions to the new republics.

Appropriately, Rodney became the first formal diplomatic agent accredited to them by the United States. From the time of his mission to South America he had kept his faith in the patriot cause, even in 1820, when political strife was followed by anarchy in Buenos Aires, a civil war instigated by Carrera. "We shall soon see the sun breaking thro' the clouds that now overshadow B. Ayres, or I am greatly mistaken," the ex-commissioner had assured Brackenridge,[34] a prediction which came true. Elected to Congress, Rodney took his seat in the House of Representatives in December, 1821. But the following January the Delaware legislature chose him to fill a vacancy in the Senate. The next year he resigned his seat to accept appointment as the first minister plenipotentiary of the United States to Buenos Aires, where he arrived in mid-November, 1823, a few weeks before the declaration of the Monroe Doctrine. On this auspicious note the good Rodney, the father of fifteen children, began his diplomatic career, which was cut short by his death in June, 1824. Mourned alike by his own countrymen and the South Americans, he was buried in the English cemetery in Buenos Aires.[35]

"We went there independent of *all* factions or parties & acted accordingly as the friends of the people their cause & their country," Rodney once had reminded Brackenridge. "Your book must have gained you their affections & applause. You have taken strong root in the country & no event can affect you."[36]

Brackenridge sent a copy of the *Voyage* to a young officer named Álvarez, whom he had met in Buenos Aires. According to Brackenridge, his acquaintance had seemed much interested in the United States and in the work of the three commissioners. Álvarez, the husband of a beautiful and accomplished niece of General Manuel Belgrano, stood high in the patriot ranks in Buenos Aires.[37] When he thanked Brackenridge for the *Voyage,* he advised him, also, that the civil war was over and independence from Spain finally achieved, a victory gained without the aid of any other power.[38] But then he wrote that his fellow South Americans could never forget their friends, in whose number Brackenridge would hold the first place, followed by Rodney, Clay, and others who had supported the cause in the gazettes of the United States. They were the three men who found the warmest spot in the hearts of the patriots—not Monroe nor George Canning, the British foreign secretary. Brackenridge and

Clay and Rodney had demonstrated a sincere concern for their brothers to the South.

For his indifference to the patriot cause, Graham, the ex-commissioner, received a reward. "Graham is gone to Brazil," Brackenridge had informed Shaler disgustedly in 1819. "Good enough for that place; an ambassador is of as about as much use at that place, as at Tombuctoo. He can then vegetate—eat, sleep, and grow fat."[39] Monroe had appointed Graham the minister plenipotentiary to Portugal, with residence in Rio de Janeiro, to succeed Thomas Sumpter, who was anxious to return home.[40] Graham, however, spent less than a year at his post, dying in 1820.[41] "Poor Graham has paid the debt of nature—may he be the inhabitant of a better world," Brackenridge observed to Rodney at the time of their former colleague's death.[42]

On the mission and afterward Brackenridge was unable to form a liking for Graham, whose unimaginative nature he despised. Although Graham had never tried to injure him, as far as Brackenridge knew, he had done little, if anything, to ease the burden when the break with Bland occurred. But in the months after the end of the voyage Brackenridge had come to detest Bland and the Carreristas: "It is mortifying that in this country, a man of letters, an honest and disinterested American, should be at the mercy of these wretches, so far as respects his standing with the chief magistrate of his country."[43]

Exactly how much Monroe appreciated Brackenridge's services on the mission and his subsequent conduct in comparison with Bland's was apparent when the post of United States judge for the Maryland District fell vacant. E. Glenn, the district attorney at Baltimore whom Secretary of State Adams believed "incompetent to his office,"[44] became an applicant for the federal judgeship. Rodney now queried Brackenridge about the matter: "Should however, the present District Attorney (who is an old friend of mine & married to an old friend) be promoted to the seat, how would you like his post? I should presume it was profitable in Baltimore."[45] But Brackenridge sought a higher office than that of district attorney—he aspired to the judgeship. As it happened, Glenn had asked Brackenridge to prepare a letter of recommendation for signing by the members of the Maryland bar. Then, as Brackenridge explained in a letter to Adams, after he had complied with Glenn's request, he learned that his own name was mentioned for the office by Baltimoreans of both political parties: "From the part I have taken in favor of Mr. Glenn delicacy forbids that I should go about to procure recommendations for the office, although nothing forbids my acceptance of the office should the President think proper to honour me with the appointment."[46] On August 11, 1819, Brackenridge called at Adams' house and the President's, although he did not actually solicit the appointment at either place.[47] The same day, however,

Adams discovered in conversation with Monroe that only one applicant was being considered for the post—Judge Bland—and that "He did not indeed know that there was any other candidate." Although Adams at once apprised Monroe of the other applicants, Bland received the appointment to the federal bench.

His appointment was indefensible. Not even the considerations of domestic politics was a sufficient excuse. There was, of course, pressure on the administration for Bland's appointment;[48] but so opposed to it was Adams that he talked against it until the last possible moment, when he had to accept Monroe's decision and to make out a commission for the successful candidate.[49] Adams, also, was required to give a commission to John Adams Webster, who, three months earlier, was a lieutenant on a Buenos Aires privateer. "With Webster for captain of the revenue cutter, and Bland for District Judge, the Baltimore pirates will have their elbows free enough," the Secretary of State wrote in protest in his diary, the pages of which contained a detailed account of the nauseating affair.

Brackenridge, the unsuccessful candidate, needed employment. When the *Voyage* was finished, he had hoped to further his law career in Baltimore, although the financial outlook was not encouraging. "All are willing to acknowledge my capacity as a lawyer, but no one will employ me, and I must do something to live," he complained, frustrated, to Peter S. Du Ponceau.[50] The ordinary steppingstones to prosperity in the law profession were unavailing in Baltimore, he still found—"law *knowledge,* or law *mind,* is totally useless" for drawing clients, nor did an excellent speech serve much as a recommendation. "I have *volunteered* every term these five years," Brackenridge confided to Du Ponceau, "and I assure you with applause, but have never yet received a single fee." Surely nothing could have been more disheartening than his present situation for the son of Hugh Henry Brackenridge, for his father easily could have amassed a fortune in the law if he had wished. The younger Brackenridge noticed that William Pinkney did well in the profession although he appeared only a few times a year in the Baltimore courts; but he knew, too, that Pinkney's business lay chiefly at Annapolis and in the Supreme Court of the United States. Secretary of State Adams indicated the secret of Pinkney's success and his eminence in the law, also, when he scornfully described him as "the counsel of all the pirates and the dictator of the Maryland bar."[51] Pinkney, moreover, was Bland's counsel when the ex-commissioner was accused of complicity in privateering—piratical—ventures.[52] Was this connection between Bland and Pinkney at least part of the explanation for Brackenridge's lack of paying clients?

On April 1, 1820, Brackenridge visited Adams and unburdened his mind by relating the "history of his misunderstanding with Judge Bland on their South American mission."[53] Adams faithfully, and sympathetically, recorded the details in his diary. Brackenridge stated how Bland, Skinner, and their friends had lent the Carreras money in return for "stipulations for exclusive privileges of commerce for ten years." It was this cabal which had obtained Bland's appointment as a commissioner:

. . . These connections of Bland, not without links of attachment to the Baltimore privateering piracies, influencing and pervading his conduct as a Commissioner, Brackenridge says were the only causes of his quarrel with him. Brackenridge had not hesitated to give him his opinion that they were improper. Rodney, he says, had done the same. Rodney being a brother Commissioner of equal rank with himself, Bland let it pass off smoothly with him; but the disapprobation of a subaltern, more galling and less dangerous, he had set at defiance, and had indulged his resentment by every effort in his power to disgrace him—one of which efforts was an attempt to palm on the mission another interpreter, on the pretence that Brackenridge was incompetent.

The ex-secretary gave Adams an account of the controversy with Bland as it had developed after the return of the mission and, as if for good measure, a characterization of Baptis Irvine, "not at all advantageous to him." Irvine was now seeking a government appointment, Adams noted, adding the information that "Brackenridge is also himself a suitor for office."

Socially, however, Brackenridge retained his popularity in Baltimore. Publication of the *Voyage* and his service in the legislature had increased his fame at the very time he worried about his inability to attract clients with money in their wallets and to win the federal judgeship. Convivial men sought his company. In November, 1819, he received an invitation[54] to join a "Conversariom" of twenty-one Baltimoreans, numbering men like General Robert Goodloe Harper, who planned to meet once a week at their homes for literary and scientific talk, "conducted with ease and good fellowship." Heading the list of proposed members was the name of "Mr. Pinkney"!

But the Delphians were the men whose companionship had sustained Brackenridge during the dark days of his controversy with the Carreristas, especially in the fall of 1818. After his long absence abroad Peregrine Bochinjochelus had rejoined the Delphians on September 19, and was greeted cordially.[55] On November 14, he acted as host for the members. That Saturday William Gwynn, as was his custom, published a notice of the meeting in his *Federal Gazette & Baltimore Daily Advertiser* to serve as a reminder for forgetful Delphians or for those who had missed the previous session:

Delphian Club.
The VIII. Session of the Thirteenth Delphiad will be held THIS EVENING at the house of Peregrine Bochinjochelus PDC. The Tripod will be taken at SEVEN o'clk precisely.
By order,
VON CRAMBOGRATH, STLPCPO. &c.

When the Delphians gathered at the "Hall" of Peregrine Bochinjochelus that night, only Precipitate Pasquin (Edward Denison), the sub-tripod (vice-president) and professor of punology, was absent.[56] Von Crambograph read the minutes of their last meeting. Then Odopoeus Oligostichus (Gwynn), the master of ceremonies, the Delphian flamen, and professor of impromptology, presented his essays on the subjects previously assigned him. Aimless conversation followed the reading until Opechancanough Sulekouqui (General William H. Winder) recalled during some talk about Oligostichus's "faculty of epigrammatick versification" that the Delphian flamen had once memorialized the Baltimore City Council in waggish verse. The Delphians asked for a specimen and received one, a fragment of verse which Oligostichus recited until his memory failed him.

Jehu O'Cataract (John Neal) distinguished himself by his remarks on painting. A conceited and tempestuous writer who later shocked Baltimoreans with his novel, *Randolph,* in which Pinkney was treated unkindly, he excelled in clever talk and clever writing, although frequently both his talk and his writing were absurd. Brackenridge himself eventually became the subject of his guest's tart comments when, in England in 1824, Neal began publishing his insulting, but amusing, essays on "American Writers" in *Blackwood's Magazine.*[57] But now in the lodgings of Peregrine Bochinjochelus, Solomon Fitz Quizz (Paul Allen) interrupted the desultory conversation on painting to say that Dr. Samuel Johnson wrote nonsense occasionally like other people. Then the Delphians discussed Pinkney, William Wirt, William H. Crawford, and President Monroe, all of whom "escaped better than could have been expected."

The conversation, becoming livelier, turned to the subject of pigs—learned pigs. Odopoeus Oligostichus was responsible for the change, for he offered a conundrum which no one could answer:

> Why may a pig with curl'd tail boast,
> That he is like Hamlet's father's ghost?
> Answer.
> The reason is by Shakspeare told—
> Because he "could a tale unfold!"

After Oligostichus had satisfied the Delphians by giving them the answer, there was sprightly talk about erudite pigs, "which, very naturally led to that of Judges, when Peregrine Bochinjochelus very appropriately remarked that the best comparison that could be found to a grave judge, was a boar pissing in a puddle and listening to the sound occasioned by it!"

" 'Apropos!' exclaimed Opechancanough Sulekouqui," as the Delphians waxed hilarious, " 'that puts me in mind of an anecdote, which, although you may have heard it, and although I was fined at the last meeting for telling

one, I am determined to run the risk of telling.' " He regaled the company
with one about Pinkney in court—and this time he was not fined. Noisy conversation ensued on the subject of "Junius," the anonymous writer who had
not hesitated to attack the great figures of his day in England. "The Club next
partook of the Bochinjochelian refreshments," after which the members discussed poetry—and not entirely in a serious vein. The hour of midnight arrived
and then was gone. Half an hour later the meeting was adjourned, but not
until His Ludship Pertinax Particular had given his host three questions as
subject matter for an essay—the first was, "What is the strongest argument in
favour of Sir Philip Francis being the authour of Junius?"

At the next meeting,[58] held at the home of Opechancanough Sulekouqui on
November 21, Peregrine Bochinjochelus presented his answer.[59] Oddly, one
month after the Delphians debated the identity of Junius, Francis died. But
each meeting had its high light comparable to the discussion of the Francis-
Junius question. On November 28, for example, all the Delphians present
correctly answered a Fitz Quizzian conundrum after Peregrine Bochinjochelus
had told an anecdote about Baptiste Legendre, an Acadian, who "was one day
suddenly aroused from a nap, by a large snake, which had coiled himself
around his neck, after having swallowed his cue, which was tied with an eel
skin."[60] Solomon Fitz Quizz pronounced the Bochinjochelian solution of the
conundrum the best:

> Why is American citizenship like a shirt?
> Solutions.
> By His Ludship: Because it is put off and on at pleasure.
> By His SubLudship: Because it hangs loosely on its wearer.
> By the Secretary: Because it is often polluted.
> By J. O'Cataract: Because always found near the heart of freemen.
> By O. Oligostichus: Because it fits every body.
> By Op. Sulekouqui: Because they are inseparable.
> By Bochinjochelus: Because it is the last shift of oppressed foreigners.

Had he been a guest of the Delphians at this meeting, the freedom-loving
Dr. Baldwin would have applauded Brackenridge's answer. As it happened,
within a few months Dr. Baldwin did see his companion on the voyage to
South America at the home of Dr. Robert Patterson in Philadelphia, where a
number of savants, including members of the American Philosophical Society,
had gathered to drink tea on a March evening in 1819—". . . I was happy to
meet my friend BRACKENRIDGE."[61] This was probably their last meeting,
for Dr. Baldwin soon departed for the West, having received an appointment
as surgeon and botanist for Major Stephen H. Long's expedition to the Rocky
Mountains. Then, on September 1, at the age of forty-one, the frail surgeon-
botanist died at Franklin, Missouri.[62] Long after his death, Dr. Baldwin's cor-

respondence was edited and published as a memorial to him by Dr. William Darlington, who sent a copy of the small volume to Brackenridge— ". . . as I had opportunities of knowing," Dr. Darlington wrote in an accompanying note, he "was *your* sincere friend, as well as mine."[63]

Brackenridge did not lack sincere friends, it is certain. He found them, moreover, in all walks of life, as his Delphian membership and his election to the legislature indicated. He was most attracted by men of his own high caliber, men like Shaler and Rodney and Dr. Baldwin and Dr. William Gibson, a native of Baltimore, who at the age of twenty-three had become the professor of surgery at the University of Maryland. In fact, Brackenridge wrote Peter S. Du Ponceau a letter recommending Dr. Gibson for the chair of surgery at the University of Pennsylvania when ill health forced Dr. Philip Syng Physick to resign.[64] But Brackenridge, too, was the officer of a company in one of the military organizations of Baltimore, at one time being invited to join it to the command of W. Pinkney, Jr.[65]

According to his sister, Cornelia, Brackenridge did not lack female companionship either during his residence in Baltimore. At least she possessed evidence that her brother was popular with the eligible young ladies of the town—evidently one of them in particular:

> I am informed by a correspondent in Hanover, that you are captivated with a young lady of Baltimore. A miss Anna Maria—something, I forget what I am told she is quite a beauty.
> She also says that a very common conclusion to the letters she receives from Baltimore is, "pray excuse me Mr Brackenridge is below" or "I must dress for a party where Mr B. is to be this evening." I think after such flattering attention if you remain an old batchelor it is your own fault.[66]

In March, 1820, when Henry apparently was no nearer the altar than ever, Cornelia reminded him that Mary Hamilton was "yet unmarried, I think she has her eye upon you. She frequently speaks of you."[67] Then, in June, Cornelia chided her brother for his indecision in the matter of marriage:

> . . . If you write again about pots, and pans, I shall think you are to be married in good earnest, for you have no doubt already thought of the articles necessary for house keeping. In a matter of so much consequence, a moment's delay may prove fatal; if you will not believe me, I could give you the very best authority to prove that the marriage state is the happiest; reminding you in the mean time of the old adage "Faint heart ne'er won fair lady," and the honest clown's decision, "I can't be worse,—so 'Ill 'een tak Jenny."[68]

Cornelia, a convalescent at the time of her writing, closed her letter on a somewhat beseeching note: "We live in the expectation of a visit from you this summer, do not disapoint us."

In the fall, however, Cornelia undoubtedly saw her brother again, as he must have passed through Carlisle on his way to the West. Quitting Baltimore as a hopeless place in which to build a law career, he had headed westward anxious to obtain a passage down the Ohio without delay. "Since I saw you at this place I have come to the determination of seeking my fortune to the West," he had advised Rodney before leaving Baltimore. "There is no opening for me here, and it is a foolish thing to loose the best years of my life as a miserable hanger on. St. Louis is the place I have chosen, and it is possible the govt. may give me some appointment there." [69] No matter what his feelings were at leave-taking, Brackenridge was not a failure in Baltimore; he was too ambitious to remain there.

A ready welcome awaited him in St. Louis, where his coming was the subject of a newspaper editorial:

> It is stated that Hugh M. Breckenridge Esquire, formerly of Pittsburg, is now on his way to Missouri, and means to settle in this State and follow the practice of the law. Mr. Breckenridge was in this country some eight or nine years ago, and by his writings contributed to make known abroad the high character of Missouri. In the short space of his absence he has seen much of the world, and filled many important stations. He has been a Judge in the state of Louisiana, Secretary to the commissioners to South America, and a member of the General Assembly in Maryland. In each situation prospects were flattering before him, but he returns to Missouri, and in doing so gives a decisive proof of his opinion of the superiority of Missouri over any country which he has yet seen.—Missourians may well exult in such an opinion from a man of Mr. Brackenridge's talents and opportunity of observation and comparison between different countries. [70]

When Brackenridge set out for St. Louis, he was thirty-four years old.

XVIII
Andrew Jackson's Private Secretary

Brackenridge arrived in St. Louis without definite plans for the future, undecided whether to establish a law practice there or to return to New Orleans, also once the scene of personal success.[1] His unrest was as great as ever, for the United States had acquired Florida, a new land of opportunity for the enterprising, although the Spanish authorities still had to surrender it to the American government.

St. Louis, which now extended almost two miles along the bank of the Mississippi, promised to fulfill Brackenridge's prophecy that it would someday become "the MEMPHIS of the American Nile."[2] The town had flourished in his absence—its growth[3] excited him. He could count, if he wished, eight streets paralleling the river and twenty-three others intersecting them. There were more than six hundred houses, over two hundred of them constructed of brick and stone. The inhabitants, numbering about 5,500, engaged in a variety of occupations, although the forty-six mercantile establishments had made their town the commercial metropolis of the Upper Mississippi. St. Louis was large enough to support three weekly newspapers and even a bookstore. The glory of the St. Louisans was the Roman Catholic cathedral, built of brick and not yet completed; but it already contained rare paintings and embroideries collected by Bishop Louis Guillaume Valentin Du Bourg, whose private library of eight thousand books was in itself an ornament for the town. The Baptists and the Episcopalians worshipped in their own edifices; the Methodists and the Presbyterians held their services in courtrooms. As for the children of St. Louis, they attended ten schools.

St. Louis was not a sleepy town when Brackenridge arrived late in 1820, despite the business stagnation, which had actually stopped construction of the new brick theater after the laying of the foundation. The surveyors, the army officers, and the Indian agents and traders who outfitted there kept the place in a bustle and cash in circulation. The water front was noisy, for there before the town were gathered the keels, the barges, and the steamboats which made extraordinary inland voyages. The activities of the new Missouri Fur Company, organized in 1819 by Manuel Lisa, were much in evidence about the town and at the riverside. Lisa, however, had died[4] almost on the eve of Brackenridge's arrival. Less than two months after Lisa's death, on September 26 to be exact, Daniel Boone died.[5] Now Brackenridge could never meet the legendary pioneer. William Clark still maintained the museum of Indian curiosities. But for Brackenridge and the St. Louisans the spot for recreation and relaxation was Colonel Elias Rector's Mound Garden with its flowered walks, adjacent to the huge Indian mound nearest town.

As soon as Brackenridge had arrived in town, he sought the whereabouts of old Schewe, who once had taught him German in Pittsburgh. Where was Schewe's shop? No one seemed to know: "I found him, after considerable search, in a back alley, the occupant of a miserable board shanty, without floor or windows, and in the lowest degree of poverty and destitution, and almost in rags."[6] Brackenridge ministered to him as best he could and promised to return later.

Brackenridge decided to spend at least the winter in St. Louis practicing law, undeterred by the presence of over twenty lawyers[7] already established there. He rented an office and inserted a notice[8] in the papers:

H. M. BRACKENRIDGE,
Attorney at Law.

MAY be consulted at his Office in the buildings of Mr. Buseron, a few doors from Main-street. He will attend the courts of St. Charles, and Edwardsville, in the state of Illinois, &c. &c.
St. Louis, Nov. 18.

On the basis of his previous experience as an attorney at law in the West, Brackenridge could now hope to attract paying clients. A surfeit of lawyers in St. Louis did not mean that he would have no business, for, after all, St. Louis was not Baltimore.

Into the office one day came a wealthy speculator, named John Melanthy, whom Brackenridge barely knew, although well acquainted with his reputation.[9] According to Brackenridge, his visitor had cleared a million dollars in cotton at the end of the War of 1812. Brackenridge estimated Melanthy's age at sixty-five or so— "a large coarse looking man, with a rough red face, a carbuncled nose, showing his habits of life to incline more to the liquids than the solids." Melanthy, who speculated in lands and buildings in the vicinity of St. Louis, invited Brackenridge to dinner.

It was an unusual repast, topped off with a surprising dessert, which Brackenridge enjoyed as Melanthy's guest. He located his host in the back room of an unfurnished brick house, where he sat comfortably before a fire watching two catfish heads broiling on two chips of wood: " 'There,' said he, 'you see your dinner; that head is yours, and this is mine; we must each do the cooking.' "
As he himself expressed it, Brackenridge was now treated to a Barmecide feast, the catfish heads served with bread and butter and an "exquisite" Madeira. Their conversation became animated as each tried to outdo the other in clever talk. Brackenridge soon had to admit to himself that Melanthy possessed a vigorous mind. In turn, Brackenridge favorably impressed Melanthy, whose

rule of life was always "to move in a contrary direction from the crowd," for he brought from his safe a bag of dollars and put it on the table and said, "There is a retaining fee, if I should want your professional services."

In his office on a blustery December night somewhat later, Brackenridge, who was seated cheerfully before his wood fire, recalled his promise to Schewe and resolved to visit him at once.[10] A lantern in his hand, he sloshed through the mud to Schewe's hut, where he found his former teacher dozing in his bunk. Brackenridge awakened him, ordered him to put on his clothes, including his well-worn surtout, and led him to a barbershop for a shave and a bath. From there Brackenridge took Schewe home with him and gave him a laundered shirt to wear. Brackenridge had food for supper and bottles of ale delivered from a restaurant. There in his room and without any other company he watched his friend undergo a transformation: the warmth, the food, and the ale made Schewe his jovial self again.

Brackenridge did not let Schewe slide back into his sluggish life. The next day he introduced his shaven friend to various acquaintances as *"Professor SHEWE, from Berlin,"* a ruse which had worked on a previous occasion years before. In better lodgings Schewe had a new outlook on life and took his rightful place in society again. Thus, in 1821, in his *St. Louis Directory and Register,* John A. Paxton listed this singular resident of St. Louis as follows: "Schewe Christopher Frederick, painter and glazier, south Church, above C." Schewe, in addition to his painting, taught school again; that is, he gave lessons in French. One of his students was Thomas H. Benton, the leading lawyer of St. Louis and the coeditor of the *St. Louis Enquirer,* who, in 1817, had killed Charles Lucas, a son of Brackenridge's former guardian, in a duel.

It was the good fortune of Timothy Flint, the New England clergyman who once had marveled at the boats and the boatmen at Pittsburgh, now, five years later, to observe both Benton and Brackenridge in action in court across the Mississippi. There was no doubt in Flint's mind that Benton stood at the head of the bar: "He is acute, laboured, florid, rather sophomorical, to use our word, but a man of strong sense. There flashes 'strange fire' from his eye, and all that he does 'smells of the lamp.' "[11] But Brackenridge, likewise, made a vivid impression on Flint: "There was a young gentleman, Mr. B., who gave strong promise of future excellence. He was the only member of the bar, whom I heard plead, that showed in his manner the fruit of classical taste and discipline. He was happy in his arrangement and choice of words, and concise and condensed; and had a suavity in his manner."[12] But Flint realized that frequently Brackenridge's attainments were wasted "upon the jury in a region, where noise and flourish are generally mistaken for sense and reason."

In the late fall and early winter of 1820, however, Benton and Bracken-ridge were personally unacquainted. They could not vie against each other in the courtroom because Benton was in the national capital where he had gone as a senator-elect with David Barton, his cosenator-elect, and John Scott, the representative-elect, to push the admission of Missouri into the Union. On July 19, 1820, the Missourians had adopted a constitution,[13] which prohibited the immigration of free negroes and mulattoes into the state. "The Missouri question is coming up again," Benton wrote Isaac N. Henry, his coeditor of the *St. Louis Enquirer*, from Washington on November 22. "The old restrictionists are rallying for another struggle. That part of the constitution which is intended to exclude free negroes and mulattoes from settling in the state, is the part laid hold of, though some boldly rely upon the old ground, disdaining all pretences."[14] But he told how he and his two colleagues had studied the laws of the different states and discovered that "free as well as slave-holding, have provisions in their laws to exclude free blacks and mulattoes." Nevertheless, Benton knew that the "portentous struggle" of the previous winter was about to recommence. Henry published the letter, cautioning his fellow citizens to assert their rights in a dignified manner: "What shall Missouri do, if rejected? Fall back into the territorial grade? we hope not. Set up for herself? we hope not. . . . Eventually, Missouri must succeed, and good may grow out of evil; the men who have raised this portentous storm, may yet perish in it."[15] Missouri must keep all her friends, Henry stressed.

Brackenridge sympathized with his Missouri friends in their predicament. In Baltimore, indeed, he had denounced the so-called humanity of the sponsors of a resolution against the admission of Missouri without restriction on slavery at a public meeting arranged by the Quakers in the courthouse: "your motives are humanity—if Missouri should be rejected, your humanity may have cause to shudder for the part you have had in it . . . ."[16] He had gone subsequently to Washington to hear the debate on the floor of Congress, there actually sitting beside Henry Baldwin, his Pittsburgh friend, as he spoke similarly on the same subject. At that time, also, Brackenridge had given all the encouragement he possibly could to Scott, who was then the territorial delegate of Missouri.

It was Scott, the late territorial delegate and the representative-elect, who presented to Congress the Missouri constitution and the application for admission and on whose motion the matter was referred to a select committee.[17] But Scott was in an anomalous position, it seemed, in which he refused to act, or be recognized as the Missouri delegate at the very time that the Speaker of the House refused to recognize him as a member of that body. At home in Missouri some of his constituents forthwith calumniated him by saying that

249

"Col. John Scott, representative from this state, presented himself to Congress and *acted as Delegate of the Territory of Missouri!*"[18] Such an accusation was nothing but a canard—politics. Scott denied the charge to Brackenridge:

> The papers will have informed you of the different steps taken in *our affair,* I say *our* because I have now the pleasure to hail you not only as a fellow Citizen of the *Union,* but a fellow Citizen of the *State of Missouri,* yes a *State,* for as such alone I hail, and will be hailed from henceforth, they were mistaken in Missouri in supposing I had acted as *Delegate.* I never did, I took my seat as a Member, on the authority derived from Illinois and Indiana, presented our charter, & moved the reference of the Land Law, being asked in what capacity I acted, and answering as a Member, I was told that as such I could not be heard, I then declined acting at all, because I would not by any act of mine compromit the smallest right of the State, or justify inferences which I did not admit.[19]

In this letter to Brackenridge, written early in February, 1821, Scott indicated how treacherous was the road Missouri had to follow to gain admission. Every proposal submitted in Congress for resolving the problem for her admission had failed—a select committee now sought a solution:

> . . . I have but small hopes from their deliberations, and if it does result in any thing it will be about this, that the Legislature of Missouri shall as matter of compact agree, that no Law shall ever be passed under that clause of the constitution, which shall operate a prohibition to free persons of coleur, who are *Citizens* of the United *States* or the Several *States* from going to Missouri to settle, and this we can but Settle for, as those persons seldom select a *Slave State* to settle in where they are placed on a Level only with the slaves, but naturally resort to free states to settle there. This will perhaps be the final issue of all this Business.

But if Missouri were admitted on that basis, or any other, Scott added, no time would remain before the end of the session for accomplishing any business for the new state.

Scott was happy that Brackenridge had settled in Missouri and promised to help him in his writing "now and at all times." But Scott appended a postscript to his letter: "Look a little into the Editing of the *enquirer* Mind this—." For more than a month the *St. Louis Enquirer* had lacked an active editor, for Benton's coeditor, Henry, had died unexpectedly in his twenty-fourth year—a "chilling illness" had "hurried him to his grave. . . ."[20] It was difficult, of course, for Benton in Washington to manage the affairs of his gazette published so far away.

"Our acquaintance is not yet personal, but I know you enough to wish it, and to begin a correspondence for the benefit of our country," an agitated Benton, almost thirty-nine years old and now on his way to greatness in the annals of the United States, wrote Brackenridge from Washington, soliciting his friendship.[21] As Benton described it to him, the outlook for the admission of Missouri was bleak at the end of January, 1821:

The fate of Missouri, and of the Union, is verging to a crisis. The present struggle is kept up by two sets of politicians. 1. Those who opposed the purchase of Louisiana, and the erection of N. O. Territory into a state. 2. Those who seek offices by the means of the new parties which will be created.

On Friday, 26th. there was a fair prospect that Missouri would be admitted, that several men from Ohio and Conn. would vote for her. On Saturday a restriction caucus was held, at which it is said that Sergeant and J. W. Taylor were present. The result of their deliberations was unknown until yesterday evening when Sergeant is supposed to have annswered it in the house, by way of watch word to his party. You will see it in this days paper, and seems to me a most insidious plan for keeping Missouri out. By voting for every amendment which brings the Senates resolution nearer to their views, they make it more unpalatable to the people of the south, whereby more of them will vote against it; then all the restrictonists voting against it, will reject it by a great majority, and the the restrictonists be kept in countenance by southern votes, tho given on such different principles.

When Brackenridge read the letter, he could see the earmarks of an angry man writing, and one in a hurry, in the misspelled words and the repetition of the word "the." But he could see, also, the space which his correspondent had left on the paper as he turned to another subject. The admission Benton made next and the request, too, was proof for Brackenridge that authorship was not without satisfying reward. Benton called Brackenridge's attention to John Floyd's bill authorizing the occupation and territorial organization of the Oregon country: "Thus an effort to open an intercourse with China, Japan, and the Indian Archipelago is commenced. The first idea I had of it was from your book on Louisiana. Since then I wrote some pieces in favor of it. I should be glad that you, to whom I owe my first idea, should enforce its advantages, and unite if possible the valley of the Mississippi in its favor." The *Views*, therefore, had furnished the spark igniting Benton's lifelong interest in the Northwest—Benton, an expansionist as well as a true-blue Missourian, wanted Oregon for the United States of America.[22]

At this juncture, when the fate of Missouri was in doubt and the Oregon Bill a new issue for the public to ponder and debate, the mails to St. Louis first became irregular and then failed. No language was adequate to express the indignation of the St. Louisans who denounced "this gross delinquncy of the post office establishment."[23]

In Washington, meanwhile, Benton had penned another earnest letter[24] to Brackenridge, dated March 1. A favor Benton asked of his correspondent:

You will see in the papers the resolution which was passed for the admission of Missouri. It was not what we wished, but the best that could be got, and it would be a great triumph to our enemies and a cruel mortification to our friends here, whose exertions have been incessant and prodigious, to see it badly received in Missouri. I wish therefore, if consistent with your views of correct policy, that you would write some pieces and have them published in support of the resolution, so as to give the tone to sentiment at home, and gratify expectation abroad, for anxiety is on tiptoe every where to see how the Missouri people will take it, and as what is written will be universally republished by other papers, I wish it to be creditable to the literary character of the State as well as agreable to our friends.

Benton insisted that Brackenridge should write articles backing the project to occupy the Columbia. "The ministers of Russia and England are against it," Benton pointed out, hopeful that the information might serve as a challenge to Brackenridge. "The latter causes pieces to be inserted in the National Int. some signed Maguina and one signed a Virginian. I wish you had leisure to answer them. You first began that business, and are most able to conclude it."

Brackenridge complied with Benton's request—"and with good success."[25] At least that was the way Brackenridge, forty-three years later, reviewed his efforts to popularize the final Missouri settlement, which actually admitted the state, a compromise engineered by Clay.[26] Missouri had to agree to interpret her constitution in a way that would never impair the rights and immunities of citizens of the United States. The first week of March thus saw the Missouri controversy ended, although the new slavery agitation persisted. Benton's gazette quickly published editorials supporting the compromise, like the one entitled "THIRD 'GRAND DIVISION' (THE WEST) AND MISSOURI TRIUMPHANT!"[27]

On the last day of March the *St. Louis Enquirer* carried an item copied from the *National Intelligencer* of March 10, announcing the appointment of General Andrew Jackson as the governor of the territory of Florida, a bit of fateful intelligence for Brackenridge. No longer could he remain even halfway content in St. Louis among his friends, who were now so conscious of Missouri's statehood, for he contemplated an opportunity, perhaps a government post, opening for him in the Spanish territory about to be relinquished to American authorities. In April, therefore, he boarded a steamboat for New Orleans,[28] while his unclaimed mail began to gather dust in the St. Louis post office.[29]

Florida, finally, was soon to become American territory. Long a matter of controversy between the United States and other governments, especially Spain and Great Britain, Florida had been the subject of much rumor during the period of protracted negotiations over its purchase. Although the Transcontinental Treaty with Spain was signed on February 22, 1819, rumors still abounded in November, prompting Selleck Osborn to headline an editorial on the various reports about the cession as follows: "THE FLORIDAS—AGAIN & AGAIN."[30]

There were some Americans who protested the signing of the treaty. The early expansionists like Benton were not happy at the thought of losing Texas, and they believed that Florida was destined to become an American possession anyhow—the very arguments which Clay used in his speeches in the House. But what irked Clay the most about the signing of the treaty was this, as he himself declared to Brackenridge: "As for me, its rejection or ratification will not excite one single emotion of pleasure or regret. Whether the one or the other takes place, Spain will have effected the main object of her policy as it regards us, which was to amuse us by negociation, and to prevent any demonstration, on the part of our Government, of interest to the Patriot success."[31] Clay, nevertheless, led unsuccessfully the opposition in Congress against the ratification of the treaty. In the meantime, Spain continued to procrastinate, withholding ratification. At last, however, ratifications were exchanged on February 22, 1821, precisely two years after the signing of the treaty.[32]

But President Monroe had decided to appoint Jackson to the governorship of Florida before the ratification process was completed. Indeed, already in 1819, Monroe had broached the matter to this major general who had electrified the nation by his campaign in Florida the year before. Now, in January, 1821, Monroe offered the post again to Jackson.[33] In the opinion of Secretary of State Adams, the chance to appoint Jackson to the office was a lucky thing, for Congress had just reduced the army, an arrangement which would have put the hero of New Orleans out of the military service by June 1—the appointment would "save the nation from the disgrace of even appearing to discard without compunction a man to whom they are so deeply indebted."[34]

Jackson, however, was reluctant to accept the appointment. Once he had decided affirmatively. But his wife, Rachel, whom he adored, found the thought of going to Florida disagreeable. Jackson declined the appointment, for with him Rachel's wishes weighed heavily whenever he made a decision involving her in any way. At the time he rejected the offer, Jackson believed that there was a chance for "a great spec" at Pensacola and St. Augustine in the purchase of slaves from persons leaving the territory because of its surrender to the United States; and he advised Dr. James C. Bronaugh, an army doctor who was his personal physician, to investigate the matter.[35]

Jackson's friends, many of whom stood to lose personally if he left the public service, importuned him to reconsider the appointment. Senator John Henry Eaton, of Tennessee, reported that Jackson's followers in Congress insisted on his appointment despite his wishes.[36] But Jackson's letters of rejection were already in the post office at Nashville when his friends in town won a promise from him—that if the letters were still there, not having been sent on to Washington, he would write the President another accepting the office. The letters were there; and Jackson had to keep his part of the agreement, although he hoped in vain that somehow the appointment would not be given him. But in his letter Jackson wrote that he accepted the governorship providing he could "resign as soon as the Government is organized and in full operation."[37] He was aware, he informed Monroe, that enemies—and Jackson had them in plenty—would now insinuate "the Seminole Campaign was but a struggle for the present appointment. . . ."

Jackson's appointment was well received by the American people. Most thought it appropriate that the general who had twice occupied Pensacola with his troops, in 1814 and 1818, should be the official to whom the Spanish surrendered Florida in 1821. Secretary of State Adams, in fact, forwarded[38] two commissions to Jackson, one "to receive possession of the Floridas" and the other to act as the governor of the newly acquired territory, both dated March 10. Jackson's compensation as governor was set at five thousand dollars a year. Actually, when his military command ended, his salary as governor was to begin. There was another commission,[39] dated March 20, empowering him to carry into effect the treaty stipulations. In his Baltimore publication Niles commented favorably on Jackson's appointment—"We are truly glad of this" —in the belief that he would put an end to the practice of smuggling in Florida, particularly to the illegal importation of slaves.[40]

An act of Congress, passed on March 3, had provided for the reception of the two Floridas and their temporary government, granting the authority embodied in Jackson's commissions. After taking possession of the Spanish territory and issuing proclamations announcing the cession, Jackson could wield almost dictatorial power over the inhabitants, although his authority was comparable to that given the governor of Louisiana in a similar situation. Jackson could exercise all the powers which had been vested in the captain general of Cuba and in the governors of East and West Florida, but he could not lay taxes or grant public lands or confirm titles and claims to land. As the new governor it was Jackson's responsibility to safeguard the rights of the inhabitants of the former Spanish provinces as well as those of American citizens who might settle there. It was, in short, his task to begin the transformation of a Spanish land into an American territory.

Before leaving Nashville, Jackson realized the difficult nature of his assignment. He anticipated various problems which would soon confront him, as he immediately notified[41] the Secretary of State. What, he asked, should be his policy concerning the Creeks who had fled to Florida during the War of 1812 and from there continued their struggle against the United States until conquered in 1818? There was, also, the problem of the fugitive slaves whom the Indians protected in Florida. Jackson wanted to remove the Creek settlements from the region to add to the security of the American frontier. He requested instructions from Adams. Jackson would need judicious advice day by day to cope with the problems arising in the administration of Florida affairs.

But on the voyage down-river to New Orleans Jackson added an unofficial adviser to his party—Brackenridge. Their meeting was accidental. In a note,[43] dated April 12, Jackson had informed the Secretary of State of his plan to leave Nashville for Florida that afternoon, although the readers of *Niles' Register*[43] learned subsequently that the departure occurred two days later. Jackson had sent Captain Richard K. Call, his aide-de-camp, ahead to Montpelier, Alabama, and hoped himself to reach there by the first of May. On the Mississippi, however, the steamboat carrying the general and his suite, including Rachel, was disabled and shortly overtaken by another on which Brackenridge was a passenger bound for New Orleans.[44] Jackson's party transferred to the other boat, a lucky circumstance for Brackenridge, who had set out for Florida on President Monroe's assurance that he would not be overlooked in the distribution of the offices there.[45] The general summoned Brackenridge and asked him to volunteer his services as a civilian secretary and translator.[46] Brackenridge thus continued his journey to Florida as a member of the Jackson party.

On April 22, they reached New Orleans, which Rachel viewed with awe and where, naturally, Jackson and his staff readied themselves for the final stages of the trip. "I will give you a faint description of this place," Rachel wrote to her Nashville friend, Eliza Kingsley, the wife of an army captain. "It reminds me of those words in Revelations: 'Great Babylon is come up before me.' Oh, the wickedness, the idolatry of this place! unspeakable the riches and splendor."[47] The populace idolized Jackson, as Rachel observed wonderingly: "They conducted him to the Grand Theater; his box was decorated with elegant hangings. At his appearance the theater rang with loud acclamations, Vive Jackson. Songs of praise were sung by ladies, and in the midst they crowned him with a crown of laurel." There was a public dinner in his honor, too, attended by two hundred people.[48] There was a discordant note in the laudation, however, for Eligius Fromentin unexpectedly showed Jackson a commission, dated 1819, granting the authority not only to receive the Floridas but also to take charge of the public archives at Pensacola and St. Augustine. Fromentin agreed that Jackson's commission to accept delivery of the territory superseded his, but he insisted on the right of safekeeping the archives himself. Fromentin's claim to office did not upset Jackson, who simply reported the situation to the State Department and at the same time refused to appoint him the public archivist.[49] But evidently Jackson assigned Brackenridge the task of studying the Spanish judicial system, about which he already knew a great deal, for, several weeks later, Edward Livingston, who was Jackson's confidant in New Orleans, forwarded "to Mr. Breckenridge some spanish books, which will be of use to him in the organization of your Courts."[50] As he informed Jackson, Livingston had fortunately found a publication of Governor Alexander O'Reilly, who had established Spanish authority in Louisiana in 1769—"... I should think it would be worth Mr. Breckenridges while to translate it for your use."

On April 27, Jackson's party left the hubbub of New Orleans,[51] embarking on Lake Pontchartrain for the short voyage to Mobile Bay and landing there at the town of Blakely, in Alabama,[52] two days later.[53]

Here Jackson decided to contact Don José Callava, the governor of West Florida and commandant of Pensacola since 1819. Jackson was anxious to expedite the transfer of the territory, for reports indicated the existence of associations for the smuggling of slaves into Florida before its surrender. On the morning of May 1, therefore, he sent Dr. Bronaugh and Brackenridge posthaste to Pensacola to investigate the matter as well as the truth of a complaint made to Jackson, first in New Orleans and then in Blakely, "that the Spanish subjects in Pensacola are in the habit constantly of pulling down the houses of non-resident Americans for fuel."[54]

Jackson's emissaries conducted their mission with dispatch, although the information which they gained was not entirely to his liking. "Dr. J. C. Bronaugh, surgeon general of the southern division, and my friend, and one of my private secretaries, Judge Brackenridge, will present you this letter; they are the bearers of a communication to you on the subject of a treaty between the United States and His Catholic Majesty, and also of all the documents with which I have been furnished to authorize me to receive possession of the Floridas," an astonished Callava read as he unsealed the letters[55] from General Jackson which the two Americans had brought to the government house in Pensacola. The Spaniard now learned that Jackson was not only desirous of preventing unnecessary delay in the act of delivery but expected him likewise to operate expeditiously. Callava bridled; and then he protested his lack of authority to make any arrangements concerning the treaty, for his superior, the captain general of Cuba, had not communicated with him about the transfer. Although he sympathized with Jackson's wish to move speedily, Callava refused to do anything until he received orders through the proper channels. By inquiry and observation, however, Dr. Bronaugh and Brackenridge found that less than five hundred and fifty Spanish troops and officials were to leave the country upon its surrender. They noted that the soldiers were drilled irregularly and that the public buildings were in disrepair—"The governor, we were told, is personally desirous to be gone; he is a frank, candid soldier, and we have no doubt that any difficulties or delays which may occur will be occasioned by the captain general." There appeared to be no substance, they reported, to the accounts regarding the smuggling of slaves into Florida. The soldiery, they learned, damaged the untenanted houses belonging to Spanish subjects besides the property of citizens of the United States. But most dwellings were dilapidated, and almost one-half unoccupied, although nearly everyone was reserved by persons awaiting the change of government—"We suspect there is a great deal of very valuable public property in and about Pensacola." On their return to Blakely, Jackson's emissaries had to report, also, that the "Hornet" had not yet reached Pensacola.

The nonappearance of the vessel at Pensacola disappointed Jackson. It meant that Colonel James G. Forbes, commissioned[56] to convey to the governor general of Cuba the order from his government for the transfer of the two provinces to the United States, was unable to conclude his business readily. Forbes had arrived in Havana harbor on board the sloop of war "Hornet" on April 22, but he experienced one frustrating delay after another in trying to obtain the delivery order, and the delivery of the archives, from the illustrious Don Nicolas Mahy, the captain general and governor of the island of Cuba and of the Floridas. Not until May 30 did the "Hornet" sail for Pensacola with Forbes aboard carrying the necessary order for Callava to act, a copy also being dispatched to the governor of East Florida. This delay in the arrival of the "Hornet" disrupted Jackson's timetable because he could not obtain Callava's cooperation. But Jackson expected the vessel soon, for he sent Major Henry Stanton, the quartermaster, to New Orleans to arrange for the transports and supplies needed to take away the Spanish officers and soldiers after the United States had received possession of the land.[57] Jackson, furthermore, wanted to move his troops as quickly as possible from Fort Gadsden, an unhealthy place for them, and to march them proudly into Pensacola. The rumors circulating in Blakely and elsewhere made him wonder if the delay of the "Hornet" was not due to an understanding between the merchants and the captain general causing him "to withhold the order for the delivery of the Floridas until the last moment, to give time for the arrival of large shipments of goods for Pensacola."

The delivery of the Floridas was to occur within six months after the exchange of ratifications on February 22, or sooner if possible. But as the days passed without the arrival of the "Hornet" at Pensacola, Jackson became suspicious of the Spanish authorities. "I am fearfull that the Governor Genl of Cuba has discovered in the Colo. too much of the swaviter et modo, and is practising upon him a little of the Spanish policy, procrastination and delay for purposes not calculated to promote our interest, but to gain time for his friends to introduce large quantities of merchandize, and africans," Jackson reported[58] to Secretary of War Calhoun after reaching Montpelier with his party, voicing a distrust of the Spaniards which time and events never effaced. Jackson blamed Colonel Forbes for a lack of energy in his negotiations—unfairly. The general, however, could never wait with folded arms when he thought action was in order. He fumed and fussed and was cantankerous. Informed of Callava's attitude by Dr. Bronaugh and Brackenridge, Jackson addressed a curt note to him on May 11, stating that transportation and supplies were ready for the evacuation of the Spanish from Pensacola.[59] On the same day Jackson wrote his friend, Brigadier General John Coffee, about the delay of the "Hornet" and of his determination to expose everyone who might be a partner in any speculation with the captain general—even if Forbes himself were involved.[60] Already Jackson regretted accepting his appointment, as he advised a sympathetic Coffee: "I will see you in the fall or winter for believe me I can never descend to become a governor of a Territory, after the offices I have filled. you may therefore rest assured after congress meets I am a private citizen." While at Blakely, Jackson also said, he had been ill, "which has debilitated me very much," but he felt better now.

Five miserable weeks, however, Jackson tarried in Montpelier awaiting the arrival of the "Hornet" at Pensacola.[61] At this cantonment in Alabama on May 31, he delivered a farewell address[62] to his troops, who composed the Division of the South—sadly he gave up his command. The retirement, severing his military connection so abruptly, was not conducive to his peace of mind. He had, in fact, grown more irritable as the fateful day approached. One letter after another he had written to Adams[63] complaining about the lack of information from Colonel Forbes, whose absence was inexplicable to him— ". . . I am induced to believe that every delay will be experienced that the Spanish officers think will be submitted to by the American Government," he stated in a dispatch written the day before his retirement from the army. But he promised to be firm and cautious in his policy and to do nothing rash.

President Monroe now dealt Jackson a humbling blow. Not planning to remain long in Florida after the cession, Jackson intended to reward his favorites before his departure with satisfactory posts in the territorial government. In May, for instance, he asked Calhoun to remind the President that Dr. Bronaugh was a suitor for the office of receiver of public money in West Florida.[64] But at the moment Jackson sought to promote this candidacy, Monroe and his Secretary of State were writing him letters about the Florida appointments just made. There was not a single Jackson adherent on the list which Adams forwarded on May 22: Eligius Fromentin, of Louisiana, was appointed judge of the United States for West Florida; Alexander Anderson, of Tennessee, attorney of the United States for West Florida; James Grant Forbes, of New York, marshal of the United States in and for East and West Florida; and George Walton, of Georgia, secretary in and for West Florida.[65] Also appointed were officials for East Florida and collectors of the customs in the three revenue districts established by the President. Minor offices were left for Jackson to fill.[66] Monroe defended his appointments in an unctuous letter to Jackson.[67] "Past experience shows that neither of us are without enemies," Monroe warned him. "If you still have any, as may be presumed, they will watch your movements, hoping to find some inadvertent circumstance to turn against you. Be therefore on your guard."

But when the list of civil officers in Florida came to hand, Jackson had reason not to regard the President as a friend. Monroe had ignored all of Jackson's recommendations, as was instantly apparent when a copy of the *National Intelligencer* arrived at the Montpelier cantonment on June 8. Fromentin, one of the appointees, later testified to Jackson's mortification upon seeing the names of the successful candidates in the paper: "Mr. Brackenridge told me, himself, that the general was raving when he first saw the list of appointments which had been made for both the Floridas."[68] Although he was "very ill" that night, Jackson recovered enough the next day to send word of the appointments to Dr. Bronaugh, who had gone to Pensacola: "had I anticipated this I should have adhered to my first determination not to have accepted the Goverment, but I will close my official duties with the next congress as I am determined, never to be associated with such men as some of those who are appointed. say to my friend Call not to despond."[69] Then, late in the evening of June 12, the communications from Adams and Monroe reached Montpelier by express. Jackson acknowledged their receipt in a frigid note to the Secretary of State: "They have been placed on file, and their contents duly noted."[70] Monroe and his appointments be damned! was Jackson's attitude.

He was too busy to think much about them anyhow, for, on the evening of June 9, the "Hornet" had arrived at Pensacola.[71] Callava no longer could refuse to assist in preparing for the delivery of West Florida. Accordingly, Jackson proceeded to the estate of Manuel González, about fifteen miles from Pensacola, reaching it on June 15.[72] There he worked out the arrangements for the transfer, finding immediately, however, that negotiating with Callava was not a simple matter. Callava wanted to remove the Spanish artillery from the fortifications before the American occupation; whereas Jackson insisted that the cannon be left behind by the departing troops. Such disputes, some important and some trivial, produced a massive correspondence with Callava, engrossing Jackson's time and that of his translators. Complicating the situation was the loss of the transport "Cora" in a gale on the way from New Orleans to Pensacola. "We are at a Spanish gentleman's, waiting the exchanging of flags, and then we go into that city of contention," Rachel described Pensacola and the feeling of its Spanish inhabitants to Eliza Kingsley while her husband negotiated furiously with a ruffled Callava. "Oh, how they dislike the idea! They are going to the Havana—don't like the Americans, nor the government."[73]

No matter how angry Jackson and Callava made each other, they always had to compromise their differences. They did not dare reach an impasse in their negotiations, a circumstance which failed to deprive Callava of the pleasure of constantly introducing new conditions certain to exasperate the thin-skinned Jackson. Although they had agreed to defer the exhibition of credentials until later, Callava requested the possession of Jackson's commission: ". . . the operation demands solely that I should be perfectly assured of the person who is to receive said Province."[74] But on other occasions Callava agreed instantly to Jackson's proposals: "I am advised of the appointment of Capt. R. K. Call, Your Excellency's secretary and aid, Dr. J. C. Bronaugh, and Judge H. M. Brackenridge to unite with an equal number of persons, whom I shall name for the purpose of examining and comparing the Inventory of the Archives, public papers, etc. as exhibited by me; all of which has my approbation, and shall be opportunely executed."[75]

Jackson depended on Brackenridge for the management of such business. His secretary's knowledge of Spanish and legal training proved indispensable. Jackson deputed Brackenridge to work with the Spanish in preparing the procès-verbal, the document which would authenticate the transfer of West Florida. "Judge Brackenridge is possessed of my views and opinions on the subject, in case any further explanation should be necessary: he is also directed to unite with your Secretary to prepare the document in a suitable manner to receive our signatures," Jackson notified Callava on July 1.[76]

Jackson and Brackenridge, assisted by Captain Call and Dr. Bronaugh, functioned as an efficient team throughout the negotiations preliminary to the transfer of West Florida—how they operated was well illustrated in this instance by an exchange of communications. On July 8, Brackenridge, who was in Pensacola, reported to Jackson:

dear General, We have been at work all morning, in marking and signing the publick records according to the idea you have suggested. But without occular examination it is difficult to have a correct notion of what they are. I have sent with Captn. Call merely the notes of the marks etc. put upon them, intending to make a formal paper to be signed by us. The records relate only to transactions between citizen and citizen; bills of sale, transfers, and protests; the United States government is no further interested than to see the citizen protected in his rights. There is not a single originial grant among them. You will perceive that these consist of unbound books containing from five to one hundred pages, for the first years one unbound book yearly was sufficient, afterwards three or four a year were required: these last are put up in separate pakages intended to form a book, and are numbered 1, 2 and 3. They are so different from any records that we are accustomed to that we had to adapt our plan according to their pecul[i]ar character. On some we have put both the letter of the alphabet and the number, when one or the other would have sufficed, but we thought it prudent abundanti cautela. The marks we have put are sufficient to identify the unbound books —it will scarcely be possible to substitute another for any one of them. This precaution is taken by us for the interests of the people here, for the United States have no interest further than this.

The Governor appeared somewhat out of humor on the subject of the Process verbal, but on explanation changed his tone. The fault was committed by his secretary. It is all rectified. The papers are prepared exactly according to the form sent to him, word for word.

The wind is now favorable and we may expect the vessels from St. Marks, this evening or tomorrow.[77]

Although suffering from chronic diarrhea, Jackson did not neglect official business, replying at once to Brackenridge's letter:

Sir

I have recd. your note of yesterday by Capt Call, the plan of identifying the records, to be receipted for by me is approved, it was certainly necessary that these should be so identified, so that no fraud should be practised on the honest citizen or subject by the roguish—and altho the record only relates to the transfer of property from one individual to another, still it is a debt due from the Goverment, to protect the honest citizen in his rights—This will do it as far as we have it in our power.—

I am truly astonished to find that the Governor should be out of humour as it respected the process verbal, it was plainly written & in due form, consistant with the custom of all nations in like cases, and by his letters to me fully approved, if his secratary imposes upon him a false translation that is no fault of mine, and if an attempt is made to impose upon me through such means, I can assure them they will be disappointed.—however I am in this case as I was in the dispute about the right to the ordinance, very happy that the Governor now understands it as he advised me by letter he did, and as I allways understood it, and that all things are now harmoniously concluded on—that possession will be had as soon as the Amelia arives.—as soon as a safe opportunity offers, I will be happy to see the two copies of the process verbal prepared —and on the arival of the Amelia I wish to have the earliest notice that I may (if the Governor does not forthwith set a day for emberkation & giving possession) write him on the subject, as I am truly wearied with delay. present me to Doctor Bronaugh & tell him I am better, but very much debilitated, that by the advice of Doctor Elliot I have commenced this morning his tonic—of its effects I will advise him.[78]

Jackson's affliction made him more short-tempered than ever. Upon learning that Rachel's maid, Betty, was "putting on some airs" and acting impudent, he had ordered her taken to the public whipping post and given fifty lashes if she persisted in her conduct—"I am determined to cure her. . . ."[79] Callava's attitude now caused a similar outburst of Jackson's temper. On July 9, the transports bringing the Spanish garrison from St. Marks reached Pensacola. Jackson, consequently, saw no reason for further delay in the delivery of the province. But Callava, who was in no hurry to complete the transaction, casually informed Jackson that on July 14 the decision would be made whether the delivery was to occur on Monday or Tuesday, July 16 or 17.[80] Two other matters remained to be settled, one concerning rations for the Spanish troops going on board the transports and the other about the subject of deserters, Callava reminded Jackson. When he read the Spaniard's communication, Jackson exploded: "I have used the utmost frankness with Your Excellency in all our correspondence. It becomes me now to speak with the same frankness."[81] Jackson ordered that the Spanish troops be aboard the transports by eleven o'clock on Sunday morning, July 15, according to a previous pledge given by Callava, "unless a tender in money be made of the daily demurrage on the two Transports, on which they shall be detained two days and no longer." Jackson could not stomach further delay: "The subject of the rations has long since been put to rest." The matter of deserters was not a subject for negotiation either: "I have no powers to treat about deserters." Then he announced the removal of his troops to Galvez Spring, only two miles from Pensacola.

This eruption of impatience did not cow Callava. Jackson's communication had astounded him, however, especially the uncalled-for attack on his good faith, the Spaniard declared in his reply.[82] He advised Jackson that the time of delivery was set for ten o'clock on the morning of July 17. "I must beg of Your Excellency that these unpleasant discussions may cease, since prudence in every point of view requires that they should be avoided." Certainly this unpleasantness should end, Jackson responded. "Your Excellency tells me, that you have been a soldier from your cradle," he continued. "Such has also been my lot, and I have never failed, Sir, to comply with my promise."[83] But Jackson accepted the date fixed for the delivery and, furthermore, waived the claim of demurrage on the transports.

Jackson and Callava suddenly became the incarnation of graciousness. On July 15, Jackson wrote a note[84] to the Spanish governor denying any intention to hurt his feelings during the negotiations, although that night he played a different tune in a message to Dr. Bronaugh: "The scripture says return good for evil, in this feeling I intend asking the Govr. and his secrataries to dine with me, he is as I suppose, very sore, and if he was devoid of urbanity I mean to shew him I at least possess magnanimity by which I will heap coals upon his head."[85] Callava did feel slighted that Jackson had not paid him an official visit. On July 16, Callava explained his conduct at length to Jackson and at the same time gently lectured him on the etiquette of diplomacy.[86] Callava recapitulated their proceedings to prove convincingly that Jackson was in the wrong by not visiting him to present his credentials. The Spaniard feigned illness as an excuse for not paying the first call himself. "My feelings as a soldier, I suppose correspond with yours, death before an undue condescension," Jackson excused himself in turn. "It is what I ask of no one It is what I will not render to any."[87] However, he invited Callava to the American camp that night of July 16; and if the weather were inclement, he asked him to breakfast instead the next morning in Pensacola in Rachel's presence: "Should we not meet each other before 10. o'clock tomorrow on the stair case, I shall then take you by the hand as a soldier and friend, and I am certain after further acquaintance we will know how to appreciate each other."

They did not meet, of course, until the ceremony the following day, Tuesday, July 17. "The whole town was in motion," it appeared to Rachel. "Never did I ever see so many pale faces. I am living on Main street which gave me an opportunity of seeing a great deal from the upper galleries."[88] Early in the morning the American troops had arrived in town from their encampment and marched to the public square where they drew up opposite the Spanish guard and exchanged salutes.[89] Then four companies of infantry were detached from the American line to take possession of Fort Barrancas below the town. An hour or two later, at ten o'clock, Jackson and his suite crossed the common; passed between the two lines of troops, receiving their salute; and entered the government house, where the formal delivery[90] of West Florida to the United States occurred. An American guard relieved the Spanish guard stationed at the gate. Governor Jackson and Colonel Callava, the late commandant, and their suites soon emerged from the building and proceeded to the rented house in which Rachel had been living for several weeks, passing first between the two lines of troops. The Spanish soldiers marched off to embark on the transports as salutes were fired and the regimental band of the Fourth Infantry, and the "Hornet's" too, played the "Star-Spangled Banner." The Stars and Stripes now flew from the flagstaff.

During the day the inhabitants of Pensacola waited on Governor Jackson to felicitate him, for at last West Florida belonged to the United States. The formal cession of East Florida had taken place a week earlier, on July 10, at St. Augustine.[91] Jackson's duties as the commissioner for receiving possession of the Floridas were concluded. Now he had to organize their government. In this task his right-hand man was Brackenridge, his private secretary, whose service as a volunteer aid merited a reward.

XIX: The Alcalde of Pensacola

"Thrice have I seen the Spanish coulours lowered and the american coulours waving over this place, and my fatigue has been greater this, than at any other period," Governor Jackson wrote General Coffee the day after the surrender of West Florida. "I am engaged establishing some rules and regulations by which a good police may be established, and the health of the place preserved. its police is wretched, the whole town inundated, it has rained for two months, and continues still every day to rain."[1] At that moment Pensacola seemed a gloomy place to Jackson, who could still see in the distance the transports convoyed by the "Hornet" and recall poignantly the sad parting of friends as the Spanish troops embarked. But he thought the melancholy atmosphere was only "a momentary thing, and I will have the pleasure to be enabled to lay the foundation of permanent happiness to the people, and lasting prosperity to the city." Jackson was sincere in professing this wish, for as soon as he completed the organization of the government he intended to retire from public life: ". . . I am contented that this will terminate my political career, and that I will have the pleasure to see you at your house in all the month of October next, fully satisfied with the Hermitage to spend the rest of my days." That Jackson did not pass quietly into retirement but withdrew from the public service as a controversial figure was the unlooked-for result of rewarding Brackenridge with the alcaldeship of Pensacola.

Before the actual delivery of West Florida Jackson had planned for the day when he would take the reins of government in his hands. Accordingly, on July 17, he had ordinances "for the better government of the town and province" ready for promulgation.[2] But, as he explained later to Adams, Jackson also needed officers of government for Pensacola, where only one office was filled, that of the alcalde, "who was the only civil provincial officer, properly speaking, in West Florida. To limp along in this maimed and imperfect state, seemed to me intolerable."[3] As the time of the delivery approached, the Spanish administration of the province had fast deteriorated. While waiting impatiently for the day of the transfer to arrive, Jackson had sought advice on the problem of providing a government for the territory about to be acquired: "On consultation with an eminent lawyer from Orleans, who was present at the change of government there, and also with Judge Brackenridge, a gentleman of high legal acquirements, who was in Louisiana some time after, I resolved, without going as far as I understood the Governor of that province had gone, to fill up those offices which I found vacant, and to make such alterations as seemed to me absolutely called for by the mere circumstance of the cessation of the government of Spain, and the extension of that of the United States over the country." Although none of the Monroe appointees to the top territorial posts had arrived, Jackson filled the vacant offices in Pensacola immediately upon receiving West Florida from Callava. Jackson wanted to appoint inhabitants of the town to as many places as possible but found them reluctant to accept, for they were unwilling to jeopardize their rights as Spanish subjects—the "former alcalde was a half-pay officer, and, of course, could not be continued." Jackson appointed Brackenridge the alcalde and notary of the town and gave the lesser offices to intimate friends (Dr. Bronaugh becoming the resident physician), to old residents (John Innerarity, an alderman), and to mere place seekers with nothing to recommend them.[4] George Bowie received the mayoralty, an unimportant post in comparison with the alcaldeship.

It was Brackenridge who occupied the key position in the government at Pensacola. The governor ordered the new alcalde to investigate the nature of his office and to apprise him promptly of the result. "Besides the Governor of West Florida, there was but one provincial officer actually in the exercise of any civil functions: this was the *alcalde,* whose place you have appointed me to supply," Brackenridge informed Jackson at the beginning of his masterful report,[5] dated July 26. ". . . I have taken pains to ascertain the duties of this office, but I assure you that it is with great difficulty I have been able to procure any thing of a certain and definite nature." Brackenridge was unable to describe the office positively, for his predecessors had acted as notary public, chief of police, superintendent and inspector of prisons, and sheriff. He could not determine precisely the jurisdiction, the duties, and the powers, which the alcalde possessed for each function: "I have been able to procure but little information from my predecessor in office; what he said was summed up by the remark that I had more power than the Governor." Brackenridge talked with Callava, too; he studied the Spanish constitution and various decrees of the Cortes; he noted past practice in Spanish towns. Then he advised Jackson to fill the vacant offices himself as an election was out of the question—". . . there is no proper officer *to hold* an election, and there is no way of ascertaining who would have a right to vote." Brackenridge made concrete recommendations to improve the administration of justice. He had discovered amazing facts in his investigation: "Another, and a very obvious inconvenience of the present state of things, is, that the powers of the different officers, and the course to be pursued to obtain redress, *are unknown to the people.* I have endeavored, without success, to procure even the fee-bill." Before the delivery of West Florida, according to Brackenridge, government under the Spanish had ceased to exist in Pensacola.

Jackson cited Brackenridge's report in an account[6] of the proceedings in West Florida, which he submitted to the Secretary of State before the end of July. Jackson indicated his reliance on Brackenridge's recommendations, not hesitating to give him credit for an assignment done well. "In this uncertainty," Jackson stated to Adams, referring to the difficulty of determining the exact nature of the Spanish administration, "I have contented myself with merely organizing a Government from the materials at hand, with as little change as possible; promulgating the same by way of ordinance, in order that the people may have some knowledge of the system to which they must conform." But Brackenridge and Abner L. Duncan, the New Orleans lawyer, actually framed the ordinances of government which Jackson signed as governor of the provinces of the Floridas.

On July 18, the day after the delivery, the inhabitants of Pensacola suddenly found that their town had a new government upon the promulgation of the first sweeping ordinance.[7] The town corporation, to be known as the city council, was to consist of a chief officer, the mayor, and six subordinate officers, the aldermen, all seven of whom were declared annual appointees of the governor. The council possessed all the powers necessary for the "good government" of Pensacola, including the levying of taxes. There were sections in this ordinance empowering the council to make regulations required for the proper observance of the "Christian Sabbath," fixing the limits of the town, shutting the gaming houses and prohibiting gambling (except billiards), and forbidding the sale of liquor to soldiers in the service of the United States. However, as Jackson emphasized to Adams, the powers of the city council conformed "to those which they would have possessed under the Spanish Government."[8]

Other ordinances to complete the organization of the provisional government followed in rapid succession. The ordinance of July 19, "for the preservation of health in the city of Pensacola,"[9] created a board of health authorized to enforce the quarantine and to establish a lazaretto at the Barrancas or at any other suitable point. Two days later Jackson promulgated an ordinance[10] erecting the counties of Escambia and St. Johns in the ceded territories. It provided for the administration of justice in each county, even the police of the roads and the bridges beyond the limits of Pensacola and St. Augustine. Another ordinance,[11] dated July 26, outlined the procedure to be followed in the county courts. The last section, significantly, was a list of fees to be "received by the officers, and no other." Thus hardly a week had passed before the Floridians had the promise of an efficient system of local government to replace the haphazard administration of the Spanish. But the Spanish machinery of government was retained as much as possible, for it was expected that at the next session of Congress a more permanent form would be provided.

Jackson, however, had not issued his last ordinance. One,[12] dated July 21, he deemed especially important after his experience in Louisiana during the war when he had seen persons "claiming exemption as foreigners, and the privileges of citizens, as it suited their convenience."[13] He intended to nip the practice in the bud if it appeared now in Florida. The ordinance, relating to the sixth article of the treaty, provided for the registering of names of Floridians who hoped to secure the rights of American citizenship. As late as September 6, the governor promulgated an ordinance[14] which declared that the Pensacola board of health was empowered to regulate the practice of medicine in the town, including the licensing of qualified practitioners.

As he promulgated one ordinance after another, happy in the thought that he was giving the Floridians a better government, Jackson had no idea what the repercussions of his action might eventually be. After all, he anticipated an early retirement from the public service; he did not seek a higher office, an ambition which required a regard for the political implications of every word and deed. Someday, however, enemies would attack him for his erection of a government in the Floridas—the ordinances became an issue in presidential politics! Brackenridge would publicly absolve Jackson of responsibility for the ordinance-making! An historian, excessively legalistic, would pronounce Jackson "guilty of high crimes and misdemeanors!"[14] Dictatorial but wise was Jackson's organization of the government.

His measures proved instantly efficacious, jolting the easy going inhabitants out of their lethargy. He found the government house, a frame building, in such disrepair that he decided not to occupy it himself but turned it over to his officers for quarters. After a thorough cleaning of the blockhouses—"the most filthy and disgusting places imaginable," Jackson assured Adams[16]—they were rendered fit for the quartering of the American troops. The barracks, originally constructed by the British at a great cost, needed repairs badly, although the prison was in a fair condition. Rachel Jackson watched the whole scene from her galleries as American initiative manifested itself marvelously:

Three Sabbaths I spent in this house before the country was in possession under American government. In all that time I was not an idle spectator. The Sabbath profanely kept; a great deal of noise and swearing in the streets; shops kept open; trade going on, I think, more than on any other day. They were so boisterous on that day I sent Major Stanton to say to them that the approaching Sunday would be differently kept. And must I say the worst people here are the cast-out Americans and negroes? Yesterday I had the happiness of witnessing the truth of what I had said. Great order was observed; the doors kept shut; the gambling houses demolished; fiddling and dancing not heard any more on the Lord's day; cursing not to be heard.

What, what has been done in one week! A province delivered to the American people; the laws of the land we live in they are now under.[17]

Rachel was not bigoted. "There is a Catholic church in the place, and the priest seems a divine looking man," she confessed to Eliza Kingsley. "He comes to see us. He dined with us yesterday, the Governor, and Secretary, French, Spanish, American ladies, and all."[18] Although the priest no doubt

267

was troubled by the provision in the first ordinance which empowered the city council to make regulations concerning the observance of the Sabbath, the purpose of the ordinance was not to threaten his church but to legalize any measures required for securing quiet Sundays in Pensacola. After some weeks of exemplary conduct in the observance of the Sabbath, did the townsmen grow heedless and lapse into their former ways to the disappointment of Rachel and her friends? In mid-September there appeared in the local gazette a list of precepts under the heading, "THE SABBATH." The first two were:

> Make the Sabbath the market day for thy soul.
> Sunday is not a day to feast our bodies, but our souls.[19]

To dictate the morals of the inhabitants was now hopeless, for almost over-night the lazy town of Pensacola had become a roaring American community, as Rachel herself could see. In the beautiful bay appeared vessel after vessel loaded with people, all coming to the little Spanish town where the public squares, long neglected, were grown over with shrubbery— "There are fewer white people far than any other, mixed with all nations under the canopy of heaven, almost in nature's darkness."[20] Rachel, however, had some reason to be happy: ". . . I think the sanctuary is about to be purged for a minister of the gospel to come over to the help of the Lord in this dark region."

There was no lack of entertainment in Pensacola. Early in September E. Hathway opened his Eagle Tavern located opposite the theater on the public square. Not only did his establishment have a bathhouse, where both hot and cold baths could be taken at any time, but also a bowling alley—"an elegant ten pin alley."[21] One month later Peter Mullen advertised *"the best oysters & porter under the sun"* at his new tavern, which catered to "the lovers of good eating and drinking. . . ."[22]

The professional entertainers came to town, also. The circus, consisting of an equestrian troupe from Havana, scheduled its first performance for August 22, a Wednesday, advertising "a variety of astonishing Feats of Horseman-ship."[23] But scarcely two weeks later the circus was put up for sale.[24] It had faced stiff competition from the Jacksonian Commonwealth Theater, managed by Andrew Allen, who removed to New Orleans for the winter season there.[25] For over two months he had offered the theatergoers of Pensacola lively enter-tainment. At each performance he presented both a play and a farce according to the custom of the day—"Admittance, Box $1, Pit 75 cents—Children 50 cents."[26] The performance which closed the season on October 22 was given for the benefit of the musicians in the band, who had received no other com-pensation for their devoted service to the drama in Pensacola.[27]

There were even a few hopeful souls who tried to eke out a living by serving the educational needs of the community. W. Davison was a bookseller who not only carried law books in his stock but also a variety of other works like Aaron Bancroft's *An Essay on the Life of George Washington* and Alexander von Humboldt's *New Spain*.[28] But his stock also included copies of Brackenridge's two-volume work on South America and his *History of the Late War*. A teacher named Henry Hill advertised his intention to start an English school as soon as he received sufficient encouragement from the public to warrant the venture. He planned to teach reading, writing, grammar, arithmetic, and bookkeeping, "both single and double entry."[29] Soon, however, Pensacola boasted another pedagogue in the person of Christopher Frederick Schewe, who had followed Brackenridge to Florida from St. Louis. That Brackenridge took his eccentric friend in charge was apparent from the notice which was inserted in the local paper:

DR. SHEWE,
Offers his services as a Teacher of the
FRENCH LANGUAGE.

HE has taught in some of the principal places of the United States—His method is calculated to enable his scholars to speak the language, as well as to read it. Tuition, Six Dollars per month—attendance one hour each day.[30]

One month after the delivery of West Florida, Pensacola had a newspaper in which such notices as Schewe's were printed. The *Floridian,* a weekly established by two partners named Cary Nicholas and George Tunstall, was delayed in its appearance when the press and type arrived late from Philadelphia. But it was not their fault, for they had ordered the equipment from Philadelphia in April. On August 10, the impatient publishers at last received the press and type—eight days later the first issue of their gazette was presented to the public. The delay in the establishment of their printing office was the subject of the first editorial, in which they promised to make the paper "useful and interesting."[31]

Their policy was reflected in the first issues of the *Floridian* to come off the press. On the first page of the very first issue of the paper, they printed the treaty of 1819 and the documents of ratification, which readers could save for future reference. In editorials the publishers soon demonstrated a concern for the development of West Florida, in one[32] analyzing the mail service to Pensacola and suggesting means of improvement. Although the last mail received from Washington had taken seventeen days to reach the town, a distance of 1,136 miles by the route in use, there was reason to hope that the time might be shortened to eleven days. The same was true of the mails to New Orleans and Nashville. "We could enlarge on this subject, but decline it for the present—we are seeking information, and will publish all we can procure," they advised their subscribers.

As they insisted in an editorial published on September 29, Nicholas and Tunstall were determined to print only reliable information concerning the territory. They were disappointed that official topographical descriptions of the Floridas were nonexistent and that topographical engineers had not yet arrived to survey the region. But resident in Pensacola was a student of topography who had already undertaken the task of preparing a popular description of Pensacola and the surrounding country for publication in the *Floridian*—he was Alcalde Brackenridge.

His articles, signed "B," appeared under the heading of "TOPOGRAPHY." In his first article, published on August 25, Brackenridge described Pensacola and its situation. According to him, the town extended a mile along Pensacola Bay but was less than a half mile in depth. Small orchards dotted the area. There were many kitchen gardens, too, largely neglected although sure to be productive if tended. Brackenridge estimated the number of houses as sufficient for a population of four thousand people. The population, however, was about twenty-five hundred or three thousand, having almost doubled in the last few months. He believed that Americans constituted a third of the inhabitants. There was little hard cash in the town—the capital consisted of houses and lots. Since the delivery of the province the residents of Pensacola had industriously repaired the dilapidated buildings: "they have been so patched, and painted, and white-washed as to be scarcely recognized." Behind the town fresh water issued from springs at the base of a hill, forming rivulets which emptied into the bay. Brackenridge concluded that Pensacola itself needed much improvement, and he recommended experimentation to determine whether any use could be made of the sandy and "apparently sterile" soil around the town. The climate, however, was salubrious. The country adjacent to Pensacola and the bay Brackenridge described in his second article, published in the *Floridian* of October 15. In his third article, printed the following week, he mentioned the live oak, so valuable in shipbuilding, which had formerly flourished in the neighborhood. In the last article, appearing on November 5, the author tried to answer a question: "A stranger on looking around on the sands of Pensacola, and the neighboring sterile pine lands, very naturally asks where is the back country to support this place?" The reader of the four articles could tell that Brackenridge was imbued with public spirit and a faith in the future of Pensacola and West Florida; that is, if he knew the identity of correspondent "B."

With zest Brackenridge had plunged into the life of the community, not holding himself aloof by reason of his office of alcalde. By mid-August he was practicing law as a partner in the firm of Brackenridge and Call. He had realized the advantage of becoming associated with Captain Call, Governor

Jackson's protégé and former aide-de-camp. They published a notice in the first issue of the *Floridian*[33] announcing their intention to practice not only in West Florida but also in Alabama. In the meantime Brackenridge had acquitted himself in the alcaldeship to Jackson's satisfaction. "He has given great satisfaction to all, and particularly to the Spanish population of this place; and I can, with truth, say that as much order at present prevails in Pensacola as I ever saw in any town," the governor reported to Adams sometime in August.[34]

Information reaching the North from Florida confirmed Jackson's report of the situation in Pensacola. "We learn, generally, that gov. Jackson is zealously employed to organize the administration of justice in this newly acquired territory, and that, so far, all things are well," Niles informed his subscribers in September.[35] Unfortunately, a calm always precedes the storm.

About ten days after the delivery of West Florida, a free quadroon woman, Mercedes Vidal Palao, had entered the office of Alcalde Brackenridge to seek the redress of a grievance.[36] She asked him to help recover the testamentary papers of her father, Nicolas Maria Vidal, a former judge at Pensacola who had died about 1806, in his will naming her one of his heirs. His property—chiefly lands at Baton Rouge and money and personal effects now in possession of John Innerarity, the powerful local representative of the commercial house of John Forbes & Company—Vidal had willed to Mercedes, his natural daughter, and her sisters. She charged that the land was sold fraudulently and illegally and that no account was yet rendered for the money and personal property. The heirs of Vidal, in short, wanted their rightful inheritance.

Brackenridge listened respectfully to Mercedes' story and then studied the documents which she had placed in his hands—"original papers and decrees, which evidently could not be properly retained by any individual, but belonged to the archives." She had stated further that for several years her father's will and the inventories of his estate were missing from the public archives in Pensacola and that she had repeatedly petitioned the authorities for their restoration. The documents, she believed, were necessary for the prosecution of her claim under the will. The papers were alleged to be in possession of Innerarity, who, she insisted, was a debtor to the Vidal estate. Finally, after seven petitions and "many" decrees, Callava had forced Innerarity to restore the documents; and the governor had also annulled the sale of sixteen thousand acres of land at Baton Rouge and ordered him to deposit a large sum of money in the national treasury until the settlement of the estate. Several days before the delivery of West Florida, Mercedes had asked Callava for the papers in question. He had refused her request but granted her permission to have them copied one by one by a responsible person, a process which she could not afford. Brackenridge could not find the documents in his office. But a few days later

Mercedes returned to tell him that they were in the possession of the late Governor Callava, at the same time producing for Brackenridge's inspection the original will, inventories, and the record of the sales of personal property: "I then learned that they were not in the actual possession of Colonel Callava, but in the custody of a person of the name of Sousa, who had formerly been a clerk in the office." Three other documents she obtained from Domingo Sousa to show Brackenridge, who decided that all of the papers should be in his charge as the "specially commissioned keeper of the archives delivered in virtue of the treaty with Spain."

Realizing the delicacy of the situation as the ex-governor himself was involved and not knowing the best course to follow, Brackenridge consulted Jackson. Naturally the alcalde was suspicious of Innerarity, the same Hispaniolized Scot Jackson had appointed an alderman. Brackenridge told Jackson how necessary the missing documents were to the Vidal heirs for prosecuting their claim, urging him to order the papers restored to the public archives. Jackson agreed with the alcalde that justice required it and asked only that the request be addressed to him in writing, if the evidence were sufficient to warrant the action. "Some of the circumstances attending the affair are of a very peculiar nature. . . ," Brackenridge asserted in the brief application[37] filed with Jackson on August 21. "At present, I must request your excellency to authorize some one to make a regular demand of the said documents, and to *ascertain precisely what they are."*

Jackson forthwith issued an order[38] authorizing Brackenridge, George Walton, the secretary of West Florida, and John Miller, the clerk of Escambia County, to demand the documents in Sousa's possession. Jackson directed them to report to him in writing if the Spaniard refused to deliver the papers. Early that very morning of August 21 the commissioners hurried to Sousa's dwelling, where they explained the purpose of their call.[39] Startled and somewhat confused, he nevertheless produced two boxes containing mostly papers concerning courts-martial and other military matters. But some documents related to the Vidal case and three other cases; all of them seemed important for inhabitants of Pensacola and certainly belonged to the public archives there. When the commissioners demanded these papers, Sousa declined to deliver them, "declaring that he was merely the servant of the late Governor Callava, who had placed them in his hands, and that, without an order from him, they could not be given up to us." The commissioners replied by making a formal demand in writing.[40] That evening they received Sousa's refusal written in Spanish.[41] The commissioners, undismayed, then prepared a letter[42] reiterating their demand and dated August 22, which Sousa on the morrow would not accept, although he said that, "in order to relieve himself from the responsibility of keeping the papers, he was about to deliver them to the late governor." There was nothing the commissioners could do now but to submit their report.

Sousa, the underling of Callava, had reason for worry. He had told the commissioners of his communication with Callava about their demand. The commissioners, in fact, assumed that the ex-governor had dictated Sousa's note of rejection.[43] As long as the papers remained in his possession, Sousa knew the Americans would never let him alone. Therefore, the morning of August 22, at eleven o'clock, he had Manuel Domingo's negro carry the boxes of documents to Callava's house and there deliver them to Antoine Fullarat, the steward, the only person at home. Sousa accompanied the negro to Callava's residence.

This transfer of the records came to light at Sousa's interrogation before the governor in the Office of the Executive of Florida. Jackson had sent Colonel Robert Butler and Miller to seize Sousa and the papers in his possession.[44] They returned with the Spanish lieutenant but without the documents, entering the governor's office about one o'clock.[45] Fifteen questions[46] Jackson asked Sousa, eliciting the information that the papers were now at Callava's house.

Jackson, determined that the papers be restored to Brackenridge's office where they belonged, summoned the officer of the day, Captain F. L. Dade, who was in charge of the jail, to take Sousa into custody until the delivery of the documents. But Jackson permitted the frightened Spaniard to apply to Callava for their return. Consequently, Captain Dade accompanied Sousa in search of his superior.[47] They found him with Innerarity and several Spanish officers at the dwelling of Colonel G. M. Brooke, the commander of the Fourth Infantry. Callava ordered Sousa to put on his uniform and surrender himself as a prisoner. The ex-governor declared that, as the commissioner for the delivery of West Florida, he expected Governor Jackson to apply directly to him for any papers. Captain Dade and his prisoner returned to Jackson's office about three o'clock.[48]

By now the governor was in a dangerous mood—and the afternoon was only half over. Earlier in the day it was apparent that his blood was beginning to boil, for, when Sousa told him that a Spanish officer could not be imprisoned, Jackson had replied "with considerable warmth, that the papers he would have, and that he would commit Sousa, Callava, and all concerned, for seven years, or until the papers should be forthcoming."[49] Upon the return of Captain Dade and Sousa without the papers, Jackson's next move was to order Colonel Butler and Dr. Bronaugh to take Callava and his steward, Fullarat, into custody and to bring them before him for an interrogation unless the documents were delivered on demand.[50] In the same written order Jackson directed Brackenridge to accompany the two men to Callava's house.

Brackenridge assumed the management of the commissioners' business at their request.[51] About four-thirty o'clock they proceeded to Callava's dwelling and there learned he was still at the dinner party at Colonel Brooke's, several doors up the street. They moved down the street and waited for half an hour, considerately giving the ex-governor time to return home. But on inquiry at the gate, the same answer as before was received—Callava was not home. Butler and Bronaugh then deputed Brackenridge to summon Callava from the residence of Colonel Brooke: "I accordingly went, and found a number of gentlemen sitting in the dining room, and in the porch fronting the bay, after having risen from dinner; Mr. Cruzat, the Governor's secretary, was called out at my request, who immediately anticipated the object of my errand, and in a passionate manner called to Colonel Callava, who came instantly, and began with warmth to assert his rights as commissioner of Spain, and to talk of the laws of nations." Callava, José Cruzat, and the Spanish officers present retired into the house. At that moment Colonel Butler and Dr. Bronaugh approached the gate; and as they entered the yard, Callava and his friends, including Innerarity, suddenly left. Colonel Brooke berated the three Americans for disturbing his company, declaring "that he acknowledged no authority to arrest a man in his House—that he was astonished at our conduct and that it had been extremely indecorous towards him." That was how Dr. Bronaugh later reported Colonel Brooke's curious attitude to the governor.

Only a few minutes had elapsed, meanwhile, before the three Americans confronted the Spaniards on Callava's back porch. Brackenridge introduced Colonel Butler to Callava, and then he explained the purpose of the call: "The utmost delicacy was observed by Colonel Butler, but Colonel Callava expressed himself in a very vehement and passionate manner, being naturally of a choleric temper." Although the conversation lasted at least one hour, Callava could not be persuaded to deliver the papers. Now Brackenridge explained the order requiring Callava to appear before Jackson for an interrogation—"When this was made known, Mr. Innerarity exclaimed 'the die is cast!' and Colonel Callava positively refused."

Colonel Butler warned Callava that he was defying the authority of Governor Jackson, a charge which the Spaniard denied. But as the Americans were about to leave, Callava offered to deliver the documents, providing Colonel Butler gave him a list of those demanded. Butler, Bronaugh, and Brackenridge withdrew. The alcalde, however, returned with the list[52] fifteen minutes later to find Callava packing boxes in the midst of his friends: "and he said to me, himself, that he was making out a protest against the proceedings, and taking such precautions as would be taken by a person who expected every thing he possessed would be forcibly carried away." Brackenridge assured him that only a few papers were wanted. He left the list with Callava and advised him that Colonel Butler and Dr. Bronaugh would return for the documents in two hours.

Brackenridge reported this latest development to Jackson, who decided that a show of force was necessary to make Callava restore the papers. The governor refused to be balked any longer. To Colonel Brooke, who enjoyed Callava's company, went an order[53] for an officer, sergeant, corporal, and twenty men— "their arms and accoutrements complete, with twelve rounds of ammunition"— to wait on Jackson at eight-thirty o'clock that evening. Lieutenant George Mountz, the officer of the guard, was instructed[54] to bring Callava and Fullarat before Jackson if they did not surrender the documents to Colonel Butler and Dr. Bronaugh.

About nine o'clock a strange procession moved toward Callava's house— Butler, Bronaugh, and Brackenridge accompanied by the guard. Theirs was a serious mission, for Jackson awaited its result in his office. Leaving the guard in the street, they unlocked the gate to Callava's front yard and entered the garden, as Brackenridge related subsequently in his version of the affair:

. . . The house was shut up; the door locked. On our entering the porch, we heard a bustle inside resembling the rattling of arms. Admittance was three times demanded by me in Spanish, but no answer was returned. I then went round, and discovered several persons in the porch on the side fronting the bay. The guard was ordered round, and formed in front of high steps which lead up to the porch; they had a short time before been ordered into the garden, and had been drawn up before the front door. On ascending the steps, inquiries were made for Colonel Callava; they all remained silent: on the question being repeated, it was observed by some one that he did not know. The only light was a candle burning in one of the rooms. Colonel Butler ordered a candle to be brought from some of the neighboring houses. After waiting fifteen minutes, it was resolved to enter the hall, and some one brought out the candle. Two or three of the soldiers were then ordered up; we then entered the room where the candle had been burning, and Colonel Callava rose from a bed, with his coat off, and expressed great surprise at our entering his house at that time of night.[55]

When the demand for the documents was made again, Callava once more refused to deliver them. Brackenridge saw the boxes containing them in the bedroom, but the ex-governor remained adamant in his attitude. Told that he must appear before Jackson, Callava expressed fear of assassination—no one would take him from his dwelling alive! The guard received an order to prime and load, whereupon Callava agreed to go to the government house. "It was impossible to have used greater delicacy to any one under similar circumstances," Brackenridge avowed later.

Innerarity's conduct irked Colonel Butler and Dr. Bronaugh. It was not so much what the wily Scot did as what he did not do. Innerarity was never far from Callava's side. Although appointed to the city council by Jackson, Innerarity did not reciprocate the favor now by urging Callava to surrender the papers. Innerarity, it seemed, tried to stiffen Callava's resolution whenever it began to waver. On their return to the government house, consequently, Butler and Bronaugh recommended to Jackson "that your excellency will fill his place in the council with a character who will manifest a proper respect for the dignity of the laws, and you their Executive."[56]

It was nearing ten o'clock when the party escorting Callava entered Jackson's office.[57] The room was already crowded with Americans and Spaniards excitedly awaiting the interrogation of Callava by the fuming governor of the provinces of the Floridas. At Jackson's invitation Callava took a seat at a table, and Brackenridge sat at one end to act as interpreter; they faced the governor. Jackson ordered Brackenridge to explain to Callava the reason for his interrogation: "Colonel Callava on this rose, and, looking at his watch, said that it was then 10 o'clock; that at that hour he had been violently taken from his house; that he protested against the proceeding; that he was commissioner of Spain, and was not answerable as a private individual." Jackson, refusing to entertain such a protest against his authority as he sat in his judicial capacity, directed Brackenridge to put the questions[58] to the Spaniard. But Callava, maintaining that he was a sick man hauled from his bed, declined answering the questions, "except in the manner he considers proper—in his own language, and with his own hand."

In his role of interpreter Brackenridge was in a ticklish situation, for, as the tempers of Jackson and Callava frayed and their expressions became warmer and warmer, his translating satisfied neither party.[59] Finally, Jackson allowed the Spaniard to write his answer to a question. Callava wrote several lines and stopped, complaining that his eyes were too weak to continue; but he received permission to dictate the remainder to Cruzat, his secretary. When it was discovered after five or six lines that Callava was really dictating a protest, Jackson turned his wrath upon Brackenridge: "The Governor, on this, with considerable warmth, striking on the table, and addressing himself to me, said, 'Why do you not tell him, sir, that I will not permit him to protest?' and which was intended as a reprimand to me for suffering Colonel Callava to proceed in this way, when he was repeatedly told that such a course would not be allowed." Again Jackson tried to interrogate Callava without success. The Spaniard refused to answer any question unless he could answer in his own way. During the proceedings Brackenridge had requested Cruzat to assist in the interpreting to eliminate the possibility of a misunderstanding—Cruzat declined the invitation. At times the argument between the parties was so heated that Brackenridge could only convey its substance.

But he deliberately toned down much of the provocative language he was called upon to interpret.[60] Although Callava objected to the interrogation of Fullarat because of his youth, Jackson examined the steward successfully, establishing the fact that the disputed papers were in Callava's possession. The governor ordered Brackenridge to tell Callava that he must surrender the documents and that he had permission to send some person to bring the boxes for opening there in the room before many witnesses. To make sure that Callava understood the demand made of him, Jackson asked the friends of the ex-governor, including Innerarity who knew both languages, to explain it carefully; and occasionally, Edward A. Rutledge assisted Brackenridge in the interpreting. Brackenridge was certain that Callava understood the demand, although the "conversation, as is natural, was warm on both sides, and some expressions were softened by me in the interpretation, and others, tending only to irritate and provoke, omitted altogether."

In his ill-humor Jackson again chided Brackenridge, who, attributing the matter to fatigue, was not offended.[61] The incident occurred when the governor

reminded Colonel Callava of his having promised to deliver the papers if found in the boxes. Here Colonel Callava exclaimed "it is false!" meaning that he had never made any such promise, but which was mistaken by the by-standers. I stated that Colonel Callava denied the promise, and that it was possible that I might have misunderstood him, which drew from the Governor an expression of displeasure. In a strong tone of voice, he asked, "Why then, sir, were you not more cautious?"—words which proceeded only from the irritation of the moment, while he was almost sinking with fatigue. It was then midnight, and he had been sitting, with scarcely any interval, from ten or eleven o'clock in the forenoon.

After two hours of contention Jackson stood up and declared that Callava must deliver the papers or suffer the consequences.[62] Once more his situation was explained to the Spaniard, who refused to comply again with the request. Now Jackson signed a blank commitment,[63] prepared in advance for such an eventuality as this, confining Callava and Fullarat to the dirty brick jail in Pensacola, where Sousa was already a prisoner in the company of a New Jersey youth, arrested for shooting a snipe on the common in violation of a municipal regulation.[64] Accompanied by Spanish officers, Lieutenant Mountz escorted Callava and his steward to the calaboose, where, in the early hours of the morning, the Spaniards got uproariously drunk upon the arrival of a supply of claret and champagne.

The morning of August 23, Jackson awoke with the satisfaction that Callava had spent the night ignominiously in the calaboose. But he was more than ever determined to obtain the documents still in Callava's possession and to restore them to the public archives. Brackenridge provided the solution to the problem by petitioning the governor for the appointment of responsible persons to open the boxes in Callava's house and to examine their contents.[65]

277

Jackson then issued a search warrant,[66] which empowered George Walton, John Miller, David Shannon, and Thomas Brownjohn, accompanied by the alcalde, to visit the Callava dwelling for the purpose of seizing the papers if found in any of the boxes there. They had no trouble at all in finding the documents, which were given to the alcalde for restoration to his office.[67]

Meanwhile, the same morning, Callava's friends waited on Eligius Fromentin, who had recently arrived in Pensacola to assume his post of judge of the United States for West Florida. Monroe's appointee was a queer personality—a bad choice for a judgeship.[68] A French priest educated by the Jesuits, Fromentin had left his country and his church during the Revolution, emigrating to the United States, where he obtained a position teaching in a Maryland school. After his marriage into a prominent family in that state, he had moved to New Orleans, practiced law there, and even represented Louisiana in the United States Senate for one term. Upon the Bourbon restoration in France, Fromentin had deserted his wife and sailed for his native land in the hope of winning preferment in the church he had once abandoned. When reports of his marriage ruined this plan, Fromentin had returned to his wife in America and resumed his practice of the law in New Orleans—but now his Louisiana friends spurned him. It was then that his wife's relatives had prevailed upon the President to give him the Florida judgeship, a temporary appointment[69] which required Monroe to ignore John Haywood, a Tennessean recommended by Jackson. The President knew nothing about Fromentin's unsavory past, however. In Pensacola, on August 11, the renegade priest received his commission as judge and was therefore ready to perform the duties of his office, although the United States attorney had not arrived and the marshal had set off for St. Augustine without appointing a deputy.[70] Immediately, Judge Fromentin and Governor Jackson had clashed over the extent of their respective jurisdictions.[71] Thus Fromentin sensed trouble when he learned early in the morning of August 23 that "Colonel Callava had been arrested the preceding night in his own house, and carried to jail. Soon after, my house was filled with people of all descriptions and languages."[72]

After the hubbub had quieted and the crowd had dispersed, four of Callava's friends reappeared at Fromentin's dwelling.[73] It was about eleven o'clock in the morning. Innerarity, of course, was one of these men who applied verbally to Fromentin for a writ of *habeas corpus* in an attempt to free Callava from the calaboose. The judge demanded security for the production of the disputed papers, and he got it in the amount of forty thousand dollars. Fromentin next issued the writ,[74] which Dr. John Brosnaham, one of the four callers, agreed to serve on the officer of the prison guard, Lieutenant Mountz. But upon receipt of the writ Mountz advised Brosnaham that no action would be taken and at the same time handed the paper to Captain P. Wager, the officer of the day, who carried it to Jackson.

This challenge to his authority infuriated the governor, and he bellowed like a wounded bull. But before dealing with Fromentin, Jackson signed an order[75] for the discharge of the three Spaniards from the calaboose. Captain Wager accompanied Callava to his house, where they examined the two boxes which had contained the documents and also his personal effects. Everything seemed to satisfy Callava, the officer reported to Jackson: "I then dismissed the guard from his house, and left him in peaceful possession of it."[76]

Because Brackenridge placed the documents in the public archives, the Vidal heirs could take their case to court. Callava, the ex-governor, no longer was in the calaboose. But the story—a comedy which James Parton called "Much Ado about Less than Nothing"[77]—had not ended, for, out of West Florida upon an unsuspecting nation, there suddenly poured charges and counter-charges, accusations and explanations. For his subscribers Niles offered this interpretation of what had happened in the South:

FLORIDA. It is well said by the *Richmond Enquirer,* that our newly acquired territory of Florida "is very productive of—documents." We now add several to the mass of matter hitherto given, to present, if possible, "a view of the whole ground." We wonder that so great a fire has been kindled by the OLD *Spanish-like* proceedings of two individuals—by which we mean to insinuate, that the door of common justice was only to be opened by a golden key. But Jackson determined that "justice is—justice," and used his great powers as "captain-general" to demonstrate it. [78]

But now Jackson could not retire to the "Hermitage" in peace. Did he rue his appointment of Brackenridge as alcalde of Pensacola?

XX
Judge Brackenridge of West Florida

Jackson dealt sternly with Fromentin. To Colonel Walton he gave a written order[1] for delivery to the judge, who was directed to appear in the governor's office at five o'clock that very day, August 23, to explain why he had acted "in open contempt" of Jackson's orders and decrees, issued in his capacity of "supreme judge" over the Floridas and "as chancellor thereof." Fromentin, however, refused to appear before Jackson at the designated hour, for he was so indisposed that only force could get him out of his house that day; as he insisted to Walton, and later assured[2] Secretary of State Adams, a "severe" case of rheumatism prevented him from walking. The indisposition was fortunate, as Fromentin knew, because time was necessary for Jackson to calm himself. But Jackson received the news of the judge's condition reasonably enough and moved the time of the meeting ahead to three o'clock the next afternoon.

Fromentin had prepared a brief reply[3] to the summons, announcing his indisposition and stating his reason for granting the writ of *habeas corpus* to Callava's friends. But Walton advised Fromentin not to send it to the governor, a recommendation which was followed.[4] The judge passed an uncomfortable night, plagued by the thought of meeting with Callava's fate; but no soldiers came to take him into custody. About noon the next day Walton returned to tell Fromentin that Jackson was anxious to have a report of their affair ready for the Washington mail and, therefore, requested him to come to an interview the following morning. The invitation puzzled Fromentin—"I determined to go there that very afternoon. . . ." Rheumatic pains did not keep the judge from entering the governor's office about four o'clock, August 24.

The meeting between the hero of New Orleans and the apostate priest was tempestuous, for they hated each other. Jackson did most of the talking; he lectured Fromentin severely.[5] "The conversation, as you may suppose, was nearly all on one side, not unmixed with threats of what he said he had a right to do for my having dared to interfere with his authority," the judge protested to Adams.[6] But before he left Jackson's office quivering with rage, Fromentin signed a statement[7] admitting that he had granted the writ only upon a verbal application made by Callava's friends. The judge, moreover, had to acknowledge the fact that he did not even know the name of the person to whom he had delivered the writ! After Fromentin's departure Jackson discovered that through inadvertence the word "verbal" was missing from the memorandum which the judge had signed. The following day Colonel Walton waited on Fromentin to have him insert the word in the proper place, "that every thing may appear as it was transacted. . . ."[8]

What transpired in Jackson's office on that afternoon of August 24 was, of course, a fertile subject for rumor in Pensacola. One story had Fromentin apologizing to the governor for issuing the writ. When Fromentin heard this rumor, he wrote Jackson on September 3, demanding his aid in contradicting it.[9] His note "truly astonished" the governor, who replied instantly, reminding Fromentin of their conversation point by point—"If this, sir, was not an apology, I know not what is."[10] Now it was Fromentin's turn to be astonished at Jackson's answer. Let a higher authority decide the issue between them, Fromentin replied.[11] "I have this moment received your second note of this day," the governor answered. "The first excited my astonishment, it is true; but the second my indignation and contempt; for I did not suppose, until your note now before me furnished conclusive evidence, that you were capable of stating a wilful and deliberate falsehood."[12] Fromentin did not pick up the gantlet which Jackson thus threw down before him.

Fromentin appealed to the Secretary of State for support in the controversy. In letter after letter the judge defended his granting of the writ and assailed Jackson. Fromentin damned the governor as a tyrant who claimed unlimited powers and whom everyone in Pensacola feared. Fromentin believed Jackson hoped to deprive him of his office to make room for John Haywood, whom Jackson had originally recommended to the President as a candidate for the judgeship:

> I understand that, with this view, a memorial has been sent by the last mail to the President, purporting to be signed by persons who call themselves members of the bar. What the precise purport of that memorial is, I know not. Of all the persons who profess themselves to be lawyers in this place, I know nobody even by name, but Mr. Brackenridge, with whom, for fifteen years, I have been on terms, if not of intimacy, at least of familiar acquaintance. Whether he has signed that memorial or not, I am not informed. But if he has, it affords an additional proof of what rapid progress the gangrene of the most abject slavery can make, even in a few hours, when the *vultus instantis tyranni,* by striking terror in every soul, compels men to do that which, under every other circumstance, they would hold most in abhorrence.[13]

As he felt his indignity more and more, Fromentin became hysterical in his protests to Adams; and he denied signing the statement which Jackson had deemed an apology.[14] Pensacola he called a "Jacksonian Commonwealth" and cited evidence to substantiate his charge: "Since the taking possession of Pensacola, all the play-bills were headed Jacksonian Commonwealth. I send one enclosed."[15] The judge, furthermore, accused Alcalde Brackenridge of abetting the Jacksonian tyranny, and the "notorious" Abner L. Duncan too, for, according to the governor's own admission, they had advised him on the establishment of the new government in West Florida. In Fromentin's opinion, Jackson was a usurper.

Adams dutifully submitted the judge's letters to President Monroe. The result was an official rebuke to Fromentin, whose jurisdiction applied only to the laws of the United States concerning the revenue and its collection and the slave trade. They were the only laws, Adams reminded him, which Congress had extended to the Floridas during this period of temporary government.[16] "In the different view which you have taken of the subject," the Secretary of State concluded, "[the President] is persuaded that your motives and intentions were entirely pure, though he deeply regrets the collision of authority and misunderstanding which has arisen between the Governor of the Territory and you." This reprimand, it was hoped, would end the affair.

Until news of the incident reached Monroe he had congratulated himself upon his appointment of Jackson as governor of the Floridas. In mid-September the President wrote Jackson praising his conduct of affairs in Pensacola.[17] Monroe explained the appointment of Fromentin as judge, denying, however, any knowledge of his offensive past except the desertion of his wife, "but seeing him afterwards with his Lady, and he being supported by the senators from Louisiana, and many, from other States, I had presumed that he had cleared the matter up to their satisfaction." The President approved of Jackson's appointment of Brackenridge, calling it "proper." Indeed, Monroe actually described Jackson's management of Florida affairs as "judicious." Stay in Florida, was the theme of the President's message to Jackson: "You may for years, render most essential service there."

Then reports of the imprisonment of Callava and of Fromentin's attempt to obtain his release reached the State Department. It was, in fact, the painful duty of Hilario de Rivas y Salmon, the new Spanish chargé d'affaires, to begin his service with a complaint by transmitting[18] Callava's official protest to the Secretary of State. Although he sent Jackson a copy of the letter reprimanding Fromentin, Adams wanted more information about the whole Callava case before addressing a reply to the Spanish government. Four circumstances needed explanation, Adams believed. One was that during the Spaniard's interrogation "neither the questions asked of him, nor his answers were correctly interpreted."[19]

The charge was an attack upon Brackenridge's work as the interpreter during the mad proceedings in the governor's office the night of August 22. Two days later six of Callava's friends had signed a statement[20] characterizing the alcalde's interpreting as "extremely faulty." They noticed that Brackenridge had interpreted only a very little of Callava's testimony. But as the alcalde explained in a subsequent defense of his work, a widely published statement,[21] he had done this deliberately in the hope of softening the most inflammatory language and thereby averting an explosion of temper on Jackson's or Callava's part. There was no reason why Callava's friends could not have supplied any deficiencies in Brackenridge's interpreting had they noted any, for Innerarity, Cruzat, and others present at the interrogation knew both English and Spanish. In a statement[22] dated September 30, 1821, Rutledge, who had assisted Brackenridge in the interpreting, confirmed the truth of the alcalde's defense. The irate Spaniards maligned Brackenridge for a difficult task well done during "two of the most painful hours of my life. . . ."

The friends of Callava, in truth, used one pretext or another on which to base declarations, made upon oath, to justify his conduct and to protest his treatment in the hands of the American governor. Six of them, for example, did not like what they saw in Callava's house after accompanying him home from the calaboose.[23] They found the dwelling open but troops on guard; and, on a table which served Callava as a desk, they observed bundles of un-sealed papers. The two boxes which the Americans had examined, they noticed, bore new wax seals alongside broken ones of the same color but of a different figure—evidence that the boxes had been opened! They watched Callava unlock his strongbox and count his gold and silver pieces—not one was missing! The Spaniards, however, protested such injustice done to their friend.

They did not realize that Jackson would stand no more of their nonsense. Twelve Spaniards and Innerarity had signed a declaration[24] on August 23— their version of what had occurred the night before in the governor's office. "The governor, Don Andrew Jackson, with turbulent and violent actions, with disjointed reasonings, blows on the table, his mouth foaming, and possessed with the furies, told the Spanish commissary to deliver the papers as a private individual," their account ran. But Jackson's sincerity in wishing justice done to the Vidal heirs was apparent in his report of the events of August 22 to the Secretary of State.[25] The governor maintained that his conduct was "dictated by the imperious rules of justice, to save the unprotected orphan from being ruined by the most cruel oppression, by the most corrupt, and wicked combination, I ever investigated." Jackson believed Callava to be merely the tool of the villainous Innerarity. Consequently, Fromentin's interference in the affair was outrageous as well as unjustifiable. The spirit animating Jackson's measures he himself described to Adams: "I did believe, and ever will believe, that just laws can make no distinction of privilege between the rich and the poor, and that when men of high standing attempt to trample upon the rights of the weak, they are the fitest objects for example and punishment. In general, the great can protect themselves, but the poor and humble, require the arm and the shield of the law."

Therefore, when Callava's friends publicly challenged his authority, Jackson reacted swiftly and in an unexpected fashion. H. Bigelow had published an account of the occurrences of August 22 in the *Louisiana Advertiser* of August 28, a statement which did not treat Callava kindly. To present the other side of the story to the inhabitants of West Florida and the United States, eight Spaniards prepared a statement[26] for publication in the Pensacola newspaper and signed it as "THE SPANISH OFFICERS, Resident in this place." At once the governor issued a proclamation,[27] dated September 29, expelling them from the Floridas. It stated that the officers had remained in town without the permission of the American authorities in violation of the seventh article of the treaty between Spain and the United States. Their publication, calculated to foment discontent, in Jackson's opinion was a "gross abuse of the lenity and indulgence heretofore extended to them." Withdraw from the Floridas before October 4, or face arrest, Jackson warned the Spaniards. As he reported to Adams, the governor could not allow his court and its officers to suffer any indignity.[28] Jackson thought Fromentin instigated the Spaniards to publish the statement—a "false, scandalous, and indecent publication."

Callava, in the meantime, had gone north to protest his treatment to the Spanish minister. Before leaving the South, however, he gave a statement, signed "CALLAVA," to the New Orleans papers, spurning the *Floridian* as a medium for presenting his case to the public. "We suppose he did not consider this a *free Press,* and that it was under the control of the government," the publishers of the Pensacola gazette commented editorially as they reprinted his declaration, which, as they observed, had suffered alteration, the "original having been written in Spanish, translated into French, & from that rendered in English."[29] Dr. Bronaugh read the statement when it first appeared in the New Orleans press and was so astonished by its contents that, in a communication[30] to the *Floridian* publishers, he pronounced it "a tissue of falsehoods and distortion of facts from the commencement to the end" and promised to prepare more of his own views for publication. Alcalde Brackenridge appended his signature to Bronaugh's declaration, certifying to its accuracy, "having had a personal acquaintance with the whole transaction."

The Callava affair was now a matter of public record in the American press. In two more articles, written for the *Floridian* and printed with official documents of the case, Dr. Bronaugh continued his presentation of Jackson's side of the controversy.[31] But the policy of the *Floridian* was pro-Jackson, for the publishers shared the governor's view of the administration of justice: "In the case in question, (as in all others) the decision was either right or wrong—and if founded on reason and law—it was fully and sufficiently found—regardless of precedent."[32] For months Nicholas and Tunstall noticed the editorial comment of other papers on the case,[33] while Niles, in Baltimore, relied on their gazette for information to print in his own repository of news, although he borrowed from other sources, also.[34] Niles, however, strove to be impartial in his handling of the affair: "It is not at all our intention to enter into a discussion of the right of certain proceedings in Florida—but it is necessary that the facts belonging to them should be *registered*."[35]

The governor's friends did not want him to become embroiled in a newspaper controversy with Callava. Jackson's situation, as one anonymous supporter stressed in a communication to the *Floridian*,[36] was too "exalted" for him to stoop to such a thing or to render an explanation of his conduct as a judge to anyone except "his immediate superior the President of the United States." Worshipful Jacksonians, like this *Floridian* correspondent, saw a chance in the Callava case to deify their hero: ". . . we who know all the circumstances attending the arrest and imprisonment of Callava and which gave rise to the publication, cannot help considering, that it will redound as much to his credit as any act of his life, and the facts need only to be known to throw a halo around and sanctify his name."

The Secretary of State stood foursquare behind Jackson and defended him in an exchange of views with the envoy of the Spanish government. Adams certainly could not have been surprised by the emotional nature of Callava's protest,[37] in which the Spaniard related how he had departed for Washington as a sick man on August 27 to protest formally to the Spanish minister. But Adams wanted Jackson's explanation of Callava's charges before he was willing "to pronounce definitively on the subject," as he informed the envoy, Joaquin de Anduaga, newly arrived in the United States.[38] Adams used this opportunity, however, to discredit part of Callava's story, particularly his allegation of mistreatment while ill, having obtained the evidence from the Spaniard's protest itself. In reply the minister applauded the prudence of the President and his Secretary of State and refrained from answering the paragraphs in Adams' note "which seem to defend the conduct of General Jackson. . . ."[39]

It was now the middle of November, 1821. At this time the Spanish minister was amazed to read Jackson's proclamation expelling the eight officers of His Catholic Majesty from Pensacola and the Floridas.[40] The envoy was doomed to eventual disappointment no matter how vigorous his protest, for Jackson had prepared an able defense of his own conduct in the Callava affair, supported by depositions[41] which Dr. Bronaugh himself conveyed to the Department of State. Jackson likewise was careful to forward to Adams copies of all the documents[42] pertaining to the clash with Fromentin along with a sarcastic attack on the judge.[43] In a letter of November 22 to Adams, written in Nashville, Jackson detailed the considerations which determined his treatment of Callava

285

and warned the Secretary of State to beware of forgeries in studying the documents displayed by the Spanish—if not forgeries, ". . . John Innerarity has perjured himself. . . ."[44]

After receiving this letter from Jackson, Adams still hesitated to reply definitively to the Spanish minister's protest in Callava's behalf. On New Year's Day, 1822, he forwarded to Jackson the translations of two more letters which the envoy had sent to the State Department. He would defer his official answer, Adams wrote, until Jackson had an opportunity to submit any remarks he cared to make on these letters from the Spanish minister.[45] When he did state the American case in mid-April, Adams could, therefore, be confident in his presentation, which proved to be a thoroughgoing and spirited defense of Jackson and, naturally, of Brackenridge, too.[46] The President had instructed Adams to say that the transactions of which the envoy had complained were "attributable entirely to the conduct of the Governor and Captain General of Cuba, and of the subordinate officers of Spain, in evading and refusing the fulfilment of the most express and positive stipulations of the treaty, both of evacuating the province within six months from the exchange of the ratifications of the treaty, and of delivering the archives and documents relating directly to the property and sovereignty of the provinces." This assertion the Secretary of State backed up with telling argumentation, reviewing the whole proceedings. The minister read Adams' note and was aghast—immediately he requested instructions from his government![47] But Adams' forceful note officially concluded the controversy with Spain.

The hurly-burly over Callava had not caused Jackson to neglect the petition[48] of Mercedes Vidal Palao for a settlement of her father's estate. He ordered Innerarity to appear before him the morning of August 29 to show cause why Callava's decrees in the Vidal case should not be enforced.[49] Innerarity later asked John Coppinger Connor, the clerk of the "Executive Court of West Florida," to identify the different handwritings in which the two documents were written: ". . . I do hereby certify that the original petition in this cause appears to be in the handwriting of R. K. Call, one of the counsel for the plaintiff; and the order, in the handwriting of H. M. Brackenridge, the other counsel for the plaintiff; and it is signed by Governor Jackson, with his own hand."[50] Undoubtedly the defendant believed that justice in his case could not have been served by such a combination against him.

At eleven o'clock on the morning of August 29, however, the case of *The Heirs of Nicolas Maria Vidal* v. *John Innerarity* had begun when the defendant appeared before Jackson and John C. Mitchell, appointed by the governor to sit with him during the proceedings. The case excited intense public interest, for it had been in litigation for fifteen years.[51] Jackson and Mitchell, sitting as a court of chancery, overruled Innerarity's objection to the petition of Mercedes Vidal and her right to sue but granted him a continuance of the case that he might make a full defense—he received an extension of time to September 6.[52] Also, when the defendant gave Alcalde Brackenridge a suitable receipt, the court allowed him to remove from the archives the papers and books relating to the case.

Innerarity sought to delay the progress of the suit. He petitioned Jackson to require Brackenridge and Call to legalize their representation of the Vidals conformably to Spanish law.[53] Through his attorney, Samuel Acre, the defendant argued, moreover, that the court had no jurisdiction in the case, contending that Callava's decrees were not binding in law and that, even if legal, they could not be enforced in good conscience.[54] On September 6, Acre petitioned successfully that more time be granted him to prepare his client's defense—Jackson postponed the proceedings until September 10.[55]

But the governor's judicial opinion,[56] pronounced by Mitchell in court in the role of law adviser according to the Spanish practice,[57] forestalled any attempt by Innerarity to evade the legal process. When the court met on the appointed day, Acre challenged its right to entertain the suit and denied the existence of any tribunal in the Floridas competent to try the case; but "Mr. Brackenridge, on the part of the petitioners, contended that the Spanish Government, of which the judiciary is part, has ceased, although the laws and usages are still in force. The error of opinion on this subject, he said, arises from not distinguishing these things." Brackenridge argued that the Spanish constitution was inapplicable in the Vidal case. "The very able and satisfactory discussion this question has undergone by the gentlemen of the bar, by which the court was not only delighted, but instructed, has stripped it, in a great measure, of its difficulty," Jackson and Mitchell declared in their opinion which overruled Acre's plea and demanded the defendant to explain why Callava's decrees ought not to be executed. In great detail but with a try at succinctness, the judges reviewed all the proceedings in the case and then ordered Innerarity to produce "exact" accounts concerning the Vidal estate, "supported by legal documents," to the auditors appointed by the court and to post security to satisfy any possible decree which the court might pass against him. The defendant had twenty days in which to submit his accounts. The judges, also, granted the Vidal heirs permission to prosecute their claims relating to 16,000 acres of land in dispute.

Sitting as the supreme court of judicature of West Florida when they delivered the decree against Innerarity on September 17, Jackson and Mitchell afterward appointed a board of three auditors to settle the estate.[58] The auditors received the power to compel the appearance of necessary witnesses and the production of required documents.[59] After a study of the statements submitted to them, the auditors reported to the court a balance of $496 in favor of the estate.[60] But disallowing two claims, the court ordered the defendant to pay $1,027.19 to the alcalde within thirty days.[61] Brackenridge was required to insert a notice[62] in the *Floridian* for two months to give creditors of the estate sufficient time to present their claims. If no substantiated claims were made, he was to pay the money in his hands to the Vidal heirs.

Although Innerarity had safely ignored the Spanish decrees against him in the case, he could not defy Jacksonian justice with impunity nor even elude it. But he tried to postpone it by submitting petition after petition[63] to Jackson's court, constantly reminding the Americans of the Spanish laws. In December his counsel, Acre, wrote an opinion[64] on the auditors' report maintaining that the Vidal estate owed $157[65] to the house of Forbes: "Hence, there is neither principal nor interest belonging to the estate of Vidal in the hands of John Innerarity, the attorney of Forbes." Acre complained that the defendant had no chance of appeal because West Florida lacked an appellate court but insisted that the "same power which did the injury can repair the wrong."

Jackson, however, was no longer in Pensacola serving as governor of the Floridas. He could have no part in further litigation in the Vidal case, should there be any.[66] But it was his administration of justice, as prompted by Brackenridge, which had given the Vidal heirs their day in court. The operation of Spanish justice was too easily impeded by an influential person like Innerarity.

By the beginning of October, 1821, the tranquillity of the "Hermitage" had become an irresistible lure for the dog-tired and ailing Jackson. As Rachel assured her brother already in August, "There never was a man more disappointed than the General has been."[67] He could not appoint his friends to the highest offices in the Floridas. The Spaniards exasperated him beyond measure, as his wife knew: "He has had terrible scenes; the governor has been put in the calaboose; which is a terrible thing, really. I was afraid there would be a rebellion, but the Spanish troops were all gone to the Havannah. . . ." In August, too, the Jacksons hoped to return to Tennessee by the first of October. Knowing the governor's desire to leave Pensacola, the officers stationed there and at the Barrancas united with the townsmen to arrange a fete in his honor at Austin's Tavern on Thursday, October 4.[68] A festive affair it was—eighty gentlemen partook of the dinner (the fifth toast: "The state of Alabama— We love her as a sister, but we would not be wed.") and in the evening their ladies joined them for the ball. The weather that night was bad—"all gloom and rain." The next day Jackson wrote the President of his intention to take a respite from his duties as governor, promising, however, to return to Pensacola if necessary.[69] But he informed Monroe of his determination to resign

288

the governorship when Congress met. Jackson planned to leave Florida affairs in charge of the secretaries, W. G. D. Worthington of East Florida and Walton of West Florida.

This intention to go home the governor announced publicly in his farewell address, "To the Citizens of the Floridas,"[70] dated October 6. In the first sentence Jackson proclaimed the completion of the temporary organization of the Florida government. Then he explained to the Floridians the spirit which had animated his official conduct:

> . . . I have made no discrimination of persons—my house has been surrounded by no guards, no one has been kept at a distance by repulsive formalities, all have had free admittance, and found a ready ear, when they required my aid for the protection of their rights. The American government, at the same time that it is the freest, is perhaps the strongest in the world; because, the most wealthy and most powerful in society, are as weak in opposition to it, as the most humble and obscure. It knows no distinction between an ex-governor and a peasant.

Only one case had occurred, he stated, which required him to exercise "that authority which is no respecter of persons." In discussing the Callava affair Jackson did not refer to the Spaniard by name but left no doubt whom he meant. Jackson had contended, he advised the Floridians, that Callava's diplomatic privileges, such as they were, had ceased upon the surrender of West Florida. Therefore, he had viewed Callava as an ordinary person without special rights and had treated him accordingly when he refused to deliver the documents. Although Jackson did not detail the consequences of Callava's attitude, he presented a dignified defense of his own conduct and accused the expelled Spanish officers of having published "a most indecent libel" against the proceedings of the highest court in the Floridas. The governor informed the Floridians of his continued respect for them—the misconduct of a few had not lessened his regard for the many—and of his placing their government in the hands of Worthington and Walton.

Niles, who had published Jackson's address and the Spanish documents as well, no longer could remain impartial in his presentation of the Florida news. He had become a Jackson partisan: "The governor's address presents a powerful justification of his conduct. He seems to hold a pen or the sword with equal ability. We think that he has done the *right*—but some believe, or at least say, that it was done in a *wrong* way."[71] But the governor was not as facile with the pen as Niles thought because Brackenridge had written the farewell address for Jackson besides many other important communications.[72] In Pensacola the alcalde was Jackson's ghost writer. As a matter of fact, Brackenridge acted as Jackson's "commissary of ideas"!

On October 6, also, the governor addressed a letter[73] to the Secretary of State to provide him with information which might be useful to Congress in preparing a more permanent form of government for the Floridas. Jackson's communication answered a request[74] of Adams for such intelligence. The governor recommended a disposition of the Indian problem in the Floridas by reserving a tract of land for the Creeks who did not wish to return to their former abode. If the Indians were concentrated safely at one point, he advocated the union of the two Floridas under one territorial government with a view to their early admission into the Union as a state. Jackson did not recommend the retention of the Spanish laws and customs, for the Spanish inhabitants were a minority group in the population—"the sooner they become American, the better." Congress, he also suggested earnestly, must give the most careful attention to the settlement of land titles, particularly to the establishment of a board of commissioners which could function without corruption. His special concern, however, was the appointment of an honest and able judiciary, for he considered it "by far the most important branch of the territorial government."

Jackson was now ready to leave Pensacola, although it was thought official duties might detain him several days after the departure of his family on October 8.[75] But that Monday they departed together when the expected difficulties did not arise[76] and reached the estate of Manual González the same day. Here the governor found time to write Brackenridge a letter:

DEAR SIR: I had a great desire to have had a few minutes' private conversation with you before I left Pensacola; but this, from the business with which I was surrounded, *was prevented me.*

I had a wish personally *to say to you the gratitude* I feel for the aid I have received from you in the organization and administration of the Government, and to know of you *if* there was any way in which I could render you any service—As you have made Pensacola your residence, you can render much good to your country *and to yourself* in a public capacity. And as far as my influence will extend, it will afford me much pleasure in using it in your behalf. I therefore *will* be gratified to receive a letter from you *adressed* to Nashville, Tennessee, stating whether you would prefer a seat in the Judiciary, *or any other office* within the Floridas, that would enable you to attend to the duties thereof, and pursue the practice of the law;—It will afford me great pleasure to forward by Dr. Bronaugh letters in your behalf to obtain such appointment as may be most *agreeable* to you—therefore I request you to write me soon upon this subject.[77]

As a favor in return, though not put that baldly, Jackson asked Brackenridge to aid Walton, a young man who faced the task of administering the West Florida government in the governor's absence.

Early in November the Jacksons reached the "Hermitage" and received a warm welcome from the people of Nashville.[78] The governor needed rest for his tired body and time to restore his dwindling fortune. But determined to resign his office in the Floridas, Jackson sent Dr. Bronaugh to Washington the middle of the month as the bearer of the resignation to Monroe.[79]

To help rally support in Congress for Jackson's cause Brackenridge wrote his friend Rodney, who was about to take his seat in the House of Representatives, informing him of Dr. Bronaugh's mission to Washington—"His information on the subject of the Floridas will be useful."[80] Brackenridge provided Rodney with his own view of Jackson's collision with Callava:

> The affair of Col. Callava of which I wrote to you some time ago appears to be making some noise; and the old enemies of the General are endeavoring to make a handle of it. But you may rest assured that old Hickory will come out right. The pompous don may find sympathy with Robert Walsh, and a few such, but every honest man will be with him. Callava had no official character, and the merit of his case turns upon that fact. Acting on the ground that he had no different rights from other inhabitants, the general pursued the course he ought to have pursued—He is a stern old Roman who does what he thinks his duty requires. I can scarcely imagine a greater contrast than that which exists between his private and publick character in the first remarkably forbearing and gentle, in the other, as unyielding and rigid as Cato. He is the most scrupulous in his regard to individual rights of any man I ever knew. . . .

Brackenridge expressed astonishment at Fromentin's efforts to attract public notice because the judge was "so vulnerable." In this letter the alcalde commented on one other subject—the difficulty Congress would have in organizing the territorial government. Although he had first favored a union of the Floridas, Brackenridge now believed that for the present two governments, the seat of one at Pensacola and the other at St. Augustine, were "unavoidably necessary."

But by an act of March 30, 1822, Congress erected the Territory of Florida. Before the passage of that law, however, the legislators had debated Jackson's conduct as governor. As John H. Eaton hastened to inform Jackson, the talk about Callava had died in Washington by the end of December: ". . . if any assault is meditated a few days more will I suppose shew it. . . ."[81] Then, several days later, the House of Representatives did pass a resolution asking the President for information on Florida affairs, a request which he complied with by submitting all the pertinent documents for its consideration.[82]

In Nashville Jackson read about the resolution in the *National Intelligencer* of January 2 and immediately posted a note[83] to the President. Behind the resolution was the threat of his impeachment, Jackson reminded Monroe, whom he requested peremptorily not to accept his resignation as governor of the Floridas until there had been a full investigation of his administration. The Florida business oppressed Jackson—that day, too, January 22, he wrote a long letter[84] to the Secretary of State defending himself against the charges of the Spanish minister.

Jackson really had nothing to fear from Congress. Although the members ordered the documents printed, they were unwilling to debate any resolutions censuring him for his conduct of Florida affairs. In Washington Dr. Bronaugh studied the political maneuvering and in February predicted the outcome:

"Indeed no man in Congress who is not completely under the influence of W. H. Crawford will be against you."[85] Some congressmen who had originally considered Jackson's actions in Florida rash, even violent, Dr. Bronaugh reported, now "declare that you are the most astonishing man that the nation has ever produced—that you always act correctly let the situation in which you are placed be ever so difficult." The Jackson enemies were afraid to censure Old Hickory whom the American people had already begun to idolize.

Dr. Bronaugh distrusted the President. Monroe, who did not appreciate Jackson's popularity which eclipsed his own standing as the chief magistrate of the United States, had moved cautiously when information about the uncommon proceedings in Florida first arrived—he solicited the advice of Calhoun and other members of the administration.[86] However, the President averred privately that Fromentin was wrong in his clash with Jackson. In his annual message to Congress,[87] dated December 3, Monroe referred to the incident without mentioning either of the principals by name; and he neither upheld Jackson nor rebuked Fromentin. Monroe dismissed the incident as regrettable. But his attitude was malicious in the opinion of ardent Jacksonians. In mid-February, 1822, Dr. Bronaugh warned Jackson to beware of Monroe's professions of friendship—". . . he is a base infamous hypocrite."[88]

The friends of Jackson were pushing him into the whirlpool of presidential politics, from which there would be no escape. Few people in the United States questioned his treatment of the Spaniards in Florida, observing that patience with Callava might have achieved what force finally did.[89] Whether right or wrong, Jackson's conduct had increased his stature in the eyes of his countrymen—he was presidential timber! Before the Callava affair, on August 1, 1821, Samuel R. Overton had written Jackson about the matter: ". . . I think very little doubt can be entertained of your election. I think as little doubt can be entertained too, that you should consent to be considered a candidate for that office."[90] But according to Brackenridge, Jackson had considered himself unfit for the office:

> I shall never forget the evening, when in presence of Mr. Henry Wilson and some other gentlemen, he took up a New York newspaper, in which he was mentioned as a probable candidate for the office of President of the United States. After reading it, he threw it down in anger: "Do they think," said he, "that I am such a d....d fool as to think myself fit for President of the United States? No, sir; I know what I am fit for; I can command a body of men in a rough way; but I am not fit to be President." We were silent, but all gave him credit, as I afterwards found, for this proof of good sense. He had resolved to retire from public life, and pass the remainder of his days in peace and quiet on his farm.[91]

At this period when Jackson retired to the "Hermitage," he was needed in Florida. The Floridians respected him; they feared him. His attitude was sometimes callous, as Brackenridge saw. The alcalde never forgot how the governor once had permitted a duel to occur between two young officers. Dr. Bronaugh served as the physician. "I was present when the Doctor returned to communicate the result to the General, who was waiting impatiently to hear it," Brackenridge recalled later. "Poor Hull was shot through the heart; his pistol, which was a hair trigger, had stopped at half cock. The General was much displeased. 'D--n the pistol!' said he; 'by G-d, to think that a brave man should risk his life on a hair trigger.' He was sufficiently generous not to arrest Randal, but gave him an intimation instantly to quit the town which might have been given before the affair had taken place."[92] Jackson, however, never shirked a responsibility. As governor of the Floridas, his power was so great, he believed, that no man in a republic ought to possess it; and as he himself remarked to the Floridians, its exercise involved him "in heavy personal responsibilities. It has been my fortune to be thus circumstanced on other occasions in my various relationships as a public servant, yet I never have and never will shrink from the discharge of my public duties from any apprehension of personal responsibility." The *Floridian* editors applauded[93] his statement, which he had made during the proceedings in the Vidal case.

Jackson's departure had thus created a void which Walton as acting governor could not fill. After Jackson had left Pensacola, Walton wrote the Secretary of State to assure him no disturbances had marked the governor's absence and the Spanish inhabitants of West Florida had even manifested a friendlier feeling toward the Americans.[94] Walton, whose father was a signer of the Declaration of Independence and a United States senator, lacked the moral strength to administer West Florida effectively, however.

Brackenridge thought Walton was a wastrel. "I assure you our situation at this moment is truely deplorable, and if there could be any doubt of the necessity of having such a man as General Jackson, clothed with ample powers, at the head of our government, a single glimpse of our present state would remove that doubt," Brackenridge notified Rodney confidentially in mid-December, 1821. "The person who fills the Office of Governor, is a young Georgian who has run through a handsome fortune, without capacity or habits of business. I have been compelled to do everything for him since General Jackson went away."[95] Brackenridge characterized Walton as a despicable creature: ". . . unfortunately he is totally wanting in that weight of character, and dignity of manners which become the station he fills. No one has respect for him or confidence in him. His companions are persons of no character, or the subalterns of the army with whom he passes almost every night over the gaming table. . . . He is in truth an object of universal contempt."

A few days before his writing Rodney, Brackenridge had witnessed an incident indicative of the alarming situation in Pensacola since Jackson's departure. Impassioned, he described the occurrence to Rodney:

... A young officer Lt. [William] Lear, a *parvenu* of the army, one of those who are raised from the ranks on account of desperate and ferocious deeds, but who can never acquire the feelings of a gentleman, and ever disposed to abuse the power entrusted to them—Such bull dogs in a garrison town like this ought to be—muzzled—this Gent. after becoming generally odious to the inhabitants, by his violent and overbearing conduct, has lately committed an outrage which in my view, and that of every citizen here is a most enormous kind. For some cause of offence which I have never yet been able accurately to ascertain, he waylaid Mr. Hanum [W. L. Hannum] as he was going from his dinner to his office, and assailed him with a cowskin. It happened to be directly opposite my office, and I shall never forget the sensation of horror I felt when I saw the ruffian laying on with this instrument of disgrace on the bare, bald, bleeding head of one of our most respectable inhabitants, a man advanced in life, the father of an amiable family, the attorney General of the Province, and one of the Aldermen of the city. A thousand worthless lives like that of Lt. Lear could not atone for the abominable act. I have had both parties arrested and bound over, but I think it probable the business will not end here. The inhabitants are struck with terror, and are afraid to speak. The officers, whose conduct in general has been unexceptionable, have on this occasion, impudently made a common cause with their brother officer, and being in the midst of a garison we must submit, but I presume a hundred private letters will by this mail blow the "tab in every eye." The poor man who has been the victim appears to be lost and bewildered, and knows not what to do—He is a harmless inoffensive man, but occasionally somewhat blustering and morose. Dr. Bronaugh can give you the characters of both.

Walton's reaction to the news of Lear's detestable deed filled Brackenridge with loathing. But as the alcalde wrote Rodney, Walton's attitude was not surprising in afterthought. In the company of his cronies when he received word of the incident, Walton had gleefully called it "the greatest news in the world—Lear has whipped Hanum." Brackenridge had expected the acting governor not only to protest the act to Lear's superior officer but also to demand Lear's arrest and an investigation of the entire affair. In Brackenridge's opinion, Lear had committed a heinous crime: "The usefulness of Mr. Hanum is entirely destroyed—it is a removal from his office—it is a kind of murder." In vain Brackenridge remonstrated with Walton.

Therefore, when Walton refused to take appropriate action in the case, the alcalde himself had proceeded against Lear. The superior officers took no official notice of the offense although Colonel Duncan L. Clinch posted security for the lieutenant. At first Brackenridge had intended to write the Secretary of War a letter which the mayor, sheriff, and the presiding judge of the county court would sign with him; he had abandoned the idea after consulting some friends about the matter. "But I can foresee from the panic which prevails that Lear cannot be brought to justice," Brackenridge confided to Rodney, for after Jackson's departure the military was not content to be subordinate to the civil authority. Dangerous though his position was ("I am compelled to act with great caution as my situation is not safe."), Brackenridge finally decided to bring the outrage to the President's attention. Monroe acted promptly upon receipt of the intelligence, ordering Colonel J. R. Fenwick, the commanding officer at Pensacola, to investigate the affair and to arrest Lear for trial if necessary. As Colonel James Gadsden, the adjutant general of the army, informed Brackenridge, the President wanted the incident "adjusted to the honour of the Army, & to the satisfaction of the Citizens of Florida."[96]

As the assault on Hannum proved, the need for a permanent territorial government in the Floridas was desperate. Brackenridge appealed to Rodney, the new congressman: "Such Sir, is the situation of this country. To you as one of the guardians of Americans I look for some remedy, from Jannisaries, swindlers, debauches, and factionists."[97] The Floridians, he added, did not generally favor annexation to Alabama. At the moment they even lacked a judge of the United States in West Florida, for Fromentin, appointed president of the college in New Orleans, had left Pensacola.

Despite this discouraging state of affairs in West Florida, Brackenridge did not wish to leave if he could fashion a career there, although there was one position in government which he coveted but which was beyond his expectation. To Rodney he confessed his ambition: "I should glory in accompanying you to Mexico as your Secretary of embassy, the first ever sent to an American republican government."[98] They supported the South American cause as enthusiastically as ever and rejoiced in its success. In Pensacola, however, Brackenridge tried to view his prospects sensibly and to adjust himself accordingly, as he told Rodney:

> I beleive I am settled here for life, unless the government should think proper to send me to Mexico or some where else in S. America, of which there is no probability— And being thus settled it is natural that I should try to make myself comfortable. I have therefore made application for some appointment under the territorial organization—My name is probably on the list, but how many are there before me? I think my chance ought to be good. I have applied for the Office of Register not knowing very well what appointment there would be to fill, but it is the opinion of my friends that I would have a better chance for a judgeship. A word from you will serve me most essentially, and for this act of friendship if it shall ever be in my power, you and yours will not be forgotten by me.

When writing Rodney again ten days later, Brackenridge was not so vague about the office he sought in West Florida: "If a U.S. district court is established here, that is the appointment I should prefer to all others."[99] Would such a high office be beyond his reach?

Brackenridge had a powerful ally working in his behalf—Jackson, who was anxious to reward his former private secretary with an appointment more important than the alcaldeship of Pensacola. Jackson appreciated his loyal service as the alcalde. After his return home Jackson received a flattering letter from the President, who spoke well of Brackenridge and approved his appointment to the alcaldeship.[100] The time seemed propitious for Brackenridge's advancement in public office. "I shall take great pleasure in naming you to the president in the terms I think you deserve—& enclose it to our mutual friend Doctor Brunaugh to hand to him at a proper period—and permit me to say to you, that it will afford me great gratification to learn that my letter is attended to by the president," Jackson promised in November, 1821. But when the vacancy in the judiciary of West Florida remained unfilled as late as July of the next year, at least to his knowledge, Jackson began to doubt whether the alcalde would win the post.[101] Again it appeared that Monroe intended to ignore a Jackson recommendation for a territorial office.

That winter and spring Brackenridge had carried on his duties as alcalde and practiced law with Call, his partner. The work of alcalde Brackenridge did not find demanding. As keeper of the archives, for example, he appointed administrators to settle the estates of deceased persons.[102] When two of the Spanish officers whom Jackson had expelled from the Floridas returned unexpectedly to Pensacola and petitioned Walton for permission to remain long enough to settle their affairs and remove their families to the Spanish dominions, he consulted Brackenridge as well as the military officers before confining the Spaniards in their own homes until disposition of the case.[103] Now and then Brackenridge performed a service for the city council of Pensacola, on one occasion transmitting a memorial from it to Rodney in Congress.[104] However, on June 15, 1822, Brackenridge and Call dissolved their partnership[105] by mutual consent, inserting a notice in the *Floridian* of that day to inform the public of their action. But in the same issue of the paper, each attorney announced his own intention to continue to practice in the courts of Pensacola, Mobile, and Blakely.

One week before the dissolution of their partnership the *Floridian*[106] had announced to the people of Pensacola the appointment of Brackenridge and Call to the Legislative Council of the Territory of Florida. Among the thirteen members of the legislative branch of the government were Dr. Bronaugh and Joseph M. White, who forthwith took up his residence in town and began the practice of the law in an office opposite the public buildings.[107] White eventually became a stanch friend of Brackenridge, remaining steadfast in his time of trouble. But now, in the spring of 1822, the alcalde was a disappointed man, for, having aspired to the judgeship, he was not content with membership in the territorial council. Monroe had named John Branch the judge of West Florida.

The new government of Florida, established by the organic law of March

30, began functioning when Governor William P. Duval, a Kentucky lawyer and an ex-congressman, administered the oath to uphold the Constitution to the members of the Legislative Council present at the first meeting, held on July 22.[108] The following day the members unanimously elected Dr. Bronaugh their president. Brackenridge was not present at either meeting.

He had resigned his council seat when suddenly elevated to the bench by Monroe. Branch, the aristocratic North Carolinian, did not want the judge-ship of West Florida, although he sat in the legislature of his own state in 1822. In Branch's place the President appointed Brackenridge "Judge in and over that part of the Territory of Florida, known as West Florida." On June 11, Adams forwarded[109] Brackenridge's commission, dated June 5.

"The appointment of Judge Brackenridge, has given universal satisfaction here, and we congratulate the country, on this happy event, satisfied as we are, that it is [the] very best appointment which could have been made," commented the *Floridian*[110] in Pensacola. *Niles' Register*[111] in Baltimore echoed the sentiment. The appointment was popular, as evidenced by the toast volunteered by Captain Joseph Shomo at a celebration of the anniversary of the annexation of the Floridas, July 17: "H.M. Brackenridge, Esq.—His appointment as Judge of the U.S. for West Florida, meets our highest approbation."[112]

Brackenridge now emerged from Jackson's shadow to become the most respected individual among the inhabitants of West Florida.

XXI: *Freedonia*

Cornelia Brackenridge wrote her brother Henry in the spring of 1821 and mailed the letter to St. Louis, where she thought he was still living. Cornelia felt as if she were writing "to an inhabitant of another world," for he lived so far away. "I am pleased to hear of your success, it would be mortifying, if you did not succeed after leaving Baltimore," she wrote candidly.[1] The letter followed Brackenridge to Pensacola, where he had reached the highroad to success.

Upon receiving the news of his appointment to the judgeship, Brackenridge had announced through the *Floridian*[2] his intention to organize the court without delay, although the first session was not to be held until October, 1822. In his mind there was no time to spare. He was merely anxious to undertake the duties of his office. As it happened, however, many inhabitants of Pensacola were then living on borrowed time.

The calamity which befell them was unexpected. From April until mid-August, the time of the visitation of the yellow fever, they had striven to make their town a pleasant community in which to live. There were concerts and a ball for the socially inclined.[3] The bookstore opened a circulating library for the reading public.[4] L. Patrick, the new owner of the Pensacola Reading Rooms, planned to add forty or fifty newspaper files to the publications already available to his subscribers.[5] Occasionally a visiting clergyman preached in town,[6] and by mid-August the Sunday School Society held regular meetings in the schoolrooms under the residence of Eugene Lavalette.[7]

Then the yellow fever arrived to desolate the town. A year before a false report had circulated in New Orleans that the disease was ravaging Pensacola.[8] Now, a year later, the *Floridian* pooh-poohed the danger of an epidemic, although at least five persons had succumbed within a week: "It is utterly inconceivable, how any infection can rage here, as long as our bay continues salt, and the Gulph stream *breeze,* continues in its daily, luxurious office."[9] The paper urged any individual alarmed by the situation to leave town immediately: "We suspect that the greatest danger, attends those who are most apprehensive—fear, is the greatest possible, predisposing cause to fever—and we implore all that are so affected—to relieve us from the danger of their longer continuance amongst us—such is the advice of the doctors, and such is the earnest entreaty of all others interested." As late as August 17, the fever had not struck in the ranks of the laborers or of the battalion of the Fourth Infantry quartered in town. Soon after that, however, the fever raged unchecked.

Perhaps it was a lucky circumstance which saved Brackenridge, as he explained to Thomas Butler, whom he considered his "best friend in the world."[10] Returning from a trip to New Orleans, Brackenridge had fallen ill from the violent attack of a bilious fever and had not become convalescent until the onset of the epidemic—"To this circumstance I ascribe my escape." When he wrote Butler in mid-October, Brackenridge was staying at Walton's home in the pine woods six miles from Pensacola, where about three hundred out of the four hundred American inhabitants had died. The fever had carried entire families away.

His horror of the pestilence Brackenridge described the best he could to Butler. After five or six deaths in the town Brackenridge decided to take refuge on Santa Rosa Peninsula, where he owned a piece of land and now had men employed erecting several buildings. Brackenridge wanted to prepare a retreat on the seashore for his friends and himself. A young Philadelphian, named Lee, accompanied him to the island. That evening Lee complained of not feeling well and detemined to return to the mainland to see a doctor:

. . . I sent him over with my boat which was directed to return next day. To my astonishment ten days elapsed, without my hearing a word from town, except from some stupid fishermen who could only tell me that the fever was raging. The first certain accounts brought an account of the death of all my friends, and acquaintance, in Pensacola, with the exception of two or three who had fled. Such was the panic which had been occasioned, that after the death of poor Lee, (which together with my boat hand occurred in three days after their return) his cloak an elegant one which had been thrown out of his room into the street was suffered to remain four or five days without being touched by even the most desperate thief. The effect produced by this dreadful intelligence I am unable to describe. My only relief was in hard work in improving my place.

It was here on Santa Rosa Peninsula that old Schewe died.[11] He no longer had his school of several French scholars when he found a refuge with Brackenridge, who observed an odd expression appear on Schewe's face and persist there. One night the Prussian strolled along the beach to enjoy the cool breeze and did not return. Late in the evening Brackenridge and some friends staying with him, apprehensive by now, searched for Schewe, shouting and firing guns as they looked. A furious storm broke and lasted most of the night. In the morning, peaceful and cloudless, the searchers espied three vultures circling in the sky; and fearfully they watched one of the horrid birds light on a tree: "We hastened to the spot; and there, his umbrella on one side and his Bible on the other, lay all that was mortal of *Frederick Shewe!*" Grief-stricken, Brackenridge buried his former teacher there on Santa Rosa Peninsula.

Jackson, too, lost a dear friend in the epidemic—Dr. Bronaugh. Since August, 1821, the physician had practiced medicine in partnership with Dr. John V. D. Voorhees in an office located next door to the Governor's.[12] As Jackson's adviser in political matters and his personal physician Dr. Bronaugh found the location convenient, for he was almost in constant attendance on

299

him. It was Dr. Bronaugh whom Jackson sent to Washington to settle the
accounts of his governorship. On his return to Pensacola Dr. Bronaugh succumbed to the fever while busy attending the sick of the town.[13] Out of respect for their late president the members of the Legislative Council wore
crepe for sixty days. Not until March of 1823 did Walton, the administrator,
attempt to settle Dr. Bronaugh's estate, mute testimony of the derangement
of affairs by the plague.[14] The plague disrupted the work of the commissioners for ascertaining claims and titles to land in West Florida, who had to
resume their important duties later.[15] It also wiped out the first session of
Brackenridge's court, causing an accumulation of business upon the dockets.[16]

But the new judge was used to the appearance of vexing problems as he
organized the administration of justice there. When Tipton B. Harrison, the
district attorney for West Florida, died, Brackenridge appointed Joseph M.
White to replace him during the January term of court.[17] White prosecuted
sixteen persons charged with piracy, three for felony, and four for misdemeanors. Brackenridge doubted whether any act of Congress authorized him
to appoint a federal marshal, however.[18] Soon after his own appointment as
judge, he had received a letter of inquiry from Benjamin Robertson of North
Carolina, to whom Monroe had given the office of marshal. Robertson obviously hesitated to accept the post. Thus, although Brackenridge had organized
his court by August of 1822 before the outbreak of yellow fever, there was a
marshal needed in West Florida. Then Monroe himself appointed William
Sebree of Kentucky to fill the office, thereby solving Brackenridge's problem.[19]

At the height of the fever in Pensacola an interesting case of piracy had
come under Brackenridge's jurisdiction, which was that of the Superior Court
of West Florida.[20] At Galvez Spring, the encampment of the Fourth Regiment,
he examined the master and crew of the schooner "Carmen." The prisoners
admitted their vessel was armed; they could not produce their commission to
cruise. They had boldly challenged the cutter "Louisiana" off Cuba in a vicinity
"notorious as the rendezvous of piratical vessels." Realizing their mistake too
late, they were captured. Brackenridge studied the evidence presented to him:
"These circumstances formed to my mind the strongest presumption of guilt,
and were considered by me, as abundantly sufficient to justify their arrest and
commitment for trial." The judge was reasonable, for he later released the
captain and mate on bail and arranged for the decent treatment of the other
prisoners left in jail. Their case was tried at the January term of court. The
evidence was substantially the same as presented previously except fuller.
However, several "respectable" witnesses testified that the "Carmen" belonged
to a wealthy merchant of Havana and often sailed in and out of the port as
an armed vessel.

The jury arrived at a verdict of not guilty after two hours of deliberation.

"Although from the peculiar mildness and humanity of our laws, I did not conceive the evidence sufficient to warrant a conviction, yet I considered the facts disclosed much more than sufficient to justify the arrest and capture of the Schooner Carmen and her crew," Brackenridge reported to the State Department.[21] His attitude betokened a more perilous life for the pirates of the Bay of Honda. In his examinations in cases like that of the "Carmen" he was vigilant for evidence of trickery. For example, in April, he libelled the schooner "Trial" and cargo for what seemed a breach of the laws regulating Indian trade, setting the trial for the ensuing May term.[22]

In May, 1823, Brackenridge presided over the Superior Court which had crowded dockets. Although the sitting began on the first Monday of the month, it was soon apparent that the session would be long and arduous.[23] The court adjourned finally on May 23. The next day the *Floridian*,[24] prompted by a correspondent, observed as follows about the session: "Much important business has been done, and the patient, dignified, and impartial deportment of the Judge, has left on the public mind a deep impression of respect and gratitude." Deserved though this encomium was, one reader of the gazette took cross exception to it.[25] Such praise of a public officer he called unjustifiable— puffing, in this instance, was especially censurable, for many people were of a different opinion from the correspondent: "And again the writer should have anticipated that a judge who had any respect for himself; would strive to avoid having the ermine of his robe soiled by such foul plasterings." Brackenridge had at least one enemy, if not more, in Pensacola.

His chief antagonist was the new district attorney for West Florida, William F. Steele, who had opened his office in Intendencia Street in April.[26]

The trouble began during the May term of court when Steele offended the members of the grand jury, whose foreman was John Innerarity, and enraged Brackenridge by presenting twenty-three bills of indictment, only one of which led to a conviction. In a letter to the *Floridian*[27] an anonymous correspondent, "CIVIS," accused Steele of "malicious prosecution" and of leaving the civil docket "one wide scene of wreck and ruin." If word leaked out to other parts of the United States that the grand jury had remained in session for eleven juridical days in Pensacola, he asserted, "it is reasonably to be apprehended, that the *morals* of our community may suffer in their estimation." Therefore, he wanted it understood that the grand jury had made only one voluntary presentment during the term: "The learned and benevolent judge intimated oftner than once, in open court, to the Attorney of the United States, that the detention of the jury was complained of. The reply still was, that he had several, or many important bills to lay before it, and would not consent to their discharge." At last in the case of *United States* v. *Riley* the judge reprimanded Steele for insisting he could hold the defendant in custody without permission of the court. Brackenridge discharged the prisoner, for there was no ground for his detention; and he reduced his verbal opinion in the case to writing at Steele's request. On May 31, the *Floridian* published the opinion, rebuke and all, with the letter of Civis.

Naturally the quarrelers resorted to the columns of the *Floridian*, where the controversy quickly became hot and dangerous. "U.S.A." wrote a sizzling letter[28] addressed to John Fitzgerald & Company, the new owner of the gazette, accusing Samuel Myers ("a Jew—not the worse because of *that nation*, but because he has proved himself one compared to whom, Shylock was a Christian. . . .") of publishing articles slandering the district attorney over the signatures of "Civis" and "A Subscriber." According to this anonymous correspondent, Myers had barely escaped being convicted for murder in a trial at Norfolk, Virginia; and he had just had charges of swindling and extortion preferred against him by Steele at the May term of court in Pensacola. When the district attorney returned from attendance at the United States District Court in Mobile, Alabama, he himself replied to the newspaper attacks by publishing his "Answer to the 'opinion of the Court,' "[29] which Brackenridge had delivered in the George Riley case. Steele defended his conduct, disclaiming any desire to offend the court or to censure the members of the grand jury.

In his publication Steele had mentioned John Lee Williams, a magistrate and Riley's counsel in court, derogatorily and leveled unfounded charges at him. But Williams answered immediately by publishing an open letter[30] to Steele, signed with his own name, reluctantly appearing before the public as a controversialist—hating to be "exposed to the glare of public notoriety." In his reply Williams deliberately insulted Steele: ". . . in the whole course of your prosecuting career, the innocent alone have suffered, and not one criminal by your exertions, has been convicted. This you must acknowledge to be a discouraging circumstance." "CANDIDUS," however, read Williams' letter and swore[31] that "such a palpable effusion of insanity" had "not appeared in print since the days of Rabelais. . . ."

In a small and isolated community like Pensacola such publications spelled trouble, for sooner or later someone was certain to issue a challenge. Calumny, in particular, goaded its victims to commit rash deeds. However, Steele had to contend with another problem: responsible persons might report his actions to the State Department in Washington.

By the end of the May term of Brackenridge's court rumors circulated that the grand jury had, in fact, made "a *private* presentment" against Steele, a copy of which was sent to one of the government departments in the national capital.[32]

Brackenridge himself brought Steele's conduct to the President's attention. But Alexander Scott, Jr., the deputy collector at Pensacola, was responsible for the action, for he had officially notified the judge of Steele's refusal to prosecute an offense committed against the United States government.[33] Steele's attitude, Scott charged, jeopardized the operations of the collector's office—its work must be suspended unless the judge remedied the situation. The district attorney had refused to institute a suit against James Forsyth, the master of the schooner "Thomas Shields," who had violated the provisions of an act of Congress by landing slaves at Pensacola without permission. ". . . I consider it a duty imperatively incumbent upon me as the Deputy Collector of this port to *insist* that an Attorney be appointed pro tem by the court to prosecute all suits arising from infractions of the Revenue Laws & those relating to the Slave trade," the incensed Scott demanded of Brackenridge. As evidence for his case against Steele, Scott enclosed copies of several letters[34] in his communication to the judge, who, in turn, forwarded them to the Secretary of State with a terse covering note—"I consider it my duty to inform the President, that the official deportment of Mr. Steel has been such as to give great dissatisfaction. . . ."[35]

To a *Floridian* subscriber, having no other source of information, Steele had become an enigma by October. Was he a despicable person—a disgrace to his profession of the law? Or was there a contemptible combination against him, an upright man? In October Steele inserted a notice in the paper[36] announcing his determination to prosecute rigorously all persons charged with committing depredations upon the public lands, specifically the cutting and transporting of public timber. In the same issue of the *Floridian,* that of October 11, there was a letter, signed "AMICUS," emphatically denying any neglect of duty on Steele's part. Amicus declared that Steele was not negligent by his nonattendance in court when Brackenridge conducted an examination of the claims against the United States under the ninth article of the Florida treaty, for the judge had not officially notified the district attorney of the proceedings nor did he hold them in open court.

The Steele affair, however, reached its climax in the May, 1824, term of Brackenridge's court. What really occurred there was difficult for an outsider to ascertain, for the newspaper accounts were as contradictory as ever. In the *Pensacola Gazette and West Florida Advertiser* of July 24, "SPECTATOR" indicated how letters written in Pensacola and printed in newspapers throughout the United States had spread untruths afar, insisting that one such communication contained five falsehoods about the events of the May term as they had involved the district attorney. Why did editors, Spectator wished to know, print letters or extracts from letters received from anonymous writers? But he overlooked the fact that he himself used a pseudonym.

Spectator, nevertheless, was as much an enemy of Steele as John Lee Williams, who did not hesitate to press his attack in the open. When a letter, signed "AN EYE WITNESS," appeared in the *National Intelligencer* of August 17, giving a contemptuous account of the occurrences in Brackenridge's court, he asked the editors, Joseph Gales and William W. Seaton, to reveal the correspondent's name. They replied[37] that the writer was William F. Steele, as Williams probably suspected.

Steele's letter so angered W. Hasell Hunt, the editor-publisher of the *Pensacola Gazette and West Florida Advertiser,* that he wrote an editorial,[38] which illuminated like a bright lamp the goings on in Brackenridge's courtroom. When he published his comments on the Steele affair, Hunt avowed he did not know the identity of An Eye Witness but that he, also, had witnessed the proceedings there:

> At the last May Term of the Superior Court of West Florida, a rule was entered against Wm. F. Steele, Esq. an Attorney of said Court, to shew cause why he should not be expelled or suspended from the bar of said court, on six charges preferred against him by John Lee Williams Esq and read in open Court, after Mr. Steele had made his appearance in Court, being then on the Piazza, and when Mr. Williams was asked by the Court if he had any motion to make (it being the regular practice to put that question to each Attorney every morning before taking up other business). On the second morning after the rule was entered, the Attorney came into Court and moved to strike said rule from the record on several grounds which he proceeded to read, one of which was "that the Judge of this Court is the personal enemy of the said Wm. F. Steele;" when he came to this ground he was interrupted by the Court, and ordered to sit down, which he refused to do, persisting that he could prove what he had stated by affidavits, and had a right to be heard; it was not 'till after he had been repeatedly ordered to sit down, (which he peremptorily refused to do) that an order of imprisonment for three hours was entered against him. Before the time had elapsed the Marshal was sent for the Attorney, and having left the Court, returned and said that Mr. Steele refused to leave the prison until the time had expired for which he was committed. The Court then proceeded in its business, until about to adjourn, when the Marshal was instructed to go for the Attorney, and if he still refused to come, to bring him by force, and to summon assistance if necessary. Mr. Steele then made his appearance in Court, with a small pocket pistol in his waistcoat pocket (the muzzle of which was visible) a cigar in his mouth and a cane in his hand, and said "You sent for me, Sir, here I am," in a manner much more insulting and contemptuous than the matter. Judge Brackenridge then proceeded to admonish him, to which he began a reply which the Judge informed him could not be heard, and he was directed to sit down, on his persisting in his attempt to answer the court, he was fined fifty dollars, and still refusing to be silent, the Marshal was ordered to take him from the room and the Court then adjourned.

Hunt suggested his subscribers might check the accuracy of both statements. A good reporter, Hunt did not rely solely on his memory in describing the scene but consulted the court records, too.

In their Washington paper Gales and Seaton had printed letters presenting different accounts of the affair, sensibly making no attempt to decide which was the correct version. The letters, however, inspired a thoughtful editorial, entitled "The Doctrine of Contempts," in which the editors declared "From what we know of Judge B. we should not have expected from him any thing despotic or derogatory to the rights of the Bar."[39] They wondered whether the doctrine was sometimes "carried too far. . ." and cited examples to make the point. Certainly Brackenridge had not abused the doctrine by his treatment of Steele, at least as Hunt related it.

Steele's downfall was imminent. His defiance of Brackenridge in open court resulted in an immediate suspension from office. Public opinion was so strong against the district attorney that by September he had left Pensacola on the revenue cutter "Florida," leaving his friends who had acted as his sureties responsible for the payment of the judgment against him.[40] Steele also had friends in the Legislative Council who later permitted a bill[41] to pass lifting his suspension from the bar of the Superior Court—a disgraceful interference with Brackenridge's administration of justice in West Florida. Afterward, in 1825, the President removed Steele from his post and replaced him with Albert J. Claggett of Maryland,[42] who arrived in Pensacola in May.[43] But an attack of bilious fever soon killed "this interesting young stranger."[44]

The Steele affair proved Brackenridge's fearlessness in his role as judge. But his reputation as an outstanding member of his profession rested already on a broader base. That he was wise and honest his neighbors testified on July 4, 1825, when they gathered at the store of John H. and James M. Stone to celebrate the holiday by drinking toasts and singing patriotic songs.[45] These celebrators were hardy citizens of Jackson County who lived along Chipola Creek. Their fourth toast was this: *"Henry M. Brackenridge, Judge of the Western District*—Wisdom and Justice have characterised his proceedings."

It had not been easy to achieve such a reputation in a few years, for all the time Steele and his friends, jealous and mean, sought to wreck Brackenridge's high standing with the public. In every instance when they tried to hurt him professionally, admirers had rushed to his aid. No better example could be found than the declaration[46] of the members of the grand jury of Escambia County, written in Pensacola on September 20, 1823, and signed by N. H. Allen, the foreman:

It having been represented to the Grand Jury . . . that several publications have appeared, in which the official conduct of the Hon. H. M. Brackenridge, the Judge of the Superior Court for this part of the Territory, as well as some acts of the Grand Jury which preceeded the present, have been arraigned before the public; they take this opportunity to declare, that it is their positive opinion and sincere conviction, that all the proceedings of Judge Brackenridge since he has presided on the bench of West

Florida, have been those of an enlightened and upright magistrate; that they know of no act of his, in his present public capacity, which they deem in the least calling for censure, but on the contrary; and they will more especially name his patriotic resistance, against the tyranical mode of prosecution, by filing ex officio informations, as meriting the highest encomiums.

Such praise, of course, was not sufficient by itself—presented to the judge in a sealed envelope, it could have no effect on public opinion. Consequently, when the Steele abuse persisted into 1824, Brackenridge released the document for publication but refrained from remarking on the matter. Ironically, Steele's friends had forced Brackenridge to the action by accusing him of withholding an important presentment of this same grand jury. The supposed presentment was the declaration commending him—he published it in self-defense!

Uneasy though his seat on the bench might be, Brackenridge found his position interesting. His court possessed the powers of a United States District Court as well as the powers of a territorial court. As a result of such sweeping jurisdiction there was a fascinating variety in the causes tried before him. There was the case of John Harris and Michael McCarty accused of mayhem: in a scuffle they had bitten off the ear of John Graves.[47] There was the case of Ambrosio, a slave convicted of grand larceny for stealing thirty-five dollars.[48] Although the territorial law defined the crime of larceny and provided certain punishments for its commission, it did not prescribe any penalty at all for the stealing of money. This defect in the legal system caused Brackenridge to free the prisoner, for otherwise he had to sentence the slave to death under the common law.

The dual nature of Brackenridge's court perplexed the uninitiated in the law. On one occasion, that of the May term, 1825, Sebree, the marshal, did not summon petit jurors for what he called "the United States' side of the Superior Court."[49] Although the grand jury was impaneled and sworn, the district attorney did not attend court. Because the jury had no business, the judge discharged it. The upshot was no court on the territorial side. There was no reason, Sebree explained in the press, why he should have summoned petit jurors on the territorial side when no need for them existed on the other. As a matter of fact, however, an act of the Legislative Council forbade him to call a petit jury on the territorial side; and on the side of the United States he would have incurred unnecessary expense for the federal government. With some justice a "Countryman" blamed Sebree for neglecting to summon the petit jurors at this time: "How often have the people been dragged, from the extreme parts of the County, to Pensacola to attend Courts, for no earthly purpose but to send them home again after expending the few hard-earned dollars they have collected for the support of their families; and this too at seasons of the year when their crop most needed attention."[50]

But the majority of the citizens of West Florida respected the court and esteemed Brackenridge's decisions. In March of 1823, Congress authorized the judges of the two Superior Courts in Florida, the one at Pensacola and the other at St. Augustine, to receive and adjust the claims submitted by the inhabitants of the territory in accordance with the ninth article of the Spanish treaty. The claims related chiefly to losses of property as a consequence of the operation of American troops in Florida in 1814 and 1818. In June Brackenridge announced his readiness to receive claims, drawn in the form of a petition and supported by depositions.[51] Having studied the first claims submitted, he decided by the first of September to require from each claimant a declaration on oath that no compensation for losses claimed had yet been received and testimony from impartial witnesses about the price of cattle at the time the losses had been sustained.[52] Early in 1824 Brackenridge sent William H. Crawford, the secretary of the treasury, transcripts of the petitions, the accompanying depositions, his decisions, and his report as the commissioner assigned the task in West Florida.[53] Brackenridge's examination of the claims created a stir among the inhabitants of Pensacola, many of whom had suffered losses from the American operations. The *Pensacola Gazette and West Florida Advertiser,* therefore, carried his report and abstract of claims in an extra edition on Monday morning, September 13, 1824, a month earlier[54] having expressed satisfaction with his handling of a most onerous assignment.

Brackenridge's examination of the claims was a task imposed by Congress. As he stated in his official report to Crawford, Brackenridge had considered himself as the Superior Court judge "acting in the character of Commissioner." But in studying the claims presented to him, he needed the wisdom of Solomon to distinguish the fraudulent from the honest.

Occasionally a case equally difficult reached him in the Superior Court— one like that of *William M. Loftin* v. *William S. Mooring,* in which two men both claimed the right to exercise the office of sheriff in Jackson County. "A correct decision of this question is of great importance to the Country, inasmuch as the interests of parties may be seriously affected by the acts of an illegal officer, and in this point of view it assumes a much higher interest than a mere question of right between two individuals," Brackenridge declared in deciding the issue in favor of Loftin. On March 4, 1826, Hunt's paper printed the judge's opinion in the case *in toto.* In four months a group of Floridians assembled at Loftin's house on St. Andrews Bay in honor of the anniversary of American independence.[55] "*Judge Brackenridge*—Indefatigable in the discharge of his duties," was their twenty-first toast!

But the judge and his legal associates labored under a depressing handicap —the absence of a treasury upon which to draw for expenses necessary in their work.[56] There was no money for the payment of magistrates, jurors, witnesses, constables, or jailers in criminal prosecutions. The situation threatened a breakdown in the administration of territorial justice. Jurors and witnesses who in the past had given freely of their time in expectation of being paid now refused their services in court. The marshal startled the inhabitants when he suddenly discharged several persons from prison without public explanation, although he had first obtained Brackenridge's opinion on the matter:

Pensacola, Aug. 10th, 1824.

Dr. SIR—I find myself much embarrassed in replying to your letter of this date, because of the novelty of the subject, and because it seems to require a judicial opinion from me, when such an opinion would only be proper in a matter submitted to me in a regular way for judicial decision. On mature consideration however, and under the peculiar circumstances of the case, I have determined to comply with your request.

I am clearly of opinion that the Marshal is not bound to maintain the prisoners at his own expense. It has been usual in States and Territories, to provide for the support of prisoners, or to allow a compensation to the Marshal, and if no provision has been made by the Legislative Council, it was a great oversight. It is not to be expected that the United States will pay all county or territorial expenses, it has not been done elsewhere, and it is not probable that it ever will be done.—It was therefore the duty of the territory to lay a tax for this purpose.

There being no provision for the support of the prisoners, I am of opinion that you are not required to support them at your own expense, and that they being committed for safe custody, all that can be expected of you is to keep them as safely as is consistent with the feelings of humanity. Rather than suffer them to perish of hunger, you will be justifiable in turning them out of prison, but if it be possible to secure their bodies so as to answer the accusations against them, you would be perfectly justifiable in pursuing any course which would not be oppressive or cruel, towards the prisoners, for the purpose of keeping them in custody, and at the same time providing for their subsistence. They ought not to be suffered to escape, and at the same time, they ought not to be suffered to perish of hunger. The case is one, in which you may safely act according to the best of your judgment, and if you act with good intentions, there is no danger of injurious reflection or responsibility.

At the moment there was no other solution to Sebree's problem. He retained custody of only one prisoner, John Chatburn, charged with murder, because a friend of the person whom Chatburn had murdered offered to support him until justice was done.

Despite the lack of funds for the support of prisoners, the West Florida district boasted a new jail in Pensacola.[57] It was a room located in the basement of the old government house, which now served as the courthouse after undergoing some repairs. Escambia County, however, not only needed a jail but also a jailer. It was not astonishing that, in his letter to Brackenridge requesting advice about the prisoners, Sebree noted "the disordered state of society" in Pensacola and West Florida. Such a condition bred violence by the disreputable part of the populace. Even the high-placed in society were apt to be hotheaded. After Joseph M. White, one of the commissioners for ascertaining land claims, had discovered his fraudulent dealing, Peter Alba, Jr., the mayor of Pensacola and a giant physically, attacked him with a bludgeon and a stiletto as he walked to his home on Palafox Street.[58] It was a vicious assault and premeditated. Their enmity was rooted in local politics, also. Shortly after the assault upon him, which had occurred in January, 1825, White announced his candidacy for the territorial office of delegate to Congress to succeed General R. K. Call, the incumbent.[59] After a heated campaign against James Gadsden and J. M. Hernandez, White won the election[60] in May and soon began a long and eminent career in Congress working assiduously for the betterment of the territory.

The deplorable state of affairs in Florida was improvable. From the beginning of its existence the Legislative Council was a force for the development of the territory despite the rough-and-ready politics played by its members. It early petitioned[61] the President and Congress to order the corps of engineers to explore the country and to mark out a road from Pensacola to St. Augustine, to consider a permanent seat for the territorial government, to correct flaws in the judicial system of the territory, and to improve the handling of land claims. The petitioners recommended the erection of lighthouses at Pensacola and St. Augustine and the establishment of a naval station at Pensacola. One by one the territorial improvements came. By 1825, Tallahassee, the new capital of Florida located in a land of sugar cane and sea-island cotton, was a reality,[62] the first house not being constructed until the spring of 1824. The following winter the Legislative Council met there for the first time. In the neighborhood of Tallahassee were situated the plantations of the leaders of capital society, which was graced by the beauty of "Florida" White, the delegate's wife, and the conversation of Achille Murat. The Tallahassee country—Middle Florida —was rich, but a wilderness separated the capital from Pensacola.

The slowness of its growth disappointed many residents of Pensacola. The town, and the district too, simply did not attract settlers like the rest of the territory. But in 1823, the year John Innerarity advertised for sale the extensive premises of John Forbes & Company on the shore of the bay,[63] the inhabitants of Pensacola joyously watched the launching of the schooner "General Call."[64] Built of live oak and red cedar, the beautiful ship was destined to operate as a regular packet between Pensacola and New Orleans. In recording the event, the *Floridian* was guilty of punning shamefully: "This being the first act of enterprize of the kind, since the cession of Florida, we cannot but wish her most prosperous voyages, and that there may be a *General Call* for her services." Statistics compiled at the customhouse revealed a gradual increase in the exports of Pensacola, indicating a healthy economy if not robust.[65] Bricks, cotton, sawed lumber, and cedar logs were the chief exports during this period. More and more planters in the vicinity, however, were turning to the cultivation of cotton for export.

The great asset of Pensacola was the harbor. The American government realized its strategic importance and upon the surrender of West Florida by Spain viewed it as a likely site for a navy yard and depot. The people of the district favored the selection of Pensacola by the Navy Department rather than Tampa or any other place on the Gulf. The choice of a site for the station became an issue in the election of a delegate to Congress in 1825. From the first, however, Brackenridge's neighbors had recognized him as a leader in this movement to exploit the one big advantage Pensacola had over rival Gulf towns. Therefore, when Commodores William Bainbridge, Lewis Warrington, and James Biddle arrived to investigate Pensacola as a possible site for the station, the most distinguished citizens of the town arranged a public dinner in their honor to be held at the Commercial Hotel on Wednesday, November 2, and chose Brackenridge to be president of the affair, assisted by John Jerrison, the mayor of Pensacola, as vice-president.[66] But not until 1830 was the yard established, for Congress was reluctant to appropriate the funds required for its construction.

"FLORIDA has had a greater accession of population, and made more progress in improvement during the few years that it has belonged to the United States, than would have happened in 100 years, had it remained under the dominion of dull and gloomy Spain," sang Niles in a paean to his subscribers in 1825. "The very land seemingly shews itself as if emancipated, and the 'wild wood notes' of freemen are heard in its gigantic forests, which yield up their sovereignty and are submitted to the plough."[67] There was evidence to support Niles' contention—the Americans in Florida were men of enterprise, aggressive and confident. Thus, in 1824, the Pensacola merchants, "wishing to encourage the trade in Wagons to their place, as also to obtain Cotton of the best quality, and being aware that many small planters, who can bring but a small quantity to market at a time, deserve encouragement," subscribed two hundred dollars to be offered as premiums for the two best loads delivered by January, 1825.[68] Examine the pieces of furniture built of red bay by McRae and Staples on the Choctawhatchee, now displayed in town, the *Pensacola Gazette and West Florida Advertiser*[69] once advised all who felt "a pride in seeing the growth of our soil manufactured in such a manner as to supercede the necessity of seeking elegant furniture from abroad. . . ."

Brackenridge was an early leader in this march of progress. Already in 1823, he was actively engaged in the movement to utilize the natural resources of West Florida in the most practical manner. "I make no apology for addressing you without the honour of an acquaintance, and requesting some information on subjects which are interesting to several of my friends and to myself, who are attempting to make something of our *barren* sands in this neighbourhood," he wrote one person. "I have been under an impression that there is a great resemblance in the lands along the seacoast in South Carolina and Georgia, to those on the coast of Florida, and the kind of culture which may have been productive in the former may become so with us."[70] He described the country about Pensacola and particularly his own tract of land on Santa Rosa Peninsula with its poor soil and occasional hammocks covered with magnolia, hickory, and live oak—"the ground in spots fertilized by decomposed oyster shells."

Brackenridge's interest in the improvement of Florida agriculture was keen. It was not a passing enthusiasm, for he associated with the prime movers in the undertaking—men like James Gadsden, who sent him from Tallahassee in January, 1826, a report[71] of the principles to be embodied in the constitution of the proposed Florida Institute of Agriculture, Antiquities, and Science. To encourage scientific inquiry and to promote the advancement of agriculture, the institute would sponsor annual exhibitions and distribute premiums for various achievements in husbandry. "I shall expect to meet you in April at our next quarterly meeting at which time I hope you will be prepared with a constitution for the Institute," Gadsden wrote in the letter[72] accompanying the report.

Brackenridge had a practical interest in this movement, for he had become a farmer in his spare time.[73] He spent much money and labor in the improvement of his place on Santa Rosa Peninsula. On seven acres of land enclosed with paling, he cultivated peas, beans, corn, pumpkins, sweet potatoes, and watermelons. In 1824, he raised about three thousand watermelons for market, a crop worth sixty or seventy dollars. The melons were enormous, one weighing as much as twenty pounds. He used another four or five acres for pasture. He experimented with fertilizers to improve the sandy soil, at first scattering decayed oyster shells over the land. He raised pigs, although he met with discouraging setbacks in this experiment; but he persisted until his luck turned for the better. In a letter to Thomas Butler in 1824, he described his life on the peninsula:

As to my domestic arrangements they are very simple. At first I was obliged to hire three or four hands and make one of them act as cook. They were chiefly discharged soldiers or Irish, lazy worthless and drunken, I was obliged to be with them continually, and then they did but little. The expence of wages and subsistence greatly exceeded my calculations. I was also exposed to a great many calls from people cast away, or wind bound and out of provisions. After six months I found this would not answer. I then tried two negro men; with the wife of one of them, I had to take the grandmother and children into the bargain, and during this time had to employ a couple of carpenters. All which together with my own expences so far from leaving me any thing at the end of the year left me in debt. I at length fell on another plan, I found a new married man, a farmer, who had no home to go to, and who agreed to take my place and instead of wages to receive one half of what he could make. His wife is a decent young woman, of respectable but poor parentage who made out to give her the usual outfit with the addition of a black girl big enough to sweep the house, make the beds, and help in the kitchen. They occupy one end of the house and I the other, they bring me my meals, and leave them with as much silence as if they were feeding a ghost. My room has two neat beds, one for a friend, besides two or three cots for extra company. My *ripe corn* is full of poultry, so that I can have a chicken now and then; fresh fish I have whenever I want merely the trouble of throwing my hook into the water. Yesterday evening in three quarters of an hour, two of us caught ten redfish and six trout.

This establishment on the peninsula, the expenses of which had prevented Brackenridge from liquidating his debt to Butler, provided an excuse to borrow more.[74] But Brackenridge had arranged that, if an accident befell him, his property would go to Butler—"and if I succeed in establishing my orange grove, although I may not live to taste the fruit, perhaps some of your children may bless the man who planted it." To borrow any more money from Butler was unthinkable, Brackenridge assured him, unless it be used for completing the house and improving the property. The trouble with Brackenridge was that he consistently overspent his salary, buying more property and unexpectedly encountering old demands against him. As he frankly stated at the end of his letter to Butler, Brackenridge wished much to complete his house, "such as plastering, laying the upper floor, and building the shed rooms, and completing the gallery &c.—this would cost from two to three hundred dollars."

A trifling sum it was, seemingly, for a man whom President Monroe, satisfied with his services, twice reappointed judge of West Florida.[75] Hard pressed for cash, Brackenridge, neverthless, had risen high in the estimation of his fellow citizens. They esteemed their learned judge, whom they asked to deliver an appropriate oration on July 4, 1826, the fiftieth anniversary of American independence. As the committee of arrangements knew, there was no other person in Pensacola so well fitted to commemorate the day.

What a gala day the national jubilee proved to be in Pensacola![76] A salute, fired by a gun captured by General Lafayette at Yorktown, ushered in the day, followed at sunrise by the raising of the Stars and Stripes, the firing of the gun again, and a pealing of bells. At ten o'clock that morning a crowd gathered at the courthouse to hear a reading of the Declaration of Independence and to listen to Brackenridge's oration[77] which was to follow. After paying tribute to the Fathers of their country, Brackenridge delighted his audience with a reference to the territory in which they lived: "But Florida, too, in her turn will join the confederacy, and add another star to the azure banner of Freedonia. Yes, our territory is complete, its limits have been fixed, and may they be as lasting as time." Indeed, this day, their political jubilee, was a proper time for the orator, filled with gratitude and pride, to summarize the state of national and territorial affairs. It was the day of Liberty, an inspiration to the oppressed everywhere. At noon after the oration a grand salute reverberated through the town. Two hours later Brackenridge presided at a public banquet where many toasts were drunk. Finally the gun was fired at sunset and the flag lowered.

It was an awesome moment when Brackenridge reverently named the surviving patriots of the Revolution in his oration—Lafayette, Adams, Jefferson, Carroll, and their companions who still lived. "Venerable men! You will this day receive the warm and enthusiastic gratulations of twelve millions of freemen, who owe to you their political existence; but who can justly estimate the searching and expansive influence of the great moral lesson your example has taught?" he asked. Alas, as Brackenridge spoke those words in Pensacola, elsewhere in the United States Thomas Jefferson and John Adams lay dying! The two patriots expired before the day was over.

Their death on the day of the national jubilee was a dramatic occurrence, of which fact the inhabitants of Pensacola were sensible as they sadly read the news reports. On July 29, the *Pensacola Gazette and West Florida Advertiser* announced Jefferson's death, the information contained in a black-bordered box. Not until August 4, however, did the newspaper publish an announcement of the death of Adams, having just received the news in the last mail to Pensacola. Quickly Mayor Jerrison had acted upon receipt of the information, for the same issue carried a public notice signed by him, in which he requested the citizens of Pensacola to meet at the courthouse the following day, a Saturday, to adopt measures for honoring the memory of the two sages of the Revolution.

A goodly crowd attended the meeting, held at five o'clock in the afternoon.[78] The mayor served as chairman. The first step in the order of business was the appointment of a committee of six, which left the room to frame resolutions as a tribute of respect to Jefferson and Adams. Upon the return of the committee the meeting unanimously adopted a preamble expressing the sorrow of the Pensacola citizenry and resolutions enjoining them to wear crepe on the left arm for a period of thirty days and to abstain from the conduct of business on the appointed day of mourning, when, it was hoped, Judge Brackenridge would deliver a eulogy on the lives and characters of the deceased. Jerrison communicated the committee's request to the judge, who, much honored, accepted the charge.

Despite the solemnity of the occasion the scene of Brackenridge's oration in the courthouse on Tuesday, August 15, was the most colorful in the history of Pensacola.[79] Badges of mourning covered the rostrum and part of the

313

ceiling. Copies of the Declaration of Independence were suspended at opposite ends of the room. Above the copy hanging behind Brackenridge there was placed a portrait of George Washington. On the orator's right hung a portrait of Adams; and on the left, one of Jefferson. The audience overflowed the hall: ". . . some, it is believed, could not procure even a situation on the galleries within an audible distance of the orator." On his right sat navy officers; on his left, army officers; and seated in front of him were the ladies and gentlemen of Pensacola. The Stars and Stripes floated at half-mast "high from the second story of the building."

The ceremonies began with music played by a band from the frigate "Constellation." Then Brackenridge addressed a rapt audience, according to eyewitnesses:

> The most perfect decorum and harmony prevailed on the occasion. All seemed sincerely to feel their loss and to unite in mingling together their grief and sorrow, in consequence of an afflicting visitation of an all-wise Providence. Such an audience was calculated to flatter the individual who addressed them, and we can safely say, that he amply repaid them for the profound attention which they bestowed upon his oration. We have rarely met with so rich an intellectual treat. It combined an appropriate sketch of the lives and characters of the deceased, enlarged philosophical reflections, the most touching pathos, with all the embellishments of the accomplished orator.[80]

The oration revealed an intimate knowledge of American history on Brackenridge's part. But he had long been a student of history. He had grown into manhood during the administrations of Adams and Jefferson. He had watched his father establish the Jeffersonian party in Western Pennsylvania. He himself had even corresponded with the Sage of Monticello. Thus the orator did not mouth meaningless expressions but could impart to his auditors a feeling of great personal loss. The widow of George Walton, a signer of the Declaration of Independence, sat not far from the orator and listened attentively to what he said.[81]

"Every heart melts at the names of the SUCCESSORS OF WASHINGTON, every tongue endeavours to pronounce their eulogy," Brackenridge declared near the beginning of his oration. "But that eulogy will be no episode in the history of our nation, for their actions will constitute the very materials of that history. If Washington be the rock on which our liberties are built, these are the corner-stones of the edifice. Bear with me, then, for a moment, while I dwell on the virtuous actions of these great men, although I feel that my words must be cold, compared with the warmth which animates your hearts."[82] So elevated were his sentiments—they had to be, considering their subjects—that a passage in his eulogy was like the one in the eulogy delivered by Governor John Tyler of Virginia. But as Hunt explained to the subscribers of his *Pensa-*

cola Gazette and West Florida Advertiser,[83] "we had the pleasure of knowing that judge Brackenridge's Eulogy was completed, before he had an opportunity of perusing that of Gov. Tyler."

Hunt printed Brackenridge's entire eulogy in his paper, calling it "a rich literary treat." The eloquent production was also struck off in the form of a pamphlet and put on sale at the Pensacola bookstore.[84]

XXII

Judge and Mrs. H. M. Brackenridge

Brackenridge distributed copies of his eulogy among his relatives and friends. "I received your address delivered in commemoration of Thos Jefferson & Jno Adams," wrote his brother Alexander, now the attorney of the United States[1] for the western district of Pennsylvania. "The perusal gave me much pleasure, and the fact that you were selected by your fellow-citizens, upon that sad yet important occasion, gave me more—It is also gratifying to find that you have not altogether forgotten us."[2] Alexander, who wondered why his brother did not visit him and other relatives oftener ("I would suppose, that you possess leisure."), had reached the "middle walks" of their profession, able to support a family and save a hundred dollars or so every year. Their brother William, Alexander reported, having failed to establish a law practice in Cincinnati, Ohio, had gone to Meadville, Pennsylvania, to try to establish himself there—"William's star is unfortunate." Henry's star, however, was still in the ascendant.

Of that fact William Magruder was positive.[3] Brackenridge's old Baltimore friend had read the eulogy approvingly, pleased by its merit. He was pleased, too, that Brackenridge had sent him a copy. "The whole production does you credit and indicates that intellectual improvement which I know you were always ambitious should appear as you advanced in life," Magruder complimented him. Then the Baltimorean confessed he had not married yet:

... I am still "Benedick the bachelor"—with little or no prospect of ever being "Benedick the married man." Your own state is one too, if I am not mistaken, of "single blessedness" still—at least the last accounts I had of you made it so. Miss Owings, your old favorite, told me a good while ago that you were married but it seems she was misinformed. Let us persuade ourselves that we are happier, each of us, as the first-mentioned Benedick than the last.

His life was sedate, Magruder admitted. He was now unambitious, content to read "nothing in Law and almost nothing in Literature."

Brackenridge was of a different mind and temperament. Aged forty, he at last stood on the threshold of marriage. He was fast approaching the age at which his father had married Sabina Wolf. The younger Brackenridge was incapable of idling away his time; like his father he never lacked something to occupy his leisure. The younger Brackenridge was more than ever a thinker as well as a doer.

Three weeks after the delivery of his eulogy in mid-August, 1826, a scandal in the administration of Florida affairs shocked the inhabitants of Pensacola. If rumors were to be believed, it seemed that Walton had absconded with a sum of money belonging to the territorial treasury. The news[4] infuriated the people, for supposedly the treasury had always been empty—prisoners had been released from jail for want of support. Early in the year, however, the secretary had reported to the governor the receipt of almost ten thousand dollars for the needs of the territory, but, apparently, had then disappeared with the funds from the public eye. According to Hunt's editorial in his Pensacola paper, here was a situation demanding an investigation by the Legislative Council. Why had Walton not deposited the money in the treasury? Where was he?

A remorseful man, Walton had gone to Washington after trying to raise money in New York, Philadelphia, and Baltimore to replace the territorial funds which he had squandered. As secretary of Florida, and acting also as treasurer, he had collected the money at Key West for the territory. Because his unsavory reputation had preceded him north, he could not borrow a dollar. Now in the national capital he was a despairing man, desperate for a friend to sympathize with him or at least to listen to his tale of woe.

Walton described his predicament in a letter[5] meant for no other eyes than Brackenridge's and requested him to befriend his suffering family. Walton wrote no one else in the territory. He evinced a determination to return to Florida to satisfy every demand against him, although he thought few persons were disposed to help him. Walton declared his intention to resign the office of secretary of the territory. Finally, he implored Brackenridge to understand his misfortune. Overwhelmed with grief, Walton wrote: "The last request, that I shall ever make—I now make to you—*Be in truth and reality, a friend to my illfated and* wretched suffering family."

The letter touched Brackenridge's heart. Walton's predicament confirmed the judge's opinion of him—that he was a wastrel. Brackenridge had, nevertheless, tirelessly assisted him in the duties of his office as secretary in compliance with Jackson's wish. As time passed, however, Brackenridge and Walton had become friends. Perhaps the judge realized that Walton was really an immature individual—a spoiled child of a good family—caught in the toils of bad company. Brackenridge did not abandon Walton now in 1826, and befriended his family too. Time would prove that the judge earned the undying gratitude of Walton's gifted daughter, Octavia.

Hunt, the vigilant editor, kept watch on Walton's movements, allowing him no peace. It was his duty, Hunt insisted, to publish the facts of the case for his subscribers. He printed the sorry facts; he dealt not in insinuations. "We must, however, protest against the idea, that the *station* or *ancestry* of a person ought to induce us to consider him of 'high standing'; with us 'WORTH makes the Man; and *want of it* the fellow,'" he opined as he published the statement of particulars against the fallen secretary, who was unable to proclaim his honesty.[6] The editor, whom Brackenridge had recently appointed the clerk of his court,[7] was a Floridian proud of the territory and eager to protect it from the unscrupulous officeholder. Hunt, however, disclaimed any intent to hurt the feelings of Walton's family.[8] But already Hunt had had the satisfaction to learn that the secretary had resigned his office and that the President appointed William M. McCarty, a Virginian, to succeed him.[9]

The effect of Walton's defalcation was seen in the administration of justice in West Florida. During the November term of Brackenridge's court in 1826, convictions were obtained in three cases.[10] The judge sentenced Antonio Escovar, who had stolen about fifty watches from the trunk of John White, a Pensacola watchmaker, to imprisonment until he received ten lashes, restored the stolen property, and paid a fifty-dollar fine and court costs. The judge did give Escovar the chance to appeal to the governor for a remission of the corporal punishment. Escovar's accomplice, Juan B. Salgado, received the same sentence except the lashes. There was the case, also, of an Indian named John, who had murdered his wife Polly, in a state of drunkenness having beaten her to death. Convicted of involuntary manslaughter, the Indian was fined five dollars by Brackenridge, ordered to pay the costs of prosecution, and given thirty lashes, which were administered without delay. The case of Benjamin Donica, accused of murdering Major Saunders Donoho, was continued until the next term of court. The military authorities at Cantonment Clinch, however, kept Donica in custody. But what was in store for the other three offenders? The session of the court had scarcely ended when Hunt's paper carried the news that "the Marshal has turned out of prison the Indian John and Juan B. Salgado *in preference to allowing them to starve, no provision having been made for their support!*" After restoring most of the watches to the owner, Escovar escaped from jail.

On this note of frustration—this defeat of justice—Brackenridge departed for Washington as soon as the November term of court was over. It was fortunate that he left Florida for a time, for political factions were displaying much ill will in their jockeying for power. In fact, Governor Duval, a Jackson satellite, had just written Brackenridge about certain articles in the press: "I saw a letter of yours to Majr. Allen a few days since, in which the recent and abusive publications, which appeared in the Pensacola paper against myself and others were mentioned—no man who is acquainted with you could do you the injustice to ascribe them to your pen."[11] He had heard reports, Duval added, that the judge was the author and had immediately scotched them. In the territorial capital, however, a political calm had settled which Duval hoped could last. Of course, in his high office it was difficult for Brackenridge to remain aloof from politics or to avoid embroilment in party disputes, especially when the governor expressed a wish to consult him on territorial affairs, as he did in this letter.

Brackenridge went straight to Havana. James Innerarity, the brother of John, gave him letters of introduction to residents of the city. In letters[12] to Robert Morison and Colin Mitchel, Innerarity requested aid be given the judge to facilitate his journey to Matanzas, Cuba, where he wanted to go by an overland route to see something of the country. To James H. Simpson, a merchant at Matanzas, Brackenridge carried a letter of introduction[13] from Robert Mitchell of Pensacola. Brackenridge's next stop was at Charleston.

There was nothing mysterious about his movements. He was not a mere sight-seer on vacation, for there was purpose to his traveling. He collected information for the use of White, the territorial delegate to Congress. White planned to introduce a bill authorizing the construction of a canal from the Apalachicola to the Choctawhatchee, to be financed by an incorporated company. White intended, also, to introduce a resolution instructing the Committee of Roads and Canals to investigate the merit of opening a communication for steamboats between Mobile and Pensacola bays. The busy delegate asked Brackenridge to write the committee chairman a letter pointing out "the advantages to all the States West of the Allegany. . . ."[14] White foresaw a strenuous winter ahead for himself as he tried "to counter act the efforts of the Tallahassee Junta—You have not much to do & one of your best efforts will be of great service to me." But to C. F. Mercer, the committee chairman, White himself addressed a long letter on Florida canals. In his communication, written in Washington in December, White obviously incorporated information supplied by Brackenridge. The *Pensacola Gazette and West Florida Advertiser* printed the whole letter on February 9, 1827. The letter was much quoted.

In December Brackenridge had spent some time in Charleston. Here he found a copy of William Roberts' work, *An Account of the First Discovery, and Natural History of Florida. With a Particular Detail of the Several Expeditions and Descent. Made on That Coast,* published in London in 1763. Jubilantly he wrote Samuel R. Overton about the discovery, which revealed an incident of Florida history little known. Overton, the navy agent at Pensacola, at once suggested to Brackenridge that he write another book:

I am very curious to know the details of the destruction of the settlements about Tallahassee, by the Governor of S. Carolina in 1702-4 & 6. The extracts you have taken from the work of Roberts, printed in 1763, ought to be published, if you think they can be relied upon as authentic. It is a subject of more than ordinary interest, and any thing of a satisfactory character, written in relation to it, would be read with avidity. The history of these settlements, together with the other wonderful things you have seen, would, no d[oubt] make a book worthy of perusal, and f[or the com]position of which, no one is better qualified [than] yourself.[15]

For the moment Brackenridge lacked the time to write a book, no matter how desirous he was to be an author again. Instead, this new historical material he used in a letter which he wrote to White after arriving in Washington. His communication, dated January 14, 1827, was a reply to White's request for a brief topographical and historical sketch of the country about Tallahassee. "In appearance, it is entirely unlike any part of the United States, so near the seaboard," Brackenridge began. His description of the region was vivid: "The soil of the uplands bears a strong resemblance to the best part of Prince George's county, Maryland; and the face of the country is not unlike the south side of the Potomac, opposite Washington city. In the valleys, there is a much heavier growth of timber, and frequently deep cane-brakes." The land about Tallahassee he pictured as an oasis, "which appears to have been formed by nature, in one of her most sportive and fantastic humours." His brief account of Florida history was likewise colorful. He presented a solution to a problem about the Tallahassee region which had interested him: "The appearances of a dense population, which seems at one time to have covered this country, has induced me to make some inquiry. While at Havana, I could learn nothing. . . ." In Charleston, however, he had discovered Roberts' work on Florida which provided an answer. Brackenridge stated that the first notice Americans had received of the Tallahassee region was the result of Jackson's march into it in pursuit of the Seminoles in 1818.

The letter to White, a memoir on the Tallahassee country, was made public with gratifying results for Brackenridge. The *National Intelligencer* called it "instructive": "If we are not mistaken, were the Judge to trace the history of this territory, in the days of Hernando Soto, more minutely, it would increase, instead of diminish in interest." The *Pensacola Gazette and West Florida Advertiser*[16] reprinted this complimentary notice with the entire letter. John Lee Williams, furthermore, included the letter in his useful compendium, *A View of West Florida, Embracing Its Geography, Topography, &c. with an Appendix, Treating of Its Antiquities, Land Titles, and Canals. And Containing a Map, Exhibiting a Chart of the Coast, a Plan of Pensacola, and the Entrance of the Harbour.*[17]

Brackenridge himself was the chief critic who reviewed Williams' small book, published in 1827. He wrote an unsigned essay on the general subject of Florida for Edward Everett's *North American Review*[18] of April, 1828, discussing Williams' work with a pamphlet containing letters of special interest to inhabitants of the territory. For his essay Brackenridge received a modest fee.[19]

The article was an important addition to Florida historiography, for Bracken-ridge noted the writers before Williams besides reviewing his contribution itself. In his graceful style of writing Brackenridge quickly led the reader through a discussion of "the beautiful name of *Florida*" and "the space which Florida has always occupied in the history of America, apparently so dispro-portioned to its intrinsic importance," to the attempt of his day toward obtain-ing accurate information about the territory, a movement of which Williams' *View* was a manifestation. He liked Williams' book, but not unreservedly. He criticized the brevity of the account of the Florida boundaries because the subject had been for years a matter of contention between Spain and the United States: "A labored argument in favor of the right of the United States, is found under the title of 'The Florida Question stated, by H. M. Brackenridge,' in Mr Walsh's 'Register,' for 1816. The author is at present one of the judges of the territory, and the writer of the letter in the Appendix to Mr Williams's book." After thus noticing his own work, Brackenridge com-mented on various topics suggested by Williams' memoir and from it selected generous extracts for the reader of the review. Brackenridge pronounced the *View* a work on the whole "creditable to its author," whose next production ought to be a similar account of East Florida. Williams had published some letters of White, the territorial delegate, in the appendix of his book. In dis-cussing them, Brackenridge paid high tribute to White's character and his zeal for the improvement of Florida. Brackenridge, however, believed the letters of David B. M'Comb, published in the form of a pamphlet, provided the reader with an exaggerated description of the Tallahassee country—"It may be a paradise, but its inhabitants are not angels."

Not long after writing the Tallahassee memoir for White, Brackenridge had left the national capital for Philadelphia, where he arrived before the end of January, 1827. The judge was bent on the completion of a mission—after many visits to Philadelphia in the past, when he had not taken the time to visit his family at Carlisle, he was now determined to marry Caroline Marie without further delay. Their marriage meant the fulfillment of her mother's wish, made when the little wanderer, Henry, had returned from Ste. Genevieve in 1796. When Jane Marie fled from Pittsburgh in 1804, upon losing her home, she had gone to Philadelphia, where, four years later, she sent Caroline to the Moravian Seminary for Young Ladies at Bethlehem, Pennsylvania, as the ward of B. R. Morgan, a Philadelphian.[20] In 1827, ten years younger than her suitor, Caroline was an attractive lady of culture.

She was not easily won. "I thought myself of a forgiving temper, I thought it impossible for you of all other persons in the world to offend me, but I am sorry to inform you that this is altogether a mistake; for after sleeping about fourteen hours I awoke this morning much out of humor," Brackenridge complained, teasingly, in a note written the morning of January 30. "Fourteen hours! You will no doubt consider this a strange confession, but then I was dreaming all that time that I heard your music, accompanied by such changes of scenes, so regardless of chronology and place, as would almost rival the creative fancy of Shakespear."[21] Caroline, as he reminded her, had slighted an engagement with him the previous evening. He had much to tell her, but he was afraid of offending her—"or of touching on a subject that might give you pain." But he must marry her:

> . . . Although as successful in my pursuits, as a moderate ambition could desire, possessing reputation, numerous and ardent friends, & the means of living, yet my life is joyless and unhappy. For scenes of dissipation and folly I never had much relish, and now that the flower of my youth has faded away, should I be forbidden to hope for the enjoyment of those pleasures which have their seat and center in the heart, existence itself will seem but a cold, and dank, and dreary way. Adieu
> H. M. Brackenridge

He had a good argument, a time-honored one, to present Caroline—no two persons could be better suited for marriage than they were. His persistence soon brought him victory, noticed by the Philadelphia press in March:

> MARRIED,
> On Thursday evening, 22d inst. at Dr. Gebhard's, in this city, by the Rev. Jacob C. Sears, the Hon. HENRY M. BRACKENRIDGE, of West Florida, to Miss CAROLINE MARIE, of this city.[22]

They hurried back to Pensacola, for Brackenridge had to preside at the May term of his Superior Court when Benjamin Donica's case was due to come before him. In November Donica had been indicted for the murder of Major Donoho at Cantonment Clinch. After the examination of many witnesses at the trial, the jury, deliberating about an hour and a half, returned a verdict of guilty with a recommendation for mercy.[23] Brackenridge sentenced Donica to death by hanging, although he promised to send immediately a copy of the record to the governor for review and a possible pardon: "It is not the intention of the court to harrow up your feelings, but it is its duty to characterize your crime in the terms which it merits, and to exhibit your conviction as an awful warning to others."[24] Condemning the soldier to death was not a pleasant duty for the bridegroom—Donica was hanged near Pensacola on June 20.[25]

Some people might have wondered how such a cause could be tried in the Superior Court and a conviction obtained when, evidently, no criminal law for the territory had been authentically published. The editor of the *Pensacola Gazette and West Florida Advertiser,* however, had procured a copy of an act for the punishment of crimes and misdemeanors when in Tallahassee during the winter and had now produced it in court.[26] Although the law was not certified, Brackenridge decided to act under it, as Hunt explained in an editorial, "taking upon himself the risk of any errors which it might contain."

But Brackenridge was unwilling to risk the health of his wife by keeping her in Pensacola after she had fallen sick, although she was now better. He anxiously waited for the chance to send her back to Philadelphia, although a separation would cause him anguish. Then, into the Pensacola harbor sailed a "fine packet vessel" by accident.[27] This was his opportunity. His wife returned north on the schooner while he prayerfully studied the weather, especially the winds. "It affords me some consolation, that thus far heaven seems to favor our designs; there is every reason to believe, that the winds have been light, but sufficient to waft you along witht. sea-sickness, and that you are now almost through the guelph stream, and have left Florida behind you," he wrote her hopefully on July 10.[28] Some of their friends, he added, were ill, notably Major Overton's family, their suffering aggravated by the dry weather and terrible heat.

The abominable sun! Despite the excessive heat Brackenridge had acquired an irksome cold, although, when he wrote Caroline again a week later, he was feeling better.[29] Was she well? he asked. "How anxious," he exclaimed, "yet how much afraid to hear from Philadelphia!" The time dragged maddeningly until he should learn of her safe arrival there. His cold had confined him indoors, making the heat seem more stifling than ever. He reminded her of childhood scenes when he mentioned his present plight:

. . . O, how I should like to wander up some of the cool shady streams of the Allegheny, along some deep glen enclosed by high hills, which keep out the rays of the sun! I dare not indulge in these pleasing dreams—they approach too near what I should imagine to myself of worldly happiness; "Man proposes but God disposes."

On the morrow, which was July 19, Brackenridge wrote Caroline about his sudden decision to proceed to Tallahassee aboard the cutter "Florida," thereby saving him the tedious journey by land.[30] The only objection to this plan was that more time would elapse before he could possibly receive the letter announcing her arrival in Philadelphia. The Overtons had lost their son, he told her, and the major appeared more distraught than his wife: "His affections were perhaps too strongly fixed on his little boy; it is perhaps in itself a misfortune to set our hearts too much on any terrestrial thing, for to what keen disappointments, to what bitter anguish does it lead? I am something of the stoic, in theory, at least." Brackenridge, also, informed Caroline of his practice now of drinking nothing but water, having read the opinion of a medical authority on the use of liquor. Then he gave her some advice: "Be cheerful, and endeavor to make the time pass pleasantly, for this is one of the great secrets of health." This letter he signed "Yours affectionately—H. M. Brackenridge."

After his arrival at Tallahassee his letters became longer and chattier. During the voyage he had "nursed the pleasing idea" that Caroline had reached her destination in good health while at the same time fears for her health plagued him.[31] "The cold bath, constant exercise, a cheerful mind," he insisted, were the means for restoring her health; she must not neglect them. He harped on the matter. As a newly married man, he was much interested in the subject of jealousy, relating in detail the shameful flirting of Mrs. White with a naval hero in her husband's presence—and Brackenridge's too. Brackenridge did not appreciate the spectacle nor the good nature of his friend in this instance. Such an incident made him miss Caroline more than ever. He had begun to repent sending her to Philadelphia for the recovery of her health: "By keeping continually in motion, I contrive to drown reflection."[32] Fortunately, he was finding Tallahassee a more congenial place than Pensacola. There were shady walks where he did not have to fear the sun. No mosquitoes bedeviled him. The few ants were not troublesome. His health was better: "Since my arrival I have not once felt the least inclined to be billious, while at Pensacola this was experienced every eight or ten days." He was careful about his health, for he hiked five or six miles every morning and bathed frequently at the cascade, where he found the impact of the cold water resembling an electric shock— "I am less corpulent, but the muscles are more firm and rigid." Finally, in mid-August, he received the joyful word of her arrival at Philadelphia: "I could annihilate space and time to press my dear Caroline once more to my heart."[33] Do not be surprised, he added, if he joined her there in a month or two instead of returning to Pensacola. Meanwhile, he had to unburden his heart:

Do not give yourself any uneasiness, my dear wife, about your giving me pain by your not being pleased with Pensacola. I knew well how to make my allowance; I felt for you, perhaps blamed a little, but my affection was not diminished. You were a young and inexperienced traveller, you recoiled like the sensitive plant from the approach of my hand, however friendly, you magnified any danger and difficulty, and the bad state of your health caused you to view everything through a deceptive medium. It is wonderful how differently we view the same object, in health and spirits, and in sadness and sickness. The difference, is, nevertheless, in *ourselves,* and not in those objects. What a blessing it is to possess a cheerful and contented disposition! It gilds the gloom of life, it lightens the weight of misfortune, and mitigates the pains of disease. Our separation at the time was necessary and unavoidable; that it has pleased the Almighty safely to bear you to the end of the voyage is a circumstance which should fill us with gratitude for his beneficence, and make us in future confide in his providence. The idea which hung so heavily on your spirits, that you were condemned to a perpetual exile at Pensacola, I hope has now been expelled from your mind, and instead of it, a conviction that the difficulties are more imaginary than real, has taken place. You are now quite a traveller my dear Caroline, by land and by sea. I have no doubt you will find your mind much enlarged, by more expanded views of the world.

Caroline's gloom, however, was catching. It was inevitable that Brackenridge became dispirited, particularly after two mails passed without a letter from his wife. "Your first, and the only, letter from you placed my mind much at ease, at the same time, like a taste of spirits to the drunkard, made me the more thirsty for another draught," he chided her.[34] On the morrow, August 29, he planned to set off for Chipola, in Jackson County, to hold court, where, according to a newspaper report,[35] he was to declare unconstitutional two acts of the Legislative Council respecting the Florida Indians. He held his court at the settlement of Webbville. Here he received distressing intelligence from Pensacola, the loss of his friends Overton and Sebree who were victims of the yellow fever in its first visitation since 1822. The news of their death cast a pall over everything—"Pensacola will henceforth be almost a deserted place to me."[36]

From Pensacola Overton had written Brackenridge a cheerful enough letter[37] on August 18. The rainy season still continued there; but instead of discomforting everyone, in Overton's opinion, it was an occurrence conducive to the health and comfort of the inhabitants. Bilious complaints among them were common, nevertheless. He himself had just recovered from an attack: "It was not violent; not much fever; but I had more bile in my system, than I think has been in it for ten years. I discharged a large quantity, and it demonstrates a sensible change in my health, no doubt for the better." On August 31, he was dead![38] Sebree, the marshal, followed Overton to the grave the next day.

On the strength of Overton's letter and other similar reports coming to hand, Brackenridge tried hopefully to believe that the common bilious fever had killed Overton and Sebree.[39] But by late September, when Brackenridge left Chipola for Tallahassee, there were dreadful reports about the plague emanating from Pensacola. Brackenridge was relieved to learn that Colonel Walton's family had left town in time to escape the scourge.[40] In Tallahassee, however, he was disheartened to hear that Caroline had been ill again—"I had a presentment of bad news. . . ." In his reply he actually mentioned quitting Florida forever, although, as he said, a salary of fifteen hundred dollars a year "in a very respectable station" was not lightly abandoned. Cheer up, he counseled his wife. He now decided to go to Philadelphia as quickly as possible.

His decision was wise. The wish to quit Florida forever was not an ephemeral thought. He was restless, and profound melancholy had seized him: "It appears to me, that I am now, the most lonesome, solitary, being in the world—deprived of the pleasures of friendship, and affection, it is all a blank, a gloomy wilderness to me."[41] The yellow fever in Pensacola, surely wiping out his November term of court, gave him the chance to escape this land of gloom for a few months at least.

But his decision to go north and not to hold the November term of court in fever-stricken Pensacola did not meet with general approval there. Hunt objected in an editorial[42] as soon as he received word of Brackenridge's intention. Hunt maintained that the judge had formed an erroneous impression of the seriousness of the epidemic, derived from false statements sent to Tallahassee. Letters to correct Brackenridge's mistaken notion about the situation in Pensacola were posted to him without avail. To one he had replied with asperity, as Hunt quoted him: "The accounts from every other source are much less favorable than yours, and I fear your zeal for the welfare of the Town, has somewhat influenced your judgment." The court met as scheduled, only to be adjourned until the next term, owing to the absence of the judge.[43] The news that he had left Tallahassee for Philadelphia on October 6 shortly reached Pensacola. Evidently he was convinced that to hold the court in Pensacola would be unsafe.

The affair was not concluded, of course. Papers in Florida and elsewhere commented on Hunt's editorial to the effect that the citizens of Escambia County were dissatisfied—"very much dissatisfied"—with their judge.[44] Chagrined by the inference drawn from his remarks, Hunt called the statement "a most egregious mistake," adding "Nor has any thing ever been published in our paper, to make a 'justification of the Judge' necessary."[45] But as Hunt emphasized, the yellow fever had quitted Pensacola by mid-October—anyhow, it had caused no deaths since October 9. He considered Brackenridge "rather too credulous" of the alarming reports from Pensacola. When Brackenridge saw Hunt's editorial, he was furious and wrote in a letter to the editor[46] that the entire statement was false: "If the November term has failed through my fault, it is the only failure at Pensacola during the many years I have been on the bench; and if this *were* the case, the cause of my absence, to a generous mind, would plead some excuse; at least, the necessity of a newspaper paragraph on the subject, would not appear the most urgent."

Brackenridge had left Tallahassee on the long journey to Philadelphia apprehensive for his wife's health.[47] As he advised her time and again, her spirits must be cheerful and she must not hesitate to meet people. Caroline was altogether too shy for her own good. She could conquer her feeling of inferiority if she persevered—"your adventures the last six months, I have no doubt produced a change already." To get her out into the world and away from her sheltered life with intimate friends, he directed her to obtain lodgings for the two of them in a genteel but cheap boardinghouse. In this frame of mind he traveled through the heart of Georgia to Milledgeville, which he reached on October 10.[48] He had passed through a region where most of the population was sick—the condition of the inhabitants appalled him. At Washington, Georgia, he became ill and had to tarry there for days, not arriving at Greensboro, in North Carolina, until the end of October. "I have suffered much in body, but much more in mind," he wrote Caroline from that place.[49]

According to a letter Brackenridge wrote Hunt from the national capital on November 14, he had not recovered his health and appetite by the time of his arrival there.[50] But in Washington gladsome news had awaited him—his wife's health was much improved, intelligence which was like a tonic for him. On November 14, also, he replied to Caroline's letter, expressing his pleasure over a brave attempt to overcome her aversion to making acquaintances.[51] He did not want her to engage in the follies of fashionable society, but he did wish her to cultivate "a polite, friendly, and affable deportment." Brackenridge described his feelings as he had lain ill in Georgia without friends to nurse him: he had realized then "the value of religious consolations—but I have no faith in *the religion of a moment,* it must rest on firm conviction, and it must be tried by our lives."

While in Washington, Brackenridge applied for the position of reporter for the United States Supreme Court, which Henry Wheaton had vacated upon his appointment as chargé d'affaires to Denmark by President John Quincy Adams in 1827. Wheaton had sailed for Copenhagen in July. If Brackenridge could obtain this honorable post, life would be simpler for him, the problem of frequent trips between Philadelphia and Pensacola eliminated. After all, he could not condemn Caroline to the isolation of a Florida residence.

But he was not to become the eminent Wheaton's successor. Richard Peters, who had published reports of cases in the Circuit Court of the United States for the Third Circuit, was also an applicant for the post. Chief Justice John Marshall candidly informed Brackenridge of his backing of Peters: "I know that three Judges are pledged to support him. Whether he will succeed with a fourth I am unable to say."[52] There were, furthermore, many other applicants worthy of consideration. Judge Joseph Story was equally discouraging in his reply[53] to Brackenridge's application. Story recalled having once met Brackenridge, as did Judge William Johnson. No less a person than Judge Fromentin's wife had introduced Johnson and Brackenridge at one of her evening parties in Washington years before. Johnson was interested in aiding Brackenridge's candidacy, but he foresaw no chance of success: "I presume you know that even in a Supreme Court there may be Parties, & can not be uninformed of the Triumvirate that is supposed to exist in ours."[54] Despite his qualifications for the post of reporter, Brackenridge lost in his candidacy to the well qualified Peters, although that fact was no consolation.

By late November Brackenridge had reached Philadelphia where he found Caroline in fair health but of delicate constitution, incapable "of bearing much either in mind or body."[55] The state of her health was a constant worry for him. Consequently, he could not plan their future confidently. How disturbed he really was, he revealed in a letter[56] written to Thomas Butler early in January, 1828. Brackenridge was now anxious about the condition of his property on Santa Rosa Peninsula, fearing especially some harm befalling his trees: "And one source of my anxiety is always connected with yourself; for I always flattered myself with the hope that it would one day, be the means of discharging the debt of gratitude I owe you." Brackenridge had planted the orange seed himself and later transplanted the trees from his nursery. Three and four years old, they were now four to six feet high. He planned a grove of one thousand trees. Brackenridge had fig trees and some peach trees, too. All this he told Butler and then made him a proposal:

... it is this to become jointly interested in the property with me in consideration of the debt I owe you, and to furnish an old negroman & woman to live at the place, take care of the trees, and do little things about it, and I would share the expence of supporting them, and superintend the management of the trees with an occasional hand. I think in [five or six] years, we might have a thousand bearing orange trees, which ought to yield three or four dollars a tree—The prospect is indeed distant, but you have children, it may benefit them, and it may be a pleasant retreat for us in old age. I have a strange affection for the spot—it is not likely I shall have anyone to inherit my share, and there is no one that I would rather see it occupied after me than by you and yours. I wish you would think seriously of this proposal. Could you not make an excursion to Pensacola in April?

As he informed his friend, Brackenridge was at this time in January intending to return soon to Florida, for his court sat in Jackson County in March. He knew already that Caroline would remain in Philadelphia "to come on in the spring or fall," a dreary prospect for him.

Brackenridge stopped awhile in Washington before continuing the journey south to Florida, lodging in the same house as the Whites.[57] With other lodgers the three of them formed what was called a mess, numbering about twelve persons. It was a pleasant company, although Mrs. White's presence annoyed Brackenridge as he disliked her coquetry. On one occasion when he tried to interest her conversationally, she could not listen because "Mr. ---------- *was playing with her finger ring!*"[58] She had never liked Overton and Brackenridge, the very men who were the "major props" by which her husband had acquired his present rank and success, for they did not approve of her flirtatious conduct. Brackenridge became so disgusted that he remained in his room instead of joining the other lodgers in the parlor. He himself was not offended, but he was troubled seeing the shameful treatment accorded his friend.

Brackenridge reached Savannah after a rough voyage during which he was often seasick.[59] Whiling away the time he had frequently recalled the scenes of his childhood and youth in his native state and wished that Caroline and he might sit by their own fireside there someday. Now, however, he was thankful to have the "greatest of earthly blessings, an affectionate wife"; and he was thankful, too, that his feelings were different "from those in days when I was like a weed torn from a rock and drifting wherever the winds and waves might carry it careless of its fate." At Savannah he was fortunate to find a steamboat ready to leave for Augusta, where his journey overland began.[60] He arrived at Flint River, Georgia, only three days distant from Webbville, in the best of health.[61] But the farther he traveled the more he missed Caroline's company, as his letters to her attested.

On Tuesday evening, March 18, Brackenridge reached his plantation on Santa Rosa Peninsula,[62] the same day Hunt, disliking sectional distinctions, dropped the word "West" from the title of his paper. Hunt believed that the citizens of East and West Florida should be united as the inhabitants of Florida—all were Floridians. In the past a stanch Floridian without strong sectional feeling, Brackenridge now more and more considered abandoning the country forever. But invariably a new thought occurred to him, like his suggestion to Caroline that for a few years a small cottage and a little garden at Webbville, where some amiable families lived, might not be unpleasant.[63]

Brackenridge, however, was glad to be in Pensacola again and at his place on the peninsula, which he found in good order. At Webbville where he held court, he had received a report that his orange trees were in blossom and his lemon tree covered with fruit.[64] But there were other things which cheered him. "I find," he wrote Caroline, "that the accounts of publick disatisfaction with my conduct, were shamefully exaggerated. . . . The old Spanish inhabitants appeared very much rejoiced to see me."[65] Everybody seemed to welcome the judge cordially, except Hunt and Adam Gordon, a lawyer who eventually became marshal. Hunt, who still thought the November term of the Superior Court ought to have been held despite the yellow fever, affected a cold manner toward Brackenridge.

Distant though Hunt was, he printed complimentary notices of Brackenridge's next term of court in Pensacola, which began on the first Monday in May.[66] The middle of the month saw the court still in session. "Much business has been done, and we have seldom seen more determination to get through the Docket, as efficiently as possible, evinced by the Court, than at this Term," Hunt commented in an editorial paragraph as if to atone for the embarrassment he had caused the judge.[67] When Brackenridge adjourned the court after a laborious session of thirteen days, the editor not only praised the work of the grand jury but by request published "with much pleasure" the opinion which Brackenridge had pronounced on the motion for a new trial in the case of *Bates* v. *Read,* Superior Court of West Florida, January, 1823.[68] The brief opinion was certain to be instructive for the members of the Florida bar.

329

There was other evidence in the spring of 1828 to convince Brackenridge that his career as a judge in Florida was not in jeopardy. The influential John Innerarity regarded him as highly as ever, indeed ranking him "foremost among my most distinguished friends. . . ." [69] With that introduction Innerarity invited the judge to the wedding of his daughter, Maria Henrietta, with Captain Henry Wilson. Brackenridge thus retained his social position among the old inhabitants of Pensacola. In Washington, furthermore, on June 4, a friend of longer standing than Innerarity, Secretary of State Henry Clay, officially notified [70] Brackenridge of his reappointment as judge for the District of West Florida and transmitted his commission.

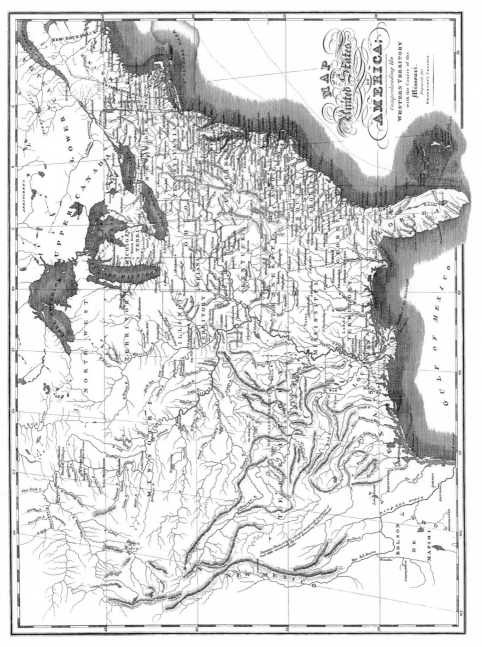

MAP OF MISSOURI RIVER REGION, a territory sparsely settled when Henry
Marie Brackenridge and John Bradbury took their trip in 1811. Map
engraved for Bradbury's *Travels in the Interior of America.*

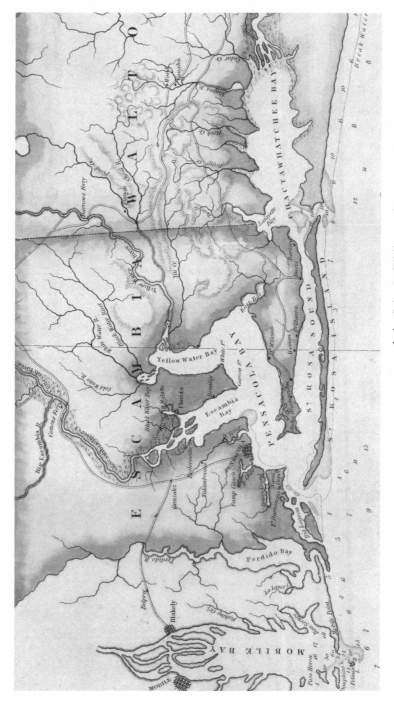

MAP OF THE WESTERN PART OF FLORIDA made by John L. Williams about 1827 showing
Brackenridge's property on Santa Rosa Peninsula across from Pensacola

XXIII: Deer Point and Tarentum

The spring of 1828 there were great plans afoot for the improvement of Florida. Hunt, in fact, predicted that fifty thousand bales of cotton would be brought to Apalachicola Bay during the year, easily transportable to Pensacola instead if a canal or railway connected the Chipola River with the eastern end of St. Andrews Bay.[1] The Floridians were aware of the facilities existing along their coast for the development of an inner coastwise navigation.

But despite the uncertainty of his future, for which the state of Caroline's health was responsible, Brackenridge himself was agitating the most original of all the plans. As a result, Brackenridge became the first forester for the United States and the superintendent of the first American forest experiment station.[2]

For almost thirty years officials of the federal government had realized the expediency of preserving for the navy the supply of live oak timber on the public lands. In 1799 Congress had passed a law authorizing the President to purchase land with valuable stands of live oak. The acquisition of Louisiana and Florida added to the supply of this timber under the control of the United States. In 1817 a surveyor and two agents were appointed to examine and then select live oak and red cedar lands for use of the navy. The government, however, had experienced difficulty in preventing the plunder of the public lands, especially in Florida, where depredations were common. It was Colonel White's motion[3] in the House of Representatives on January 12, 1827, which prompted an inquiry into the matter of preserving the supply of live oak and of increasing it by the establishment of plantations for raising the trees. His resolution, referred to the Navy Department,[4] elicited a reply[5] from Secretary Samuel L. Southard containing an historical account of past measures taken for the preservation of the timber and recommending the purchase of new tracts of land, the establishment of reservations in Florida and Louisiana, and the cultivation of the tree on government property—from the seed and by transplanting. Southard was concerned particularly about the needs of the navy in time of war.

According to Southard, the most advantageous site on the Florida coast for a reservation was a large tract of land belonging to the United States near the navy yard at Pensacola.[6] His department had ascertained that fact in executing the law of March 3, 1827, for improving the navy. Near the center of that part of the tract situated on Santa Rosa Peninsula, however, were sixteen hundred arpents—about fourteen hundred acres—of private land, which Southard requested authorization to buy: "The whole together would form very far the best plantation for live oak which can be found in Florida."

White and Brackenridge owned most of this land wanted by the Navy Department to form an unbroken tract for the reservation. As the Florida delegate to Congress, White undertook to act as the agent for selling to the government the land on the peninsula besides some other land adjoining the navy yard itself, an involved transaction.[7] It was complicated by the determination of the Adams administration to secure a transfer of title so airtight that political opponents could never challenge it. The Secretary of the Navy even asked Congress for specific authority to make the purchase. While they were in Washington in late January, 1828, White and Brackenridge had begun their negotiations with Southard to give the government the sole possession of the peninsula. It was not until fall, however, before the deeds were duly executed, authenticated, and registered—the transaction completed.

Carelessly estimating the worth of his establishment situated four miles below Deer Point on the peninsula, Brackenridge had agreed to sell it at a price which he immediately regretted.[8] He had originally offered the four hundred arpents of land, including the live oak, improvements, and buildings, for only $2,200. But upon reflection he had repented the bargain, for, before the mail route changed and "the road ceased to be traveled, I valued the property at five thousand dollars." Brackenridge promised to honor the agreement, however, if the Secretary of the Navy believed any change in it unwise— "It is certainly not common for people to ask too little for their property, but those who know me, I think, will do me the honor to say that, if such a blockhead can be found, it is more likely to be myself than any other." Nevertheless, White, serving as Brackenridge's attorney, received[9] $2,200 for the whole property on March 21.

In Pensacola that same day Brackenridge wrote Southard an extraordinary letter.[10] "On my arrival here, I found my orange trees, together with a variety of exotic fruit trees, from the West Indies, which I had not seen for a year, had grown beyond my most sanguine hopes, and are become exceedingly interesting and valuable, but, if removed, I fear, will perish," he began. "Having reared them from the seed while a solitary hermit, it is not surprising that I should have an attachment to them; they are my children." To think of parting with them was distressing. Again he asked for a reconsideration of their contract to enable him to retain the several acres on which stood his house and favorite trees: "I fear, sir, I may appear whimsical and ridiculous, but we are strange beings, fearfully made, and the happiness or misery of our lives is very differently compounded. There are associations connected with this spot which render it extremely painful for me to think of leaving it. What they are would be fitter for the story of romance."

Next Brackenridge declared that having a person resident there would be an advantage to the government, for he could keep the fires out of the thickets. At least he hoped for sufficient time to remove his trees and shrubs to another place should the Navy Department not grant his request. Then he made a bold proposition in his own inimitable way:

> . . . Perhaps an agent may be wanted by the government to superintend and direct the plantation of live oak, who has made the subject of the cultivation of trees his study; and, if I might speak of myself, I will venture to say that none has been more successful in this country. I have imported from England some of the works on *plantations,* as they are called, and the study and practice has, for several years, been my favorite amusement. Although I do not pretend to be equal to Solomon, for this would be vanity and vexation of spirit, yet I may say, with truth, that there is no tree or shrub in this country with whose history, properties, and habits I have not an acquaintance. If I could be permitted to remain in possession of my little Elysium as the agent, or an agent to superintend the noble experiment of preserving the live oak, I shall be content. I know nothing of speculation; I have no desire to sell to individuals; my only wish is the privilege of passing the few gliding years of a life already half accomplished, amid the harmless creation of my own hands. The superintendence would be an amusement to me, sufficient to compensate for the trouble. You may think this letter somewhat singular, and my request unreasonable, and founded on considerations which, as a man of business and official station, you can hardly act upon. Under the pre-emption act of Congress, I am entitled to a quarter section of land below the tract I purchased, having improved it in 1822, but I have never asserted my claim, which I might do if I were avaricious.

A few months at the beginning of 1828 thus saw Brackenridge experience a revealing change of heart. When he offered Butler an interest in the Santa Rosa property, Brackenridge was in Philadelphia with Caroline. He hated the thought of returning to Florida without her, although he worried about the condition of his trees. Before receiving a reply from Butler, Brackenridge had proceeded to Washington where White and he began their negotiations with Southard. "In a few days I think I shall be able to learn the decision of the Secretary of the Navy, respecting the purchase of my place," he informed Caroline in a letter written on January 20. "It is too desireable a thing to be very sanguine about."[11] But upon his return to Pensacola Brackenridge no longer found Florida a land of gloom. "I begin to regret my rather hasty determination to sell the place, in fact the impression I was under as to the state of my improvements, and their prospects was so very gloomy, that at the time, I thought it the best thing I could do," he confessed to her in mid-April. "But I was mistaken, the orange trees are becoming very valuable; they have grown since Mr. Davis came here, for he has taken care of them, so much that I could scarcely have believed it. I wrote to the Sec: of the Navy requesting a reconsideration of the bargain...."[12]

Before the year was over Brackenridge and Southard reached a satisfactory agreement in this matter, although a retransfer of land proved impossible. In March, three days after applying for the superintendency of the reservation, Brackenridge asked Southard's permission to remain in possession of his place until he could remove his trees to a spot prepared for them and reminded him of the application to manage the live oak experiment.[13] The judge, also, offered to communicate everything he knew about the cultivation of the trees. The final decision on the fate of his orange grove—that it would remain permanently in his control—Brackenridge learned from Southard's letter[14] of December 13.

The Secretary of the Navy did not require half a year or more, however, to ask Brackenridge to present his views on the culture of the live oak. Southard was eager to have them: "Will you express to me your opinion of the best mode of clearing out and planting the whole tract with live oak?"[15] Brackenridge could not comply at once with the request, for it came during his May term of court in Pensacola. But he promised to undertake the agreeable task as soon as the session was over.[16]

Here was Brackenridge's chance to demonstrate his fitness for the superintendency, which, as the days passed, he desired more and more. Precisely why he now fought to hold a piece of his property he confided to Caroline: "My object in wishing to retain this place, is for the purpose of having a foothold somewhere, in case the resignation of my office, at the end of three years, should threaten to render me dependant upon circumstances—*fifty bearing orange trees* would suffice for my support, without the horrors of slavery, or the necessity of looking to my profession. By having a little anchor of this kind to hold by, I shall feel more confidence in any future plan."[17] With Caroline pregnant in Philadelphia, Brackenridge needed an anchorage. In early May he ordered her to "throw away all false delicacy, and in every thing unusual consult the doctor."[18] Consequently, what he wrote the Secretary of the Navy four days later was self-explanatory, although Southard, unknowing, perhaps laughed at this evidence of his correspondent's eccentricity: "I make the offer of my services without any expectation of emolument or compensation; and should any moderate compensation be deemed proper by the President, it will only be accepted by me in order that I may engage an assistant, who may be constantly on the spot when my duties shall require my absence at court."[19]

Dated Santa Rosa, June 1, Brackenridge's letter[20] to Southard on the culture of the live oak was divided into two parts—one being a description of the tree itself and the other a plan for operating the proposed reservation. "The live oak, *quercus vivus,* is one of the most valuable timber trees our country produces, and is unequaled for the frames of vessels," Brackenridge asserted. "There is no wood superior, if equal to it, in strength, buoyancy, and durability." He also described the live oak as one of the noblest shade trees in the world. But all this was common knowledge. His account of the properties of the tree, or of its natural history, however, contained information gained by much reading and personal experiment—little known but important facts he brought to Southard's attention: "I can, therefore, speak with the confidence derived from experience on the advantages of nursing the trees which we find already set by the hand of nature; for they often have the advantage of a root a hundred or perhaps five hundred years old." Brackenridge knew of no other forest tree which improved with care as much as the live oak.

Deer Point Brackenridge considered an ideal spot to make a "fair" experiment in the cultivation of the tree. One advantage was its proximity to the navy yard, and another was the availability of water transportation for the heavy wood. In planning the experiment, he paid strict attention to the matter of economy; therefore, he recommended an expenditure of about sixty-four hundred dollars for the first year of operation. This estimate included the hire of twenty laborers and the salaries of a superintendent and an overseer. Brackenridge suggested steps to be taken for establishing the plantation, such as confining the first operations to the tract of four or five thousand acres where he himself resided. Later, in two or three years, subordinate establishments could be created.

Brackenridge had not exhausted his subject in this letter to Southard, for he wrote[21] him again on June 10. Brackenridge wished to correct his estimate of the number of young trees which could be cleared from surrounding thickets; but he reported, too, that a fire had just destroyed thousands of young trees which he had intended to replant in the pine flats. The fire hazard was much on his mind as he asked help "to prevent mischievous lime burners and wood cutters from continuing their depredations" and to drive off the Indians, whose campfires were a constant menace. Although not authorized by the federal government, Brackenridge had already employed a laborer to prune the live oak and to clear trees from the undergrowth. In concluding this second communication to Southard, Brackenridge informed him that a boat would be necessary "to the establishment, at any rate, and the one which I have is very crazy and unsafe."

The first letter, that of June 1, was a pioneering piece in American forestry literature. A century later it could command the respect of an authority[22] in the field, who recommended it to the foresters of his day. Despite its serious subject, the letter was interesting. Brackenridge obviously understood the importance of fire prevention. An optimist as he viewed the projected plantation, he naturally tended to exaggerate here and there. However, the letter not only impressed Southard favorably but also President Adams, whose hobby was arboriculture.

The President and the Secretary of the Navy thoroughly discussed the letter upon its receipt in Washington. After breakfast on July 5, Southard called upon his chief. When the conversation turned to Brackenridge's letter, Adams approved his appointment as superintendent of the live oak experiment at Deer Point, which Southard had recommended.[23] Adams, an avid experimenter in his own summerhouse nursery, ordered the planting of acorns on the reservation, a step which Brackenridge in his letter on the cultivation of the live oak had said was unnecessary. "But the natural history of the live-oak has many singularities, and has not been duly observed," the President insisted.

Therefore, when Southard replied to the letters of June 1 and 10, he stressed the President's concern about the planting of the acorn. But this letter[24] of appointment to Brackenridge the Secretary of the Navy did not write until December 6, after the election of Jackson as President of the United States. Despite the victory of his opponent, Adams had decided to launch the experiment at Deer Point under Brackenridge's superintendency. According to Southard's letter, Brackenridge's annual salary was fixed at four hundred dollars, precisely what he had originally suggested the post pay. Southard authorized him to employ an overseer, to hire not more than twenty laborers for one year, and to procure whatever supplies and accommodations were required. Brackenridge was permitted to carry out his ideas on the culture of the live oak exactly as he had presented them, except for the matter of the acorns.

The arrangement suited Brackenridge, for he had won not only the superintendency but also permission to keep his orange grove and the other improvements. Although Brackenridge received the news of his appointment at Tallahassee, he began the undertaking at once by writing Samuel Davis, his caretaker on Santa Rosa Peninsula, to appoint him the overseer.[25] Brackenridge hired laborers to work on the reservation. Despite his absence from Pensacola, he was confident that operations could begin by January 10. He was enthusiastic about the experiment, not even questioning Adams' order concerning the planting of acorns, "which, I find, also accords with the opinion of Commodore Woolsey, who is well informed on such subjects, and enters into the views of the President with judgment and zeal." In his letter of acceptance to Southard, dated January 5, Brackenridge had one request to make—he desired a copy of his letter on the culture of the live oak be sent him.

Brackenridge had long contemplated the publication of another book. What he had intended to publish was not an original work but a collection of several of the best speeches, including his own, made over the years on the Jew Bill in the House of Delegates in Maryland. He wished to perpetuate some evidence of the struggle waged there for the freedom of conscience. Now, in 1829, Brackenridge decided to include other pieces in the publication, which was the reason why he had asked Southard for a copy of the live oak letter. The slim 236-page volume, ponderously entitled *Speeches on the Jew Bill, in*

*the House of Delegates of Maryland, by H. M. Brackenridge, Col. W. G. D.
Worthington, and John S. Tyson, Esquire. Together with an Argument on the
Chancery Powers, and an Eulogy on Thomas Jefferson and John Adams, &c.
By H. M. Brackenridge,* was published in the late summer in Philadelphia.
Besides the speeches noted in the title the volume contained the live oak letter;
Brackenridge's letter to Jefferson written in 1813 on the subject of western
antiquities; his report on commemorating the defense of Baltimore against
the British, adopted by the city council; and an oration which his father had
delivered on July 4, 1779, in the German Calvinist Church, Philadelphia,
memorializing all who had fallen in the Revolutionary War. Not to be overlooked is Brackenridge's statement in a footnote to the live oak letter: "I shall
feel proud of being instrumental in a work of such vast national importance,
as that of securing a permanent supply of the only kind of timber fit for ships
of war."[26]

Tyson had furnished Brackenridge with the last copy of his own Jew speech,
happy to go down with him "to posterity in the bark you have provided or are
providing. . . ."[27] The book was noticed satisfactorily by the press. The editor,
Niles, approved the publication of the speeches on the Jew Bill in particular,
for they involved "a subject of great interest, and are altogether worthy of
the reason and liberality of the age."[28] Surely the most satisfying reaction to
Brackenridge's latest publication was the comment of Peleg Sprague, the eminent United States senator from Maine, who perused it in its entirety despite
failing eyesight:

> . . . I have read it with great pleasure & advantage—and hope that the lawyers of our
> country may imitate the research, and be instructed by the original & comprehensive
> views of the argument on the Chancery powers—and that all may imbibe something of
> the truly liberal & republican spirit of the speech upon the Jew-bill—and be impressed
> with a profounder reverence for the great-founders-and invaluable institutions of our
> Republic by the perusal of the Eulogy upon Adams & Jefferson and the Oration upon
> the Anniversary of our national Independence.[29]

The publication of the book had not interfered with Brackenridge's supervision of the live oak plantation. The experiment had an auspicious beginning, for, true to his word, his men—fifteen laborers—were already at work
by mid-January.[30] So enthusiastic about starting operations was Brackenridge
that he paid the initial expenses himself until he could draw on government
funds. He bought oxen, a cart, a boat, and tools. As authorized by his agreement with Southard, Brackenridge negotiated for the purchase of pre-emptions
on the peninsula—he recommended that the reservation eventually encompass
all of it.[31] "I feel perfectly confident that I shall be able to clear out thirty
thousand trees, from ten to thirty feet high, in the course of the year," he
advised Southard early in February. The superintendent had employed young

men only—seventeen to twenty years old—"who have no bad habits, who can
be perfectly contented, and who will remain contented on this insular spot."

Brackenridge's report for the first quarter, ending April 18, was a record
of the surprising progress achieved in a few months. He submitted his accounts
to John Branch, the new secretary of the navy, the North Carolinian who had
resigned his Senate seat to serve in Jackson's Cabinet. The report was impressive, for, according to Davis,[32] the overseer at Deer Point, 22,202 trees—from
full grown to under two inches—had been cleared from other growth; in fact,
that was the number of live oaks on a tract of two hundred acres. Under the
direction of Davis the hands had cut roads to aid the work of fire prevention
and erected quarters for themselves. As Brackenridge emphasized to his superior at Washington, the work accomplished exceeded the original estimate at
no additional expense to the government.[33] "The groves already assume a
beautiful appearance," he wrote Branch. "We have transplanted only a few
trees, and as there were no acorns last year—the live oak bearing only every
other year—it was impossible to commence a nursery from them, which,
according to the opinion of some writers, is most advisable." Using the British
principle of annuities, Brackenridge estimated the value of the trees cleared
at $10,920.

There was a discordant note in his optimistic report, however. The work
of the whole quarter Brackenridge carried at his own expense and by his
credit. He hoped Secretary Branch would promptly place funds at his dis-
posal for the operation of the reservation.[34] The judge had reason to worry
about the state of his finances, for he was now a father. Benjamin Morgan,
whom he had not yet seen, had been born in Philadelphia on November 5,
1828. Once he knew of his son's birth, Brackenridge was tortured by doubt
and fear concerning the health of Caroline and the baby whenever the mail
arrived without a letter from her—and whether he was happy or despondent
in this regard, his imagination was lively![35] "Do not my dear Caroline stint
yourself in any expence, our means are sufficient, and they are improving,"
he advised her soon after the birth of his son. "Spare no expence that may
contribute to your comfort, and to the safety of our little boy."[36] Despite the
demands upon him, which he detailed for Caroline, Brackenridge had just
purchased a tract of land at the settlement of Alaqua, which was a journey of
a day and a half from Santa Rosa—"I am no speculator, but a small sum
judiciously invested under such circumstances produces an increase which it
is impossible to obtain in any other way."

Now Brackenridge discovered to his dismay that he had no friend at court
in the person of Branch. Was it possible that the new Secretary of the Navy
viewed the live oak experiment with a jaundiced eye? On April 7 he had

written the unsuspecting superintendent a peremptory note informing him that the Board of Navy Commissioners was about to visit the reservation on Santa Rosa Peninsula. "You will be pleased to suspend all operations commenced under former instructions, relating to that tract which is under your immediate superintendence, until you shall hear further from the Department," Branch ordered without explanation.[37]

The commissioners under the presidency of Commodore John Rodgers conducted their investigation with dispatch. On July 3, Rodgers was ready to write his report[38] in Washington! He had found about a fourth of the tract purchased from Brackenridge to be hammock land, on one hammock of which grew a hundred or more large live oaks. The other hammocks contained sizable stumps, "thus furnishing, if not conclusive, strong presumptive evidence that a soil that had once given growth to such timber might, with care and proper management, be made to produce it again, if not by transplanting young and thrifty trees, at least by sowing acorns taken from trees of large growth, while in a sound, healthy state." But the commodore thought the rest of the land worthless for the purpose of cultivation. He had seen Brackenridge's improvements—the one-story frame dwelling ("not plastered") with six rooms, a central hall, and porticoes at the front and back; the log kitchen, the stable, and other outhouses; the two log buildings commodious enough to accommodate twenty negro laborers; and the two gardens. Davis, the overseer, had accompanied Rodgers over the entire reservation; they had watched the hired hands at work. Rodgers was inclined to believe that Davis's count of 22,202 trees on the lands cleared to be "nearly, if not quite correct." Although the commodore's report was far from enthusiastic, it did not indicate in any way that White and Brackenridge had fleeced the government.

Commodore Rodgers had not seen Colonel White, who was at Tallahassee; nor had he conversed with Brackenridge, who was on his way to Philadelphia.

Brackenridge had first headed for Pittsburgh where he planned to remain long enough to inspect Caroline's property on the Allegheny at the mouth of Bull Creek, twenty-one miles distant from town. He had sailed for New Orleans on May 12.[39] Early in June he reached Pittsburgh after a pleasant voyage up the Mississippi and the Ohio.[40] There he visited his brother Alexander, who managed Caroline's property.

Years before, John Woods, the aristocratic lawyer and the political rival of Hugh Henry Brackenridge, had provided for Caroline's support by executing an unusual deed of trust[41] on November 17, 1815, when she was about nineteen years old. At last Woods had acknowledged a responsibility for her welfare, which, however, he had not wished to admit in his will,[42] dated September 20, 1816. For a consideration of one dollar he had deeded nine tracts of land—about two thousand acres—with the appurtenances to James Ross and John McDonald of Pittsburgh and to Josiah Espy of Bedford as trustees charged with leasing the property to tenants and applying the rents collected to Caroline's support. The land was situated on the west side of the Allegheny River at and near the mouth of Bull Creek.

Woods' designation of his brother-in-law, Ross, as a trustee was ironical, for it was he who had once dispossessed little Caroline and her mother of their home on Grant's Hill. But with age Ross had mellowed and had undertaken the charge conscientiously. After his marriage Brackenridge himself testified to this in a letter to Thomas Butler, written in Philadelphia: "Mr. Ross . . . called to see us, and is disposed to render us any assistance. He looks remarkably well for one of his age, and much better than in Pittsburgh, where every ones face is begrimed with coal smoke. I thought he appeared ten years younger."[43] Ross and his fellow trustees surrendered possession of the Bull Creek property to Caroline and her husband upon their marriage and wrote an order for the agent to pay them the rents due.[44]

Brackenridge, nevertheless, had not long before studied the deed of trust and believed it imperfect and also doubted the sincerity of Ross. From the moment of his marriage Brackenridge had dreamed a "golden dream"[45] of someday residing at Bull Creek, where he could live independently by attending the neighboring courts and making "a few hundred dollars" to supplement whatever income the property provided. The state of Caroline's health had precluded even the discussion of such a plan. But Brackenridge advised her early in their marriage of his concern about the deed:

. . . I have been engaged in studying that important deed of trust, for I have been revolving plans of future life, but I dare not encourage them too much. The result of my investigation has been to fix the first impression which I took respecting the deed—that a court of chancery would compel the trustees to settle the estate at once—and further that under the act of assembly of Pennsylvania, a deed of conveyance and reconveyance, acknowledged by you in open court, would even now change the title, the happening of one contingency being sufficient—But these are law questions which you do not understand. I intended to have drawn up an opinion on the instrument and have submitted it to several of the most eminent lawyers in the United States, and when fully satisfied as to our rights boldly demanded them. I am strongly inclined to think that Mr. Ross has overreached himself by his excessive *skill*.

Brackenridge's interest in the deed of trust resulted not only in a thorough examination of the instrument itself but in the production of a legal treatise, *An Essay on Trusts and Trustees,* a small volume of value both to the student and the practitioner. In the spring of 1828 he had consulted Roger B. Taney and R. B. Magruder for their opinion of the deed and found their views in accord with his own—as he explained the matter to Caroline, Taney held that it was "an estate *tail,* and therefore can be barred as we express it, that is

340

turned into a fee simple, by a simple conveyance by us to some one, and by another deed receiving it back. . . . It is laughable to see the simplicity of Mr. Taney in ascribing the obscurity of the deed of trust to *want of skill*—when it was by consummate skill, abused, that it was rendered obscure on purpose."[46] To prove his thesis that the deed was imperfect, Brackenridge finally went to the length of publishing an analysis of it—his scholarly *Essay*—in Washington fourteen years later. He was, therefore, convinced that the deed was "a barrable estate tail" in Caroline.

His doubts about the deed and his mistrust of Ross, however, did not prevent Brackenridge from proceeding with the improvement of the Bull Creek property. In fact, Caroline and he held possession of the land without the interference of the trustees, although an agreement was made for laying out town lots on part of it to repay the sum advanced for her support before her marriage.[47]

Brackenridge's mind was filled with plans for the improvement of the property as he went upriver from Pittsburgh in June, 1829. Months before he had added to the land by purchasing a little island in the river for two hundred dollars.[48] He had the plan of the house, too—a "very simple and perhaps common" house—to be built on a beautiful site, on the second bank about three hundred yards from the Allegheny. "It is a two story framed house, on a brick foundation four feet high, cellar under it, and a back building also, two stories, but not so high," he had informed Caroline. There would be closets in this eight-room house, he assured her.

Brackenridge reached Bull Creek on June 9 and the next day wrote Caroline. He expected to

be engaged two days in examining the land, and fixing on a spot for future improvement. Alexander has done the best in his power, some decent log houses and good barns have been built, and better tenants procured; the improvements to [be] paid out of the rent. The farms were in such a wretched state that it will take all the rents to accomplish this. I have been at Freeport, six miles from this place—it is a very pretty village, and is likely to grow rapidly. This is a most beautiful country, and the improvements within the last two years have much exceeded my expectations. The canal is not yet in operation —they have attempted to let the water into it, but they find a greater number of weak and defective places, than was supposed.[49]

Their property was ideally located for improvement. The site Brackenridge fixed upon for future development bordered in part on the land of Felix Negley. In 1829 the population of the district was still sparse; and the inhabitants of the log cabins dotting the countryside led lives reminiscent of the frontier. But the Pennsylvania Canal, into which the water was first let the previous year, was soon to be a boon to the farmer and the businessman of the Allegheny Valley. Brackenridge envisaged the rise of a thriving town on the property. Under his direction W. Martin surveyed the spot chosen for improvement in the fall of 1829. Brackenridge named the town which he founded here on the bank of the river, Tarentum, perhaps after the ancient city of southern Italy, for he was a classical scholar.[50] In March, 1832, Brackenridge, as the proprietor, recorded the ground plot[51] of Tarentum, which showed the town situated on the Allegheny River and the Pennsylvania Canal at the aqueduct and locks, near the mouth of Bull Creek. Tarentum reached from the river to the Pittsburgh-Kittanning road. It was an excellent location for the establishment of manufactures, for coal abounded in the neighboring hills and water power was available at the lock. Adjoining the town were a steam gristmill, a sawmill, and a fulling mill.

In June, 1829, Brackenridge did not tarry long at Bull Creek, for he was anxious to see Caroline and his son in Philadelphia. But when he inspected Caroline's land and launched an ambitious plan for its improvement, he must have thought his dream nearer realization than ever. Sometimes he wondered whether he deserved a residence on the Allegheny, although he knew that was what he needed: "I found that I was not well suited to a laborious, dependent, slavish life. It is very hard to be poor and dependent. . . . Although not devoid of industry, my industry is too much of that kind which the busy world calls idleness—it is too contemplative, disinterested, and abstract."[52] He entertained no doubts about his love for Caroline and Benjamin Morgan, however. "Let us so live, if possible, as not to be too much elevated or depressed by worldly events," he once adjured his wife. "Yet I confess that that little infant next to yourself is the nearest and dearest object to me on this earth. Every thought of this world is inseparately mingled with the idea of our little boy."[53]

But shortening his reunion with Caroline was the imperative need for Brackenridge to hurry to Washington on Florida business. From Philadelphia he went to Baltimore and left there for Washington on June 29.[54] After his arrival he immediately met with delay in the conduct of his business, for Secretary Branch was too much engaged to see him.[55] Brackenridge, therefore, had ample time to observe the state of affairs in the national capital. What he saw and what he sensed made him uncomfortable, as he told Caroline:

There is a great deal of unhappiness here in those who have lost their offices. There is a painful uneasiness with every person, which looks indeed like the effect of despotism. I fear the mild administrations of an Adams, a Monroe, or a Madison, are never again to be seen. Office will be the reward of successful partisans, and hence the struggle will be embittered. I have heard of no representations against me, and I think Jackson is friendly to me, but I am convinced the sooner I quit the territory of Florida, the better. My feelings are all against this harsh administration of the government, and I fear it will be continued.

Evidently Brackenridge did not wish to worry Caroline by mentioning representations made against him, for, the day before writing her, on July 1, he had solicited [56] a statement from William M. McCarty, the late secretary of Florida who was now in Washington an unwell man. Brackenridge put three queries to McCarty, which, if answered correctly, would be proof that the lands at Deer Point abounded in young live oak of a thrifty growth, appeared adapted to a live oak plantation, and were not extravagantly priced at two dollars an acre. McCarty's reply, [57] written the next day, favored the purchase of the Brackenridge land and the establishment of the plantation.

However, in a communication [58] to the Secretary of the Navy, dated July 16, Thomas F. Cornell, the late agent of the department in West Florida, stated a contrary opinion. Cornell asserted that the idea of buying land in Florida to establish a live oak nursery seemed "very singular" to the inhabitants when the federal government already owned better lands elsewhere. He condemned the purchase of land from White: "Sir, when this information was first communicated in Florida, it was received with astonishment, and could not be believed; and the doubts of many were not removed until seeing extensive operations commenced, negroes hired at enormous wages, and the grand scheme of supplying our navy with a future supply of live oak put into active and extensive operation." The tracts obtained through White he described as the "most worthless and miserable" ones in the entire territory, "all of which, I venture to say, could not at this moment command 9,000 cents, except for the buildings erected by Judge Breckenridge, one of the former proprietors, and some other little improvements, of no use to the government, put on one of the tracts by him previously to the sale of it to the government." The campaign to discredit the experiment at Deer Point was under way!

Meanwhile, Brackenridge had written Branch a letter, [59] being unable to obtain an interview. As concisely as possible the judge explained how he had followed the instructions of Secretary Southard, "not aware that there would be any hesitation in settling the accounts." He mentioned Southard's assurance regarding the fruit trees. "I have not the remotest interest in the establishment, never having owned but one slave in my life, and those who know me will inform you that avarice forms no part of my character," he asserted in defense of his integrity. If Branch should decide to terminate operations on the reservation, Brackenridge requested a prompt notification, although he offered to remain as superintendent with or without compensation as the President might determine. It was a humbling letter to write, a letter which Brackenridge believed Branch might not read for some time—"they usually file such things away, and look at them in their turn some six months afterwards!" [60]

Brackenridge, nevertheless, did see the President and Secretary Branch before returning to Florida. The morning of July 30 he was able to converse with both. He talked first with Branch, who promised to speak to Jackson in his behalf. Brackenridge again explained the arrangement concerning his orange grove and denied any intention of defrauding the government in the sale of land for the live oak establishment. Later that day he reported the result of his conversations to Caroline: "The Secretary seems very friendly to me, and declared that he knew from my character, I could have no possible interest in the matter, or speculative views."[61]

Heartened, Brackenridge returned to his family in Philadelphia and shortly prepared for the journey south. On September 1 he forwarded to Branch the report[62] of the overseer, Davis, for the quarter ending July 18. In his letter[63] transmitting the report and the accounts to the Navy Department, Brackenridge praised the zeal of Davis, who had four of his own laborers at work on the experiment. The report showed that the expense of the quarter was less than that of the previous one and the work accomplished greater. Altogether, more than forty thousand trees had been pruned and cleared, ten thousand more than Brackenridge had expected for the whole year. Two weeks after submitting his accounts, Brackenridge arranged for the collection and deposit of the money due him as the superintendent of the live oak plantation.[64] Then he was ready to return to Pensacola.

During the ensuing months, as revealed by the quarterly reports[65] of the overseer made regularly to Brackenridge in 1830, work on the reservation at Deer Point progressed steadily. They could inspect their plantation with pride —it was a model for other reservations which might be established. Their hands grubbed the thickets and the protecting roads; they cleared new roads. They erected a three-rail post fence and in one of the enclosures planted acorns. Another enclosure was reserved for the experimental transplanting of young trees. Pruning and grubbing—that was the chief occupation of the hands, however. The summer heat slowed operations, but by now the cultivated trees were extremely thrifty as compared with those encumbered still with thickets. But the experiment of planting acorns proved Brackenridge's contention that the formation of nurseries was unnecessary when a vast number of young trees were already thriving and possessed old roots. Enthusiastically Davis offered his superintendent suggestions for future operations.

But on August 30, in Washington, Secretary Branch had written Brackenridge an icy note[66] which spelled ruin for his plans for the reservation. Branch ordered that operations end as soon as practicable, "with the understanding that they positively terminate with the present year." Brackenridge, in turn, transmitted the order to his overseer, who confined the work to the groves already cleared, hoping to place the establishment in the best possible condition before the operations ceased on January 18, 1831. "The trees are in a most flourishing state; they have continued to grow, notwithstanding the extraordinary drought we have experienced," Davis noted in his report[67] for the quarter ending October 18. The overseer had successfully attended to the problem of fire prevention during the dry spell. It was, therefore, with a heavy heart that Brackenridge sent his accounts for the quarter to Washington. His sincerity was unmistakable in the proposition he now made to Branch:

> If a few hands will be allowed, say from two to *five,* (but I think the latter number at least,) I will undertake, for the sum which has been allowed me as superintendent, to continue the care of the trees for the next year, and will, *out of that sum,* engage a white laborer, who can, at the same time, act as overseer of the hands. I should feel great regret to see the work abandoned when it is so promising, and after so much expense and labor have been bestowed. The space now occupied can sustain at least sixty thousand trees, the whole of which, in less than twenty years, and many much sooner, will be fit for most purposes for ship-building.[68]

The insinuation that he, as well as White, had defrauded the government disheartened Brackenridge, although it was only a by-product of Florida politics. For more than a year White and Call, Brackenridge's former law partner, had hurled charge and countercharge at each other in the Florida press[69] over the transactions by which the tracts of land composing the reservation were purchased for the United States. Call accused White of profiteering at the expense of his constituents: "Did he speculate on his Constituents? No, the Colonel is not 'skilled in the arts of speculation,' but he *gleaned* a little." Call described the property sold the government as worthless—"arid sands." As Call accused him of doing, White had bought the tracts for a small sum and sold for a larger. But that fact had nothing to do with Brackenridge's role in the affair.

In a letter[70] to Michael Hoffman, chairman of the House Naval Affairs Committee, White now defended Brackenridge from the imputation of wrongdoing as made by Branch in his annual report to Congress, wherein he had announced his intention to end the Santa Rosa experiment. The Florida delegate held that a continuance of the experiment was not only indispensable to the existence of the navy but also to the general prosperity of the country. "The report seems exclusively designed to make an unfavorable impression in relation to the purchase of the land," White charged. He reviewed the whole involved transaction with Secretary Southard to prove the government had not made a "bad bargain." Finally, White clarified Brackenridge's part in the business in a striking way:

> I have considered this hasty detail due to a gentleman of as pure and unsullied character as any in this nation; a man who, at the moment when party clamor discolored even the most innocent transactions, sent a petition to rescind his contract, to save his reputation from its malignant attacks. His petition was unanimously refused by your

committee. The United States would neither give him back his land, nor cease to complain of the purchase.

I have, then, shown the land was well adapted to the object for which it was purchased; that the purchase was made after the contract was submitted to Congress, and that it was made for a sum far below its value, in the opinions of the most respectable and honorable men in this country. I have further shown that, as soon as Judge Breckenridge was informed that there was any complaint, or likely to be any, he petitioned Congress to rescind the contract, which was refused.

I show by the statement presented, that the live oak now upon his land is worth, at contract prices, deducting all expenses, more than ten thousand dollars.

I think it must be apparent that *he,* and not the United States, had made a bad bargain, and that Congress ought to make an appropriation for the value of *his* land and live oak, as it is evident that he sold it for only one-fifth of its value.

White himself had initiated an official investigation of the Santa Rosa experiment by his motion of December 16, 1830, in the House of Representatives. Branch was required to submit to that body all the pertinent documents in possession of his department. In his report,[71] dated January 7, he called the deeds from White to Southard faulty and disparaged the lands acquired. Branch, of course, had interpreted the documents[72] in a manner calculated to suggest the advisability of stopping the culture of the live oak. His report did not end the investigation, for the House of Representatives referred it to the Naval Affairs Committee for action.[73]

The report[74] of Hoffman's committee to the House of Representatives, communicated on February 26, was a curious document. It was noncommittal on the important issues. Because the evidence concerning the value of the lands in question and their fitness for a live oak nursery was so contradictory, the committee recommended more examinations. Refer all conveyances and title deeds to the attorney general for his opinion, the committee advised. Although the committee approved the establishment of live oak reservations, it did not advocate Adams' idea of growing the trees from acorns, no doubt much to his chagrin.

Adams, who would take his seat in Congress in December to begin an astonishing period of legislative service, was already in Washington and upset about the apparent fate of his favorite project. After church on February 20 he had visited White at his lodgings.[75] While they were conversing, Brackenridge arrived. The ex-President thus received the details of the affair firsthand. But Adams had his own views, too. "The report of the Secretary of the Navy . . . is remarkable at once for gross ignorance and wilful misrepresentation; and he has been guilty of a dishonorable suppression of a report from the Commissioners of the Navy, because it would have refuted and falsified his own," he stated in his diary. Adams believed the attack on the reservation was directed at him: "The malicious pleasure of destroying everything of which I had planted the germ, and the base purpose of representing as wasteful

THE BRACKENRIDGE HOME, "Oak Grove," Tarentum, Pennsylvania
Courtesy of Helen Brackenridge Painter

HENRY MARIE BRACKENRIDGE in the late years of his life

prodigality the most useful and most economical expenditures, are the motives that act upon the Secretary of the Navy and the present Administration." The ex-President was bitter: "The plantation, both of young trees growing when I commenced it and of those from the acorn which I had caused to be planted, is now in a condition as flourishing as possible, and more than a hundred thousand live-oaks are growing upon it. All is to be abandoned by the stolid ignorance and stupid malignity of John Branch and of his filthy subaltern, Amos Kendall."

But perhaps all was not lost, for the downfall of Branch was imminent. Involved in the uproarious Eaton affair, he was forced to resign his cabinet post, to be succeeded by Levi Woodbury, of New Hampshire, in May. Before retiring from office, however, Branch instituted a system for the protection of the live oak by the employment of seven superintendents, or agents, to supervise seven districts. In the press there had appeared warnings against this precipitate abandonment of the plantation system as represented by the Santa Rosa experiment.[76]

As a proponent of scientific agriculture Woodbury was interested in giving the superintendent of the plantation a hearing. Brackenridge did not wait until invited to give his views; but, on July 27, he wrote the new Secretary of the Navy, promising to continue to take care of the trees—eighty thousand of them—and to furnish any information desired.[77] The entire matter, Brackenridge averred, had "received an improper color and magnified importance, from its connection with the local politics of the Territory." He wished that Woodbury would study *all* the documents in the case. Brackenridge was obviously not satisfied with this effort to win Woodbury's support, for he wrote him another letter[78] a week later, communicating a list of facts about the culture of the live oak. Brackenridge condemned Branch's system of protecting the live oak as "an idle thing, a useless expense" and called it "an electioneering contrivance, to operate upon individuals to the prejudice of Colonel White." In its place he recommended the establishment of several reservations like his own at Deer Point ("which I am now taking care of at my private expense").

Woodbury's prompt reply[79] was encouraging. The Secretary of the Navy, however, ordered the operations to be confined to the preservation of what had already been accomplished. This was a sensible directive for the present, at least until he had received the report of General John Clark, whom Branch had appointed one of the agents for live oak. On September 26, five days after writing Brackenridge, Woodbury dispatched an order[80] to Clark to examine the plantation at Deer Point—"a critical examination" to be made "without delay."

Apart from certain reservations—as the "experiment . . . has not yet advanced sufficiently to enable me to form an opinion as to the probability of the production paying for the labor expended"—Clark's report[81] was favorable to Brackenridge. It was really a vindication of White and Brackenridge. The live oaks, Clark noted, were thrifty and numbered between fifty and eighty thousand. The proximity of the plantation to the navy yard was also a point in its favor. All in all, Clark decided to "recommend the continuance of the cultivation, with an increase of five more laborers."

The experiment at Deer Point was, nevertheless, doomed to a quick end. In the fall of 1831 White had attacked[82] Branch's system not without some effect, for, by the end of another year, Woodbury was liquidating it.[83] Early in 1832, in fact, White and Branch, now serving in the House of Representatives, had engaged in "a very sharp debate" on the live oak issue.[84] Meanwhile, on January 24, Brackenridge had transmitted the plantation accounts to Woodbury: "The progress has been equal to my expectations, although the work was somewhat retarded by the excessive cold of the winter. I do not advise the increase in the number of hands for the present."[85] But in this same year, 1832, Brackenridge left Florida forever as a disillusioned man and fighting mad, the victim of Jacksonian politics. Secretary Woodbury, willing to give the noble experiment in forestry a further trial, placed the plantation under the superintendency of the commander of the Pensacola navy yard[86] after the judge had returned to Pennsylvania—and Tarentum. Actually, Brackenridge's departure concluded the experiment.

XXIV: The Fall from Grace

As a judge, Brackenridge had never truckled to anyone. He had preserved his independence amid the skirmishing of the territorial politicians. In 1828, when he attended a dinner at Tallahassee in honor of his friend White, Brackenridge reminded the company of a signal fact before toasting the memory of Dr. Bronaugh and Major Overton—"It is true, I am one of the small number of those Americans yet remaining, who came to Florida immediately on its surrender to the United States. . . ."[1] He declared his embarrassment at being an invited guest to this dinner, for he tried "to avoid every thing which may turn upon me the public eye. The judiciary should keep aloof from whatever is calculated to agitate or excite the public mind, and in the wisest and the best, it is no easy task to preserve that equanimity, without which, it is impossible to hold the scales of justice with a steady hand." Brackenridge had maintained the independence of the judiciary while, at the same time, he had labored zealously for the improvement of Florida. Jesse H. Willis, indeed, volunteered a fitting toast to "Our distinguished Guest, The Hon. H. M. BRACKEN-RIDGE.—His useful exertions for our Territory when in infancy, deserve the gratitude of her citizens."

A year later the *Pensacola Gazette and Florida Advertiser* documented the sentiment expressed by Willis in his toast. The readers of the paper were not left in doubt about Brackenridge's role in territorial progress:

. . . We have in our possession an interesting document of which Judge B. is known to be the author, written in 1822. A document which points out with clear forecast, all the important measures proper to be taken for the organization of the Territory. Such as the great road from Pensacola to St. Augustine, the establishment of a seat of Government east of Appalachicola, the organization of a Court of Appeals, and many others subsequently carried into effect, and for which great credit has been claimed for other prominent individuals by their friends. The Judge has been content to see the effect of his public spirit, leaving the credit to others; but justice ought to be rendered where it is due, without detracting from the merits of other public men who have also done their duty, although not solely and exclusively entitled to the praise.[2]

The paper, moreover, reprinted Brackenridge's articles[3] on the topography of Pensacola and its vicinity, which had appeared in the *Floridian* eight years earlier, pronouncing the first, a description of the town, as "the most correct and graphic we have seen. . . ."

Brackenridge had always been the man of culture in Pensacola. His reputation had not diminished with the passage of time. When a "gentleman of great intelligence"[4] of Havana purchased a rare book concerning Florida history, he wanted Brackenridge to know about it. When the eminent Dr. Thomas Cooper, formerly a professor of chemistry in Carlisle College (Dickinson) and now president of the South Carolina College, tired of his post and a body of captious trustees and toyed with the idea of removing to a richer land

("I see the blast of poverty sweeping over this country: her resources are diminishing, and our salaries here will be retrenched, even in the face of the most strongly implied contract."), he sought information from Brackenridge about the advisability of establishing "a Collegiate School of a high class" in Florida.[5] Write soon, he requested Brackenridge: "I bring a library worth 10,000 dollars, a little money, an excellent chemical apparatus, & I possess young & old about 12 negroes." There was the possibility that Brackenridge himself had even founded a fellowship modeled after the Delphian Club, as the following notice in the *Pensacola Gazette and Florida Advertiser* of December 12, 1829, might indicate:

> The annual meeting of the "R.A." society will take place at Santa Rosa Island, on the 25th inst; those members at a distance are particularly requested to take notice of it and govern themselves accordingly, as the laws of the society will be strictly, and rigidly enforced against such as absent themselves—business of the utmost importance, not only to the well being of the society, but to the world at large, will be laid before this meeting, for the particular consideration of the members of the same.
>
> By Order of
> R.T.W.X.L.M.Z.HUMBUG NOSIBUS.
> *President.*
> QUIZZEM QUANTI.
> *Recording Secretary.*

Never did Brackenridge lose his zeal for the betterment of the territory. Despite his concern about Caroline's health, his interest in the development of her property at Bull Creek, and the dissension over the live oak experiment, he could still preside interestedly over a meeting of Pensacola citizens to consider the state of the roads between their town and Alabama.[6] Some of the roads in Escambia County were almost impassable, in particular the mail route from Pensacola to Burnt Corn in Alabama.

Brackenridge's reputation as a wise judge had increased year by year. His opinions and even his charges to the jury were consistently newsworthy. "Judge B. delivered to the Grand Jury an able and impressive charge, pointing out in a clear and lucid manner, the important duties which devolved upon them," reported the *Pensacola Gazette* on November 6, 1830. "The Grand Jury we learn, have applied to the Judge for a copy for publication, if he consents, we shall endeavor to present it to our readers next week." The following issue of the paper, that of November 13, carried Brackenridge's charge *in toto*.

Of course, his opinions made him some enemies as well as friends. Did Peter G. Williamson, convicted of the inhuman treatment of his slave, Katy, appreciate the sentence[7] Judge Brackenridge handed him? Intoxicated, Williamson had tied her behind a wagon—"by a chain fastened to her neck by a leather string, and with her arms tied fast behind her"—and had ordered the driver to drag her through the streets full of puddles. This brutal treatment of a runaway slave had aroused the citizens of Pensacola, who applauded the sentence as justifiable. Certainly John and James Innerarity were not happy when, in 1830, Brackenridge rejected their petition in an opinion[8] pronounced in Superior Court at a special term for adjudicating land causes. The Inneraritys and the heirs of John Forbes, deceased, had claimed a tract of about one million acres situated between the Apalachicola and the Choctawhatchee.

The enemies of Brackenridge were naturally concentrated in the legal profession. On the bench he had offended many a practitioner by his independence and incorruptibility—he had not brooked forever the malicious conduct of William F. Steele, the district attorney for West Florida! On the bench or off Brackenridge refused to be party to the schemes of men of little natures, corrupt lawyers and avaricious place seekers who had long abounded in Florida. In 1827, when he hurried to Philadelphia and failed to hold the November term of court, Robert Mitchell had sent him a warning from Pensacola: ". . . it is true, that it is not of much consequence, but you are well aware, of what kind of materials your enemies are composed, and that they will avail themselves of every opportunity to injure you; I would therefore ascertain, if any, and what attempts have been made, and counter act them before you return; you know they work in the dark, and that it is impossible for us here to discover their movements."[9]

Independent though he tried to be, Brackenridge could not divorce himself from politics. His fair-mindedness caused him to plunge into the presidential campaign of 1828 in defense of Jackson. After seeing evidences of an attempt in the press to injure Jackson's candidacy by unfavorable references to the Florida ordinances promulgated in 1821, Brackenridge addressed a letter[10] to the editors of the *National Intelligencer* in July, relating the background of the ordinance-making and claiming the authorship for himself and the late Abner L. Duncan. "It is not my intention to undertake a defence of the ordinances, but to explain their history and origin," Brackenridge stated. His sole purpose was to accept his share of the responsibility for whatever might be censurable in the ordinances. However, he had no intention of favoring one candidate or the other in the present contest: ". . . I feel a strong attachment to General Jackson, from personal intimacy and a sense of obligation, but it is also well known that I entertain a high respect for Mr. Adams, and approve the principles on which he has administered the Government." But intentionally or not, Brackenridge had implied a flaw in Jackson's character, a trait already recognized by enemies—a tendency to depend upon the judgment of friends for guidance in his official conduct. Brackenridge, in truth, had not relieved Jackson of his legal responsibility as governor in issuing the ordinances, although his gesture was manly.

In this election year of 1828 the citizens of Pensacola gave a dinner to White as a tribute of their respect for his service as the territorial delegate, a function to which Brackenridge was invited as a guest.[11] It was significant that in his reply to the letter of invitation White alluded to the propriety of a territorial policy calculated to keep Florida on a neutral course in national politics. In his labors for the welfare of the Floridians, White had always sought bipartisan support. Brackenridge approved his friend's policy.

Jackson feeling was evident at this dinner in honor of White. When called upon to speak, Governor Duval destroyed the nonpartisan spirit of the affair by his political remarks. The rabid Jacksonians could not tolerate indifference to their candidate. White, however, was so popular with the Floridians that he served five successive terms as the delegate to Congress,[12] thriving on the animosity which the Jacksonians generated against him. Brackenridge likewise was the target of Jacksonian abuse. "It is unfortunate that our enemies in this country, are generally favorites of Gen: Jackson, but I am so much in the way of most of them, that possibly they may try to get rid of me by sending me back to Pittsburgh as the successor of Wilkins," Brackenridge conjectured in a letter to Caroline in 1829. "But this is not likely, as there are no doubt many applicants for that office. I do not count upon it."[13] There was no chance that he would succeed William Wilkins as judge of the United States district court for Western Pennsylvania.

Only Jacksonians could expect preferment. In 1831, in Florida, so intense had political feeling become that apparently there was an equality of votes in the election for territorial delegate after Governor Duval had rejected many votes from various precincts as defective—he wanted a new election and the defeat of White.[14] White accused federal officers of interfering in the election to prevent his winning. The situation in the territory was scandalous, for terror prevailed among White's friends, who, according to Brackenridge, feared denunciation by officers of government for their loyalty to the delegate. When Brackenridge described this frightful state of affairs to Edward Livingston, newly appointed secretary of state in the Jackson administration, he was nonplused and frankly did not know what to say in reply—"You give a very dark picture of the State of Society with you."[15] He promised the judge that the Jackson administration would not countenance the designs of unprincipled men. Livingston reminded him of the brighter side of the picture: "Whatever may be the State of public opinion in your part of the US. be assured my good friend that in every other there never was a period when there was so much private happiness and public prosperity and that very generally it is attributed to the wise measures pursued by the first Magistrate whose popularity is greatly on the increase." It was a warning when, in conclusion, Livingston expressed the greatest confidence in Brackenridge's judgment besides his "attachment to the President."

Now it required a courageous, or foolhardy, official to maintain any semblance of independence in the conduct of his office, for, if he did not demonstrate unwavering loyalty to the President, the Jacksonians demanded his scalp. The administration had a potent vehicle for attacking dissent and disseminating its views in the *Globe,* Francis P. Blair's daily newspaper established in Washington in December, 1830, in opposition to Duff Green's *United States Telegraph.*[16] Jackson had, meanwhile, severed relations with Calhoun, the vice-president; and in the spring of 1831, he reorganized his cabinet to eliminate Calhoun supporters. A reluctant Roger B. Taney, in poor health, became the attorney general of the United States. "The manner in which the new appointments have been received is gratifying and encouraging," he advised Brackenridge in answer to a letter of congratulation. "And it will I am sure give you pleasure to know that the most perfect unity of principles and cordiality of feeling exists between the President and the present members of his Cabinet, —and if he should in any respect fail to accomplish what his friends expect of him—the failure will not be occasioned by a want of confidence & concert between him and his advisers—nor by discord & disunion among ourselves."[17]

Jackson's policy of removal from office, be that office high or low, was called "reform." His adherents used the spoils system without apology to strengthen their party. In announcing the dismissal of Alexander Brackenridge from the office of prosecutor in the United States District Court, the *Statesman,*[18] of Pittsburgh, commented acidly that the terms "removal" and "reform" were "neither synonymous, or convertible," as was obvious from a comparison of his qualifications with those of his successor. Thus, late in 1830, Brackenridge's half brother lost his office without a reason given him for the action.

How long could Brackenridge, who had offended many Jackson partisans, retain his own post in Florida? Once, in 1830, he had written Caroline a letter in which he hopefully set a time for his leaving the territory: "The year '31, should it please the will of providence, I look to as the period of my finally quitting this country."[19] Despite the fact that his town of Tarentum had become a post office[20] and his house[21] there ready for occupancy before the end of October, 1830, Brackenridge remained in Florida to serve as superintendent of the live oak plantation. But the experiment became enmeshed in the politics of the day. As reported by the *Niles' Register* of March 31, 1832, the announcement that Brackenridge and Joseph L. Smith had been superseded as Florida judges was neither unexpected nor startling to the public at large.

A few days before, Brackenridge had written[22] Caroline from Louisville, which he had just reached on his voyage home. The high waters and an accident to its water wheel had delayed the boat. It was more than an anxious voyage for him, for he was now the father of a girl, Cornelia, of whose birth he had learned in February.[23] Cornelia was fated to die in her infancy. Here at Louisville, Brackenridge could no longer keep a secret from his wife:

> I did not inform you before I left Pensacola, that I had just received a letter from Col. White, stating that General Jackson had nominated a Mr. Biddle, formerly a broken merchant of Philadelphia, and of no repute, and no lawyer, to succeed me after the expiration of my term of office. I think it probable I should not have wished to return—but the bad faith of General Jackson, after his solemn promise, shocked me. It is said the merit of Biddle lies in having paid the first visit to Mrs. Eaton, and having given her a large tea party. It is a pleasing reflection, that as soon as doubts were expressed of my reappointment, memorials were circulated, and signed by almost *every inhabitant* of the district in my favor. Great dissatisfaction has been expressed by the People, and on leaving there I recd. an expression of respect and esteem from them, which few individuals have obtained, after discharging such an office. They say I have the good wishes of every honest man—and they now unanimously recognize me as a publick and private benefactor. These are crushing reflections.

Brackenridge was upset by the turn of events, for he had trusted the word of Old Hickory. When in Washington the past year Brackenridge had visited him at the White House; he had been received cordially and treated to a family dinner.[24] Then the President, smoking his pipe in the best of humor, retired with Brackenridge and showed him his nomination by the New York legislature, "as a child exhibits his bauble." Brackenridge reminded him that his commission as a Florida judge needed renewing at the next session of Congress. "Upon my word I never thought of it," Jackson exclaimed. "Appoint *you*, certainly, sir.—*When I know a man, sir*, my opinion is not to be changed by any one." He assured Brackenridge of reappointment to the bench. Before his departure the judge mentioned his intention of resigning before the expiration of his next term of office and his consequent desire to have a successor pleasing to the Floridians, whereupon Jackson replied, "Ah, sir, I will take care of that. I have already fixed upon a gentleman, a Mr. ———!" The slip of tongue, the insincerity seemingly manifest in this revelation, chilled Brackenridge's heart. Yet he had not expected Jackson to break his pledge.

Resentful, Brackenridge attacked the President in the public press in the election year of 1832. As his father once had unmercifully castigated William Findley in print, Brackenridge derided the popular idol of his own day. He was revengeful now; and he never ceased to despise Jackson, who had sacrificed him to the patronage machine. Brackenridge's attack, sustained and vituperative, provoked widespread comment. Such conduct, however, did not befit him—it was undignified. Niles reported that many of "the judge's friends (and he had many in Baltimore), regretted that he descended from the bench to take a part in the *presidential* mele—but still believing that he is an upright man, also regret that he has been dismissed from his place."[25]

By appealing to the public Brackenridge hoped to vindicate his own cause and to destroy the immense popularity of the President. The publication of *Judge Brackenridge's Letters,* a pamphlet, was a powerful blast directed at Jackson, in which the nature of the assault was best revealed, for the brief work contained not only letters the judge had written to the *United States Telegraph* and the *National Union* of Washington but also letters from his own private correspondence. Coalition members of Congress under their frank could send copies to constituents to stir enmity against the tyrant in the White House. The influence of this pamphlet was lasting, for, in his *Life of Andrew Jackson,* James Parton made free use of it as a source.[26]

Brackenridge avowed that he obtained no satisfaction in exhibiting the President in an odious light. Once he had been his friend. He respected the office which Jackson held. "But, when a citizen, comparatively obscure and humble, has been treated with gross injustice, and when, in that injustice, one of the most sacred principles of our free government has been violated, it behooves him to speak out boldly, and without regard to consequences," he declared.[27] He charged the President with violating inexcusably his personal promise. He charged the President with undermining the independence of the judiciary by nominating unfit persons for the Florida judgeships. He charged the President with ignoring the wishes of the Floridians. Brackenridge insisted that the tenure of his judgeship was generally believed lasting during good behavior, although limited by Congress to four years—reappointment had always been considered a mere formality. The crux of the matter was this: "I ask what judge after this, holding his commission at the pleasure of Gen. Jackson, will dare to decide in favor of, or against a citizen, whose cause has been prejudged by him or his favorites?"[28]

Jackson, in Brackenridge's opinion, was not fit to hold a magistracy of any kind. The President was illiterate: "He was at the bar without practice or reputation; he was on the bench at a time, when any body might be a Judge, and he has been in legislative bodies, without having prepared a single report or taking part in the most trivial debate."[29] Jackson was a tyrant with an ungovernable temper, but also a ready instrument in the hands of unscrupulous men. "Personal hate, or personal partiality, are his only incentives to public measures: all virtue consists in attachment to his person, and all iniquity in being opposed to him," Brackenridge asserted. "He pursues his enemies with a cruel vengeance, which knows no bounds, and is restrained by no generosity, while he rewards his friends, because he is rewarding himself."[30] Old Hickory was qualified only for arbitrary command, not for "the exercise of civil authority, under our mild and peaceful institutions"; he was "formed for action."

Brackenridge related how, in his own presence in Florida, Jackson had vehemently pronounced himself unfit for the presidency.

In the pamphlet Brackenridge took care to document his assertions. He refuted the contention of the *Globe*,[31] as stated in a blistering editorial entitled "An Honest Judge," that he was nothing but a "miserable copyist" and a "wretched scribbler" when Jackson's secretary and translator in Florida. In denial he claimed authorship of the controversial ordinances and even Jackson's farewell address to the army. He referred the reader to his publication on the ordinances, prepared during the presidential campaign of 1828. "It was intimated to me by a friend, that the General, on his electioneering visit to New Orleans, complained of my indifference, and spoke with some chagrin of my not defending him from attacks in relation to the ordinances, and the affair of Callava, and particularly as to the former which were drawn up by me," Brackenridge recalled. "I did not hesitate, on this intimation, to make the publication which I have said *operated* favorably on the General's election, although I disclaimed at the time all party views, and avowed my predilection of Mr. Adams. It was treated by me as a matter of history."[32] Besides two letters of 1821 from Jackson, thanking him for aid in the organization and administration of the Florida government, he printed Colonel White's letter[33] to the United States Senate, dated Washington, February 21, 1832, which was a remonstrance against the supersedure of Brackenridge and Smith as Florida judges and the nomination of two incompetents to succeed them.

It required courage to direct an attack like this at Jackson. "I find myself at length engaged in immediate encounter with the President of the United States," Brackenridge had announced boldly, heedless of danger.[34] The thought that he thereby exposed himself and his family to vilification had not deterred him. He could expect immediate retaliation by the Jacksonian press. But he had faith in the American public, hoping that his revelations would end the idolization of Old Hickory, whom he considered a despicable man. Brackenridge, however, craved no sympathy, only a fair hearing as he discharged a duty owed to his country and to himself by "exposing the conduct of the highest functionary in the Government."[35]

The administration organ, the *Globe,* was quick to reply to Brackenridge's publication in the *United States Telegraph* of April 17. Now began a concerted campaign by the Jacksonian editors to demean him and so to vitiate his charges. The first *Globe*[36] editorial was a masterpiece of political writing—it put Brackenridge in such an unfavorable light that the subscriber might well laugh at his embarrassment:

H. M. BRECKENRIDGE

An attack of this ex-Judge upon the President has found its way to the public through the appropriate columns of the United States Telegraph. If any thing were wanting to prove the utter unfitness of this gentleman for a judicial station, it is found in this appeal to the public. In ill-nature, want of dignity, and destitution of truth, it is equalled only by the fanciful Editorials of the journal in which it appears. The ex-dignitary descends even to detailing pretended private conversations with the President, and to the publication of certain hastily written private letters in which some of the A's look like O's, the I's are not dotted and the T's not crossed!

What does the honorable ex-Judge plead in justification of conduct so strange and so dishonorable? Why, he *has been* a Judge; his time was out; the President *did not re-appoint him!* This is the great injury and wrong of which he complains! He is not permitted to hold an office *for life* which the law has *expressly limited to a term of years.*

Had Mr. Breckenridge any *right* to the office he held beyond the limit prescribed by law? Did it not just as much belong to any other man in the nation? Or does he maintain, that it was the President's *duty* to appoint and re-appoint him as long as he lives? On no other ground has he any apology for his appeal to the people. The President has made no charge against him; he has uttered no imputation upon his character, his temper or his conduct; he has done nothing but *fail to re-appoint him.* Not giving him the office again which he had once held, is a justification, in the eyes of this dignitary, for forgetting, not only the respect which is due to the Chief Magistrate, but even *self-respect.*

The *lordlings* of America and the *lords* of Europe are exactly alike. Touch their offices and their sinecures, their pensions and their places, deprive them of the means of living upon the labor of the people, and they denounce the democrat that does it as a tyrant and a robber! The people of Europe are turning out their lords to earn their own living; the people of America will not regret to see their *lordlings* share the same fate. Mr. Breckenridge has the same opportunity to earn his living as any other citizen; let him do like the thousands of freemen around him, who have more cause to complain that they *never had an office,* than he has to complain that he *has lost one which he long enjoyed.*

To the editorial Blair appended an anonymous communication charging Brackenridge with great unpopularity in Florida and describing him as "an eccentric man, inconsistent in his decisions, and by no means a man of business." When Brackenridge continued his assault on the President, the *Globe*[37] returned the fire by maligning him in other long editorials.

Before the controversy ended, Niles himself had turned on Brackenridge. Originally the editor was sympathetic with the judge's predicament although regretful of his ill-tempered attack on the President. In one issue of his *Weekly Register*[38] Niles had printed Brackenridge's reply to Thomas Ritchie, of the Richmond *Enquirer,* who had assaulted him editorially and then had denied him space for his answer. But the *Constitutional Whig* of Richmond had first opened its columns to Brackenridge with the comment that the publication of his letter to Ritchie was "due to the liberty of the press." Niles' interest in Brackenridge's cause was not sincere, for he soon printed[39] a shabby jest about "Judge Brackenridge who has lately made some stir in the political world, and who is a comical son of a comical father"—and entitled it "In spite of your teeth."

In the spring of 1832, however, Neville B. Craig, the editor of the *Pitts-*

357

burgh Gazette, had coined a happier phrase, describing Brackenridge as the "gifted son of a gifted sire."[40] Having just received the first contribution to his paper from the son, Craig noted that forty-six years earlier the father had begun his contributions in the very first number and continued them for many years. The editor hoped that the "assiduity and perseverance" of the son would equal his father's. Brackenridge had sent Craig an extract from his *"future"* book, his memoirs, entitled *Recollections of Persons and Places in the West* and eventually published both in Philadelphia[41] and Pittsburgh[42] in 1834. The passage Brackenridge selected from his manuscript for publication was a charming description of Pittsburgh as it was when he had been a boy and as it appeared to him now—"What a change in the appearance of Pittsburg since that day!—since the time, when I used to roll over and over on the smooth velvet side of Grant's Hill."

Brackenridge—"A Native of the Ohio" he styled himself as the author of the *Recollections*—had not returned to Western Pennsylvania a beaten man. When he reached Pittsburgh on April 1,[43] he had still to launch his direct attack upon the President. But his self-confidence was shaken, for he wrote Caroline that he was unregretful about his misfortune if she could "be contented to settle down on the Allegheny, in an humble and retired way. I feel confident you can exert a proper self command, and acquire the necessary strength of mind, to reconcile yourself to a situation which is now unavoidable. There is no possibility of my obtaining any employment in Philadelphia, so as to justify our settling there." Trying to restore his self-respect, Brackenridge had begun his memoirs in leisure moments before arriving in Pittsburgh.

His book was a narrative of the happiest years of his life—"a life somewhat out of the common track, up to the age of twenty-three or four. . . ."[44] A work of nineteen chapters, the book was not long. Someday he might lengthen it, Brackenridge apprised the reader in his foreword, for "the subject is not exhausted, but only begun." He stated that nothing could be found in his *Recollections* that was not "strictly true." He related the events of his childhood when he was the hapless wanderer, outlined his course of study for the bar, and discussed his first attempts at advancement in the legal profession. Significantly, he ended this fragment of an autobiography with the recollection of his romantic reunion with the Beauvais family in Ste. Genevieve. Although admitting he was not a Goldsmith writing with a pen of magic, Brackenridge offered no apology for presenting the work to the public, if his readers could overlook the frequent repetition of the personal pronoun.[45]

The *Recollections* was egotistical, naturally. But Brackenridge wrote with a pen of magic, making up for this fault—if it be a fault—which really did not irritate the reader. The reader might be inconvenienced or annoyed, how-

ever, by the author's apparent reluctance to use precise dates—"To begin with
my birth, where men generally begin: that event took place about the year
1786, at the very fountain or source of the noble river Ohio (that is, if we
consider such the spot where its name first attaches), where stood the village
of Fort Pitt, now Pittsburgh."[46] Whenever Brackenridge lacked facts about
his life, he indulged in description which his lively imagination rendered
vivid. He thus still excelled in the use of description, a talent which he had
evidenced previously in his *Views*, the *Journal*, and the *Voyage*. His characterization of persons like his father or Madame Beauvais was first-rate. His style
was simple and clear, enlivened by the frequent quotation of verse and the
employment of dialogue. The *Recollections*, filled with humorous anecdotes,
was a delightful book to read.

The work was the production of a scholar. Van Wyck Brooks, who described the *Recollections* as "charming," believed Brackenridge was "a man
of all but universal cultivation and curiosity. . . ."[47] Certainly Brackenridge's
vast knowledge was manifest in his book. Often he digressed to philosophize
a bit. At times he seemed to parade his knowledge, but somehow never offen-
sively. He had, furthermore, an opinion to offer on every subject. In his well-
known description of Pittsburgh, he suggested the idea of erecting a gaslight
on a hill overlooking the town to take the place of the sun. "I claim the merit
of being the first to give this hint, for I have never yet heard of any one
proposing to light a city by towers and elevated lamps," he added.[48] In this
instance, however, his claim was not justified, for a few years before a man
named Jacob Smith of Philadelphia had advanced the same proposal for
illuminating that city.[49] Brackenridge, nevertheless, possessed an inventive
mind.

What did a contemporary critic think of the *Recollections?* James Hall's
*Western Monthly Magazine, a Continuation of the Illinois Monthly Maga-
zine*[50] carried a lengthy notice of the book in the May number, 1834. "The
writer is a man of genius, with much strength of character, and a marked
peculiarity of mind, which is not so discernible in his style, as in the views
which he takes of life," the critic remarked. "He has seen more of life than
most men, and has told more of his own experience than the pride of most
men would permit them to divulge." He referred to Brackenridge's description of himself in childhood as a neglected orphan. The critic liked Brackenridge's "graphic" account of his life with the Beauvais family in Ste. Genevieve. In his opinion, Brackenridge's education, as supervised by his father,
was "most defective"—"Between his father, who was never wearied of heaping
tasks upon him, and 'Joe,' who would fain have allured him to the haunts of
youthful dissipation, he was in a fair way to be spoiled." This first part of

359

the book, the story of Brackenridge's childhood, the critic considered not only "curious" but also "instructive." He found the anecdotes of persons and places, particularly the author's reminiscences of Pittsburgh and its inhabitants, "exceedingly interesting." No higher praise could the critic give than to say he would now wait impatiently for Brackenridge to publish a continuation of his fascinating *Recollections*.

The work, especially the enlarged second edition of 1868, was destined to become a valuable source book on the West for the historian. Despite its air of boastfulness, the *Recollections* is authentic. No one had a better right than the author to call himself "A Native of the West," as he did on the title page of the new edition. From the moment of its original publication, the book has been much quoted, a perennial favorite of editors and historians. Occasionally, a scholar has found the *Recollections* indispensable as a source.[51]

In the continuation of his reminiscences Brackenridge did not relate the events of his Florida career, for the wound inflicted by Jackson was too deep. In 1833, while still smarting from his removal as a judge, he had received an infuriating letter from Louis McLane, the secretary of state. McLane, citing a law of 1827, intimated that the volumes of reports, transmitted from his department, Brackenridge should deliver to his successor in Florida. Not only did Brackenridge refuse to comply with the request but he took the opportunity to argue again the legality of his expulsion from office: "As I am not dead, and have not resigned, I conclude that you consider me as having been *dismissed from office*. Will you be so good, sir, as to inform me, when, by whom and for what cause, I have incurred this ignominy?"[52] That no investigation had been instituted in his case galled him. That other territorial judges had also lost their offices was no salve for his wound.

Brackenridge became an active Whig, determined to oppose the Jacksonians to the end. In the campaign of 1836, he supported the unsuccessful candidacy of William Henry Harrison[53] against Martin Van Buren, whose nomination for the presidency Jackson had dictated. But the result in 1840 was different, for the military hero—"Tippecanoe and Tyler too"—decisively defeated Van Buren. Whiggism was triumphant. In this campaign Brackenridge had addressed his neighbors at Freeport in September in Harrison's behalf and proved himself still a capable stump speaker.[54] Brackenridge, himself a Whig candidate[55] for the seat in the national House of Representatives which Richard Biddle had resigned, was likewise victorious and took his place on December 10.[56]

His brief service of one session in Congress was unexceptionable, but not distinguished. A member of the standing committee on Public Expenditures, he made only one speech—on the Treasury Note Bill, delivered on February

3, 1841. But he had no real desire for an elective office which kept him from his family at "Oak Grove" on the Allegheny. A Florida acquaintance, Adam Gordon, had once admonished him not to be satisfied with one term in Congress: ". . . you are somewhat altered from former times, if you do not give the *public* the preference over your *private* wishes."[57]

Separation from his family was not pleasant for Brackenridge. But in Washington there was much to interest him, more so as the session of Congress drew to a close and Inauguration Day approached. "I could have wished you had been here to see and hear Mr. Clay, and Mr. Webster," he wrote his son, Morgan. "They both spoke in their best style, and two such orators are not to be found either in England or America. Their speeches and their manner, would give you some idea of true eloquence, especially when contrasted with so many bad speakers in both houses of Congress, who exhibit examples to be avoided, and to shew what is not eloquence."[58] He stressed the nobility and the rarity of eloquence as a hint to Morgan, comparing the talents of two preachers heard in the House chamber. There was fatherly advice, too: "You must be extremely careful in getting in and out of the cars. I saw an account the other day of a person being crushed between two of them, where they are joined together—When you get in, stay in, and when you get out, get entirely out of the way of the track." Brackenridge encouraged his son to copy pictures by giving him a portfolio—"There is no name on it but it can have yours put in gold letters, at a book binders."—and promising to buy him some secondhand prints—"after copying them, you can, if you choose through them aside." This letter of an affectionate father ended with a teasing problem: "Suppose an acre of ground be two hundred and ten feet square, and I plant it with corn the hills six feet apart, how many hills, will there be on an acre? And how many hills on ten acres?" Brackenridge was not the gruff and heartless parent old Hugh had often been.

Appointed[59] a member of the Mexican Claims Commission by President John Tyler on August 23, 1841, Brackenridge brought his family to Washington to live during the period of his service. This was the very time when Walter Forward, the new secretary of the treasury, entered upon the discharge of his official duties. Thus, the coming winter was almost certain to be a happy one for Brackenridge. He obtained lodgings in a good boardinghouse and sent Morgan to school.[60] The expense of living in the capital in this fashion was not great, for Brackenridge had half his salary left and could save something. The work of the commission was exacting, however: "In fact my whole time is taken up with the claims. We meet in the forenoon, sit for some hours and then go home to examine papers and write opinions until we meet again."

His service as a judge in Louisiana and Florida had fitted Brackenridge for this work[61] of adjudicating the claims of American citizens upon the Mexican government under the Convention of April 11, 1839. He had not solicited the post, but as "a point of duty" had accepted appointment to the vacancy on the commission created by the resignation of Judge John Rowan.[62] There was general satisfaction with the appointment, which the Senate confirmed unanimously. The claimants rejoiced, knowing Brackenridge's reputation for impartiality while on the bench. He was, moreover, not likely to tolerate procrastination by his Mexican colleagues.

But in the meantime Brackenridge had nursed his grudge against Jackson. Before the end of 1842, but after his service on the commission, Brackenridge again assaulted him in the press.[63] Perhaps it was unkind of Brackenridge to continue the attack now that Jackson was a feeble old man whose friends sought to have Congress refund him the thousand-dollar fine imposed by Judge Dominick Hall for contempt of court in the last days of the defense of New Orleans and to expunge from the record the imputation of illegal action. Brackenridge, however, hoped to destroy the Jackson Legend which he had helped to create. "The man who acquitted himself well in the situation for which he was fitted, became unfortunately for us, invested with ideal attributes," Brackenridge maintained. "He was permitted, like the rough soldier Marius, to do things that no other citizen would have dared to do, thus familiarizing us with the possibility of certain acts which our minds could not before have conceived, and more pernicious to the constitutional freedom of our country than the loss of a hundred battles." Brackenridge praised the moral and physical courage of Judge Hall for "ordering this conqueror to the bar. . . ." Brackenridge had known the judge well: "he was a modest, single-hearted, retired student, deeply learned, of unsuspected integrity, and as innocent as a child of all party intrigue or faction." After reviewing the facts of the case, Brackenridge concluded his argument:

I have no objection to restoring the fine to Gen. Jackson, and I am perfectly satisfied with the ground on which it has been placed in the late message of Mr. Tyler. But I am much deceived if the general will be satisfied with it. Although he loves money as well as most men, that is not his strongest passion; the gratification of vindictive feeling is his "ruling passion strong in death;" he will not be satisfied without placing a stigma on the memory of Judge Hall.

To aid the cause of procuring the remission of Jackson's fine, William Darby, the geographer, wrote a letter to Henry A. Wise, the Virginia congressman, who had requested his testimony on the controversial events in New Orleans in 1815. Wise gave the letter to the *Daily Madisonian* of Washington for immediate publication.[64] A well-written and interesting letter upholding Jackson's conduct, it occupied six full columns in the paper. Darby answered Brackenridge's publication point by point.

362

The same day Darby's letter appeared in the *Daily Madisonian*, January 10, 1843, Major William B. Lewis forwarded a copy of the paper to the "Hermitage." Gratefully Jackson read the defense in his behalf:

> Should Mr. Wm. Darby be in the City on the receipt of this, I pray you to present him my thanks for this act of Justice to me, and for the scurging he has given that worthless lying scamp Brakenridge, who I found in Neworleans on my way to Pensacola to receive the Government of Florida, without mony or friends, took him into my family, bear all his expences, appointed him alcade and sworn translator of the Spanish language, found him an imperfect translator, and made young Mr. Rutledge translator, never having the least idea of his treachery until, after the charge was made against him of leaving the Bench in the midst of a cause without his hat and leaving the jury in their box and not returning to adjourn the Court, and would not reapoint him Judge. He came out with an abusive pamphlet against me, acknowledging, that he had given a false translation of Govr. Calava address to me, least I might have treated him harshly, acknowledging that he had perjured himself to hold forth my ungovernment of temper. *What an ingrate of baseness?* And these are the tools, that Wiggery hires to abuse me.[65]

In 1844, Old Hickory received the refund of his fine with interest, totaling $2700, and celebrations occurred throughout the land.[66]

XXV: The Sage of Tarentum

When Brackenridge returned to Pennsylvania in 1832, his great adventures were over. Now his dream of a quiet and contemplative life on the Allegheny —the life of a country gentleman—was about to be realized. He practiced law,[1] although he never attended the courts regularly. He capped his career in the public service by sitting in one session of the state legislature in 1846 as a representative from Allegheny County.[2] When not occupied by the business of his estate, or by the law, he devoted his time to literature. Until his death after the Civil War, Brackenridge was a cultural force in Western Pennsylvania.

His native town, once an outpost of civilization, had become a prosperous city surrounded by growing villages. Far and wide people called Pittsburgh the "Birmingham of America." Several hundred steamboats arrived every year without creating a stir; whereas forty years earlier, the arrival of a pirogue caused a bustle. To the visitor, however, the blasts of a steamboat reverberating from the hills was startling—the vessel itself seemed a great panting beast.[3] The Pennsylvania Canal and Portage Railroad linked the city to the east coast. Twelve dollars was the passenger fare between Philadelphia and Pittsburgh— twenty-five cents from Tarentum.

As the founder of a town on the canal Brackenridge had a personal interest in such progress. In March, 1834, the packet, "General Lacock," brought the first lot of goods to Pittsburgh from Philadelphia by way of the Portage Railroad in thirteen days.[4] Three years before, a steamboat had ascended the Allegheny to Franklin and Warren with twenty-seven tons of freight and forty-odd passengers.[5] But the river needed improvement to be fit for regular steamboat traffic. Engineers generally did not believe navigation could be made easier without prohibitive cost. However, as Brackenridge wrote to Neville B. Craig, the Pittsburgh editor, "if fifty engineers say nay, a sixtieth may be able to accomplish what they deem impossible. Some things are difficult, very difficult, but I am scarcely a believer in impossibilities, where the subject is not absolutely beyond the limits of human genius."[6] Then, showing his concern in the matter, Brackenridge suggested ways of improving the natural channel of the river at little expense and proposed a change be made in the structure of the boats. "The part of the Allegheny, which I have seen, bears a strong resemblance to the Ohio," he added. "I think it the continuation of that noble river."

The Pittsburghers were progressive. Not all their energy was spent on the creation of wealth. Although lying beneath dense clouds of smoke their city was not impervious to change. In 1828, J. R. Lambdin had opened his museum and art gallery at Fourth and Market Streets and shortly had it illuminated by gas every evening.[7] Not until 1837 were a few streets and buildings lighted in this way—"Thus has the standing reproach of the intolerable gloom and insecurity of our streets at night been in a measure wiped from the character of our city."[8] The face of the city changed rapidly with the constant demolition of old buildings and the construction of new—in some instances, cast iron pillars and window sills replaced those of stone and wood.[9] In the spring of 1836, construction of the new courthouse, Doric in style, began on Grant's Hill on the property formerly owned by James Ross. The architect was John Chislett.[10] Alas, the lovely hill itself, attacked by powder and spades and pick-axes, slowly disappeared![11]

Before the completion of the courthouse Brackenridge stood before it one day in admiration and in his mind contrasted it with the humbler structures of another day, that of his childhood and youth. To him the view was magnificent: "With what a lofty pre-eminence it seems to overlook the busy city below, rolling its clouds of smoke to its base, its hum of life and industry ascending above it, the noble rivers rolling along, and the green and swelling landscape fading in the distance!" He espied the old temple of justice, a brick building with a steeple, and could not refrain from reminiscing about the one it likewise had superseded, the courtroom occupying the third story of William Irwin's house, which also doubled for the village theater. Humble were the structures of that early day, but Brackenridge recalled the greatness of the minds which shone in them. He thought of his father: "I could name one, whose reach and sublimity of thought, electric eye, and fascinating voice, could never be forgotten by those who witnessed his powers." Brackenridge later recorded his thoughts in the form of an essay, "Pittsburgh in the Olden Time," which was published in the first number of the *Literary Examiner, and Western Monthly Review*[12] in May, 1839.

E. Burke Fisher, the editor of the *Pittsburgh Saturday Evening Visiter*, and William H. Burleigh launched this new western magazine with the claim that it would be the "Largest Literary Work in the Union."[13] Each number, they promised, would contain eighty pages; and six numbers would constitute a volume—two volumes a yearly subscription. It was the editors' hope to provide the reader with original writing by the best authors of the West: "it will be our sole aim to make the EXAMINER the depository of Western genius, the treasure-house of Western literature."[14] A brave hope this was, considering the number of western journals which had already foundered. "Will the return of another May find us strong in the renewed Spring of thy affections, or a ruin on the stark plain of Winter!" the editors wondered.

But their magazine expired before the year was over. The last number was that of February, 1840. Aside from the financial, the most difficult problem facing the editors from the first was the acquisition of an adequate budget of articles for publication to uphold their promise to the subscribers. The magazine soon contained the lectures which had been delivered before the Wirt Literary Society, an organization which was in Pittsburgh the first manifestation of the lyceum movement sweeping the country and to which Brackenridge himself was invited to speak.[15] The lectures, however, were not original matter written especially for the magazine. Except Brackenridge ("our valuable and valued friend"), Dr. William Elder, and A. W. Marks, the local writers were reluctant to contribute their work: "Why do you refuse us your aid? Why, when so much real benefit would result to our city and our name as a community from your occasional assistance, do you seem to regard the effort to send out from your midst a respectable literary journal as beneath your consideration?"[16]

Besides his article on Pittsburgh in the *Examiner,* Brackenridge contributed a biographical essay published in three parts and entitled "Pedro Menendez de Aviles, First Spanish Conqueror and Adelantado of Florida."[17] The Florida career of Menéndez provided the author with the opportunity to inveigh against religious bigotry, which he detested. The theme of the work was the harm intolerance can do to a man otherwise great. Brackenridge, however, characterized the Spaniards as always having been a "barbarous, blood-thirsty people, and are still the same at this day in Spain." Brackenridge continued his narrative in three more parts,[18] entitled "The Chevalier de Gourges." This continuation was not a biographical notice of the avenger of the Huguenots murdered by Menéndez, but it was rather a comparative study of the conduct of two men: "There is this difference between him and Menendez; in the case of the latter, it was an error of the *heart*—in that of De Gourges, it was an error of the *head.*"

The same time Brackenridge contributed to the *Examiner,* 1839, he had prepared the second edition of his father's *Modern Chivalry,* revising and correcting it for the press of John I. Kay & Co. of Pittsburgh. There was need for a new and improved edition, for, as Fisher noted in his *Examiner,*[19] it was now impossible to procure a copy of the first issue, as he himself had learned upon investigation.

It was Fisher who persuaded Brackenridge to continue his *Recollections.* As editor of the *Pittsburgh Saturday Evening Visiter* in 1837, Fisher had solicited him to furnish the paper with articles continuing the subject of the little book published three years before. Therefore, in the number of December 16, 1837, Brackenridge appeared again before the public. In a prefatory note to the first chapter, as the essay was denominated, the author described his new work as a distinct effort, an entity in itself, although it did continue his personal narrative: "It will be found to contain more incident, more egotism, and less moralising." He refreshed the reader's memory by summarizing the events of the volume already published. The second chapter was printed in the *Visiter* of January 13, 1838, additional chapters appearing on into the spring. Brackenridge titled the series "Adventures and Recollections." Fisher realized that he had scored a notable success in getting the essays of this author gratis and sometimes advised his subscribers not to overlook a particular contribution: "To the many who have read the earlier Recollections of Mr. Breckenridge, we need scarce prefer a request that they give an attentive perusal to the inimitable article on our first page. It will be found an ably written defence of such authors as from parity of ideas sometimes incur unjustly the suspicion of having plagiarized."[20] Brackenridge had originally intended to publish this series as a second volume of the *Recollections*. Instead, he added the chapters to the 1834 edition, which came off the press as the enlarged second edition many years later—in 1868.

"Our esteemed friend, H. M. Brackenridge, Esq., has promised us some further favors," Fisher jubilantly announced to the subscribers of his *Visiter* on July 14, 1838. "Our readers may anticipate a rich repast." In the *Second Quarterly Supplement* of the paper the following January were collected five new chapters of Brackenridge's memoirs. The author related the adventures of his voyage up the Missouri as a member of Manuel Lisa's party. At the beginning of the twelfth chapter Brackenridge made a curious admission: "I have been somewhat neglectful of dates in these memoirs, and I have thought proper to be more particular on this occasion, for reasons which are satisfactory to myself."

Brackenridge, a literary light, an orator, and above all a man of adventure, was an attractive personality to the college student of 1838. Especially appealing was the touch of eccentricity so obvious to the reader of the *Recollections*. Brackenridge was honored by an invitation[21] to address the Philo and Franklin Literary Societies of Jefferson College at commencement on Thursday, September 27. Having himself once participated as a student in their activities, he returned to the college in a nostalgic mood. In his address,[22] delivered after the awarding of degrees, Brackenridge recalled his own teachers at the institution and reminded his listeners that someday they, too, might face a task similar to his in addressing them. But the theme of his address was apparent in his opening statement: "The future may be compared to a vast field without definite boundaries—to an immense ocean, or rather to an undiscovered country within it, which every one fashions and peoples according to his fancy. It is the prospect of that undiscovered region, which governs all our thoughts and actions, directs our journey through life, and opens the door to eternity."

Brackenridge did not condemn the urge to get ahead in the world, although he warned his audience against vainglory and "inordinate" ambition; but he denounced "the selfish idleness and inanity which mark the useless in human Society." He recommended a "virtuous and useful life" as possibly "the best preparative to the life to come." With the gentlemen of the literary societies Brackenridge gazed momentarily at "the glorious vision of the future."

No Pittsburgher, however, could envision the conflagration which destroyed what Brackenridge considered "the best half of the city" on April 10, 1845, the most terrible day in Pittsburgh's history. That Thursday about noon a woman had kindled a fire to wash her clothes in the backyard of some frame buildings at the corner of Second and Ferry.[23] The wind, blowing like a gale, swept the flames to an icehouse on Ferry and thence across Second, where the cotton factory of Colonel James Woods was soon a smouldering ruin. The fire sped from structure to structure. Brackenridge, who happened to be staying at the elegant Monongahela House, walked the streets after the alarm was given: "When in Smithfield street, which runs to the bridge, I discovered, in looking across the city, that the air was filled with flying pieces of wood in a state of combustion, for a piece of shingle as large as my hand, still blazing, fell at my feet, and was crushed out by me." By two o'clock every man hurried to his own home to save it if possible, and Brackenridge grabbed his carpetbag and struggled against the wind and dust up Smithfield to the Allegheny.

About three o'clock he reached Allegheny City across the river. "At this time the whole part of the town destroyed was one sheet of fire," Brackenridge reported to the *National Intelligencer* in a letter written four days later, a communication many Pittsburghers believed the best published account of the conflagration.[24] "The cupola of the University burnt for a few moments like paper, and went down." In three hours, Brackenridge estimated, twelve thousand men, women, and children were rendered destitute by the fire—"a sheet of flame three hundred yards wide, driven before the fiercest wind!" But he emphasized that these unfortunate people were not "homeless," for their fellow citizens whose houses had escaped destruction gave them shelter. The next morning Brackenridge picked his way through the smoking ruins: "Although familiar with the spot for fifty years, having seen almost every house erected, it was with difficulty that I could recognise the places where once stood the most familiar dwellings." The part of Pittsburgh destroyed was the original town.

Brackenridge was an excellent reporter. But he was more than a reporter of interesting events in which he had played a part—he was ever an indefatigable commentator on the American scene. Therefore, when a state of war with Mexico was declared to exist in May, 1846, Brackenridge could not remain silent. Beginning in June, he contributed articles to the *Daily Commercial Journal* of Pittsburgh, which were later collected and with notes and corrections republished as the *Mexican Letters Written during the Progress of the Late War between the United States and Mexico.*[25] He disagreed with his fellow Whigs on the issue of the war by insisting that it was just, that it had to be fought, and that the United States must be victorious. Writing the letters also gave Brackenridge the chance to indulge his interest in the history of the American Southwest and of Mexico itself. In fact, to the letters he appended an article entitled "The Early Discoveries of the Spaniards in New Mexico" and a note on the "Destruction of the Indians by Smallpox."

As it happened, Brackenridge spent the winter of 1850 in Washington, where he was privileged to use Peter Force's invaluable collection of materials on early American history to investigate the Spanish explorations in New Mexico.[26] Force personally aided the research, for Brackenridge had acquired the reputation of being a serious student of American antiquities. Brackenridge's interest in the ancient remains dated back to his youth when he had observed them on his travels. When Ephraim G. Squier and Edwin H. Davis published their classic account of the *Ancient Monuments of the Mississippi Valley: Comprising the Results of Extensive Original Surveys and Explorations*[27] in 1848, a work sponsored by the Smithsonian Institution, they acknowledged a debt to Brackenridge's research and writing in this field of study, styling him "one of the most accurate of the early explorers of the West."[28] They described his remarks on American antiquities, found in his letter to Jefferson on the population and tumuli of the North American aborigines and in his *Views,* as "distinguished for their comprehensiveness and sound philosophical spirit." Ethnologists like George R. Gliddon, who was famous for his popular lectures on Egyptian archaeology,[29] were acquainted with Brackenridge's contributions to their field of scholarship. In 1851, when Gliddon had to interrupt his lectures temporarily at Pittsburgh, he rented a cottage across the Allegheny at Sharpsburg and invited Brackenridge to visit him: "I need not say, my dear Sir, if your rides can extend as far as my shantee, I will give you an Arab's welcome to 'bread & salt,' and we can talk *archaeology* to our full content."[30]

The result of Brackenridge's research was the production of a pamphlet, the *Early Discoveries by Spaniards in New Mexico: Containing an Account of the Castles of Cibola, and the Present Appearance of Their Ruins,* which he signed as a member of the "Antiquarian Societies of Copenhagen and Boston, and of the Historical Societies of New York and Pennsylvania." The work was not dull, for there was a dash to his writing and a challenge to the reader in his argument. In Force's collection Brackenridge had found old maps to aid his study. His first difficult problem was to disentangle the narratives mixed up in Gomara and Hakluyt: "What struck me as most extraordinary, was, that after the expeditions of Coronado and of Espejo, between 1540 and 1583, a country so interesting, filled with large towns and *singularly constructed castles,* should have been lost sight of for nearly a hundred years!"[31] In his preface Brackenridge revealed why the study of American antiquities had always enthralled him:

It will strike most readers as a singular fact, that there should be found in America *a land of castles,* built on successive platforms like that of Babylon, as restored by Major Rawlinson, and rising to seven stories, in some instances, in the manner of the Chinese pagoda. These castles, it is true, were constructed of perishable materials—of sun-dried earth, mixed with gravel, and the terraces formed of layers of pine or cedar, and covered with clay hardened by the sun. How interesting would have been the minute description of these edifices and their inhabitants, in the time of Coronado! But these castles were not permanent works, like those of the Rhine or the Danube; nor were they the abodes of feudal chiefs, often robbers of the unprotected and defenceless. These, on the contrary, were places of defence, occupied by an industrious agricultural population, under *republican governments,* ruled by councils of elders, and exposed to the depredations and attacks of the warlike nomadic tribes of Cibola, who lived on the buffalo which swarmed in the vast regions further north. I hope some future Humboldt may arise, to pursue the subject of American antiquities, with the wide range of philosophical inquiry which has distinguished the writings of that great man. He has, it must be admitted, done more than any other, to lay the foundation; but there is much yet to be done in rearing the superstructure. There is a moral sublimity in such studies, which can be felt, but not described.[32]

In his pamphlet Brackenridge, always citing his sources of information, discussed the first Spanish expeditions into New Mexico and described the houses, or "castles," of Cibola, particularly their ruins as observable in his own day. Sometime between 1583 and 1694, according to the author, there had occurred an amazing depopulation of the country, which he attributed to the ravaging of the smallpox. Following the opinion of Humboldt on the matter, Brackenridge believed the people of Cibola were likely Asiatic in origin. The advancement of the Cibolians in agriculture he considered a striking fact, although the tribes, or nations, north of the Rio Grande were not as civilized as those to the South. "What I have written may be regarded as merely suggestive, to those who have taste, leisure and opportunity to engage in a pursuit *more curious than utilitarian,*" he concluded his essay.[33]

This work on the Pueblo civilization led Brackenridge into a lively correspondence with the leading ethnologists of his time. Alexander von Humboldt, the renowned naturalist and explorer, praised Brackenridge's research on the ancient civilizations of the Southwest. "Your observations are full of sagacity and of historical impartiality," Humboldt wrote.[34] Humboldt had read with discernment the pamphlet Brackenridge sent him. Brackenridge sent a copy, also, to Brantz Mayer, lawyer, historian, and ethnologist—"I could have made a big book, but find printing too expensive, like the young lawyer who found the *practice* to be so."[35] Residing at Tarentum away from libraries, Brackenridge admitted, made it hard for him to continue his inquiry on the differences and similarities between Cibola, Yucatan, Peru, and Babylonia. But he had lately "read Herodotus with great care—it leaves the question still in doubt with me, *whether the civilization of Greece was Egyptian, or the latter Grecian.*" In his correspondence with Mayer, Brackenridge conjectured that Quivera must have been on the Mississippi, "perhaps the great mound of Cahokia opposite St. Louis."[36] After he had distributed copies of his pamphlet to friends, he told Mayer, Harper & Brothers published *El-Gringo; or, New Mexico and Her People* by W. W. H. Davis: "If I had seen the work of Mr. Davis my pamphlet would have been different." The more Brackenridge read on the subject of American antiquities, the more opinions he had to change, only to have important new reflections.[37] In the fall of 1857, he asked Mayer, an authority on Mexican history, to suggest a particular part for study—"The field *is so vast,* that I do not know what topic to select for observation."[38]

Ephraim G. Squier, coauthor of the *Ancient Monuments of the Mississippi Valley,* obtained several copies of Brackenridge's pamphlet directly from the publisher, Henry Miner & Co., of Pittsburgh.[39] Brackenridge had stated carelessly that in the work of Squier and Davis no notice had been taken of the Cahokia mounds, "which I regard as the most interesting yet discovered in the West. . . ."[40] To correct this mistake, Squier wrote Brackenridge to draw his attention to a brief account of the tumuli, which somehow he had overlooked in studying the large volume. Squier, however, complimented Brackenridge: "I visited them in May last, & can witness to the accuracy of your description." Squier agreed with everything Brackenridge had written about the early Spanish discoveries in New Mexico and offered to show him some unpublished accounts of the region going back to the sixteenth century, a real treat should he ever visit New York. In his reply,[41] Brackenridge expressed the belief that the aborigines of America were indigenous, as was "the development of their faculties, or approach to civilization"—a theory which he had already advanced in his pamphlet as being not impossible.

His ethnological studies did not engross Brackenridge's leisure, for he had time to engage in a prolonged and acrimonious controversy with Neville B. Craig over the role of the elder Brackenridge in the Whisky Insurrection. As a boy, the younger Brackenridge was aware of the enmity existing between his father and "the Neville connection." Now, as a man, he became the champion of his father, whose honor was again at stake.

Brackenridge had first attempted to vindicate his father's conduct in an unsigned article, the "Biographical Notice of H. H. Brackenridge, Late of the Supreme Court of Pennsylvania," published in the January, 1842, number of the *Southern Literary Messenger.*[42] Brackenridge had completed the essay in the fall of 1841, intending it as "a precursor to the publication of a new and improved edition of 'Modern Chivalry,'" in which it would be reprinted.[43] F. W. Thomas, the lame novelist and journalist and loyal friend of Edgar Allan Poe, arranged the publication of the essay in the *Messenger,* first offering it, however, to Poe, now the literary editor of *Graham's Magazine*—"If it does not suit your Magazine, let me know frankly and I will send it to the Southern Literary Messenger."[44]

At once the essay became the chief source of biographical information on Hugh Henry Brackenridge. "I think it an excellent bit of biography," Thomas advised Poe. The essay was a scintillating defense of the elder Brackenridge's actions in the rebellion and turned mostly on that crisis in his life. The son argued that his father's part was important, dangerous, and honorable, misrepresented by enemies and so for a time misunderstood. After relating the principal events of the affair, he discussed his father's effort to recover his popularity with the people of Western Pennsylvania. The son ended his essay with this declaration of faith: "Such was Hugh Henry Brackenridge, a man but imperfectly appreciated in his own day, because, like others of an original cast of intellect, he was ahead of the age; but whose fame is destined to increase, as it becomes more removed from the times in which he lived."

Brackenridge thought "the best monument" he could erect in his father's memory was the publication of a complete edition of *Modern Chivalry.*[45] In 1846, the Philadelphia firm of Carey and Hart issued the second edition (after the author's death). Having read that Louis Philippe, the King of the French, still remembered the author of *Modern Chivalry* and sometimes spoke of him, Brackenridge sent him a copy of the work through his friend Robert Walsh, who now resided in Paris and served as the consul general of the United States. "Fifty years ago I saw Your Majesty at my father's house in Pittsburgh, with your Majesty's estimable brothers," Brackenridge wrote the king. "The recollection is as distinct as if it were yesterday."[46]

Brackenridge's erection of a monument in his father's honor did not remain long unchallenged. In his monthly publication, *The Olden Time,* a repository of documents concerning the colonial history of the Pittsburgh region, Craig introduced materials relating to the Whisky Insurrection in the last number ever published (December, 1847) and admittedly out of their chronological order, with this barbed comment: "Some other accounts heretofore published are, in fact, excuses or defences, prepared by persons more or less closely implicated in the criminality of the transactions narrated; and, of course, partake more of the character of the advocate than of the historian."[47] In 1851, Craig published his *History of Pittsburgh;* and in treating the rebellion,[48] he borrowed liberally from Alexander Hamilton's report on the affair and from Richard Hildreth's *History of the United States*—all in all, a thoroughly Federalist, anti-Brackenridge version of the proceedings.

Immediately Brackenridge resorted to the columns of the *Daily Commercial Journal* with a rejoinder and then determinedly continued the argument in eighteen more articles in the same paper.[49] In the sixth installment of his "Review of Craig's History," Brackenridge declared that another object besides the vindication of his father was responsible for a continuation of the series: "I have a further and higher aim in defending my countrymen, the people of the West, from the injustice done them. . . ." He believed that no event in American history had ever been so unfairly misrepresented as the Whisky Insurrection. Craig defended his views in five numbers in the *Journal,* to which his opponent responded with ten more. But, as Craig once put the matter: "I added a rebutter, as the lawyers style it, of four numbers. I then thought that the controversy was ended; I even hoped so. Both H. M. Brackenridge and myself have passed beyond our three score and twelfth years, and might, as well as ought to, be thinking of something else than such controversy."[50]

Craig ought to have known better, for with Brackenridge the defense of his father had become almost an obsession. The honor of the two families was in jeopardy, although the dueling in this instance would involve only words—thousands of them. That Brackenridge had no intention of ending the controversy at this point was evidenced by a letter[51] written to Peter Force in the fall of 1852, requesting some extracts be made from William Findley's *History of the Insurrection, in the Four Western Counties of Pennsylvania: in the Year M.DCC.XCIV,* published in 1796.[52] While engaged in the newspaper controversy with Craig, Brackenridge had vainly tried to procure a copy of the book—"Findly and Gallatin were both unfriendly to my father, having been opposed to each other on the question of the adoption of the federal constitution; no justice could therefore be expected from them."

About five years after the end of the journalistic conflict Brackenridge finished his *History of the Western Insurrection in Western Pennsylvania, Commonly Called the Whiskey Insurrection. 1794* and gave the manuscript to the Historical Society of Pennsylvania in the hope that organization would publish it.[53] However, the large, documented, 336-page book was published by the Pittsburgh firm of W. S. Haven in 1859. In this work Brackenridge tried to prove—and did so convincingly—that his father had acted an important part "in preventing a dreadful civil war, and in saving the town of Pittsburgh from destruction."[54] He cast the elder Brackenridge in the role of mediator between the people and the federal government. The author's notes, appended to each chapter, made interesting reading, especially one like the explanation of the term "The Neville Connection."[55] In his introduction, entitled "To Alexander Brackenridge, Esq.," the author outlined the history of his controversy with Craig and explained the reason for writing his latest work— "Neville Craig, in his book, insinuates that our father was the secret instigator of every unlawful act done by the mob!"[56]

Brackenridge had concluded the presentation of his case—the public had ample evidence to judge between him and Craig, he believed.[57] Craig, a grandson of General John Neville, the inspector of the excise at the time of the rebellion, had the last word in the controversy by promptly counterattacking with a small 79-page book pretentiously entitled *Exposure of a Few of the Many Misstatements in H. M. Brackenridge's History of the Whiskey Insurrection*. The oldest male descendant of Neville then living, Craig was harsh with the Brackenridges, the "slanderers" of his family.[58] But Craig was not sporting when he attacked[59] the younger Brackenridge, in language as vicious as Pentland's in the *Commonwealth,* years before, assailing the integrity of the Brackenridge family. Such was the bitterness of nineteenth century politics! Pittsburgh's battle royal, nevertheless, had at last ended!

There was a humorous side to the controversy. At its height Pittsburghers celebrated the centennial of the evacuation of Fort Duquesne. As part of the ceremonies, the stage manager of the Pittsburgh Theater recited a poem called "Suc-co-tash,"[60] composed by William H. Denny in honor of the occasion. This was the first stanza:

> A HUNDRED YEARS AGO! what sylvan beauty
> Did Nature on this almost island crowd;
> Where Art now, from her altars grim and sooty,
> "Doth overcome us like a winter cloud."

The fourth stanza went like this:

> But long ago the picture was defaced;
> The trees are gone—the green round hill is level;
> And hardly can the outlines be retraced,
> By those old scene-restorers, BRACK and NEVILLE.

When Denny published his poem, he appended a footnote[61] to explain the reference to "BRACK and NEVILLE," a felicitous compliment to the controversialists for setting an example for other Pittsburghers to follow by preserving historical materials. Besides inspiring the composition of "Suc-co-tash," the centennial led to the formation of the third Historical Society of Western Pennsylvania. At a meeting in January of 1859, when the organization of the society was completed, three men were chosen as vice-presidents representing

374

Allegheny County. The names of two of them were H. M. Brackenridge and Neville B. Craig.

Brackenridge favored James Parton with a copy of his *Insurrection*. Parton, busy completing the second volume of his Jackson biography in New York City, soon had a third of the book read, finding it "a light in a dark place. It is curious, interesting & picturesque, and draws the veil from a region little known to us here."[62] Parton also had a word for Morgan Brackenridge: "Your son will find food for his antipathy in my second volume, which goes to the printer this week. I go dead against Jackson on every controverted point— from the Six militia men to the comedy of Callava in the Calaboose. It was both just and necessary to set forth the good deeds & traits of Jackson in a bright light. But after the 8th of Jan - 1815, there is little brightness in his career." The astute Parton thought he had hit upon the reason why: "Among the 'casualties' of the battle, there was one not mentioned in the official report, namely, the Commanding General lost his head."

Undoubtedly Morgan had been reared on the family antipathy for Old Hickory. Father and son were very close, although on one occasion Morgan neglected to comply with a parental request. In 1844, Henry Clay had written Brackenridge about his southern tour: "Mrs. Levert, the Lady of Dr. Levert at whose house I tarried in Mobile, is your old friend Octavia, and a most fascinating and talented lady she is. She is now the mother of three little daughters, and she continues to cultivate the Spanish and French which you taught her, to which she has added Italian."[63] Octavia Walton, the little girl Brackenridge befriended after her father had squandered the territorial funds of Florida, had become the loveliest of all the Southern belles. When Morgan came of age and made his grand tour, he neglected to visit the Le Verts of Mobile, as Octavia informed his father: "We regret exceedingly, that we did not see your Son. Dr. Le Vert, says, he did not present your letter to him. I am sure, he could not have tarried more than a day here for we were on the 'qui vive,' and often sent to the Hotels, to find if he had arrived. We should have given him a welcome warm from the heart."[64]

Octavia still remembered Brackenridge as her "first friend":

... Oh! my friend, how often, then, has my memory dwelt upon you, and I have blessed you, for the love of learning, you instilled into my young mind, when as a little child, I sat at your feet, and listened to the eloquent words, which made instruction, from your lips so enchanting, and awakened a pride in my heart to be learned like you. Often have I said to my Octavia, "Thus did my friend Judge B. teach me, when I was only ten, and I can never fancy any other method as good." "The good, men do, live after them," some wise man has said, but the good, you have done my beloved friend, exists now, while health & intellect are still yours.

In 1850, when he received this letter from Octavia Walton Le Vert, Brackenridge's health was capital. Caroline, however, had scarcely two years more to live, dying in September, 1852. Her health had always been delicate and her greatest concern in later years was Morgan's welfare. Always beset by doubts and fears, she might not have understood the ways of a boy become man. That she doubted his love was expressed in her dying message for him: "Tell him from me, to turn to the Lord with all his heart, and entreat him to remember his poor mother with that warmth of affection he formerly felt for her."[65] After her death, Morgan married the accomplished daughter of Dr. Edward Stieren, chemist for the Pennsylvania Salt Manufacturing Company plant at Natrona, built, incidentally, on land cut from the Brackenridge property. They had three children. But Morgan's health was uncertain like his mother's had been—his career as a chemist never developed.[66]

Morgan's health now caused his father anxiety, as evident in his correspondence with Evert A. Duyckinck, who was preparing a *Cyclopaedia of American Literature* in the 1850's. For this work, historical in treatment rather than critical,[67] Duyckinck desired biographical notices for Hugh Henry Brackenridge and his son, to be published with portraits and autographs. Because the work proceeded chronologically, the matter of perpetuating the memory of Old Hugh was finished first—the plates even made before a sketch of the younger Brackenridge's career was required.[68] According to his father's wish Morgan undertook to write a notice for him.[69] Morgan ambitiously wanted to furnish a portrait of his father for the *Cyclopaedia* but had much difficulty securing a faithful likeness, "as it seems to be impossible for him to sit long enough to obtain a good photograph. . . ."[70] In the new art, or science, of photography, Morgan was a perfectionist. In the end his father prepared a notice of himself[71] and sent it to Duyckinck with an apology for its egotistical nature.[72] Morgan, Brackenridge wrote later to Duyckinck, felt mortified "that he should not have prepared a memoir after informing you that he would do it, but not succeeding to his satisfaction in obtaining a photograph, which he has ascertained to be the fault of one of the lenses of the camera, he delayed the undertaking, and fears that without this explanation he may have suffered in your estimation."[73]

In 1855, the year of this correspondence with Duyckinck, Morgan was already suffering from an incurable affliction—an anal fistula. The fall of the next year Brackenridge accompanied his son to New York, where it was hoped a successful operation might be performed.[74] Brackenridge visited Duyckinck while there, but had to return to Tarentum without Morgan, who had not yet had an operation, "from which alone he can expect a cure."[75] Morgan spent the winter in Philadelphia and in the spring went back to New York to see, wrote his father disconsolately to Duyckinck, "what surgical miracle can be wrought in his favor. It is a dreadful state to be in. He bears up with much fortitude, but such a situation is calculated to cast a gloom over every thing in life."[76]

Aged thirty-four, Morgan died in 1862, during the Civil War. Until his death he had assisted his father in the management of the estate at Tarentum. In September, 1860, they had held a notable sale of bottom land, advertised as ideal for market gardens and vineyards and residences. There were splendid sites for rolling mills and tanneries.[77] The Brackenridges offered for sale farms and detached lots and two sawmills and salt wells. By now Tarentum was a flourishing town with a population of about twelve hundred. East Tarentum, laid out on the Brackenridge property, was a bustling village containing the largest plant for the manufacture of chemicals west of the Allegheny Mountains.

There Tarentum stood as the fulfillment of Brackenridge's dream of closing his life on the Allegheny. His wife and his son ("my usual companion")[78] were no longer with him, but his daughter-in-law, Phillipine, and the little grandchildren could bolster his spirits whenever necessary. Without them life would have been "truly miserable," as he had discovered it might have been the winter Morgan spent in Philadelphia.

To his grandchildren, Henry Morgan and Cornelia Caroline, Brackenridge once expressed in writing a wish that the beautiful natural spring in Tarentum, which he had preserved from private exploitation, be improved tastefully for the pleasure of the townspeople.[79] He still remembered the "City Spring" of Baltimore as a favorite haunt of his youth. But now it was his hope that fifty dollars, appropriated from a fund to be established by the churches, by those who used the water, and perhaps by voluntary subscription, be awarded every year as a prize to the best reader among the boys from twelve to fourteen in the Tarentum public schools. He told his grandchildren how he himself as a boy had won a toy set of cups and saucers at a public exhibition in Ste. Genevieve. The winner of the contest in Tarentum would be required to read publicly at the spring, on the Fourth of July, Brackenridge's eulogy on Adams and Jefferson, originally delivered in Pensacola in 1826.

This wish was a display of vanity, as Brackenridge feared—however, a desire "at least harmless." But rightfully proud of his own oratorical ability, he wanted to foster the cultivation of eloquence among the youth of Tarentum. He prized the eulogy on Adams and Jefferson as the best of his orations. William Wirt had admired it:

. . . It was one evening at his fireside, in his family, several gentlemen and ladies present. Said he, "Mr. Brackenridge, I have been desirous of saying to you that I regard your oration on Jefferson and Adams, the best that has been delivered, not excepting my own, of course. But I except no one. That I am sincere in this, I will appeal to Mrs. Wirt, to whom I have repeatedly said the same thing. Mine was delivered after all the others, and yours is the only one from which I have quoted—it is that part in which you speak of the declaration of independence."[80]

Not greatly inferior to that oration, if at all, was Brackenridge's eulogy on John Quincy Adams, delivered at the schoolhouse of the sixth ward in Pittsburgh on May 11, 1848.[81] His orations, if collected, Brackenridge estimated, would fill several volumes, "not to speak of those things, which I gave away to help the reputations of others, who put their names to them."[82]

Brackenridge's last important speech, delivered in the presidential campaign of 1864, was entitled "Sixty Years in the North and Twenty Years in the South." After its delivery he prepared it for publication from his notes, making changes here and there. The speech in its pamphlet form is a valuable source of information for details of Brackenridge's career as related to the growth of the United States from a fledgling nation into a powerful Union disrupted by a fratricidal war. Although he advocated the election of General George McClellan over Lincoln, calling for the success of "the great conservative Democratic party,"[83] his speech was not a party speech: "it was intended for the philosopher and the historian who honestly seek out the causes of events."[84] Anecdotes and historical examples abounded in the speech, many derived from personal experience—his life spanned the whole history of the Union! A fine biting humor pervaded the work. But the published speech was wordy and repetitious. There were frequent digressions.

The cause of the war, in Brackenridge's opinion, was the existence of slavery in the South, a local institution with which no authority had a right to interfere. How he hated the "demon of abolition"![85] To him *Uncle Tom's Cabin* was a "slanderous novel."[86] In fact, he had denounced[87] the book upon its publication in 1851-52, only to be flayed promptly by Pittsburgh's antislavery editor, Jane G. Swisshelm.[88] Although Brackenridge did not approve of slavery on any ground, he did condemn the abusers of the South: "For thirty years I have never ceased to warn my countrymen against the never ceasing abuse of the South, which must necessarily lead to alienation of feeling and mutual hatred, civil war, bloody, destructive civil war, and endangering the existence of the noblest political fabric ever erected by man."[89] The lot of the negro, Brackenridge contended, had been immeasurably improved by being sold as a slave in America. He favored the gradual emancipation of the slaves. Decidedly not a secessionist, he knew that, in 1864, conciliation was the only policy for the North to pursue.

"I have lived twenty years in the South and sixty in the North, and claim to know something of both," he reminded his listeners. "I was born in Pennsylvania, and went to the South with all my prepossessions against slavery; but experience, a wise instructor, has pointed out to me the difficulties of

dealing with a subject so complicated."[90] It was a wise voice speaking, for Brackenridge lived long enough to see the end of the war and the commencement of congressional reconstruction with all its evils.

Brackenridge saw, however, the preservation of the Union—the new nation, whose

> Renowned characters, and glorious works
> Of high invention and of wond'rous art

his father had envisioned as a student at the College of New Jersey and he himself, the son, had done so much to record for the pleasure and instruction of his fellow Americans.

Brackenridge died near his birthplace in Pittsburgh at the home of his daughter-in-law, Phillipine, on January 18, 1871. He was then the oldest native-born Pittsburgher.[91] But he was buried next to Caroline at Tarentum, their town. On his stone in Prospect Cemetery[92] an inscription notes that Brackenridge was a "Traveler, Author, and Jurist" and "A Man of Honor."

Notes

Chapter I: BIRTHRIGHT

1. Fred Lewis Pattee (ed.), *The Poems of Philip Freneau: Poet of the American Revolution* (Princeton: The University Library, 1902), I, 82-83.

2. For full text of the original poem, published in Philadelphia in 1772, see Pattee, *ibid.*, I, 50-83; account of Freneau and Brackenridge at Princeton, I, xvi-xxi.

3. [H. M. Brackenridge], "Biographical Notice of H. H. Brackenridge, Late of the Supreme Court of Pennsylvania," in H. H. Brackenridge, *Modern Chivalry, or the Adventures of Captain Farrago and Teague O'Regan* (2d ed. after author's death in 1816; Philadelphia: Getz & Buck, 1851), II, 151-53. The essay originally appeared in the *Southern Literary Messenger*, VIII (January, 1842), 1-19. Hereafter cited as "Biographical Notice."

4. Alexander Brackenridge to William M. Darlington, Pittsburgh, December 22, 1866, Darlington Collection (MSS in the Darlington Memorial Library, University of Pittsburgh. Hereafter cited as Darlington MSS.)

5. "Biographical Notice," p. 154.

6. April 1, in *Letters and Other Writings of James Madison, Fourth President of the United States* (Philadelphia: J. B. Lippincott & Co., 1865), I, 13.

7. Madison to Bradford, Virginia, Orange County, January 20, 1775, in *ibid.*, I, 18.

8. "Biographical Notice," p. 154.

9. Later published in Philadelphia by Robert Bell, 1776.

10. "Biographical Notice," p. 154.

11. *Ibid.*, pp. 154-55.

12. Hugh Montgomery Brackenridge, *Six Political Discourses Founded on the Scripture* (Lancaster: Francis Bailey, [1778]), p. 16.

13. Printed and sold by Francis Bailey.

14. Pattee, *op. cit.*, I, xxvii-xxx.

15. "Biographical Notice," pp. 155-56.

16. Hugh Henry Brackenridge, *Law Miscellanies: Containing an Introduction to the Study of the Law; Notes on Blackstone's Commentaries, Shewing the Variations of the Law of Pennsylvania from the Law of England, and What Acts of Assembly Might Require to Be Repealed or Modified; Observations on Smith's Edition of the Laws of Pennsylvania; Strictures on Decisions of the Supreme Court of the United States, and on Certain Acts of Congress, with Some Law Cases, and a Variety of Other Matters, Chiefly Original* (Philadelphia: P. Byrne, 1814), p. 511.

17. Brackenridge to the Citizens of Greene, Washington, and Allegheny Counties in *Pittsburgh Gazette*, July 21, 1798.

18. See extract from Arthur Lee's Journal in *The Olden Time; a Monthly Publication, Devoted to the Preservation of Documents and Other Authentic Information in Relation to the Early Explorations, and the Settlement and Improvement of the Country around the Head of the Ohio*, II (July and August, 1847), 339-40.

19. *Ibid.*

20. In *Incidents of the Insurrection in the Western Parts of Pennsylvania, in the Year 1794* (Philadelphia: John M'Culloch, 1795), III, 13.

21. "Biographical Notice," p. 156.

22. H. H. Brackenridge, *Gazette Publications* (Carlisle: Alexander & Phillips, 1806), p. 7.

23. For Brackenridge's description of Pittsburgh in 1786, see *ibid.*, pp. 7-19.

24. Evert A. and George L. Duyckinck, *Cyclopaedia of American Literature; Embracing Personal and Critical Notices of Authors, and Selections from Their Writings. From the Earliest Period to the Present Day; with Portraits, Autographs, and Other Illustrations* (New York: Charles Scribner, 1866), I, 668; H. M. Brackenridge, *Recol-

lections of Persons and Places in the West (2d ed., enlarged; Philadelphia: J. B. Lippincott & Co., 1868), pp. 10-11. The latter work does not give the precise date of birth.

25. Brackenridge, *Gazette Publications,* pp. 23-24.

26. *Pittsburgh Gazette,* September 9, 1786.

27. *Ibid.,* October 14, 1786.

28. *Ibid.,* November 4, 1786.

29. *Ibid.,* January 6, 1787.

30. Brackenridge, *Incidents of the Insurrection,* III, 13.

31. *Pittsburgh Gazette,* March 17, 1787.

32. *Ibid.*

33. *Ibid.,* March 24, 1787.

34. April 12, in *ibid.,* April 14, 1787.

35. April 21, 28; May 5, 12, 19, 26; June 2 and 9, 1787.

36. July 21, 28; August 18, 25; September 1, 8, 15, and 22, 1787.

37. August 3 and 11, 1787.

38. Both letters dated September 30, 1787, in *ibid.,* February 23, 1788.

39. April 14, 1787.

40. Extract of a letter from a gentleman in Philadelphia, to his friend in this place in *ibid.*

41. Reprinted in *ibid.,* May 26, 1787.

42. *Ibid.,* October 27, 1787.

43. *Ibid.,* November 3, 1787.

44. *Ibid.,* November 3 and 10, 1787.

45. Brackenridge, *Incidents of the Insurrection,* III,14.

46. *Ibid.*

47. *Pittsburgh Gazette,* October 21, 1787.

48. *Ibid.,* November 10, 1787.

49. December 1, 1787.

50. *Ibid.,* June 2, 1787. "This account is taken from a journal kept by the adjutant at Fort Harmar, on Muskinghum."

51. For the whole story of this institution, see Agnes Lynch Starrett, *Through One Hundred and Fifty Years: The University of Pittsburgh* (Pittsburgh: University of Pittsburgh Press, 1937).

52. "On the ROAD BILL" in *Pittsburgh Gazette,* April 26, 1788.

53. For the entire description of this event, see account in *ibid.,* June 28, 1788.

Chapter II: FATHER AND SON

1. Brackenridge, *Recollections,* p. 10. All references to this work are to the 1868 edition unless otherwise indicated.

2. *Ibid.*

3. Henry Adams, *The Life of Albert Gallatin* (Philadelphia: J. B. Lippincott & Co., 1879), p. 68.

4. Brackenridge, *Recollections,* p. 10.

5. *Ibid.*

6. *Ibid.,* pp. 10-11.

7. *Pittsburgh Gazette,* December 5, 1789.

8. *Ibid.,* February 9, 1793.

9. *Ibid.,* January 24, 1795.

10. Notice dated November 8, 1797, in *ibid.,* November 18, 1797.

11. Brackenridge, *Recollections*, p. 11.

12. *Ibid.*

13. *Ibid.*

14. *Ibid.*, p. 42.

15. "Biographical Notice," p. 158.

16. Brackenridge, *Recollections*, pp. 11-12.

17. Brackenridge, *Gazette Publications*, p. 90.

18. For text, see *ibid.*, pp. 86-93.

19. *Pittsburgh Gazette,* September 9, 1786.

20. January 17, 1789.

21. *Ibid.*, April 25, 1789.

22. John Pope, *A Tour through the Southern and Western Territories of the United States of North-America; the Spanish Dominions on the River Mississippi, and the Floridas; the Countries of the Creek Nations; and Many Uninhabited Parts* (Richmond: John Dixon, 1792; reprinted with index for Charles L. Woodward, New York, 1888), p. 5.

23. *Ibid.*, pp. 12-14.

24. *Ibid.*, p. 17.

25. For text of the poem and account of Brackenridge's marriage, see *ibid.*, pp. 14-17.

26. "The Population of Pittsburgh and Contiguous Territory, Including the Names of Heads of Families as Shown by the United States Census of 1790," in *Western Pennsylvania Historical Magazine*, II (July, 1919), 168; Brackenridge, *Recollections*, p. 12.

27. Pope, *op. cit.*, pp. 15-16.

28. Brackenridge, *Recollections*, pp. 12-13.

29. First volume (4-29 September, 1787) printed by Daniel Humphreys in Philadelphia, 1787; second volume (22 October-29 November, 1787), Joseph James, Philadelphia, 1787.

30. Brackenridge, *Incidents of the Insurrection*, III, 13.

31. See, for example, the account of the Meeting of the Inhabitants of Pittsburgh on the Evening of the 25th Instant in *Pittsburgh Gazette*, November 29, 1788.

32. Brackenridge, *Incidents of the Insurrection*, III, 29-30.

33. For date and text, see Brackenridge, *Gazette Publications*, pp. 311-40.

34. *Ibid.*, p. 311.

35. See Postscript to *Modern Chivalry: Containing the Adventures of Captain John Farrago, and Teague ORegan, His Servant* (Philadelphia: John M'Culloch, 1792), I, 150.

36. *Ibid.*, I, 152.

37. *Ibid.*, I, 156.

38. Printed and sold by John M'Culloch, Philadelphia.

39. *Ibid.*, I, 82-83.

40. *Ibid.*, I, 5-6.

41. *Ibid.* (1793 ed.), III, v.

42. *Ibid.*, I, 8-9.

43. *Ibid.*, I, 152-53.

44. P. xi.

45. P. xiii.

46. Pp. xvii-xxiv.

47. P. xvii.

48. Pp. xxx-lxiii.

49. *Ibid.*, I, 150.

50. *Ibid.*, I, 12.

51. *Ibid.*, I, 16.
52. *Ibid.*, I, 22-24.
53. *Ibid.*, I, 27.
54. *Ibid.*, I, 31.
55. *Ibid.*, I, 35.
56. *Ibid.*, III, 61.
57. *Ibid.*, III, 100.
58. *Ibid.*
59. *Ibid.* (1792 ed.), II, 51.
60. See notice of new edition of *Modern Chivalry* in the *Literary Examiner, and Western Monthly Review*, I (June, 1839), 159.
61. *Main Currents in American Thought: An Interpretation of American Literature from the Beginnings to 1920* (New York: Harcourt, Brace and Company, 1930), I, 390-95.
62. Brackenridge, *Recollections*, p. 188.
63. *Ibid.*, p. 13.
64. *Pittsburgh Gazette*, March 23, 1793.
65. Brackenridge, *Recollections*, p. 13.
66. *Ibid.*, p. 14.

Chapter III: STE. GENEVIEVE

1. Brackenridge, *Recollections*, pp. 13-14.
2. *Pittsburgh Gazette*, July 6, 1793.
3. For text, see Brackenridge, *Gazette Publications*, pp. 121-24.
4. André Michaux, "Journal of André Michaux, 1793-1796," in Reuben Gold Thwaites (ed.), *Early Western Travels, 1748-1846: A Series of Annotated Reprints of Some of the Best and Rarest Contemporary Volumes of Travel, Descriptive of the Aborigines and Social and Economic Conditions in the Middle and Far West, during the Period of Early American Settlement* (Cleveland: The Arthur H. Clark Company, 1904), III, 28.
5. *Ibid.*, III, 32.
6. February 22, in Neville B. Craig, *The History of Pittsburgh, with a Brief Notice of Its Facilities of Communication, and Other Advantages for Commercial and Manufacturing Purposes* (Pittsburgh: John H. Mellor, 1851), p. 216.
7. For example, see notice in *Pittsburgh Gazette*, February 16, 1793.
8. *Ibid.*, May 18, 1793.
9. October 19, 1793.
10. *Dunlap's American Daily Advertiser*, August 16, 1793.
11. *Ibid.*, August 19, 1793.
12. Voucher of Lucas, sworn before A. Addison, in Brackenridge, *Incidents of the Insurrection*, III, 104-108.
13. H. H. Brackenridge to Lucas, Carlisle, March 25, 1805, Lucas Papers (MSS in the Missouri Historical Society, St. Louis).
14. *Pittsburgh Gazette*, May 4, 1793.
15. In Lucas Papers, see the trader's account book for 1793-94 with entry for "Henry Brakenridge" and other references to him.
16. In Thwaites, *op. cit.*, III, 31.
17. Brackenridge, *Recollections*, pp. 14-16.
18. *Ibid.*, p. 14.
19. *Ibid.*, p. 17.

20. *Ibid.,* pp. 17-18.
21. *Ibid.,* pp. 18-19.
22. *Ibid.,* pp. 19-27.
23. Power's narrative and deposition respecting his mission in 1795, in *American State Papers: Miscellaneous* (Washington: Gales and Seaton, 1834), II, 96.
24. Brackenridge, *Gazette Publications,* pp. 275-76.
25. See entry for March 27, 1800, Jefferson's "Anas," in Thomas Jefferson Randolph (ed.), *Memoirs, Correspondence, and Private Papers of Thomas Jefferson, Late President of the United States* (London: Henry Colburn and Richard Bentley, 1829), IV, 527.
26. James Wilkinson, *Memoirs of My Own Times* (Philadelphia: Abraham Small, 1816), II, 88.
27. Brackenridge, *Recollections,* pp. 28-29.
28. *Ibid.,* pp. 29-31.
29. *Ibid.,* pp. 31-33.
30. *Ibid.,* pp. 34-40.
31. *Ibid.,* p. 41.
32. *The Journal of Andrew Ellicott, Late Commissioner on Behalf of the United States during Part of the Year 1796, the Years 1797, 1798, 1799, and Part of the Year 1800: for Determining the Boundary between the United States and the Possessions of His Catholic Majesty in America, Containing Occasional Remarks on the Situation, Soil, Rivers, Natural Productions, and Diseases of the Different Countries on the Ohio, Mississippi, and Gulf of Mexico, with Six Maps Comprehending the Ohio, the Mississippi from the Mouth of the Ohio to the Gulf of Mexico, the Whole of West Florida, and Part of East Florida* (2d ed.; Philadelphia: William Fry, 1814), p. 6.
33. Brackenridge, *Recollections,* p. 42.

Chapter IV: THE STUDENT

1. Brackenridge, *Recollections,* p. 56.
2. *Ibid.,* p. 57.
3. *Ibid.,* pp. 57-58.
4. H. M. Brackenridge, *History of the Western Insurrection in Western Pennsylvania, Commonly Called the Whiskey Insurrection. 1794* (Pittsburgh: W. S. Haven, 1859), p. ix.
5. *Incidents of the Insurrection,* I, 86; III, 25.
6. In *Ibid.,* II, 51-52.
7. *Ibid.,* II, 77.
8. Notice dated October 8, in *Pittsburgh Gazette,* October 11, 1794.
9. October 18, 1794.
10. See, for example, Leland D. Baldwin, *Whiskey Rebels: The Story of a Frontier Uprising* (Pittsburgh: University of Pittsburgh Press, 1939), p. 292.
11. *Modern Chivalry* (1797 ed.), IV, 112.
12. *Ibid.,* IV, 116.
13. *Ibid.,* IV, 101.
14. *Ibid.,* IV, 102.
15. Brackenridge, *Recollections,* p. 43.
16. *Ibid.,* pp. 43-45.
17. *Ibid.,* pp. 45-47.
18. *Ibid.,* pp. 44, 47-49.
19. *Ibid.,* pp. 50-51.
20. *Ibid.,* p. 44.

21. *Ibid.*, pp. 53-54.

22. *Ibid.*, p. 47.

23. *Ibid.*, p. 54.

24. *Ibid.*, pp. 48-49.

25. Joseph Smith, *History of Jefferson College: Including an Account of the Early "Log-Cabin" Schools, and the Canonsburg Academy: with Biographical Sketches of Rev. Matthew Brown, D.D., Rev. Samuel Ralston, D.D., Rev. Matthew Henderson, Rev. James Ramsey, D.D., Rev. John H. Kennedy, and Rev. Abr'm. Anderson, D.D.* (Pittsburgh: J. T. Shryock, 1857), pp. 38-39.

26. Charles W. Dahlinger, "Rev. John Taylor: The First Rector of Trinity Episcopal Church of Pittsburgh and His Commonplace Book," in *Western Pennsylvania Historical Magazine*, I (January, 1918), 11; Brackenridge, *Recollections*, pp. 49-50, 55.

27. *Recollections*, pp. 51-53.

28. See notice dated January 16, 1796, in *Pittsburgh Gazette*, January 23, 1796.

29. Brackenridge, *Recollections*, p. 55.

30. *Ibid.*, pp. 55-56.

31. *Pittsburgh Gazette*, January 9, 1796.

32. *Ibid.*, March 28, 1795.

33. *Ibid.*, November 21, 1795.

34. *Ibid.*, March 5, 1796.

35. May 14, 1796.

36. Brackenridge, *Recollections*, pp. 62-63.

37. George Swetnam, a student of folk song, questions Loughy's authorship and Brackenridge's recollection of the verse. Whether Brackenridge's remembrance of the exact words was imperfect or not, the fact remains that he left to posterity the only detailed—and vivid!—description of this blind poet. See Swetnam's "Singing Pittsburgh," in *Western Pennsylvania Historical Magazine*, XXXV (March, 1952), 25-36.

38. H. M. Brackenridge, "Pittsburgh in the Olden Time," in the *Literary Examiner, and Western Monthly Review*, I (May, 1839), 28.

39. *Tree of Liberty*, September 6, 1800.

40. *Ibid.*, March 28, 1801.

41. *Pittsburgh Gazette*, November 18, 1797.

42. *Ibid.*, November 16, 1799.

43. Brackenridge, *Recollections*, p. 67.

44. *Ibid.*, p. 66.

45. *Ibid.*, p. 67.

46. See notice by the administrators of his estate, Mary Murphy and Ebenezer Denny, in *Pittsburgh Gazette*, February 4, 1797.

47. *Ibid.*, November 2, 1799.

48. Brackenridge, *Recollections*, p. 66.

49. See notices of Republican meetings at John Marie's house in *Tree of Liberty*, August 30 and October 11, 1800; July 4, 1801.

50. *Pittsburgh Gazette*, November 2 and 30, 1799.

51. *Ibid.*, July 5, 1800.

52. Brackenridge, *Recollections*, p. 53.

53. *Ibid.*, p. 68.

54. See his advertisement, dated December 19, in *Pittsburgh Gazette*, December 22, 1798.

55. *Ibid.*, May 4, 1799.

56. Brackenridge, *Recollections*, p. 68.

57. *Ibid.*, pp. 68-69.

Chapter V: *THE LAW IS A JEALOUS MISTRESS*

1. H. M. Brackenridge, *A Speech Delivered by H. M. Brackenridge, in the Presidential Campaign of 1864: Sixty Years in the North and Twenty Years in the South* (Pittsburgh: Barr & Myers, 1865), pp. 11-12.

2. Brackenridge, *Recollections*, pp. 69-70.

3. *Pittsburgh Gazette*, November 18, 1797.

4. In *ibid.*, July 21, 1798.

5. Brackenridge's "Sketch of the ground of my opposition to the Election of John Woods as a Representative in Congress," in *ibid.*, September 29, 1798.

6. See account of the meeting in *ibid.*, August 11, 1798.

7. *Ibid.*, September 8, 1798.

8. *Ibid.*, September 22, 1798.

9. *Ibid.*, September 29, 1798.

10. *Ibid.*

11. *Ibid.*, October 20 and November 10, 1798.

12. Brackenridge, *Recollections*, p. 70.

13. *Pittsburgh Gazette*, January 19, 1799.

14. *Ibid.*, August 29, 1800.

15. *Ibid.*, March 23, 1799.

16. *Ibid.*, March 30, 1799.

17. *Ibid.*, September 14, 1799.

18. *Ibid.*, October 5, 1799.

19. *Ibid.*, November 2, 1799.

20. *Ibid.*, November 30, 1799.

21. See Brackenridge's letter in *ibid.*, December 7, 1799.

22. See Scull's answer in *ibid.*

23. Brackenridge, *Recollections*, p. 70.

24. *Pittsburgh Gazette*, August 23, 1800.

25. *Ibid.*, September 26, 1800.

26. *Tree of Liberty*, September 20, 1800.

27. Brackenridge, *Recollections*, pp. 71-72.

28. The article cannot be identified in the extant files of the paper, which are incomplete.

29. *Pittsburgh Gazette*, December 21, 1799.

30. *Tree of Liberty*, October 4, 1800.

31. Brackenridge, *Recollections*, p. 72.

32. *Pittsburgh Gazette*, January 25, 1800.

33. Brackenridge, *Recollections*, pp. 72-73.

34. *Pittsburgh Gazette*, March 29, 1800.

35. December 16, 1798—January 24, 1800. The Historical Society of Western Pennsylvania, Pittsburgh, possesses a photostatic copy of the original.

36. *Pittsburgh Gazette*, March 29, 1800.

37. "Biographical Notice," p. 188.

38. In *Law Miscellanies*, p. 523.

39. *Tree of Liberty*, August 22, 1801.

40. Brackenridge, *Recollections*, p. 72.

41. *Ibid.*, pp. 73-74.

42. *Ibid.*, pp. 74-75.

43. *Ibid.*, pp. 88-89.

44. *Tree of Liberty*, February 19, 1803.
45. *Ibid.*, March 5, 1803.
46. Brackenridge, *Recollections*, p. 89.
47. *Ibid.*, p. 88.
48. *Ibid.*, pp. 87-88.
49. *Commonwealth*, July 2, 1806.
50. Brackenridge, *Recollections*, p. 85.
51. *Ibid.*, p. 76.
52. *Ibid.*, p. 81.
53. *Tree of Liberty*, May 16, 1801.
54. Brackenridge, *Recollections*, p. 81.

Chapter VI: THE BAR OF PITTSBURGH

1. See pp. vii-xxvi.
2. *Tree of Liberty*, July 23, 1803.
3. Brackenridge, *Recollections*, p. 76.
4. *Ibid.*, pp. 76-78.
5. *Ibid.*, pp. 78-81.
6. R. C. Brown (ed.), *History of Butler County, Pennsylvania* (Chicago: R. C. Brown & Co., 1895), p. 137.
7. Brackenridge, *Recollections*, p. 81.
8. *Ibid.*, p. 82.
9. *Ibid.*, p. 81.
10. *Ibid.*, pp. 82-83.
11. [Jane Marie], *The Case of Jane Marie, Exhibiting the Cruelty and Barbarous Conduct of James Ross, to a Defenceless Woman. Written and Published by the Object of His Cruelty and Vengeance, and Addressed to the PUBLIC OF PHILADELPHIA and the Whole of PENNSYLVANIA* ([Philadelphia], September, 1808; reprinted in *Select Pamphlets* [Duane's Collection], Philadelphia, 1814). Unless otherwise indicated, the facts related concerning this affair are drawn from the pamphlet as the chief source of information.
12. In Lucas Papers.
13. April 21, 1797. Recorder's Office, Allegheny County, Deed Book F-6, pp. 448-49. Reprinted in *Case of Jane Marie*, pp. 3-4.
14. Deed Book M-12, p. 62.
15. *Case of Jane Marie*, p. 11.
16. *Ibid.*, p. 12.
17. In *ibid.*
18. See the documents in *ibid.*, pp. 5-8.
19. *Ibid.*, p. 20.
20. *Ibid.*, p. 21.
21. *Ibid.*, pp. 22-23.
22. Recorder's Office, Allegheny County, Deed Book O-14, pp. 489-90.
23. *Commonwealth*, July 1, 1807.
24. Brackenridge, *Recollections*, p. 84.
25. *Ibid.*, p. 83.
26. *Commonwealth*, December 4, 1805.
27. *Ibid.*, November 6, 1805.
28. *Ibid.*, December 4, 1805.

29. *Ibid.*, January 1, 1806.

30. Brackenridge, *Recollections*, p. 89.

31. Smith, *Jefferson College*, pp. 54-55.

32. Brackenridge, *Recollections*, p. 89.

33. *Ibid.*, pp. 89-90.

34. For an interesting collection of documents pertaining to this whole affair, see Mrs. Elvert M. Davis, "The Bates Boys on the Western Waters," Part III, in *Western Pennsylvania Historical Magazine*, XXX (March-June, 1947), 34-48.

35. From the statement in the *Pittsburgh Gazette* which Pentland reprinted in the *Commonwealth*, January 15, 1806, as an authentic report of the duel.

36. Brackenridge, *Recollections*, p. 90.

37. *Ibid.*, p. 91.

38. *Ibid.*, pp. 91-94.

39. *Ibid.*, pp. 96-97.

40. *Pittsburgh Gazette*, April 9, 1796.

41. *Ibid.*, May 7, 1796.

42. *Commonwealth*, February 25, 1807.

43. Brackenridge, *Recollections*, p. 97.

44. *Ibid.*, p. 96.

45. *Ibid.*, p. 103.

46. *Ibid.*, p. 104.

47. *Ibid.*, p. 103 fn.

48. *Commonwealth*, August 27, 1806.

49. *Ibid.*, December 24, 1806.

50. *Ibid.*

51. Records of the Allegheny County Bar Association, Pittsburgh.

52. Brackenridge, *Recollections*, p. 97.

53. *Ibid.*, p. 98.

54. *Ibid.*, p. 102.

55. *Case of Jane Marie*, p. 9.

56. *Ibid.*, p. 24.

57. See deed books in Recorder's Office, Allegheny County.

58. Brackenridge, *Recollections*, p. 99.

59. *Ibid.*

60. *Ibid.*, p. 100.

61. *Ibid.*, p. 101.

62. *Ibid.*, pp. 101-102.

63. *Ibid.*, p. 103.

Chapter VII: THE ATTORNEY AT LAW

1. Brackenridge, *Recollections*, pp. 105-107.

2. *Ibid.*, pp. 107-109.

3. F. Cuming, *Sketches of a Tour to the Western Country, through the States of Ohio and Kentucky; a Voyage down the Ohio and Mississippi Rivers, and a Trip through the Mississippi Territory, and Part of West Florida. Commenced at Philadelphia in the Winter of 1807, and Concluded in 1809* (Pittsburgh: Cramer, Spear & Eichbaum, 1810), pp. 31-33.

4. Brackenridge, *Recollections*, p. 109.

5. *Gazette Publications*, p. 4.
6. *Ibid.*, pp. 347-48.
7. Brackenridge, *Law Miscellanies*, p. 571.
8. *Ibid.*, p. 572.
9. Brackenridge, *Recollections*, pp. 109-10.
10. *Ibid.*, p. 110.
11. *Ibid.*, p. 107.
12. *Ibid.*, p. 110.
13. *Ibid.*, p. 111.
14. *Ibid;* Brackenridge, *Law Miscellanies*, p. 575.
15. Brackenridge, *Recollections*, p. 112.
16. *Ibid.*, pp. 113-14.
17. *Ibid.*, pp. 114-15.
18. *Ibid.*, pp. 115-16.
19. Carlisle, June 4, 1807, Dunning McNair Collection (MSS in the Darlington Memorial Library, University of Pittsburgh).
20. Brackenridge, *Recollections*, pp. 116-17.
21. *Ibid.*, pp. 118-20.
22. *Ibid.*, pp. 120-21.
23. *Ibid.*, pp. 121-22.
24. *Ibid.*, pp. 122-27.
25. *Ibid.*, pp. 127-28.
26. *Ibid.*, pp. 127-28; 134-35.
27. *Ibid.*, pp. 128-29.
28. "Letter to Walter Forward," September 29, 1817, in *ibid.*, Appendix, pp. 275-77.
29. *Ibid.*, pp. 135-36.
30. *Ibid.*, pp. 133-34.
31. *Ibid.*, pp. 129-31.
32. *Ibid.*, p. 131.
33. *Ibid.*, p. 130.
34. *Ibid.*, pp. 132-33.
35. *Ibid.*, pp. 142-46.
36. *Commonwealth*, May 11 and June 1, 1808.
37. Brackenridge, *Recollections*, p. 146.
38. *Ibid.*, pp. 137-41.
39. "Letter to Walter Forward," p. 277.
40. Brackenridge, *Recollections*, p. 146.
41. *Ibid.*, pp. 147-48.
42. *Ibid.*, pp. 149-50.
43. *Ibid.*, pp. 150-51.
44. *Ibid.*, pp. 151-52.
45. *Ibid.*, pp. 152-54.
46. *Ibid.*, p. 163.
47. *Ibid.*, p. 162.
48. *Ibid.*, pp. 164-65.
49. *Ibid.*, pp. 169-72.
50. *Ibid.*, p. 164.
51. *Ibid.*, pp. 161-64.

Chapter VIII: *SKETCHES OF THE TERRITORY OF LOUISIANA*

1. Brackenridge, *Recollections,* pp. 172-74.
2. "Roll of Attorneys Admitted to Practice at the Westmoreland Bar," in George Dallas Albert (ed.), *History of the County of Westmoreland, Pennsylvania, with Biographical Sketches of Many of Its Pioneers and Prominent Men* (Philadelphia: L. H. Everts & Co., 1882), p. 330.
3. Brackenridge, *Recollections,* pp. 174-75.
4. *Ibid.,* pp. 173-75.
5. *Ibid.,* pp. 175-76.
6. *Ibid.,* pp. 176-83.
7. *Ibid.,* pp. 183-84.
8. *Ibid.,* pp. 184-86.
9. *Ibid.,* pp. 186-87.
10. *Ibid.,* pp. 187-90.
11. *Ibid.,* pp. 190-95.
12. *Ibid.,* pp. 195-99.
13. *Ibid.,* pp. 199-200.
14. *Ibid.,* pp. 200-201.
15. *Ibid.,* pp. 201-205.
16. *Ibid.,* pp. 205-207.
17. *Ibid.,* pp. 207-208.
18. *Ibid.,* pp. 209-15.
19. *Ibid.,* pp. 215-28.
20. *Ibid.,* pp. 229-30.
21. *Sketches of a Tour,* p. 69.
22. Brackenridge, *Recollections,* pp. 215-16.
23. February 24, 1808.
24. *Commonwealth,* March 9, 1808.
25. *Missouri Gazette,* January 11 and February 1, 1809.
26. Brackenridge, *Recollections,* p. 215.
27. *Ibid.,* p. 230.
28. *Ibid.,* pp. 233-35.
29. *Ibid.,* pp. 229; 260.
30. *Ibid.,* pp. 260-66.
31. *Ibid.,* p. 265.
32. *Louisiana Gazette,* January 2, 1811.
33. Brackenridge, *Recollections,* pp. 235-42.
34. *Ibid.,* p. 241.
35. *Louisiana Gazette,* January 16, 1811.
36. Brackenridge, *Recollections,* p. 232.
37. *Ibid.,* p. 231.
38. *Ibid.*
39. *Ibid.,* pp. 232-33.
40. *Louisiana Gazette,* October 11 and 17, 1810.
41. The anonymous nature of the letter does not prevent its identification as the product of Brackenridge's pen, for he incorporated this material in his *Views of Louisiana; Together with a Journal of a Voyage up the Missouri River, in 1811* (Pittsburgh: Cramer, Spear and Eichbaum, 1814). For example, see pp. 120-24.

42. Brackenridge, *Recollections,* pp. 230-31.

43. *Louisiana Gazette,* January 16, 1811.

44. The "New Orleans."

45. *Louisiana Gazette,* August 30, 1810.

46. *Ibid.,* October 31 and November 7, 1810. Brackenridge used this material in the *Views of Louisiana* (1814 ed.), pp. 193-95.

47. H. M. Brackenridge, *Early Discoveries by Spaniards in New Mexico: Containing an Account of the Castles of Cibola, and the Present Appearance of Their Ruins* (Pittsburgh: Henry Miner & Co.,1857), p. 41.

48. Brackenridge, *Recollections,* p. 260.

49. Brackenridge, *Early Discoveries by Spaniards,* p. 41.

50. See the article, "Cantine Mounds, and the Monastery of La Trappe," in *Louisiana Gazette,* January 9 and 31, 1811; *Views of Louisiana* (1814 ed.), pp. 186-89; 287-91.

51. *Louisiana Gazette,* January 24, 1811. Brackenridge incorporated this material in the first two chapters, Book I, of the *Views of Louisiana* (1814 ed.).

52. *Louisiana Gazette,* February 7 and 14, 1811.

53. *Ibid.,* February 14, 1811.

54. *Ibid.,* February 21, 1811.

55. *Ibid.,* February 21, 28; March 7, 1811.

56. *Ibid.,* March 7 and 14, 1811.

57. *Ibid.,* March 14 and 21, 1811.

58. *Ibid.,* April 4 and 11, 1811.

59. *Ibid.,* June 20 and 27, 1811.

60. *Ibid.,* April 18 and 25, 1811.

61. *Ibid.,* October 26, 1811.

62. *Kline's Weekly Carlisle Gazette,* May 24 and 31, 1811.

63. *Niles' Register,* October 12 and December 7, 1811.

64. Herzog to Christian Wilt, Philadelphia, May 23, 1811, Herzog Letterbook (MS in the Missouri Historical Society).

65. Wash to Jefferson, St. Louis, June 20, 1811, in Clarence Edwin Carter (comp. and ed.), *The Territorial Papers of the United States* (Washington: Government Printing Office, 1934-1952), XIV, 455.

Chapter IX: THE RACE TO THE ARIKARA VILLAGE

1. But he wrote No. XI after his return to St. Louis.

2. John Bradbury, *Travels in the Interior of America, in the Years 1809, 1810, and 1811; Including a Description of Upper Louisiana, together with the States of Ohio, Kentucky, Indiana, and Tennessee, with the Illinois and Western Territories, and Containing Remarks and Observations Useful to Persons Emigrating to Those Countries* (2d ed.; London: Sherwood, Neely, and Jones, 1819), p. 18.

3. Washington Irving, *Astoria; or Anecdotes of an Enterprise beyond the Rocky Mountains* (Author's revised ed.; New York: G. P. Putnam, 1865), pp. 42-45.

4. *Ibid.,* pp. 124-32.

5. *Ibid.,* pp. 134-39.

6. *Ibid.,* pp. 140-43.

7. *Louisiana Gazette,* March 14, 1811.

8. Irving, *Astoria,* pp. 143-44; Bradbury, *Travels,* pp. 19-22.

9. Bradbury, *Travels,* pp. 20-21.

10. Brackenridge, *Views of Louisiana* (1814 ed.), p. 4.

11. *Ibid.,* p. 200.

12. "Letter to Walter Forward," p. 278.

13. *Second Quarterly Supplement of the Pittsburgh Saturday Evening Visiter,* January, 1839.

14. *Ibid.*

15. Compare statement in *ibid.,* with the following: ". . . being solicited by this gentleman to accompany him, my wish to visit those countries was so strong, that I did not hesitate. . . ." (*Views of Louisiana,* 1814 ed., p. 4).

16. *Views of Louisiana* (1814 ed.), p. 199.

17. *Ibid.,* pp. 200-201.

18. *Ibid.,* p. 201.

19. *Louisiana Gazette,* April 11, 1811.

20. *Ibid.*

21. Brackenridge, *Views of Louisiana* (1814 ed.), pp. 200-202.

22. *Ibid.,* pp. 202-208.

23. Bradbury, *Travels,* p. 24.

24. *Second Quarterly Supplement of the Pittsburgh Saturday Evening Visiter,* January, 1839.

25. Brackenridge, *Views of Louisiana* (1814 ed.), pp. 208-14.

26. *Ibid.,* pp. 214-18.

27. See his table of distances, printed in *ibid.,* pp. 265-68.

28. *Ibid.,* p. 219.

29. *Ibid.,* pp. 220-24.

30. *Ibid.,* pp. 224-26.

31. *Ibid.,* pp. 227-29.

32. *Ibid.,* pp. 229-33.

33. *Ibid.,* pp. 233-35.

34. *Ibid.,* p. 235.

35. *Ibid.,* pp. 235-38.

36. *Ibid.,* p. 238.

37. Bradbury (*Travels,* p. 105) fixes the day of the meeting as June 3, and Irving (*Astoria,* pp. 191-92) gives it as July 3.

38. Irving, *Astoria,* pp. 175-76, 192; Brackenridge, *Views of Louisiana* (1814 ed.), p. 242 fn.

39. Bradbury, *Travels,* p. 108.

40. Brackenridge, *Views of Louisiana* (1814 ed.), p. 238.

41. *Ibid.,* p. 239.

42. Bradbury, *Travels,* p. 54.

43. Brackenridge, *Views of Louisiana* (1814 ed.), p. 240.

44. *Ibid.,* pp. 241-42; Bradbury, *Travels,* pp. 110-12; Irving, *Astoria,* pp. 193-94.

45. Bradbury, *Travels,* pp. 113-14.

46. *Ibid.,* p. 116; Brackenridge, *Views of Louisiana* (1814 ed.), pp. 242-43.

47. Bradbury, *Travels,* p. 118; Brackenridge, *Views of Louisiana* (1814 ed.), pp. 244-45; Irving, *Astoria,* pp. 197-98.

48. Brackenridge, *Views of Louisiana* (1814 ed.), pp. 245-46; Bradbury, *Travels,* pp. 118-23; Irving, *Astoria,* pp. 198-204.

49. Brackenridge, *Views of Louisiana* (1814 ed.), p. 247.

50. Bradbury, *Travels,* p. 124.

51. Brackenridge, *Views of Louisiana* (1814 ed.), p. 249.

52. Bradbury, *Travels,* pp. 129-30.
53. *Ibid.,* pp. 123-34; Brackenridge, *Views of Louisiana* (1814 ed.), pp. 247-58.
54. Bradbury, *Travels,* p. 135.
55. *Ibid.,* pp. 147-48.
56. *Ibid.,* p. 151.
57. Brackenridge, *Views of Louisiana* (1814 ed.), p. 260.
58. Bradbury, *Travels,* pp. 158-60.
59. *Ibid.,* p. 163; Brackenridge, *Views of Louisiana* (1814 ed.), p. 261.
60. Bradbury, *Travels,* p. 164.
61. Brackenridge, *Views of Louisiana* (1814 ed.), pp. 261-62.
62. *Ibid.,* pp. 262-64; Bradbury, *Travels,* pp. 164-98.
63. "List of Letters, Remaining in the Post office St. Louis, La. quarter ending June 30, 1811," in *Louisiana Gazette,* July 11, 25; August 1, 1811.
64. See letter to Charless, in *ibid.,* August 8, 1811.

Chapter X: A MAN OF SOME IMPORTANCE

1. *Travels,* p. vi.
2. *Ibid.,* p. 183.
3. *Louisiana Gazette,* August 8, 1811.
4. September 28, 1811.
5. See news account in *Louisiana Gazette,* October 26, 1811.
6. Irving, *Astoria,* pp. 219-329.
7. For example, see *Niles' Register,* June 26, 1813.
8. See Irving, *Astoria,* pp. v-viii.
9. *Ibid.,* p. 200.
10. *Louisiana Gazette,* June 20, 1811.
11. *Ibid.,* May 30, 1811.
12. Compare Charless' report of the trial in *ibid.,* August 22, 1811, with Brackenridge's own account in his *Recollections,* pp. 242-52.
13. Brackenridge, *Recollections,* pp. 253; 256-57.
14. *Louisiana Gazette,* October 12, 1811.
15. Brackenridge, *Recollections,* p. 267.
16. Gratiot to Poydras, St. Louis, November 3, 1811, Gratiot Letterbook (MS in the Missouri Historical Society).
17. Brackenridge, *Views of Louisiana* (1814 ed.), p. 4.
18. Brackenridge, *Recollections,* p. 267.
19. Bradbury, *Travels,* pp. 199-217.
20. *Louisiana Gazette,* December 21, 1811.
21. H.M.B., "Biography," in *Cramer's Pittsburgh Magazine Almanack, for the Year of Our Lord 1816* (Pittsburgh: Cramer, Spear, and Eichbaum, [1816]), p. 65.
22. Brackenridge, *Views of Louisiana* (1814 ed.), p. 4.
23. *Ibid.,* p. 3.
24. *Ibid.,* pp. 3-4.
25. *Ibid.,* pp. 6-7.
26. *Ibid.,* p. 7.
27. *Ibid.,* p. 4.
28. *Ibid.,* p. 7.
29. *Ibid.,* p. 198.

30. *Ibid.*, p. 6.

31. *Ibid.*, p. 5.

32. *Ibid.*, p. 32.

33. *Ibid.*, p. 198.

34. *Ibid.*, p. 258.

35. *Ibid.*, p. 139.

36. *Ibid.*, p. 146.

37. *Ibid.*, p. 227.

38. H.M.B., "Biography," pp. 64-65.

39. See, for example, the sixth edition, published in 1808.

40. *Commonwealth*, August 25, 1812.

41. Brackenridge, *Views of Louisiana* (1814 ed.), p. 2.

42. *Commonwealth*, February 23, 1814.

43. See "DEATHS," in *Cramer's Pittsburgh Magazine Almanack, for the Year of Our Lord 1816*, p. 72.

44. H.M.B., "Biography," p. 65.

45. *Ibid.*

46. *A Geographical Description of the State of Louisiana: Presenting a View of the Soil, Climate, Animal, Vegetable, and Mineral Productions; Illustrative of Its Natural Physiognomy, Its Geographical Configuration, and Relative Situation: With an Account of the Character and Manners of the Inhabitants. Being an Accompaniment to the Map of Louisiana* (Philadelphia: John Melish, 1816), p. iv.

47. Published in New York by James Olmstead, 1817.

48. For the whole story, see *Niles' Register*, October 18 and November 22, 1817.

49. Joseph Sabin (comp.), *A Dictionary of Books Relating to America, from Its Discovery to the Present Time* (New York: J. Sabin & Sons, 1869), II, 387, no. 7178.

50. XXXII (July, 1819), 241.

51. Jefferson to Brackenridge, Monticello, March 16, 1814, Jefferson Papers (MSS in the Library of Congress, Washington, D. C.), CC, 35698. The document is a polygraphic copy.

52. Brackenridge to Jefferson, Baton Rouge, May 30, 1814, in *ibid.*, CCI, 35786-87.

Chapter XI: GRASS IN THE STREETS OF NEW ORLEANS

1. "Letter to Walter Forward," p. 278.

2. Duyckinck and Duyckinck, *Cyclopaedia*, I, 669.

3. "Letter to Walter Forward," p. 278.

4. *Ibid.*, pp. 278-79.

5. *Ibid.*, p. 279.

6. *Ibid.*

7. In *Transactions of the American Philosophical Society, Held at Philadelphia, for Promoting Useful Knowledge* (Philadelphia: A. Small, 1818), New Series, I, 151-59.

8. September 20, 1813, Jefferson Papers (MSS in the Library of Congress), CXCIX, 35458. (Polygraphic copy.)

9. See Part 3, *Proceedings of the American Philosophical Society Held at Philadelphia for Promoting Useful Knowledge* (Philadelphia: M'Calla & Stavely, 1885), XXII, 441.

10. *Ibid.*, XXII, 452.

11. XI (April, 1818), 311.

12. *Analectic Magazine*, XI, 319.

13. Supplement to Volume XVI [March to September, 1819], pp. 89-91.

14. H. M. Brackenridge to John Graham, New Orleans, March 20, 1814, General Records of the Department of State, Miscellaneous Letters (MSS in the National Archives, Washington, D. C.).

15. "Letter to Walter Forward," p. 280.

16. In Shaler Papers (MSS in the Historical Society of Pennsylvania, Philadelphia).

17. Baton Rouge, December 8, 1813, in *ibid.*

18. Brackenridge to Shaler, Baton Rouge, December 16, 1813, in *ibid.*

19. *Ibid.*

20. New Orleans, March 20, 1814, General Records of the Department of State, Miscellaneous Letters (MSS in the National Archives).

21. Brackenridge to Shaler, Baton Rouge, December 16, 1813, Shaler Papers (MSS in the Historical Society of Pennsylvania).

22. H. Yoakum, *History of Texas from Its First Settlement in 1685 to Its Annexation to the United States in 1846* (New York: Redfield, 1855), I, 175 fn.

23. Everett S. Brown (ed.), "Letters from Louisiana, 1813-1814," in *Mississippi Valley Historical Review,* XI (March, 1925), 570-79.

24. *Ibid.,* p. 579.

25. *Ibid.,* p. 571.

26. *Ibid.,* p. 573.

27. "Letter to Walter Forward," pp. 279-80.

28. *Ibid.,* p. 280.

29. In General Records of the Department of State, Miscellaneous Letters (MSS in the National Archives).

30. Baton Rouge, October 30, 1813, in *ibid.*

31. Baton Rouge, December 16, 1813, Shaler Papers (MSS in the Historical Society of Pennsylvania).

32. Brackenridge to John Graham, New Orleans, March 20, 1814, General Records of the Department of State, Miscellaneous Letters (MSS in the National Archives).

33. *Ibid.*

34. "Letter to Walter Forward," p. 280.

35. H. M. Brackenridge, *Views of Louisiana; Containing Geographical, Statistical and Historical Notices of That Vast and Important Portion of America* (Baltimore: Schaeffer & Maund, 1817), p. 8.

36. Duyckinck and Duyckinck, *Cyclopaedia,* I, 669.

37. *The Pittsburgh Directory for 1815: Containing the Names, Professions, and Residence of the Heads of Families and Persons in Business, in the Borough of Pittsburgh, with an Appendix, Containing a Variety of Useful Information* (Pittsburgh: James M. Riddle, 1815), p. 13.

38. Brown, *Butler County,* p. 158.

39. *Recollections of the Last Ten Years, Passed in Occasional Residences and Journeyings in the Valley of the Mississippi, from Pittsburg and the Missouri to the Gulf of Mexico, and from Florida to the Spanish Frontier; in a Series of Letters to The Rev. James Flint, of Salem, Massachusetts* (Boston: Cummings, Hilliard, and Company, 1826), p. 13.

40. *Ibid.,* p. 16.

41. *Ibid.,* pp. 17-18.

42. September 16, 1811.

43. *Commonwealth,* February 18, 1815.

44. See the advance notice in *ibid.,* February 11, 1815.

45. In *ibid.,* March 4, 1815.

Chapter XII: THE GARRET

1. Pp. 37-39.
2. Pp. 63-66.
3. "Letter to Walter Forward," pp. 280-81.
4. *Federal Gazette & Baltimore Daily Advertiser,* February 13, 1815.
5. *Ibid.,* February 27, 1815.
6. Signed "H.M.B." in *ibid.,* September 11, 1815.
7. The cornerstone of the Washington Monument was laid July 4, 1815.
8. "Letter to Walter Forward," p. 281.
9. See Peale's notice in *Federal Gazette & Baltimore Daily Advertiser,* August 2, 1815.
10. *Ibid.,* June 12, 1816.
11. "Letter to Walter Forward," pp. 282-84.
12. *Ibid.,* p. 284.
13. See preface to the second edition, an 1816 copy of which is reprinted in Thwaites, *Early Western Travels,* VI, 21-166.
14. In *ibid.,* VI, 42-43 fn. Compare with version in *Second Quarterly Supplement of the Pittsburgh Saturday Evening Visiter,* January, 1839.
15. IV (November, 1816), 114.
16. *North-American Review and Miscellaneous Journal,* IV, 117.
17. VII (February, 1816), 142.
18. *Analectic Magazine, and Naval Chronicle,* VII, 148.
19. *Ibid.,* VII, 142-43.
20. June 8, 1816.
21. In *Niles' Register,* June 22, 1816. Compare with version printed in Brackenridge's *Views of Louisiana* (1817 ed.), pp. 316-23.
22. H. H. Brackenridge to Alexander Brackenridge, Carlisle, February 27, 1816, Dreer Collection-American Lawyers (MSS in the Historical Society of Pennsylvania).
23. *Kline's Weekly Carlisle Gazette,* June 26, 1816.
24. Baltimore, November 10, 1816, Thomas Butler and Family Papers (MSS in the Department of Archives, Louisiana State University, Baton Rouge, La.).
25. "Biographical Notice," p. 188.
26. Brackenridge's Last Will and Testament, Office of Register of Wills, Cumberland County, Pa. Will Book H, p. 407.
27. Brackenridge to Butler, Baltimore, November 10, 1816, Thomas Butler and Family Papers (MSS in Department of Archives, Louisiana State University).
28. *History of the Western Insurrection,* p. 77.
29. "Biographical Notice," p. 188.
30. Pittsburgh, September 24, 1816, Henry Marie Brackenridge Letterbook (MSS in the Darlington Memorial Library, University of Pittsburgh. Hereafter cited as Brackenridge Letterbook.).
31. "Letter to Walter Forward," p. 281.
32. *Federal Gazette & Baltimore Daily Advertiser,* September 28, 1816.
33. "Letter to Walter Forward," p. 282.
34. Sixth ed.; Philadelphia: James Kay, Jun. and Brother, 1839, pp. 27-28.
35. *Life of Andrew Jackson* (New York: Mason Brothers, 1861), I, 564-65.
36. *Ibid.,* I, xvi.
37. Paris, January 25, 1820, in *Niles' Register,* April 1, 1820.
38. In *ibid.*
39. "Letter to Walter Forward," pp. 281-82.

40. Pittsburgh, October 28, 1816, in Brackenridge Letterbook.

41. Forward to Brackenridge, Pittsburgh, September 24, 1816, in *ibid.*

42. Baltimore, November 10, 1816, Thomas Butler and Family Papers (MSS in Department of Archives, Louisiana State University).

Chapter XIII: PEREGRINE BOCHINJOCHELUS

1. Carlisle, November 24, 1816, in Brackenridge Letterbook.

2. Carlisle, March 17, 1817, in *ibid.*

3. Archives of the Delphian Club, Year I, pp. 77-78, in Delphian Club Minute Book I (MSS in Maryland Historical Society, Baltimore, Md.).

4. For an excellent account of the club and a description of its records, see John Earle Uhler, "The Delphian Club: A Contribution to the Literary History of Baltimore in the Early Nineteenth Century," in the *Maryland Historical Magazine*, XX (December, 1925), 305-46.

5. See John C. French, "Poe's Literary Baltimore," in *ibid.*, XXXII (June, 1937), 101-12.

6. "End of the Proceedings of Year I of the Delphian Club," in Delphian Club Minute Book I.

7. Session XXII, Delphian Club Minute Book I.

8. Session XXXI, *ibid.*

9. Session XXXIII, *ibid.*

10. Session XXXVI, *ibid.*

11. Session XXXVII, *ibid.*

12. For the questions and the complete answers, see Archives, Session XXXVII, May 10, 1817, in *ibid.*

13. Session XXXIX, *ibid.*, pp. 145-55.

14. *Ibid.*, p. 148.

15. In *ibid.*

16. Brackenridge to Thomas Butler, Baltimore, April 10, 1817, Thomas Butler and Family Papers (MSS in Department of Archives, Louisiana State University).

17. Brackenridge later published it in a collection entitled *Speeches on the Jew Bill, in the House of Delegates of Maryland, by H. M. Brackenridge, Col. W.G.D. Worthington, and John S. Tyson, Esquire. Together with an Argument on the Chancery Powers, and an Eulogy on Thomas Jefferson and John Adams, &c.* (Philadelphia: J. Dobson, 1829), pp. 1-58.

18. *Ibid.*, p. 1.

19. *Ibid.*, p. 13.

20. *Ibid.*, p. 18.

21. Brackenridge to Thomas Butler, Baltimore, April 10, 1817, Thomas Butler and Family Papers (MSS in Department of Archives, Louisiana State University).

22. *Ibid.*

23. Ross to Brackenridge, Pittsburgh, February 15, 1817, in Brackenridge Letterbook.

24. See Alexander to Henry, Pittsburgh, October 23, 1818, in *ibid.*

25. *Ibid.*

26. For the career of Correa, see Joseph Eugene Agan, "Correa da Serra," in the *Pennsylvania Magazine of History and Biography*, XLIX (1925), 1-43.

27. John Francis McDermott believes that this second edition was first issued in 1816, and then reissued in 1817, although he admits having never seen a copy of the earlier issue, or any reference to it. See McDermott's "Henry Marie Brackenridge and His Writings," in the *Western Pennsylvania Historical Magazine*, XX (September, 1937), p. 192. His bibliography is incomplete.

28. Philadelphia: Robert Walsh, 1817, I, 128-48.
29. In Thomas Butler and Family Papers (MSS in Department of Archives, Louisiana State University).
30. May 30, 1817, in Brackenridge Letterbook.
31. Washington, May 6, 1817, in *ibid.*
32. In General Records of the Department of State, Instructions to Consuls, II, 31 (MSS in the National Archives).
33. Session XLV, Delphian Club Minute Book I.
34. Session XLVI, *ibid.*
35. Session XLVII, *ibid.*
36. Session XLVIII, *ibid.*
37. Baltimore, July 16, 1817, in General Records of the Department of State, Special Agents, South American Missions, 1815-18, Vol. I (MSS in the National Archives).
38. See, for example, E.S. Sergeant to Brackenridge, Philadelphia, July 22, 1817, in Brackenridge Letterbook.
39. In *ibid.*
40. Baltimore, July 19, 1817, in General Records of the Department of State, Special Agents, South American Missions, 1815-18, Vol. I (MSS in the National Archives).
41. Washington, July 21, 1817, in General Records of the Department of State, Instructions to Consuls, II, 45 (MSS in the National Archives).
42. Washington, July 21, 1817, in *ibid.,* II, 44.
43. Brackenridge, *Recollections,* pp. 51-52.
44. See M. Young to Brackenridge, Washington, July 22, 1817, in General Records of the Department of State, Instructions to Consuls, II, 62; Brackenridge to Rush, Baltimore, July 23, 1817, in Special Agents, South American Missions, 1815-18, Vol. I (MSS in the National Archives).
45. In Special Agents, South American Missions, 1815-18, Vol. I.
46. See Richard Rush to C. A. Rodney, Washington, July 29, 1817, in General Records of the Department of State, Instructions to Consuls, II, 49 (MSS in the National Archives).
47. *Ibid.*
48. Washington, July 29, 1817, in Brackenridge Letterbook.
49. In *ibid.*
50. Session XLIX, Delphian Club Minute Book I.

Chapter XIV: THE SECRETARY OF THE MISSION TO SOUTH AMERICA (1)

1. "One might even claim that Brackenridge, the pamphleteer, was the first professional student of Latin America in the United States, the forerunner of the *Hispanistas* of our own day." Laura Bornholdt, *Baltimore and Early Pan-Americanism: A Study in the Background of the Monroe Doctrine* (Northampton, Mass.: Smith College, 1949), p. 81.
2. *American Watchman,* July 30, 1817.
3. July 18, 1817, in General Records of the Department of State, Instructions to Consuls, II, 34-39 (MSS in the National Archives). The instructions, the supplementary instruction of November 21, 1817, and letters to be delivered to Thomas Sumpter, the United States minister to the Portuguese Court in Brazil, are printed in William R. Manning (comp. and ed.), *Diplomatic Correspondence of the United States concerning the Independence of the Latin-American Nations* (New York: Oxford University Press, 1925), I, 41-49.
4. Brackenridge to Thomas Butler, New York, August 10, 1817, in Thomas Butler and Family Papers (MSS in Department of Archives, Louisiana State University).

5. *Ibid.*

6. Session LIV, Delphian Club Minute Book II.

7. Brackenridge to Butler, New York, August 10, 1817, in Thomas Butler and Family Papers (MSS in Department of Archives, Louisiana State University).

8. Washington, November 8, 1817, in General Records of the Department of State, Special Agents, South American Missions, 1815-18, Vol. I (MSS in the National Archives).

9. M. Young to Brackenridge, Washington, November 13, 1817, in General Records of the Department of State, Instructions to Consuls, II, 61 (MSS in the National Archives).

10. Dated November 11, 1817, in *ibid.*, II, 62-63.

11. See Daniel Brent to Captain James Biddle, Washington, October 6, 1817, in *ibid.*, II, 60-61.

12. See the statement prefacing the list in *ibid.*, II, 62-63.

13. Biddle to Brackenridge, New York, October 3, 1817, in Brackenridge Letterbook.

14. "Letter to Walter Forward," pp. 285-86.

15. Baltimore, April 21, 1819, in Shaler Papers (MSS in the Historical Society of Pennsylvania).

16. *South America:* A Letter, p. 9.

17. *Ibid.*, p. 4.

18. *Ibid.*, p. 8.

19. *Ibid.*, p. 9.

20. *Ibid.*, p. 10.

21. *Ibid.*, p. 11.

22. *Ibid.*, p. 13.

23. *Ibid.*, p. 14.

24. *Ibid.*, p. 15.

25. *Ibid.*

26. *Ibid.*, p. 22.

27. *Ibid.*, p. 23.

28. *Ibid.*, p. 26.

29. *Ibid.*, p. 32.

30. *Ibid.*, p. 34.

31. *Ibid.*, p. 35.

32. *Ibid.*, p. 36.

33. *Ibid.*, p. 34.

34. *Ibid.*, p. 35.

35. *Ibid.*, p. 37.

36. *Ibid.*, p. 38.

37. *Ibid.*, p. 42.

38. *Ibid.*, p. 46.

39. *Ibid.*, p. 50.

40. Bornholdt, *Baltimore and Early Pan-Americanism*, p. 85.

41. See *ibid.*, p. 27.

42. Bagot to Lord Castlereagh, December 2, 1817, cited in Charles Carroll Griffin, *The United States and the Disruption of the Spanish Empire, 1810-1822: A Study of the Relations of the United States with Spain and with the Rebel Spanish Colonies* (New York: Columbia University Press, 1937), p. 122.

43. See Brackenridge, *Recollections*, Appendix, p. 286.

44. See *ibid.*

45. For brief comment on this work, see Bornholdt, *Baltimore and Early Pan-Americanism,* p. 86 fn.

46. See Brackenridge, *Recollections,* Appendix, p. 286.

47. Philadelphia: J. F. Hurtel, 1817.

48. C****, *Reply to the Author of the Letter,* p. 4.

49. *Ibid.,* p. 7.

50. Washington, October 26, 1817, in Brackenridge Letterbook.

51. *American Watchman,* November 1, 1817, from the *Richmond Enquirer.*

52. See Bornholdt, *Baltimore and Early Pan-Americanism,* pp. 62-63; 75-77.

53. *Niles' Register,* November 15, 1817.

54. *Ibid.*

55. Darlington (comp.), *Reliquiae Baldwinianae: Selections from the Correspondence of the Late William Baldwin, M.D., Surgeon in the U.S. Navy. With Occasional Notes, and a Short Biographical Memoir* (Philadelphia: Kimber and Sharpless, 1843), p. 10.

56. *Ibid.,* p. 13.

57. Baldwin to Darlington, Wilmington, October 30, 1817, in *ibid.,* pp. 244-45.

58. Baldwin to Darlington, Wilmington, November 10, 1817, in *ibid.,* pp. 246-48.

59. Baldwin to Darlington, Norfolk, November 20, 1817, in *ibid.,* p. 250.

60. *Ibid.*

61. Manning, *Diplomatic Correspondence,* I, 42.

62. *Ibid.,* I, 47-49.

63. Session LXV, Delphian Club Minute Book II.

64. *Niles' Register,* November 29, 1817.

65. H. M. Brackenridge, *Voyage to South America, Performed by Order of the American Government, in the Years 1817 and 1818, in the Frigate Congress* (Baltimore: Published by the Author, 1819), I, 101.

66. *American Watchman,* December 17, 1817.

67. *Voyage to South America,* I, 101-102.

68. December 3, 1817, in *Reliquiae Baldwinianae,* p. 252.

Chapter XV: THE SECRETARY OF THE MISSION TO SOUTH AMERICA (2)

1. Baldwin to Darlington, U.S. Ship "Congress," Harbor of Rio de Janeiro, January 30, 1818, in *Reliquiae Baldwinianae,* pp. 252-53; Brackenridge, *Voyage to South America,* I, 103-13.

2. *Voyage to South America,* I, 107.

3. *Ibid.,* I, 115-17.

4. *Ibid.,* I, 117-33.

5. *Ibid.,* I, 134.

6. *Ibid.,* I, 134-40.

7. Baldwin to Darlington, U.S. Ship "Congress," at Sea, February 11, 1818, in *Reliquiae Baldwinianae,* p. 260.

8. *Voyage to South America,* I, 149-53.

9. Rio de Janeiro, February 7, 1818, in Delphian Club Minute Book II, pp. 345-49.

10. For example, see *Niles' Register,* May 23, June 13, June 20, and July 25, 1818.

11. *American Watchman,* May 23, 1818.

12. *Niles' Register,* May 30, 1818.

13. *Voyage to South America,* I, 183-208.

14. *Ibid.,* I, 208-13.

15. *Ibid.,* I, 216-30.
16. *Ibid.,* I, 230-40.
17. *Ibid.,* I, 264-69.
18. *Ibid.,* I, 269-77.
19. In *Reliquiae Baldwinianae,* p. 263.
20. *Voyage to South America,* I, 277-81.
21. *Ibid.,* I, 281-94.
22. *Ibid.,* I, 295-305.
23. *Ibid.,* I, 305-308.
24. *Ibid.,* I, 308-11.
25. *Ibid.,* I, 311-13.
26. *Ibid.,* II, 5-6.
27. *Ibid.,* II, 6-41.
28. *Ibid.,* II, 41-60.
29. *Ibid.,* II, 301-302.
30. *Ibid.,* II, 301.
31. *Ibid.,* II, 60-63.
32. *Ibid.,* II, 301.
33. See the Report on Theodorick Bland, on the Condition of South America in *American State Papers: Foreign Relations,* IV, 291-95.
34. *Voyage to South America,* II, 303-305.
35. *Ibid.,* II, 306-308.
36. *Ibid.,* II, 308-11.
37. In *Reliquiae Baldwinianae,* pp. 272-73.
38. May 30, in *ibid.,* p. 270.
39. *American Watchman,* July 25, 1818.
40. *Niles' Register,* August 22, 1818.
41. Charles Francis Adams (ed.), *Memoirs of John Quincy Adams, Comprising Portions of His Diary from 1795 to 1848* (Philadelphia: J. B. Lippincott & Co., 1874-77), IV, 117.
42. *Ibid.,* IV, 119.
43. Baltimore, April 21, 1819, in Shaler Papers (MSS in the Historical Society of Pennsylvania).
44. *Ibid.*
45. *American Watchman,* July 18, 1818.
46. Read to Brackenridge, New Castle, March 17, 1820, in Brackenridge Letterbook.

Chapter XVI: *IF I ERR, I WILL ERR WITH THEM*

1. J. Q. Adams, *Memoirs,* IV, 117-18.
2. *Ibid.,* IV, 119.
3. *American Watchman,* July 18, 1818.
4. *Ibid.*
5. For example, see items in *Niles' Register,* May 2 and July 18, 1818.
6. *Ibid.,* April 4, 1818.
7. Calvin Colton (ed.), *The Works of Henry Clay, Comprising His Life, Correspondence and Speeches* (New York: G. P. Putnam's Sons, 1904), VI, 138-62.
8. Lexington, August 4, 1818, in Brackenridge Letterbook.
9. See letter in *ibid.*

10. "Letter to Walter Forward," p. 285.

11. See election details in *Niles' Register,* October 10, 1818.

12. Baltimore, April 21, 1819, in Shaler Papers (MSS in the Historical Society of Pennsylvania).

13. *Ibid.*

14. Correa to Brackenridge, Washington, October 12, 1818, in Brackenridge Letterbook.

15. August 14, 1818, in *Reliquiae Baldwinianae,* pp. 278-79.

16. October 23, 1818, in *ibid.,* p. 286.

17. Washington, November 4, 1818, in General Records of the Department of State, Special Agents, South American Missions, 1815-18, Vol. I (MSS in the National Archives).

18. J. Q. Adams, *Memoirs,* IV, 155-56.

19. *Niles' Register,* October 24, 1818.

20. In *American State Papers: Foreign Relations,* IV, 217-24.

21. J. Q. Adams, *Memoirs,* IV, 159.

22. *Niles' Register,* November 14, 1818.

23. J. Q. Adams, *Memoirs,* IV, 27.

24. *Ibid.,* IV, 159.

25. In *American State Papers: Foreign Relations,* IV, 224-27.

26. *American Watchman,* November 28, 1818.

27. In *Pittsburgh Gazette,* December 8, 1818.

28. In *American State Papers: Foreign Relations,* IV, 270-312.

29. J. Q. Adams, *Memoirs,* IV, 388.

30. *American Watchman,* October 17, 1818.

31. *Ibid.,* October 21, 1818.

32. *Ibid.,* November 4 and 7, 1818.

33. *Ibid.,* September 2, 1818.

34. *Ibid.,* September 30, 1818.

35. *Ibid.,* November 18, 1818.

36. Washington, April 28, 1818, in Stanislaus Murray Hamilton (ed.), *The Writings of James Monroe, Including a Collection of His Public and Private Papers and Correspondence Now for the First Time Printed* (New York: G. P. Putnam's Sons, 1898-1903), VI, 50-51.

37. In *American State Papers: Foreign Relations,* IV, 324-48.

38. In *ibid.,* IV, 213-16.

39. See "Sketch of Instructions for Agent for South America—Notes for Department of State," in Monroe, *Writings,* VI, 92-102.

40. *Niles' Register,* November 14 and 21, 1818.

41. See Brackenridge to J. Q. Adams, Baltimore, August 1, 1819, General Records of the Department of State, Miscellaneous Letters (MSS in the National Archives).

42. See *Niles' Register,* October 30, 1819.

43. For the entire story, see the *American Watchman,* November 25, 1818.

44. In *Federal Gazette & Baltimore Daily Advertiser,* November 16, 1818.

45. *American Watchman,* August 25, 1819.

46. "Letter to Walter Forward," p. 285.

47. Greensburg, January 13, 1819, in Brackenridge Letterbook.

48. Brackenridge, *Recollections,* Appendix, p. 291 fn.

49. *Ibid.,* p. 288.

50. For three versions, see *ibid.*, pp. 293-317; *Niles' Register*, May 29, 1819; and Brackenridge, *Speeches on the Jew Bill*, pp. 59-100.

51. *Niles' Register*, Supplement to Vol. XV, pp. 9-10.

52. January 22, 1819, in Brackenridge Letterbook.

53. *Niles' Register*, May 29, 1819.

54. *Sketch of Proceedings in the Legislature of Maryland, December Session, 1818, on What is Commonly Called The Jew Bill; Containing the Report of the Committee Appointed by the House of Delegates "To consider the justice and expediency of extending to those persons professing the Jewish Religion, the same privileges that are enjoyed by Christians:" together with the Bill Reported by the Committee, and the Speeches of Thomas Kennedy, Esq. of Washington County, and H. M. Brackenridge, Esq. of Baltimore City* (Baltimore: Joseph Robinson, 1819).

55. Brackenridge, *Speeches on the Jew Bill*, p. 59 fn.

56. *Niles' Register*, October 14, 1826.

57. *Memoirs*, IV, 388.

58. Baltimore, September 25, 1819, in American Literary Duplicates (MSS in the Historical Society of Pennsylvania).

59. Rodney to Brackenridge, Wilmington, April 4, 1819, in Brackenridge Letterbook.

60. Baltimore, April 21, 1819, in Shaler Papers (MSS in the Historical Society of Pennsylvania).

61. U.S.S. "Franklin," Gibraltar, July 5, 1819, in Brackenridge Letterbook.

62. Clay to Brackenridge, Lexington, August 28, 1819, in *ibid.*

63. *American Watchman*, April 10, 1819.

64. *Niles' Register*, April 17, 1819.

65. *Voyage to South America*, II, 307.

66. *Niles' Register*, October 30, 1819.

67. See Brackenridge to Adams, Baltimore, August 1, 1819, General Records of the Department of State, Miscellaneous Letters (MSS in the National Archives).

68. *Voyage to South America*, I, v.

69. *Ibid.*, I, vi.

70. For a review of this work, see *Analectic Magazine*, XI (January, 1818), 21-23.

71. *Voyage to South America*, I, vii.

72. *Ibid.*, I, viii.

73. *Ibid.*, I, viii-ix.

74. *Ibid.*, I, ix.

75. *Ibid.*, I, x.

76. *Ibid.*, I, xi.

77. *Ibid.*, I, xii.

78. *Ibid.*, I, xv.

79. See the list of errata appended to the first volume.

80. *Voyage to South America*, I, 67 fn.

81. *Ibid.*, I, 168.

82. *Ibid.*, I, 307.

83. *Ibid.*, II, 255.

Chapter XVII: RETURN TO MISSOURI

1. Clay to Brackenridge, Lexington, August 28, 1819, in Brackenridge Letterbook.

2. *American Watchman*, April 17, 1819.

3. Wilmington, July 25, 1819, in Brackenridge Letterbook.

4. See *Niles' Register,* April 13, 1839.

5. Brobson to Brackenridge, Wilmington, August 14, 1819, in Brackenridge Letterbook.

6. May 13, 1819, in *ibid.*

7. Du Ponceau to Brackenridge, Philadelphia, August 7, 1819, in *ibid.*

8. See Pleasonton to Brackenridge, Washington, October 27, 1819, in *ibid.*

9. Washington, October 23, 1821, in *ibid.*

10. Monticello, January 2, 1820, Rodney Collection (MSS in the Historical Society of Delaware, Wilmington, Del.).

11. Annapolis, February 5, 1820, Jefferson Papers (MSS in the Library of Congress), CCXVII, 38694-95.

12. Baltimore: Richard J. Matchett, 1820.

13. J. Q. Adams, *Memoirs,* V, 57.

14. *Strictures,* p. v.

15. *Ibid.,* p. 9.

16. *Ibid.,* p. 34.

17. See *ibid.,* pp. 173-74.

18. *Analectic Magazine,* I (March, 1820), New Series, 190.

19. *Ibid.,* pp. 190-91.

20. Bornholdt, *Baltimore and Early Pan-Americanism,* pp. 103-104.

21. *Ibid.,* pp. 104-105.

22. Rodney to Brackenridge, Wilmington, May 18, 1820, in Brackenridge Letterbook.

23. London, December 4, 1820, in *ibid.*

24. Brackenridge to Rodney, Baltimore, May 15, 1820 (MS in the Missouri Historical Society).

25. See Rush to Brackenridge, London, December 4, 1820, in Brackenridge Letterbook.

26. XCIII (September, 1820), 89-94.

27. Wilmington, August 14, 1819, in Brackenridge Letterbook.

28. Washington, March 7, 1820, in *ibid.*

29. See Clay, *Works,* VI, 238-44.

30. Baltimore, May 15, 1820 (MS in the Missouri Historical Society).

31. Rodney to Brackenridge, Wilmington, May 18, 1820, in Brackenridge Letterbook.

32. Baltimore, May 15, 1820 (MS in the Missouri Historical Society).

33. In James Monroe Papers (MSS in the New York Public Library, New York, N.Y.).

34. Wilmington, July 2, 1820, in Brackenridge Letterbook.

35. See *Niles' Register,* August 14 and October 2, 1824.

36. Wilmington, May 18, 1820, in Brackenridge Letterbook.

37. Brackenridge, *Voyage to South America,* II, 8.

38. Buenos Aires, October 14, 1821, in Brackenridge Letterbook.

39. Baltimore, April 21, 1819, in Shaler Papers (MSS in the Historical Society of Pennsylvania).

40. *Niles' Register,* January 9, 1819.

41. *Ibid.,* August 12, 1820.

42. Baltimore, September 20, 1820 (MS in the Missouri Historical Society).

43. Brackenridge to Shaler, Baltimore, April 21, 1819, in Shaler Papers (MSS in the Historical Society of Pennsylvania).

44. J. Q. Adams, *Memoirs,* IV, 308.

45. Wilmington, July 25, 1819, in Brackenridge Letterbook.

46. Baltimore, August 1, 1819, General Records of the Department of State, Miscellaneous Letters (MSS in the National Archives).

47. J. Q. Adams, *Memoirs*, IV, 408.

48. For example, see *ibid.,* IV, 416, 426.

49. *Ibid.,* IV, 445.

50. Baltimore, September 25, 1819, in American Literary Duplicates (MSS in the Historical Society of Pennsylvania).

51. J. Q. Adams, *Memoirs*, IV, 413.

52. *Ibid.*

53. *Ibid.,* V, 56-57.

54. David Hoffman to Brackenridge, Baltimore, November 15, 1819, in Brackenridge Letterbook.

55. Session CVIII, Delphian Club Minute Book III.

56. Session CXVI, *ibid.*

57. For the life of Neal and the essays conveniently reprinted with notes, see Fred Lewis Pattee (ed.), *American Writers: A Series of Papers Contributed to Blackwood's Magazine (1824-1825) by John Neal* (Durham: Duke University Press, 1937). For the material on Brackenridge, see pp. 41-42.

58. Session CXVII, Delphian Club Minute Book III.

59. In Archives, Session CXVII. *ibid.*

60. Session CXVIII, *ibid.*

61. Baldwin to Darlington, Philadelphia, March 14, 1819, in *Reliquiae Baldwinianae,* p. 305.

62. Obituary in *American Watchman,* October 13, 1819.

63. West Chester, September 16, 1843, in Brackenridge Letterbook.

64. Baltimore, July 15, 1819, in American Historians (MSS in the Historical Society of Pennsylvania).

65. See Pinkney, Jr. to Brackenridge, Baltimore, September 12, 1819, in Brackenridge Letterbook.

66. Cornelia to Henry, Carlisle, [?], in *ibid.*

67. Carlisle, March 15, 1820, in *ibid.*

68. Carlisle, June 23, 1820, in *ibid.*

69. Baltimore, September 20, 1820 (MS in the Missouri Historical Society).

70. *St. Louis Enquirer,* October 7, 1820.

Chapter XVIII: ANDREW JACKSON'S PRIVATE SECRETARY

1. Brackenridge, *Recollections,* p. 267.

2. *Ibid.,* p. 269.

3. For the statistics on St. Louis, see John A. Paxton (ed.), *The St. Louis Directory and Register, Containing the Names, Professions, and Residence of All the Heads of Families and Persons in Business; together with Descriptive Notes on St. Louis; the Constitution of the U. States, and State of Missouri; with Other Useful Information* (St. Louis: Printed for the Publisher, 1821).

4. See *Missouri Gazette & Public Advertiser,* August 16, 1820.

5. *Ibid.,* October 4, 1820.

6. Brackenridge, *Recollections,* p. 268.

7. For their names, see Paxton, *St. Louis Directory and Register.*

8. In *St. Louis Enquirer,* November 18, 1820; *Missouri Gazette & Public Advertiser,* November 22, 1820.

9. Brackenridge, *Recollections,* pp. 269-71. A John Mullanphy advertised two houses for rent—one a new brick and the other a two-story stone almost finished—in the *Missouri Gazette & Public Advertiser,* August 9, 1820; and a plantation for rent in the issue of December 20, 1820. Possibly Brackenridge's Melanthy and this John Mullanphy were the same person. Neither name, however, is listed in Paxton's directory.

10. Brackenridge, *Recollections,* pp. 271-72.

11. Flint, *Recollections of the Last Ten Years,* p. 184.

12. *Ibid.,* pp. 184-85.

13. See *Missouri Gazette & Public Advertiser,* July 19 and 26, 1820.

14. In *St. Louis Enquirer,* December 23, 1820.

15. *Ibid.*

16. Brackenridge, *Sixty Years in the North and Twenty Years in the South,* pp. 29-30.

17. See Thomas Hart Benton, *Thirty Years' View; or, A History of the Working of the American Government for Thirty Years, from 1820 to 1850* (New York: D. Appleton and Company, 1854-56), I, 9.

18. See editorial in *St. Louis Enquirer,* April 28, 1821.

19. Washington, February 8, 1821, in Brackenridge Letterbook.

20. Obituary in *St. Louis Enquirer,* January 6, 1821.

21. January 30, 1821, in Brackenridge Letterbook.

22. Significantly, Floyd's bill and the committee report accompanying it were printed in the *St. Louis Enquirer,* April 21, 1821, with an editorial advocating the occupation and settlement of the Columbia River.

23. *Ibid.,* March 3, 1821.

24. In Brackenridge Letterbook.

25. Brackenridge, *Sixty Years in the North and Twenty Years in the South,* p. 31 fn.

26. Benton, *Thirty Years' View* I, 10.

27. *St. Louis Enquirer,* March 24, 1821.

28. Duyckinck and Duyckinck, *Cyclopaedia,* I, 670.

29. "List of Letters Remaining in the Post Office at St. Louis, Mo., June 30, 1821," in *St. Louis Enquirer,* July 7, 1821.

30. *American Watchman,* November 27, 1819.

31. Lexington, August 28, 1819, in Brackenridge Letterbook.

32. For the treaty and ratifications, see *American State Papers: Foreign Relations,* V, 127-33.

33. Washington, January 24, 1821, in John Spencer Bassett (ed.), *Correspondence of Andrew Jackson* (Washington: Carnegie Institution of Washington, 1926-35), III, 38.

34. J. Q. Adams, *Memoirs,* V, 322.

35. "Hermitage," February 11, 1821, in Jackson, *Correspondence,* III, 39.

36. See Jackson to Brigadier General John Coffee, "Hermitage," March 1, 1821, in *ibid.,* III, 40-41.

37. Jackson to Monroe, "Hermitage," February 11, 1821, in *ibid.,* III, 39.

38. Washington, March 12, 1821, in *American State Papers: Foreign Relations,* IV, 750-52.

39. In *ibid.,* IV, 752.

40. *Niles' Register,* March 17, 1821.

41. Nashville, April 2, 1821, in *American State Papers: Foreign Relations,* IV, 755.

42. In *ibid.,* IV, 756.

43. May 5, 1821.

44. Duyckinck and Duyckinck, *Cyclopaedia,* I, 670.

45. Parton, *Jackson,* II, 615.

46. Duyckinck and Duyckinck, *Cyclopaedia*, I, 670.

47. Parton, *Jackson*, II, 595.

48. *Niles' Register*, May 26, 1821.

49. Jackson to Adams, New Orleans, April 24, 1821, in *American State Papers: Foreign Relations*, IV, 756.

50. Livingston to Jackson, New Orleans, May 14, 1821, in Jackson, *Correspondence*, III, 56.

51. *Niles' Register*, May 26, 1821.

52. See Rachel Jackson to Eliza Kingsley, West Florida, June 21, 1821, in Parton, *Jackson*, II, 597.

53. Jackson to Adams, Blakely, May 1, 1821, in *American State Papers: Foreign Relations*, IV, 756-57.

54. *Ibid.*

55. For these and other documents relating to the mission, see *ibid.*, IV, 757-60. Note especially the report of Dr. Bronaugh and Brackenridge to Jackson, dated Blakely, May 7, 1821.

56. For the documents pertaining to Forbes' assignment, see *ibid.*, IV, 740-49.

57. See Jackson to Adams, Blakely, May 7, 1821, in *ibid.*, IV, 758.

58. May 22, 1821, in Jackson, *Correspondence*, III, 58.

59. *Ibid.*, III, 54.

60. *Ibid.*, III, 55-56.

61. See Rachel Jackson to Eliza Kingsley, West Florida, June 21, 1821, in Parton, *Jackson*, II, 597.

62. In Jackson, *Correspondence*, III, 62-65.

63. For this correspondence, see *American State Papers: Foreign Relations*, IV, 760-62.

64. Montpelier, May 22, 1821, in Jackson, *Correspondence*, III, 59.

65. In *American State Papers: Foreign Relations*, IV, 753-54.

66. See Adams to Jackson, Washington, May 23, 1821, in *ibid.*, IV, 754.

67. Washington, May 23, 1821, in Monroe, *Writings*, VI, 180-85.

68. Fromentin to Adams, Pensacola, October 28, 1821, in *American State Papers: Miscellaneous*, II, 844.

69. Montpelier, June 9, 1821, in Jackson, *Correspondence*, III, 65.

70. Montpelier, June 13, 1821, in *American State Papers: Foreign Relations*, IV, 763.

71. See Jackson to Adams, Montpelier, June 10, 1821, in *ibid.*, IV, 762.

72. See Jackson to Adams, Manuel's, June 29, 1821, in *ibid.*, IV, 763-64.

73. West Florida, June 21, 1821, in Parton, *Jackson*, II, 597.

74. Pensacola, June 22, 1821, in Jackson, *Correspondence*, III, 74-75.

75. Pensacola, June 30, 1821, in *ibid.*, III, 84.

76. In *ibid.*, III, 85.

77. In *ibid.*, III, 90-91.

78. Manuel's, July 8, 1821, in Brackenridge Letterbook.

79. See Jackson to Andrew J. Donelson, Manuel's, July 3, 1821, in Jackson, *Correspondence*, III, 87.

80. Pensacola, July 11, 1821, in *ibid.*, III, 92.

81. Jackson to Callava, Manuel's, July 12, 1821, in *ibid.*, III, 92-94.

82. Pensacola, July 13, 1821, in *ibid.*, III, 94-98.

83. Galvez Spring, July 13, 1821, in *ibid.*, III, 98.

84. In *ibid.*, III, 100.

85. In *ibid.*, III, 100-101.

86. *Ibid.*, III, 101-103.

87. Galvez Spring, July 16, 1821, in *ibid.*, III, 103-104.

88. Rachel Jackson to Eliza Kingsley, Pensacola, July 23, 1821, in Parton, *Jackson,* II, 604.

89. For description of the ceremony, see *Niles' Register,* August 25, 1821.

90. For the procès-verbal, see *American State Papers: Foreign Relations,* IV, 764-65.

91. "Act of Cession of East Florida," St. Augustine, July 10, 1821, in *ibid.*, IV, 749-50.

Chapter XIX: THE ALCALDE OF PENSACOLA

1. Pensacola, July 18, 1821, in Jackson, *Correspondence,* III, 105.

2. See Jackson to Adams, Pensacola, July 17, 1821, in *American State Papers: Foreign Relations,* IV, 764.

3. Pensacola, July 30, 1821, in *American State Papers: Miscellaneous,* II, 900.

4. See "A list of appointments by his Excellency Governor JACKSON," in the *Floridian,* August 18, 1821.

5. In *American State Papers: Miscellaneous,* II, 902-904.

6. Dated Pensacola, July 30, 1821, in *ibid.*, II, 896-901.

7. In *ibid.*, II, 904-905.

8. Pensacola, July 30, 1821, in *ibid.*, II, 900.

9. In *ibid.*, II, 905.

10. *Ibid.*, II, 906-907.

11. *Ibid.*, II, 907-908.

12. *Ibid.*, II, 905-906.

13. Jackson to Adams, Pensacola, July 30, 1821, in *ibid.*, II, 900.

14. In *Floridian,* September 8, 1821.

15. David Yancey Thomas, *A History of Military Government in Newly Acquired Territory of the United States* (New York: Columbia University Press, 1904), p. 75. For a criticism of Thomas's argument, see John Spencer Bassett, *The Life of Andrew Jackson* (2d ed., 2 vols. in 1; New York: The Macmillan Company, 1928), pp. 316-17.

16. Pensacola, July 30, 1821, in *American State Papers: Miscellaneous,* II, 901.

17. Rachel Jackson to Eliza Kingsley, Pensacola, July 23, 1821, in Parton, *Jackson,* II, 604.

18. *Ibid.*, II, 605-606.

19. In *Floridian,* September 22, 1821.

20. Rachel Jackson to Eliza Kingsley, Pensacola, July 23, 1821, in Parton, *Jackson,* II, 605.

21. See notice in *Floridian,* September 8, 1821.

22. *Ibid.*, October 8, 1821.

23. See notice in *ibid.*, August 18, 1821.

24. *Ibid.*, August 18, 1821.

25. See Allen's notice in *ibid.*, October 8, 1821.

26. See notices in *ibid.*, August 18, September 8, and October 8, 1821.

27. *Ibid.*, October 22, 1821.

28. *Ibid.*, September 1, 1821.

29. *Ibid.*, September 15, 1821.

30. *Ibid.*, November 5, 1821.

31. *Ibid.*, August 18, 1821.

32. *Ibid.*, September 8, 1821.

33. August 18, 1821.

34. In *American State Papers: Miscellaneous*, II, 909.

35. *Niles' Register*, September 15, 1821.

36. Affidavit of Mercedes Vidal, August 23, 1821, in *American State Papers: Foreign Relations*, IV, 784-85; Brackenridge to Jackson, Pensacola, August 24, 1821, in *American State Papers: Miscellaneous*, II, 811-12; and Affidavit of H. M. Brackenridge, October 22, 1821, in *ibid.*, II, 828-31.

37. In *American State Papers: Foreign Relations*, IV, 779.

38. Pensacola, August 21, 1821, in *ibid.*

39. See Walton, Brackenridge, and Miller to Jackson, Pensacola, August 22, 1821, in *ibid.*, IV, 779-80.

40. *Ibid.*, IV, 780.

41. *Ibid.*

42. *Ibid.*, IV, 780-81.

43. See Brackenridge's affidavit, October 22, 1821.

44. Jackson to Miller and Butler, August 22, 1821, in *American State Papers: Foreign Relations*, IV, 781.

45. Brackenridge's affidavit, October 22, 1821.

46. In *American State Papers: Foreign Relations*, IV, 781-82.

47. See Dade to Jackson, Pensacola, September 25, 1821, in *American State Papers: Miscellaneous*, II, 824.

48. Brackenridge's affidavit, October 22, 1821.

49. Affidavit of John Coppinger Connor, October 3, 1821, in *American State Papers: Miscellaneous*, II, 825.

50. Order to Butler and Bronaugh, August 22, 1821, in *American State Papers: Foreign Relations*, IV, 782.

51. Brackenridge's affidavit, October 22, 1821; report of Butler and Bronaugh to Jackson, August 22, 1821, in *American State Papers: Foreign Relations*, IV, 782-83; and Bronaugh to Jackson, Pensacola, August 23, 1821, in Jackson, *Correspondence*, III, 112.

52. In *American State Papers: Foreign Relations*, IV, 783.

53. In *ibid.*, IV, 782.

54. See order in *ibid.*

55. Brackenridge's affidavit, October 22, 1821.

56. Report of Butler and Bronaugh to Jackson, August 22, 1821, in *American State Papers: Foreign Relations*, IV, 783.

57. Brackenridge's affidavit, October 22, 1821.

58. Minutes of the examination of Colonel Callava and Fullarat, August 22, 1821, in *American State Papers: Foreign Relations*, IV, 783-84.

59. Brackenridge's affidavit, October 22, 1821.

60. *Ibid.*

61. *Ibid.*

62. *Ibid.*

63. Order for the imprisonment of Domingo Sousa, Colonel José Callava, and Antoine Fullarat, August 22, 1821, in *American State Papers: Foreign Relations*, IV, 784.

64. Parton, *Jackson*, II, 632.

65. Pensacola, August 23, 1821, in *American State Papers: Foreign Relations*, IV, 784.

66. August 23, 1821, in *ibid.*, IV, 785.

67. See return of Walton, Miller, Shannon, and Brownjohn to the search warrant, August 23, 1821, and Brackenridge's receipt to Walton for the documents, August 25, 1821, in *ibid.*, IV, 785-86.

68. Parton, *Jackson*, II, 616-17.

69. For Fromentin's commission, see *American State Papers: Miscellaneous*, II, 833.

70. See Fromentin to J. Q. Adams, Pensacola, August 12, 1821, in *ibid.*

71. See Fromentin to Adams, Pensacola, August 20, 1821, in *ibid.*, II, 833-34.

72. Fromentin to Adams, Pensacola, August 26, 1821, in *ibid.*, II, 834.

73. *Ibid.*

74. In *ibid.*, II, 809-810.

75. August 23, 1821, in *American State Papers: Foreign Relations*, IV, 785-86.

76. August 24, 1821, in *ibid.*, IV, 786.

77. *Jackson*, II, 617.

78. *Niles' Register*, November 3, 1821.

Chapter XX: JUDGE BRACKENRIDGE OF WEST FLORIDA

1. August 23, 1821, in *American State Papers: Miscellaneous*, II, 810.

2. Pensacola, August 26, 1821, in *ibid.*, II, 835.

3. Pensacola, August 23, 1821, in *ibid.*, II, 836.

4. See Fromentin to Adams, Pensacola, August 26, 1821, in *ibid.*, II, 835.

5. Jackson to Adams, Pensacola, August 26, 1821, in Jackson, *Correspondence*, III, 115.

6. Pensacola, August 26, 1821, in *American State Papers: Miscellaneous*, II, 835.

7. August 24, 1821, in *ibid.*, II, 810.

8. Jackson to Fromentin, Pensacola, August 25, 1821, in *ibid.*, II, 842.

9. In *ibid.*, II, 820.

10. *Ibid.*

11. *Ibid.*, II, 821.

12. *Ibid.*

13. Fromentin to Adams, Pensacola, August 31, 1821, in *ibid.*, II, 837.

14. Fromentin to Adams, Pensacola, September 6 and 8, 1821, in *ibid.*, II, 838-41.

15. Fromentin to Adams, Pensacola, October 28, 1821, in *ibid.*, II, 844-48.

16. Washington, October 26, 1821, in *ibid.*, II, 848.

17. Oak Hill, Loudon County, Virginia, September 16, 1821, in Jackson, *Correspondence*, VI, 475-77.

18. Philadelphia, October 6, 1821, in *American State Papers: Foreign Relations*, IV, 767-68.

19. Adams to Jackson, Washington, October 26, 1821, in Jackson, *Correspondence*, III, 126.

20. In *American State Papers: Foreign Relations*, IV, 776-77.

21. In *Floridian*, October 22, 1821.

22. *Ibid.*

23. See their statement, dated August 24, 1821, in *American State Papers: Foreign Relations*, IV, 786-87.

24. In *ibid.*, IV, 777-79.

25. Pensacola, August 26, 1821, in Jackson, *Correspondence*, III, 112-16.

26. In *Floridian*, September 29, 1821.

27. *Ibid.*, October 8, 1821.

28. Pensacola, September 30, 1821, in *American State Papers: Miscellaneous*, II, 813.

29. *Floridian,* September 29, 1821.

30. In *Ibid.*

31. *Ibid.,* October 8, 15, and 22, 1821.

32. *Ibid.,* September 29, 1821.

33. *Ibid.,* November 5 and December 10, 1821; April 13, 1822.

34. See *Niles' Register,* September 29, October 6 and 27, November 3, 1821.

35. *Ibid.,* October 27, 1821.

36. September 22, 1821.

37. Philadelphia, October 3, 1821, in *American State Papers: Foreign Relations,* IV, 768-76.

38. Washington, November 2, 1821, in *ibid.,* IV, 787-88.

39. Joaquin de Anduaga to Adams, Philadelphia, November 14, 1821, in *ibid.,* IV, 788.

40. Joaquin de Anduaga to Adams, Philadelphia, November 18, 1821, in *ibid.,* IV, 789.

41. In *American State Papers: Miscellaneous,* II, 823-26.

42. In *ibid.,* II, 820-23.

43. Nashville, November 13, 1821, in Jackson, *Correspondence,* III, 126-29.

44. In *American State Papers: Miscellaneous,* II, 826-28.

45. Washington, January 1, 1822, in *ibid.,* II, 832.

46. Adams to Joaquin de Anduaga, Washington, April 15, 1822, in *American State Papers: Foreign Relations,* IV, 802-807.

47. See Joaquin de Anduaga to Adams, Philadelphia, April 26, 1822, in *ibid.,* IV, 808.

48. In *American State Papers: Miscellaneous,* II, 850.

49. Order in *ibid.*

50. Certificate in *ibid.,* II, 851.

51. *Floridian,* September 22, 1821.

52. Proceedings in *American State Papers: Miscellaneous,* II, 852-53.

53. Petition in *ibid.,* II, 853.

54. Plea and petition in *ibid.,* II, 853, 854.

55. Proceedings in *ibid.,* II, 854-55.

56. In *ibid.,* II, 814-18.

57. See *Floridian,* September 15, 1821.

58. John Coppinger Connor to F. H. Nisbet, J. De la Rua, and William Davidson, Pensacola, September 17, 1821, in *American State Papers: Miscellaneous,* II, 818.

59. Order to auditors in *ibid.,* II, 854.

60. See *ibid.,* II, 855-65.

61. Decision, dated October 8, 1821, in *ibid.,* II, 867.

62. In *Floridian,* October 15, 1821.

63. In *American State Papers: Miscellaneous,* II, 865-67.

64. In *ibid.,* II, 873-75.

65. Sum used by Parton in *Jackson,* II, 639.

66. See Thomas, *Military Government,* p. 84; Bassett, *Jackson,* p. 310; Marquis James, *Andrew Jackson: The Border Captain* (Indianapolis: The Bobbs-Merrill Company, 1933), p. 414, fn. 15.

67. Pensacola, August 25, 1821, in Parton, *Jackson,* II, 610.

68. *Floridian,* October 8, 1821.

69. Pensacola, October 5, 1821, in Jackson, *Correspondence,* III, 122-24.

NOTES

70. In *Floridian,* October 8, 1821, and reprinted in *Niles' Register,* November 10, 1821.

71. *Niles' Register,* November 10, 1821.

72. See H. M. Brackenridge, *Judge Brackenridge's Letters* (Washington, 1832), pp. 8-9.

73. In *American State Papers: Miscellaneous,* II, 909-11.

74. Adams to Jackson, Washington, August 20, 1821, in *American State Papers: Foreign Relations,* IV, 754-55.

75. *Floridian,* October 8, 1821.

76. *Ibid.,* October 15, 1821.

77. October 8, 1821, in *Judge Brackenridge's Letters,* p. 6

78. *Floridian,* December 10, 1821.

79. Jackson to Monroe, "Hermitage," November 14, 1821, and Jackson to R. K. Call, "Hermitage," November 15, 1821, in Jackson, *Correspondence,* III, 129-31.

80. Pensacola, November 4, 1821 (MS in the Missouri Historical Society).

81. Washington, December 30, 1821, in Jackson, *Correspondence,* III, 142.

82. See *American State Papers: Miscellaneous,* II, 799-801.

83. January 22, 1822, in Jackson, *Correspondence,* III, 143.

84. In *American State Papers: Foreign Relations,* IV, 793-96.

85. February 8, 1822, in Jackson, *Correspondence,* III, 145-48.

86. Monroe to Calhoun, Highland near Milton, September 24, 1821, in Monroe, *Writings,* VI, 198-201.

87. In *American State Papers: Foreign Relations,* IV, 736-40.

88. Washington, February 16, 1822, in Jackson, *Correspondence,* III, 151.

89. Parton, *Jackson,* II, 640-42.

90. Nashville, in Jackson, *Correspondence,* III, 105-106.

91. *Judge Brackenridge's Letters,* p. 8.

92. *Ibid.,* p. 9.

93. *Floridian,* September 22, 1821.

94. Pensacola, October 29, 1821, in *American State Papers: Miscellaneous,* II, 896.

95. Pensacola, December 20, 1821, in American Historians (MSS in the Historical Society of Pennsylvania).

96. Washington, January 23, 1822, in Brackenridge Letterbook.

97. Pensacola, December 20, 1821, in American Historians (MSS in the Historical Society of Pennsylvania).

98. Pensacola, December 10, 1821, in Mitten Collection (MSS in the Indiana Historical Society, William Henry Smith Memorial Library, Indianapolis, Indiana).

99. Pensacola, December 20, 1821, in American Historians (MSS in the Historical Society of Pennsylvania).

100. See Jackson to Brackenridge, "Hermitage," November 22, 1821 (MS in possession of Mrs. Helen Brackenridge Painter, Washington, Pennsylvania); letter printed in *Judge Brackenridge's Letters,* p. 7.

101. Jackson to Bronaugh, "Hermitage," July 18, 1822, in Jackson, *Correspondence,* III, 169.

102. See *Floridian,* November 5, 1821.

103. See *American State Papers: Foreign Relations,* IV, 800-802; *Floridian,* March 30, 1822.

104. See Brackenridge to Rodney, Pensacola, December 30, 1821, in Simon Gratz Collection (MSS in the Historical Society of Pennsylvania).

105. For some notices of their cases, see the *Floridian,* January 7 and February 4, 1822.

413

106. June 8, 1822.
107. *Floridian,* July 20, 1822.
108. *Ibid.,* July 27, 1822.
109. Washington, in Brackenridge Letterbook.
110. July 20, 1822.
111. August 24, 1822.
112. *Floridian,* July 27, 1822.

Chapter XXI: *FREEDONIA*

1. Carlisle, May 18, 1821 (MS in possession of Mrs. Painter).
2. July 20, 1822.
3. *Floridian,* April 27, 1822.
4. *Ibid.,* April 6, 1822.
5. *Ibid.,* June 8, 1822.
6. *Ibid.*
7. *Ibid.,* August 10, 1822.
8. *Ibid.,* September 1, 1821.
9. *Ibid.,* August 17, 1822.
10. "Near Pensacola," October 13, 1822, in Thomas Butler and Family Papers (MSS in Department of Archives, Louisiana State University).
11. Brackenridge, *Recollections,* pp. 272-73.
12. *Floridian,* September 1, 1821.
13. *Niles' Register,* October 19, 1822.
14. *Floridian,* March 8, 1823.
15. *Ibid.,* March 8 and August 2, 1823.
16. *Ibid.,* May 17, 1823.
17. See Brackenridge's certification of White's account as acting U.S. attorney for January term, 1823, dated Pensacola, September 6, 1823, General Records of the Department of State, Miscellaneous Letters (MSS in the National Archives).
18. See Brackenridge to J. Q. Adams, Pensacola, August 4, 1822, in *ibid.*
19. See Sebree to Brackenridge, Georgetown, Kentucky, February 6, 1823, in Brackenridge Letterbook.
20. See Brackenridge's judicial report on Schooner "Carmen" Case, dated Pensacola, June 1, 1823, General Records of the Department of State, Miscellaneous Letters (MSS in the National Archives).
21. *Ibid.*
22. See notice in *Floridian,* May 10, 1823.
23. *Ibid.,* May 17, 1823.
24. May 24, 1823.
25. See *Floridian,* May 31, 1823.
26. *Ibid.,* June 14, 1823.
27. May 31, 1823.
28. In *Floridian,* June 14, 1823.
29. *Ibid.,* June 21, 1823.
30. *Ibid.,* June 28, 1823.
31. *Ibid.,* July 5, 1823.
32. See letter signed "AMICI" in *ibid.,* May 31, 1823.
33. Pensacola, September 2, 1823, General Records of the Department of State, Miscellaneous Letters (MSS in the National Archives).

34. Bev. Chew to Scott, New Orleans, June 26, 1823; Scott to Steele, Pensacola, July 19, 1823; and Steele to Scott, Pensacola, July 20, 1823, in *ibid.*

35. Brackenridge to Adams, Pensacola, September 12, 1823, in *ibid.*

36. *Floridian,* October 11, 1823.

37. See *Pensacola Gazette and West Florida Advertiser,* October 30, 1824.

38. *Ibid.,* September 11, 1824.

39. *National Intelligencer,* August 17, 1824.

40. See *Pensacola Gazette and West Florida Advertiser,* September 4 and October 2, 1824.

41. See *ibid.,* January 8, 1825.

42. *Ibid.,* April 16, 1825.

43. *Ibid.,* May 21, 1825.

44. *Ibid.,* October 22, 1825.

45. *Ibid.,* July 23, 1825.

46. In *ibid.,* March 13, 1824.

47. *Floridian,* November 15, 1823.

48. *Pensacola Gazette and West Florida Advertiser,* November 19, 1825.

49. See *ibid.,* May 14, 1825.

50. *Ibid.,* May 7, 1825.

51. *Floridian,* June 28, 1823.

52. *Ibid.,* September 13, 1823.

53. *Pensacola Gazette and West Florida Advertiser,* March 20, 1824.

54. August 14, 1824.

55. *Pensacola Gazette and West Florida Advertiser,* August 21, 1824.

56. See *ibid.,* August 14 and 21, 1824. The letters exchanged by Sebree and Brackenridge on this question are printed in the issue of August 21.

57. *Ibid.,* August 7, 1824.

58. *Ibid.,* January 8, 1825.

59. *Ibid.,* January 22 and 29, 1825.

60. *Ibid.,* June 11, 1825.

61. See memorial in *American State Papers: Miscellaneous,* II, 1025-27.

62. See *Pensacola Gazette and West Florida Advertiser,* January 8 and April 23, 1825; *Niles' Register* October 1, 1825.

63. *Floridian,* March 8, 1823.

64. *Ibid.,* August 30, 1823.

65. *Niles' Register,* September 24, 1825.

66. *Pensacola Gazette and West Florida Advertiser,* November 5, 1825.

67. *Niles' Register,* October 29, 1825.

68. *Pensacola Gazette and West Florida Advertiser,* September 25, 1824.

69. January 22, 1825.

70. Brackenridge to (?), Pensacola, September 12, 1823, in Brackenridge Letterbook.

71. In *ibid.*

72. January 12, 1826, in *ibid.*

73. See Brackenridge to Thomas Butler, Pensacola, August 13, 1824, in Thomas Butler and Family Papers (MSS in Department of Archives, Louisiana State University).

74. See *ibid.*

75. See J. Q. Adams to Brackenridge, Washington, January 8, 1824, in Brackenridge Letterbook; *Pensacola Gazette and West Florida Advertiser,* July 24, 1824.

76. *Pensacola Gazette and West Florida Advertiser,* July 8, 1826. The program planned for the day was published in *ibid.,* July 1.

77. In *ibid.;* also printed in a slightly revised form in the appendix of Brackenridge's *Recollections,* pp. 318-25.

78. *Pensacola Gazette and West Florida Advertiser,* August 11, 1826.

79. See description of the event in *ibid.,* August 18, 1826.

80. In *ibid.*

81. Brackenridge, *Speeches on the Jew Bill,* p. 170 fn.

82. For text of the oration, see *ibid.,* pp. 157-82; *Pensacola Gazette and West Florida Advertiser,* August 25, 1826.

83. August 25, 1826.

84. See *ibid.*

Chapter XXII: JUDGE AND MRS. H. M. BRACKENRIDGE

1. *Niles' Register,* January 29, 1825 and February 28, 1829.

2. Pittsburgh, January 8, 1827, in Brackenridge Letterbook.

3. Magruder to Brackenridge, Baltimore, December 21, 1826, in *ibid.*

4. See editorial in *Pensacola Gazette and West Florida Advertiser,* September 8, 1826.

5. Washington, December 11, 1826, in Brackenridge Letterbook.

6. *Pensacola Gazette and West Florida Advertiser,* June 22, 1827.

7. *Ibid.,* February 18, 1826.

8. *Ibid.,* August 24, 1827.

9. *Ibid.,* March 30, 1827.

10. See *ibid.,* November 23, 1826.

11. Tallahassee, November 30, 1826, in Brackenridge Letterbook.

12. Both dated Pensacola, November 25, 1826, in *ibid.*

13. November 22, 1826, in *ibid.*

14. St. Augustine, November 4, 1826, in *ibid.*

15. Pensacola, January 28, 1827, in *ibid.*

16. March 23, 1827.

17. Philadelphia: Printed for H. S. Tanner and the Author, 1827, pp. 105-10.

18. XXVI, 478-97.

19. See Everett to Joseph M. White, Washington, April 23, 1828, in Brackenridge Letterbook.

20. William C. Reichel, *A History of the Rise, Progress, and Present Condition of the Moravian Seminary for Young Ladies, at Bethlehem, Pa. With a Catalogue of Its Pupils. 1785-1858* (2d ed., revised and enlarged by William H. Bigler; Philadelphia: J. B. Lippincott & Co., 1870), p. 361.

21. MS in possession of Mrs. Painter.

22. *National Gazette and Literary Register,* March 23, 1827.

23. *Pensacola Gazette and West Florida Advertiser,* May 18, 1827.

24. *Ibid.,* May 25, 1827.

25. *Ibid.,* June 22, 1827.

26. *Ibid.,* May 25, 1827.

27. Brackenridge to Thomas Butler, Philadelphia, January 6, 1828, in Thomas Butler and Family Papers (MSS in Department of Archives, Louisiana State University).

28. MS in possession of Mrs. Painter.

29. Santa Rosa, July 18, 1827, in *ibid.*

30. In *ibid.*

31. Tallahassee, July 27, 1827, in *ibid.*

32. Tallahassee, August 12, 1827, in *ibid.*

33. Tallahassee, August 18, 1827, in *ibid.*
34. Tallahassee, August 28, 1827, in *ibid.*
35. *Pensacola Gazette and West Florida Advertiser,* November 9, 1827.
36. Brackenridge to Caroline, Webbville, September 8, 1827 (MS in possession of Mrs. Painter).
37. In Brackenridge Letterbook.
38. *Pensacola Gazette and West Florida Advertiser,* October 8, 1827.
39. Brackenridge to Caroline, Webbville, September 8, 1827 (MS in possession of Mrs. Painter).
40. Brackenridge to Caroline, Tallahassee, September 24, 1827, in *ibid.*
41. Brackenridge to Caroline, Tallahassee, September 25, 1827, in *ibid.*
42. In *Pensacola Gazette and West Florida Advertiser,* October 26, 1827.
43. *Ibid.,* November 9, 1827.
44. See *ibid.,* December 7, 1827.
45. *Ibid.*
46. *Ibid.,* January 4, 1828.
47. Brackenridge to Caroline, Tallahassee, October 2, 1827 (MS in possession of Mrs. Painter).
48. Brackenridge to Caroline, Milledgeville, October 12, 1827, in *ibid.*
49. October 31, 1827, in *ibid.*
50. *Pensacola Gazette and West Florida Advertiser,* December 7, 1827.
51. MS in possession of Mrs. Painter.
52. Richmond, November 19, 1827, in Brackenridge Letterbook.
53. Salem, November 28, 1827, in *ibid.*
54. Charleston, December 5, 1827, in *ibid.*
55. Brackenridge to Thomas Butler, Philadelphia, January 6, 1828, in Thomas Butler and Family Papers (MSS in Department of Archives, Louisiana State University).
56. *Ibid.*
57. Brackenridge to Caroline, Washington, January 20, 1828 (MS in possession of Mrs. Painter).
58. Brackenridge to Caroline, Washington, January 23, 1828, in *ibid.*
59. Brackenridge to Caroline, Savannah, February 16, 1828, in *ibid.*
60. Brackenridge to Caroline, Augusta, February 18, 1828, in *ibid.*
61. Brackenridge to Caroline, Flint River, February 26, 1828, in *ibid.*
62. *Pensacola Gazette and Florida Advertiser,* March 21, 1828.
63. Webbville, March 7, 1828 (MS in possession of Mrs. Painter).
64. *Ibid.*
65. Pensacola, March 24, 1828, in *ibid.*
66. *Pensacola Gazette and Florida Advertiser,* April 25, 1828.
67. *Ibid.,* May 16, 1828.
68. *Ibid.,* May 23, 1828.
69. Innerarity to Brackenridge, Pensacola, May 15, 1828, in Brackenridge Letterbook.
70. See letter in *ibid.*

Chapter XXIII: DEER POINT AND TARENTUM

1. See *Niles' Register,* April 19, 1828.
2. Jenks Cameron, *The Development of Governmental Forest Control in the United States* (Baltimore: The Johns Hopkins Press, 1928), p. 49.

3. In *American State Papers: Naval Affairs,* III, 50.

4. Henry R. Storrs, chairman of Naval Committee of House of Representatives, to Samuel L. Southard, secretary of the navy, Washington, January 18, 1827, in *ibid.*

5. Southard to Storrs, Washington, January 29, 1827, in *ibid.,* III, 47-50.

6. Southard to George McDuffie, chairman of Committee of Ways and Means of House of Representatives, Washington, January 29, 1828, in *ibid.,* III, 945.

7. For all the pertinent documents, see *ibid.,* III, 931-50.

8. See letters to Southard, dated Washington, January 28 and January 29-February 1, 1828, in *ibid.,* III, 937-38.

9. Statement of White's accounts with the United States, in *ibid.,* III, 934.

10. In *ibid.,* III, 920-21.

11. MS in possession of Mrs. Painter.

12. Santa Rosa, April 16, 1828, in *ibid.*

13. In *American State Papers: Naval Affairs,* III, 921.

14. In *ibid.,* III, 925.

15. Washington, April 12, 1828, in *ibid.,* III, 921.

16. Brackenridge to Southard, Pensacola, May 9, 1828, in *ibid.,* III, 922.

17. Santa Rosa, April 29, 1828 (MS in possession of Mrs. Painter).

18. Pensacola, May 5, 1828, in *ibid.*

19. In *American State Papers: Naval Affairs,* III, 922.

20. In *ibid.,* III, 922-25.

21. In *ibid.,* III, 925.

22. Cameron, *Governmental Forest Control,* pp. 49-50.

23. J. Q. Adams, *Memoirs,* VIII, 51.

24. In *American State Papers: Naval Affairs,* III, 946.

25. See Brackenridge to Southard, Tallahassee, January 5, 1829, in *ibid.,* III, 926.

26. *Speeches on the Jew Bill,* p. 224.

27. Tyson to Brackenridge, Baltimore, August 27, 1829, in Brackenridge Letterbook.

28. *Niles' Register,* October 3, 1829.

29. Sprague to Brackenridge, Hallowell, Maine, September 18, 1830, in Brackenridge Letterbook.

30. Brackenridge to Southard, Deer Point, January 27, 1829, in *American State Papers: Naval Affairs,* III, 946.

31. Brackenridge to Southard, Santa Rosa, February 4, 1829, in *ibid.,* III, 945.

32. See his quarterly report, dated April 18, 1829, in *ibid.,* III, 928.

33. Brackenridge to Branch, Deer Point, April 18, 1829, in *ibid.,* III, 926-27.

34. *Ibid.,* III, 927.

35. See Brackenridge to Caroline, Pensacola, December 8, 1828 (MS in possession of Mrs. Painter).

36. Tallahassee, December 26, 1828, in *ibid.*

37. In *American State Papers: Naval Affairs,* III, 926.

38. In *ibid.,* III, 943-44.

39. Brackenridge to Caroline, Pensacola, May 11, 1829 (MS in possession of Mrs. Painter).

40. Brackenridge to Caroline, Pittsburgh, June 4, 1829, in *ibid.*

41. Recorder's Office, Allegheny County, Deed Book 23, pp. 61-63.

42. In Office of Register of Wills, Allegheny County, Will Book 2, pp. 107-109.

43. January 6, 1828, in Thomas Butler and Family Papers (MSS in Department of Archives, Louisiana State University).

44. Brackenridge, *Trusts and Trustees*, pp. 152-53.

45. Brackenridge to Caroline, Tallahassee, September 25, 1827 (MS in possession of Mrs. Painter).

46. Santa Rosa, April 29, 1828, in *ibid.*

47. Brackenridge, *Trusts and Trustees*, p. 153.

48. Brackenridge to Caroline, Tallahassee, January 4, 1829 (MS in possession of Mrs. Painter).

49. In *ibid.*

50. See A. Howry Espenshade, *Pennsylvania Place Names* (State College: The Pennsylvania State College, 1925), p. 186.

51. Recorder's Office, Allegheny County, Plan Book I, Part I, pp. 16-17.

52. Brackenridge to Caroline, Santa Rosa, July 4, 1828 (MS in possession of Mrs. Painter).

53. Tallahassee, January 12, 1829, in *ibid.*

54. See Richard Raynal Keen to Brackenridge, Baltimore, June 29, 1829, in Brackenridge Letterbook.

55. Brackenridge to Caroline, Washington, July 2, 1829 (MS in possession of Mrs. Painter).

56. In *American State Papers: Naval Affairs*, III, 958.

57. In *ibid.*

58. In *ibid.*, III, 939.

59. Washington, July 6, 1829, in *ibid.*, III, 927.

60. Brackenridge to Caroline, Washington, July 8, 1829 (MS in possession of Mrs. Painter).

61. In *ibid.*

62. In *American State Papers: Naval Affairs*, III, 929-30.

63. In *ibid.*, III, 930-31.

64. See Brackenridge to Richard Smith, cashier of the Office of Discount and Deposit of the Bank of the United States of Washington, D. C., Philadelphia, September 14, 1829 (MS in possession of Rare Book Department, Boston Public Library, Boston, Massachusetts).

65. In *American State Papers: Naval Affairs*, III, 928-30.

66. In *ibid.*, III, 928.

67. In *ibid.*, III, 929.

68. Pensacola, October 24, 1830, in *ibid.*, III, 950.

69. See *Pensacola Gazette*, December 4, 1830.

70. Washington, January 22, 1831, in *American State Papers: Naval Affairs*, IV, 112-17.

71. In *ibid.*, III, 918-20.

72. In *ibid.*, III, 944 and 950-51.

73. See Hoffman to Branch, Washington, February 1, 1831, in *ibid.*, III, 951-52.

74. In *ibid.*, III, 917-18.

75. J. Q. Adams, *Memoirs*, VIII, 322-23.

76. *Niles' Register*, February 12, 1831.

77. In *American State Papers: Naval Affairs*, IV, 119.

78. Pensacola, August 4, 1831, in *ibid.*, IV, 119-21.

79. Washington, September 21, 1831, in *ibid.*, IV, 119.

80. In *ibid.*, IV, 123.

81. Holmes' Valley, December 4, 1831, in *ibid.*, IV, 107-108.

82. See White to Woodbury, Washington, October 11 and 23, 1831, in *ibid.*, IV, 111-12.

83. See Woodbury's annual report, dated December 3, 1832, in *ibid.*, IV, 161.

84. *Niles' Register,* March 3, 1832.

85. In *American State Papers: Naval Affairs,* IV, 122.

86. See Woodbury's annual report, dated November 30, 1833, in *ibid.*, IV, 356.

Chapter XXIV: THE FALL FROM GRACE

1. See report of the White dinner in *Pensacola Gazette and Florida Advertiser,* October 21, 1828.

2. In *ibid.,* December 5, 1829.

3. In *ibid.,* December 5, 12, and 19, 1829; January 9, 1830.

4. See extract of his letter in *ibid.,* February 6, 1830.

5. Columbia, South Carolina, April 12, 1829, in Brackenridge Letterbook.

6. *Pensacola Gazette and Chronicle,* October 22, 1831.

7. *Ibid.,* March 10, 1829.

8. In *ibid.,* November 6, 1830.

9. December 1, 1827 (MS in the Historical Society of Western Pennsylvania).

10. Reprinted in *Pensacola Gazette and Florida Advertiser,* September 9, 1828.

11. *Ibid.,* October 21, 1828.

12. *Niles' Register,* November 23, 1839.

13. Webbville, April 10, 1829 (MS in possession of Mrs. Painter).

14. See *Niles' Register,* July 30, 1831.

15. Washington, September 30, 1831, in Brackenridge Letterbook.

16. *Niles' Register,* December 18, 1830; Benton, *Thirty Years' View,* I, 128-30.

17. Washington, September 10, 1831, in Brackenridge Letterbook.

18. November 10, 1830.

19. Pensacola, February 10, 1830 (MS in possession of Mrs. Painter).

20. See Brackenridge to Caroline, Pensacola, October 10, 1830, in *ibid.*

21. Brackenridge to Caroline, Pensacola, October 24, 1830, in *ibid.*

22. March 26, 1832, in *ibid.*

23. See Brackenridge to Caroline, Pensacola, February 26, 1832, in *ibid.*

24. *Judge Brackenridge's Letters,* pp. 4-5.

25. *Niles' Register,* April 28, 1832.

26. *Jackson,* I, xviii.

27. *Judge Brackenridge's Letters,* p. 1.

28. *Ibid.,* p. 2.

29. *Ibid.,* p. 3.

30. *Ibid.,* pp. 8-9.

31. May 11, 1832.

32. *Judge Brackenridge's Letters,* p. 8.

33. In *ibid.,* pp. 13-15.

34. *Ibid.,* p. 11.

35. *Ibid.,* p. 5.

36. April 27, 1832.

37. May 11 and June 9, 1832.

38. June 23, 1832.

39. October 6, 1832.

40. See *Hazard's Register of Pennsylvania,* April 21, 1832.

41. James Kay, Jun. and Brother.

42. John I. Kay and Co.

43. Brackenridge to Caroline, Pittsburgh, April 2, 1832 (MS in possession of Mrs. Painter).

44. *Recollections* (1834 ed.), p. iii.

45. *Ibid.,* p. 10.

46. *Ibid.*

47. *The World of Washington Irving* (New York: E. P. Dutton & Company, Inc., 1944), p. 98.

48. *Recollections* (1834 ed.), p. 70.

49. See *Hazard's Register of Pennsylvania,* May 25, 1833 and July 12, 1834.

50. II, 274-77.

51. See H. Fouré Selter, *L' odyssée Américaine d'une Famille Francaise. Le Docteur Antoine Saugrain. Etude Suivie de Manuscrits Inédits et de la Correspondance de Sophie Michau Robinson* (Baltimore: The Johns Hopkins Press, 1936), pp. 23-35.

52. Tarentum, September 28, 1833, in *Niles' Register,* November 30, 1833.

53. See Harrison to Brackenridge, Cincinnati, February 2, 1836, in Brackenridge Letterbook.

54. The manuscript of his speech is in possession of Mrs. Painter.

55. *Niles' Register,* October 10, 1840.

56. *Ibid.,* December 19, 1840.

57. Key West, September 29, 1840, in Brackenridge Letterbook.

58. Washington, January 29, 1841, in *ibid.*

59. Commission in possession of Mrs. Painter; *Niles' Register,* September 4 and 25, 1841.

60. Brackenridge to George Haslet, Washington, December 15, 1841, in Brackenridge Letterbook.

61. For a detailed study, see John Bassett Moore, *History and Digest of the International Arbitrations to Which the United States Has Been a Party, Together with Appendices Containing the Treaties Relating to Such Arbitrations, and Historical and Legal Notes on Other International Arbitrations Ancient and Modern, and on the Domestic Commissions of the United States for the Adjustment of International Claims* (Washington: Government Printing Office, 1898), II, 1209-86.

62. See John Baldwin to Brackenridge, Washington, August 23, 1841, in Brackenridge Letterbook.

63. See *Niles' Register,* January 14, 1843.

64. January 10, 1843.

65. Jackson to Lewis, "Hermitage," January 20, 1843, in Jackson, *Correspondence,* VI, 182-83.

66. *Niles' Register,* February 24, 1844.

Chapter XXV: THE SAGE OF TARENTUM

1. For example, see *Argument of H. M. Brackenridge, before the Supreme Court, in the Case of Edmund Greer, et. al. Ads. Commonwealth of Pennsylvania, Ex. Rel. Att'y. Gen'l. Messrs. Brackenridge & Palmer, for appellants. Delivered the 8th of October, 1849* (Pittsburgh: Johnston & Stockton,1849).

2. *Journal of the Fifty-Sixth House of Representatives of the Commonwealth of Pennsylvania* (Harrisburg: J.M.G. Lescure, 1846), I, 4.

3. See extract of a letter to the editors of the New York *Observer,* dated Pittsburgh, October 30, 1830, in *Hazard's Register of Pennsylvania,* December 4, 1830.

4. *Ibid.*, March 29, 1834.

5. *Ibid.*, May 21, 1831.

6. Tarentum, July 26, 1835, in *ibid.*, August 8, 1835.

7. *Statesman,* June 10, 1829.

8. *Pittsburgh Saturday Evening Visiter,* April 8, 1837.

9. *Statesman,* May 4, 1831.

10. *Pittsburgh Saturday Evening Visiter and Galaxy of Western Literature and Science,* August 18, 1838.

11. *Ibid.*, December 24, 1836.

12. Pp. 27-29.

13. See their huge, full-page advertisement in *Third Quarterly Supplement of the Pittsburgh Saturday Evening Visiter,* May, 1839.

14. *Literary Examiner, and Western Monthly Review,* I (May, 1839), 80.

15. William Elder to Brackenridge, Pittsburgh, March 5, 1840, and R. H. Forrester, Robert Tener, Jr., W. M. Wright, and J. Schoonmaker to Brackenridge, Pittsburgh, March 6, 1840, in Brackenridge Letterbook.

16. *Literary Examiner, and Western Monthly Review,* I (August, 1839), 320.

17. *Ibid.*, I (June-August, 1839), 99-104; 180-84; 261-65.

18. *Ibid.*, I (September, 1839), 333-35; *Examiner and Hesperian,* II (January-February, 1840), 50-52; 83-86.

19. I (June, 1839), 159.

20. *Pittsburgh Saturday Evening Visiter,* April 14, 1838.

21. Henry Snyder, William Mathiot, and J. R. Thompson to Brackenridge, Jefferson College, July 21, 1838, in Brackenridge Letterbook; *Pittsburgh Saturday Evening Visiter,* September 22, 1838.

22. *The Annual Address Delivered before the Philo and Franklin Literary Societies of Jefferson College, Canonsburg, Pa. on the Day of the Annual Commencement, September 27, 1838* (Washington, Pa.: Uriah W. Wise, 1838).

23. J. Heron Foster (comp.), *A Full Account of the Great Fire at Pittsburgh, on the Tenth Day of April, 1845; with the Individual Losses, and Contributions for Relief* (Pittsburgh: J. W. Cook, 1845), p. 3.

24. *Ibid.*, p. 7. For letter, see *ibid.*, pp. 7-9; or *Daily National Intelligencer,* April 19, 1845.

25. Washington: Robert A. Waters, 1850. His first letter, dated Tarentum, June 24, 1846, appeared in the July 2 issue of the paper.

26. Brackenridge, *Early Discoveries by Spaniards,* p. 4.

27. New York, Bartlett & Welford.

28. Pp. xxxi-xxxii.

29. *Niles' Register,* November 4, 1843.

30. Sharpsburg, July 19, 1851, in Brackenridge Letterbook.

31. *Early Discoveries by Spaniards,* p. 4.

32. *Ibid.*, pp. 5-6.

33. *Ibid.*, p. 40.

34. Potsdam, May 24, 1857, in Brackenridge Letterbook.

35. Brackenridge to Mayer, Tarentum, February 1, 1857, Darlington MSS.

36. Tarentum, March 11, 1857, *ibid.*

37. Brackenridge to Mayer, Tarentum, October 15, 1857, *ibid.*

38. Tarentum, October 27, 1857, *ibid.*

39. New York, January 22, 1858, in Brackenridge Letterbook.

40. *Early Discoveries by Spaniards,* p. 38.

41. Tarentum, February 2, 1858, in E. G. Squier Papers (MSS in possession of Frank Squier, New York, N.Y.).

42. Pp. 1-19.

43. Brackenridge to F. W. Thomas, Washington, November 6, 1841, in Griswold Collection (MSS in Rare Book Department, Boston Public Library).

44. Washington, November 6, 1841, *ibid.*

45. Brackenridge to Messrs. Kay Brothers, Harrisburg, April 10, 1846 (MS in possession of Rare Book Department, Boston Public Library).

46. Pittsburgh, April 22, 1846 (MS copy in Harvard College Library copy of 1846 edition of *Modern Chivalry*).

47. P. 547.

48. Pp. 233-73.

49. For the newspaper phase of the controversy, see the files of this paper for 1851-52, although those extant are incomplete.

50. *Exposure of a Few of the Many Misstatements in H.M. Brackenridge's History of the Whiskey Insurrection* (Pittsburgh: John S. Davison, 1859), p. 10.

51. Tarentum, November 5, 1852, Darlington MSS.

52. Philadelphia, Samuel Harrison Smith.

53. Brackenridge to P.A. Browne, Tarentum, March 11, 1857, in American Literary Duplicates (MSS in the Historical Society of Pennsylvania).

54. *Ibid.*

55. Pp. 31-36.

56. P. ix.

57. P. 332.

58. *Exposure,* p. 79.

59. *Ibid.,* p. 12.

60. Pittsburgh: W.S. Haven, 1858.

61. P. 18.

62. Parton to Brackenridge, New York, November 28, 1859, in Brackenridge Letterbook.

63. Ashland, June 18, 1844, in *ibid.*

64. Mobile, March 11, 1850, in *ibid.*

65. Rachel C. Smith to B. M. Brackenridge, Philadelphia, October 16, 1852, in *ibid.*

66. *History of Allegheny County Pennsylvania* (Chicago: A. Warner & Co., 1889), II, 436.

67. Duyckinck and Duyckinck, *Cyclopaedia,* I, v-vi.

68. See Evert A. Duyckinck to H.M. Brackenridge, New York, March 31, 1855, in Brackenridge Letterbook.

69. B. M. Brackenridge to Duyckinck, Pittsburgh April 19, 1855, in Duyckinck Collection (MSS in New York Public Library).

70. B.M. Brackenridge to Duyckinck, Tarentum, June 1, 1855, in *ibid.*

71. In Duyckinck and Duyckinck, *Cyclopaedia,* I, 668-73; for notice of Hugh Henry Brackenridge, see *ibid.,* I, 288-99.

72. See H. M. Brackenridge to Duyckinck, Tarentum, May 26 and June 10, 1855, in Duyckinck Collection (MSS in New York Public Library).

73. Tarentum, June 15, 1855, in *ibid.*

74. Tarentum, October, 1856, in *ibid.*

75. Tarentum, December 18, 1856, in *ibid.*

76. Tarentum, April 6, 1857, in *ibid.*

77. *Pittsburgh Post,* September 10, 1860.

78. H. M. Brackenridge to Duyckinck, Tarentum, April 6, 1857, in Duyckinck Collection (MSS in New York Public Library).

79. Undated MS in possession of Mrs. Painter.

80. Brackenridge to Duyckinck, Tarentum, June 19, 1855, in Duyckinck Collection (MSS in New York Public Library).

81. Pittsburgh: Johnston & Stockton, 1848.

82. Brackenridge to Duyckinck, Tarentum, July 10, 1855, in Duyckinck Collection (MSS in New York Public Library).

83. *Sixty Years in the North and Twenty Years in the South*, p. 72.

84. *Ibid.*, p. viii.

85. *Ibid.*, p. 12.

86. *Ibid.*, p. 50.

87. See MS essay, "Uncle Tom's Cabin," in possession of Mrs. Painter.

88. For example, see *Saturday Visiter*, November 27, 1852.

89. *Sixty Years in the North and Twenty Years in the South*, p. 34.

90. *Ibid.*, p. 20.

91. Obituary in *Pittsburgh Daily Gazette*, January 19, 1871.

92. Actually the cemetery is in Brackenridge, about one block beyond the Tarentum line.

Bibliography

This is a selected list of the sources consulted, both manuscript and printed. The first editions of the works of H. M. Brackenridge are listed chronologically with his most important pamphlets and essays. Other writings of his, particularly newspaper, are discussed in this biography, cited fully in the notes, and listed in the index. So prolific was Brackenridge's pen that no attempt has been made to incorporate in the text or in the bibliography everything he wrote. Otherwise, all sources cited in the notes are given below with a few additional works perhaps of some special interest to the reader. Standard reference aids, to which every conscientious researcher or writer owe a great debt, are not named.

A. THE WORKS OF H. M. BRACKENRIDGE.

Books

Views of Louisiana; Together with a Journal of a Voyage up the Missouri River, in 1811. Pittsburgh: Cramer, Spear and Eichbaum, 1814.

History of the Late War, between the United States and Great Britain. Containing a Minute Account of the Various Military and Naval Operations. Baltimore: Joseph Cushing, 1816.

Voyage to South America, Performed by Order of the American Government, in the Years 1817 and 1818, in the Frigate Congress. 2 vols. Baltimore: Published by the Author, 1819.

Speeches on the Jew Bill, in the House of Delegates of Maryland, by H. M. Brackenridge, Col. W. G. D. Worthington, and John S. Tyson, Esquire. Together with an Argument on the Chancery Powers, and an Eulogy on Thomas Jefferson and John Adams, &c. By H. M. Brackenridge. Philadelphia: J. Dobson, 1829.

Recollections of Persons and Places in the West. Philadelphia: James Kay, Jun. and Brother, 1834. Pittsburgh: John I. Kay and Co., 1834.

An Essay on Trusts and Trustees: In Relation to the Settlement of Real Estate—The Power of Trustees—and Involving Many of the Most Abstruse Questions in the English and American Law of Tenures. Washington: William M. Morrison, 1842.

History of the Western Insurrection in Western Pennsylvania, Commonly Called the Whiskey Insurrection. 1794. Pittsburgh: W. S. Haven, 1859.

Pamphlets

South America: A Letter on the Present State of That Country, to James Monroe, President of the United States. Washington: The National Register, 1817.

A Eulogy, on the Lives and Characters of John Adams & Thomas Jefferson. By the Hon. H. M. Brackenridge. Delivered at the Courthouse in Pensacola, on Tuesday, 15th August, 1826, in Compliance with a Request from the Citizens, in Town-meeting Assembled. Pensacola: W. H. Hunt, 1826.

Judge Brackenridge's Letters. Washington, 1832.

The Annual Address Delivered before the Philo and Franklin Literary Societies of Jefferson College, Canonsburg, Pa. on the Day of the Annual Commencement, September 27, 1838. Washington, Pa.: Uriah W. Wise, 1838.

Eulogy on John Quincy Adams, Delivered May 11th, 1848. At the School House of the Sixth Ward, Pittsburgh. Pittsburgh: Johnston & Stockton, 1848.

Argument of H. M. Brackenridge, before the Supreme Court, in the Case of Edmund Greer, et. al. Ads. Commonwealth of Pennsylvania, Ex. Rel. Att'y. Gen'l. Messrs. Brackenridge & Palmer, for appellants. Delivered the 8th of October, 1849. Pittsburgh: Johnston & Stockton, 1849.

Mexican Letters Written during the Progress of the Late War between the United States and Mexico. Washington: Robert A. Waters, 1850.

Early Discoveries by Spaniards in New Mexico: Containing an Account of the Castles of Cibola, and the Present Appearance of Their Ruins. Pittsburgh: Henry Miner & Co., 1857.

A Speech Delivered by H. M. Brackenridge, in the Presidential Campaign of 1864: Sixty Years in the North and Twenty Years in the South. Pittsburgh: Barr & Myers, 1865.

Essays

"The Florida Question Stated," *American Register; or, Summary Review of History, Politics and Literature,* I (1817), 128-48.

"On the Population and Tumuli of the Aborigines of North America," *Transactions of the American Philosophical Society, Held at Philadelphia, for Promoting Useful Knowledge,* New Series, I (1818), 151-59.

"Pittsburgh in the Olden Time," *Literary Examiner, and Western Monthly Review,* I (May, 1839), 27-29.

"Pedro Menendez de Aviles, First Spanish Conqueror and Adelantado of Florida," *Literary Examiner, and Western Monthly Review,* I (June-August, 1839), 99-104, 180-84, 261-65.

"The Chevalier de Gourges," *Literary Examiner, and Western Monthly Review,* I (September, 1839), 333-35; *Examiner and Hesperian,* II (January-February, 1840), 50-52, 83-86.

"Biographical Notice of H. H. Brackenridge, Late of the Supreme Court of Pennsylvania," *Southern Literary Messenger,* VIII (January, 1842), 1-19.

B. MANUSCRIPT SOURCES.

American Historians. Historical Society of Pennsylvania, Philadelphia.

American Literary Duplicates. Historical Society of Pennsylvania.

Brackenridge, Henry Marie, Family Papers. In the possession of Mrs. Helen Brackenridge Painter, Washington, Pa.

Brackenridge, Henry Marie, Letterbook. Darlington Memorial Library, University of Pittsburgh.

Butler, Thomas, and Family Papers. Department of Archives, Louisiana State University, Baton Rouge, La.

Constitution and Proceedings of the Delphian Club. Maryland Historical Society, Baltimore.

Craig Collection. Neville B. Craig Papers. Carnegie Library of Pittsburgh.

Darlington Collection. Darlington Memorial Library.

Deed Books. Recorder's Office, Allegheny County, Pittsburgh.

Dreer Collection—American Lawyers. Historical Society of Pennsylvania.

Duyckinck Collection. New York Public Library.

Gilkison Account Book. Photostat. Historical Society of Western Pennsylvania.

Gratiot Letterbook. Missouri Historical Society, St. Louis.

Gratz, Simon, Collection. Historical Society of Pennsylvania.

Griswold Manuscripts. Rare Book Department, Boston Public Library.

Herzog Letterbook. Missouri Historical Society.

Instructions to Consuls, General Records of the Department of State. National Archives.

Jefferson, Thomas, Papers. Library of Congress.

Lucas Papers. Missouri Historical Society.

Manuscript Copy of H. M. Brackenridge to King of the French, Pittsburgh, April 22, 1846. In copy of 1846 edition of H. H. Brackenridge's *Modern Chivalry.* Harvard College Library, Cambridge, Mass.

McNair, Dunning, Collection. Darlington Memorial Library.

Miscellaneous Letters, General Records of the Department of State. National Archives.

Miscellaneous Letters. Historical Society of Western Pennsylvania.

Miscellaneous Letters. Missouri Historical Society.

Miscellaneous Letters. Rare Book Department, Boston Public Library.

Mitten Collection. Indiana Historical Society, Indianapolis.

Monroe, James, Papers. New York Public Library.

Plan Books. Recorder's Office, Allegheny County, Pittsburgh.

Records. Allegheny County Bar Association, Pittsburgh.

Rodney Collection. Historical Society of Delaware, Wilmington.

Shaler Papers. Historical Society of Pennsylvania.

Special Agents, South American Missions, 1815-1818, General Records of the Department of State. National Archives.

Squier, E. G., Papers. In the possession of Frank Squier, New York City.

Will Books. Office of Register of Wills, Allegheny County, Pittsburgh; Cumberland County, Carlisle, Pa.

C. PRINTED SOURCES.

ABERNETHY, THOMAS PERKINS. *The Burr Conspiracy.* New York: Oxford University Press, 1954.

ADAMS, CHARLES FRANCIS (ed.). *Memoirs of John Quincy Adams, Comprising Portions of His Diary from 1795 to 1848.* 12 vols. Philadelphia: J. B. Lippincott & Co., 1874-77.

ADAMS, HENRY. *The Life of Albert Gallatin.* Philadelphia: J. B. Lippincott & Co., 1879.

AGAN, JOSEPH EUGENE. "Correa da Serra," *Pennsylvania Magazine of History and Biography,* XLIX (1925), 1-43.

ALBERT, GEORGE DALLAS (ed.). *History of the County of Westmoreland, Pennsylvania, with Biographical Sketches of Many of Its Pioneers and Prominent Men.* Philadelphia: L. H. Everts & Co., 1882.

American Watchman [Wilmington, Del.], 1817-19.

Analectic Magazine. Comprising Original Reviews, Biography, Analytical Abstracts of New Publications, Translations from French Journals, and Selections from the Most Esteemed British Reviews. 16 vols. Philadelphia: M. Thomas [etc.], 1813-20.

ANDREWS, J. CUTLER. *Pittsburgh's Post-Gazette: "The First Newspaper West of The Alleghenies."* Boston: Chapman & Grimes, 1936.

BALDWIN, LELAND D. *Whiskey Rebels: The Story of a Frontier Uprising.* Pittsburgh: University of Pittsburgh Press, 1939.

BASSETT, JOHN SPENCER (ed.). *Correspondence of Andrew Jackson.* 7 vols. Washington: Carnegie Institution of Washington, 1926-35.

———. *The Life of Andrew Jackson.* 2 vols. in 1. New York: The Macmillan Company, 1928.

BECK, VIRGINIA. "The Evolution of Government in Allegheny County, 1788-1808," *Western Pennsylvania Historical Magazine,* XXIV (December, 1941), 209-28.

BEIRNE, FRANCIS F. *The War of 1812.* New York: E. P. Dutton & Co., Inc., 1949.

BENTON, THOMAS HART. *Thirty Years' View; or, A History of the Working of the American Government for Thirty Years, from 1820 to 1850.* 2 vols. New York: D. Appleton and Company, 1854-56.

BORNHOLDT, LAURA. *Baltimore and Early Pan-Americanism: A Study in the Background of the Monroe Doctrine.* ("Smith College Studies in History," Vol. XXXIV.) Northampton, Mass., 1949.

BRACKENRIDGE, H. H. *Gazette Publications.* Carlisle, Pa.: Alexander & Phillips, 1806.

———. *Incidents of the Insurrection in the Western Parts of Pennsylvania, in the Year 1794.* 3 vols. in 1. Philadelphia: John M'Culloch, 1795.

———. *Law Miscellanies: Containing an Introduction to the Study of the Law; Notes on Blackstone's Commentaries, Shewing the Variations of the Law of Pennsylvania from the Law of England, and What Acts of Assembly Might Require to Be Repealed or Modified; Observations on Smith's Edition of the Laws of Pennsylvania; Strictures on Decisions of the Supreme Court of the United States, and on Certain Acts of Congress, with Some Law Cases, and a Variety of Other Matters, Chiefly Original.* Philadelphia: P. Byrne, 1814.

———. *Modern Chivalry: Containing the Adventures of Captain John Farrago, and Teague Oregan, His Servant.* 4 vols. Philadelphia and Pittsburgh: John M'Culloch, John Scull, 1792-97.

BRACKENRIDGE, HUGH MONTGOMERY (H. H.). *Six Political Discourses Founded on the Scripture.* Lancaster, Pa.: Francis Bailey, [1778].

BRADBURY, JOHN. *Travels in the Interior of America, in the Years 1809, 1810, and 1811; Including a Description of Upper Louisiana, together with the States of Ohio, Kentucky, Indiana, and Tennessee, with the Illinois and Western Territories, and Containing Remarks and Observations Useful to Persons Emigrating to Those Countries.* London: Sherwood, Neely, and Jones, 1819.

BRIGHAM, CLARENCE S. *History and Bibliography of American Newspapers, 1690-1820.* 2 vols. Worcester, Mass.: American Antiquarian Society, 1947.

BROOKS, VAN WYCK. *The World of Washington Irving.* New York: E. P. Dutton & Company, Inc., 1944.

BROWN, EVERETT S. (ed.). "Letters from Louisiana, 1813-1814," *Mississippi Valley Historical Review*, XI (March, 1925). 570-79.

BROWN, R. C. (ed.). *History of Butler County, Pennsylvania.* [Chicago]: R. C. Brown & Co., 1895.

CAMERON, JENKS. *The Development of Governmental Forest Control in the United States.* (Institute for Government Research, "Studies in Administration.") Baltimore: The John Hopkins Press, 1928.

Carlisle Gazette [Pa.], 1801-19.

CARTER, CLARENCE EDWIN (comp. and ed.). *The Territorial Papers of the United States.* 18 vols. Washington: United States Government Printing Office, 1934-52.

CLELAND, HUGH G. "John B. C. Lucas, Physiocrat on the Frontier," *Western Pennsylvania Historical Magazine*, XXXVI (March, 1953), 1-15.

CLEVEN, N. ANDREW N., "Henry Marie Brackenridge, Diplomat,"*Pennsylvania History*, V (October, 1938), 213-22.

COLTON, CALVIN (ed.). *The Works of Henry Clay, Comprising His Life, Correspondence and Speeches.* 10 vols. New York: G. P. Putnam's Sons, 1904.

Commonwealth [Pittsburgh], 1805-15.

COX, ISAAC JOSLIN. "Monroe and the Early Mexican Revolutionary Agents," *American Historical Association Annual Report for the Year 1911*, I, 199-215.

CRAIG, NEVILLE B. *Exposure of a Few of the Many Misstatements in H. M. Brackenridge's History of the Whiskey Insurrection.* Pittsburgh: John S. Davison, 1859.

———. *The History of Pittsburgh, with a Brief Notice of Its Facilities of Communication, and Other Advantages for Commercial and Manufacturing Purposes.* Pittsburgh: John H. Mellor, 1851.

———. (ed.). *The Olden Time; a Monthly Publication, Devoted to the Preservation of Documents and Other Authentic Information in Relation to the Early Explorations, and the Settlement and Improvement of the Country around the Head of the Ohio.* 2 vols. Pittsburgh: J. W. Cook, 1846-48.

[CRAMER, ZADOK, comp.]. *The Navigator: Containing Directions for Navigating the Monongahela, Alleghany, Ohio, and Mississippi Rivers; With an Ample Account of These Much Admired Waters, from the Head of the Former to the Mouth of the Latter; And a Concise Description of Their Towns, Villages, Harbours, Settlements, &c. With Accurate Maps of the Ohio and Mississippi. To Which Is Added an Appendix, Containing an Account of Louisiana, and of the Missouri and Columbia Rivers, as Discovered by the Voyage under Captains Lewis and Clark.* Pittsburgh: Cramer & Spear, 1808.

Cramer's Pittsburgh Magazine Almanack, for 1815 and 1816. Pittsburgh, Cramer, Spear and Eichbaum.

CUMING, F. *Sketches of a Tour to the Western Country, through the States of Ohio and Kentucky; a Voyage down the Ohio and Mississippi Rivers, and a Trip through the Mississippi Territory, and Part of West Florida. Commenced at Philadelphia in the Winter of 1807, and Concluded in 1809.* Pittsburgh: Cramer, Spear & Eichbaum, 1810.

DAHLINGER, CHARLES W. "Rev. John Taylor: The First Rector of Trinity Episcopal Church of Pittsburgh and His Commonplace Book," *Western Pennsylvania Historical Magazine,* I (January-April, 1918), 3-25, 85-96.

Daily Commercial Journal [Pittsburgh], 1846-52.

Daily Madisonian [Washington, D.C.], 1843.

DARBY, WILLIAM. *A Geographical Description of the State of Louisiana: Presenting a View of the Soil, Climate, Animal, Vegetable, and Mineral Productions; Illustrative of Its Natural Physiognomy, Its Geographical Configuration, and Relative Situation: With an Account of the Character and Manners of the Inhabitants. Being an Accompaniment to the Map of Louisiana.* Philadelphia: John Melish, 1816.

DARLINGTON, WILLIAM (comp.). *Reliquiae Baldwinianae: Selections from the Correspondence of the Late William Baldwin, M.D., Surgeon in the U. S. Navy. With Occasional Notes, and a Short Biographical Memoir.* Philadelphia: Kimber and Sharpless, 1843.

DAVIS, (MRS.) ELVERT M. "The Bates Boys on the Western Waters," *Western Pennsylvania Historical Magazine,* XXIX-XXX (June, 1946-December, 1947), 1-34, 85-138; 15-67, 107-44.

DAVIS, MATTHEW L. (ed.). *Memoirs of Aaron Burr. With Miscellaneous Selections from His Correspondence.* 2 vols. New York: Harper & Brothers, 1836-37.

DELAFIELD, JOSEPH L. "Notes on the Woods Family, of Bedford, Pennsylvania," *Pennsylvania Magazine of History and Biography,* XXXII (1908), 335-44.

DENNY, WILLIAM H. *Suc-co-tash.* Pittsburgh: W. S. Haven, 1858.

Dunlap's American Daily Advertiser [Philadelphia], 1793.

DUYCKINCK, EVERT A., and GEORGE L. *Cyclopaedia of American Literature; Embracing Personal and Critical Notices of Authors, and Selections from Their Writings. From the Earliest Period to the Present Day; with Portraits, Autographs, and Other Illustrations.* 2 vols. New York: Charles Scribner, 1856.

Edinburgh Review, or Critical Journal. Vols. 1-250. Edinburgh [etc.], 1802-1929.

ESPENSHADE, A. HOWRY. *Pennsylvania Place Names.* State College, Pa.: The Pennsylvania State College, 1925.

EVERETT, EDWARD. "Jeffersonian Democracy and the Tree of Liberty, 1800-1803," *Western Pennsylvania Historical Magazine,* XXXII (March-June, 1949), 11-44.

———. "John Smilie, Forgotten Champion of Early Western Pennsylvania," *Western Pennsylvania Historical Magazine,* XXXIII (September-December, 1950), 77-89.

Federal Gazette & Baltimore Daily Advertiser, 1815-18.

FERGUSON, RUSSELL J. *Early Western Pennsylvania Politics.* Pittsburgh: University of Pittsburgh Press, 1938.

FINDLEY, WILLIAM. *History of the Insurrection, in the Four Western Counties of Pennsylvania: in the Year M.DCC.XCIV. With a Recital of the Circumstances Specially Connected Therewith: and an Historical Review of the Previous Situation of the Country.* Philadelphia: Samuel Harrison Smith, 1796.

FLINT, TIMOTHY. *Recollections of the Last Ten Years, Passed in Occasional Residences and Journeyings in the Valley of the Mississippi, from Pittsburg and the Missouri to the Gulf of Mexico, and from Florida to the Spanish Frontier; in a Series of Letters to The Rev. James Flint, of Salem, Massachusetts.* Boston: Cummings, Hilliard, and Company, 1826.

Floridian [Pensacola], 1821-23.

FOSTER, J. HERON (comp.). *A Full Account of the Great Fire at Pittsburgh, on the Tenth Day of April, 1845; with the Individual Losses, and Contributions for Relief.* Pittsburgh: J. W. Cook, 1845.

FRENCH, JOHN C. "Poe's Literary Baltimore," *Maryland Historical Magazine,* XXXII (June, 1937), 101-12.

Globe [Washington, D. C.], 1832.

GRIFFIN, CHARLES CARROLL. *The United States and the Disruption of the Spanish Empire, 1810-1822: A Study of the Relations of the United States with Spain and with the Rebel Spanish Colonies.* ("Studies in History, Economics and Public Law," No. 429.) New York: Columbia University Press, 1937.

GRIFFITH, THOMAS W. *Annals of Baltimore.* Baltimore: William Wooddy, 1833.

HAMILTON, STANISLAUS MURRAY (ed.). *The Writings of James Monroe, Including a Collection of His Public and Private Papers and Correspondence Now for the First Time Printed.* 7 vols. New York: G. P. Putnam's Sons, 1898-1903.

HAZARD, SAMUEL (ed.). *The Register of Pennsylvania. Devoted to the Preservation of Facts and Documents, and Every Other Kind of Useful Information Respecting the State of Pennsylvania.* 16 vols. Philadelphia: William F. Geddes, 1828-35.

HEARTMAN, CHARLES F. (comp.). *A Bibliography of the Writings of Hugh Henry Brackenridge Prior to 1825.* New York: The Compiler, 1917.

History of Allegheny County Pennsylvania. Including Its Early Settlement and Progress to the Present Time; a Description of Its Historic and Interesting Localities; Its Cities, Towns and Villages; Religious, Educational, Social and Military History; Mining, Manufacturing and Commercial Interests; Improvements, Resources, Statistics, Etc. Also Portraits of Some of Its Prominent Men, and Biographies of Many of Its Representative Citizens. 2 parts in 1 vol. Chicago: A. Warner & Co., 1889.

History of Cumberland and Adams Counties, Pennsylvania. Chicago: Warner, Beers & Co., 1886.

HODGE, FREDERICK WEBB (ed.). *Handbook of American Indians North of Mexico.* (Smithsonian Institution: Bureau of American Ethnology, Bulletin 30.) 2 parts. Washington: Government Printing Office, 1907-10.

[IRVINE, BAPTIS]. *Strictures on a Voyage to South America, as Indited by the "Secretary to the [Late] Mission" to La Plata: Including Observations on the Capability of the Spanish Americans for Civil Liberty.—On the Principal Events (Civil and Military,) of the Revolution in Buenos Ayres, Chili, the Oriental Banda, Etc. And on the Importance of Friendly Relations, Political and Commercial, with the Independent States of South America. In a Series of Letters, Addressed to a Gentlemen* [sic] *of Distinction at Washington.* Baltimore: Richard J. Matchett, 1820.

IRVING, WASHINGTON. *Astoria; or Anecdotes of an Enterprise beyond the Rocky Mountains.* New York: G. P. Putnam, 1865.

JACOBS, JAMES RIPLEY. *Tarnished Warrior: Major-General James Wilkinson.* New York: The Macmillan Company, 1938.

JAMES, MARQUIS. *Andrew Jackson: The Border Captain.* Indianapolis: The Bobbs-Merrill Company, 1933.

———. *Andrew Jackson: Portrait of a President.* Indianapolis: The Bobbs-Merrill Company, 1937.

JAMESON, J. FRANKLIN (ed.). "Correspondence of John C. Calhoun," *American Historical Association Annual Report for the Year 1899,* II, 93-1212.

Journal of the Fifty-Sixth House of Representatives of the Commonwealth of Pennsylvania. Harrisburg: J. M. G. Lescure, 1846. Vol. I.

KELLER, WILLIAM F. "A Gifted Son of a Gifted Sire," *Pitt* (Winter, 1952-53), pp. 26-29.

———. "A Glimpse of the Life and Letters of Henry Marie Brackenridge," *Western Pennsylvania Historical Magazine,* XXXVII (March, 1954), 1-17.

KUSSART, (MRS.) S. *The Allegheny River.* Pittsburgh: Burgum Printing Company, 1938.

LANMAN, CHARLES (comp.). *Dictionary of the United States Congress, Compiled as a Manual of Reference for the Legislator and Statesman.* Washington: Government Printing Office, 1866.

Letters and Other Writings of James Madison, Fourth President of the United States. 4 vols. Philadelphia: J. B. Lippincott & Co., 1865.

Literary Examiner, and Western Monthly Review. 2 vols. Pittsburgh: Whitney & M'Cord, 1839-40.

LLOYD, THOMAS (comp.). *Proceedings and Debates of the General Assembly of Pennsylvania.* 2 vols. Philadelphia: Daniel Humphreys, Joseph James, 1787.

MANNING, WILLIAM R. (comp. and ed.). *Diplomatic Correspondence of the United States concerning the Independence of the Latin-American Nations.* 3 vols. New York: Oxford University Press, 1925.

[MARIE, JANE]. *The Case of Jane Marie, Exhibiting the Cruelty and Barbarous Conduct of James Ross, to a Defenceless Woman. Written and published by the object of his cruelty and vengeance, and addressed to the PUBLIC OF PHILADELPHIA and the Whole of PENNSYLVANIA.* September, 1808. In *Select Pamphlets* (Duane's Collection). Philadelphia, 1814.

MARTIN, SIDNEY WALTER. *Florida during the Territorial Days.* Athens: The University of Georgia Press, 1944.

McDERMOTT, JOHN FRANCIS. "Henry Marie Brackenridge and His Writings," *Western Pennsylvania Historical Magazine,* XX (September, 1937), 181-96.

———. "John B. C. Lucas in Pennsylvania," *Western Pennsylvania Historical Magazine,* XXI (September, 1938), 209-30.

———. "Schoolmaster—Early Western Model," *Western Pennsylvania Historical Magazine,* XXII (December, 1939), 237-44.

———. (ed.). *The Early Histories of St. Louis.* St. Louis: St. Louis Historical Documents Foundation, 1952.

MELLON, THOMAS. "Reminiscences of Hon. James Ross," *Western Pennsylvania Historical Magazine,* III (June, 1920), 103-8.

MICHAUX, ANDRE. "Journal of André Michaux, 1793-1796," in Reuben Gold Thwaites (ed.), *Early Western Travels, 1748-1846: A Series of Annotated Reprints of Some of the Best and Rarest Contemporary Volumes of Travel, Descriptive of the Aborigines and Social and Economic Conditions in the Middle and Far West, during the Period of Early American Settlement.* 32 vols. Cleveland: The Arthur H. Clark Company, 1904-7.

MILLER, BEN ROBERTSON. *The Louisiana Judiciary.* ("University Studies," no. 9.) Baton Rouge: Louisiana State University Press, 1932.

Missouri Gazette [St. Louis], 1809-11, 1820.

Monthly Review; or Literary Journal, Enlarged. 2d Series: vols. 1-108. London, January, 1790-November, 1825.

MOORE, JOHN BASSETT. *History and Digest of the International Arbitrations to Which the United States Has Been a Party, Together with Appendices Containing the Treaties Relating to Such Arbitrations, and Historical and Legal Notes on Other International Arbitrations Ancient and Modern, and on the Domestic Commissions of the United*

States for the Adjustment of International Claims. 6 vols. Washington: Government Printing Office, 1898.

National Gazette and Literary Register [Philadelphia], 1827.

National Intelligencer [Washington, D. C.], 1824.

NEWLIN, CLAUDE M. (ed.). *Modern Chivalry by Hugh Henry Brackenridge.* ("American Fiction Series.") New York: American Book Company, 1937.

———. *The Life and Writings of Hugh Henry Brackenridge.* Princeton: Princeton University Press, 1932.

NILES, H. (ed.). *The Weekly Register: Containing Political, Historical, Geographical, Scientifical, Astronomical, Statistical, and Biographical Documents, Essays and Facts; together with Notices of the Arts and Manufactures, and a Record of the Events of the Times.* 75 vols. Baltimore [etc.], 1811-49.

North-American Review and Miscellaneous Journal. Boston: Vols. IV (November, 1816), XXVI (April, 1828).

PARRINGTON, VERNON LOUIS. *Main Currents in American Thought: An Interpretation of American Literature from the Beginnings to 1920.* 3 vols. in 1. New York: Harcourt, Brace and Company, 1930.

PARTON, JAMES. *Life of Andrew Jackson.* 3 vols. New York: Mason Brothers, 1861.

PATTEE, FRED LEWIS (ed.). *American Writers: A Series of Papers Contributed to Blackwood's Magazine (1824-1825) by John Neal.* Durham: Duke University Press, 1937.

———. (ed.). *The Poems of Philip Freneau: Poet of the American Revolution.* 3 vols. Princeton, N. J.: The University Library, 1902-7.

PATTERSON, BURD S. "The Historical Society of Western Pennsylvania. Its History, Objects and Achievements," *Western Pennsylvania Historical Magazine,* II (January, 1919), 1-4.

PAXTON, JOHN A. (ed.). *The St. Louis Directory and Register, Containing the Names, Professions, and Residence of All the Heads of Families and Persons in Business; together with Descriptive Notes on St. Louis; the Constitution of the U. States, and State of Missouri; with Other Useful Information.* St. Louis: Printed for the Publisher, 1821.

Pensacola Gazette and West Florida Advertiser, 1824-31.

Pittsburgh Gazette, 1786-1804, 1818-20, 1822-25, 1871.

Pittsburgh Post, 1860.

POPE, JOHN. *A Tour through the Southern and Western Territories of the United States of North-America; the Spanish Dominions on the River Mississippi, and the Floridas; the Countries of the Creek Nations; and Many Uninhabited Parts.* Richmond: John Dixon, 1792. Reprinted—With index for Charles L. Woodward, New York, 1888.

PRESTON, JOHN HYDE. *A Gentleman Rebel: The Exploits of Anthony Wayne.* New York: Farrar & Rinehart, 1930.

Proceedings of the American Philosophical Society Held at Philadelphia for Promoting Useful Knowledge. Vol. XXII. Philadelphia: Printed for the Society by M'Calla & Stavely, 1885.

RANDOLPH, THOMAS JEFFERSON (ed). *Memoirs, Correspondence, and Private Papers of Thomas Jefferson, Late President of the United States.* 4 vols. London: Henry Colburn and Richard Bentley, 1829.

RASMUSSEN, WAYNE D. "Diplomats and Plant Collectors: The South American Commission, 1817-1818," *Agricultural History,* XXIX (January, 1955), 22-31.

REICHEL, WILLIAM C. *A History of the Rise, Progress, and Present Condition of the Moravian Seminary for Young Ladies, at Bethlehem, Pa. With a Catalogue of Its Pupils. 1785-1858.* Philadelphia: J. B. Lippincott & Co., 1870.

REID, A. B. "Early Courts, Judges, and Lawyers of Allegheny County," *Western Pennsylvania Historical Magazine,* V (July, 1922), 185-202.

BIBLIOGRAPHY

Reply to the Author of the Letter on South America and Mexico, By an American, Addressed to Mr. James Munroe [sic], President of the United States, Printed at Washington, in This Present Year, 1817. Philadelphia: J. F. Hurtel, 1817.

SABIN, JOSEPH, EAMES, WILBERFORCE, and VAIL, R.W.G. (comps.). *A Dictionary of Books Relating to America, from Its Discovery to the Present Time.* 29 vols. New York: Joseph Sabin [etc.], 1868-1936.

SAFFORD, WILLIAM H. *The Life of Harman Blennerhassett. Comprising an Authentic Narrative of the Burr Expedition: And Containing Many Additional Facts Not Heretofore Published.* Chillicothe, O.: Ely, Allen & Looker, 1850.

Saturday Evening Visiter [Pittsburgh], 1834-55.

SELTER, H. FOURE. *L'odyssée Américaine d'une Famille Francaise. Le Docteur Antoine Saugrain. Etude Suivie de Manuscrits Inédits et de la Correspondance de Sophie Michau Robinson.* (Institut Francais de Washington.) Baltimore: The Johns Hopkins Press, 1936.

SHETRONE, HENRY CLYDE. *The Mound-Builders: A Reconstruction of the Life of a Prehistoric American Race, through Exploration and Interpretation of Their Earth Mounds, Their Burials, and Their Cultural Remains.* New York: D. Appleton and Company, 1930.

Sketch of Proceedings in the Legislature of Maryland, December Session, 1818, on What Is Commonly Called The Jew Bill; Containing the Report of the Committee Appointed by the House of Delegates "To consider the justice and expediency of extending to those persons professing the Jewish Religion, the same privileges that are enjoyed by Christians:" together with the Bill Reported by the Committee, and the Speeches of Thomas Kennedy, Esq. of Washington County, and H. M. Brackenridge, Esq. of Baltimore City. Baltimore: Joseph Robinson, 1819.

SMITH, JOSEPH. *History of Jefferson College: Including an Account of the Early "Log-Cabin" Schools, and the Canonsburg Academy: with Biographical Sketches of Rev. Matthew Brown, D.D., Rev. Samuel Ralston, D.D., Rev. Matthew Henderson, Rev. James Ramsey, D.D., Rev. John H. Kennedy, and Rev. Abr'm. Anderson, D.D.* Pittsburgh: J. T. Shryock, 1857.

SQUIER, E. G., and DAVIS, E. H. *Ancient Monuments of the Mississippi Valley: Comprising the Results of Extensive Original Surveys and Explorations.* New York: Bartlett & Welford, 1848.

STARKE, AUBREY. "Books in the Wilderness," *Journal* of The Illinois State Historical Society, XXVIII (January, 1936), 258-70.

STARRETT, AGNES LYNCH. *Through One Hundred and Fifty Years: The University of Pittsburgh.* Pittsburgh: University of Pittsburgh Press, 1937.

Statesman [Pittsburgh], 1823-31.

St. Louis Enquirer, 1820-21.

SWETNAM, GEORGE. "Singing Pittsburgh," *Western Pennsylvania Historical Magazine,* XXXV (March, 1952), 25-36.

TAYLOR, M. FLAVIA. "The Political and Civic Career of Henry Baldwin, 1799-1830," *Western Pennsylvania Historical Magazine,* XXIV (March, 1941), 37-50.

The Journal of Andrew Ellicott, Late Commissioner on Behalf of the United States during Part of the Year 1796, the Years 1797, 1798, 1799, and Part of the Year 1800: for Determining the Boundary between the United States and the Possessions of His Catholic Majesty in America, Containing Occasional Remarks on the Situation, Soil, Rivers, Natural Productions, and Diseases of the Different Countries on the Ohio, Mississippi, and Gulf of Mexico, with Six Maps Comprehending the Ohio, the Mississippi from the Mouth of the Ohio to the Gulf of Mexico, the Whole of West Florida, and Part of East Florida. Philadelphia: William Fry, 1814.

The Pittsburgh Directory, for 1815: Containing the Names, Professions, and Residence of the Heads of Families and Persons in Business, in the Borough of Pittsburgh, with an Appendix, Containing a Variety of Useful Information. Pittsburgh: Printed for James M. Riddle, Compiler and Publisher, 1815.

"The Population of Pittsburgh and Contiguous Territory, Including the Names of Heads of Families as Shown by the United States Census of 1790," *Western Pennsylvania Historical Magazine*, II (July, 1919), 161-73.

THOMAS, DAVID YANCEY. *A History of Military Government in Newly Acquired Territory of the United States.* ("Studies in History, Economics and Public Law," Vol. XX, No. 2.) New York: Columbia University Press, 1904.

Tree of Liberty [Pittsburgh], 1800-4.

UHLER, JOHN EARLE. "The Delphian Club: A Contribution to the Literary History of Baltimore in the Early Nineteenth Century," *Maryland Historical Magazine*, XX (December, 1925), 305-46.

U. S. CONGRESS. *American State Papers. Documents, Legislative and Executive, of the Congress of the United States.* 38 vols. Washington: Gales and Seaton, 1832-61.

Valley Daily News [Tarentum], 1952.

WARREN, HARRIS GAYLORD. *The Sword Was Their Passport: A History of American Filibustering in the Mexican Revolution.* Baton Rouge: Louisiana State University Press, 1943.

Western Monthly Magazine, a Continuation of the Illinois Monthly Magazine. 4 vols. Cincinnati: Corey & Fairbank [etc.], 1833-35.

WHITE, J. W. F. "The Judiciary of Allegheny County," *Pennsylvania Magazine of History and Biography*, VII (1883), 143-93.

WILKINSON, JAMES. *Memoirs of My Own Times.* 3 vols. Philadelphia: Abraham Small, 1816.

WILLIAMS, JOHN LEE. *A View of West Florida, Embracing Its Geography, Topography, &c. with an Appendix, Treating of Its Antiquities, Land Titles, and Canals. And Containing a Map, Exhibiting a Chart of the Coast, a Plan of Pensacola, and the Entrance of the Harbour.* Philadelphia: Printed for H. S. Tanner and the Author, 1827.

YOAKUM, H. *History of Texas from Its First Settlement in 1685 to Its Annexation to the United States in 1846.* 2 vols. New York: Redfield, 1855.

D.   UNPUBLISHED SOURCES.

KELLER, WILLIAM F., "American Politics and the Genet Mission, 1793-1794." Ph.D. dissertation, University of Pittsburgh, 1951.

McQUEEN, RAY A., "The Role of Andrew Jackson in the Acquisition of the Floridas." Ph.D. dissertation, University of Pittsburgh, 1942.

ZIMMERMAN, LUCINDA, "Henry Marie Brackenridge: Author, Traveler, Jurist." M.A. thesis, University of Pittsburgh, 1932.

Index

Account of the First Discovery, and Natural History of Florida, An (William Roberts), 319

Acre, Samuel, 287, 288

Adams, John, 313, 314

Adams, John Quincy, 153, 180, 185, 186, 187, 196, 210, 214, 218, 219, 220, 221, 222, 224, 225, 226, 227, 229, 232, 237, 239, 240-41, 253, 254, 255, 258, 259, 265, 266, 267, 271, 280, 281, 282, 283, 284, 285, 286, 290, 293, 297, 318, 327, 332, 334, 335, 336, 342, 346, 347, 351, 356

Addison, Judge Alexander, 56

Aeneid (Vergil), 46

Alabama, State of, 271, 288, 295

Alaqua, Fla., 338

Alba, Peter, Jr., 309

Aldao, Carlos A., 236

Alexander & Phillips, 83

Alien and Sedition Acts, 55, 58

Allegheny County, Pa., 7, 8, 13, 44, 59, 79, 364

Allegheny Mountains, 3, 5, 19, 26, 82, 93, 155

Allegheny River, 3, 4, 7, 51, 339, 340, 342, 364, 368

Allen, Andrew, 268

Allen, N. H., 305

Allen, Paul, 170, 242, 243

Allen, W. O., 131, 133

Allman, F. and J., 236

"Alodia," 32

Alvarez, 238

Alvarez de Toledo, José, 146, 147, 148

Ambrosio Case, 306

Amelia Island, 196

American bottom, 108

American Philosophical Society, 26, 30, 145

American Register; or, Summary Review of History, Politics and Literature, 178

American Watchman (Wilmington, Del.), 184, 195, 210, 214, 220, 221

"AMICUS," 303

Analectic Magazine, 145, 160-61, 162, 234-35

Ancient Monuments of the Mississippi Valley (Squier and Davis), 369, 371

Anderson, Alexander, 258

Andes Mountains, 208, 209

Anduaga, Joaquin de, 285, 286

"AN EYE WITNESS," 304

Anglophiles, 29

Annapolis, Md., 187, 222, 224

Anticonstitutionalists, in Pa. assembly, 8

Anti-Federalists, opponents of Constitution of 1787, 11-12

Anti-Federalists, opponents of Hamiltonian policies, 29

Apalachicola Bay, 331

Apalachicola River, 319

Arikaras, 121, 122, 123, 124, 125, 126, 129, 136

Artigas, José, 202, 208, 212, 217, 220, 229, 236

Artigas y Carrera (H. M. Brackenridge), 236

Askmava, 131-33

Assiniboin, 128

Assumption, 209

Astor, John Jacob, 112, 129

Astoria, 129

Astoria; or Anecdotes of an Enterprise beyond the Rocky Mountains (Irving), 129

Attakapas, 150

Aurora (Philadelphia), 91, 220-21, 222

Austin, Moses, 102

Austin's Tavern, Pensacola, 288

Ayres, William, 69, 73

Ayres Hill, Pittsburgh, 4

Bagot, Sir Charles, 191

Bainbridge, Commodore William, 310

Baird, John, 13

Baird, Thomas, 61

Baldwin, Dr. William, 195, 196, 197, 199, 200, 201, 204, 205, 207, 209, 210, 213, 214, 217, 218, 243, 244

Baldwin, Henry, 70, 72, 74, 80-81, 167, 249

Baldwin, Thomas, 195

Baltimore, Md., 3, 84, 86, 87, 88, 89, 90,
91, 92, 93, 157-59, 162, 164, 167, 168,
169, 170, 176, 177, 179, 184, 186, 196,
216, 217, 218, 224, 240, 244, 245, 249,
377

Baltimore Patriot, 220, 232, 234

Banda Oriental del Uruguay, 202

Bank of North America, 8, 9

Barr, James, 6, 13

Barrett, Mrs., 154

Barton, David, 249

Bastille, 77

Bates, Frederick, 105, 108

Bates, Tarleton F., 62, 63, 65, 66, 74, 75,
104, 105

Bates v. *Read,* 329

Bates-Stewart duel, 75, 104

Baton Rouge, La., 143, 145, 146, 147, 151

Bay of Honda, 301

Beard, James, 131

Beauvais, Mme., 35, 36, 100, 137, 359

Beauvais, Vital, 34, 35, 36, 101, 137

Beauvais, Zouzou, 35, 100

Beauvais family, 358, 359

Bedford, Dr. Nathaniel, 17

Bedford, Pa., 82

Belgrano, Gen. Manuel, 238

Benton, Thomas H., 248, 249, 250, 251,
252

Biddle, a Jacksonian, 354

Biddle, Capt. James, 181, 185, 187, 310

Biddle, Richard, 360

Bigelow, H., 284

Big Sioux River, 120

Blackbird Hill, 120, 127

Blackfeet, 113, 116, 128

Black Shoe, 126

Blackwood's Magazine, 242

Blair, Francis P., 353, 357

Blakely, Ala., 256, 257, 258

Bland, Theodorick, 182, 184, 193, 194,
195, 196, 201, 202, 206, 209, 210, 211,
213, 214, 215, 216, 217, 218, 219, 220,
227, 229, 232, 234, 239, 240, 241

Blennerhassett, Island of, 97

Bloody Run, 82

"Blossom," 201

Board of Navy Commissioners, 339, 346

Bolivar, Gen., 185

Bonaparte, Jerome, 90

Bonaparte, Mme., 90

Bonpland, Aimé, 207

Boone, Daniel, 117, 246

Bowie, George, 265

Boyd, John, 7, 8, 9

Brackenridge, Alexander, 84, 163, 164,
178, 316, 339, 341, 353, 374

Brackenridge, Benjamin Morgan, 338, 342,
361, 375-77

Brackenridge, Cornelia (daughter of
H.M.), 354

Brackenridge, Cornelia (sister of H.M.),
84, 163, 168, 169, 180, 244, 298

Brackenridge, Cornelia Caroline, 377

Brackenridge, Henry M.: Life
HM born, 5; possible presence at Pittsburgh celebration (1788), 15; mother,
friendship with "Joe," 16; life with the
Maries, 16-17; stepmother, 20; step-
grandfather, 20-21, 27; father's decision
to send him to Louisiana, 28; beginning
of voyage to Louisiana, 33; life with
the Beauvais family, 34-36; begins return to Pittsburgh, 38-39; sojourn in
Gallipolis, 40-41; arrival in Pittsburgh,
42; meets future wife, 43; a student of
his father, 46-49; Pittsburgh Academy,
49; Pittsburgh, an exciting place for a
boy, 50-54; grandmother, 54; Gilkison's
student, 54-55; learns politics early, 56,
58; at age of fifteen, he becomes a writer,
60-61; begins law apprenticeship, 62,
63; hobbies, 64-65; friendship with
Nicholson, 66-67; why he reads law in
Butler, 68-70; college student, 74-75;
law studies, 75-76; studies German with
Schewe, 76; Burr's design, 77-79; passes
bar examination, 79; admires Pittsburgh
lawyers, 79-81; journey to Carlisle, 82;
preparation for a law practice in Baltimore, 83-86; as a young lawyer in Baltimore, 87-92; practices law in Somerset,
92-94; the return to Ste. Genevieve,
96-101; in St. Louis, 102-105; a promising writer, 106-111; why he undertakes
the Missouri voyage, 112-16; ascent of
the Missouri, 116-21; the rival expeditions joined, 121-26; descent of the
Missouri, 126-27; achievement upriver
recognized, 128-30; wins a law case,
130-33; goes to New Orleans, 134-35;
publishes his first book, 135-41; studious
but active life in Louisiana—becomes a
judge, 142-45; friendship with Shaler—
they plan a book on Texan revolution,
145-48; reports defenseless situation of
Louisiana to the federal government,

148-51; returns to Pittsburgh, 151-54; reaction to War of 1812—memorializes Cramer, 155-56; goes to Washington, Philadelphia, and Baltimore, 157; begins second residence in Baltimore, 157-59; authorship lures him again, 159-61; a plan for New Orleans, 161-62; his father's death, 162-63; an astonishing hack, 164-67; the Delphian, 169-76; the struggle to get ahead in Baltimore, 176-79; receives a government appointment, 179-83; preparations for the South American mission, 184-87; writes famous pamphlet on South America, 187-95; his mission sails, 195-97; the voyage to South America, 198-210; defended against charges of misdoing on the mission, 210-13; the struggle for South American recognition, 214-16, 217-22, 230-41, 253; elected to Md. legislature, 217; the Jew Bill, 222-25; reports to the nation on his South American mission, 225-29; a popular Delphian, 241-44; leaves Baltimore for the West again, 244-45; decides to practice law in St. Louis, 246-48; the Missouri question, 249-52; leaves St. Louis for Florida, 252; becomes an unofficial adviser to Jackson, 255-63; role in organizing the Florida government, 264-67; Schewe arrives in Florida, 269; law partner of Call, 270-71; the Vidal case—Callava, 271-79, 281-84, 286-88; Jackson appreciates his aid in organizing the Florida government, 289-97; yellow fever in Pensacola, 298-300; the new judge, 300; the Steele affair, 301-306; the administration of territorial justice, 306-308; a leader in Florida progress, 310-12; the Walton affair, 316-18; trip north and marriage to Caroline Marie, 318-22; the first months of marriage, 322-28; the return to Florida and reappointment as judge, 328-30; sells land to Navy Department and wins superintendency of live oak experiment, 331-36; trouble with Secretary of the Navy Branch, 338-39, 342-48; Caroline's property at Bull Creek, 339-42; a leading Floridian with friends and enemies, 349-51; the Jacksonians, 351-53; loses his judgeship and attacks Jackson, 353-58, 360, 362-63; Congress—Mexican Claims Commission, 360-62; notes changes in the Pittsburgh scene, 364-65; addresses the literary societies at Jefferson College, 367-68; reports the Pittsburgh fire, 368; corresponds with important ethnologists, 370-71; the controversy with Neville B. Craig, 371-75; concern for his son, 375-77; comment on his orations, 377-78; death, 379.

Brackenridge, Henry M.: Writings
"Biographical Notice of H.H. Brackenridge, Late of the Supreme Court of Pennsylvania," 372
"Chevalier de Gourges, The," 366
"Dubukes Mines," 130, 134
Early Discoveries by Spaniards in New Mexico, 369-71
Essay on Florida in *North American Review*, 320-21
Essay on Trusts and Trustees, An, 73, 340-41
Essays in defense of his father, *Daily Commercial Journal*, 373
Eulogy on Adams and Jefferson, 313-15, 316, 337, 377
Eulogy on John Quincy Adams, 378
"Florida Question Stated, The," 178-79, 321
Floridian articles, 270
History of the Late War, between the United States and Great Britain, 164-67, 179, 180, 183, 269
History of the Revolution of Texas, The, 146-48, 225
History of the Western Insurrection in Western Pennsylvania, Commonly Called the Whiskey Insurrection. 1794, 373-74, 375
Jubilee Oration, 312-13
Judge Brackenridge's Letters, 355-56
Letter on the culture of the live oak, 334-36, 337
Letter to Jefferson on tumuli of North American aborigines, 143-45, 337, 369
"Lines on an Unfortunate Female Maniac, Seen on the Missouri, beyond the White Settlements," 159-60
Louisiana Gazette articles, 106-109, and "Sketches of the Territory of Louisiana," 109-11, 112, 127, 130, 135, 178
Mexican Letters Written during the Progress of the Late War between the United States and Mexico, 369
"Observations on a passage in Dr. Robertsons America," 133-34
"Ode on Jackson's Victory, 8th January, 1815," 154, 155

"On the Monumental Procession," 157-58

"Pedro Menendez de Aviles, First Spanish Conqueror and Adelantado of Florida," 366

"Pittsburgh in the Olden Time," 365

Recollections of Persons and Places in the West, 358-60, 366-67

Report on commemorating the defense of Baltimore, adopted by the city council, 337

Sixty Years in the North and Twenty Years in the South, 378-79

South America: A Letter on the Present State of That Country, to James Monroe, President of the United States, 188-95, 196, 215, 229, 235

Speeches on the Jew Bill, 336-37

"The Genius of the Hills, an Elegy," 172-76

"To a Lady Who Advised Him to Take a Wife," 168-69

Views of Louisiana; Together with a Journal of a Voyage up the Missouri River, in 1811, 135-41, 142, 143, 148, 159-61, 178, 179, 251, 359, 369

Voyage to South America, 225-29, 230, 231, 232, 233, 234, 235, 236, 238, 240, 241, 269, 359

"Western Country, The," 155

Brackenridge, Henry Morgan, 377

Brackenridge, Hugh Henry: Life

HH an immigrant to American colonies, schoolteacher, student at Princeton, changes name, 1; master of Md. school, chaplain, editor of United States Magazine, student of theology and law, lawyer, 2; leading lawyer in Pittsburgh, 3; birth of son, interest in Pittsburgh Gazette, 5; elected to state assembly, 6; conduct there, 7-9; legislative activity offends Western Pa. colleagues and constituents, 8-9; newspaper controversy with Findley, 9-10; supporters in assembly, 11; champion of federal constitution in Western Pa., 11-14; a stern parent, 16-17; sermon on talebearing, 17-18; marriage, 20; surrenders ambition to win elective office, 21; plans education for son, 28; a Francophile, 29-30; sees Michaux, 31; friendship with Lucas, 33; opinion of Genet, 37; attitude toward conspiracy endangering Union, 37-38; meeting with son, 42; role in Whisky Insurrection, 43-45; adds a fourth volume to Modern Chival-

ry, 45-46; supervises son's education, 46-49; helps start a bookstore, 54; establishes Jeffersonian party in Western Pa., 56-61; establishes the Tree of Liberty, 59-60; justice of Pa. Supreme Court, 61-63; moves to Carlisle, 63; dislike of the theater, 65; attacked by Pentland, 74; description of Woods, his political rival, 80; son describes his legal talent, 81; advises his son to practice law in Baltimore, 83-84, 86; 89, 91, 92, 93, 102, 105, 135, 157; death, 162-63, 166; 177-78, 180, 182, 223, 224, 229, 240, 316, 337, 339, 354, 358, 359, 361, 365, 371, 372, 373, 374, 376, 379

Brackenridge, Hugh Henry: Writings

Gazette Publications, 83

Incidents of the Insurrection in the Western Parts of Pennsylvania, in the Year 1794, 45

Law Miscellanies, 68

"Modern Chevalier, The," 21-22

Modern Chivalry: Containing the Adventures of Captain John Farrago, and Teague O'Regan, His Servant, 22-27, 45-46, 48, 56, 58, 84, 98, 163, 177-78, 235, 366, 372

"On the Popularity of ....," 13, 21

"On the Situation of the Town of Pittsburgh, and the State of Society at That Place," 4

"Rising Glory of America, The," 1, 5

"To the INHABITANTS of the WESTERN COUNTRY"—"NOTES on the OBSERVATIONS of WILLIAM FINDLEY," 10

Brackenridge, Mrs. Phillipine, 377,379

Brackenridge, William, 84, 163, 230-31, 316

Bradbury, John, 112, 114, 115, 117, 122, 123, 124, 125, 126, 127, 128, 134-35, 136

Braddock's Field, 43

Bradford, William, Jr., 1

Branch, John, 296, 297, 338, 339, 342, 343, 344, 345, 346, 347, 348

Brazil, 185, 189, 190, 191, 192, 199, 239

Brent, Daniel, 219

Brison, James, 61

Brobson, William P., 230, 236

Bronaugh, Dr. James C., 253, 256, 257, 258, 259, 260, 261, 262, 265, 273, 274, 275, 276, 284, 285, 290, 291, 292, 293, 294, 296, 297, 299, 300, 349

Brooke, Col. G. M., 273, 274, 275
Brooks, Van Wyck, 359
Brosnaham, Dr. John, 278, 279
Brownjohn, Thomas, 278
Buenos Aires, 185, 196, 202, 203, 204, 205, 206, 207, 208, 209, 210, 212, 213, 214, 215, 216, 218, 219, 220, 222, 228, 238
Buffon, 134
Bull Creek, 339, 340, 341, 342, 350
Burlamaqui, Jean Jacques, 85
Burleigh, William H., 365-66
Burning Bluffs, 120
Burnt Corn, Ala., 350
Burr, Aaron, 77-79, 83
Butler, Col. Robert, 273, 274, 275, 276
Butler, Pa., 69
Butler, Thomas (of Pittsburgh), 64, 78
Butler, Thomas (of St. Francisville, La.), 163, 167, 168, 179, 186, 298, 299, 311, 312, 328, 333, 340
Butler County, Pa., 152

Cahokia mounds, 108-109, 371
Calhoun, John, 214, 231, 257, 258, 292, 353
Call, Capt. Richard K., 255, 259, 260, 261, 270, 271, 286, 287, 296, 309, 345
Callava, Col. José, 256-63, 265, 271, 272, 273, 274, 275, 276, 277, 278, 279, 280, 282, 283, 284, 285, 286, 287, 288, 289, 291, 292, 356, 363, 375
"CANDIDUS," 302
Canning, George, 238
Canonsburg, Pa., 74, 75
Canonsburg Academy, 49
Cantonment Clinch, 318, 322
Cape Disappointment, 129
Cape Frio, 198
Cape Girardeau, Mo., 100, 104
Caracas, 185
Carey and Hart, 372
Carey, Mathew, 157
Carlisle, Pa., 63, 82, 83, 85, 86, 88
Carlisle College (Dickinson), 83, 87, 349
"Carmen," 300-301
Carrera, José Miguel, 191, 193, 194, 201, 202, 203, 208, 212, 213, 221, 227, 229, 234, 238, 241

Carreristas, 194, 196, 209, 211, 212, 214, 215, 217, 220, 222, 227, 228, 229, 232, 233, 239, 241
Carroll, Charles, 313
Carthagena, 185
Case of Jane Marie, The, 73
Castor, 117
Chambersburg, Pa., 82
Charette, 117
Charless, Joseph, 104, 106, 107, 109, 112, 116, 127, 128, 130, 132, 134
Charleston, S. C., 30
Chase, Mary, 90
Chase, Samuel, 2, 89-90
Chatburn, John, 308
Cheves, Langdon, 156
Cheyenne River, 123, 126
Cheyennes, 125
Chile, 188, 190, 191, 193, 194, 196, 203, 208, 209, 219, 220, 221
Chipola, Fla., 325
Chipola River, 331
Chislett, John, 365
Choctawhatchee River, 319
Choctaws, 150
Chouteau, Auguste, 105, 108, 131
Chouteau, Pierre, 130
Cibola, 370-71
Cicero, 66
Cincinnati, O., 32, 33, 34, 41, 97, 106, 153
Civil War, 378, 379
"CIVIS," 301, 302
Claggett, Albert J., 305
"Clapboard Democracy," 61
Clark, Gen. John, 347, 348
Clark, George Rogers, 30, 31, 37, 38
Clark, James, 87
Clark, William, 105, 108, 118, 136, 246
Clay, Henry, 153, 215, 216, 220, 221, 222, 225, 226, 230, 236, 237, 238, 239, 252, 253, 330, 361, 375
Clinch, Col. Duncan L., 294
Coal Hill, Pittsburgh, 27
Coale and Maxwell, 159
Code Napoléon, 143
Coffee, Gen. John, 258, 264
Cohen, J. I., 224
Coke, 135
College of New Jersey (Princeton), 1

Collins, Thomas, 72
Columbia River, 112, 114, 125, 128, 129, 187, 252
Columbian (New York), 139
Columbus, 134
Commentaries (Blackstone), 68, 69, 70
Commercial Hotel, Pensacola, 310
Commonwealth (Pittsburgh), 74, 75, 128, 153, 154
Conemaugh River, 11
"Congress," 187, 194, 195, 196, 197, 198, 199, 200, 201, 202, 209, 210
Connecticut, State of, 14
Connor, John Coppinger, 286
"Constellation," 314
Constitution of 1787, 11-14, 224
Constitutional Whig (Richmond), 357
Constitutionalists, in Pa. assembly, 8
Continental Divide, 129
Cooper, Braxton, 117
Cooper, Dr. Thomas, 349-50
"Cora," 259
Cordelle, 119
Cornell, Thomas F., 343
Cornplanter, Seneca chief, 19
Coronado, 370
Corpus Juris Civilis, 143
Correa da Serra, Abbé José Francisco, 178, 196, 217
Cote sans Dessein, 116, 117
Coulter, Richard, 75
Council Bluffs, 119
"Countryman," 306
Coureur des bois, 112
Craig, Maj. Isaac, 31
Craig, Neville B., 357, 358, 364, 371-75
Cramer, Zadok, 62, 135, 137, 138, 156
Cramer, Spear and Eichbaum, 137, 138, 140
Cramer's Pittsburgh Magazine Almanack, for the Year of Our Lord, 1815, 138
Cramer's Pittsburgh Magazine Almanack, for the Year of Our Lord, 1816, 155, 156
Crawford, William H., 242, 292, 307
Creeks, 148, 150, 151, 153, 254, 290
Crooks, Ramsay, 113, 122, 123, 125, 129
Crowder, 52
Crows, 128
Cruzat, José, 274, 276, 283
Cumberland County, Pa., 83

Cuming, Fortescue, 102
Cushing, Joseph, 164
Custom of Paris, 101
Cyclopaedia of American Literature, 376

Dade, Capt. F. L., 273
Daily Commercial Journal (Pittsburgh), 369, 373
Daily Courier (Petersburg, Va.), 157
Daily Madisonian (Washington, D. C.), 362-63
Dalmas, A. de, 166
Darby, William, 138-40, 362-63
Darlington, Dr. William, 195, 196, 197, 200, 204, 209, 210, 217, 218, 244
Davenport, R., 50
Davis, Edwin H., 369
Davis, Samuel, 333, 336, 338, 339, 344, 345
Davis, W. W. H., 371
Davison, W., 268
Day, John, 113
Decatur, Commodore Stephen, 185
Declaration of Independence, 58, 312, 314
Deer Point, 332, 335, 336, 343, 344, 347, 348
Delaware, State of, 14
De Lisle, 50
Delphian Club, 169-76, 179, 180, 183, 186, 196, 197, 200, 241-44, 350
Democratic-Republican party, 56, 58, 59, 60, 61, 63, 74, 79
Denison, Edward, 170, 242, 243
Denny, William H., 374
De officiis (Cicero), 64
Description de la Louisiane (Hennepin), 105
Doddridge, Philip, 94
Domingo, Manuel, 273
Donica, Benjamin, 318, 322
Donoho, Maj. Saunders, 318, 322
Don Quixote (Cervantes), 24, 27, 46, 115
Dorion, Pierre, 114-15, 123, 129
Duane, William, 91, 220-21, 222, 230
Dubac, Chevalier Gabriel, 53
Du Bourg, Bishop Louis Guillaume Valentin, 246
Dubuque, Julien, 130
Duncan, Abner L., 264, 266, 281, 351

Duncan, David, 14
Duncan, Thomas, 85
Du Ponceau, Peter S., 225, 231, 240, 244
Duval, William P., 297, 318, 352
Duyckinck, Evert A., 376

Eagle Tavern, Pensacola, 268
Earle, Mrs., 65-66, 70, 74, 75, 77, 79, 90
Eaton, John Henry, 253, 291
Eaton, Margaret, 354
Eaton affair, 347
Edinburgh Review, 140
Eichbaum, William Peter, 54
Elder, Dr. William, 366
Elegant Extracts in Prose and Verse, 64
El-Gringo; or, New Mexico and Her People (W. W. H. Davis), 371
"Eloquence" (Abbé Maury), 64
Embarras, 117
Escambia County, Fla., 266, 308, 326, 350
Escovar, Antonio, 318
Espejo, 370
Espy, Josiah, 340
Essay on Population (Malthus), 96
Essay on the Life of George Washington, An (Aaron Bancroft), 269
Etting, S., 224
Everett, Edward, 320
Ewalt, Samuel, 59
Exposure of a Few of the Many Misstatements in H. M. Brackenridge's History of the Whiskey Insurrection (Neville B. Craig), 374

Fallen Timbers, battle of, 41
Fauchet, Citizen, 37
Fayette County, Pa., 3
Federal Gazette & Baltimore Daily Advertiser, 157, 241
Federalist, The, 74
Federalists, followers of Hamilton, 29, 30, 56, 57, 58, 59, 60, 61, 63, 79, 80, 91
Fell's Point, Baltimore, 91
Fénelon, Francois de Salignac de La Mothe, 42
Fenwick, Col. J. R., 295
Ferdinand VII, king of Spain, 192
Fergusson, Robert, 54
Fifteenth Congress of U. S., 214, 215, 216, 220, 221, 222, 237

Findley, William, 6, 8, 9, 10, 11, 12, 13, 21, 25, 27, 354, 373
Finley, Capt. John, 31
Fisher, E. Burke, 365-67
Flint, Timothy, 152-53, 248
"Florida," 305, 323
Florida, Spanish territory, 29, 246, 252, 253, 254, 255, 256, 257, 259, 260, 263, 321
Florida, Territory of, 252, 258, 259, 263, 264, 265, 266, 267, 269, 270, 279, 282, 284, 285, 288, 289, 290, 291, 293, 295, 296, 297, 305, 307, 308, 309, 310, 311, 312, 317, 319, 326, 329, 331, 342, 347, 349, 350, 352
Florida Institute of Agriculture, Antiquities, and Science, 311
Florida Legislative Council, 296, 297, 300, 305, 306, 308, 309, 317, 325
Floridian (Pensacola), 269, 270, 271, 284, 285, 288, 296, 297, 298, 301, 302, 303, 309, 349
Floyd, John, 251
Forbes, Col. James G., 257, 258
Forbes, John, 351
Force, Peter, 369, 373
Forks of the Ohio, 33
Forsyth, James, 303
Fort Barrancas, 263, 266, 288
Fort de Chartres, 101
Fort Duquesne, 4, 374
Fort Fayette, 58
Fort Gadsden, 257
Fort Mandan, 116, 125, 126
Fort McHenry, 157, 158
Fort Osage, 118, 127
Fort Pitt, 4, 19, 31
Fort Washington (modern Cincinnati), 33
Forward, Walter, 70, 74, 75, 76, 79, 80, 93, 94, 163-64, 167, 361
France, 29, 30, 37, 146
Francis, Sir Philip, 243
Francophiles, 29
Franklin, Benjamin, 47
Franklin, Pa., 364
Franklin Library, Philadelphia, 157
Frederick the Great, 77
Freeport, Pa., 341, 360
Freneau, Philip, 1, 2

Fromentin, Eligius, 142, 255, 258, 259, 278, 279, 280, 281, 282, 283, 284, 285, 291, 292, 295, 327
Fullarat, Antoine, 273, 275, 277
Funes, Dr. Gregorio, 207

Gadsden, Col. James, 295, 309, 311
Gales, Joseph, 304, 305
Gallatin, Albert, 16, 56, 57, 58, 153, 373
Gallipolis, O., 40, 41, 97, 100
Galveston, Tex., 196
Galvez Spring, Fla., 262, 300
Gasconade River, 117, 159
Gauchos, 202, 205
Gebhard, Dr., 322
Gellert, 85
"General Call," 309
"General Lacock," 364
Genet, Edmond Charles, 29, 30, 31, 37, 44, 220
Georgia, State of, 14, 327
Geographical Description of the State of Louisiana . . . Being an Accompaniment to the Map of Louisiana, A (William Darby), 139
German Lutheran Church, Pittsburgh, 77
Gibson, Dr. William, 244
Gibson, John, 85
Gil Blas (Le Sage), 46
Gilkison, John, 54-55, 61, 62, 69, 135
Glade Run, 69
Glenn, E., 239
Gliddon, George R., 369
Globe (Washington, D. C.), 353, 356, 357
Goethe, 85
Gomara, 370
Goncalves da Cruz, Antonio, 192
Gonzalez, Manuel, 259, 290
Gordon, Adam, 329, 361
Graham (college roommate of H. M. Brackenridge), 75, 102-104, 108
Graham, John, 147-48, 181, 182, 183, 184, 194, 195, 196, 210, 211, 216, 218, 219, 220, 229, 239
Graham's Magazine, 372
Grand River, 117
Grand Saline, 118
Grant's Hill, Pittsburgh, 4, 14, 16, 17, 29-30, 51, 54, 70, 71, 72, 96, 340, 358, 365
Gratiot, Charles, 134

Great Bend of the Missouri, 121, 126
Great Britain, 29, 30, 31, 32, 146, 148, 149, 150, 151, 153, 155, 157, 165, 191, 214, 252
Greaves, 96, 97, 98
Green, Duff, 353
Greensburg, Pa., 94
Grotius, 27, 66
Gutiérrez de Lara, José Bernardo, 146
Gwynn, William, 157, 170, 222, 241, 242, 243

Hakluyt, 370
Hall, James, 359
Hall, Joseph, 4, 5, 7
Hall, Judge Dominick, 362
Halsey, Thomas L., 205, 207
Hamilton, Alexander, 12, 29, 44, 373
Hamilton, Judge James, 85
Hamilton, Mary, 168, 244
Hamiltonian excise law, 30, 44
Hampton Roads, 197
Hanckel, Frederick, 76
Hannum, W. L., 294, 295
Harmar, Gen. Josiah, 31
Harper, Robert G., 92, 176, 241
Harper & Brothers, 371
Harris and McCarty Case, 306
Harrison, Tipton B., 300
Harrison, William Henry, 360
Hathway, E., 268
Haven, W. S., 373
Haywood, John, 278, 281
Heirs of Nicolas Maria Vidal v. *John Innerarity,* 286, 287, 288, 293
Helvetius, 66
Henry, Andrew, 113, 120, 128, 129
Henry, Isaac N., 249, 250
Henry Miner & Co., 371
Herald of Liberty (Washington, Pa.), 60
"Hermitage," 264, 279, 288, 290, 292, 363
Hernandez, J. M., 309
Herodotus, 371
Herzog, Joseph, 110
Hickey, Capt., 201
Higgenbotham, Ralph, 99
Hildreth, Richard, 373
Hill, Henry, 269

Histoire et description generale de la Nouvelle France (Charlevoix), 105

Historical Society of Pennsylvania, 373

Historical Society of Western Pennsylvania, 374

History of America, The (William Robertson), 133

History of England (Hume), 47

History of Pittsburgh (Neville B. Craig), 373

History of Spain (Mariana), 143

History of the Decline and Fall of the Roman Empire (Gibbon), 74

History of the English Law (John Reeves), 70

History of the Insurrection, in the Four Western Counties of Pennsylvania: in the Year M.DCC.XCIV (William Findley), 373

History of the Reign of the Emperor Charles the Fifth (William Robertson), 74

History of the United States (Richard Hildreth), 373

Hobson's Choice, 33, 34

Hoffman, Michael, 345

"Hornet," 257, 258, 259, 263, 264

Horseshoe Bend, battle of, 153

Hudibrastic verse, 12, 13, 21, 23, 24

Hulings, Bill, 99

Hull, Gen. William, 151

Humbert, Gen. Jean, 146, 147

Humboldt, Alexander von, 370

Humphreys, 98-99

Hunt, W. Hasell, 304, 314, 315, 317, 318, 322, 326, 327, 329, 331

Hunt, Wilson P., 112-26, 128, 129, 160-61

Iliad (Homer), 49

Imlay, George, 96

Independent and Revolutionary Legion of the Mississippi, 30

Indian Queen, Baltimore hotel, 86

Innerarity, James, 319, 351

Innerarity, John, 265, 271, 272, 273, 274, 275, 276, 277, 278, 283, 286, 287, 288, 301, 309, 319, 330, 351

Innerarity, Maria Henrietta, 330

Institutes, 143

Irvine, Baptis, 224, 232-34, 241

Irving, Washington, 129

Irwin, John, 13

Irwin, William, 365

Israel, John, 60, 61, 63, 67

Isthmus of Panama, 190

Jackson, Andrew, 138, 148, 153-54, 155, 157, 166, 252-63, 264-67, 271-79, 280-97, 299, 300, 317, 318, 320, 336, 338, 342, 343, 344, 351-58, 362, 363, 375

Jackson, Rachel, 253, 255, 259-60, 261, 263, 267, 268, 288

Jackson County, Fla., 307

Jackson Legend, 155, 362

Jacksonian Commonwealth Theater, 268, 281

Jay, John, 12

Jay-Gardoqui negotiations, 6

Jefferson, Thomas, 29, 31, 53, 67, 74, 78, 79, 90-91, 109, 110, 111, 133-34, 140-41, 142, 143-45, 187, 231-32, 234, 313, 314

Jefferson College, 74-75, 76, 367

Jennings, 92

Jerrison, John, 310, 313

Jew Bill, 222-24, 336-37

"Joe" (boyhood companion of H. M. Brackenridge), 16, 28, 33, 42, 43, 66, 359

John Fitzgerald & Company, 302

John Forbes & Company, 271, 288, 309

John I. Kay & Co., 366

John VI, king of Portugal, 199, 200

Johnson, Dr. Samuel, 242

Johnson, Judge William, 327

Johnston, John, 72

Jones, Walter, 179

"Junius," 243

Kansas River, 119

Kaskaskia River, 38

Kell, Thomas, 92, 224

Kendall, Amos, 347

Kemper, Reuben, 148

Kemper, Samuel, 147

Kennedy, Thomas, 224

Kentucky, 3, 13, 19, 31, 34, 37, 38, 39, 156

Key, Francis Scott, 157

Kickapoos, 26, 36, 132-33

King's Artillery Gardens, Pittsburgh, 4

Kingsley, Eliza, 255, 260, 267

Kline, George, 162
Kline's Carlisle Weekly Gazette, 91, 110

La Araucana (Ercilla), 143
Lacock, Abner, 152
Lafayette, 166, 312-13
Lake Champlain, battle of, 153
Lambdin, J. R., 364
Latrobe, John H. B., 169
"LAUTARO" letters, 193, 194
Lavalette, Eugene, 298
Lavater, Johann Kaspar, 64
Lear, Lt. William, 294, 295
Learned, Joseph D., 170
Le Borgne, 126
Lecor, Gen. Carlos Frederico, 201, 202
Lectures (Hugh Blair), 64
Lee, a Philadelphian, 299
Lee, Arthur, 3
Lee, Gen. Henry, 61
Le Gauche, 124
Legion of the United States, 31
Legionville, 31, 33, 97
Letters on the United Provinces of South America, Addressed to the Hon. Henry Clay (Vicente Pazos), 230
Le Vert, Dr., 375
Lewis, Maj. William B., 363
Lewis, Meriwether, 105, 126
Lewis, Reuben, 126, 129
Lewis and Clark expedition, 111, 126, 138
Library of Congress, 187, 195
Life of Andrew Jackson (James Parton), 355
Life of George Washington, The (John Marshall), 74
Limestone, Ky., 32
Lincoln, Abraham, 378
Lisa, Manuel, 113-26, 128, 129, 160-61, 246
Literary Examiner, and Western Monthly Review, 27, 365, 366
Little Cedar Island, 121
"Little Democrat," 32
Little Osage band, 118
Live oak, 331-39, 343-48, 350, 353
Livingston, Edward, 255-56, 352
Livingston, Robert R., 67
Lloyd, Thomas, 21

Locke, John, 66
Logan, 90
Lois civiles dans leur ordre naturel (Jean Domat), 143
Long, Maj. Stephen H., 243
Lopez, Juan, 143, 145
Loughy, Dennis, 52-53
Louis Philippe, king of France, 53, 372
Louis XVI, king of France, 29, 54
"Louisiana," 300
Louisiana, Spanish territory, 29, 31, 33, 37, 67
Louisiana, State of, 135, 136, 139, 141, 142, 143, 148, 149, 150, 151, 152, 266
Louisiana Territory of, 107, 109, 110, 112, 132, 138
Louisiana Advertiser (New Orleans), 284
Louisiana boundary question, 178-79
Louisiana Gazette (St. Louis), 104, 105, 106, 110, 111, 114, 128, 130, 134, 135, 136
Louisiana Purchase, 67, 77, 111, 136
Louisville, Ky., 34, 38, 39, 98, 153
Lucas, Charles, 248
Lucas, John B. C., 33, 34, 36, 38, 39, 40, 56, 72, 101, 131, 132, 248

McCarty, William M., 318, 343
McClellan, Gen. George, 378
McClellan, Robert, 113, 122, 123, 124, 129
M'Comb, David B., 321
McCoskry, Mrs., 168, 180
M'Culloch, John, 22, 45, 46
McDonald, a Pittsburgh law student, 75
McDonald, John, 340
Macdonough, Thomas, 153
McHenry, Dr. James, 89
McHenry, John, 89
McJunkin, John, 69
McKean, Thomas, 53, 58, 59, 61, 74
M'Kean v. *Bruff,* 177, 337
McKeesport, Pa., 51
McKenzie, Donald, 112, 129
Mackinaw, 113
Mackintosh, Sir James, 235
McLane, Louis, 360
McNair, Dunning, 86
McRae and Staples, 310

Madison, James, 112, 149, 152, 157, 180, 191, 221, 229, 231, 342
Magee, Christopher, 49
Magruder, Richard, 88, 340
Magruder, William, 316
Maha village, 120, 127
Mahy, Nicolas, 257, 258
Maine, State of, 237
Maipu, battle of, 208, 209, 212
"Malacabada," 203, 204
Maldonado, 209
Mandan village, 120, 125, 126, 128, 136
Margarita, 209
Marie, Caroline (Mrs. H. M. Bracken-ridge), 43, 54, 72, 73, 80, 321-29, 331, 333, 334, 338-44, 350, 352, 353, 354, 358, 376, 377, 379
Marie, Jane, 16, 17, 43, 54, 71-73, 80, 91, 321, 340
Marie, John, 16, 71-73
Marietta, O., 97
Marius, 362
Marks, A. W., 366
Marshall, Judge John, 327
Marshallton Botanic Garden, 195
Martens, 85
Martin, Luther, 88, 92
Martin, W., 342
Maryland, State of, 14
Maryland Censor (Baltimore), 220
Maryland House of Delegates, 217, 222, 223, 224
Mascouten tribe, 131
Massachusetts, State of, 14
Mayer, Brantz, 371
Melanthy, John, 247
Mercer, C. F., 319
"Meridian Hill," 193
Mexican Claims Commission, 361
Mexican revolutionists, 145, 146, 147, 148, 150, 151
Mexico, 77-78, 127, 133, 144, 146, 151, 188, 189, 214, 237, 362, 368-69
Michaux, André, 30, 31, 33, 37
Michilimackinac, 113
Mifflin, Thomas, 10
Miller, John (clerk of Escambia County, Fla.), 272, 273, 278
Miller, John (London publisher), 235, 236
Miller, Joseph, 113

Miller, Samuel, 74-75
Miller, W. G., 213
Mine a Burton, 101
Mingo Creek democratic society, 44
Mississippi, Territory of, 150, 156
Mississippi question, 6-7, 11
Mississippi River, 6, 30, 34, 38, 67, 101, 106, 107, 108, 130, 134, 144, 149, 150, 161-62, 246, 255
Missouri, State of, 245, 250, 252
Missouri, Territory of, 136, 156, 237, 249, 250, 251
Missouri Fur Company, 246
Missouri question, 222, 237, 249, 250, 251, 252
Missouri River, 30, 105, 112-27, 128-29
Mitchel, Colin, 319
Mitchell, John C., 286, 287
Mitchell, Robert, 319, 351
Mobile Bay, 319
Moeurs des Sauvages Ameriquains (Lafitau), 105
"Monongahela Farmer," 67
Monongahela House, Pittsburgh, 368
Monongahela River, 3, 4, 19, 28, 31, 51, 75, 96
Monroe, James, 67, 146, 149-51, 157, 178, 179, 180, 181, 184, 188, 191, 192, 210, 211, 214, 216, 217, 218, 219, 221, 222, 225, 226, 229, 231, 234, 237, 238, 239, 240, 242, 253, 254, 255, 258, 259, 264, 278, 281, 282, 285, 286, 288, 289, 290, 291, 292, 295, 296, 297, 300, 303, 312, 342
Monroe Doctrine, 190, 191, 235, 238
Monroe's tavern, Canonsburg, Pa., 57
Montevideo, 185, 201, 202, 203, 209
Montpelier, Ala., 255, 257, 258, 259
Monthly Review, 236
Monticello, 141
Montreal, 112, 113
Moore, Judge Jesse, 69
Morales, Juan Ventura, 67
Moravian Seminary for Young Ladies, Bethlehem, Pa., 321
Moreno, Manuel, 232
Morgan, B. R., 321
Morison, Robert, 319
Morning Chronicle (Savannah), 139
Mountain, James, 49, 70, 73, 79, 80, 81, 162

Mountz, Lt. George, 275, 277, 278, 279
Mullen, Peter, 268
Murat, Achilles, 77, 309
Murphy, Mary, 54, 80
Murphy, Patrick, 54
Myers, Jacob, 32
Myers, Samuel, 302

Napoleon, 67
Napoleonists, 149
Nashville, Tenn., 253
Nassau Hall, Princeton, 1
Natchez, 134, 146, 149
Natchitoches, La., 147, 151
National Intelligencer (Washington, D. C.), 252, 259, 291, 304, 305, 320, 351, 368
National Register (Washington, D. C.), 188
National Union (Washington, D. C.), 355
Natrona, Pa., 376
Naturalization Act, 55
Naval Affairs Committee, U. S. House of Representatives, 346
Navigator, 138
Navy Board, 193
Navy Department, 195
Neal, John, 170, 242, 243
Negley, Felix, 341
Neville, Col. Presley, 57, 78
Neville, Fayette, 49
Neville, Gen. John, 43, 374
Neville, Morgan, 50, 64, 78, 220
"Neville Connection, the," 57, 371, 374
New Hampshire, State of, 14
New Jersey, State of, 14
New Madrid, Mo., 27, 34, 98-99, 105
"New Orleans," 137
New Orleans, battle of, 154, 166
New Orleans, La., 30, 32, 37, 67, 101, 134, 135, 138, 141, 142, 149, 150, 154, 161-62, 199, 246, 255, 256, 362, 363
New Spain (Alexander von Humboldt), 269
New Voyages to North-America (Lahontan), 105
New York, State of, 14
Nicholas, Cary, 269, 270, 285, 293

Nicholson, John, 66-67, 70
Niglos, 213
Niles, Hezekiah, 110, 139, 140, 145, 161, 166, 194, 195, 196, 200, 201, 210, 215, 219, 222, 224, 226, 254, 271, 279, 285, 289, 310, 337, 354, 357
Nisbet, Alexander, 87
Nisbet, Dr. Charles, 87
Norfolk, Va., 196, 197, 210, 214
North-American Review and Miscellaneous Journal, 160, 320
North Carolina, State of, 14
North Point, battle of, 157
Northwest Company, 112, 113
Northwest Territory, 31
Notes on the State of Virginia (Jefferson), 110, 143
Nuttall, Thomas, 112, 114, 115, 122-23, 126

"Oak Grove," 361
O'Hara, James, 49, 78, 79
O'Higgins, Bernardo, 193, 208
Ohio, State of, 156
Ohio River, 4, 13, 14, 31, 32, 34, 38, 39, 96, 97, 98, 144, 359, 364
Olden Time, The, 372
Old Indian Queen, Philadelphia inn, 8
Omaha, Neb., 137
"Ontario," 181, 185, 186, 187, 194
Opelousas, 150
Oregon Bill, 251
O'Reilly, Gov. Alexander, 256
Orleans Territory, 142
Osage River, 117
Osborn, Selleck, 184, 195, 200, 210, 211, 214, 215, 219, 220, 221, 226, 230, 252
Othepya, 131-32
Ottawa River, 113
Otto village, 114
Outline of the Revolution in Spanish America, 227
Overton, Samuel R., 292, 319, 323, 325, 328, 349
Owings, Miss, 316

Pacific Fur Company, 112, 115
Pacific Ocean, 30, 112, 128, 187
Paine, Thomas, 66

Palao, Mercedes Vidal, 271, 272, 286, 287

Pamphleteer, 192

Panic of 1819, 156

Paraguay, 203

Parrington, Vernon Louis, 27

Parrot's Head, 199

Partidas, 143

Parton, James, 166, 279, 355, 375

Passamonte, 50

Patrick, L., 298

Patterson, Dr. Robert, 243

Paxton, John A., 248

Pazos, Vicente, 230

Peale, Rembrandt, 158

Peninsular War, 150

Pennsylvania, State of, 14

Pennsylvania Canal, 341, 342

Pennsylvania Canal and Portage Railroad, 364

Pennsylvania legislature (assembly), 5, 7, 8, 10, 11

Pennsylvania Salt Manufacturing Company, 376

Pensacola, Fla., 138, 254, 255, 256, 257, 258, 259, 260, 262, 263, 264, 265, 266, 267, 268, 269, 270, 271, 272, 277, 278, 281, 288, 291, 294, 296, 298, 299, 300, 302, 308, 309, 310, 312, 313, 314, 316, 317, 318, 324, 325, 326, 331, 349, 350

Pensacola Bay, 319

Pensacola Gazette and West Florida Advertiser, 303, 304, 307, 310, 313, 314, 319, 320, 329, 349, 350

Pentland, Ephraim, 74, 75, 77, 78, 79, 102, 128, 374

Pernambuco, 185, 191, 192

Perry family, 102

Peru, 188, 190

Peters, Richard, 327

Peyroux, 105

Philadelphia, Pa., 2, 3, 5, 6, 7, 12, 14, 22, 26, 31, 32, 73, 97, 157, 364

Phillips, R., 236

Philo and Franklin literary societies, Jefferson College, 75, 367-68

Physick, Dr. Philip Syng, 244

Pierpont, John, 170

Pinkney, William, 158-59, 172, 240, 241, 242, 243

Pinkney, W., Jr., 244

Pittsburgh, Pa., 3-5, 6, 7, 13, 14, 16, 17-18, 19, 23, 27-28, 31, 32, 33, 34, 41, 42, 43, 44, 45, 50-51, 52, 53, 54, 57, 59, 63, 64, 65, 73, 74, 75, 77, 78, 79, 80, 82, 83, 88, 96, 134, 137, 140, 152-53, 154, 358, 359, 360, 364, 365, 368, 373, 379

Pittsburgh Academy, 7, 11, 13, 14, 51, 77

Pittsburgh Directory, for 1815, The, 152

Pittsburgh Federalists, 14

Pittsburgh Gazette, 4, 5, 6, 7, 8, 9, 10, 11, 12, 13, 14, 18, 19, 20, 23, 44, 45, 51, 52, 53, 54, 59, 60, 61, 357-58

Pittsburgh-Kittanning road, 342

Pittsburgh racecourse, 51-52

Pittsburgh Races, 18

Pittsburgh Saturday Evening Visiter, 365, 366, 367

Pittsburgh Theater, 154

Plata River, 181, 185, 201, 203, 209

Platte River, 118, 119, 127

Pleasonton, Stephen, 231

Plumer, William, Jr., 148

Plutarch's Lives, 69

Poe, Edgar Allan, 170, 372

Poinsett, Joel, 193, 221

Point, the, Pittsburgh, 4, 96

Poncas, 120, 122, 126

Pope, Alexander, 188

Pope, John, 19-20

Porter, Commodore David, 193, 194, 202, 233

Portico, 170

Power, Thomas, 37, 38

Poydras, Julien de Lalande, 134, 142

Pradt, Abbé de, 192

Presbyterian Congregation, Pittsburgh, 7, 8-9, 11, 13

Princeton, N. J., 1

Princeton Whigs, 1

Proceedings and Debates of the General Assembly of Pennsylvania (Thomas Lloyd), 21

Prospect Cemetery, 379

Pueyrredon, Juan Martin de, 191, 196, 203, 206, 207, 210, 212, 213

Pufendorf, 85

Purviance, 92, 219

Quarry Hill, Pittsburgh, 4

Quivera, 371

Randolph, John, 80
Randolph (John Neal), 242
Ramsay, Allan, 54
"R.A." Society, 350
Rasselas (Dr. Johnson), 64
Read, William T., 197, 199, 200, 211, 212, 213, 215
Readel, Dr. John D., 169, 170, 171, 176, 183, 241, 242, 243
Rector, Col. Elias, 247
Red River, 142
Redstone Creek, 19
Reply to the Author of the Letter on South America and Mexico, By an American, Addressed to Mr. James Munroe, President of the United States, Printed at Washington, in This Present Year, 1817, 192
Rhode Island, State of, 14
Richmond, Va., 19
Richmond Enquirer, 194, 214, 279, 357
Rio de Janeiro, 185, 198, 199, 200, 201, 204, 205, 209, 221, 239
Rio Grande, 370
Ritchie, Thomas, 194, 357
Rivas y Salmon, Hilario de, 282
Robertson, Benjamin, 300
Robertson, Thomas B., 152
Robertson, William, 133-34
Robinson, Dr. John Hamilton, 146
Robinson, Tully, 152
Robinson, William, 78
Robinson Crusoe (Defoe), 46
Rocky Mountains, 112, 113, 129
Rodgers, Commodore John, 185, 339
Rodney, Caesar A., 182, 184, 185, 194, 195, 196, 197, 206, 211, 214, 218, 219, 220, 221, 222, 224, 225, 227, 229, 230, 231, 234, 235, 236, 237, 238, 239, 241, 244, 245, 291, 293, 294, 295, 296
Rodney, Thomas, 197, 214
Ross, James, 12, 58, 61, 71-73, 78, 79-80, 81, 91, 177-78, 340, 341, 365
Rosso, L. J., 236
R. Patterson & Lambdin, 178
Rowan, Judge John, 362
Rush, Richard, 179, 180, 181, 182, 183, 184, 185, 193, 196, 235-36
Rutledge, Edward A., 277, 283, 363

St. Andrews Bay, 331
St. Anne's, 113

St. Augustine, Fla., 255, 263, 266, 291, 309
St. Charles, Mo., 114, 116
St. Clair, Arthur, 31
St. Johns County, Fla., 266
St. Louis, Mo., 37, 101, 102, 103, 104, 105, 106, 107, 108, 109, 112, 113, 114, 115, 116, 126, 127, 128, 129, 130, 131, 134, 245, 246, 247, 248, 251, 252
St. Louis Directory and Register, 248
St. Louis Enquirer, 248, 249, 250, 252
St. Louis Missouri Fur Company, 113-14, 115, 120, 125, 128
St. Pierre, Pere, 35
Ste. Genevieve, Mo., 29, 34, 35, 36, 37, 99, 100, 101, 102, 104, 107
Salgado, Juan B., 318
Sample, David, 19
San Antonio, battle of, 151
San Martin, José de, 191, 193, 203, 207, 208, 209, 212
Sans Oreille, 118
Santa Rosa Peninsula, 299, 311, 312, 328, 329, 331, 332, 333, 336, 338, 339
Santiago, 208, 209
Sao Salvador, 185, 209, 210
Saugrain, Dr. Antoine, 40, 41, 97, 102
Saunders, 51
Scachi, Francis, 66
Schaeffer and Maund, 178
Schewe, Christopher Frederick, 76-77, 85, 102-103, 134, 247, 248, 269, 299
Schiller, 85
Scott, Alexander, Jr., 303
Scott, John, 249, 250
Scott, Sir Walter, 48
Scull, John, 4, 5, 7, 8, 9, 19, 23, 26, 27, 51, 56, 58, 59, 60, 61, 65
Sears, Rev. Jacob C., 322
Seaton, William W., 304, 305
Sebree, William, 300, 304, 306, 308, 318, 325
Second Bank of the U. S., 156
Seminoles, 320
Semple, Mrs. Steele, 71
Semple, Steele, 70, 71, 72, 80, 81
"Senator Ross," 58
Shakespeare, 172
Shaler, William, 145-48, 151, 188, 211, 217, 225, 233, 239, 244
Shannon, David, 278
Sharpsburg, Pa., 369

She-he-ke (Le Gros Blanc), 126

Shippensburg, Pa., 82

Shomo, Capt. Joseph, 297

Short Practical Narrative of the Diseases Which Prevailed among the American Seamen, at Wampoa, in China, in the Year 1805; with Some Account of Diseases Which Appeared among the Crew of the Ship New Jersey, on the Passage from Thence to Philadelphia, A (Dr. William Baldwin), 195

Sibley, George, 118, 127

Sign of General Butler, Pittsburgh tavern, 54

Sign of the Bell, Marie tavern in Pittsburgh, 16, 54

Sign of the Indian Queen, Pittsburgh tavern, 54

Simpson, James H., 319

Sinclair, Commodore Arthur, 187, 198, 199, 201, 228

Sinclair, William, 169

Sioux, 113, 116, 120, 121, 122, 125, 126, 128, 129

Skinner, John Stuart, 193, 194, 210, 211, 217, 219, 220, 227, 232, 241

Sloan, James, 89

Smilie, John, 10

Smith, Jacob, 359

Smith, Joseph L., 353, 356

Smith, Samuel, 73

Smithsonian Institution, 369

Smur, Capt. John, 54, 59

Snake River, 129

Snyder, Simon, 74, 91

Society of the Cincinnati, 24

Somerset, Pa., 92-94, 96

Sousa, Domingo, 272, 273, 277

South American mission (1817-18), 184-88, 193, 194, 196, 197, 198-213, 214, 215, 216, 218, 219, 220, 221, 222, 225, 226, 227, 228, 234, 235, 236, 238, 239, 241

Southard, Samuel L., 331, 332, 333, 334, 335, 336, 337, 343, 345, 346

South Carolina, State of, 14

South Carolina College, 349

Southern Literary Messenger, 372

Spain, 30, 31, 32, 37, 146, 150, 151, 178-79, 184, 188, 189, 190, 192, 203, 208, 215, 221, 222, 237, 252, 253, 264, 266, 282, 286, 310, 321

Spanish American independence movement, 146-48, 151, 184, 188, 189, 190, 191, 192, 193, 194, 196, 200, 202, 203, 204, 205, 206, 208, 212, 214, 215, 216, 217, 218, 219, 220, 221, 222, 225, 227, 228, 229, 231, 232, 234, 235, 237, 238, 239, 253, 295

Spanish Conspiracy, 38

Spanish Main, 181, 185, 237

"SPECTATOR," 303-304

Spectator (Addison and Steele), 46

Speeches (John Philpot Curran), 64

Spooner, Alden, 139

Sprague, Peleg, 337

Squier, Ephraim G., 369, 371

Stanton, Maj. Henry, 257, 267

Stars and Stripes, 312, 314

"Star-Spangled Banner," 157

Statesman (Pittsburgh), 353

Steele, William F., 301-306, 351

Stewart, Thomas, 75

Stieren, Dr. Edward, 376

Stone, James M., 305

Stone, John H., 305

Story, Judge Joseph, 327

Strictures on a Voyage to South America, as Indited by the "Secretary to the [Late] Mission" to La Plata, 232-34

Stuart, Robert, 129

"Suc-co-tash" (William H. Denny), 374

Sugarloaf Mountain, 198

Suke's Run, 17

Sumpter, Thomas, 185, 199, 221, 239

Superior Court of West Florida, 300, 301, 302, 303, 304, 305, 306, 307, 318, 322, 326, 328, 329, 330, 334

Supreme Court of the U. S., 22, 132, 327

Susquehanna River, 7

Swisshelm, Jane G., 378

Tagle, Gregorio, 205, 206, 210, 213

Tallahassee, Fla., 309, 319, 320, 321, 324

Tallahassee Junta, 319

Tamerlane, 120

Taney, Roger B., 340-41, 353

Tannehill, Adamson, 152

Tannehill, Wilkins, 49

Tarentum, Pa., 342, 353, 364, 371, 377, 379

Tavern Rocks, 117

Taylor, Rev. John, 49, 138

Télémaque (Fénelon), 42, 46
Tennessee, State of, 156
Texas, 142, 146, 147, 148
Thespian Club, Pittsburgh, 64-65
Thomas, F. W., 372
"Thomas Shields," 303
Thorn, Capt. Jonathan, 112
Three Forks of the Missouri, 113
Tod, 46
Todd, Dr. William A., 195
Todd, William, 13
Tombigbee River, 150
Tom Jones (Fielding), 46
"Tonquin," 112
Transactions, American Philosophical Society, 145
Transcontinental Treaty, 221, 237, 252, 253, 254, 267, 272, 284, 303, 307
Trappists, 108-109
Treasury Note Bill, 360
Treaty of Ghent, 153, 155, 166
Treaty of Greenville, 41
Treaty of San Lorenzo, 67
Tree of Liberty (Pittsburgh), 60-61, **63**, 67, 70, 74
"Trial," 301
Trinity Episcopal Church, Pittsburgh, 49
Tuesday Club, 170
Tumuli of North American aborigines, 108-109, 143-45
Tunstall, George, 269, 270, 285, 293
Turner, Mrs. Emma, 154
Tyler, John, 314-15, 361, 362
Tyson, John S., 337

Uncle Tom's Cabin (Stowe), 378
United Provinces of Rio de la Plata, 190, 191, 215, 226, 230
United States Magazine: A Repository of History, Politics and Literature, 2, 5
United States Telegraph (Washington, D. C.), 353, 355, 356, 357
United States v. *Riley,* 302
University of Pennsylvania, 195
University of Pittsburgh, 13
"U.S.A.," 302

Valparaiso, 209, 218
Van Buren, Martin, 360
Vattel, 85

Vicar of Wakefield (Goldsmith), 46
Vidal, Nicolas Maria, 271, 286
View of West Florida, A (John Lee Williams), 320-21
Vinton, Samuel F., 41
Virginia, State of, 14
Visinier, 46
Voltaire, 66
Voorhees, Dr. John V. D., 299
Voyages (Cook), 47
Voyageurs, 113, 114
Wabash River, 98
Wager, Capt. P., 279
Wallace, George, 64
Walsh, Robert, 291, 372
Walton, George, 258, 272, 273, 278, 280, 289, 290, 293, 294, 296, 299, 300, 316, 317, 318, 325, 375
Walton, Mrs. George, 314
Walton, Octavia, 317, 375
War Hawks, 153, 165
War of 1812, 129, 138, 148, 153-54, 155, 156, 157, 162, 164, 165, 254
War of 1812, The (Francis F. Beirne), 165
Warm Springs, Va., 3
Warren, Pa., 364
Warrington, Capt. Lewis, 185, 310
Wash, Richard, 111
Washington, D. C., 153, 157, 165, 177, 187
Washington, George, 26, 31, 37, 44, 52, 191, 314
Washington administration, 29, 31
Washington County, Pa., 3, 44
Watkins, Dr. Tobias, 169, 170, 171, 176, 180, 186, 200, 243
Watson's Hill, Pittsburgh, 76, 96
Watts, David, 85
Wayne, Gen. Anthony, 31, 34, 41, 51, 113
Webbville, Fla., 325, 329
Webster, Daniel, 361
Webster, John Adams, 240
Weekly Register (Baltimore), 110, 128, 139, 140, 161, 215, 222, 225, 255, 297, 353, 357
Weimar, 140
Western Monthly Magazine, 359
Westmoreland County, Pa., 3, 5, 12, 13, 96
Wheaton, Henry, 327
Wheeling, W. Va., 97

Whetstone Point, Baltimore, 158
Whiggism, 360, 363
Whisky Insurrection, 43-45, 56, 59, 61, 371-74
White, Bishop, 71
White, "Florida," 309, 324, 328
White, John, 318
White, Joseph M., 296, 300, 308, 309, 319, 320, 321, 324, 328, 331, 332, 333, 339, 343, 345, 346, 347, 348, 349, 352, 354, 356
White River, 121, 126
White Wolf, 126
Wilkins, Charles, 76
Wilkins, James C., 49
Wilkins, John, Jr., 78
Wilkins, William, 64, 70, 76, 81, 352
Wilkinson, Gen. James, 38, 41, 42, 90
Wilkinson, Joseph Biddle, 42
William M. Loftin v. *William S. Mooring*, 307
Williams, John Lee, 302, 304, 320-21
Williamson, Peter G., 350
Willis, Jesse H., 349

Wilmington, Del., 196, 200, 214, 217, 218
Wilson, Henry, 292, 330
Winder, William H., 92, 242, 243
Windship, John, 148, 149
Wirt, William, 242, 377
Wirt Literary Society, 366
Wise, Henry A., 362
Witherspoon, Dr. John, 1
Wolf, Jacob, 20-21, 27
Wolf, Sabina (Mrs. H. H. Brackenridge), 20, 61, 84, 91, 163, 178, 316
Woodbury, Levi, 347, 348
Woods, Col. James, 368
Woods, John, 57, 80-81, 339, 340
Woolsey, Commodore, 336
Worthington, W. G. D., 224, 289, 337

"X Y Z Affair," 56

York County, Pa., 1
Yorktown, battle of, 2
Young, Judge John, 93, 94, 223-24
Young White Hairs, 118

This book was composed in Linotype Garamond Light text with
Ludlow Garamond Light heads; printed on sixty pound
White Strathmore Impress Text by the Herbick and
Held Printing Company of Pittsburgh; and
bound by Russell Rutter Company, Inc.
in natural finish Novelex for the
University of Pittsburgh Press.